THE LIFE OF
HILAIRE BELLOC

BY

ROBERT SPEAIGHT

LONDON

HOLLIS & CARTER

MADE AND PRINTED IN GREAT BRITAIN BY
SPOTTISWOODE, BALLANTYNE AND CO. LTD., LONDON AND COLCHESTER, FOR
HOLLIS AND CARTER LIMITED,
25 ASHLEY PLACE, LONDON, S.W.I

First published 1957

Hilaire Belloc: Portrait by James Gunn, 1939,
in the possession of the artist

TO
TERESA

who met Hilaire Belloc when he was very
old and she was very young, this story of
his life is affectionately dedicated.

Les Chrétiens ont raison, les Paiens ont tort.
Chanson de Roland.

Il allait hériter de l'école stoïque,
Il allait hériter de l'héritier romain,
Il allait hériter du laurier héroïque,
Il allait hériter de tout l'effort humain.
Charles Péguy.

Almighty God will surely cry,
  " St. Michael! who is this that stands
With Ireland in his dubious eye
  And Périgord between his hands,

" And on his arm the stirrup-thongs
  And in his gait the narrow seas,
And in his mouth Burgundian songs,
  But in his heart the Pyrenees ? "
Hilaire Belloc.

Militia est vita hominis.

CONTENTS

CONTENTS

vii

ILLUSTRATIONS

The names are as follows—*Left*: P. Belloc; J. J. Hall; R. A. Jebb; T. Michael Pope; James Gunn; D. B. Wyndham Lewis; F. vanden Heuvel; Douglas Woodruff; Christopher Hollis; Gerald Barry; H. S. Mackintosh; A. D. Peters; C. Wilkinson; Jerrard Tickell; E. S. P. Haynes; Edward Shanks; J. B. Morton. *Right*: A. P. Herbert; Robert Lynd; J. C. Squire; H. Belloc; Maurice Baring; Duff Cooper; E. C. Bentley; G. K. Chesterton.

The author's thanks are due to Mr. James Gunn, A.R.A., Mr. James Hall, Mr. H. S. Mackintosh, Miss Miranda Mackintosh, Sir John Rothenstein and to P. A.-Reuter Features Ltd. for making available the originals of the illustrations, and to the Earl of Carlisle for permission to quote from the privately printed memoirs of Hubert Howard.

The author also acknowledges his indebtedness for quotations to the publishers of reminiscences and earlier studies of Hilaire Belloc and to the very many publishers of Hilaire Belloc's varied output.

PREFACE

I MUST express my thanks to the literary executors of Hilaire Belloc—Mrs. Raymond Asquith, Monsignor R. A. Knox, and the late Viscount Norwich—for asking me to write this book; and to Mrs. Asquith and Monsignor Knox for their help and encouragement during the two years that I have been at work. I am deeply conscious of the high trust they reposed in me. I am further indebted to Monsignor Knox for allowing me to reproduce the panegyric that he preached at Belloc's Requiem in Westminster Cathedral.

The materials for the life of Belloc fall under four headings:

1. His private papers. Belloc did not keep many private letters, but his business correspondence was carefully filed. His earlier Press cuttings were collected in albums by his wife, but a great number were left unsorted, and of the later ones by far the greater number have disappeared. He kept a strictly factual diary from 1912 to 1920. To this and to certain other papers at King's Land I have been given access through the courtesy of his daughter, Mrs. Reginald Jebb. Both she and Mr. Jebb have been prompt in replying to the numerous questions I have put to them, and I wish to extend to them my thanks. I must also thank Miss Elizabeth Belloc for inviting me to draw upon her memories.

2. His correspondence. Belloc was an untiring letter writer, and I am especially grateful for the many collections which their recipients or present owners have placed at my disposal. I have not been able to use more than a fraction of this fascinating material, but it is hoped to bring out, later, a volume of Selected Letters, and much that I have not found space for in the biography will be included in it. Meanwhile I must thank the following persons, without whose help this book could not have been written: Mrs. Raymond Asquith; Lady Dorothy Charteris; Mrs. Frank Collin; Miss Dorothy Collins; Lady Diana Cooper; Mrs. Guy Dawnay; Lady Juliet Duff; Mrs. Charles Goodwin; Mrs. E. S. P.

Haynes; The Hon. Mrs. Mervyn Herbert; Mrs. Charles Goodwin, Captain Alan Hillgarth, R.N.; The Countess of Iddesleigh; Laura, Lady Lovat; Mr. Dermot MacCarthy; Mrs. Ogilvie-Forbes; Mrs. J. S. Phillimore; Lady Phipps; Mrs. A. Hungerford Pollen; Lady Reid; Mrs. R. T. Sheppard; Mrs. Wansbrough; Captain E. L. Warre; the Librarian of Princeton University, and the Editor of *Studies*.

3. The reminiscences of those who knew him. Most of his immediate contemporaries are now dead, but Belloc was a man of many friendships and many more acquaintances, and I have benefited greatly from correspondence and conversation with those who had met him at different stages of his life, or held views about him to which I listened with respect. Some of these also had letters which they showed to me. Here the list of my indebtedness is too long for separate mention, though much of it will be apparent to the reader of the book. I am particularly grateful to the Hon. Mrs. Herbert for allowing me to draw on the memories of her long friendship with Belloc; to Lord Henley and Professor Eccles for many reminiscences of the Balliol years; to Mr. Douglas Jerrold for light on *Land and Water*, and to Mr. Maurice Reckitt for a sympathetic estimate of distributism; to Brother Sylvester Humphries, O.P., for a great deal of information and research; to the Reverend Timothy McCarthy of the Birmingham Oratory and Dom Adrian Morey, O.S.B., Headmaster of the Oratory School, for helping me to reconstruct Belloc's schooldays; to Mr. John Somers Cocks for filling in the picture of Belloc's friendship with his uncle; to Miss Ruby Goldsmith for the vivid picture she gave me of what it was like to be Belloc's secretary; to Mr. A. D. Peters and Mr. W. N. Roughead for giving me access to their files, which show what it was like to be his literary agent; to Mr. and Mrs. Sheed for always having the answer to a great variety of questions; and to Mr. Peter Watts for solving the riddle of the *Ode to the West Wind*. Two people deserve a special word of thanks: Mr. Douglas Woodruff for the care with which he has read my MS., and for the valuable criticisms he has made upon it; and Miss Hilda Coe for the rapidity, intelligence and skill with which she has typed a very complicated script.

4. His books, pamphlets and contributions to journalism. A bibliography of books and pamphlets by Belloc, and also of books about him, will be found at the end of this volume. The importance of this material does not, of course, need underlining. When I was starting work on the life of Belloc someone who had known him well remarked to me: 'I hope you will concentrate on Mr. Belloc's opinions'. In so far as one cannot write the biography of a very opinionated man without discussing his opinions, the advice was unnecessary; in so far as it suggested I should discuss nothing else but that, it was absurd. The purpose of a literary biography is to get at the man behind the books. A biography is at once more and less than criticism, although criticism must naturally be included in it. Separate books, almost as long as this one, might be devoted to Belloc's views on history, economics, or religion. They might discuss him as a poet, a traveller, or a political theorist. They might debate his failure as a practical politician. Mr. E. C. Bentley's clerihew is well known:

> Mr. Hilaire Belloc
> Is a case for legislation *ad hoc;*
> He seems to think nobody minds
> His books being all of different kinds.

And Sir John Squire once said, with no exaggeration, that 'the man who attempts to survey the writings of Belloc will think he is undertaking to write the literary history of a small nation'. I sympathize with that feeling. The survey attempted here does not pretend to be exhaustive; there will always be plenty more to say. If I had tried to discuss, or even to summarize, everything that Belloc had written, there would have been no room for anything else. The man would have been left out; and it is the man with whom I have been principally concerned.

Some of his books I have discussed in detail; others I have not discussed at all. I am not a professional historian, and where Belloc's views on history are in question I have not attempted to compete with scholarly opinion. His fiscal theories, though I have not omitted them altogether, are quite beyond my competence. Some readers will miss the mention of their favourite poem, or

the inclusion of their cherished quotation. I can only crave their
indulgence. If I had included everything which deserved to be
quoted, the result would have been not a biography but an
anthology. Here again, an anthology would be easy to compose
from any single department of Belloc's writing.

There were two further problems: one of treatment and the
other of proportion. Up to the end of the First World War it was
easy to follow Belloc's life in more or less chronological sequence,
but after that the themes were so interwoven that it would have
been confusing to attempt to trace them through their annual
repetitions. It seemed to me better to treat them separately; and
that is what I have done from Chapter XVII to XX.

In the days of lavish biography a life so full as this might well
have run to a second volume. I have, however, no complaint of
the space allotted to me; but it has imposed upon me a choice of
emphasis. Those who wish for a fuller picture of Belloc's childhood and family background should turn to the memoirs of his
sister, Mrs. Belloc-Lowndes: *I, too, have lived in Arcadia* (1941),
Where Love and Friendship Dwelt (1943) and *The Young Hilaire
Belloc* (1956). These are an indispensable source. Where I have
been able to add to them (generally through the courtesy of
Belloc's niece, Lady Iddesleigh) I have done so; but they have
given me a great deal of essential information, and direct quotation from them has in each case been acknowledged. Certain
aspects of Belloc's later years have been covered by Mr. J. B.
Morton in his admirable Memoir [1] and by Mr. and Mrs. Jebb in
their *Testimony to Hilaire Belloc* (1956). Mr. Morton wrote from
a personal knowledge of his subject to which I can lay no claim;
and I take this opportunity of thanking him, not only for the
vivid and affectionate portrait he has drawn, but for the many
conversations we have had together and for the generosity with
which he has allowed me to draw upon his memory. I should
also mention Lord Stanley of Alderley's introduction to the last
edition of *The Cruise of the 'Nona'* (1955). This gives a lively
picture of Belloc at sea by one who often sailed with him after
the First World War. It has seemed to me, however, that for the

purposes of the present biography, the greater emphasis should be laid upon those years—1893 to 1918—when Belloc was forming his opinions and developing his personality, and when his impact upon English life and letters was most considerable. It has seemed to me, too, that we shall understand him better if we see him in a certain setting of time.

I first met Belloc in the autumn of 1938. It was at a luncheon in the Brompton Road—I think at the *Speranza*—and there were several others present. Of these I only now remember Mr. Christopher Hollis. Belloc swept in, all sails flying, and talking about the effects of the Reformation in Scandinavia. I did not meet him again until the summer of 1942, when my friend, Douglas Woodruff, took me down to King's Land, and we drank the last bottle of a miraculous Vermouth. Belloc was then recovering from a serious illness, and his memory and physical strength were both gravely impaired. He was like a great wind that had blown itself out into the calm of a summer evening. After that I saw him fairly constantly and I spent the Christmases of 1943 and 1944 at King's Land. For a long time I do not think he knew who I was. He seemed to imagine that I was a member of the Foreign Office and, since we both had a liking for diplomats, I did not disabuse him. But I never pretended to a close acquaintance, and the personal note has been generally excluded from these pages. Others had a right to speak of him as a friend, where I had not. They have spoken of him already, and will no doubt speak of him again. Wherever possible, I have allowed them to speak of him here.

One last word. Belloc had a unique power of inspiring affection in those who knew him well. I hope that his friends will pardon me for any note of criticism that may from time to time have crept into this book. Such criticism is hardly to be avoided in dealing with a highly controversial figure. Human judgments are fallible; but justice is the least tribute we can pay to the immortal dead.

Benenden: 1956.

CHAPTER I

UNQUIET HOMES

I

ALTHOUGH the village of La Celle St. Cloud is only a few miles from the centre of Paris, it still leaves an impression of repose. Neither railway nor arterial road passes within earshot of its lazy streets. In the summer of 1870, long before the great new highway was driven through the hill just to the east of the gardens of St. Cloud, the peaceful impression must have been even more marked than it is today. Now, the wide tarmac takes you in a few minutes to Versailles or to Vaucresson, or, in an hour or so, to Vernon and to Mantes. Then, you would have had to skirt the Palace which the Prussians burned down after the war of 1870, and climb the hill dominating the north bank of the Seine before gaining the open country beyond. La Celle St. Cloud lies clustered at the foot of a fairly steep hill, about four miles to the north of the present main road.

The village is pretty without being picturesque. If you stand with your back to the church, you see two roads forking out to right and left at a gentle angle from the square. The one leads up on to the side of the hill dotted with villas and small châteaux; the other follows the line of the valley. Go down this second road for a hundred yards and you will perceive a nondescript building on your left, rather too rambling to be called a villa and rather too cramped to be called a château. An iron gate, from which the paint is now flaking off, gives directly on to the road: the house stands only two or three feet back. If you penetrate the unkempt garden, you will notice on the western side of the building a bronze plaque fixed to the wall. This represents a woman's head of unusual strength and beauty, Greek in its proportion, and underneath it is inscribed the name—Louise Swanton Belloc. For the house had once been the property of Hilaire Belloc, the celebrated academic painter, and his wife, Louise Swanton. It was here that Louise continued to live with her semi-invalid son, Louis, after her husband's death in 1865. It was here, to the small châlet adjoining the main house, that Louis brought his English bride, Bessie Parkes, after their marriage in London on September 19, 1867. And it was here, in the long salon temporarily furnished as a bedroom, that on July 27, 1870, Bessie Belloc sat quietly awaiting the birth of her second child.

She had never known her father-in-law, for he had died before she was first brought to La Celle St. Cloud in the spring of 1867. But she knew him by reputation. A pupil of Géricault, he was considered a fine teacher in his day, and several museums in France showed examples of his work. He was short, gay and fat, with a square beard and a broad forehead, conservatively Republican and conventionally anti-clerical, until he became reconciled to the Church a year before he died. He would generally take a *fiacre* from the Gare St. Lazare to the Ecole des Beaux Arts, and his grandson had the story that if the cabman overcharged him he had no hesitation in pulling him from his seat and beating him insensible. 'We have always been a family of guts.'[1] Numbers of interesting people had come to La Celle St. Cloud when he was alive, notably Michelet and Barthélemy St. Hilaire. For a short time Michelet was tutor to his only son and the great historian was shocked one day to find Madame Belloc teaching him his catechism. He regarded this as yet another straw in a strangely contrary wind, for so many of his friends were just then returning to the practice of the Faith. Madame Belloc herself, we are told, would assist at the sermons '*du beau et riche M. de Consey, éloquent et poitrinaire*'. The phrase renders vividly a certain well-padded clericalism, rather too prosperous and self-assured.

Madame Belloc's origins were romantic. The Swantons were Irish Protestants from Co. Cork, where the place now known as Ballydehob used to be called Swantonstown. Her father was one of the last Colonels of the Berwick (Stuart Irish) Brigade, before its

---

[1] Letter to the Hon. Mrs. Mervyn Herbert: Feb. 7, 1939.

dissolution, and Dean of the Order of St. Louis. Colonel Swanton's uncle had killed his opponent in a duel, and fled to the Continent, where he became a Catholic and afterwards a priest. The nephew had begun his military career in the Royalist army, but he afterwards fought in Napoleon's early campaigns, and held Rocroi during the hundred days. While he was still a lieutenant he married a Chassériau of La Rochelle, and it was there, in her mother's ancestral home, that Louise Swanton was born.

She was a girl of strong intelligence and character, evidently no blue-stocking. After the marriage of her two elder sisters she settled in Paris with her father and it was here that she met Hilaire Belloc. The Bellocs had for two generations been large shipowners in Nantes, and in 1665 a certain Moses Belloc had been attorney-general of Languedoc under Louis XIV. But these antecedents were altogether too bourgeois for Colonel Swanton, and a painter, to his sense of protocol, was a good deal worse than a shipowner. He stiffly opposed the marriage, and only became fully reconciled to his son-in-law a few years before his own death. Meanwhile in 1823 Louise had published a French translation of the Irish Melodies, and by the time she was thirty she had published a life of Byron with a preface by Stendhal. Afterwards she wrote books for children and translated into French the novels of her English and American contemporaries. She was described by Myles Byrne as 'a fine girl of the highest merit, who by one of her books won the Monthyon Prize of the French Academy,'[1] and Tom Moore is quoted by Lord John Russell as receiving, on July 15, 1823, 'a letter . . . informing me that Madame Belloc, besides being so clever, is young and pretty'.[2] Certainly her beauty in later life is attested by Hilaire Belloc's admirable sketch, reproduced as the frontispiece to *Where Love and Friendship Dwelt*, and by his portrait in the Louvre. Such was the woman whose personality, so rich and yet so reserved, once presided over the house in La Celle St. Cloud.

[1] *Memoirs of Myles Byrne*, Vol. II (1907).
[2] *Memoirs, Journals and Correspondence of Tom Moore*, edited by Lord John Russell.

Although she had warmly reciprocated the devotion of Bessie Parkes, the prospect of Bessie marrying her son caused her considerable disquiet. To begin with, Louis, though qualified as a barrister, was too delicate to work and it was doubtful whether he ought to marry at all. Bessie had only known him for a few months, but she had discovered a deep affection for him in spite of a previous attachment which had obsessed her unhappily for many years. She was thirty-nine, a little older than he was; old enough, certainly, to know her own mind; of the same religion, for she had been received into the Catholic Church in 1864; but of a milieu very different from his. She came of Unitarian stock. Her father, Joseph Parkes, was a Birmingham solicitor, and manager for the Liberal Party in that city; the historian of the Chancery Bar and also a founder of the Reform Club. Bessie's mother was the grand-daughter of Joseph Priestley, the scientist who discovered oxygen, sometimes described as the founder of modern chemistry. Mrs. Parkes would recall Priestley's love of music, and she remembered him teaching her to read. Her daughter Bessie was reared in the cradle of English Radicalism, and became devoted to all the progressive causes of the day, particularly to the rather vague cause of Women's Rights. In 1861, for example, we find her attending the Congress for the Advancement of Social Science in Dublin. It was then she became interested in the Irish Sisters of Mercy and Sisters of Charity and saw something of their work; and no doubt it was these contacts, with her close friendship for Sara Atkinson, which hastened her conversion to Catholicism. 'What religious feelings I possess', she had written immediately afterwards to this remarkable and saintly woman, 'are, as they always have been, rather deep and conscientious than warm. I have very little power of religious enthusiasm in my nature, at least of the kind that enables people to wave flags. . . . Just now, I am *sore* with the fearful effort I have made. Sunday morning I was so cold that tho' one of the hottest days of the year I had to go down to the kitchen and sit by the fire.' [1]

Joseph Parkes moved to London while Bessie was still quite

[1] Letter to Sara Atkinson: July 20, 1864.

young, and this brought her into contact with almost everyone worth knowing in the literary and political worlds. Her father was a friend of Brougham, Grote, and J. S. Mill, and she was invited to Samuel Rogers' famous breakfasts. She was on close terms with George Eliot and Elizabeth Barrett Browning, and she corresponded with George Sand. When Mrs. Gaskell was working on her life of the Brontës, Bessie Parkes accompanied her to Yorkshire. She knew Thackeray and Trollope well. Thackeray would often dine at their house in Wimpole Street, because he liked meeting Liberal politicians, and Bessie always ascribed to him the following translation of Horace's famous line:

> Eheu fugaces, posthume, posthume,
> Oh for the years that are lost to me, lost to me.

She may well have thought them lost when she looked at the pale, thin man who sat beside her in the long salon; the man whom she had met only on the threshold of middle age and with whom she was to know so brief and so intense a happiness.

The two windows of the salon opened on to a rose-twined balcony, from which steps led down to a narrow strip of garden. Beyond the garden was a lane, and on the other side of this ran the wall of the great park surrounding the Château of La Celle St. Cloud. This had once been owned for a short time by Madame de Pompadour. The park contained many beautiful trees, and although a great number of them were cut down by the Germans in their successive occupations of the place, they would all have been standing when Bessie looked out of her windows on July 27, 1870, and some of them are standing today. She would have seen, quite close at hand, some noble firs and a pair of weeping willows, and between them, shrunk to a trickle by the summer drought, a little running stream. Beyond the park were the woods of Marly and the long crest of Louveciennes.

It was a day of intense heat and the heavy silence was broken at one moment by a terrific thunderstorm, the worst that had been known for fifty years in that part of France. Louis and Bessie, with the young Quaker midwife Mercy Baker whom they had brought over from England, and their French maid Adeline, were alone in the house. The Bellocs' daughter, Marie, had been born in London two years before; but Louis, ardently hoping for a son, was determined that he should be born in France. Rumours of war were in the air and this was not their only anxiety. Both Louis and his wife were nervous lest the unborn child should have suffered from a tour they had undertaken in France only three months earlier. So they waited on through the sultry afternoon, ready to summon Dr. Lemaire when he was needed—an old man who had been physician to Louis XVIII. But the doctor was not to be found, and Mercy Baker was alone when she brought Hilaire Belloc into the world. Within a few days of his birth war had broken out between France and Germany.

Owing to the national emergency the boy was christened privately. René Millet, his cousin, was there in uniform, and his aunt Lily Ballot. He was named Jean-Hilaire after his paternal, and Joseph after his maternal, grandfather. Then, as he was being held at the font, Louis Belloc called out: 'I should like him to be called Pierre.' It was a happy and prophetic afterthought. Mrs. Belloc-Lowndes tells us [1] that his aunt also called out 'René', but this name does not seem to have stuck so well as the others.

By the time Bessie was able to walk after her confinement, officers had made a survey of the hills round the village of La Celle St. Cloud and a gun had been placed on the top of the aqueduct. So it was thought best that the family should leave for Paris, where Louis had an apartment. But Bessie expected to be back quite soon. A week after Hilaire's birth she had arranged the miniatures above the mantelpiece in the salon, and when they left she did not trouble to put anything away. It took them five hours to reach Paris in the stifling August heat, and here they remained through the cumulative disasters of the war—Sedan, the flight of the Empress Eugénie from the Tuileries, and the fall of the Empire on September 4. Finally, in response to urgent appeals from Mrs. Parkes and from Madame Swanton-Belloc, who had already left the country, Louis agreed to remove his wife and children to England. They left Paris by the last train for Dieppe. As it puffed its way through the lush countryside, they could see the soldiers

---

[1] *I, too, have lived in Arcadia* (1941).

shovelling the earth on to the rails behind them. And when they reached Southampton—for the Newhaven route had not yet been opened—they remarked bitterly that the German ships in the harbour were dressed with flags in honour of the Prussian victory.

The winter of the siege of Paris, during which almost every child under three years old perished from malnutrition, was spent by the Bellocs in Mrs. Parkes' London house. Madame Swanton-Belloc, with her daughter Louise, had gone first to the Isle of Wight and afterwards taken a furnished house on Richmond Green. By degrees the painful news from Paris trickled through. They learned from *The Times* that the houses in Bougival and La Celle St. Cloud were 'fast disappearing'. The neighbourhood was constantly being shelled from Mont Valérien, which was in Prussian hands; not even the château had escaped damage. Early in the following spring Bessie persuaded Madame Swanton-Belloc to occupy the house of her uncle, Josiah Parkes, which was standing furnished but empty in Great College Street, Westminster. The two women and Louis settled there, but owing to the smallness of the house, they left Hilaire, his sister, and Adeline with Mrs. Parkes in Wimpole Street. Meanwhile, the new baby grew apace to the tune of *Au Clair de la Lune*, which his sister had learned to sing to him, and it was already remarked that he seemed to notice everything that was going on around him.

In June 1871, Bessie and Louis returned to France and saw for themselves the damage that had been done to their house in La Celle St. Cloud. The châlet where they normally lived had been reduced to a skeleton, and the house alongside had been barbarously pillaged. Bessie's books, hidden in a cupboard in the salon, were safe, but most of Madame Swanton-Belloc's manuscripts and papers had been destroyed or defaced. In the bedroom upstairs were some eighteenth-century engravings, and on to the faces of these elegant women the Prussian soldiery had amused themselves by adding moustaches and beards. Such drawings and engravings as their clownish humour had no mind to improve upon they merely tore up; and such paintings as they could not take away they used for target practice. A portrait of Madame

Swanton-Belloc's mother was found stuffing up a broken
window, its painted breast riddled with bullets. Only three or
four pictures, which a neighbour had rescued in the early days of
the occupation, remained of the family collection. Two letters
from Victor Hugo and three from Michelet were discovered
among the mounds of filth in the garden. Nor was it enough for
the *furor teutonicus* to destroy the works of man. The chestnut
grove on the other side of the road had been levelled to the
ground. Only the fruit trees survived in the orchard, and a single
poplar to which Bessie was particularly attached. Such vandalism
in war is not confined to Germans, but Hilaire Belloc grew up
under its shadow, and as the years went by its details would have
been burned upon his mind.

Neither house nor châlet being as yet habitable, the Bellocs
stayed with the nuns near by, but in August Louis and Bessie
were brought back to London by the death of Josiah Parkes. He
bequeathed to Bessie the substantial sum of £20,000 and the lease
of the house in Westminster. It was here, at 11 Great College
Street, that the family settled in December of the same year.

2

By the time they paid their next visit to the stricken home, in
the following summer, Hilaire was already beginning to talk. On
August 6 his parents left him with his sister and nurse to visit some
friends in Auvergne. Nowhere in France is the heat so intolerable
as in the Massif Central, and it was seemingly on account of this
that they decided to cut short their stay. They arrived back in
the evening of Sunday, the 18th, two days before they were
expected. Louis was greatly fatigued by the long journey and the
pitiless sun; at one point they had met a funeral procession and he
had stood with his hat off for a quarter of an hour, waiting for it
to go by. He did not dine with the others but retired to his room
in the châlet. He slept late the next morning and on into the
afternoon; efforts were made to awaken him and the doctor and
priest were sent for; but he died shortly before midnight without
regaining consciousness. He was forty-two years old.

Louis Belloc was buried on August 22, in the cemetery of La Celle St. Cloud. His widow, holding Hilaire by the hand (he was just two years old) walked immediately behind the coffin. Madame Swanton-Belloc, with little Marie, followed after. When the coffin had been lowered into the grave Madame Swanton-Belloc moved away to shake hands with those who had attended the funeral. But Bessie, with her two children and Adeline, remained apart until the others had left the cemetery. A cross was in due course erected over the grave, but it bore no inscription. To see the beloved name engraved upon the memorial whenever she went to pray beside it was a prospect that Bessie could not face. It was only fifty years later, after her own death in 1925, that, by order of her son, the name of Louis Belloc was added to it.

It is a characteristic, and even at times a weakness, of the French people that they live more intimately with their dead than do the races of the Protestant tradition. What appears morbidity to the foreigner is simple fidelity to them. But no Frenchwoman, widowed after a few years of married life, ever lived more continuously with the memory of her husband than did Bessie Parkes Belloc. Other women, even though such memories haunt them, are strengthened and increased by sorrow. They become more, not less, than themselves. But Bessie, from all that we are given to understand, was not a woman of this kind. Her active, energetic and disinterested youth had been fulfilled by a sudden, supreme experience. When that experience was cut short, she was never the same person again. Madame Swanton-Belloc compared her to 'an exquisite watch whose mainspring had been broken'. She moved through the next four years in a trance of melancholy; her judgment in matters great and small was seriously affected; and the balance of her temperament was disturbed.

The bereavement and its aftermath cannot have been without effect upon her son. Not only had he lost a father, but he had also lost the mother that he might have had. His duty and devotion would always respond to the care and affection she lavished on him, but we have the impression that they corresponded through a gauze of absent-mindedness. Her mind was permanently rooted in the years of perfect happiness she had known. Had Louis Belloc survived, his son would have been a Frenchman with an English mother instead of being an Englishman with a French father. How far his English mother succeeded in transmitting to him the memory she cherished, how far he inherited his father's qualities, these questions are difficult to determine. Sensitive and strongly sympathetic, yet not very sharply defined, Louis Belloc passes sadly away from the biography he might have helped to build.

Immediately after her husband's death Bessie Belloc took the children to stay with relatives at Villebouzin, and they remained in France until after the *Jour des Morts*. Once again Hilaire was led by the hand up the cemetery path, carrying a little nosegay of flowers, picked from the garden of the châlet, to lay upon his father's grave. A friend of the family, Anatole Dunoyer de Segonzac, was appointed guardian to the children, but he never played a very active part in their lives. Soon afterwards Bessie returned to London with Hilaire and his sister. Mrs. Parkes wanted them to go to Wimpole Street, but Bessie preferred to settle down in Westminster.

She now resumed her acquaintance with Cardinal Manning, whom she had known before she became a Catholic. Manning, Hilaire Belloc would write later, 'had more in him than the rest of the Oxford converts put together—a great love-affair and a great death'.[1] But Mrs. Manning had been dead for a long time, and the ageing Archbishop was fixed in the habits of asceticism and power. He rebuked Bessie for luxuriating in a grief whose poignancy he might have been expected to understand.

Intense though her suffering was, it did not freeze the social charity which had always been quick in her. She gave both her money and her personal attention to the Paris *communards* who had fled from the vengeance of the Versailles government, and we find her escorting a priest to an Irish prostitute who lay dying in a brothel in Great Peter Street. But she sometimes quailed before the thought of what her children would expect of her, of the strength which was hardly, as yet, hers to give. Louis had been her refuge and protection, but now—

[1] Letter to Duff Cooper: March 22, 1938.

I must stand steady for *them* to dash up against *me*. Hilaire would ride on my shoulders this evening, just as if I had been the father I am not; and at last I had to put the poor little creature down on the floor. My strength had given way, and I felt as if it were symbolical of the whole position.[1]

To the same correspondent she wrote of her French sisters-in-law, of what she called the 'Belloc quality'. She described them as

full of power . . . dowered with a sort of profusion of nature which must have come from the gay, brilliant old father whom, to my great regret, I never saw. Louis had something of it . . . I never usually see in Hilaire any likeness to him but this morning I was sitting on the grass in the early sunlight, and the little lad standing, so that our faces were just on a level, and all of a sudden he flashed at me a look so like his father that I called out in surprise.[2]

It was probably about this time that Hilaire began to go regularly to Mass. His parents had always frequented the Church of Notre Dame de France, just off Leicester Square, the parish church of the French colony in London, and Bessie continued to take the children there. At home he would listen to his elders debating the rights of the Tichborne claimant, and he used to say in later life that the Tichborne verdict, given on February 28, 1874, was the first thing that he remembered.

My nurse, who was excited in the matter, as all folk were, rich and poor, took me into the press of people in Westminster Hall to hear the result.[3]

Bessie gave much thought to the education of the children. She would read chapters of the Bible to them every day, but she could not awaken in Hilaire any deep attachment to the Hebrew Scriptures. She was torn between the Puritan and the Catholic ideals, and sometimes felt as if she 'was trying to grow hawthorns under the equator'.[4] When they returned to London, Hilaire

[1] Letter to Miss Merryweather, March 1873: quoted in *I, too, have lived in Arcadia* (1941).
[2] *Ibid.*   [3] *The Cruise of the 'Nona'* (1925).
[4] Letter to Mrs. Parkes, quoted in *I, too, have lived in Arcadia* (1941).

was sent to school with Mrs. Shiel in Great College Street; the
other pupils, boys and girls, were mostly children of the Canons of
Westminster. Hilaire was astonishingly mature, learning with
quickness and accuracy, and composing verses on any event that
stirred him. The loss of H.M.S. *Eurydice* in March 1878, which
inspired Gerard Manley Hopkins to one of his finest poems, also
moved the young Belloc to an impassioned lament.

> While it was snowing
> And the wind was blowing
> And the ship was going
>   The Frigate Eurydice;
> While prayers were being offered from the deck
> On came that cruel cloud to wreck
>   The Frigate Eurydice;
> Just passing round
> By Ventnor town
> The ship went down,
>   The Frigate Eurydice! [1]

It may have been these verses which prompted the following
letter from Lucy Field to Madame Belloc a few weeks afterwards.
Lucy Field had taught her at school and she was now watching
Hilaire's progress.

> I do not wonder that you are proud of your Boy's talents,
> and it is almost incredible he could manage sense, sentiment
> and metre as he has done in the little poems you send us . . . I feel
> quite alarmed at his precocity and cannot help wishing he was
> the companion of other boys and induced to make mud pies,
> or otherwise to be as much stultified as possible. Such a mind is
> indeed a grave charge for you, though you will have the reward
> of the glow of maternal pride. [2]

By the time he was six, Hilaire was equally at home in French
and English. His mother did her best to retard a development
which she regarded as precocious, although his French relations
were not particularly impressed by it. But she took him to

[1] Printed in *The Young Hilaire Belloc* (1956).   [2] April 11, 1878.

exhibitions and museums. Remembering his grandfather, she hoped that he might become an artist and already, at the age of four or five, he would cover his letters with drawings. He also displayed a talent for topography. He could draw a map of La Celle St. Cloud with every street and even every house accurately marked upon it. He was evidently of a practical turn of mind and used the three outdoor taps in the garden to build lakes, canals and diminutive streams. This fascination with water would easily translate itself later into an abiding and no less practical love of the sea.

In the November of 1874, Madame Belloc decided to let the house in Great College Street and to live with her mother while she was in London. Mrs. Parkes was now seventy-eight and she craved the society of her grandchildren. At the same time Bessie engaged for them a more permanent and efficient nurse than any she had discovered or retained hitherto. Sarah Mew was a rigid Wesleyan who found it hard to understand how a woman so virtuous as Bessie Belloc could hold, and instil into the minds of her children, the doctrines of the Catholic Church. But she became deeply devoted to Hilaire, or 'Master Hilary', as she insisted on calling him. It was this grave Puritan who read *The Pilgrim's Progress* aloud to him when he was recovering from measles. It was never among his favourite books, and all he remembered of it in after life were 'some few parts . . . excellent in rhythm, but the rest dull, and all false in philosophy'.[1] As to Sarah's persistent anglicization of his Christian name, he seems to have been in two minds about this all through his boyhood and early youth. 'If my name were Hilary', he writes to Father Matthew Russell, S.J., Editor of the *Irish Rosary*, 'I should be delighted. It is a pretty name and many people whom I love have called me by it. But as the other, Hilaire, is my name, dubs me as belonging to the perfect nation, and is moreover an echo of my father's father . . . I sign myself and *am* that name.'[2] In practice he became Hilary to the English members of his family and to most, though not all, of his friends.

---

[1] Letter to Mrs. Raymond Asquith: May 22, 1925.
[2] October 8, 1888; quoted in the *Irish Monthly* from a lecture by the Editor, February 1910.

Sarah Mew replaced what remained of evangelical influences in Bessie Belloc. The Bible readings had ceased but she now resumed them. She taught the children Moody and Sankey hymns and read to them *Line upon Line* and *The Peep of Day*. But she did not neglect their lighter reading, and had copies of the *Boy's Own Paper* bound up for the nursery. If either Marie or Hilaire were disobedient, they were made to sit upon a chair until she released them. Considering the barbarous punishments then in vogue both in nursery and school-room, this penalty has an almost frivolous ring. But Mrs. Belloc-Lowndes assures us that it was extremely effective. When Hilaire's strong temperament erupted, his mother would call him 'old thunder' in reminiscence of the storm which had preceded his birth.

Soon after the move to Wimpole Street he was sent to Mrs. Case's preparatory school in Hampstead. But the summers continued to be spent at La Celle St. Cloud, and it was undoubtedly the French background with its natural beauties and historical associations which made the stronger impression on the boy's mind. He would remember the army manœuvres and the cavalry riding past at dawn; the coloured troops and the friendly welcome they received in the village; visits to Paris and the Jardin des Plantes; luncheons with his Aunt Lily in her old-fashioned apartment. His grandmother's friend, Mlle de Montgolfier, would have described to him how, as a girl, she had watched the storming of the Bastille. So the years from 1874 to 1877 slipped by, his mother devoted but still numb with grief; Sarah Mew, no less faithful and affectionate, but sterner and assuming more and more authority; his sister Marie; and his grandmother, Mrs. Parkes, 'seated by the fire of what was called the boudoir at 17, Wimpole Street', wearing 'a full black-silk dress, with a small lace collar, and lace frills coming down over her still pretty hands'.[1]

In the autumn of 1877 Mrs. Parkes died and Bessie was thrown more and more upon the companionship of Madame Swanton-Belloc. There was a perfect understanding between the two, but the mere presence of her mother-in-law nourished Bessie's

---

[1] *I, too, have lived in Arcadia* (1941).

memories of the past. On the material plane, also, she was beset
with troubles. A stockbroker friend of her mother's came to live
in Wimpole Street, and lost £20,000 of Bessie's money in rash
speculations. This plunged the family in a decisive poverty, the
extent of which—Hilaire always maintained—was never fully
revealed to him. So Bessie sold the lease of the house and early
in the following year rented 'Slindon Cottage', four miles from
Arundel, in a fold of the South Downs. This was the Dower
House of the Slindon Estate and a good deal more substantial
than it sounds. While it was being got ready, Hilaire and his
nurse were installed in country lodgings before moving in on
July 22. All the household gods, by which Bessie meant 'Dr.
Priestley, Burke, Fox, Jeremy Bentham', were still 'whirling in
a saturnalia about the rooms',[1] when Hilaire Belloc fell happily
asleep in the first of his Sussex homes.

[1] Letter quoted in *I, too, have lived in Arcadia* (1941).

CHAPTER II

CHAPTER II

GROWING PAINS

THE Bellocs' house in Slindon could be recognized by two blue jars on the gate-posts and it bore the date 1714. Hilaire took to it from the first and, unlike his sister, he fell in love with the surrounding country. There was something native and predestinate in the soil of Sussex, a sympathy in the *genius loci,* which he claimed instinctively. Even today, when the buses disgorge their huddled trippers on to the summit of Bury Hill, Slindon is reasonably undisturbed. It lies at the southern end of Fairmile Bottom, about half a mile from the main road, spreading out on a gentle slope which ends in a sharp spur clothed with beech trees—for this is chalk where the beech flourishes. Standing on the spur at the extremity of the village, you face the Nore Hill and the wooded downs which are here crossed by Stane Street. To the west is Eartham, and a mile further on in the same direction you see the hump of Halnacker Hill. Already the place-names spell out the poetry and the prose which were in the blood of Hilaire Belloc—the tramp of the legions and the slowly emerging pattern of the English past. And to the west, on the further side of Rewell Woods, are the beeches of Arundel Park, mounting a splendid guard over Amberley, Storrington and the Weald. Hilaire quickly found his legs as a walker. In 1881 he climbed the Wrekin with his mother, and not long afterwards he was walking the Downs from Petersfield to Beachy Head—a march of four or five days—sleeping by the rivers and only once descending into the Weald. Little though he guessed it, he was already at the heart of the Belloc country. It was much less celebrated then, and much less spoiled, than it is now.

Elizabeth Parkes Belloc

Louis Belloc

Hilaire Belloc's Birthplace at La Celle St. Cloud

Arundel Castle, governed with a wise charitable benignity by
Henry, fifteenth Duke of Norfolk, was 'the perfect symbol of
grandeur as the nineteenth century understood it'.[1] It also
enshrined all that was most prominent in the tradition of a
national minority. Against the social and political assertions of
this tradition Hilaire would later react with some vehemence.
('They wanted to make me a paid man of the Howards', he was
once heard to exclaim.) But the authority of Arundel would have
dominated all his early years. He would have seen it, as Turner
saw it, through a golden glow. As the years drew on towards the
Jubilee of 1887, the castle fringed by the river seemed an image of
impregnable aristocracy quietly resolving within its own domain
the tensions of religious difference.

Already, on the hill, the new church of St. Philip Neri, built by
the fifteenth Duke in 1870, gave notice of a Catholicism which was
active and public, without exactly being militant. Here Madame
Belloc would occasionally take the children to Mass or Benediction, although there was a Catholic church in Slindon. They
would also visit the Fitzalan tombs, and on rare visits to the castle
itself the portraits would make their impression; Philip Howard,
tense and intelligent over his ruff, the Gainsborough Dukes in
their sleek velvets, Lord Howard of Effingham, very foxy and
unflattered as Zucchero had painted him. At Arundel history, at
some of its most controversial cross-roads, hems you in, and it
was within the shadow of these associations that Madame Belloc
began to plan the future of her son.

The most pressing problem was education, and soon after the
move to Slindon she engaged a French tutor for the children.
Monsieur Leheribel, who arrived in the spring of 1879, was not a
success. Mrs. Belloc-Lowndes describes him as 'priggish, obstinate,
conceited and high-minded'.[2] He came with two large cases of
books and clearly expected to settle down in Slindon for life. He
accompanied the family to La Celle St. Cloud in the summer and
did not return. Meanwhile, Madame Belloc decided to let Slindon
Cottage and settle in lodgings in Hampstead, where Hilaire

---

[1] *Catholicism in England*, by David Mathew (1936).
[2] *The Young Hilaire Belloc* (1956).

could attend Mrs. Case's preparatory school, Heath Brow. Here he was described as 'clever, but rather idle'. But he was obviously well taught since he was able to take his place, shortly afterwards, with boys two or three years older than himself. He was given religious instruction at the same time, by Father Arden, O.P., from the Priory, Haverstock Hill.

If the family were to live in England, Hilaire must go to an English Public School. Hitherto, the Jesuit tradition, at once robust and ultramontane, had been predominant; Stonyhurst was as self-confident as Winchester. The Benedictine centres at Downside and Ampleforth had not yet made their mark. Some of the Catholic gentry sent their boys to Eton, where the social background was congenial to them, although their spiritual needs were rather casually cared for. But neither Eton nor Stonyhurst quite met the demands of the new generation which had grown up since the Oxford conversions. It was therefore appropriate that John Henry Newman, who had already founded the Oratory at Edgbaston as a centre from which he and his Community could make their distinctive contribution to Catholic life, should found a school beside it where the gentle spirituality of St. Philip Neri might be married to all that was best in the humanism of the Public Schools. The idea had begun to take shape in 1858 and the school was formally opened in the following year. Like most other English Public Schools of the period, the Oratory had a clerical headmaster and it had, of course, the firm doctrinal basis which Catholicism provides. But it was in no sense monastic. Laymen could teach on its staff (Gerard Manley Hopkins taught there for a short time) and although it only numbered between seventy and eighty boys, it would attempt to rival the scholarship—and, within limits, the sportsmanship—of its Protestant competitors.

What attracted Madame Belloc to the Oratory was the genius of Cardinal Newman. As a Victorian intellectual she recognized one of the most profound intelligences of her time. Like Bessie herself, Newman had remained incorrigibly English throughout the vicissitudes, painful and disappointing as they generally were, of his Catholic years. Now, with the election of Leo XIII in 1878, he was soon to enter into the undisputed glory of his last phase. Trinity had given him an Honorary Fellowship in 1877, and this was the sign that Oxford had made her peace with the lost leader. Two years later he was created a Cardinal Priest of the title of San Giorgio in Velabro, and this was the sign that Rome's lingering suspicions were at least temporarily allayed. Cardinal Newman was now at peace with everyone except Cardinal Manning.

It was this figure—sensitive, fragile, reflective and august—who presided, a little remotely, over the fortunes of the Oratory School. The boys would normally only meet him when he came down to the Latin class; or on Speech Day if they had won a prize, for it was always he who gave away the prizes; and again, when they left, to receive a signed copy of *The Dream of Gerontius*. On weekdays they heard Mass in the School Chapel, but on Sundays and greater Feasts they occupied a gallery over the Hagley Road entrance to the old church. This was a Byzantine oblong, quite fine in its way, over and around which the present church was built in 1903. Madame Belloc gives her impression of the place on a visit to Birmingham in 1884.

> We went last Sunday for the first time to the new Oratory which might have walked out of Rome, so like is it to some of the Roman churches. But it looks too new and has not a comfortable air of old prayers about it, and being very bare of ornament I do not like it so well as many modern Gothic churches and chapels. The music was wonderful. I seemed to hear a harp constantly. The sermon was a very gentle discourse on Holy Poverty and made me long to say to the young preacher 'Now do say the truth'. Everybody dislikes poverty and everyone is more or less ashamed of it.[1]

Here, at Pentecost or Corpus Christi or on All Saints' Day, the boys would see the Cardinal preside or pontificate in the Sanctuary. Apart from these sacred and ceremonial occasions, he remained for them a presence rather than a power; but schoolboys are not easily overawed, and the pen almost falters to record that they called him 'Jack'.

[1] Letter to Sara Atkinson: Dec. 28, 1884.

It was in September 1880 that Madame Belloc wrote to the
Cardinal, asking him to take her son under his care. She received
an encouraging reply and went down to see him. As a result of this
interview Belloc (as we shall now call him) entered the school at
the beginning of the autumn term. The total cost of his education
at the Oratory was borne by a wealthy relative of his mother
who lived in Edgbaston.

Father John Norris was Headmaster during the whole of
Belloc's schooldays. Belloc would quote him in after life as an
example of the 'good man', and the quality of his goodness is
conveyed by Mr. J. P. Boland who was Captain of the school
from the beginning of the summer term 1888 until the end of the
summer term 1889. He was therefore a close contemporary of
Belloc.

He was not a great scholar nor a great teacher, but he exerted
a fine moral influence over the whole school, and that I think
was his greatest quality. His rule was strict enough, but it was
the good-humoured strictness of a tolerant man who knew the
ways of boys and could make allowances. Some characteristics
stand out. He did not repel; he invited confidence. In those days
Father Richard Bellasis was the usual confessor, but Father John
also heard confessions in his own Headmaster's room (opposite
the school library). That was a good test of confidence. I
usually went to him; so did others. There was less of a queue for
him than there was for Father Richard in the school chapel.
Perhaps that weighed with us. Anyhow once you had got over
the hurdle of going to confession to your headmaster, he had
gained your full confidence for your school life. He wasn't
wanting in humour. Far from it, though it might take a teasing
turn. Once when I was Captain of the school, something
important had happened—perhaps it was a new honour conferred on Cardinal Newman—and, greatly daring, I knocked
on Father John's door and plunged right into a request for a
half-holiday that afternoon to celebrate the event. I wasn't
invited to sit down but stood with my back to the door, as if
to indicate that I wasn't going to leave the room till I got the
half-holiday. He played with me for a bit—upset to the whole

of an afternoon's work—the masters had got no notice. So I had to argue; and at last he gave way. I think he had enjoyed playing the fish.[1]

Father Norris was assisted by twelve Oratorian Fathers, and on the lay staff were Paul Eaglesim, who had once edited the *Cornhill* and was later to become a Father of the Oratory, and Mr. Tydd, a convert, who instilled into the Upper School a devotion to Trollope and Disraeli. There was also a nervous and difficult Cornishman called Tregenna, and a French master, Meunier, of the traditional type, rather easy to caricature.

Belloc was placed in the First Form under Mr. Allequist. At first he was acutely miserable. He found himself 'at ten years old and shrivelled for my age' among

a mass of boys some of whom were 17 or 18 and looked to me like enormous giants. It was fearfully rough and I suffered heavily. . . . They . . . gave us uneatable food and there was bad bullying and as for the attitude towards the outside world, it was that of the Old Catholic clique. Yet I fitted in at last.

In fact, there is no reason to suppose that the Oratory was any more unpleasant than other Public Schools of the period, and in some respects it may have been pleasanter, for there was no fagging. Also, Belloc was put in the choir and this meant 'a bean-feast on the Licky Hills which, at that age, were to me paradise'.[2] The boys rose at 6.30; heard Mass at 7; and worked till 9. Classes began again at 9.30 and continued till 1; except on half-holidays they were resumed at 2.30 and went on till 9 with only an hour's break for tea and recreation—a gruelling schedule. Father Denis Sheil remembers Belloc—from the distance of the Upper School—as 'a small, self-possessed, calm, detached lad'.[3] One day he was found examining a wall of the old church, and when asked what he was doing he explained that he was measuring its height by methods incomprehensible to the older boy. But there was 'no show off', Father Denis writes; only a quiet self-confidence. The

[1] Note to the Author: April 16, 1955.
[2] Letters to Mrs. Raymond Asquith: Oct. 10 and Nov. 22, 1929.
[3] Note to the Author: April 14, 1955.

boy already had that passion for accuracy, which he was afterwards so widely criticized for lacking. He could also be impetuous. Once during the school sports he refused to follow the prescribed routine of climbing through an empty barrel, hollow at both ends. He attempted to dive through, with disastrous results. He was not always, it seems, as placid as he appeared that day to Denis Sheil, for the School Alphabet of 1880 opened as follows:

A is for Allequist, heavy and fat,
B is for Belloc, a cheeky young brat.

The boys normally walked nearly two miles to Ravenshurst for their games, at which Belloc never excelled. Only those certified by the Matron as 'delicate' went by cab, although there was a horse omnibus running part of the way at intervals of half an hour. A swimming-bath was installed at the school in 1883, and Belloc was relieved to find a 'large part all in my depth'.[1]

One of his most distinguished contemporaries was Hugh Pope, later to be widely known as Father Hugh Pope of the Order of Preachers. They ran neck and neck up to the Sixth Form. One day, so the story runs, Cardinal Newman paid a rare and rather awe-inspiring visit to the Latin class. It appears that the conduct of the class had not been satisfactory, and the boys received the Cardinal with a good deal of apprehension. Newman called upon Pope to construe a passage from Virgil, but no sooner had the boy begun to worry out the meaning of the lines than the Cardinal burst into tears and left the room. He was easily moved by great music and great verse, and the associations of the passage —Trinity perhaps, the haunting irrecoverable past—were too much for him. Pope happened to be sitting next to Belloc, and asked him, not a little dismayed, what he had done to drive the Cardinal from the class-room. 'I don't know,' replied Belloc, 'but you've saved our bacon.'

On July 27, 1884, Bessie Belloc wrote to Sara Atkinson:

On Friday, 18, dear, my lad of 14 carried off the Second Norfolk Prize, the First English Prize of the whole school, the

---

[1] Letter to Madame Belloc: March 11, 1883.

Prize of his own form, was second in mathematical marks, and within the running zone, as it were, of two other prizes. The Duke of Norfolk stood by Cardinal Newman and gave him the books all the time.

In the following summer Belloc won the First Prize for Mathematics (this subject always had a fascination for him) and was given the first volume of *Chambers's Encyclopædia*. He was also awarded the First Norfolk Prize, for which he received the complete works of Newman—a handsome trophy indeed.

Madame Belloc had now left Slindon Cottage for another, and smaller, house in the same village, but the summer holidays, as usual, were spent at La Celle St. Cloud. There were days when Bessie was left alone with her pride and her persisting sorrow.

Today I am alone in the house; Hilary having bicycled off to his Aunt's, near Monthéry, and Mary having gone on a three days' visit to the nuns at Neuilly. I sit, I am quite alone in the house; my cook being in England, managing College Street, which I have let for the winter, and Nurse not returned from the Convent. Behind me are two fine oil-portraits, a soldier and a nun; the one is Captain Armand Swanton; the other our great-aunt Sœur St. Julienne, old Cork blood. Everything is as it was when my dear mother-in-law ruled the house.

I have made a discovery today, being so alone that I have had time to think of my appearance. It is that my once beautiful brown hair is nearly white.[1]

Belloc won the English Prize in 1886, but where he seems most to have distinguished himself was on the floor of the debating hall and on the stage. The debating prizes were awarded to Belloc and James Hope (afterwards Lord Rankeillour) 'both of whom', according to the Headmaster, had 'taken great interest in the debates and devoted considerable time and study to the getting up of the subjects on which discussion had taken place.' Belloc's success on the stage seems at first sight more surprising. He was never afterwards to take any but the slightest interest in the

---

[1] Letter to Sara Atkinson: Aug. 31, 1885.

theatre; he tried once or twice to write a play, but always confessed his incapacity; he was only a qualified admirer of Shakespeare; and, although he studied one or two Greek plays in class,
the Greek drama does not seem to have figured largely in his
private reading. Indeed the only dramatists he spoke of with
enthusiasm in later life were Molière and Racine; and his pleasure
in Racine was poetic—the mastery of metre and the occasional
great line:

> C'est Vénus toute entière à sa proie attachée.

Furthermore there was something about the theatre—a necessary
exhibitionism perhaps—which repelled him, and which he
suggested, rather absurdly, as one of the differences between
Christian and Jewish psychology. But already, in 1883, we find
him playing Pythias Ancilla in Plautus's *Pincerna*, bowdlerized
even down to its title (*Eunuchus*) by Cardinal Newman; for the
Cardinal had adapted several plays by Plautus and Terence, giving
them (how, one would like to know) a Christian slant. He had
usually directed these plays himself, but the task was now beyond
him and it was taken over by the Headmaster. Father Norris was
no actor. 'We boys could see that. But his job was to get us word-
perfect in our parts and trust to the natural genius of boy-actors
like Belloc and Arthur Pollen to make the play go. And sometimes it worked.'[1] In 1884 Belloc was Staphyla, an elderly slave-
woman in *Ambularia*; in 1885 he played Gita in *Phormio*; and in
1886 he excelled as Davus in the *Andria*. This play had not been
seen before at the Oratory, but Father Andrews and Mr. Bellasis,
both members of the Oratory School Society, had seen the
Westminster School performance in December of the previous
year. The critic of the *Birmingham Post* thought 'the parts of Davus
and Simo were the most perfectly filled, the acting herein of both
Belloc and Eaton being equal to anything yet seen on the Oratory
stage'.[2] Belloc's last part in the Latin plays was Gnatho the
Parasite in a second production of *Pincerna*; according to Hugh
Pope, he 'acted this to the life'. For a time his unbroken treble
voice would have fitted him for female parts, and a certain Gallic

---

[1] J. P. Boland: note to the author.   [2] July 21, 1886.

ease of gesture distinguished him from the ramrod reserve of the average English adolescent. The plays were given at the end of the summer term and acted in a long room with a crucifix at one end oddly presiding over Plautus, and the stage was built against the further wall. The parents were there in force, and Mr. Boland remembers Marie Belloc with her long plaits.

The habit of illustrating in ink or pencil whatever was in his mind or eye at the moment was by now well established. His text of *Antigone* is covered with sketches—some of them very lively—of dogs and cities, soldiers and schoolmasters. There are also snatches of translation:

> Not Zeus: not Justice of the gods below
> Who rule the ways of men proclaimed it.
> Methinks a mortal can scarce have the power
> T'outrun the strong unwritten laws of God
> Which are not of today, of yesterday.

The sketches in the margin did not mean that he was bored with Sophocles or Virgil or any other classical author that he was studying; they only meant that he was exasperated, at that moment, by the pedantry of the master in charge.

We are labouring through the satires of Horace [he writes to his friend Minna Hope, the elder sister of James Hope, some time in 1884]. I say 'labouring', and this shocks you for you like Horace; so do I; but you see one sits at the end of a bench with a large book and small text, and all the while our reverend preceptor, who is an Oxford man and believes in Sanskrit roots, and who moreover is horribly nervous and cries out in agony when anyone drops a pen or creaks the table, sits near and listens to someone droning out a translation far away. All this time you are supposed to be taking notes, and this goes on for one hour and a half, seasoned with occasional fits of bad temper on the part of the president and now and then a bit of wild excitement in the translation. This and bad eyes tend to depress the mind of youth.

Sophocles we are doing; Sophocles is divine; . . . we are doing the *Antigone*, and if it were not for the constant finding of æsthetical meanings on the part of the master, it would be seventh heaven. I wish you knew Greek. Now it is very rude to say that to one who knows very much more than I do; I only mean that if you knew Greek you would be able to understand *how* one likes it. It positively *sings* even in a dusty room at Birmingham.

You know they had what one called choruses stuck in here and there through the play; these choruses are songs, and these songs are simply glorious. They have always got metre, not quantity but real *metre* like a well played piece of music. They have a funny way of dropping off at the end like this: 'And it shall roll strong in all the ages, as when the blue wave strikes the tideworn rocks and cliff to beaten cliff resounds with sullen roar. Lo! Here is Oedipus coming to meet us on his two feet.'

He concludes by admitting that 'though I like Greek plays, you must know that the grammar is a caution'.[1]

One feels the throb of experience in this letter; nothing in it, neither its mature comment nor its occasional naïveté, is delivered at second-hand. Minna Hope was eight years older than Belloc, the eldest of the three Hope sisters, and he often used to stay with the family at Herons Ghyll, in East Sussex. Also living there were the Dowager Duchess of Norfolk with her daughters and grand-children. There were five Howard sisters, and one of them, Lady Philippa Stuart, remembered Belloc as 'a very rude and bad-tempered boy'. In spite of his friendship for James Hope, this was not a milieu in which he felt at home and in any case he was going through a difficult phase. He had evidently paid one of his visits during the Easter holidays of 1884, and there had been intimate talks between him and Minna, perhaps the gropings of calf-love. Her answer to the letter quoted above gives us some idea of its missing contents.

I am very glad that you say—'an ounce of pity is worth a pound of help', in spite of the misquotation, because I have often felt how useless mere words must be to you and how

---

[1] Undated and incomplete draft.

little practical good my sympathy in your difficulties. I do really feel for you more than I can well say for I know that at times it seems hardly possible to keep one's head above water so to speak. You must remember not to take anything I say to you as preaching, what I say to you would apply every bit as well to myself. Do you try, I wonder, mentally to put yourself into other people's shoes and judge things from their point of view? Would it not sometimes be the better way to try and understand and perhaps help them even though they may not understand you? One gains so much from shifting one's position and learning to look at life through other people's windows. I have found these sort of things helpful to me but I do not know how it may strike you. I am glad you have begun upon Horace, I thought you would enjoy him. I advise you to try the *Ars Poetica,* I believe it is considered to be his chief production for finish completeness etc. It is in an altogether different style to the Odes and has not their simplicity and gracefulness. Carmen XIII, *Ad Fontem Bandusium,* Lib. III is certain to please you—note the delicate characteristic swagger (?) of the last verse:

> Fies nobilium tu quoque fontium
> Me dicente cavis impositam ilicem
> Saxis, unde loquaces
> Lymphae desiliunt tuae.

Your studies ought to be a great help and yet I think if everything goes out of joint they partake of the twist . . . Do not be 'shut up on every possible occasion', are there none of your school-fellows who can make good companions if not helpers? Anyhow remember that I am always very glad to hear how you are getting on, write to me whenever you feel inclined. I do hope and believe that better, brighter days are in store for you. Do you remember the verse:

> Nam et si ambulavero in medio umbrae mortis, non
> timebo mala; quoniam tu mecum es? [1]

[1] May 6, 1884.

It is no mean tribute to Catholic education in the eighties that boys and girls should have bandied Horace and Sophocles with each other in their teens. Indeed Minna Hope may have been something of a blue-stocking, but Belloc always remembered her as the greatest friend of his youth, and he remembered her extreme beauty. He himself was no highbrow. *Tom Sawyer, Huckleberry Finn,* and Glaiser's *Travels in the Air* were already among his favourite books; he read *Masterman Ready* from a first edition; and Church's *Stories from Homer,* he tells us, 'illuminated my life from my tenth to my twentieth year'. 'Get Church's *Stories from Homer*', he afterwards advised the readers of *London Opinion.*

When you have read it (or as you read it) go to the British Museum and look closely at the archaic Greek sculptures—at the stiffness, and the astonishing realism of it, and at the fixed smile which some have thought cruel, others merely ritual. Catch the rhythm of this little book. Read twice or thrice the fainting of Andromache when she sees Hector dead; read, indeed, the whole most carefully. If you are lucky, there will happen to you what happened to me when I first read this book. The river you know best will be Scamander, and the war that dinned round Ilium will be fought in the road next your home, for believe me, when I was a boy the sacred cities stood upon the foothills of the Downs, and the sea-plain held the camp of the Greeks, and Arun was Xanthus, and the Wight a long way off, was Tenedos.[1]

He also enjoyed Dasent's *Tales from the Norse*—'a noble great book . . . a book of the solid England of the '50s which I love'.[2]

His reply to Minna Hope reveals him, now in his fourteenth year, as more lonely and more melancholy, more introspective even, than he may have appeared to the outside world.

I think you got very near what I was thinking of last holidays, only I don't think you quite know how it made me feel at the time. You see I got a little bit down in the mouth, because, you

[1] June, 1904.   [2] Letter to Mrs. Raymond Asquith: July 19, 1918.

see, when one is lonely one feels an increase of loneliness strongly . . .

You are the only person who ever helped me or whom I ever cared to be helped by, not that I shut myself up in a shell, but that I have been disappointed in a friend, not through his fault but my own. And so when your letter takes the form, I may have misunderstood it, of regret for a new state of things in a friendship, it makes me a little bit sad, for I don't see, selfish that I am, how I am going to get along alone after all. You see, it may have been my fault, but I took your friendship not as a help only, for one doesn't pick up one's friends but one's mind takes hold of them and won't let them go. I am afraid all this is great bosh to you and I only wish I could put it more clearly, I only mean that it would take me down a bit to think that our friendship was not as before.[1]

In the confusions and repetitions of this letter it is easy to detect both the pains of adolescence and the signature of a born correspondent. Generally speaking, however, we do not have the impression that Belloc's personality has as yet shown its promise. A good, quick mind; a sound scholarship; a solid, unobtrusive piety—these qualities have been inscribed on many school reports. There is no hint of genius, nor even of marked originality. He passed his London Matriculation, and in September 1886—a year before he left—he was made a prefect. Belloc, as we shall see, developed late. But he gained from the Oratory something better than even the best education; he gained at least two intimate friends. Charles Somers Cocks was his class-mate and close companion all the way up the school. At midsummer, 1886, he was top of Form Five with Belloc second and Hugh Pope fourth. At Christmas, James Hope went to the first place with Belloc third, Somers Cocks fourth and Pope fifth. They were a brilliant little band of rivals. James Hope became Deputy-Speaker of the House of Commons and Somers Cocks went into the Foreign Office. The other lifelong friend that Belloc made at the Oratory was Arthur Pollen, although they do not seem to

[1] Undated draft.

have been in the same class. We shall see them in close partnership soon after they both left school, for Pollen shared Belloc's literary tastes and also his historical curiosity.

Already, he was beginning to write—a little dreamily, after the way of literary adolescents. One long story, *Buzenval,* seems to have been composed while he was still at the Oratory, but it was not published until November 1888, when it appeared in *Merrie England.* It is a story of the war of 1870, romantic and diffuse, coloured by the associations of La Celle St. Cloud; but it showed the landscape artist that Belloc was afterwards to become.

> Up the Enghien valley to which he was turning came the mist, white and vague, rolling on towards St. Sen, and above the mist the sky in the east was darkened and night had come upon the hills; but towards the Couplans and the hills the light lingered yet, a rosy light that was caught by the slow waters of the Seine and thrown far off, so that the men in the fields beyond Hublay could see glimpses of shining water against the dark trees of the wood, a light that gleamed reddest where the trees of the forest stood up against it in the west; a gold that was changing into grey twilight on the stretching plain, and that had died already in the blue above, where the great stars were coming out most faintly and timidly, the vanguard of the thousands shining to see if the day had died and left the darkness to them.

It would be misleading to suggest that Belloc felt for the Oratory the *pietas* he was later to show for Balliol. To begin with, his respect for Cardinal Newman—for his intelligence and royal gift of expression—somehow fell short of adulation. He used to say that 'Newman was a don'; and although in 1888 he did not yet realize the enormity of dons, he may have been irked by something a little sequestered in Newman's personality. Only in one particular did he consciously imitate the Cardinal; he tried to reproduce the graceful slant of his handwriting. In this attempt he was not successful. He always claimed that he had never been taught to hold a pen properly, and that was why his handwriting was illegible, unless he laboriously separated the letters. But the legend of Belloc's illegibility, like most legends, has been considerably embroidered. His spelling, however, was always erratic. He insisted to the end of his life that 'appalling' had only one 'p'; he would frequently transpose his 'i's' and his 'e's'; 'distil' would appear with two 'l's' and he would begin 'invigorate' with an 'e'. He would probably have found it as difficult to imitate Newman's script as to imitate Newman's mind; and it was not to early impressions of Newman—it was to meetings with Manning soon after he left the Oratory—that he would more often refer in after life.

It is not easy to say how much the simple and virile piety of Hilaire Belloc owed to the Oratorian formation. He was not given to spiritual reading, or to the cultivation of special influences. He learnt the Catechism; acquired the habit of the Rosary; and frequented the Sacraments like anybody else. He made his First Communion on Maundy Thursday, 1882, and he wrote to his mother afterwards to say what a difference this had made to him. He also enjoyed the occasional Retreats, noting down in a little book the main points of the discourses. He took his religion happily, though not always easily, for granted, as he had taken it at his mother's knee. He would generally take it so. In the degree to which the atmosphere of the school reflected the circles of privilege in English Catholic society, he found it rather stuffy; and he welcomed the holidays at La Celle St. Cloud for the glimpse they gave him of grander causes and more exciting conflicts. Here more militant influences would make themselves felt, and memories already deeper than any which disturbed the average schoolboy; the shame and anger of the defeat; the despoiled home; the family graves just opposite the entrance to the cimetière (Madame Swanton-Belloc had died in 1881); and the growing pains of the Republic. Boulanger threw out his theatrical challenge in 1885, and the naïf integrity of Déroulède, with his Ligue des Patriotes, kept alive the hope of an avenging war.

The Déroulèdes lived at Croissy, not far from La Celle St. Cloud, and were on friendly terms with the Bellocs. René Millet, who did not believe in the possibility or the profit of a second Franco-Prussian War, was nervous lest this magnanimous but

monomaniac Frenchman should gain an ascendancy over the
mind of his younger cousin. His fears were justified, for Belloc
later enrolled in the *Ligue des Patriotes*. He was now fifteen, with
his eyes and ears wide open. But they were open to other things
besides politics. One day, as he was sketching on the *quais*, an old
man looked over his shoulder and remarked: 'Your work has
great interest to me, for I see in it a trick of perspective I have
never come across in anyone else, except my old teacher.'
'And what', asked Belloc, 'was his name?' 'His name was
Hilaire Belloc.' 'And that is my name too,' the boy replied. 'He
was my grandfather.'

In comparison, therefore, with his school-fellows, Belloc was
already someone with a double life. He was feeling his feet on
both sides of the Channel, standing sturdily, though still uneasily,
astride. At the Oratory, he wrote many years later:

> They taught me to fear none but God and speak the truth
> and be in everything an English Gentleman. But it never took.
> I was and am afraid of any reasonably good woman and of the
> sea—let alone dentists.[1]

But he had not forgotten one incalculable debt; the Oratory
had taught him the Classics. At Oxford, and beyond Oxford, he
would be plunged in history; but he never forgot the bitter-sweet
brevity of Catullus, the tenderness of Virgil, and the total humanity of Homer. If he sat up all night on a tramp-steamer, the
Odyssey was in his pocket; if he wrote to a friend from the edge of
the Sahara, his letter was dotted with Greek quotations. These
gave him more than a standard of literary taste, though that was
valuable enough; they gave him a memory, active and continuously creative, of the Pagan past.

> As for the Classics *all* my generation ought to thank God
> that they were well whipped into them—for Latin and Greek
> are *tasks* for boys and it is as tasks and discipline that they take
> root. Then in later life they bear a glorious fruit.[2]

---

[1] Letter to Mrs. Raymond Asquith: March 16, 1925.
[2] Letter to Mrs. Reginald Balfour: Jan. 20, 1932.

Hilaire Belloc at the Oratory School

Hilaire Belloc aged 2 years

Hilaire Belloc with Basil Blackwood during his Oxford years

Hilaire Belloc aged about 17

CHAPTER III

EXPERIMENTS AND IMPRESSIONS

I

HILAIRE BELLOC left the Oratory at the end of the summer term, 1887, with a copy of *The Imitation of Christ*, given him by Father John Norris, but without any clear idea of what he was going to do next. He was barely seventeen and he might have been expected to remain at school for a further year, to enjoy the privileges and exert the responsibilities of the Sixth Form. But his restlessness probably showed itself at home, and Madame Belloc remembered that he was a French citizen. In which country, his father's or his mother's, was he to make his career? This question had still to be decided. On the one hand were England and Sussex, with their farming attachments; on the other was France, and the swarms of French relatives, and the more dramatic possibilities of French public life.

There are not many clues as to what was really going on in the boy's mind. But here is one given many years later in a letter to Lady Juliet Duff.

When one is quite young then is the time to learn the world. One never learns it later. I have always been glad that I left school at 17, learnt to plow, reap and sow, shot a lot, went off to America from east to west, walked all over California and Colorado, went into the French Artillery and got into Balliol all before I was 22. Since then I have done nothing and those are the only years in which one lives; for one has no duties and no accursèd conscience.[1]

[1] Jan. 18, 1919.

And here is another, in a letter to Mrs. Asquith:

> It has made a great difference to my life that I went out to sea
> quite young and sailed alone almost before I was allowed to
> do anything in the way of other travel alone.[1]

Chichester harbour was not far from Slindon and it was a man
from Slindon who had first taught him to sail. Nearer home, the
Arun was navigable for the first few miles of its course; and the
Channel, which he had crossed so often in a steamer, invited more
intimate and more hazardous exploration. This may well have
given him the idea of joining the French Navy. His guardian, his
French relations and his late headmaster were all strongly opposed
to it. But the boy persisted, the decision of his character already
prompt to make itself felt; and at last, armed with testimonials
from Cardinal Newman and Father Norris, he entered the
Collège Stanislas, in Paris, in the October of 1887.

The Collège Stanislas was then run by the Marist fathers. It had
counted many illustrious men among its pupils; Gratry and
Lacordaire in the earlier part of the century and, more recently,
Edmond Rostand and Anatole France. Ferdinand Brunetière and
Paul Bourget were on the board of Trustees, and Paul Desjardins,
founder of the *décades* at Pontigny, was for many years teacher of
the fifth form. Although it was a Catholic school, Protestants as
well as Catholics attended it. A very high standard of academic
attainment was expected, and if a boy failed to reach it he was
dismissed. The Abbé Ernest Dimnet, who taught there after the
Marists had been banished by the anti-clerical government of
Combes, gives a vivid picture of the life and traditions of the place.

> The Marists had invented a system, still maintained, whereby
> every mark given in class was converted into 'points' which
> really were the college currency. Studious boys were affluent,
> lazy ones were penurious. With a given number of points you
> could buy your Sunday outing, a monthly play-day or a day or
> two extra vacation at Christmas or Easter. So was virtue
> rewarded while remissness looked on.[2]

---

[1] Sept. 13, 1919.   [2] *My New World* (1938).

There were about eighty members of the Faculty, all laymen with the exception of four or five priests. The professors were lent to the College, at the suggestion of the Headmaster, by the Minister of Education. There were fifteen hundred students and three or four hundred of these were being prepared for the Ecole Polytechnique, the military academy of St. Cyr, or the Naval College. The chief emphasis was laid on literature and mathematics, and in both these subjects the young Belloc was proficient. The boys, Dimnet tells us,

> were used to the ideal of men who, being writers, habitually bore in mind literary perfection. When an essay of theirs got 58 or 60 they were overjoyed at the exceptional piece of luck, but they were not led to imagine that their achievement could not be bettered—as they would have been in schools where it rains 95's so that the very ordinary best of a boy comes to be regarded by him as perfection.[1]

The College was situated, as it still is, in the Rue Notre-Dame des Champs, just at the point where it bisects the Boulevard Raspail. Behind the College, and forming part of its buildings, was the Pavillon Belgiojoso, an elegant 'folly' originally built as a present for Madame du Barry, where some of the professors had their quarters. A statue of the Chevalier Bayard, encircled by thin chestnut trees, reinforced the motto of the school—'*Français sans peur, Chrétien sans reproche*'—and presided over the playground. At the entrance to the chapel, hideous and sombre and unswept, hung the photographs and relics of a Marist father who had been killed in the Commune.

Belloc was immediately placed in the Naval class, with about twenty other boys. But he was not happy at the College. Although it was reputed for its freedom as well as for its thoroughness, this was not freedom as Belloc understood the sacred word. The boys were encouraged, according to the prospectus, to regard the Christian faith as something '*qui grandit la soumission*', and to regard their schoolmaster as the '*délégué de Dieu*'. This was more than Belloc could stomach. Only two minutes away were the

[1] *Ibid.*

Luxembourg Gardens, but he was only allowed to wander there
if accompanied by an escort approved by his parents or guardian.
After lunching at eleven-thirty off the bare, marble-topped tables
of the Refectory, he would long to escape into the trim alleys of
the chestnuts, now touched with autumn, for this was the moment
of the year when the gardens most powerfully distil their magic.
And only a short walk away, beyond the *Quartier Latin*, were the
quais where the boy loved to sketch or browse among the book-
stalls; here were the Sainte Chapelle, and the Louvre, and the historical heart of the city. But only on Sundays and holidays could his
guardian fetch him for a few hours' respite in an apartment on the
Ile St. Louis. The uniform worn by the Stanislas boys only emphasized their servitude. The College may have been liberal according
to its lights, but other influences were hovering in that incomparable air—the realism of Villon, the exuberance of Rabelais, the
scepticism of Voltaire, the revolt of Rousseau, and the hesitant
introspections of Montaigne. These were the things, as Belloc afterwards wrote, which 'make Paris Athenian'.[1] They beckoned him
but he could not answer their call. And so he turned up one day at
Great College Street, to the consternation of his mother and sister,
still wearing his cadet's uniform, having abandoned his Naval
examination, and resolved to have done with school for ever. He
had remained at the Collège Stanislas for little more than a term.

2

If it was not to be the sea, then it should be the land. The young
Belloc was now sent to Manor Farm at Bury, just at the foot of the
Downs in the Arundel gap, to learn how to be a land agent. He rose at
six and went to bed at nine. He bought a gun and case for only four
pounds, and had all the riding that he wanted. He was, he tells us,

> a fairly good shot by nature, but the only thing human I ever
> shot was a farmer called Halkett. It was his fault, he got out of
> place in a line on the edge of the wood, and came out suddenly
> from cover without warning. He leapt high into the air, but

[1] *Avril* (1904).

suffered no real damage except to his breeches. It stung him up, no doubt, but that did him good.[1]

This was in 1888; for the rest, Belloc did not show much aptitude for farming, although the direct experience of the soil entered deeply into his thought and feeling. He only longed, like any other literary adolescent, for the moment at the end of a long day when he could be alone with Shakespeare, and especially with Milton, for of English poets Milton was already his favourite. In later life he would point out the field where he had sat reading him. He was still writing poetry himself, and he sent his verses to Father Matthew Russell, S.J.(brother to Lord Russell of Killowen), who was then editing the *Irish Monthly* from Dublin. He had never met Father Russell, but he assures him that correspondence with an '*ami inconnu*' has certain advantages.

> When two spirits intercommunicate they have a vast pull on men in having no rough nails nor small pig's eyes, no characteristic warts, no family squints, no selfish unloveliness of speech, no shameful blushings, and above all no tailor.[2]

Father Russell printed one of his sonnets, and Belloc confessed that in the same post he had sent other poems to other editors and that he was quite sure they would 'all turn up refused'. The first of these was addressed to Paul Déroulède. 'Now Paul Déroulède's singing', he explains, 'is not Titanic in method but it is eminently so in soul and idea, and he is the singer of the *Marseillaise*. He is what our God told us to be—like a little child neither ashamed of enthusiasm nor of love, and therefore I admit him.'[3] Evidently the poems were returned, as he expected, and he now sent them to the more indulgent editor in Ireland. In the same letter he explains his reasons for trying to get into print.

> To tell you the truth my only motive in thus trying to appear at an age when one's work, if healthy, must be imperfect, was to begin to earn a little. When one has been brought up in

[1] Letter to Lady Phipps: Nov. 6, 1933.   [2] Oct. 28, 1888.
[3] Letter to Father Matthew Russell: 1888.

the way of knowing how many pence make a shilling (especially when two women have to live on the common fund) one desires at least the beginnings of gain. So that I now ask if you would read in the regular way a prose story of mine; I can quite understand how valueless Rhythm and English are on the market. But something in the way of a story sells better.

The story in question was intended for serialization. Father Russell replied with cautious encouragement.

> Everything of yours has something in it; and, please God, you will cultivate his gifts humbly and steadily. By the way, I hate all reference to the Gods; I think poets should always speak the truth . . . I must read William Yeats' poems; he is a friend of mine. In a few years we shall have a similar book from you—but do not let it be too soon.[1]

The farming experiment lasted only a few months. Belloc took a great dislike to the farmer and his wife, and expressed his feelings rather strongly in a letter to a friend in Paris. The letter was opened by the farmer who reaped the proper reward of his impertinence when he read it in translation. We may safely assume that it was spiced by illustrations as well as by satire and Belloc was sent packing. Once again he turned up unexpectedly at his mother's house, and in the August of 1888 we have record of him rowing on an Irish river. No doubt he took the opportunity of making the personal acquaintance of Father Russell. Later, he went to Paris and we find him poring over the great series of maps which hung in the Ministry of Agriculture, tracing the progress of the phylloxera. In the autumn he settled in lodgings in Bloomsbury and all through the winter of 1888–9 he was working in an architect's office. He next turned to journalism. His sister Marie was now working for W. T. Stead, editor of the *Pall Mall Gazette*, and Stead sent him down to Edgbaston to review the Oratory play. But a further letter to Father Russell, dated February 1889, shows him independent and ill-at-ease in the literary circus. He guessed,

[1] Jan. 30, 1889.

already, that he was not made to perform in it. His natural piety and his revolutionary ardour, kindled by his Boulangist acquaintances of the *Ligue des Patriotes* and by the ferment of political passion to which the French eternally prostitute their logic, were attempting to come to terms in a nature which was searching for its true direction. This was the year in which all Republicans were preparing to celebrate the centenary of the Revolution; the year of the Eiffel Tower; the year also of the *Ralliement,* when Cardinal Lavigerie invited his naval hosts to toast the Republic in the harbour of Algiers. In later years Belloc became a natural and happy Londoner, craving its society and its conflicts, but he had not yet discovered his genius for friendship and we have the impression of a lonely, gawky lad, too beset with his own difficulties to get on at all easily with other people. 'Don't you ever have a bath, Belloc?' the boys at Slindon used to call after him. 'Not at this time of the year', came the instant repartee, 'but I sometimes wash my feet in vinegar.'

He had written to Father Russell as follows, the page embellished with the drawing of a devil with a pitchfork:

I have for the last week been visiting various people of importance with a view to choosing a profession. I want to be earning soon; I believe that my mathematics and my successful pass at London will help me in engineering—but I never live except when I am on the water.

As to my writing . . . if you ask why I write as I do, I will tell you this much, that in the circle of newspapers, of criticism, of perfectly turned verses, of madly hunted ideas, I am all at sea. I would have it that no man should write who was not a zealot for something, and *when* I desire, I desire the hills and the sea, I desire the faces of men and women, not some unjust imitation, and I desire above all that free and happy forbearance and that perfection of Charity which this country is absolutely unable to give. When I first met these Rhymsters and Paragraphists and these would-be thinkers of the Reviews, I admired and feared them because they were quite strange to me, but having since then met them in the flesh, and having since then been taught the . . .

value of mental clear-sightedness, I hate and despise them. More than this, having seen something of London poverty near the Docks just lately, I cannot bear the sound of these geese who cackle in the West. Surely the spirit of '93 is not yet dead, but tell me, has it got a market? For I find that what has no market is worse than useless.

Politics were now disputing with literature for his zeal. He was undeterred, and in no way despondent, if his poetry remained unpublished. If ever he became an Editor, he wrote to Father Russell on Holy Saturday, 1889,

I shall accept everything that touches me—irrespective of merit and shall refuse all well-known names. There is in Paris a club called 'La Décadence' into which no one can be admitted whose work has not been refused three times, and they turn out such clever pictures and such delightful epigrams and they make dainty and delightful terra-cotta busts that their ancient enemies gnash their teeth with rage. Only, well understand, the things that have been rejected must be approved good by the Committee of the Club. They are all young men and Boulangists without exception.

Yesterday, Good Friday, London was yellow with primroses as though her mourning colour was yellow like the Chinese. One of the most amusing institutions on God's earth is this Primrose League. Sometimes in France one is at a loss to pin down that particular class with doing all the evil . . . but in England it is simple enough. This class waits until there comes round the great anniversary of the 'Come to me all you who are weary', and then it takes the opportunity to sport the flower and to say 'Come by all means—and I will teach you the great truths of 20 per cent. You shall be initiated in the art of stealing without risk, or thieving made easy.' And up they come, poor and rich and aristocrats and Old Names and fat city men dull-eyed with over feeding, they come and worship Law and Order.

I know where those primroses grow, in happy shades of trees in the downs, cool and unknown, in the rich bottom meadows

or in among the stunted thorn bushes, close to the rabbit
warrens in the very centre of the hills. And very often I have
gone to these places just at this time of the year and delighted
and rejoiced and looked up to Heaven, and have seen a Notice
Board 'Trespassers will be prosecuted with the utmost rigour
of the LAW . . . By Order'. Hence it is that I am a Red-Republi-
can and as you doubtless know the Red-Republicans are never
happy till they get it—but when they get it they and I believe
the whole round world will be as happy as in the old times
before ever the Jew came to the land.

The anti-Semitic germ which he had caught from French
nationalism (the Collège Stanislas with its scions of the great
military families must have been full of it) has already bitten deep,
and the letter reveals a temper little suited to the rhythm of English
politics. One feels the itch for the *levée en masse*, the Tricolor and
the barricades. The boy has travelled a long way from Edgbaston
and the tranquil holidays at Slindon or Herons Ghyll. His impatient, emotional radicalism is even more marked in the letter
that follows, written to the same correspondent on June 20.
Belloc had now moved from Bloomsbury to Brompton Square,
where he was lodging with Charles Somers Cocks.

How I long for the Great War! It will sweep Europe like a
broom, it will make Kings jump like coffee beans on the roaster,
Napoleon's Republicans and Cossacks are abroad and not all
the monarchs together can outweigh them.

For my part I keep on writing bellicose rhymes and Shrieks
of Liberty. I will enclose in this letter a whole batch of fourteen-
line compositions and I beg you choose one from amongst
them. . . .

There is going to be a monster meeting in Hyde Park to
protest against the *prospective* imprisonment of Conybeare. It
is a hot day and verily it will be a *demos* demon; a crowd on a
hot day is always more radical, more enthusiastic and more
thoroughly and more offensively powerful than on a cold one.
If they march on Brompton Square I shall hang out the Red
Flag and the Tricolor.

Father Russell must have smiled at this—or did he smile? It makes strange reading after the middle of the twentieth century. But then, in the glow of the first Jubilee, after nearly a hundred years of peace, a few people in this privileged corner of Europe were beginning to hanker after violence. They little knew what they were asking for. The novels of Charles Kingsley and even, a little later, of G. K. Chesterton showed how men, personally humane, seemed to insist on paper, if not in politics, that the blood should flow. One remembers Stevenson's outcry, 'Are we never to shed blood again?' No two men could have been more different, in character and ambition, than Hilaire Belloc and Paul Valéry. Yet in May 1891, only two years later than the letter quoted above, we find Valéry writing as follows to André Gide:

> Je désire presque une guerre monstrueuse où fuir parmi le choc d'une Europe folle at rouge, où perdre le respect de toute écriture et de tout rêve dans des visions réelles, trépignements funèbres de sabots clapotants et déchirements de fusillades, et n'en revenir! [1]

If Belloc talked like this to his mother, she may have wondered what George Eliot would have thought of it. Bessie Parkes had been a radical in her day, but the English progressives who gathered round Samuel Rogers' breakfast table came flaunting the olive-branch and not the sword. It is perhaps worth remarking that Belloc afterwards referred to this summer of '89 as a time when he was never in bed before 4 a.m. He may have been reading or he may have been talking, but the admission explains—and extenuates—a good deal.

3

In *The Cruise of the 'Nona'* Belloc tells us that during his early days in London he was often received by Cardinal Manning, who was now approaching the term of his long reign at Westminster. The Cardinal's positive character and practical ability, his outspoken sympathy for the poor, his encouragement of Christian demo-

---

[1] *Correspondance*, 1890–1942: André Gide-Paul Valéry (1955).

cracy, his crusade for social as well as political regeneration, met and influenced a mind stirred by radical theories of government. Several years before he became a Catholic, Manning had written in his Diary (1839):

The course of Europe seems to be towards a development of national life and action by calling up into political power larger numbers of the people.

This was Belloc's theory of democracy until he came to the despairing conclusion that it could only be practised successfully in small communities. In 1889 he had no such doubts, and neither had the Cardinal. Manning had inspired the Encyclical *Rerum Novarum* and prevented Henry George's advocacy of the Single Tax, *Progress and Poverty*, from being placed on the Index. The storms of the Vatican Council and its aftermath were over. Newman was too old to be dangerous and Acton had submitted, not without difficulty, to the decrees he had striven to prevent. Manning had defied the Jesuits, welcomed the Irish secular clergy into his arch-diocese, and forbidden the Catholic well-to-do to send their sons to Oxford or Cambridge. But he was happier in political than in intellectual debate. His firm, unquesting mind distrusted specula-tion, and it was when the principles of Trade Unionism rather than the limits of toleration were at stake that he rose to the height of his authority.

For all his asceticism, and for all his fear of the imaginative life, Manning knew the world. He was in close *rapport* with Cardinal Gibbons and Archbishop Ireland, who brought him news of the Church in the United States—its precarious hold over the multi-tudes of immigrants, its difficult poise between capital and labour, its poverty and its promise. If he spoke of these things to Belloc, they must have sounded a tocsin to the boy's adventurous spirit. How challenging and turbulent they sounded! How remote from the stuffy, conventional round of the English Catholic families, so quiet and tenacious in their country-houses, so well-inten-tioned and so unaware! One thing he never forgot that Manning said to him, and it was a thing that went beyond politics: 'All human conflict is ultimately theological.'

Manning's sagacity was now to be put to a searching practical test, for in the August of 1889 the London dockers revolted against the conditions of their work, and struck to obtain an extra penny to their wages of fivepence an hour. The strikers were led by Ben Tillett and John Burns, both friends of the Cardinal. Manning drove in his brougham to the Mansion House and pleaded with the Directors. For three weeks he kept the negotiations afloat and finally obtained for the men the bare justice they asked for. The Directors agreed to consider their demands 'if they came through Cardinal Manning', and on September 14 'the Cardinal's Peace' was signed. The story is told in vivid detail by Sir Shane Leslie,[1] who makes clear the eminent place which Manning had come to occupy in the public mind. His intervention was popular not only because it had secured justice, but because it had prevented disorder.

These were stormy days in London, and Belloc thumped his tub whenever he could find two or three people to listen to him. For a brief interval of crisis he was singed by the resentment of the poor. Never again, and never certainly when he was in Parliament, would he so feel the quick throb of creative conflict. Never again would the Catholic Church appear so decisively or so dramatically where Belloc then believed it should be—at the side of the despairing and the dispossessed. London, in those weeks, must have worn the look of Paris when trouble is brewing. But did Belloc realize the difference in justice and good sense between the rhetoric of Déroulède and the posturing of Boulanger, and the deep emotional murmur of primitive indignation which underlay the dockers' revolt? Looking back on it from a somewhat disgruntled maturity he wrote:

Well do I remember the fevers of that struggle! I was but nineteen years of age; it was my delight to follow the intense passions of the time; and those passions were real. It was before the socialist creed had been captured for the sham battle at Westminster. The leaders *did* desire, and *did* think they could achieve an England in which the poor should be poor no

[1] *Henry Edward Manning* (1921).

longer, and in which there should be sustenance and happiness for all. They *did* still believe the amazing proposition that what they called 'the community'—that is, in practice, the politicians —could own all we have and handle it with a superhuman justice. Great God! They believed it . . .

I have seen in those days a young man, the heir to a great fortune (later a minister of sorts) standing under the flaring naphtha lamps of a muddy London evening, calling out the new gospel and the promised land. I remember the eager, stupid, upturned faces of the men and women, who had come there from bestial depths of the slums to hear him; to go back to those depths, and there to remain . . . I remember the great mobs that followed John Burns, and how I myself would go miles through the East End to hear him; and I remember that great whirlpool of men in Trafalgar Square on the most critical day when he and others accepted imprisonment. There is nothing now for which men would act so; no one now has a creed; therefore, I call that time of my youth a better time.[1]

4

Belloc had now resumed contact with an Oratory friend—Arthur Hungerford Pollen. Pollen was four years his senior, and having come down from Oxford, was reading for the Bar. The two young men were drawn together by a common interest in literature, politics and history. They decided to found a monthly review, called the *Paternoster,* and since the first number of this appeared in 1889 the idea must have been under discussion between them for some time. The paper was financed by James Hope and a number of other friends, and Belloc and Pollen were announced as Joint-Editors. Their aims were as follows:

> To present to the public a monthly magazine, which maga-zine shall take care never to help those who are at war with the common ideas of right and wrong.
> To present to the public just about as good a sixpenny worth as can be had in the Kingdom.

[1] *The Cruise of the 'Nona'* (1925).

To make this little bundle of information clear and worth
the reading by the introduction of slight sketches illustrating
the author's thoughts.

To make it more than a series of articles by introducing a
number of abstracts with regard to the events of the month,
the books, the politics, the whole movement.

There are now a certain number of men who for mere effect
have dared to introduce into literature and into art views which
make men morbid, tired, unhappy. Against these the *Paternoster*
declares open war.

A time was, quite a little time ago, when men refused these
views as unhealthy and almost immoral. The *Paternoster* looks
back to it; but, above all, looks forward to the future time when
these views shall be regarded not as unhealthy ones to be
avoided by the individual, but as insane ones, intolerable to all.

There is nothing grotesque in the admission of matter
according to its interest and value; there is something absurd in
the admission of matter according to the mere name of its
author—a name depending often on a chance title rather than
on any tried valuable work.

OUR MANIFESTO

Fortes fortuna adjuvat

There are, we take it, in the modern Magazine literature,
two facts apparent:

(1) The absolute lack of any ethical criterion whatsoever.

(2) The existence of a small circle of names, whose sufficiency
however justly asserted, must necessarily tend to exclude new-
comers and hence to continually narrow its own limits.

The paper had its offices at 11 Clements Inn, and sixty pounds'
worth of advertisements were soon subscribed. The first issue
was ushered in by a photograph of Cardinal Newman taken
by the Reverend Anthony Pollen of the Birmingham Oratory.
This was the last photograph to be taken of the Cardinal in his
lifetime; he died on August 11, 1890. The contents of the
number were solid, but not uninteresting. There was an article on

India, a little pompous and pro-consular, by the Marquess of Ripon, an ex-Viceroy of India and convert to Catholicism; articles on the potato blight and the Primrose League (which G. Lane Fox treated with proper respect); and an interesting account by Kegan Paul of his last visit to Henry Parry Liddon. Belloc and Pollen were drawing upon their connections to make their paper readable, and Belloc's acquaintance with the Carlisle Howards seems to have dated from this time. Paul Déroulède had promised them an article, but this never seems to have reached them. The second number had a frontispiece of Thomas Carlyle by the Earl of Carlisle, who was an accomplished draughtsman; a reminiscence of the philosopher-historian by E. A. Venturi; and a poem, *The Riddle for Men* (the *Paternoster* would be manly or it would be nothing) by George Meredith. Meredith was a close friend of Wilfrid and Alice Meynell, and was thus in contact with the small group of literary Catholics in London who were united in sympathy for the social policies of Cardinal Manning. There was also, in the same number, an article by Barthélemy St. Hilaire.

The London Press had been sceptical of the Review when it was launched, but the comments on the first number were generally approving. The *St. James's Gazette* remarked that the editors had clearly aimed at actuality, and that in this they had succeeded well. Only the prospectus was criticized as 'too high-flown'. The effect of the paper on a sympathetic outsider, and also its initial circulation, can be judged by the following letter from Gertrude Bell to Arthur Pollen.

I saw it (the *Paternoster*) yesterday on a bookstall at Windermere and its attractive appearance caught my attention even before I had realised that it was *the* Review. Need I add that I fell upon it at once and found that its inner pages did not belie the promise of its outer? . . . I am glad that you have taken up such an impartial attitude; a truculent editor . . . lowers himself to the level of the *Pall Mall!* Will you allow me to give you a very impertinent and uncalled for counsel? . . . You must not be jocular: it smacks of youth and the University which, in these days, when we are sick of early promise, is unpardonable. An Editor should be judicial—I do not want to hurry you unkindly into the sixth age, nor to imply that the *Paternoster* should aim at [the] ponderousness of the *Spectator*; that would ill beseem its years: but there is a certain lightness of hand which never shows itself in jests, or in anything approaching slang. Even colloquialisms are better avoided, when you are walking on such narrow and dangerous paths. They lead, alas! too soon to a literary vulgarity which shocks the more refined, while it is not broad enough to catch the more uncivilised of your readers. And when the first freshness has passed from the pen of the writer, he falls deep into the slough of mediocrity from which there is no return.

The man at the bookstall said 'I like the look of this paper. I am sure it will sell. I am very pleased with it myself.'[1]

In the December issue appeared the first signed contribution by Belloc himself. This was a short story called *Bona Mors*. A poor woman comes to Rheims on Christmas Eve to find her father, who was the old door-keeper of the Cathedral, and dies beside the Crib. The tale is immature and sentimental, but there is evidence of a personal style. The *ego* awkwardly intrudes:

> It is a high town, a large town, a clean town, a wealthy town, yes! the best town in the world! It has merchants who live in great houses well built and curiously ornamented, and many priests serve in its many churches, and good barracks (where are soldiers, fierce men ready for war) and wine-growers who grow grapes all the way from Epernay to Ste. Germaine, and gold-beaters, and carpenters and men that work in iron, and many other kinds of artificers, and also it has an Archbishop, a holy man full of the love of the poor and so great a Republican that you may not breathe a word against the State in his presence—he lives in a great palace but has little wealth.

Belloc must also have had a hand in the editorial comment on the Parnell crisis.

[1] Sept. 28, 1890.

The papers which have shown a little gentlemanly feeling, a little sense of moderation, are the Conservative papers. They alone of the Press seem to have understood how vile a Pecksniff is. How worse than vile a cynical Pecksniff. Mr. Parnell's future attitude is undecided. His interest lies in one direction only—that of remaining at the head of his party, in spite of all that outsiders, obviously interested, may advise, and in spite of his wrong. If he stays at the head of his party he will undoubtedly have aggravated his crime, if he leaves it he has undoubtedly yielded not to conscience but to threats.

The first number of 1890 had an article by Manning, *Darkest England,* in which the Cardinal warmly commended the humanitarian work of the Salvation Army, and a contribution by W. T. Stead in which he discussed the North Kilkenny election. Here Parnell's nominee had been defeated by 1,200 votes, thanks to 'the power of the Hierarchy allied to the democratic enthusiasm of Michael Davitt'. The result was approved by Stead.

It is because the Irish Priest in these human relations is constantly trying to be what the most ultra Protestant would wish to be himself if he were a good man and planted in the Irish peasantry, that he has been able to checkmate Mr. Parnell. Why should we not recognize this, and extend a cordial right hand of fellowship across the Irish Channel to our comrades in arms, the Bishops and Priests of Ireland?

Rather strange language from the friend of John Morley; but the editors of *Paternoster* had no doubt that 'the issue of Kilkenny is all on the side of the right'.

The *Paternoster* ended rather quickly after the fashion of so many young reviews. Only six numbers appeared. No doubt, like Belloc himself, it was too conservative for some and too radical for others. The Turks paid it the high compliment of having it burnt publicly as a result of an article in defence of the Armenians. It was also in competition with more firmly established journals, like the *Dublin Review* and *Merrie England,* and it appealed to the same restricted public. How far Belloc himself

E

took part in the humdrum task of editing it is more doubtful. He
was not a natural editor. He had ideas and scattered them; but the
daily grind of administration was never to his taste. He was not
perhaps very good at handling other people, and one suspects that
these essential tasks were more and more left to Pollen. Belloc
would always be glad to launch a paper, but he soon grew bored
with sustaining it. Moreover he spent at least a part of these
months abroad. On October 30, 1889, he was writing to Father
Russell from La Celle St. Cloud.

> I have been writing some articles for the Pall Mall about the
> French elections, which articles have brought me in money; I
> have a cheque uncashed—I am rich. I am now doing them some
> work on the French Ministry of Agriculture which will give
> me another cheque—all this is very nice.
>
> Are you not delighted at the result of the French elections?
> I am. I do not like Kings, I detest reaction. As for Boulanger I
> am sorry, but it is only just that he should be beaten if he allies
> himself with the right. Déroulède said 'la Victoire est à gauche',
> and Déroulède knows a great deal about his own country. We
> all hate Kings.

Belloc had been sent by the *Pall Mall Gazette* as their 'cycling
correspondent in France' to discover what he could about public
opinion in the provinces. He bought a new bicycle for the
purpose—a Rapid, made by the St. George's Engineering
Company in Birmingham, and acquired from a dealer in Holborn.
'This beats any other bicycle of the ordinary or high type that I
have ridden', he wrote in his first despatch. 'Whether this is
because of the large hind wheel, of the saddle adjustment, or of
the tangential spokes, I do not know; but certainly no other
machine with which I am acquainted gets one up to the top so
easily and runs so smoothly.'[1]
He had been asked to talk to at least three typical Frenchmen in
each place he visited. He was to find out what they thought about
General Boulanger (who was then in London, hoping to be

---

[1] *Pall Mall Gazette:* Sept. 14, 1889.

recalled), about the chronic tension between State and Church, and about the recovery of the lost provinces. Short notes, rather than detailed analyses, were required of him. He began his tour in Calvados, not only because it was so close to England but because he thought the Norman character was more comprehensible to Englishmen than the Parisian or the Meridional. Roughly three parties were contending for power: the Royalists, the Boulangists (or *révisionistes*, as they were called) and the Republicans. The country districts inclined to the monarchy, and the towns to the General. Belloc noticed the thirty-foot high Calvaries, so well cared for, by the roadside as he cycled along; and in Caen he found much indignation against Jules Ferry's persecution of the Church. As for the war of *revanche* with Germany, the desire for this flared out in the eyes and speech of an old man whom he met in a village *bistro*. The boy was studying his map—an old map of the time of Louis Philippe—when the man pointed with shaking finger to the lost provinces and exclaimed, '*On les aura!*'

He crossed into Britanny with the impression that the Royalists he had met were not merely discontented with the Republic, but were actively devoted to the Monarchy. Boulangism, in lower Normandy, was 'the handmaid of reaction, not its mistress'. He visited Mortain, on its crag, and Rennes where the local mayor had been deposed for his Boulangist opinions, and Vilaine where all the shoemakers were happily out on strike. Nantes he found more evenly divided between the Republic and the Reaction; but the climax of his tour was Angoulême where Paul Déroulède was almost sure to be elected. His war-cry, '*A bas les Parliamentaires: Vive la République!*' was flaunted in the streets. Everyone Belloc spoke to seemed to want the *revanche*, though some did not want it just yet.

He then made his way to Clermont-Ferrand and the Puy-de-Dôme. Auvergne had once been hotly Boulangist and the General had had his military headquarters at Clermont. But his persistent absence seemed to have told against him, and the sympathies of the district were now more evenly split. Belloc noted in his third and last despatch that the Army was strongly Boulangist, but that no

soldier on active duty could vote. He also noted that Jules Ferry
was hated in inverse proportion to the size of a place; execrated in
Paris and venerated in Pontgibaud, for example, where Belloc
spent the night.

The election itself, on which the survival of the Republic depended, seems to have surprised the 'cycling correspondent'
while he was still in Auvergne. It may have surprised him in
more senses than one, for Jules Ferry's Republic was saved by
152 seats. The Royalists did much better than the Boulangists, and
the elegant General consoled himself with Mademoiselle de
Bonnemains from whom he was to be separated by death but not
by politics. The spirit of the '*prud'homme*' had once more prevailed; and all the radical reactionaries and drastic *révisionistes*,
who had infected Belloc with their zeal, were left to nurse their
memories of Bonaparte. General Boulanger had faced two ways in
his appeal to the revolutionary and the traditional temper of the
French; here he suggested in more respects than one the starry-
eyed despotisms of the twentieth century. The mantle of his
failure, later to be embroidered with the *fleur de lys*, would fall
upon the shoulders of Charles Maurras, and Belloc, in spite of
certain reservations which we shall note in their proper place,
agreed with Maurras more closely than he agreed with any other
political theorist of his time. But in 1889 he still wanted the
Republic, although it was the Republic of Danton and St. Just,
not that of Jules Ferry or Félix Faure. The hard scepticism and
calculating prudence of the French were as yet foreign to his
nature, but he shared fully their native anti-clericalism and their
inherited, their informing faith. We must never forget that he
was himself a Frenchman, and he felt these divisions not only with
his intelligence but in his blood.

5

In the early months of 1890 three American ladies were travelling
in Europe; Mrs. Ellen Hogan (*née* Barrett) and her second and
third daughters, Elizabeth and Elodie. Mrs. Hogan was the widow
of Joseph Smethwick Hogan of Napa, California. Both she and

her husband had been born in Ireland; she at Harthill, near Listowel in Co. Kerry, he at Nenagh in Co. Tipperary. They had seven children, three sons and four daughters. Neither Elizabeth nor Elodie, who was only nineteen years old, had ever been to Europe before.

The chief object of their present journey was to make a pilgrimage to Rome. Elodie already felt a vocation to enter the Order of the Sisters of Charity, and this desire was uppermost in her mind when she arrived with her mother and sister in the Eternal City. She was, however, still troubled by the attachment of a young Californian suitor, and it was in order to resolve such doubts as still remained that she sought the acquaintance of a Polish priest, Father A, to whom the ladies had been given an introduction.

From the moment of their first interview Father A had no doubts that Elodie's vocation was genuine and he did all he could to encourage it. He spared no time or trouble in showing his American visitors the sights of the city, which he knew well from a long residence in Rome. He escorted them to the catacombs and to Castel Gandolfo. He procured for them places in St. Peter's for the Beatification of Jean Giovenal Ancina, a Bishop of the Congregation of the Oratory, but refused to accompany them to the Carnival on Shrove Tuesday. Mrs. Hogan had wished to leave before Easter, but Father A persuaded her to stay on, promising to secure an audience with the Pope for herself and her daughters. This was duly obtained. Nothing had as yet been said to Mrs. Hogan of Elodie's desire to enter the religious life, but when the ladies left Rome in April Father A had no doubt that her resolution was firm. For she had adopted him as her spiritual guide and appeared to rely implicitly on his advice.

He was taking no chances, however, and as the pilgrims made their way slowly up through Europe from Florence to Geneva and from Geneva to Lourdes he pursued Elodie with letters of a formidable prolixity. He wrote in fluent and ungrammatical French, covering page after page with his precise handwriting, repeating the same thing over and over again in only a slightly different way. He was particularly concerned about the young

man from California who was still plying her with gifts, photographs and letters. As she discouraged him, the flowery compliments had given place to bitter reproaches. Father A enjoined her
to send him, unopened, any correspondence she received and
faithful copies of any letters she wrote back. Meanwhile, he sent
her no fewer than five pictures of St. Ignatius Loyola and exhorted
her to refrain from tea and coffee. This must have added considerably to the mortifications of a Continental breakfast.

But what also disturbed him was Mrs. Hogan's decision to
spend some time in London before returning to America. He
wrote to her, without any specific allusion to Elodie, urging her
to sacrifice her family to God. He was afraid that Elodie's vocation
was weakening. He accused her of *légèreté*, of reading the books
she liked and of making whatever acquaintances appealed to her.
He had no assurance that she had broken finally with her American
suitor. It was even possible that, in London, she would be tempted
to a cup of tea.

The Hogans settled for the time being in rooms in Cecil
Street, just off the Strand. Chief among their English friends was
W. T. Stead, whose acquaintance they had made in America.
One day, probably in early June, he brought the American ladies
to tea in Great College Street. No doubt the talk ran on Ireland
and Home Rule and the indiscretions of Mr. Parnell (from which
Mr. Gladstone had just taken a well-deserved holiday); on Sara
Atkinson and the Sisters of Mercy; on Cardinal Manning and the
poor. Suddenly, in the midst of the conversation, Belloc walked
into the room and was introduced. He took one look at Elodie
and determined that she should be his wife.

What happened to him in those few moments can only be
described in metaphors too worn for repetition. To understand it,
one must turn to those pages of prose, or those occasional lyrics,
where he describes the action of the 'little God'. It may be Marie
Antoinette and her desperate passion for Fersen; or Boutroux in
The Girondin, dreaming of the sunburnt face that was the spirit
of the woods; or Belinda sighing for Horatio; or some verse
inspired in later life by a friend whose beauty he admired. These
passages, where the prose takes on a studied gravity, or the verse

glows, are all translations—and they translate a unique experience. Through all the years to come, through all the dust and battle and bereavements of a crowded life, a single face stood guard over his inmost thoughts.

Elodie was described, shortly after their first meeting, as 'a beautiful creature, with hair like polished mahogany, eyes of a dark, rich blue, delicate regular features, and a "mantling colour". She had neither figure nor style, and dressed abominably, but with a face like that it little mattered, and she also possessed the twin gifts of personality and charm.' [1] Mrs. Hogan was unexpectedly recalled to America, but Elodie and Elizabeth decided to stay on in London. So Madame Belloc arranged for them to occupy the ground-floor rooms in Great College Street during the temporary absence of the tenant. Elodie and Hilaire went about together unchaperoned during the weeks that followed, for Bessie Belloc had not forgotten her education in Women's Rights. They visited the East End and moved happily among the poor of Dockland. Hilaire explained to Elodie the construction of the Blackwall Tunnel; he told her of his confused ambitions; and she, who brought with her the breath of a world so different as to be hardly intelligible—what did she think of the unkempt, love-stricken youth at her side? The answer is given in a letter to Father Russell, written from the Hôtel de la Chaine d'Or, Petit-Andely, more than twenty years later.

> Years and years ago, about the very time of these crude letters of his to you I met him; and considering my complete indifference during those days, indifference and virginal scorn for the whole masculine world, I marvel at my own insight! for I plainly foresaw all his power and I realised the greatness of his soul. As he has gone on from year to year achieving and accomplishing, I have never been surprised. It is only my girlish vision of him and faith in him being realised.

About this time Elodie wrote to Father A, explaining, quite truthfully, that her sister Elizabeth, presumably encouraged by Stead, was proposing to stay on in London and try her hand at

[1] *Adventures of a Novelist*, by Gertrude Atherton (1932).

journalism; that she, Elodie, had decided to remain with her; and
that Mrs. Hogan would return alone to the United States. At this
Father A's anger overstepped the limits of propriety. The plan,
he declared, was a monstrous one. London was a city of shameful
corruption and abominable vice. If she could not leave it on the
date originally fixed, then she must avoid all social gatherings,
all concerts, conversation, and acquaintances, all appearances
in public or in private. She must not even go out for a walk,
unless she was obliged to. What then, she may well have
asked—though there were now certain questions she no longer
put to Father A—was she to do with herself? He had already
answered her. There was one thing she could do; she could go to
confession, and ask the priest for his visiting card, so that
Father A might know that she had obeyed his injunctions.
Fortunately the Jesuits of Farm Street, to whom she went, have
always been noted for their charity and common sense, and if her
conscience had suffered in any way from the decision to remain
in London, it was immediately put at rest. When Father A
reproached her with going to a theatre and with attending a
service in a Protestant church, she had no need to excuse herself
for the first and she was able to claim her confessor's permission for the second. Once again, the Jesuits had triumphed over
Jansenism.

Elodie knew better than to breathe a word of her new attachment to Father A. But after she had been in London for six weeks,
she wrote to him expressing doubts of her vocation. She had also
recovered her own zest for journalism. But the future remained
obscure. Madame Belloc was opposed to even a temporary engagement. She argued, not without reason, that her son was only
nineteen and not yet settled in a career. Elodie herself was still
half-tempted by the religious life. There was no way of resolving
her doubts during these hectic, halcyon weeks of a London
summer; and when she and her sister returned to California at
the end of August, neither she nor Hilaire had any assurance for
the future beyond a memory that must be tested by time. Did
she guess that in the boy who loved her two qualities were
already predominant—honour and will?

6

Before Elodie Hogan had left for California, Belloc had threatened to follow her there. We must suppose that the threats continued, for Mrs. Atherton describes the girl sitting on the edge of her bed one morning and 'crying into a cup of cocoa'. She wanted, and she did not want, to become a nun. She was praying that Belloc would not come out to her, and hoping that he would. He guessed her hopes and put a liberal interpretation on her prayers.

The chief problems were money and parental opposition. The latter he could defy, but poverty does not yield to threats. Accordingly he borrowed twenty pounds from a friend of his mother's and sold all the prizes he had won at the Oratory—the calf-bound poets, the single volume of *Chambers's Encyclopædia,* and the signed complete edition of Newman. One is pleased to record that all the Newmans were seen shortly afterwards in an Oxford Street dealer's, and were bought back by Madame Belloc. With the money so raised Hilaire bought a passage in the steerage from Liverpool to New York. He had told his mother that he intended to visit his Priestley relations in America, and rather surprisingly she believed him.

He would always remember how it stank in the steerage, but his will was set and his heart was wild with hope. Every man crossing the Atlantic for the first time has had the same sensation when he is about three-quarters of the way across. It is quite strictly a sensation, for it is nothing that he can see or hear or smell. It is the awareness, psychic rather than physical, of a New World; a certainty, lifting the heart and mind, that discovery is at hand. Belloc describes it for us in the opening chapter of *The Contrast* (1923):

> After I had journeyed on the ocean many days in no great comfort, for I did not travel as the rich travel, I came to a part of the sea where all things changed.
>
> It was in crossing the Grand Banks that I discovered this new air; I was appalled and vastly intrigued. I was coming to unknown things. It was in what I breathed and in the quality of the wind. . . .

The heavens did have a new influence before the sea was crossed, and I did already perceive by every sense known and unknown that I was upon the threshold of new things.

How rapidly, how sharply did that impression grow!

The first light-ship twinkling upon the horizon was like a herald. I wondered at the coming world; and when I passed through the Narrows into New York Harbour, I saw grass and trees, contours of low hills, the houses of men, and all was utterly strange.

His Priestley cousins lived in Philadelphia and he stayed with them for a few days. He was impressed by the strangeness, and also by the slowness, of American speech; but gradually, by listening carefully and constantly repeating himself, he made himself understood. Then he set forth on the longer and more difficult stretch of his odyssey.

He had little money left and when this was exhausted he gambled his way across the plains, winning or losing in the saloons which added, at widely spaced intervals, to the hazards of a half-formed continent. Everywhere what struck him was the difference between America and anything he had ever known. The trees pointed monotonously upward; the margins of the rivers were undefined. When he came to Cincinnati, he observed that the Ohio ran through a gorge of wooded hills, but it was no more like the Meuse than a steel-engraving is like a mezzotint. And the mountains, too, were different. They were 'slow lifts of land like succeeding waves; but not bold waves'.[1] Their similarity was 'heightened by the clothing common to all. The same sparse and regular and uplifted trees everywhere; the branches rejected from the soil.'[2] He remembered twenty years later how he had made his

way on foot for lack of a railway ticket along the Denver and Rio Grande, through the deserts and threading odd and deep canyons by way of the railway embankment, seeing trains go by with people in them and sleeping out and trudging on next morning and marvelling at the rocks and the new sights and

---

[1] *The Contrast* (1923).   [2] *Ibid.*

sleeping in unexpected houses and so on, with no end but getting somehow to Denver and selling pictures on the way and wondering about things that don't matter and writing verse in one's head and losing money at cards on the Cimarron and then having none and so limping into Canyon City and then getting money again and walking over the shoulder of Pike's Peak down on to the Florente and landing up at night in a goods wagon—and so on to the end.[1]

As everyone knows who has crossed the American continent, the great central plain rises so surely, yet so imperceptibly, that when at last the Rockies come in sight they do not seem to rise abruptly but rather to grow in a vast sterile confusion, dwarfed already by the height of the plateau on which they stand. Nor are they humanized, like all but the highest Alps. Yet here, at last, were contours, sprawling and seemingly illimitable, and here and there a peak mantled in snow. On the shoulder of Pike's Peak Belloc met a solitary inhabitant who thought that a man he had seen riding about on a little donkey was God! The unaccustomed altitudes excited Belloc to no such illusion; they only spurred him to take out his sketch-book and his pen. He had lost the last of his money at cards, 'playing against more cunning and older men', and he earned his further progress by selling his drawings for a night's lodging.

> I would make a good little sketch in sepia of some peak, and this a lonely fellow on a ranch was very glad to have, giving me in exchange my supper, my breakfast and my bed; and I would go on next day to another and draw another picture and sell it for another lodging.[2]

So he continued, trudging and tired, until at last he stood upon the western precipice of the desert, and looked down upon what he described as 'a vision of Europe glorified'; upon 'the cascade of dense forests' which descended into California. In opulent and fertile profusion they beckoned him forward to the fulfilment of his heart's desire.

[1] Letter to George Wyndham: Feb. 5, 1910.   [2] *The Contrast* (1923).

Mrs. Hogan, with her family, had moved from Napa to San Francisco, where the younger boys were at Santa Clara College as day-scholars. A typical representative of the rising and prosperous middle-class, she did not welcome Belloc with open arms when he arrived on March 10. What did he expect, this tattered and penniless Frenchman who had landed uninvited on her doorstep and aspired, impertinently, to her daughter's hand? He expected the moon and the stars, and in a measure, maybe, he got them. Christian charity forbade the exasperated mother to turn him away; besides, she and Elodie had received much hospitality from Madame Belloc in London, and she could not return it with so brutal a rebuff. The impression he made on an outsider is described by Mrs. Atherton.

He was not an impressive figure in those days. His hair was long and dusty, his hands and linen were never clean, and his clothes looked as if they had been slept in, which no doubt they had.

But he was a 'dynamic personality' and his mind was so active and blazing that I was always expecting it to explode and burst through his skull. One evening he came to call on me alone, and remained until four in the morning. He sat huddled over the fire, his hands hanging between his knees, his shoulders above his ears, and talked and talked and talked. Such a flow of words I have never listened to, and every one of them sparkled. From his passion for Elodie and his determination to marry despite Church, Mothers, Youth and Poverty, he passed on to the affairs of the world, and never before or since have I heard anyone discourse so brilliantly. I sat in fascinated silence, regardless of time or of possible Grundys across the street. I still wondered how Elodie could have fallen in love with him, but when he turned on that extraordinary mind of his at full blast, I could have listened to him for ever. He almost convinced me that he knew more than any statesman in Europe.

He also told me something of his own aspirations. He intended to write, and to cultivate a style as simple as 'Mary had a little lamb'. What else was there left after the elliptical

Meredith? Yes, he would create a sensation by his pellucid simplicity.[1]

Belloc remained with the Hogans only a few weeks. Mrs. Atherton describes Elodie as more and more fixed in her determination to try her vocation for the religious life. How far, or for how long, she was shaken in it we do not know. In any event Mrs. Hogan's opposition to the marriage was implacable and, shortly before Easter, Belloc started on his homeward journey. As he saw the Sierra Nevada against the dawn of Easter Day, he was nursing a regret that was much more than a momentary disappointment. It was a regret that stayed with him to the end of his life. For he always wished that he and Elodie had married there and then, in the high spring of their affection. If they had done so, the course of his life might well have been radically changed. He might have become an American instead of a British citizen and lost, under those Californian skies, the sense of Europe which was the informing passion of his thought. The *genius loci* might have proved too strong for him. But one thing he always held to be certain: his life, in whatever other ways it might have been changed, would have been simplified. For this man, so variously gifted and subtle with so many conflicting strains of race and tradition, had a deep hunger for simplicity. The wanderer had a thirst for respose. And he had missed, as he believed, the unique and fugitive moment when he might have found them. But the vision lasted. He remembered California 'as Paradise, and Paradise never lasts long'.[2] Sadly he turned his back on the Pacific sunshine, and the Sierras whose dust he had tramped in hope. Passing quickly through the plains (for he now had money for his minimum needs) he reached his friends on the eastern coast. It was here, at Montclair, New Jersey, that he received a letter from Elodie telling him, quite finally, that she could not marry him. The decision hurt him more bitterly than he thought it possible to be hurt; and it was to his mother that he looked for comfort and advice when he reached home in the middle of May.

[1] *Adventures of a Novelist* (1932).
[2] Letter to Lady Juliet Duff: Feb. 15, 1937.

CHAPTER IV

THE CONSCRIPT

I

FOR some time a secret resolution had been forming in Belloc's mind; he wished to do his military service with the French army. If he were to remain a French citizen, this would, of course, be necessary, but there were deeper motives impelling him. The French military tradition had touched him at many points; through the forebears on his father's side, through the hotly nationalist friends he had made in Paris, through the boys he had known at the Collège Stanislas, through Déroulède and the *Ligue des Patriotes*. His mother had vigorously opposed the idea. She guessed the perilous transition to which he would be exposed, and she thought that it would brand him as a foreigner for the rest of his life. In this Belloc afterwards admitted her to have judged correctly. But Elodie had just as warmly encouraged him. Did she guess that her suitor was as yet only half-formed? Did she feel, as he did, that the experience would help him to grow up? Was she half-consciously playing for time, in case she failed in her vocation? Or did she realize, more clearly than Madame Belloc, that once Hilaire had set his mind on a thing no power on earth would stop him?

In the event nothing did stop him. His French relatives were consulted and his cousin René Millet busied himself at the Ministère de Guerre to get the boy posted where he wanted to be —with the artillery. Artillery had decided the Franco-Prussian War, but by 1872 Colonel de Bange had devised the breech action which was adopted by every other country in Europe except Germany. Soon the French would have a weapon in which the recoil was entirely absorbed and with which the rate of fire was three times that of any rival in active service. They were also leading in mobile heavy guns for use in the field. By the beginning of November Belloc was in Paris and on the 9th he received his *feuille d'appel*. On the 14th he had his marching orders for Toul, where he joined the 10th Battery of the 8th Regiment of Artillery. He asks his mother not to fret after him, and adds that it is all 'rather a novel experience'.[1]

The Prussian annexation of Alsace and Lorraine had given Toul the importance of a frontier town. It stands at the junction of the Meurthe and the Moselle in an open plain bounded by deep woods on the western side, which divide it from the valley of the Meuse, and on the eastern by the Forêt de Haye. To the north is the long blue line of hills beyond Domrémy, overhanging the birthplace of Jeanne d'Arc. Toul was the seat of an ancient bishopric, and the cathedral, with its flamboyant façade, stood out from the jumbled roofs and the *enceinte* of fortifications. There was more to these than met the eye, for much important work had been done below ground since the defeat of 1870. The town was quite small, but beside its civilian population of 7,000 there was a garrison of 16,000 men. For every adult man in Toul there were at least six soldiers. This produced, observed Belloc, 'a peculiar effect'.[2]

The garrison was continually being reinforced, and although many troops were sent there, none were ever sent away. The peace-time strength of the artillery was 100,000 men, and it could count on 400,000 reserves. Belloc was lucky in belonging to a Battery training on the frontier, for this gave an edge of emergency to what might have seemed a dull routine. He had little time for writing. From *reveillé* at 5.30 a.m. until 5 in the afternoon his time was fully occupied; at first, by the gruelling and hardening ordeal of drill. The discipline was strict and the punctuality exacting. When the day's work was over, there was so much harness to clean that little time was left for recreation or, still less, for solitude. 'Yet the rigidity required for one's daily duties', Belloc told his mother, made 'many things easy which would be impossible in civil life.'[3]

---

[1] Letter to Madame Belloc: Nov. 9, 1891.
[2] Letter to Madame Belloc: Nov. 20, 1891.   [3] *Ibid.*

In his service book the young conscript is described as 1.74
metres tall, chestnut-brown in colouring, with blue eyes, high
forehead, and nose *fort*. He was placed in the second class for
revolver shooting and fencing, and in the third for gymnastics.
It was noted that he was an excellent swimmer, and that he could
read, write and add up. At the end of his service no punishments
had been recorded against his name.

The tone of his letters is sternly, if not harshly, realistic. Being
the only son of a widowed mother, he might expect to be released
from the army after ten or twelve months' service. He showed no
desire to remain in it a day longer than was necessary, and was
advised to put in an immediate claim for his *dispense*. It was not
easy to get leave from Toul, for the garrison was perpetually on
the alert, and although he hoped to get up to Paris for the New
Year, his humble rank forbade him to take an express, and he
doubted if he could get away for long enough to make the eight
or nine-hour journey worth while. It might be better if Madame
Belloc came to Toul for Christmas; then he could get a twelve or
twenty-four hour *permission* and spend his free time with her.
Later, on December 18, he fears that in any case leave for Paris
will be refused, 'as the whole cannon got into a row just as I
asked and they may make no distinction between the old ones
who are punished and the recruits who are innocent'. Yet he is
already proud of the army to which he belongs. He would rather
come to Paris than to La Celle St. Cloud, 'because for Paris one
starts in complete uniform with sword and for the Departements
in undress'.

He is anxious, like any schoolboy, for news from the outside
world. 'I am so grateful for a letter. I have so little to read; I
would like *The Lamp* when it comes out but not anything else
just yet.' Later he asks for the *Figaro*, and we find him on stable-
guard reading *Le Mariage de Loti*, which reminds him of
California. Father John Norris writes him an affectionate letter
and encloses a copy of the Oratory School Magazine. He wants
him to contribute an article, and this eventually appeared in
July 1894. It contained nothing to indicate the writer Belloc
subsequently became; the style was stilted and there were some

rather naïve observations on the disadvantage to the French in not having any Public Schools. Belloc was still smarting from the Stanislas, and he refers to the 'perpetual spy-system' in French schools 'which has destroyed any active life among the boys themselves'. Father John had been very complimentary in his letter, and had spoken 'a great deal about religion which is odd from him'. Belloc wants to know if the *Review of Reviews,* of which Stead had recently become editor, had noticed some verse of his in a paper called *St. Nicholas.* 'Pray send me the news of our friends,' he writes, 'one is terribly exiled here after a life of great interest.'[1] And again like a schoolboy, he asks for pocket-money—the conscript only received two or three cents per day—and for eatables. 'A few tins of cheap potted meat or anchovies to put on bread would be very good.'[2] Most urgently of all—and this request is underlined—he asks his mother: '*If anything comes from America,* pray send it on at once. Do not keep anything back. I have lost here a little photograph which I had kept sixteen months and it gives me great pain.' He did not know that his mother had written to Elodie asking her to stay at Slindon, and arguing that if she really loved Hilaire there was every good reason why she should marry him.

The letters are evocative in their shorthand account of the packed days; they have a deep unselfconscious simplicity. It was a freezing winter in Toul and in January it snowed without ceasing for two days. The Battery was required to manœuvre in the snow for two hours and during the second hour it was all but dark. The cold reminded Belloc of Nebraska through which he had passed exactly a year before, on his way out to California. Since then Mrs. Hogan had died, quite unexpectedly, in May; and for Elodie, at least, there were no further obstacles. But perhaps it was as necessary for her to try the discipline of the cloister, as it was for him to endure the discipline of the guns. And in any case, he could wait—for years, if necessary. On that matter, as on all others, she knew his mind; more perfectly, perhaps, than he knew it himself.

One night in January, when the snow lay thick upon the ground and the horses were stamping in their straw, a man appeared

---

[1] Dec. 15.　　　　[2] *Ibid.*

with a lantern at the foot of Belloc's bed. His name was Frocot
and he came from the Ardennes. He stood there in his dark blue
driver's coat, staring with a fixed and haunted expression, and
declared that he had heard the dragging of the Loose Spur. There
was a superstition in the Regiment about the Loose Spur.

Our spurs were not buckled on like the officers'; they were
fixed into the heel of the boot, and if a nail loosened upon either
side the spur dragged with an unmistakable noise. There was a
sergeant who (for some reason) had one so loosened on the last
night he had ever gone the rounds before his death, for in the
morning as he came off guard he killed himself, and the story
went about among the drivers that sometimes on stable guard in
the thick of the night, when you watched all alone by the lantern
(with your three comrades asleep in the straw of an empty stall)
your blood would stop and your skin tauten at the sound of a
loose spur dragging on the far side of the stable in the dark. But
though many had heard the story, and though some had
pretended to find proof for it, I never knew a man to feel and
know it except this man Frocot on that night.[1]

The weather had not changed when the General commanding
the artillery of the Corps d'Armée came down to inspect the
Regiment. Belloc's health seems to have borne up pretty well
under the hardships and the unaccustomed fatigues, but he
developed a bad sore throat in mid-winter, and this was aggravated by having to give commands in the instruction squad. There
was talk of the 8th going up to the frontier itself in the spring—
to Lunéville or some other advanced post. 'Things are very ready
on this side of the frontier', he writes. 'I suppose they are readier
still on the other.'[2] Mobilization was in fact ordered during the
last week of March. Madame Belloc had paid a visit to Toul not
long before, and Hilaire regrets that she was not there to see the
Battery on the march. 'It was very splendid. The whole garrison
is on the frontier road, and the gates are shut in two hours.'[3] The
same letter brings news that his papers have come from the

---

[1] *The Reveillon: First and Last* (1911).
[2] Jan. 7, 1892.   [3] March 26, 1892.

Minister of War; that some special favour has been exercised on his behalf; and that he need only do a year's service. Others in similar case would only know their fates in the summer. With luck he should be free by September. The intervening months were all spent in preparation for the summer manœuvres, the climax of his training and the final test of his proficiency.

We have just finished the embarkations in which the Batteries mobilize as they would for war, with the difference that they embark in a train instead of marching. It means several nights almost without sleep, and it has partly accounted for my not writing. It is very wonderful to see all the guns and men fastening in, in the night . . .We march to camp at Châlons on July 2nd.[1]

Meanwhile he seems to have acquired a room in Toul, where he could snatch an hour or two of quiet, and his mother sends him the money for the rent. In the evenings he would saunter about the town. Here the Middle Ages, which had hitherto seemed more remote than antiquity, became immediate and palpable. Occasionally there was a dance and they were the only dances Belloc ever enjoyed. He used to look back on a particular evening at Liverdun, in a barn, when 'one had to dance with one's sword and scabbard under one's arm and take care not to tear the skirt of the wench with one's great coarse spurs . . .'[2] For the most part these companions of his service are shadowy figures, but now and then their humanity breaks through. He tells of one who lost his girl and had his foot run over by a gun in the course of the same week. Once, on a Sunday in May, he took 'a long spree up the Moselle', with some of his comrades, and this explained why he had not written home. He is always anxious to spare his mother the least anxiety on his account.

The letters are dutiful and even suggestive in their brief outline, but they do not give us the substance and colour of his experience with the French Army. They tell us nothing of the men he served with, or the technique of the science he acquired. For that we must turn to the few essays he wrote on the subject,

[1] *Ibid.*   [2] Letter to the Hon. Mrs. Mervyn Herbert: Sept. 23, 1933.

while the detail and intensity of his service were still vivid in his
mind. What, for example, were the main differences between the
French Army and other European Armies of that time? He could
only speak from his limited experience, but that experience had
'about it much of the hardship, all of the discipline, and in the
period of the manœuvres not a little of the outward experience
of a war'.

The French Army [he goes on] is peculiar in Europe for
being the most universally recruited of any. In France young
men of every social rank serve as private soldiers, and during
their period of service are merged entirely into the rank and
file: officers in the Reserve are appointed to a great extent from
the body of retired officers and non-commissioned officers of
long service, and promotion from the ranks is not only theo-
retically possible but very largely practised. Discipline loses
somewhat by the absence of that class loyalty and reverence, on
which German authorities have insisted so much, but it gains in
the possibility of raising in large numbers to commissioned rank
men of long service and sound disciplinary qualities. And it
would, I think, be the unanimous testimony of French soldiers
that officers who have seen service in the ranks are the most
constant in service and are more certain of obedience and
respect, of securing efficiency in those under them, than any
others, a result which comes largely from their personal
experience of the limits which make a discipline so valuable
and which if they are exceeded vex the men submitted to
them to no purpose.

This mixture of the different social ranks is remarkable also
in the case of the Private soldier. But here the military effect is
less marked. Whether a man proves an efficient or inefficient
soldier very much depends upon his physical strength and on
his readiness to obey and to acquire the habits demanded of him;
the first part of this is independent to a great extent of social
differences save that the peasant and artisan have in all that
involves manual labour the advantage over the product of the
wretched public school system which obtains in France. The

second part is ensured (by) a discipline pressing so hardly and so equally upon all that the habit of continual labour is acquired with an ease and rapidity that surprise the man himself who is submitted to it. The great fatigues—or rather the fatigues which seem so great after an ordinary civilian life—the long marches in full kit followed often by nights of guard duty with their lack of sleep seem at the first unendurable. All these fatigues, as is natural, press hardest on the man who has seen no active exercise to speak of . . . But it cannot be denied that the change, though it is sudden and extreme, has (as) a rule a good effect: the French Lycéen learns in the regiment an independence and a self-reliance that years in the society of men of his own stamp would never teach him, nearly always picks up health visibly in spite of the short hours of sleep, the bad food, and the perpetual labour.

This extreme amount of work which is demanded of a soldier in the Eastern Army Corps is regarded by him as a thing quite peculiar to his division. And it is evident that in a position where a little under two hours is allowed for mobilization the duties are far more rigorous than those of more sheltered places. The men who came to us from regiments lying further inland to our frontier garrison, noted at once the increase of duties, and would tantalize us after the 'soupe' round the barrack-room fire at evening with descriptions of Orléans or Clermont-Ferrand where stable guard came round every six days and where cleaning harness after hours was unknown. But the difficulties entailed by the position give a certain pride to the men of the 6th and 7th Army Corps, and a man on leave is always careful to let you know that he comes from the gates of the country, Toul, Epinal or Belfort.[1]

Here, then, is the general, the objective picture, but what of the personal experience upon which such conclusions were based? They had marched him up to barracks in the dark and the rain with a batch of other recruits, with whom he had little in common and with whom he could scarcely be on

[1] *MSS.*

speaking terms. He was faulty in his grammar and doubtful in his accent, 'ignorant especially of those things which are taken for granted in every civilization but never explained in full, and ignorant therefore of the key which alone can open that civilization to a stranger. Things irksome or a heavy burden to the young men of my age, born and brought up in the French air, were to me, brought up with Englishmen an Englishman, odious and bewildering. Orders that I but half comprehended; boasting of which I knew little, coupled with a courage that seemed ill-suited to it; a habit of fighting coupled with a curious contempt for the accident of individual superiority . . .' Everything that made up 'what was generally understood by a gentleman was subjected to the orders and the occasional insult of a hierarchy of office'. His whole nurture and upbringing were 'thought nothing but a hindrance and an absurdity'.[1] He had had wilder adventures, and experienced deeper emotions, than most boys of his age. But, for all that, the shock was brutal.

His nature, though it was strong and gaining every day in definition, was still supple, and he soon adjusted himself.

I saw (when I had long lost my manners and ceased to care for refinement) that the French were attempting a generation before any others in the world to establish an army that should be a mere army and in which a man counted only as a man. I cared more for guns than for books, I obeyed by instinct now not men but symbols of authority. My captain was a man promoted from the ranks; one of my lieutenants was an Alsatian Charity boy and the other a rich fellow mixed up with sugar; the sergeant of my piece was a poor young noble, the wheeler of No. 5 a wealthy and very vulgar chemist's son, the man in the next bed a cook of some skill and my bombardier a mild young farmer. I thought only in terms of the artillery; I could judge men for their aptitude alone, and in me, I suppose, were accomplished many things, one of Danton's dreams, one of St. Just's prophecies, the fulfilment also of what a hundred brains had silently determined 20 years before when the staff gave up

[1] *The First Day's March : Hills and the Sea* (1906).

their swords outside Metz . . . I cared little in what vessel I ate, or whether I had to tear meat with my fingers, I could march in reserve more than 20 miles a day for day upon day, I knew all about my horses, I could sweep, wash, make a bed, clean kit, cook a little, tidy a stable, turn to entrenching for emplacement, take a place at lifting a gun or changing a wheel, I took charge with a gunner and could point well . . .[1]

To drive a gun in the French Artillery was no easy matter. Three men had to control six horses, each riding one and leading another. Belloc himself was never allowed to take charge of the wheelers or the leaders—he rode, that is to say, in the middle— and no man was given control of the wheelers or the leaders who had not had at least two years' arduous training. It required considerable skill to take six horses and a gun weighing about two tons across a small ditch and through a hedge on the further side. Each man had to know his horses thoroughly and to make himself responsible for their fitness and cleanliness. Only the feeding was done by the stable guard. The losses among these trained drivers were expected to be heavy at the beginning of a war. At Sedan the battery to which Belloc was attached lost every commissioned and non-commissioned officer, except one who saved his piece.

2

All the fatigues and exaltations, all the science and comradeship, of his service were summed up in the march to Châlons-sur-Marne for manœuvres early in July. Everything in the French Artillery was designed for speed, and the gunners and reserve drivers were sent on ahead in rotation so as not to weight the limber. This practice was called 'Haut-le pied', and a rare exception to it was made when they were manœuvring on the Argonne and a rapid movement had to be executed. Belloc had charge of two horses, Pacte and Basilique. 'Basilique was a slow beast, full of strength and sympathy, but stupid and given to sudden fears.

[1] Ibid.

Pacte had never heard the guns.' But today they would go off without him. Meanwhile he prepared for the long march, with a copy of Mark Twain's *Roughing It* in his pocket. He had the sensation of great discoveries at hand; the feeling that came to him as the ship bearing him to America drew out from the docks at Liverpool.

They had risen at 2.30 a.m., and breakfasted on no more than black coffee, without sugar, and a hunk of bread left over from the day before; the diet of Napoleon's armies who had marched and fought upon it all day long. By 3.30 they were on the road. The French had adopted the German practice of halting the column for a five-minutes' rest in every hour. Then the trumpet call of the Battery—the '*quatre-vingts chasseurs*', as they called it— would sound and they were off again along the road to Commercy. As they passed through the villages, their singing and the quick rhythm of their steps drew the children on to the pavements, and above their heads the shutters opened in curiosity. To the end of his life Belloc remembered, and would still sing, the marching-songs of the French Army; the song of the Miller, and *Auprès de ma Blonde*, which had come down from the Flemish Wars of Louis XIV, and *Les Filles de Commercy*—the town which they were now approaching. 'I have heard them singing', he exclaims in the great concluding chapter of *Marie Antoinette*, as he describes the Republican charge at Wattignies. These men with whom he marched were of the same stock, and now he understood why they sang. Their songs were

> a whole expression of the barrack-room; its extreme coarseness; its steady and perpetual humour; its hatred of the hard conditions of discipline; and also these songs continually portray the distant but delightful picture of things—I mean of things rare and far off—which must ever lie at the back of men's minds when they have much work to do with their hands and much living in the open air.

The march was not an easy one, for the swords worn by the drivers got in their way, and their boots were not suited to the road. (Top-boots were not worn by drivers in the French Army.)

Beside him were the companions of his service; men he knew with difficulty and was never to meet again. Colson, the half-educated son of an ironmaster, who wanted to hear about England, and was always complaining, and wondered how he would get dry after the rain; Frocot perhaps; and others whose names have not come down to us. The rain continued and the songs ceased.

There was at last no noise but the slush of all those feet beating the muddy road, and the occasional clank of metal as a scabbard touched some other steel, or a slung carbine struck the hilt of a bayonet. It was well on in the morning when the guns caught us up and passed us; the drivers all shrouded in their coats and bending forward in the rain; the guns coated and splashed with thick mud and the horses also threatened hours of grooming.

Among them was Labbé, 'by profession a cook, and by inclination a marquis, and by destiny a very good driver of guns'. For today, by the chance of rotation, it was Labbé's turn to ride. And the marching column was not to come to Commercy, with its girls and its small provincial bustle, after all. For an orderly rode up and turned them back four miles along the way they had come and then off on to a side road, and they had to spend the night in a village.

That night I sat at a peasant's table and heard my four stable-companions understanding everything, and evidently in their world and at home, although they were conscripts. This turned me silent, and I sat away from the light, looking at the fire, and drying myself by its logs. As I heard their laughter I remembered Sussex and the woods above Arun, and I felt myself to be in exile.

They had reason, these bewildered conscripts, to call Belloc 'the Englishman'; his roots were fixed.

On the fourth day of the seven days' march the regiment met at Bar-le-Duc, but only half of it halted there. The six batteries, with their thirty-six guns, men, horses and wagons formed a splendid sight as they advanced into the valley of the Meuse. The gunners and drivers who had marched from Toul were drawn up at the side of the road to join them. The seventh Battery passed with a certain Major Chevalier, known to all by his monocle; and the ninth with Captain Levy, a mathematician, at its head. Levy was popular with the men because he would go into their kitchen and taste their soup to see if it were drinkable. These were officers, hardly known to Belloc and his comrades, of whom nevertheless many stories were told.

As the ninth battery passed us we were given the order to mount, and knew that our place came next. The long-drawn Ha–a—lte! and the lifted swords down the road contained for a while the batteries that were to follow, and we filed out of our side-road into the long gap they had left us. Then, taking up the trot ourselves, we heard the order passing down infinitely till it was lost in the length of the road; the trumpets galloped past us and formed at the head of the column; a much more triumphant noise of brass than we had yet heard heralded us with a kind of insolence, and the whole train with its two miles and more of noisy power gloried into the old town of Bar-le-Duc, to the great joy of its young men and women at the windows, to the annoyance of the householders, to the stupefaction of the old, and doubtless to the ultimate advantage of the Republic.[1]

And so they came by stages to Châlons-sur-Marne, with its Hôtel de la Haute Mère de Dieu, which Belloc was to love to the end of his life. At Châlons there were competitions between the Batteries, firing at targets seven or eight kilometres distant, and at night bivouacs by the camp fire. Two regiments of men with 144 pieces of cannon and 1,600 horse slept under canvas, ten men to a tent, or under the stars. Very soon now the nine-months' ordeal would be over. But Belloc had learnt from it how the military temper had moulded 'the French people today, putting too much knowledge and bitterness into their eyes, but a great determination into their gestures and a trained tenacity into the methods of their thoughts.'[2] The bivouac under the stars may be

---

[1] *The Guns: Hills and the Sea* (1906).
[2] *The First Day's March: Hills and the Sea* (1906).

read as an image of completion and momentary repose; an image also of exile, for in the verses which it afterwards inspired there can be no mistaking the face which there looked down upon him. It was the face whose photograph he had lost but whose every feature was graven on his mind.

> You came without a human sound,
>   You came and brought my soul to me;
> I only woke, and all around
> They slumbered on the firelit ground,
>   Beside the guns in Burgundy.
>
> I felt the gesture of your hands,
>   You signed my forehead with the Cross;
> The gesture of your holy hands
> Was bounteous—like the misty lands
>   Along the Hills in Calvados.
>
> But when I slept I saw your eyes,
>   Hungry as death, and very far.
> I saw demand in your dim eyes
> Mysterious as the moons that rise
>   At midnight, in the Pines of Var.

CHAPTER V

BALLIOL MEN

I

BELLOC received his '*certificat de bonne conduite*' at Toul in September. This described him as a '*conducteur mediocre ... ayant servi avec honneur et fidelité.*' But his future lay open and obscure. René Millet wanted him to stay on as an interpreter in the French Army; but he had had enough of the French Army, having fulfilled his duty to the 'idea' which had called him into its ranks. Then a letter from his mother brought a ray of light; an offer had been made to send him to Oxford. There was as yet no formal permission for Catholics to go to Oxford or Cambridge, but a few had taken the law into their own hands. In the case of Belloc, the opportunity was due to the generosity of his sister Marie and of Frederic Lowndes to whom she was then engaged. Marie sold her interest in the Parkes Trust Fund (£800) and gave Hilaire her share in the French property in order that he should go to the University; and for many years afterwards Lowndes paid all the taxes on this property. He also relieved Madame Belloc of the responsibility of finding a College to take her son. She was not at all a practical person and she had no experience of these things. It was too late to fix up his entrance for the October term and it might be awkward for him to go up in January, since most of the Colleges would be full. Madame Belloc would have had a natural preference for Trinity, because it had been Newman's College; and there seems to have been some prospect of Trinity when Belloc wrote to her from Luxembourg, where he had gone to stay with friends.

It will be quite impossible for me to pass any entrance examination without six weeks' reading. Hope says there is no question of my presenting myself before January; do you mean by the beginning of October that it is to be the date to begin a course of reading for the test exam at Trinity? or what? Write and tell me very clearly by *return* because if I am to hurry back I may as well know why.[1]

Trinity and at least one other College had refused him before he was accepted by Balliol. Benjamin Jowett was still Master, and Jowett had an eye for originality as well as for rank. He had met Madame Belloc at the Westminster deanery; and there was quite enough in her son's career since he had left school, and in the academic distinctions he had won at the Oratory, to recommend him. Belloc, for his part, wanted nothing better than 'the Classics and the society of my equals'.[2] He went to Oxford in November and stayed with A. M. Bell, who was coaching him. Bell sent the following report to Madame Belloc.

I am neither confident nor despondent about your son's chances of success: indeed I consider that probably he will be successful. I have found him clever and clear-minded; but *very* unequal in his work from day to day; apt to lose his self-control at trifles, so that he has not progressed as much as his abilities would have allowed. He also has a number of friends who ask him about; at one time this threatened to interfere with his duties seriously; at present it does not.[3]

He passed the entrance examination in December, mainly on his English essay about poetry. On the 12th we find him at Wilfrid Blunt's house in Sussex, failing miserably to make the groom drunk. This was a man of resolute character who afterwards became one of the very few teetotal publicans in England. Meanwhile Belloc did a little private coaching to earn some pocket money, and went up to Balliol in the Hilary term of 1893. In December of the same year he was awarded one of the two Brackenbury scholarships in History. These were the blue ribbons of History scholarships in the University, and the other was

[1] Sept. 25, 1892.
[2] Letter to Madame Belloc, quoted in *The Young Hilaire Belloc* (1956).
[3] Nov. 27, 1892.

given to Ramsay Muir. Belloc had wanted to read Greats, but Balliol thought his Classics had grown too rusty from disuse.

Balliol in the 'nineties appeared very much as it does now. The new Chapel and Dining Hall had been completed in 1876. Here the portraits of Southey and Speaker Peel, the billowing lawn sleeves of Shute Baring and John Parsons looked down upon the ranged undergraduates. Below the organ gallery the Latin inscription—*Junior fui et enim senior et non vidi justum derelictum nec semen eius quaerens panem*—must have sounded a little monkish to ears attuned to Cicero. But the panelling and decoration in the Hall had been designed by Paul Waterhouse, who used to follow the Psalms in the Vulgate when they were recited in choir, and they were the gift of Robert Younger, afterwards Lord Blanesburgh. Some people always thought the inscription an arrogant personal allusion; a few may have found it an inspiring text. Belloc had rooms on the ground floor of staircase No. 3 in the main quadrangle—the staircase that almost faces you as you come through from the Porter's Lodge. They were on the left-hand side as you go in. There was plenty of *lebensraum* at Balliol in those days. On the same staircase lived a Japanese Baron, T. Minami-Iwakura, and the son of a famous German banking family, Paul Robert Ernst von Mendelssohn-Bartholdy. Later, in the Michaelmas term of 1893, they were joined by Ernest Barker, a scholar from Manchester. The rooms opposite to Belloc were occupied by a classics don, Baron Paravicini, of whom it was written:

> Virgil shrilly I can render
> Cock-a-hoop upon the fender.

Sir Ernest Barker remembers taking Latin verses to him, and he also remembers the fender.

Belloc was on no more than nodding terms with Ernest Barker, who does not recall exchanging a single word with him. The scholars of the College, most of whom were poor and many of whom won high distinction in after-life, seem to have regarded Belloc as arrogant and snobbish because he made his friends among the fashionable set. Although he was not yet a scholar, he was certainly poor. His friend, F. Y. Eccles, who was then at Christ Church, remembers taking him along to Hall Bros. in the High to be fitted out with some decent clothes, for he had come out of the French Army with a considerably depleted wardrobe. It might have been expected, therefore, that he would find his place among those who had won their way to Oxford with their brains rather than with their money. But Belloc was innocent of either straightforward or inverted snobbery. He did not choose his friends because they came from a particular social background or because they held views on religion or politics which coincided with his own. These common interests might count, but they were not the determining factor. He chose his friends for their qualities as men—or women. As for his acquaintances, he would go to Harold (later Sir Harold) Hartley's rooms and say to him: 'You and I agree about nothing, Hartley, but you have good port and good drawing-paper.' We must remember that Belloc's military service, though it had been gregarious, had also been essentially solitary. He must have longed for companionship on equal terms. Now the 'poor scholar', seriously working for his First in Mods, is an admirable type, but he has not had time to become a man of the world. And Belloc was already at home in a world wider and rougher than any known to his Oxford contemporaries.

Balliol, with its 170 undergraduates, was large enough to be divided easily into 'sets'; and these were grouped round the College societies. The Dervorguilla, named after the 'mother' of Balliol, was aristocratic and convivial. It had its own table in Hall, at right angles to the High Table, as you faced the Gallery. Its members met in each other's rooms when the host of the evening provided port and biscuits, and where some topic of intellectual interest was lightly discussed. It had been founded in the 'eighties. The Brackenbury was more recent, less smart and social, and it discussed the same kind of thing more seriously. There was a third, newer and more highbrow discussion club called the Arnold, which had been founded in 1891 by R. J. Walker, son of the High Master of St. Paul's. And there was the Annandale, devoted exclusively to eating and drinking, whose members wore a pretty tie. Belloc was a prominent member of the 'Dervor', which sometimes held its meetings with the Brackenbury. On one of these occasions, a crisp and bright October evening, he was due to read a paper. He began by reminding his audience that they had no business to be so ecstatic about the weather, when the poor were going hungry in their rags.

Among his immediate or near contemporaries were Leo Amery, Lord Basil Blackwood, Philip and Jack Kershaw, Francis Urquhart, Anthony Henley, and Arthur Stanley, fifth Baron Stanley of Alderley. Of these Basil Blackwood, who gave him his first meerschaum pipe, the Kershaws, Henley and Arthur Stanley were to become life-long friends. He was on equally close terms with at least two men outside Balliol: Eccles and J. S. Phillimore, who were both at the 'House'. Both had come to Oxford from Westminster. Belloc very quickly became a University figure, known far outside the Balliol circle for his exuberance and wit. The impression he made is clearly conveyed by Eccles.

In our little group we never tired of getting him to tell us about his experiences, and he needed no invitation to do so. He would talk about himself without the slightest trace of boasting; but he talked, as he talked about everything else, with a frankness and a spontaneity, as admirable as they were rare. It was no doubt this marvellous facility of speech which made Hilaire Belloc's reputation at Oxford. Those who knew him superficially remarked that in whatever society he happened to be, he talked more than anybody else; they said this before realising that he talked better and more to the point, and before seeing that there was more substance in what he said. It was not, with him, a matter of mere verbal incontinence, a need to hold the floor and a desire to impose his point of view. Even when he was very young, he always respected the convictions of other people when they were sincerely held. His abundant speech not only conveyed the vividness of his impressions; it also sorted out his ideas. No one would have described him as erudite, but he knew a great many things, and there was more of reflexion than of reading in his mind. He might be talking about poetry or morality, history or gastronomy, navigation or politics, but he expressed himself with a fine decision. He thought his subject out to the end, and his judgments, which were sometimes rash or excessive, though never without foundation, hung together remarkably well. There was a sort of family air about them. The Oxford youth were not much given to general ideas, and it was this, very Latin, trait, which distinguished the conversation of my friend. However, one must not suppose that this vigorous young man of 22 was always serious. On the contrary, he was the gayest of companions ... we laughed together a great deal; our conversation was extremely free; we ragged each other; and we sang at the tops of our voices. We feasted and smoked together, we went out for walks and excursions, and nothing could have been happier or more high-spirited. Belloc was never attracted by organised games, but he was indefatigable on foot, on horseback, or in the water. He was especially keen on sailing and canoe-ing up the river—waiting until he could have a little yacht of his own ... Those were good times.[1]

The impression of physical vigour and intellectual high spirits persists in every reminiscence of Belloc in his Oxford days. He walks with Anthony Henley from Carfax to Marble Arch in $11\frac{1}{2}$ hours; and this record was not broken by the attempt of three undergraduates in 1955. He celebrates the Diamond Jubilee by walking from York to Edinburgh; and he walks by himself from Oxford to Holyhead. He is learning England by physical contact with her contours and her soil. He is probing her history by discovering how she is made. He may well have taken part in the famous expedition to Stratford when a band of Balliol men rammed with boats the dam in the Avon, which the Fairfax-Lucys had erected at Charlecote. They evidently resented this as an attack upon the freedom of the stream. Belloc especially enjoyed the Balliol practice of 'booming'; taking a canoe up river by train and coming down on the flood. His spacious and

---

[1] Preface by F. Y. Eccles to the French edition of Belloc's *Essay on the Nature of Contemporary England* : author's translation.

almost insolent approach to living is illustrated by the following letter to Mrs. Wright-Biddulph.

Talking of horses—I and four other Balliol men went out on a distant expedition down the Thames last Sunday, and at evening we found ourselves at a place called Cuddesdon with no way of getting back to Oxford. We asked the innkeeper for a trap and all he said was: 'Is the trap in the yard yours?' So we went out and saw a trap very neat, and a nice horse with the harness marked with Franklin's initial, the horse dealer in Oxford. We got in and drove back to Oxford and when we got near Oxford we got out and gave a little boy a shilling to lead it back to Franklin's yard. But who had hired the trap and whether he minded our taking it, and how he got home, or indeed whether he got back at all, these and other questions we felt no interest in—and we know nothing of it to this day, but we look askance at the Authorities people and we are frightened. Wasn't it very sporting—in a way? [1]

The impression persists of energy, eloquence and song. Belloc could regale his friends with a good many Rabelaisian refrains which he had learned in the French Army, and there was a certain unprintable eighteenth-century ditty, called *The Parson and the Crayfish,* which he was liable to sing in all but the politest company. One afternoon in May Edward Thomas was standing with a companion at the foot of Boars Hill, when they suddenly heard a high tenor voice lifted on the air:

'S'ils tombent, nos jeunes héros,
La France en produit de nouveaux,
Contre vous tous prêts à se battre
Aux armes, citoyens!'

A bicycle swept by, down a steep hill, guided, so far as it was guided at all, by the spirit of the Spring, winged by the south wind, crowned by superb white clouds, and singing that song in a whirl of golden dust. 'That was Belloc', said my

[1] Jan. 19, 1895.

companion, as he lay by the roadside trembling from the shock of that wild career. It was Belloc; and it still is.[1]

In the autumn of 1892, a few months before he went up to Oxford and before he had even matriculated, Belloc met Hubert Howard, second son of the ninth Earl of Carlisle, in the rooms of Francis Urquhart. Howard was three years older than Belloc; he had matriculated in 1889. This seniority gave a certain depth to their friendship, a dimension which hardly existed as yet between Belloc and his younger Oxford friends.

In the hour we spent together a friendship was struck which a certain lapse of time—fatally short—neither emphasized nor altered because it was graven.

... It is his figure that comes up when one recalls the fresh winds in the river valleys, the races on the February floods, the canoes on the Cher, and those glorious runs across country which he continually led with laughter and with a kind of enthusiasm for hazard and for danger. . . . He gave to Balliol a particular character for these things. It was he who attempted to break the record in walking between the University and London; to paddle the forty miles of the Cherwell from Banbury between sunrise and sunset of a February day; and he continually led us in hunts over the fields after nothing, taking jumps that led nowhere, and swimming rivers that were well bridged for those who took life easier.

Now as I write I know that the ten or fifteen of us who were nearest to Hubert Howard are thinking continually of those races over the winter grass. No one can remember him without his figure suggesting the flat meadows down to Sandford, the hedges and walls by Marston, and the risks of taking the Cherwell or of jumping the bank below the Kennington willows.

The two men differed widely not only in social background, but in political opinions and in personal taste. Hubert Howard was a teetotaller:

This temperance was with Hubert Howard a matter so dependent upon general strength of purpose that when we

[1] Edward Thomas. *The Tribune*: Aug. 10, 1906.

thought or spoke of him his teetotalism never entered our
heads; and yet that when he was with us it never entered our
heads either to offer him a glass of wine.

He was also an imperialist:

If the Empire has one quality more than another that
distinguishes it among nations it is this, that it chooses and can
find from a comparatively small circle the energy, the devotion
and the ability without which its whole character would be
changed.

Hubert Howard was killed at Omdurman on September 2,
1898, either by a stray shell or a sniping dervish; and the tribute
from which extracts have been given above, was written at the
request of his father, Lord Carlisle, and printed privately for
circulation among his family and friends. He was a man in
whom 'the power of England worked with the effect of a
great artistic presentation' and to this effect the artist in Belloc
had responded. Few men have been so fated in their death or
so fortunate in their epitaph.

2

Belloc's main platform was the Union, and he began to speak
there almost as soon as he had found his feet. It is a pity that the
Union does not publish its Hansard, so that it is rarely possible to
catch the tone of Belloc's voice in these debates, or the turn of his
phrase. Yet it was undoubtedly his performance at the Union
which made many people prophesy for him a brilliant political
career. He was competing with men like F. E. Smith and John
Simon, J. L. Hammond and F. W. Hirst. All these were masters
of debate; yet Belloc's oratory outshone them all. What was it
like? Here again Eccles gives us the answer.

His speech astonished, then captivated and dazzled his
audience. I seem to recall that on that particular evening the
motion before the house expressed the hope that the French
people would adopt a dictatorial régime. Belloc was a staunch

Republican at that time and he opposed the motion. The chief speaker on the other side was a Prussian baron—rather a piquant detail. It was not so much the substance as the tone of his speech which held the attention. The Union debates follow a ritual modelled on that of Parliament; that was enough to accentuate their unreality. Most of the young speakers, when they are not hum-ing and haw-ing, recite what they have already got by heart; and the most applauded are the dry wits who manage to introduce into a solemn context the most far-fetched allusions and the most idiotic puns. Belloc's eloquence was of quite a different sort. He spoke with great fluency, without the slightest hesitation and without any blurring of his words. There was no emphasis and no clowning. But above all there was inspiration and there was movement. Towards the end he kindled to his theme, and we were kindled by him. I can still see him, standing upright in the great debating hall. He was of medium height, but powerfully built; his features were regular, his eye clear, and his chestnut hair close-cut. He had a wide forehead and a determined chin. He was carelessly dressed and he bent forward a little as he spoke. You wondered whether he was English or French. Those who took him for a French-man on the strength of his surname were as surprised as any. The style and diction were beyond reproach, and nothing in his accent, except a slightly guttural pronunciation of his r's, betrayed his foreign birth. Only an occasional gesture, and a bell-like *timbre* in his voice at certain moments suggested that he was not of purely English blood.[1]

Another impression, equally vivid, is given by Basil Mathews in *The Young Man*.

It was one of those rare nights in the Oxford Union when new men are discovered. Simon had denounced the Turk in Thessaly and Smith had held up the Oriental to admiration. Men whispered to each other of the future Gladstone and Dizzy whom Oxford was to give the nation. No one would be fool enough to speak after such brilliant rhetoric . . . Suddenly a

[1] *Op. cit.*

young man rose and walked to the table. He was broad of
shoulder and trod the floor confidently. A chin that was almost
grim in its young strength was surmounted by a large squarely-
built face. Over his forehead and absurdly experienced eyes,
dark hair fell stiffly. As he rose, men started up and began to
leave the house; at his first sentence they paused and looked at
him—and sat down again. By the end of his third sentence,
with a few waves of his powerful hands, and a touch of unconscious magnetism and conscious strength, the speeches of
J. A. Simon and F. E. Smith were as though they had never
been. For twenty minutes the new orator, Mr. Hilaire Belloc,
who was soon to sit in the seat of Gladstone, Salisbury, Milner,
Curzon and Asquith, as President of the Union, held his
audience breathless.

Belloc tended in his speeches to ride the same hobby-horses. If
the House were being asked to decide whether the University of
Oxford encouraged the most desirable studies, he would still find
room for an explanation of Republicanism, or a defence of
democracy, or a castigation of Prussia. If the matter at issue were
the Disestablishment of the Church in Wales he would find time
to abuse the aristocracy with whose sons he consorted. The
previous speaker had made more than one disparaging reference
to the 'agricultural labourer', and this launched Belloc into a
fierce invective against the supporters of privilege. Why, asked
the *Oxford Magazine,* would he 'mar the effect of his oratorical
power by persistently deserting the question under discussion, in
order to wave the Republican flag?' On January 27, 1894, he
opposed the establishment of a School of English Literature as
'unwise and unnecessary'. This would make of English Literature
a 'thing to be hung up and framed'. Back again at grips with his
bête noire, he amused the House with a specimen of German
criticism at work on *Hamlet.* The Germans studied English, he
maintained, because they had so little literature of their own.
Nor was it true that the literature of France was formed by a
French Literature School: it was formed by the French classics.
Beautiful things were made to be revered; they should not be

touched by brutal examiners. In this debate Belloc was opposed
by F. E. Smith, whom the *Oxford Magazine* described as 'forcible,
biting and epigrammatic'.[1] He argued that there was no difference, in this respect, between English Literature and Greek or
Latin. If the one was too beautiful to touch, so were the others.

Belloc spoke frequently during 1894. He objected to the
principle of the House of Lords quite independently of what it did.
An hereditary Upper Chamber was opposed to the native right to
self-government; and there was 'no surer way of destroying the
life of a nation than by keeping up verbal as opposed to vital
distinctions.' He urged that the interests of Great Britain had
nothing in common with the Triple Alliance; maintained that the
'Revolt of the Daughters', as the motion described the agitation
for Women's Suffrage, was only an aristocratic movement in a
restricted circle; and in proposing that 'This House would
welcome any scheme for associating undergraduates with the
government of the University', he appealed to the sacred principles of 1789. Here again, logically enough, he was opposed by
F. E. Smith. On June 2, after the rejection of Gladstone's Home
Rule Bill, John Dillon came down to plead for Ireland. Of Belloc's
speech on this occasion the *Isis* remarked that 'it was as eloquent
and abstract as of old'. These *idées générales* did not always make
easy listening. But in the opinion of the *Oxford Magazine* a better
speech had not been delivered in the Union for a very long time.
In October 1894, he opposed the Bishop of Chester's licensing
scheme on the grounds that it was 'like putting a thermometer in
front of the fire to make the weather warmer. Opportunity has
little to do with drunkenness. Drunkenness is due to the desire for
getting drunk'.

Many people must have wondered why Belloc was not a
Socialist, for he stood well to the left of Liberalism. The collective
theory had, as we have seen, tempted him at the time of the
London Dock Strike; but his radicalism was French, not English,
in its origin. France had taught him what a peasantry can bring to
a nation, and there is no peasant without property. In France, too,
among so much that was uncertain, he had admired the stability

[1] Jan. 31, 1894.

of wealth evenly distributed. And so when the policy of the Independent Labour Party was under discussion, he vigorously opposed it.

'How could Collectivism work', he exclaimed, 'without a military despotism? How could it work with the existing attitude of the individual conscience unchanged? In fact, it involves Theft in its inception, and Tyranny in its execution, and for neither is Society yet ready.'

Belloc stood for the Secretaryship of the Union in November 1893 and polled 123 votes against the 203 of F. R. C. Bruce (Worcester) who was elected. At the end of the following term, however, he was elected Librarian, with 146 votes against 82 for Vernon Harcourt. A photograph of the Standing Committee shows him with large knotted tie, winged collar, crumpled coat and high waitscoat with lapels. Beside him are: F. E. Smith, President; Earl Beauchamp; the Earl of Crawford and Balcarris; and E. G. Hemmerde, afterwards Recorder of Liverpool.

'I have been to the Union for the first time as Librarian feeling very grand', he writes to Mrs. Wright-Biddulph. 'Also I have introduced a list of books as warm and vicious as I dare—but I drew the line at the book known as "Elsie" and indulged in nothing worse than George Moore's "Esther Waters".'[1]

The Presidency, the golden key which has opened so many great careers, was now well within his grasp, and the debate on which the choice of the new President largely depended, was held on November 24, 1894. It was concerned with the London School Board Election; not a very inspiring topic. But Belloc surpassed himself in his support of the Progressives against the Moderates, in whose circular, he claimed, there were words 'so distinctly theological that I should be called to order for quoting them in this house, and so controversial that they were debated for a long time in the Council of Nicaea'. His speech, according to the *Isis*, displayed 'a consistent view of almost every subject, based on intelligent and broad principles; an elaboration of forcible and easily comprehended argument; an appropriateness of phraseology adorned by an appositeness of analogy, and delivered with an irresistible

[1] April 28, 1894.

vehemence of utterance—each of these Mr. Belloc has in greater
abundance than any other member of the society. And they
were never more effectively displayed than on Thursday'.

Belloc won the Presidency with 327 votes against 196 for
F. R. C. Bruce, and J. L. Hammond was elected Secretary. This
was the summit of Belloc's Oxford fame and only the shrewder
and more cynical of those who had watched him may have had
their doubts. When the debates were over, he would walk up and
down the Union garden, restless and absorbed in conversation,
waving a pencil to illustrate his points. *Punch,* he would declare,
'has no humour and the upper classes have no manners'. 'The
trouble with you, Belloc,' F. E. Smith is said to have remarked to
him, 'is that you will insist on playing the fool.' But the difference
between Belloc and his most brilliant rival at the Union was the
difference between two men who could each be funny in his own
way, but who were each serious about quite different things.
'F. E.' won all, or nearly all, the glittering prizes that were
predicted for him, and Belloc's career, in comparison, reads like an
eccentric failure. Yet which man left the more enduring mark?
Meanwhile, the *Isis* celebrated the new President in a long
article.

. . . The Union, when it has been taken by storm, feels
afterwards a revulsion of shame that it has let itself go too
cheap. And so for a time there was a tendency to regard Mr.
Belloc as a windy rhetorician with one speech, until he proved
by happy efforts of humour, and convincing arguments
dispassionately searching the most various provinces of politics
and debate, that he was equally master of all styles and all topics.
Then he was rehabilitated, and once more the House preferred
to applaud his periods rather than to laugh at parodies of his
manner.

From Mr. Belloc you get a speech different from anything
else you will hear in the Union. He dares to be serious and to
show it; the ordinary speaker is too much afraid of being taken
to mean what he says. He loves general principles, has a perfect
lust of deduction; and it is the unity in which he comprises all
departments of politics, the consistent measure to which he

reduced them all, which gave colour to the taunt that he had one speech of all work. Of course that kind of oratory is a prey to the scoffer, but its effect outlasts the laugh; and Mr. Belloc, almost alone of Union speakers, makes converts. . . .

His heart is so ostentatiously on his sleeve that you suspect that it is large enough for some to be under his waistcoat too. But the freedom of his conversation is admirable; he scintillates with enthusiasm on all things—boats, riding, Shakespeare, running across country, Balliol—and some others *in camera*.

Among other tastes should be mentioned a liking for—Burgundy, sunshine, tobacco, music, Rabelais, good verse, non-typical Frenchmen, beggars, Irishmen, gas-lamps, pretty stories, Gothic architecture, similes, and all good fellowship; and a hatred for—Oxford tradesmen, the Proctorial system, affectation, prudery, English weather, silence, the German Emperor, modernity, hero-worship, . . . Socialists and oligarchs.

There roughly you have the President portrayed. Only one College turns out a school of men whose brains are not turned to muscle, nor their thews to flap-doodle; but even Balliol has seldom before numbered among her trophies such a combination as the familiar figure with the big dark cloak, soft hat, and bludgeon, known to his friends as 'Peter'.

3

It was natural that a man with so superb a gift of advocacy and so passionate an interest in politics should have had leanings towards the Bar. That would have been a sure entrance into the House of Commons. Belloc certainly played with the idea, and returned to it, as we shall see, a year or two later. While he was still at Oxford, he went to London to eat his dinners. Meanwhile he read his essays to the Balliol History tutor, A. L. Smith, in company with H. C. ('Fluffy') Davis, the Brackenbury scholar of 1891. Davis was to become one of Belloc's stoutest opponents and chronic *bêtes noires*. After reading 'Greats' he had now moved on to History. Belloc had taken 'Pass Mods' in the ordinary way (for the 'History Prelim' Examination had not yet been instituted) and his many extra-collegiate activities did not prevent him from working hard. He would read all the morning, only breaking off to snatch a cup of coffee at Buols, which had just opened in the Cornmarket. He was the first, at Balliol, to start this modern practice of 'elevenses', and it seems oddly out of character. Lunch was a scratch sort of meal—bread and cheese and beer; physical exercise was reserved for the afternoon, and serious conviviality for the evening. Later, as his Schools approached, he did not speak at the Union and he took to going to bed early. He now shared rooms at No. 6, St. Aldates ('Austerlitz') with Eccles, Phillimore and Malcolm Seton. This gives a key to the quatrain, which has puzzled many.

> Not even this peculiar town
> Has ever fixed a friendship firmer,
> But—one is married, one's gone down,
> And one's a Don and one's in Burmah.

At the time these lines were written, Belloc was married, Eccles had gone down, Phillimore was teaching Greek at Glasgow, and Seton was in Burmah.

Belloc seems to have worked hard, also, in the vacation, either at Slindon or in other houses where he was regarded as a somewhat unpredictable guest. He receives an invitation from Mrs. Wright-Biddulph in November and answers it in March. He then goes to her in April (1894) complete 'with a fine new leather bag beautiful to see with plated clasps and my name painted on it'. He paid several visits to Naworth, where Lord Carlisle had engaged him to tutor his son. The two young men would ride over the moors on their ponies, wrestling in the saddle to decide who should go through a gate first. In the Long Vacation he sometimes went further afield. In 1893 he wrote up his name and the number of his regiment on the spire of Strasbourg Cathedral, and in August 1895 we find him with Basil Blackwood in Scandinavia, roaming the forests for game. A woman of ravishing beauty stole 5s. off him at Elsinore.

Jowett had died in May 1893, but there had been time for him to read Belloc's essays and he once remarked to him with a characteristic appreciation of the world: 'Belloc, you are a man of no family and of no wealth, it seems to me that your talents should lead you to the Bar.' Later, he told him that he could get a Fellowship, pretty well for the asking; this was in tune with his dictum that a man is seldom more influential than when he is at the heart of some great institution. Jowett liked to invite important people down from London for the week-end and ask selected undergraduates to meet them. At other times they would be invited to the Master's house after 'Hall', and sit round his dining-table, sipping claret, speaking when they were spoken to, and eating preserved cherries.

Jowett's ascendancy at Oxford was unquestioned—least of all by himself.

> This is Balliol, I am Jowett,
> All there is to know I know it;
> I am Master of this College;
> What I don't know isn't knowledge.

Cosmo Gordon Lang remembered him as 'a little figure with its black swallow-tail coat and white shirt-front and "choker", the ruddy chubby face with its rather fretful mouth, like a chestnut out of condition, the chirpy voice'.[1] Once he asked Belloc what he regarded as the best form of government. Belloc, as one of the only four Republicans in Oxford (the others were Eccles, Phillimore and a man called Thornton), replied: 'A Republic.' 'Ah', said Jowett, 'but before you can have a Republic, you must have Republicans.' There were never enough Republicans for the Republic of which Belloc dreamed. There were enough, however, to form the Republican Club, one of the smallest, the shortest-lived, and the most famous of Oxford Societies. To qualify for membership you had to hold radical ideas of government and you had to have been fined for misconduct. The philosophy of the Club was inspired by Thomas Jefferson, whose birthday was celebrated as the principal feast of the year, although the behead-

---

[1] *Cosmo Gordon Lang*: J. G. Lockhart (1949).

ing of Charles I and Louis XVI were remembered with an almost
equal enthusiasm.

Jowett was succeeded by Edward Caird, an Hegelian philosopher from Glasgow. He used to invite women undergraduates
to his breakfast parties and, like his wife, was extremely shy.
Belloc thought at first that he was 'going the way to make
himself out of touch with the College', but a year later he 'was
growing rather more popular'.[1] Caird grew fond of Belloc, and
was able to influence him, as we shall see, at an important crisis of
his early career.

But the only Don with whom Belloc was in regular contact
was his tutor, A. L. Smith. 'A. L.' was a man of small stature and
immensely varied knowledge. He had founded the Athletic
Committee and through it produced two lob bowlers in the
same University team. He was also concerned with the College
finances.

> I am little Smith who glances
>   On disorganised finances;
> Who'd have looked for so much vigour
>   In so very small a figure?

But history was his passion and Belloc was among his favourite
pupils. Ramsay Muir, a Balliol contemporary, describes him as

a tutor of genius. . . . A good historical mind, he said, ought
not to be all precise detail, like a pre-Raphaelite picture; there
should be haze in the middle distance, as in a good landscape
painting; and this half-remembered knowledge, even if it
cannot be set down in detail, will show itself in the turn of a
phrase, in the avoidance of errors, in a right atmosphere.[2]

There can be no doubt that A. L. Smith, also, encouraged Belloc
to think that, given a good Class in his Schools, he could have a
Fellowship for the asking. Preferably at All Souls; but if not at All
Souls, then at some other College. These hopes, inspired from
such a quarter, may well have deflected his ambitions from the
Bar.

[1] Letter to Madame Belloc: May 13, 1894.
[2] *An Autobiography and Some Essays* (1943).

A glance at Belloc's notes for the Oxford History Schools reveals the width of his reading, his power of analysis, his quickness in assimilation, and the extreme precision of his method. His special period was the formative centuries of Europe between 919 and 1273. He read Bryce on the Holy Roman Empire, Sismondi on the Italian Republics, Milman on the Church, Freeman on the Norman Conquest, Zeller on France and Italy. He would go to Gibbon for the Fourth Crusade ('how admirable he is!') and to an article by Renan in *Etudes Religieuses* for the Franciscan movement. For original sources he would dip into Matthew Paris and William of Apulia, or consult the Itinerarium Ricardi Primi. For further information on France he went to Kitchin, Michelet and Lavisse, quoting with some relish Thierry's aphorism that 'the Seine had taken its revenge upon the Rhine'. The notes are set out on foolscap in small, very careful handwriting, with wide margins; the quotations and headlines are generally in red ink; and each phase of historical development is illustrated by a map, often tiny in scale, but always meticulously drawn. Most of these maps are clearly his own; but a few he had taken from Spruner's *Historische Handatlas*. His personal comments are very few. At one point he wonders if Frederick Barbarossa knew Theocritus; and his *précis* of Bryce is introduced by the picture of an elephant.

Among those lecturing on the period at that time were Charles Oman (who was Proctor in 1894–5), Frank Bright of 'Univ', A. J. Carlyle and A. L. Smith. Many of Belloc's notes were evidently taken down in the lecture-hall, or directly afterwards. Others were given him by A. L. Smith in tutorials, and these were intended to suggest the answers to likely questions by the examiners. J. A. Froude was the Regius Professor during the first two years of Belloc's residence in Oxford. In November 1892 he had given his Inaugural Lecture on 'the Professor's apology for treating history as a branch of the dramatic art'. Belloc may well have heard this, and not many years would go by before he would better Froude's instruction. For the present he was content to learn whatever the academic historians had to teach him. Only in his third year did he suspect a flaw in their presentation. Besides, his special period was not the ground upon which he

later chose to challenge them most vigorously. But he must have
got tired of the immaculate Anglo-Saxons before he was through
with Freeman.

He sat for his Schools in June 1895 and gained a First Class
Honours. There is a story that he had done some research among
the archives of a French château, and that the results of this helped
to win him the distinction. In July he sat for a Fellowship at All
Souls. He was competing with all the ablest men in Greats,
History and Law, and out of these only two were chosen. Belloc
was unsuccessful. Of the two candidates elected one was his rival,
'Fluffy' Davis, a first-rate academic scholar, and this added gall
to his defeat. There were twenty-one unsuccessful candidates;
among them E. I. Carlyle (later Fellow of Lincoln), C. A. Aling-
ton (who was elected the following year), and C. H. K. Marten
(afterwards Provost of Eton). But their company brought Belloc
no consolation in what he regarded as a personal catastrophe. He
never forgave All Souls for refusing him. Whenever he felt the
pinch of poverty or the gloom of depression, whenever he cursed
the necessity which made him grind out books for a living, he
would look back and reflect that all these burdens might have been
spared him if he had been elected to All Souls. A prize Fellowship
would have given him two hundred pounds a year, rooms in
college, and free dinners for seven years. Afterwards he might have
been given a teaching Fellowship at another college. He would
have had sufficient income to maintain his wife and family, and
sufficient leisure to write only the books he wanted to write, and
in the way that he wanted to write them.

The disappointment became an obsession; it marked all the
conversation of his later years when so many other memories had
faded. So we must ask ourselves why so brilliant a man was turned
down. The candidate for an All Souls Fellowship is not required
to answer more than two or three questions; he is generally able
to write on what interests him most. H. A. L. Fisher used to say
that Belloc injured his chances by a prolonged eulogy of St.
Louis. He was also thought to have annoyed the examiners by
placing a statue of the Blessed Virgin on the desk where he was
writing. Or it may be argued, quite simply, that he was not cut

out to be a don. But then a Fellow of All Souls is no ordinary don.
He is under no obligation to teach; he has none of the duties that
fall on the Fellow of another College; he need never meet an
undergraduate unless he wants to. But he must be *persona grata* in
the Common Room and justify his election by his scholarship.
Now Belloc always maintained that he was rejected on account of
his 'militant Catholicism'; but his Catholicism was anything but
militant at this time. He was certainly known to be a Catholic,
but Eccles tells us that this had nothing to do with his prestige
and that only a small number of his intimate friends were interested
in his religious views. It is not easy to say what exactly these were.
According to Eccles, his certitude in matters of belief only confirmed his ascendancy over those who met him. But other evidence
suggests that he had moved a long way from the piety of his
boyhood. It is probable that he still went, fairly regularly, to
Mass. He had promised his mother that he would do so; besides,
for a French nationalist, going to Mass was not necessarily a
declaration of personal belief. It was an *acte de présence* which certain
political circumstances might demand of him. It was a way of
protest against the Freemasons and the Jews. Belloc would never
at any time have dreamed of denying that he was a Catholic; he
belonged with every fibre of his being to the Catholic tradition of
Europe. But his temper, though it was ardent and romantic, was
also sceptical. The men he mixed with at Balliol had only the
vaguest religious convictions; a cloudy and conceited agnosticism
was in the air. He was at the age when faith wears thin, and the
world is too much with one. He was feeling his personality and his
powers, forming his judgments, and finding his friends. His self-
confidence was unbounded. The French Army had taught him
much, but it had not left him unscathed. He did not yet realize
how good a thing it would be 'not to have to return to the Faith'.[1]

It is more likely that All Souls rejected him because he was not
universally popular. No dominating personality ever is. But the
Fellows may well have thought twice before welcoming into
their midst a man who monopolized every conversation. Many
years later Belloc was elected to the Beefsteak Club, but he soon

[1] *The Path to Rome* (1901).

resigned from it when he found that members of the Beefsteak were expected to listen as well as to talk. His indifference towards those not in his own set must have been resented by many besides the 'poor scholars' of Balliol. And there was a further cause of unpopularity—his strident, exotic anti-Semitism. What were they to make of a radical who went about proclaiming the guilt of Dreyfus? The invective he had picked up from Drumont and the *Libre Parole* might have its place in the slanging-match of French politics; at Oxford it merely seemed offensive and silly. The young Herbert Samuel was at Balliol with Belloc, and Paul Rubens was up at the same time. These men and others of Jewish birth, like Ball the librettist and composer, were popular and respected. Nothing could have been better calculated than Belloc's phobia to frighten the dons into thinking that for all his brilliance, he was a little unbalanced; and that a young man in whose bonnet so many bees were buzzing might well become something of a bore.

Belloc's reputation for anti-Semitism was to dog him till the end of his life. We shall examine later how far it was deserved. Already, at Oxford, he was incredulous that one of his closest friends should have been in love with a Jewess. But what labelled him in the public eye as an anti-Semite was unquestionably his attitude to the great *affaire*. When he wrote that his point of view was shared by 'ninety-nine Frenchmen out of a hundred' and in particular by the 3,000,000 soldiers who were actually serving in the Army, or composed its Reserve; when he claimed that there was a greater 'percentage of men in Pittsburg today who sympathize with the Spanish cause in Cuba than you could find in Paris who entertain any doubt of Dreyfus' guilt'; when he maintained that of the men who signed the petition for the retrial only Anatole France was 'a man of reputation and well-received'; when he asserted that the agitation for a retrial was dictated by a small minority in control of the money-power—when he argued thus, he was plainly repeating the catch-cries and echoing the prejudices of those Frenchmen among whom he moved and whose general outlook he shared. He boasted that his forebears had served in the armies of France before the Revolution, and he

H

could not understand how the word of a man like Zola, who was hardly received in polite society, could be taken against the considered verdict of seven honourable judges. He pointed out the great peril to national security of disclosing the nature of the document Dreyfus was said to have betrayed and the name of the power to whom he was believed to have betrayed it. A state of 'cold' war existed between France and Germany, and if open hostilities were to break out again, France must choose the moment most propitious for her military chances.

This reasoning was set out in an article in the *Pittsburg Post* [1] and Belloc repeated the gist of it in *The Cruise of the 'Nona'*. He was not a man who easily changed his mind. Time has established the innocence of Dreyfus beyond any reasonable doubt, but it has also established a distinction between Dreyfus and the Dreyfusards. Belloc was grossly unjust when he spoke of Dreyfus as 'an officer with the worst of records'. On the contrary, Dreyfus had nothing against him but the reputation of being something of a bore and of occasionally frequenting houses of ill-fame. If this last were to be regarded as a military offence, the armies of Europe would quickly be deprived of their effectives. But Belloc was certainly right in seeing that many of the Dreyfusards were actuated by less than a pure love of justice. They did want to weaken the Army; they did want to destroy the Church. If there was prejudice on one side, there was also prejudice on the other. Where Belloc did himself infinite harm was in not seeing, or in not coming later to admit, that the great principle of *fiat justitia ruat caelum* was at stake; and that this principle, which has always been the pride of Liberalism, was one that every Christian should be proud to make his own. The Dreyfus case brought out into the open those contradictions in Belloc's political philosophy which made some people regard him as a radical and others as a reactionary. It made them wonder how disinterested was his search for truth when, in this capital instance, it was so manifestly impaired by prejudice.

The refusal of a Fellowship struck him like the tragic ending of a love-affair, and indeed it may well have dashed, for the time

[1] March 1898.

being, what hopes still remained to him that Elodie would one day be his wife. For he had loved Oxford—as she deserves to be loved—almost to the limit of idolatry. He had taken for granted that he would continue to bask in her grace and favour. But she had brusquely turned away from him. He would court her for a few years still, and then he, too, would turn away—with the fury of a rejected suitor. Yet how many of Belloc's admirers would have wished him to remain permanently in Oxford? And would he really have wished it himself? Many years afterwards he said to Cyril Clemens:

> For anyone who has important work to do in the world the temptation of Oxford is like that of the Siren in Homer's *Odyssey*. There are few greater temptations on earth than to stay permanently at Oxford in meditation, and to read all the books in the Bodleian. But sooner or later the man who succumbs to it loses his youth and finally his vitality unless he manages to throw himself whole-heartedly into a corporate existence without thought of any financial return beyond the wherewithal for a college board and lodging. Many a man, however, cannot renounce the temptations of an active business life without the incentive of a larger income and a wider scope for his ambition than the University is able to offer him.[1]

[1] Interview, from the *Mark Twain Journal*.

CHAPTER VI

MARRIAGE AND VERSE

I

HOW matters stood between Belloc and Elodie at this moment it is difficult to say. She had been deeply affected by her mother's death in 1891, and she had kept up a desultory correspondence with Father A, still telling him nothing of Belloc's attachment to her or of his visit to California in 1891. She even went so far as to reproach him for the tone of his previous letters; and he, on his side, contented himself with a formal and reasonably courteous disapproval of her delay in following what he still believed to be her vocation, and of many liberties which were apparently sanctioned in the United States. He had heard of Mrs. Hogan's death, though not from Elodie; and he had said Mass for the repose of her soul. In March 1893 Elodie wrote to say that all was ready for her admission to the convent, but that a fresh testamentary obstacle had arisen and that she must wait. She felt that she had been ungrateful to him, and sent him an article she had written for an American paper on 'Some Masters of the Ego'. Father A had rather curiously equated sanctity with *égoisme*—presumably because he was so haunted by the fear of Hell—and she had borrowed his terminology. But of these 'masters' two were Protestants and one was a Quaker, and she had not hesitated to describe the two Protestants as 'the best exponents in this century of the Christian Faith'. Such language was not at all to Father A's liking. He replied that he would much rather have read an announcement in a Catholic paper that she was taking the veil. Even from a distance of several thousand miles he still itched to control her movements, and her intention to visit the Exhibition at Chicago before entering the convent filled him with alarm.

We may reasonably suppose that Belloc and she had been corresponding all this time, and he had no doubt told her of his hopes for a Fellowship. When these were dashed, did the prospect of an early marriage seem yet further removed? Anyway, she entered St. Joseph's Central House of the Sisters of Charity at Emmitsburg, Maryland, in October 1895. All we know for certain is that she remained a postulant, contracted no obligations, and left of her own accord a month later, having decided that she had no call to the religious life. The Sisters of Charity had a Vincentian father as their priest-director, and the story persists that she showed him the letters she had received—and was perhaps still receiving—from Belloc. He is said to have remarked that any man capable of writing such letters must have been truly in love with her.

When she came out of the convent she wrote to Belloc and informed him that she had failed to prove her vocation; she did not tell him that her nerves were shattered and her health impaired. He, for his part, received the news with something of a shock, for Elodie had faded, not indeed from his thoughts, but from his expectations. He had no doubts, however, as to what he must do. On January 24, 1896, he cabled her, rather imperatively: 'Elodie write plans won't wait.' She had obviously not yet given him a definite answer as to when, or whether, they could be married. Meanwhile, he had had news of her from Gertrude Atherton who was in England. Early in March, though with what encouragement from Elodie we do not know, he sailed, accompanied by his mother, for New York. On arrival they went to Philadelphia where Hilaire lectured, later in the month, on Joan of Arc. Further lectures followed in Germantown, Baltimore, and New Orleans, bringing him twenty pounds a week. From New Orleans he wrote to his mother:

> The hotel where I am is pure French and it is striking to see how bi-lingual the town is. Even the quite newcomers get to talk French. They are very devout and bring out no Monday papers. The approach to this place was through an endless pine-forest, 200 miles at least. The ground was all swamp. All

night there were zig-zags of light through the woods, coming
from fireflies which swarm as gnats do in England. The mountains of North Carolina in the distance were almost as fine as
the Limousin Hills from Angoulême.[1]

He reached San Francisco about the middle of May, Madame
Belloc remaining behind in Philadelphia.

These are the bare facts; what lay behind them is made clear by
a letter to John Phillimore, dated May 28. First, there had been
two months of violent opposition at home. Terrible examples of
this or that *mésalliance* had been held up to him; threats about
the alteration of wills had been uttered. These had left him
quite unmoved, and he borrowed the money for his journey at
an interest of five per cent. He had given Elodie his address in
Philadelphia, but no letter was waiting for him when he got
there. He had given her other addresses across the continent,
but still there was no word. When he arrived in San Francisco
he discovered the reason. She had been dangerously ill. This
would appear to have been a nervous breakdown, brought
on by emotional strain and the austerities of her stay in
the convent. She was convalescent, however, by the end of the
month.

For Belloc, too, the strain of waiting—and of wondering—
had been too much. On finding her, he 'went to pieces. I suppose
every man does that once or twice in his life, but I hope never
again to suffer from a collapse of the kind. It is worse than drink—
one is afraid of delirium.' It was the shock of relief, but also of
revelation. It was the stunning paralysis of return. He had not
seen her for five years, and in those five years he had grown up.
He had grown, not away from her, but away from many of the
things in which she believed; things which had intimately
formed her and could never be divorced from her personality.
Chief among them was the Faith. The dazzling prestige of
Oxford, the laughter, the carousals, the physical energy, the
cutting intellectual debate—all seemed an expense of spirit and a
waste of breath beside the reality of the things he had recovered.

[1] May 3, 1896.

My intense loneliness here—the shock of readjustment after all the wreck of these five years was not helped till I got your letter. . . .

You do well to say Christian. God brings a man to knowledge in any one of a thousand paths, but I feel as though I had not understood the Mother Rome until these days. Her immense tradition and power putting into insignificance the ill-working and over-momentum of the hierarchy of the moment. That is the one thing here which is holding and moulding the new chaos they have made. The Mass and the Sacraments are the same: and I tell you it is like home to me to hear the Mumbo-Jumbo of the young priests and the venerable common sense of the old Fathers: and to be able to pray at Our Lady's altar and to find my childhood again.

I had no conception till I got here of what these five years had been. My soul had frozen—a little more and I should have done nothing with my life.

Thank you for the 100 Dollars. They will form the most useful of wedding presents for I fear the little estate over here in the hills is mortgaged past all hope (and in the present decline of values) and my work does not begin till October. But you are not a rich man and you must not drain yourself in presents of that magnitude.[1]

Hilaire Belloc and Elodie Hogan were married on June 16, in the Church of St. John the Baptist, Napa—Elodie's birthplace. An elderly Irish priest, Father Slattery, was the officiant and a nuptial Mass was celebrated. Henry and Elizabeth Hogan witnessed the register. Elodie had made her bridegroom go twice to confession before receiving Holy Communion; Father Slattery suggested to him that he should take the pledge of total abstinence, but that advice was not followed. There was a sumptuous wedding breakfast and Hilaire sent his mother a piece of the cake. The married couple went on the same evening to Geysers in Sonoma County, and if the shadow of Father A fell across the completion of that day, Elodie may have recalled a remark that he had made

[1] Letter to J. S. Phillimore: May 28, 1896.

to her in Rome—that if she did not become a Sister of Charity, she would become a very special sort of wife. But he could not have guessed how large a service to the Church she had performed in failing to fulfil his hopes of her. As Belloc had written to Phillimore:

> You must not think my intellect permanently injured because the Church looms over me here. You have it 'in open soup' where you are, but here it is like a country house planted in the wilds of West Ham, or like a decent woman in a race meeting, or like a stream of water in New Mexico. An unforgettable oasis of Discipline, and duty and right feeling and home.[1]

2

The Bellocs returned by Lake Champlain in time for the Summer Meeting of Studies at Philadelphia in July. Belloc gave the Inaugural Lecture on the Roman Basis of our Civilization, and an evening course on the French Revolution. In March his first volume of poems—*Verses and Sonnets*—had been published by Ward and Downey at 5s., and was, for some curious reason, printed on cardboard. Of this Maurice Baring wrote, in *The Puppet Show of Memory*[2]:

> I do not think that this book excited a ripple of attention at the time, and yet some of the poems in it have lived, and are now found in many anthologies, whereas the verse which at this time was received with a clamour of applause is nearly all of it not only dead but buried and completely forgotten.

Apart from a single poem, 'Homer', which Wilfrid Meynell had printed in *Merrie England* in 1888 and one or two juvenilia in the *Irish Monthly*, no verse of Belloc's had appeared anywhere and he does not seem to have been regarded as a poet. Much had happened since he sat reading Milton and Shakespeare in the Arundel gap. Life had seized him by the throat and he had been a quick learner. He had learnt, among other things, that his own

---

[1] May 28, 1896.   [2] 1922.

way of writing verse would be the slow way, chiselling and refining until he had completed a nearly perfect thing. He did not set out to astonish but to satisfy; classical rhythm rather than romantic surprise, melody rather than image, would be his *forte*. The rhyming scheme of his Sonnets to the Twelve Months was skilfully varied. It is worth remarking that in only one of the twelve did he allow himself an extra syllable in the final couplet, but that when he did so the effect was extremely beautiful.

> But in my garden all the trees have shed
> Their legacies of light, and all the flowers are dead.

There are clear Shakespearian echoes, bracing the emotion with thought.

> Youth gave you to me, but I'll not believe
> That Youth will, taking his quick self, take you.
> Youth's all our Truth: he cannot so deceive.
> He has our graces, not our ownselves too.
> He still compares with time when he'll be spent,
> By human doom enhancing what we are;
> Enriches us with rare experiment,
> Lends arms to leaguered Age in Time's rough war.

There is experience as well as craftsmanship in these poems, and there is personality as well. Now personality, disciplined to expression, is the stuff that makes poetry live. What other poet would have regarded August as

> The soldier month, the bulwark of the year—

or have evoked, in the same context, Charlemagne:

> When he with his wide host came conquering home
> From vengeance under Roncesvalles ta'en.
> Or when his bramble beard flaked red with foam
> Of bivouac wine-cups on the Lombard plain,
> What time he swept to grasp the world at Rome.

The lines are not particularly good; but you feel the personality of the man storming its way through. Equally surprising, but a

good deal more successful, is 'September', inspired by the
memory of Sedan; all the boyhood of Belloc had been spent under
the shadow of that defeat, and a good part of his manhood would
be spent in avenging it.

> I, from a window where the Meuse is wide,
>   Looked westward out to the September night;
> The men that in the hopeless battle died
>   Rose, and deployed, and stationed for the fight;
> A brumal army, vague and ordered large
>   For mile on mile by some pale general;
> I saw them lean by companies to the charge,
>   But no man living heard the bugle-call.
>
> And fading still, and pointing to their scars,
>   They fled in lessening cloud, where gray and high
> Dawn lay along the heaven in misty bars;
>   But watching from that eastern casement, I
>   Saw the Republic splendid in the sky,
> And round her terrible head the morning stars.

This is good, rousing rhetoric, if indeed it is not something more;
and no one but Belloc could have written it. Once or twice, as in
'The Poor of London', a note of indignation, deep not shrill,
makes itself heard.

> The poor of Jesus Christ along the street
> In your rain sodden, in your snows unshod,
> They have nor hearth, nor sword, nor human meat,
> Nor even the bread of men: Almighty God.

He remembered the Dock Strike and the hungry faces he had
harangued; just as in 'Auvergnat' we catch a glimpse of 'our
cycling correspondent in France'—

> The road went up, the road went down,
>   And there the matter ended it.
> He broke his heart in Clermont town,
>   At Pontgibaud they mended it.

But the sensitive ear may catch an even more intimate experience in some of these early poems. Most, if not all, of them had been written while he was waiting for Elodie; and one or two of them betray his hope and his dependence. She would give him 'Her Faith'

> Because my faltering feet may fail to dare
> The first descendant of the steps of Hell
> Give me the word in Time that triumphs there.

She had echoed like music in his memory, yet he had not known the ending of the song:

> Oh! do not play me music any more,
>   Lest in us mortal, some not mortal spell
>   Should stir strange hopes, and leave a tale to tell
> Of two belovéd whom holy music bore,
>   Through whispering night and doubt's uncertain seas,
> To drift at length along a dawnless shore,
>   The last sad goal of human harmonies.
> Look! do not play me music any more.
>
> You are my music and my mistress both,
>   Why, then, let music play the master here?
> Make silent melody, Melodie. I am loath
>   To find that music, large in my soul's ear,
> Should stop my fancy, hold my heart in prize,
> And make me dreamer more than dreams are wise.

This again is very Elizabethan in its feeling and intellectual 'conceit'. In his introduction to the last edition of *Sonnets and Verse* [1] Mr. R. A. Jebb tells us that Elodie persuaded Belloc to withdraw the first volume from circulation because it contained some poems that she did not like. In a later collection of his poems the sonnet just quoted was among the other verse (mostly satirical) which had been omitted. Did she dislike the play upon her name? Or did they both feel that it expressed a doubt which had long since been resolved?

[1] 1954.

There was a certain piquancy in the publication of *Verses and Sonnets* just before Belloc got married, for he stood, though he probably did not know it, at the parting of the ways. In so far as he wished to write at all—and he had published little while he was at Oxford—he wished to write verse. The slim volume might have been the prelude to an output as large and varied as Yeats's. But although so much of his verse has the quality of permanence—the *graven* quality which he tirelessly strove for—it only forms a fraction of his total work. It may well be that he will be remembered as a poet, but it was not as a poet that he chose to live.

> Nor even in my rightful garden lingered.

The line was often taken to mean that he ought to have remained in France, but he explained to F. J. Sheed that it did not mean that at all. It meant that he had deserted poetry for prose—'because one fights with prose'. He would always have been a fighter, but Elodie had a persuasive voice in deciding the things for which he fought. And the battle was shortly to begin.

3

Everything was going to be difficult for the Bellocs. Even before he left California Hilaire wondered how his mother would receive his bride. 'You know,' he wrote to Phillimore, 'I am still in the dark as to how far an opposition which has been so bitter will translate itself into active rudeness when I bring my wife home.' This opposition, which at one point had seemed to be relaxed, had now gathered considerable force. Then, for a young married man, the material prospects were not encouraging.

> I have a prospect of work lecturing—nothing enormous . . . I wish to God they had given me the All Souls. I earned it quite enough. Tell me, to the address in Philadelphia, when you come back to England. I must have a friend or two when the struggle begins.[1]

In September they were in Normandy and then they settled down in Oxford at 5 Bath Place. Later they moved out to rooms

---

[1] 1896.

in Littlemore, with access to a garden and orchard. Belloc would bicycle into Oxford for his work. He had now—very temporarily—abandoned wine for beer; this saved him money and gained him sleep. Finally they established themselves in the upper part of 36 Holywell. You entered through an archway from the street and went straight upstairs. From the back there was a view on to Wadham. Belloc had a regular job lecturing for the University Extension, principally in Lancashire and the north of England, and this would take him away from home for several nights at a time. He had carefully defined views on this University Extension work, believing that those attending the lectures should be encouraged to enrol themselves in classes and to pledge themselves to write at least one essay before the course was over. He thought it preferable that they should write four, and only to those who had written four did he think a Certificate should be given. Most importantly, he believed that some authority recommended by the lecturer should be read by every member of the class. It was waste of time for him to lecture on the French Revolution to people who had not read the *Contrat Social*. When the meeting was over, some member of the audience would offer him hospitality for the night. They did not always realize what they had let themselves in for.

On our return from the lecture hall he was greeted by my father, a very well-read man but too busy to attend lectures and I was firmly despatched to bed. The next morning my father complained that this very positive young man had not only kept him up talking until two o'clock but when informed that breakfast in the household was at seven-thirty had blandly announced that he always took eight hours sleep and that he would come down when he woke.

This had somewhat shaken the foundations of a very regular *menage*! [1]

In the intervals of lecturing he did private coaching. Occasionally he would address a University audience. The women students were now becoming more numerous, and Belloc is described

[1] Major-General G. G. Waterhouse: Letter to the author: April 11, 1954.

as pointing at them and exclaiming in a loud voice, 'These are not the kind of women we want to make our wives'. It was the Oxford life, as before, but with a difference. Everyone who visited the Bellocs—and it need hardly be said that they kept open house—remarked on his extraordinary tenderness and chivalry towards his wife. He gave the impression that he was thinking of her all the time. Such feelings are natural in the newly-wed, but they are not always communicated without embarrassment. Gertrude Atherton was among the friends who came to stay. She noted that Belloc was already suffering from insomnia, but that in the morning

> he was as brilliant as ever, and when he monologued . . . he shed light on every subject he pounced upon, dissected, tossed into the air, where the particles cohered in iridescent bubbles and floated off into space.[1]

He was now in touch with a new Balliol generation. Auberon Herbert (afterwards 8th Baron Lucas and Dingwall) had come up in 1895; Edmond Warre, Francis Henley (afterwards 6th Baron Henley) and E. S. P. Haynes in 1896; Raymond Asquith and Conrad Russell followed in 1897, and Aubrey Herbert in 1898. These were among Belloc's closest friends. All Souls may have turned him down, but the bounty of Balliol was a personal and spiritual thing; and it seemed to be inexhaustible.

Maurice Baring, though not himself an Oxford man, was prominent in the Balliol set about this time. He was known as the 'Balliol tosher'; 'tosher' being the Balliol slang for a man who was unattached to a college. Baring was being coached in Latin and arithmetic for the Diplomatic Service. Elegant, versatile, unpredictable and patrician, he was a contrast to Belloc in almost every way. Yet the two men became friends for life, and were associated in many of the same causes. Their first meeting in Oxford was in the summer of 1897.

> I had met him before with Basil Blackwood, but all he had said to me was that I would most certainly go to hell, and so I had not thought it likely that we should ever make friends.[2]

[1] *Op. cit.*   [2] *The Puppet Show of Memory* (1922).

Belloc admired one of Baring's sonnets and hung it up in his room on the back of a picture. Baring also showed him some parodies written in French of some French authors. Belloc would then translate these to his pupils and make them translate them back into French. Baring had rooms in King Edward Street and these were the scene of some wonderful supper-parties.

Donald Tovey, who was then musical scholar at Balliol, used to come and play a Wagnerian setting to a story he had found in *Punch* called 'The Hornets', and sometimes the Waldstein Sonata. He discussed music boldly with Fletcher, the Rowing Blue. Belloc discoursed of the Jewish Peril, the Catholic Church, the Chanson de Roland, Ronsard and the Pyrenees with indescribable gusto and vehemence.

People would come in through the window, and syphons would sometimes be hurled across the room; but nobody was ever wounded. The ham would be slapped and butter thrown to the ceiling where it stuck. Piles of chairs would be placed in a pinnacle, one on top of the other, over Arthur Stanley, and someone would climb to the top of this airy Babel and drop ink down on him through the seats of the chairs. Songs were sung; port was drunk and thrown about the room. Indeed we had a special brand of port which was called *throwing port*, for the purpose. And then again the evenings would finish in long talks, the endless serious talks of youth, ranging over every topic from Transubstantiation to Toggers, and from the last row with the Junior Dean to Pre-destination and Free-will. We were all discovering things for each other and opening for each other unguessed-at doors.

Donald Tovey used to explain to us how bad musically Hymns A. and M. were; and tried (and failed) to explain to me the Chinese Scale. Belloc would quote the Chanson de Roland and, when shown some piece of verse in French or English that he liked, say: 'Why have I not known that before?' or murmur 'Good verse. Good verse.'[1]

[1] *Ibid.*

In November 1896 *The Bad Child's Book of Beasts* was published by Alden and Co. The verses were by Belloc and the illustrations by B. T. B.—which were the initials of Basil Blackwood. This was the first of four books that Belloc and Blackwood did together, and from it may be said to date Belloc's popularity, as distinct from his reputation. The first edition of the *Bad Child's Book of Beasts* was sold out within four days, and a second printing was immediately put in hand. Sir Harold Nicolson, who was Blackwood's cousin, remembers sitting to him at Clandeboye, dressed in his Eton suit, for one of the drawings.

He was a small man rather like early pictures of his father Lord Dufferin with the dark skin and hair which the Sheridans inherited from the Lindleys. He spoke in a slow but rather positive voice and to me he seemed the very glass of fashion.[1]

The Spectator was quick to observe that 'the sparkle of Sheridan's *bon mots*' had 'found its way into his great-great-grandson's drawings'.[2]

Such were the men, and such the milieu, to whom Belloc had introduced his wife. What did she make of it all?

The answer is: not very much. As an American she would have been naturally ignorant of English society. Its humour, eccentricities, subtleties, scepticism, and hierarchies would have bewildered when they did not actively repel her. As an Irish-American, with profound memories of a persecuted past, she would have seen in many of her husband's friends the representatives of a ruling class which she had been taught to regard as oppressors—alien to her race and hostile to her faith. These were not the people that Hilary had gone about with when she first met him in 1890. One or two of them, like Maurice Baring and John Phillimore, she would get to know and appreciate when they became Catholics in the course of time. But taken as a whole, they composed a world with which she had little in common. They came to her house, made a lot of noise, and occasionally drank more than was good for them. They were her husband's friends and to that extent they were hers also; but she felt them to be inexpressibly foreign.

[1] Letter to the author: May 31, 1955.   [2] Nov. 26, 1898.

Her notebook for the autumn of 1896 gives a picture of her daily round. The rooms in Bath Place were blessed in the middle of October. John Phillimore and his wife come to dinner and she takes Mrs. Phillimore for a walk. On All Souls' Day she and Hilaire go for a drive through Bagley Woods. She dines out with Lord and Lady Morpeth, Auberon Herbert and Phil Kershaw. She lunches with E. S. P. Haynes and Wilfrid Rooke Ley. She visits Rooke Ley and Harman Grisewood[1] at the House. And then there are the household chores; on December 4 she must 'darn all stockings'. Quietly she is making her influence felt.

Belloc had not renounced any of his democratic ideals, and with these she certainly sympathized; but his Catholicism now became militant and vocal. Paul Sabatier, the Protestant historian, came to Oxford to lecture on St. Francis, and Belloc was there to heckle him. Sabatier had been speaking of 'a new Catholicism that was rising up, not animated by a spirit of revolt, but a Catholicism in which each individual soul receives religious inspiration from God'. 'Precisely,' interjected Eccles who was present, 'Protestantism.' Belloc also addressed the Newman Society on the Catholic Reaction in Modern France. When he talked of religion, his Balliol friends had always been astonished, and even shocked, by the freedom of his *blague*. But now he was liable to disconcert. One of his friends who was reading chemistry made a rather banal remark about the doctrine of Transubstantiation. Belloc, who had been talking in his usual vein, suddenly turned on him, called him a cad, and refused to speak to him for the rest of the term. The death of Hubert Howard in 1898 profoundly affected Belloc's views on the central question of immortality.

When I was young I thought the views about Death great nonsense. There we were, terminated, as all things terminate. It seemed to me no more a thing to fuss about than the end of a play or the end of a Dinner Party or the end of a dog's tail. Later on I was *intrigué* by the contrast between the sane and normal instinct about personality and the absurdly mechanical accidental way in which it was suddenly cut into by this thing

[1] H. J. G. Grisewood, 1879–1954.

I

Death . . . I only speak of *my* feeling, or mode of thought, of the time Hubert Howard's death was the first one I came across.[1]

In January 1897 the Bellocs returned to America. Belloc gave one hundred lectures in fifteen different centres through the States of New Jersey, Pennsylvania and Delaware. His subjects included the French Revolution, Representative Frenchmen, and The Crusades. On April 1 he represented the English Universities at a meeting of the Yale Alumni; and he arranged for the publication of *The Bad Child's Book of Beasts* with an American firm. Before sailing home in April Belloc summed up his impressions of America in an interview with the Press. He chiefly criticized the haste in all the smaller affairs and casual contacts of daily life which resulted in a certain disregard for human dignity; he described this as 'the lack of a lubricator to make the wheels of social converse run smoothly. . . . That the man who blacks your boots should think himself your equal seems to me a most admirable thing, but then he must pay the price of equality which is a certain studied and continuous courtesy.' But he found this roughness more than counterbalanced by the great American courtesy in larger matters. Generosity was a kind of courtesy, and generosity was the most conspicuous feature of American public life. One saw it in the size of American benefactions and in the ease with which the ordinary man was given access to people of importance. This was a direct consequence of an egalitarian social philosophy. In so far as Belloc had been able to observe the working of the political machine, he found that 'nothing could be better than a primary as the origin for a popular mandate, and if you do not go to a primary it is your fault and not the system's fault if it works badly'. He ended his remarks by saying that 'a few weeks of real intimacy with the society of England would make almost any American who had doubts of the value of his institutions a confirmed and possibly a bitter Republican'.[2]

In 1898 the Bellocs made a similar tour, going as far south as

---

[1] Letter to Maurice Baring: Dec. 26, 1909.   [2] Press interview.

Richmond, Virginia. This was still a long way from California and there was a deadly sameness between one place and another. Hilaire wrote to Mrs. Wright-Biddulph from Harrisburg, Pennsylvania:

This place is ugly. God made it the night after a debauch when His ideas were neither many nor interesting (you see I judge the Creator by myself like other theologians). Here I lecture to horrible people, kindly, of the middle class (as I am) yet, oddly enough, not congenial to me. I am bored and lonely. Also the wine is dear and bad.[1]

During this tour both Belloc and his wife became close friends with Maria Lansdale of Philadelphia. Belloc helped her with her researches for a historical guide to Paris. 'For the first time in my life,' he wrote to her,' I have been overpaid.'[2] He was, however, heavily fatigued by the lectures, describing himself (from Greensburg, Pennsylvania) as 'overworked and miserable'. On his return to England in May he seems to have collapsed and the first week in July found him still convalescing near Lowestoft.

Meanwhile *More Beasts (for Worse Children)* had been published by Edward Arnold in November 1897, and *The Modern Traveller* (for many readers the summit of Belloc's comic verse) appeared in November 1898. These books were extremely popular. *The Bad Child's Book of Beasts* had sold 4,000 copies within three months of publication and the *Academy* ranked the author as equal to Lewis Carroll and superior to Edward Lear. A good book of nonsense, it declared, was 'as rare as a visit from the angels'. *The Spectator* also devoted a long article to the book, again comparing 'H. B.' with Edward Lear and observing that 'books of nonsense are the best cures in the world for that laughter of fools which is like the crackling of thorns under a pot, and for that childish assumption of virtue and sagacity which so completely fails in concealing the vanity from which it proceeds'.[3] Indeed the whole Press was unanimous in its praise; but it generally missed the point that Belloc's comic verse is rarely quite nonsensical.

[1] Jan. 27, 1898.   [2] July 4, 1898.   [3] Dec. 26, 1897.

The Modern Traveller was very warmly reviewed by Quiller-Couch in *The Speaker*. The adventures of Commander Sin and Captain Blood were seen as something much more than high spirits; they were seen as satire. And 'Q' was not surprised that a poem which set out to expose *The Daily Menace* should have been coolly received in certain quarters of the Press.

> The exploration-business, the 'Anglo-Saxon' *entente*—can a journalist who has been watering these plants with emotion for months past be expected to welcome a book which hints that some recent and practical applications of his past creed have been absurd and others more than a little base?

Belloc's travels in America had taught him the truth about 'our Anglo-Saxon cousins'.

> Our Anglo-Saxon kith and kin,
> They doted on Commander Sin,
> And gave him a tremendous feast
> The week before we started.
> O'Hooligan, and Vonderbeast,
> And Nicolazzi, and the rest,
> Were simply broken-hearted.
>
> They came and ate and cried, 'God speed!'
> The Bill was very large indeed,
> And paid for by an Anglo-Saxon
> Who bore the sterling name of Jackson.

And there was the hint of hard blows to come in the portrait of Captain Blood.

> Like all great men, his chief affairs
> Were buying stocks and selling shares.
> He occupied his mind
> In buying them by day from men
> Who needed ready cash, and then
> At evening selling them again
> To those with whom he dined.

This laughter was cutting deep.

Meanwhile Belloc was also contributing serious poetry to *The Citizen*. *A Bivouac* was first printed here in the spring of 1897; also his sonnet to John Keats, with its lovely first line, 'Of meadows drowsy with Trinacrian bees'. When he was in Oxford he still continued to speak at the Union from time to time, and the hall was generally crowded for what became known as 'a Belloc night'. He defended popular education against Andrew Lang, and of all these later appearances the most notable was on May 6, 1897—the Jubilee Summer—when he spoke in company with F. E. Smith, F. W. Hirst, and John Buchan (B. N. C.). The House was invited to debate whether 'the progress of events in the East demonstrates the uselessness of the Concert and the incompetence of Her Majesty's Government'. Belloc argued in favour of withdrawal from the Concert. England, he said, should make a definite appeal to Europe to sympathize with her attitude against the Turks. She had nothing to fear from such a step; even the hostility of France was an imaginary peril in face of the anti-Turkish sentiment then running strongly across the Channel. Belloc went on to plead for action founded upon the truth of human feeling and not dictated by pressure of the money power. These were old hobby-horses he was riding, but he had rarely ridden them to such effect. He sat down to tumultuous applause and the *Isis* declared his speech to be 'considerably greater than any Englishman present' could 'imagine himself capable of delivering'. Many of those in the Hall that night must have felt the same exhilaration of fabulous promise which had dazzled and delighted the Oxford of 1894 and 1895; and if they were acquainted with Belloc's ambitions, they may well have wondered why the University could find no place for so rich a personality and such versatile gifts.

The measure of his influence in Oxford had been proved earlier in the same year by the publication of *Essays in Liberalism* by Six Oxford Men.[1] The book was dedicated to John Morley, commended by Herbert Gladstone, and inspired by Belloc. This is made clear in the introduction by J. S. Phillimore and F. W. Hirst. It was around Belloc's *idées générales* that the other essays

[1] Cassell.

had been gathered. 'So far as the causes are personal, Mr. Belloc has been the leading spirit; and we cannot refrain from gratefully expressing our admiration for his kindling eloquence, his liberal enthusiasm and his practical idealism.' The *Isis* was quick to detect the signature of the Republican group, and it seemed to be looking into the future when it said that 'Mr. Belloc is in all his ideas a Frenchman and has never fully appreciated the character of the English people', and that the views expressed in the book 'do not correspond to those of any recognized section of the Liberal Party'.[1] The other writers were J. L. Hammond, John Simon and P. J. Macdonnell; and both Phillimore and Hirst had contributed essays of their own. To a certain school of Liberal reformers the essays, though they claimed to be radical, would have seemed reactionary. Belloc had vied with Lecky in his respect for property, and already we find him opposing the distributist to the collectivist ideal. There was no capitalist ideal. Capitalism was an ugly reality, which most reformers were out to cure in one way or another. Belloc held that on the question of Land Reform, as on the question of Home Rule, the Liberal hierarchy had abandoned principle for detail. The book was seriously considered in the national Press. The *Academy* pointed out a strange discrepancy between Belloc's rather violent statement of first principles and the 'Manchesterian economics' of Hirst's essay which followed it; and to another critic Hammond seemed to be moving nearer to Socialism than the others. The book should be read as a first manifesto for the *Speaker,* on which all the writers were to join forces three years later.

But the charms of Oxford were beginning to wear thin. Belloc's friends were going down, many of them already started on important and lucrative careers. His early promise was coming to have a faded air; Oxford is a dangerous place in which to linger, unless one intends to make it one's home and one's profession. One quickly looks out of date. Belloc went on hoping for a Fellowship, but he found that first one college and then another turned him down, although in each case he had a friend among the Fellows who told him he was certain to be elected.

[1] March 20, 1897.

The bitterest blow of all came to him with the election of F. F. ('Sligger') Urquhart to Balliol in 1898. Urquhart, who had come to Balliol as an undergraduate from Beaumont and Stonyhurst, was the first Catholic to be elected to a History Fellowship at Oxford since the Reformation. Belloc could no longer say that the Dons would never have him because he was a Catholic; he merely said they had elected Urquhart because he was a 'tame' Catholic. The gibe, which was often repeated, was unfair to Urquhart's deep religious faith and permeating influence for good among all who knew him. There are more ways than one of making the Catholic Faith respected; and Urquhart's was the quiet way, by example and the unconscious exercise of personality. It is also true that in his concentration on the eleventh century he avoided those historical topics most likely to divide him from his academic colleagues. But Urquhart grew into a greatly loved Oxford personality. His was not the greatness of Belloc; he had no sense of a militant apostolate. But he had something which Belloc lacked to his dying day: a sympathetic understanding of the people he was hoping to persuade. And he understood, among other things, the acoustics of the Senior Common Rooms.

On September 23, 1897, a son was born to Elodie and christened Louis John. John Phillimore, Father John Norris and Mrs. Wright-Biddulph were his godparents. When Elodie had recovered from her confinement, the family took a reading-party to the Norfolk Broads, where Phillimore joined them. On July 14, 1899, a daughter, Eleanor, was born, and Elodie writes as follows to E. S. P. Haynes:

She is well supplied with Godfathers and Godmothers— the former for the most part being confirmed heretics and healthy Atheists. The Godmothers make up for this by their piety, faith and religion. The Godfathers are Lord Basil Blackwood, Philip Macdonnell of B. N. C. and M. René Millet, the French Governor of Tunis, my husband's cousin. The Godmothers (are) the Baroness de Paravicini and Madame Pescatore, a charming French lady—a playmate of my husband. You ask for Oxford gossip. There is none. Oxford is heavenly and empty except for an annual invasion of the Extension barbarian—his name is like that of the difficult Devil of Scripture—Legion—also his nationality includes all civilized people and Yankees.

Mrs. Wright-Biddulph had offered Elodie a nurse and Belloc wrote to thank her.

Elodie lies on her back and it is *my fault* that she does not write at once. It is necessary that she should sleep.

I am full of work. It is not lucrative. I earn good wine and sweetbread and caviare by the sweat of my pen, and my pen sweats 'wi' deeficulty' as the Scotchman said of his joking. You will be glad to hear that the publishers ask me for many books but sorry to hear that no man can live upon books alone; exactly 30,410 of my books are in the hands of the public and my total earnings therefrom in three years is £500! i.e. £150 to £175 a year.[1]

A week later he sent her some snapshots of her godson, with a characteristic postscript.

I have no news except that as I bicycled today I passed a public house called the Noah's Ark, and with the loud shout 'I am one of the beasts' I went in and drank honest beer.[2]

On August 15 he writes to John Phillimore:

Eleanor Philippa Mary grins like a pig and grows in weight like a walrus. The Boy Louis is wilful and violent needing taming like a wild boar, but is withal affectionate. He can just make the sign of the Cross.

Belloc went over to Paris at Christmas, 1898, and took the opportunity of informing himself more fully about the Dreyfus *affaire*.

I . . . went right into the Dreyfus business with my cousin (René Millet) who was one of his most intimate friends and

---

[1] June 26, 1899.   [2] July 11, 1899.

then with Déroulède who is the opposite and a very old friend of our family's. Neither of them could give me anything but conjectures; it was like talking theology where there are no facts but only awful threats. I wish an Angel would appear and set the matter right.[1]

Dean Inge would later reproach Belloc with being the only man in England who did not take the side of the accused. Belloc replied that he knew at least half a dozen prominent Englishmen, qualified to judge, who remained in doubt of Dreyfus's innocence. Notable among these were Lord Russell of Killowen and Henry Labouchere. Belloc admitted that of those among his intimate acquaintance who were on the spot and competent to give an opinion, a majority were for the innocence of Dreyfus; but for himself (writing in 1925) he pretended 'to no certain conclusion in the matter'. One thing, however, he always maintained: that the vindication of Dreyfus, by destroying the French Intelligence Bureau, had permitted the German surprise on Mons and Charleroi in 1914, and had thus tragically prolonged the Great War.

With a wife and two children Belloc could no longer afford to wait on the displeasure of the dons. Hearing that the Professorship of History at Glasgow was vacant, he decided to put in for it. He had more than a First in History to his name, for his *Danton* had appeared in March 1899. This will be discussed in due course, but it had proved beyond all cavil that if Belloc had lost a Fellowship England had gained an historian. He had given up his work for the University Extension in order to devote himself to serious research, wishing at first to write on English history. But the publishers, attracted by his French name, thought he would make a more popular impression with a French theme. Furthermore, John Phillimore was now installed at Glasgow as Lecturer in Greek, and that was an inducement to join him. So Belloc set about to prepare the necessary testimonials. But he received three letters from Caird, each stronger than the last, begging him not to stand. Then the Principal of Glasgow University wrote to tell

[1] Letter to Maria Lansdale : Feb. 15, 1899.

him that his religion would be an absolute bar to election. But
Belloc was still disposed to enter his name. He did not think a
failure would hurt him in a competition with so many candidates
and he thought the advertisement would do him good. However,
Mrs. Caird was then persuaded to write to Elodie, who came to
the conclusion that Glasgow was afraid of even having to consider the claims of a Catholic candidate. She felt that Belloc would
have made many enemies to no purpose; so he retreated 'for the
first time in my life. It is very sad ... I have fits of depression when
I consider that there is no future for me, but again I am merry
when I consider the folly, wickedness and immense complexity of
the world. It is borne in upon me that before I die I shall write a
play or poem or novel, for the sense of comedy grows in me
daily'.[1]

Indeed it did. For about this time Belloc was contributing
regularly to an Oxford paper called *The J. C. R.* and his articles
were published by the proprietors under the title of *Lambkin's
Remains* (1900). He sold the copyright for £10. This was the
first, and it remains the funniest, of his prose satires. The comic
verse was always full of admirable fooling, and occasionally of
something more than fooling. But *Lambkin* struck a deeper
note. It proved once again that good satire must proceed from
strong conviction. Here were many of Belloc's convictions—his
love of clear thinking, his Germanophobia, his hatred of condes-
cending snobbery, his rooted distrust of wealth, his contempt for
donnishness—all conveyed with a cutting wit. The object of his
satire was a clerical don—the Bursar of Burford College—and the
portrait is far more effective here than it is in the famous *Lines to a
Don*, inspired by an attack on Chesterton. There the indignation
became rumbustious, but in *Lambkin* all is held in control and
there is no departure from urbanity. One sees very clearly that,
in the literary sense, Belloc's home was the eighteenth century;
and this satire, so slight in form and solid in content, may be
matched without presumption against some exercise by Pope or
Swift. It was a book, said one critic, to be put beside one's
Sterne. One may argue, of course, that the joke is an Oxford

[1] Letter to J. S. Phillimore: Aug. 19, 1899.

joke, and therefore a private or at least a provincial joke. But then most of the best jokes are private; and a joke which is as large as Oxford has no need to think of becoming any bigger.

What makes *Lambkin* immortal in its minor way is the infusion of satire with affection. Lambkin 'was one of nature's gentlemen; reticent, just, and full of self-respect. He hated a scene, and was careful to avoid giving rise even to an argument. On the other hand he was most tenacious of his just rights, though charitable to the deserving poor, and left a fortune of thirty-five thousand pounds.' In politics 'his attitude was this: that we are compelled to admit the aristocratic quality of the English polity and should, while decently veiling its cruder aspects, enjoy to the full the benefits which such a constitution confers upon society and upon our individual selves'. In religion 'he was a sincere Christian in the true sense of the word, attached to no narrow formularies, but following as closely as he could the system of Seneca, stiffened (as it were) with the meditations of Marcus Aurelius, though he was never so violent as to attempt a practice of what that extreme Stoic laid down in theory. . . . Neither a ritualist nor a low-churchman, he expressed his attitude by a profound and suggestive silence. These words only escaped him upon one single occasion: "Medio tutissimus ibis." '

Lambkin was embellished by the Bursar's ineffable Newdigate Poem and it was prefaced by the Dedicatory Ode, addressed to the members of the Republican Club. This was Belloc's declaration of love for the University which would not keep him at any price.

> We kept the Rabelaisian plan:
> We dignified the dainty cloisters
> With Natural Law, the Rights of Man,
> Song, Stoicism, Wine and Oysters.

> We taught the art of writing things
> On men we still should like to throttle:
> And where to get the Blood of Kings
> At only half a crown a bottle.

> They say that in the unchanging place,
> Where all we loved is always dear,
> We meet our morning face to face
> And find at last our twentieth year . . .
>
> From quiet home and first beginning,
> Out to the undiscovered ends,
> There's nothing worth the wear of winning,
> But laughter and the love of friends.

The last quatrain has been much quoted, and Belloc came to dislike it because he said that it was not true. We may answer that it was true enough for a young man who was not so long past his twentieth year. He had not yet become the

> tremendous ghost,
> The brazen-lunged, the bumper-filler

who sang

> to an immortal toast
> The Misadventures of the Miller.

He was still part of the comradeship he celebrated; his high spirits were still untouched by melancholy; and they were certainly not dimmed by the crowning happiness of marriage. Only his precarious finances and his failure to find secure employment now caused him anxiety.

But his energy was unimpaired and he was ready to try any expedient. Embittered in some respects he may have been, but it was not in his nature to repine. He gave a second thought to the Bar and consulted John Simon. But Simon warned him of the inevitable delay before he could hope to make any money; and money was now urgent. So he returned, resolutely, to literature and journalism. His fourth volume of light verse, *A Moral Alphabet*, came out in November 1899, again with illustrations by Basil Blackwood. But the appeal of these exquisite frivolities was beginning to wear a little thin, and he had weightier stuff in hand. He had already made a start on *Robespierre*, writing fourteen hours a day, and he was working all through the summer of 1899, very slowly and carefully, at his book on Paris. The writing of three pages took him six days. 'It is in a turgid, bombastic kind of style', he mockingly (and misleadingly) informs Phillimore. 'Every verb is metaphysical and every adjective violent.'[1] In addition to all this he had fourteen pupils in for the final Schools. But Oxford was a backwater for a young writer who wanted to get on, and in the winter of 1899–1900 he moved with Elodie to London.

[1] Aug. 19, 1899.

CHAPTER VII

THE REPUBLIC

I

THE Oxford Republican Club was among the more picturesque and impermanent of undergraduate societies, but it would be altogether too facile to dismiss it as a joke. Belloc's fun was more formidable than most people's earnest, and even his anger was generally indulged to a thumping accompaniment of high spirits. These Oxford Republicans really did believe in the Republic, and they really did believe that it was an attainable ideal. What exactly did they mean by it?

They had begun by translating it correctly. For Belloc the Republic was the 'public thing', and his whole objection to privilege was that privilege was a private thing. He had already seen for himself that England was governed, and the British Empire administered, by a number of families, most of them known to one another, many of them interrelated. They shared a common outlook on religion and morals, and this might have been described as the Protestant ethic softened and civilized by the traditions of English humanism. The men who governed England during the last decade of the nineteenth century were still educated men, but they were educated within the limits of a national myth. Nor, in spite of certain warning signals, had the myth lost its vitality; that is to say, its power of moving its devotees to sustained and successful action. At the time when Belloc left Oxford for good, it was being put ruthlessly to the test in the matter of the Boer War.

But it would hardly be an exaggeration to say that, with the exception of Hilaire Belloc, the whole of England was still complacently isolationist. It did not think that it belonged, in any organic sense, to the continent of Europe. It thought of itself and its vast Dominions as a thing apart. This mood was bred of naval supremacy, geographical situation and industrial power; and we have seen a parallel to it in the mood of America between the two world wars. But there was this difference, that with the American recognition of Wendell Wilkie's 'one world', American power increased and American prosperity was recovered. England, at the close of the nineteenth century, had no need of a major war to confirm its strength. The major wars, when they came, fatally weakened it; and the country could not really afford the hostility everywhere provoked by the South African suppression nor, in the long run, the resentment of Irishmen deprived of their rights. These facts, which are plain to everyone today, were plain to Belloc in 1900. More clearly than most other men of his time, he understood the century that was coming to an end, and he had a true presentiment of the age that was waiting to be born. He perceived the isolation of his country to be a dangerous and not a glorious thing, for he had some experience of the forces that were preparing to challenge it. He had travelled widely in America and Europe. Through his wife he had learnt much of America and much of Ireland also. Through his father and his paternal fore-bears he carried France in his blood. All this he could bring to the reading, and the writing, of history.

When Belloc proclaimed himself a Republican, he was not animated by a special resentment against the House of Hanover. Certainly the Jubilee of 1897 did not move him to any transports of what it has become fashionable to call 'Balmorality'. He regarded the reigning House as German in origin and still Germanic in taste, having nothing whatever in common with Monarchy as the Middle Ages or the Renaissance had understood it. These Teutonic princelings were the tools of a triumphant oligarchy, and Belloc, though he observed the decencies of public debate, paid them scant reverence. Among the things he did not see, and which the Jubilee might have taught him, was the new mystique of Monarchy which was developing in modern England; according to this the Monarch having long ceased to be the supreme ruler was now to become the supreme representative.

He did not foresee the time when the people would invest their emotions in the Crown, as they had once invested them in the nobility. He wanted the people to invest their emotions in themselves; that is to say, in the Republic. He was never afraid of despotism, because the power of a despot was a public—and generally, in its origin, a popular—power. He never doubted that despotism could be an expression of democracy. But the power conferred by money was a secret power—and this was the real enemy of the people.

These simplifications were at the root of Belloc's political philosophy and he never deserted them. He would shift the emphasis a little, as he saw the corruptions of representative government. He came to see the value, in England at any rate, of an aristocracy of birth, rooted in popular respect and not mulcted of its wealth. He did not subscribe to any hard doctrine of class government, but he concluded that as England ceased to be governed by class it was governed by cads—and he preferred the first to the second. Even his irreverent attitude to the reigning House was modified when it married into an ancient Scottish family, and he presented a volume of his poems, through Mr. Duff Cooper, to the Queen Consort of George VI. But in his basic ideas he remained Republican. He would always have said that the perfect Republic must be democratic, and he certainly began by thinking that the perfect democracy must be republican; but as he grew older, he ceased to believe in perfectibility. No society, for example, has ever striven to realize the twin ideals of liberty and equality without being forced to sacrifice the one to the other, and with Belloc the emphasis was generally on equality. But by equality he meant nothing less (and nothing more) than the doctrine that all men are equal before God and that, as sons of God, certain equal rights should be assured to them. But this did not mean that he liked an egalitarian society. There were aspects of egalitarianism in America that he disliked very much indeed, as there were aspects of it in France that he admired. The difference was a difference of tradition, and Belloc was at home in the French tradition where he was ill at ease in the American. It was also the difference between his private preferences and his public attitudes.

Life in an English country-house was a pleasure to him and life in an American provincial town was a purgatory. But he still believed in the dogmas which were the basis of American society.

Belloc was generally regarded as a dogmatic person because he liked laying down the law, but he was a man who believed in dogmas before he believed in dogmatism. This was at the root of his political thought, as it was at the root of his religious faith and his literary practice. He believed that certain things were true and that their converse was false; and these beliefs extended down to the smallest details of daily life. We shall seize the character of his mind if we say that he was dogmatic where other men were opinionated. It was rarely, with him, a case of 'I think'; it was nearly always a case of 'this is so'. He was in a very high degree a rational man, and even his prejudices and his exaggerations were rational rather than emotional. Whether reason and emotion can ever be kept as strictly separate as Belloc tried to keep them is a doubtful question. Is any reasoning quite unemotional? Nevertheless, it was Belloc's pride to proclaim the rights of reason to a world given over increasingly to violence and instinct. He was himself a man of large heart and healthy indignations, but both his anger and his affections were controlled.

In the quest of the Republic, which remained his central preoccupation right into middle age, he could not avoid the challenge of the French Revolution. There was no matter upon which the minds of educated Englishmen were more biased. Nourished on the rhetoric of Burke and the impressionism of Carlyle, they viewed it through a cloud of prejudice which Belloc made it his business to dispel. Those who regarded him as a Defender of the Faith—as a man who would invariably take the Catholic side in any contemporary quarrel, or, more accurately, the side upon which a majority of Catholics were aligned—often expressed astonishment at his sympathy with the regicides of the Revolution. Because he was a Catholic, they expected him to defend the Ancien Régime. In his magisterial essay on the Revolution, published at the invitation of H. A. L. Fisher in the Home University Library (1911), Belloc devoted his final chapter to refuting the idea that the democratic theory of the Revolution

K

and the transcendental doctrines of Catholicism were necessarily opposed. Between the mood and mystique of the Revolution and the political assumptions of the French Hierarchy there was indeed a bitter conflict, but Belloc pointed out how far the Church in France had fallen from the height of her profession during the long 'swoon' of the eighteenth century. Or again, there had certainly been a conflict between certain acts of the Revolutionaries—the Civil Constitution of the Clergy was one of them—and the claims of Catholic authority. But these conflicts were accidental, and with better judgment on one side or the other they need not have occurred.

Belloc took his theory of democracy from Rousseau, and to a lesser extent, from Michelet. He regarded the *Contrat Social* as one of the master-books of literature, for it combined in a very brief compass the two virtues of vision and style. He had no great admiration for Rousseau as a man; his excessive sensibility and exalted temperament repelled him. But abnormal as was Rousseau's psychology, his political theory, applied to the petrified codes of the eighteenth century, was essentially a gospel of the good life; a return to normality and not in any way a departure from it.

'We cannot prove', said Belloc in a public lecture during the spring of 1897, 'that the normal is this or that; we cannot show why there is in us, nor even prove to men who disbelieve it, that there is in us at all times a constant standard of action with which material developments have nothing to do, but which must bow or break them when they come into contact with this moral and permanent standard. It is the part of all reformers to preach this whenever humanity deviates, by whatever cause, from the conditions in which it can be moral and sane, and when we see a man changing the whole of a society which had grown insane and immoral, we may be certain that he has struck this note and struck it with convincing power.'

The doctrine of the Revolution to which Belloc subscribed was simply this: that any political community pretending to sovereignty derives the civil and temporal authority of its laws, not from its rulers or its magistracy, but from itself. But it cannot express this authority unless it possess a corporate initiative, and most political dispute is concerned with how this initiative is to be exercised. Belloc argued that whenever a dictator or an oligarchy or an anointed monarch have acted in seeming defiance of the popular will, they have done so in the name of the people, claiming that the true sense of a community resides in its permanent institutions rather than in its occasional majorities. This opened the way to Maurras's famous distinction between the *pays légal* and the *pays réel*, and to his policy of seizing power '*par tous les moyens, même légaux*'. Belloc also had this conception, so very un-English, of power as something to be seized. He was impatient with constitutional purism, even in its legitimist forms, and this set him a little apart from the *Action Française* on the one hand and a long way apart from Lord Acton on the other. Indeed, we have only to think of what democracy meant to Acton and of what it meant to Belloc to realize how many meanings may be attached to a single word.

For Belloc, possessed by the mystique of the Revolution, power must be centralized, and this centralization made possible and easy the despotism which he dreaded so little. Bonaparte was the classic example of a transition that Aristotle had so well understood. For Belloc power was the natural instrument by which a community expressed itself, and it must be centralized to the highest point of efficiency. The Revolution, in 1897, appeared to him as 'the main example of successful socialism in the history of a State'.[1] For Acton power was an evil necessity, and it must be divided almost to the limits of impotence. Belloc, like Rousseau before him, believed that pure democracy—that is to say, the direct expression of the people's will—was only possible in small communities. He admitted

that large communities can only indirectly and imperfectly express themselves when the permanent government of their whole interest is concerned. Our attachment, which may be passionate, to the rights of the Common Will we must satisfy either by demanding a loose federation of small, self-governing

[1] Lecture.

states, or submitting the central government of large ones to
occasional insurrection and to violent corporate expressions of
opinion which shall re-adjust the relations between the governor and the governed.

Here, for a moment, Belloc and Acton would have found
themselves on common ground in 'demanding a loose federation
of small, self-governing states'. Acton, in writing to General Lee
after the ending of the War between the States in America, had
described the preservation of States rights as 'the redemption of
democracy'. But he, in common with the whole Liberal tradition,
would have seen in representative government a means of ensuring democracy in large states, where direct expression of the
popular will could preserve it in small ones. It was on this point
that Belloc parted company from the Liberalism to which on
certain other doctrines, such as self-determination, free trade and
anti-imperialism, he remained attached. When he wrote the
passage quoted above, he had become finally disillusioned with
representative government, as he had seen it at work in England
and France. But he never gave it more than a provisional ad-
herence. It was no part of the gospel of democracy, as he had
learnt it from Rousseau, and he had found it used, within his own
experience, as a means of frustrating and not of fulfilling the
people's will.

There was a further point upon which his general acceptance
of the Revolutionary doctrine contradicted his deeper reading of
history. He believed that the Revolution was indeed the matrix of
modern society, and that Rousseau was its father. Rousseau, he
claimed, had 'inspired the whole career of Jefferson, all the men of
the French upheaval, the entire character of Charles James Fox,
and every word that was written by Cobbett'.[1] But Belloc was
not so ignorant as to suppose that history began with the Year
One, and his reading had taught him that the schism of the
sixteenth century had resulted in the triumph of nationalism.
Nationalism, as Cecil and Richelieu understood and practised it,
was a new force in European affairs—a force destructive of unity.

[1] Lecture in America, 1897.

And Belloc, who had made so profound a study of the formative centuries, did not underestimate the regression. Now the Revolution had given a new impetus to nationalism. The doctrines which inspired it had also inspired the revolt of the American Colonies and the Irish Rising of 1798. Wolfe Tone and Jefferson were both sons of the Enlightenment. It might be argued, of course, that there was no necessary connection between nationalism and democracy; that if the kings and the oligarchies had not opposed the people, democracy might have refashioned the unity of Europe. Belloc believed that this unity might have been brought about by Napoleon, if Napoleon had not been destroyed by his exorbitance as well as by his enemies. But he was constrained to recognize that patriotism played as big a part in halting the Revolution as it had played in propelling it. Belloc believed that the political theory of the Revolution was 'universal, eternal . . . and true,'[1] and this universality justified, in his eyes, a conquest which liked to call itself a crusade. But in England and Germany, Italy and Spain, the slaves were curiously reluctant to be liberated.

This is where Belloc could have learnt a lot from Acton if he had been able to read him with sympathy. Acton's ideal of the multi-national state was much nearer to the classic conception of Christendom than any idea of political organization that emerged from the Revolutionary ferment. Rousseau had written upon a project for perpetual peace which Belloc dismissed as 'rubbish', but it is interesting to ask oneself what Rousseau would have thought of Robespierre. The answer might not be comforting for the regicides. But then it was in the genius of Rousseau not only to have made the classic apologia for democracy, but to have anticipated many of the objections to it. Of these objections the most powerful was of the philosophical and not the practical kind, and Belloc, rather strangely, did not think that it was the historian's business to answer it. It might be said that since all men are prone to corruption, a democracy tends to corrupt itself more absolutely than a despot or an oligarchy. These, in the nature of human satiety, come to the end of their satisfactions, and they have the

[1] *The French Revolution* (1911).

energy left over to devote themselves to the common good. A democracy has no such reservoir of disinterestedness. This was the argument—the argument of an ultimate cynicism—that Maurras would have used, and Rousseau replied to it by his belief in the perfectibility of man. Belloc, with his Christian belief in original sin, was precluded from this reply; but there was another answer, ready to his hand, which he did not use. It was the answer that Aquinas had taken from Aristotle; namely that the most perfect state is that in which the monarchical, the aristocratic and the democratic forces are maintained in equilibrium, each correcting the other. Each of these principles has a proportionate, none of them has an absolute, validity. It may be that at the end of his life Belloc, who never ceased to proclaim that 'truth lies in proportion', would have given this answer. But he had an obstinate and touching loyalty to his youth, and when the present writer asked him, only a few weeks before he died, how he would answer the question, 'Did the Revolution accomplish more harm than good?' he replied that it was necessary. 'Otherwise society would just have withered up.'

2

It was with these ideas fixed, or quickly forming, that Belloc began his career as an historian. He had, in equal measure, an attachment to dogma and to fact. This is not to say that he was infallible in reading the fact or in interpreting the dogma, but he knew that belief must be confirmed by experience. The historian must understand the ideas that have moved men to action, but he must also understand the stuff of which men are made. He must recover their physique, their temperament, their idiosyncrasies. He must see them in their time and place and circumstance. In a word, he must bring them to life; and here Michelet was at hand with his doctrine that 'history should be a resurrection of the flesh'.

The great historian, as we have seen, had been a frequent visitor to La Celle St. Cloud in the lifetime of Belloc's grandfather. He belonged to the memories of the place; and so it was in Michelet that Belloc first read the confused, sanguinary epic of the Revolution. What possessed him as an idea in Rousseau, possessed him as a narrative in Michelet. Dogma became passion in the men who strove, so desperately and so imperfectly, to realize the democratic dream. The reasoning of Rousseau had its own cold beauty, but it required for complement the enthusiasm of St. Just's 'The words that we have spoken shall never be lost on earth', and the defiance of Danton's 'Assailed by the Kings of the earth, we hurl at them the head of a King'. Belloc warmed to the task of reinterpreting these men to a public who had written them off as rogues.

The spirit of Michelet was congenial to him in many ways: there was in both men an admiration for the power of will, and what men admire they will generally understand. The 'unconquerable will' that Michelet loved to quote from Milton had been strong in him ever since the cold morning of the Hundred Days, when he crouched in his attic with the snow outside and resolved on the reconquest of liberty. More romantic than Belloc, and far less firmly attached to the Catholic Church, he was still penetrated by a Christian mystique which resisted all his efforts to expel it. Both would have called themselves popular humanists, their minds rooted in classical antiquity, and their hearts warming to the mass of men who were excluded from the culture which they had made their own. If the arrival of the people to power were compared to a barbarian invasion, then Michelet, who was himself a man of the people, was not ashamed to assume the comparison. 'We have a natural advantage, we barbarians', he exclaimed. 'If the upper classes have the culture, we have far more vital warmth.' He knew Virgil by heart and would speak of 'Saint Virgile, divin Homère'. He was on fire with the enthusiasm of first principles, whatever conclusions they might lead him to. The study of history, he wrote in his diary in 1820, was not enough. The discovery of facts must be vivified by the understanding of ideas; the particular must be read in the light of the universal. If he were to write the history of France, it was because 'la France était la nation où se dénouait le drame de l'histoire universelle'. He compared 'la massive Asie' with 'l'Europe articulée', and France was the most European of European things; the least fatalistic of nations and the most free.

> 'L'humanité toute entière vibre en lui. Dans cette vive sympathie est toute sa gloire et toute sa beauté. Chaque pensée solitaire des nations est révélée par la France. Elle dit le verbe de l'Europe comme la Grèce a dit celui de l'Asie. . . . Ce qu'il y a de plus jeune et de plus fécond dans le monde, ce n'est point l'Amerique, enfant sérieux qui imitera longtemps, c'est la vieille France, renouvelée par l'esprit.

The theme of the Revolution attracted Michelet because the Revolution 'est le premier essai de l'humanité pour prendre ses propres rêves et se diriger elle-même. C'est l'avènement de la réflexion dans le Gouvernement de l'humanité.'

Just as Belloc had seen the doctrine of Rousseau as a return to normality, so Michelet discerned in the Revolution a principle not of anarchy but of order.

> Seul, un vif sentiment de l'ordre fait les âmes révolutionnaires. Elles ne veulent abolir le présent qu'à cause de ses artifices et pensent par la Révolution rétablir la nature dans ses droits.

The influence of Michelet upon Belloc now becomes easy to understand. They had the same dislike for preciosity and *malaise* in literature—Belloc reacted against the *fin de siècle* with the same brusque vigour as Michelet had reacted against Chateaubriand and Bernardin de St. Pierre—and they both loved 'les deux grandes communions de la montagne et de la mer'. They both looked forward to the birth of a new humanity to match the opportunities of a new age, and in the minds of each the conservative and the radical currents ran together. The philosophy of Michelet, like that of Rousseau, was 'beneath the height of a final theory of man,'[1] but neither Michelet nor Rousseau believed that man could live without the gods. Belloc, as we have seen, had in him a strong vein of scepticism, and the men

---

[1] *The French Revolution* (1911).

of the Enlightenment were the only foemen he considered worthy of his steel. They belonged to a culture, even if they did not profess a religion, which he shared. They were on the right side of the boundary.

It was with Michelet behind him, therefore, that he attacked the story of Danton. The biography came out in 1899, and he must have been working on it for some time—all through the first years of his marriage. This was his first work in prose and it showed, at once, that he had found his style. Some critics complained that the rhetoric was to florid, but the book does not, now, give an impression of overwriting. The style is as readable and as durable as Macaulay, and the personality behind it is quite untouched by that philistinism which Mr. T. S. Eliot has described as a taint upon the historian of the Whigs. Belloc once modestly claimed of his style that it had 'rhythm', and the claim is already justified by *Danton*. The style is oratorical only in the sense that Belloc hears the rhythm of his sentences; it is the style of one who knows the effect of his own voice, and is not afraid of the grand manner. But the grand manner never becomes automatic; it is calculated and fitted to its theme. Is there in the whole of modern English writing a passage of rhetoric more appropriate in its colour and movement than his epitaph on the French monarchy?

So perished the French monarchy. Its dim origins stretched out and lost themselves in Rome; it had already learnt to speak and recognised its own nature when the vaults of the Thermæ echoed heavily to the slow footsteps of the Merovingian kings. Look up that vast valley of dead men crowned, and you may see the gigantic figure of Charlemagne, his brows level and his long white beard tangled like an undergrowth, having in his left hand the globe and in his right the hilt of an unconquerable sword. There also are the short, strong horsemen of the Robertian house, half hidden by their leather shields, and their sons before them growing in vestment and majesty, and taking on the pomp of the Middle Ages; Louis VII, all covered with iron; Philip the Conqueror; Louis IX, who alone is surrounded with light: they stand in a widening interminable procession, this great crowd of kings; they loose their armour, they take their ermine on, they are accompanied by their captains and their marshals; at last, in their attitude and their magnificence they sum up in themselves the pride and the achievement of the French nation. But time has dissipated what it could not tarnish, and the process of a thousand years has turned these mighty figures into unsubstantial things. You may see them in the grey end of darkness, like a pageant all standing still. You look again, but with the growing light and with the wind that rises before morning they have disappeared.

This is as good as Macaulay or Gibbon; and it is not only in the purple passages (of which there are not too many) that Belloc shows his mastery of the English language. The style has the more difficult and unspectacular virtues of ordonnance, precision and restraint. Nevertheless *Danton* is a young man's book. The sap is still rising and the enthusiasms are undimmed. You have only to compare the long introductory chapter on the Revolution with Belloc's later book on the same subject to realize the embittering effect of his political experience. The later essay is splendid in its clarity and conciseness, but the spring has gone out of the writing. When he was writing *Danton* Belloc was writing about his heroes, but when he resumed the theme of the Revolution in 1911 he had not many heroes left.

Every historical biographer faces the same problem: in what proportion and perspective shall he keep his principal actors and the background against which they moved? If he gives too much space to the background, he may dwarf the actors; if he concentrates too tightly on the actors, he may isolate them theatrically from the circumstances without which they cannot be understood. The difficulty will vary with the particular instance. History sometimes seems to be made by blind forces, enormous and fated; at other times it seems to be forged by the unconquerable wills or the inevitable weaknesses of men. Belloc, like his master Michelet, was the least fatalistic of historians, but he perceived this dual action.

It is in the nature of the French people . . . that their history should present itself in a peculiarly dramatic fashion. Their adventures, their illusions, their violence, their despair; these achievements seem upon a hundred occasions to centre round particular men or certain conspicuous actions, in such a fashion that those men and these actions fit themselves into a story, the plot and interest of which absorb the reader. But if we attempt to connect the whole into a series, even if we attempt to give the causes or the meaning of a few years' events, the dramatic aspect fails. This quality, which has fascinated so many, has also mistaught us and confused us, and, in the desire to 'throw the limelight' upon the centre of action, one historian after another has left in obscurity that impersonal blind force which directs the whole.

Belloc began, therefore, by defining the Revolution.

It was essentially a reversion to the normal—a sudden and violent return to those conditions which are the necessary bases of health in any political community, which are clearly apparent in every primitive society, and from which Europe had been estranged by an increasing complexity and a spirit of routine.

He compared the petrifaction of eighteenth-century France with the more supple and human society of the high Middle Ages.

New institutions, the Parliaments, the Universities, the personal tax, rose as they were demanded, and the great transition was crowned with the security and content that surrounded St. Louis. Simplicity, that main condition of happiness, was the governing virtue of the time. The king ruled, the knight fought, the peasant dug in his own ground, and the priest believed.

It was in the name of the Middle Ages that the lawyers and the privileged classes had opposed the Revolution.

They used the name of the Middle Ages precisely because they thought the Middle Ages were dead, when suddenly the spirit of the Middle Ages, the spirit of enthusiasm and of faith, the Crusade came out of the tomb and routed them.

Belloc, even in his first enthusiasm, perceived not only the origin of the Revolution, but its final, its possibly disastrous divagations.

All our modern indecision, our confused philosophies, our innumerable doubts, spring from that stirring of the depths. Is property a right? May men own land? Is marriage sacred? Have we duties to the State, to the family? All these questions begin to be raised.

On the other hand, the Revolution, for all its antagonism to the Church, had given a new impetus to the Faith. There were more clergy, more missionaries, more religious houses and more practising faithful in 1900 than there had been in 1789. Above all, the French intelligence was once more active in defence of Catholic dogma, and in adapting, not indeed the fundamentals of the Faith but their philosophical and theological expression to the mentality of the modern world. The Revolution had ensured the independence of the French peasantry. Belloc believed that under the industrial system the French character became 'like good wine turned sour'; the worst excesses of the time had been due to the army risen from the streets, patriotic but impatient, angry, ungovernable and misinformed. But when Belloc claimed that the French peasant was 'working out the necessary thing which shall put flesh on to the dry bones of the Revolution— I mean the reconciliation of the Republic and the Church' he was over-simplifying a good deal. He had found the Faith active in Normandy and Brittany, but there were tracts of the French countryside just as pagan as the proletarian quarters of Paris, Lyons or Marseilles. Belloc always tended to idealize the peasant— 'he has recreated a host of songs and he has turned all France into a kind of walled garden'—but the peasant had his sombre side; he had his pathological avarice, his civic indifference, and his crass egoism. No doubt his realism softened the crudities of political doctrinaires, but everything in his 'walled garden' was not lovely. If the French proletariat has become something of a nation apart, resentful and potentially seditious, the selfishness of the peasant is in some degree responsible for his isolation. But

Belloc was remembering the men he had served with in the French Army; he knew them better as soldiers than as civilians.

In general, however, he had an exact appreciation of the French character; he saw how it combined an excess of idealism with a passion for the positive, the objective and the certain. In the same man you would continually find some idea which pushes him to extremes, and in the ordinary affairs of life a most exact sense of reality, even sometimes an exasperating accuracy of detail. The nearest parallel to this he found among the Scots, who also delighted in the abstract problem, and who were also thrifty and independent. Belloc was always trying to explain to his country-men what it was in France that forbade the growth of oligarchic institutions. He could only describe it as

> something in the genius of the nation [which] makes for equality with the depth and silence of a strong tide at night. It is not the Roman law—all the nations had that. It is not even the Church—there is something in the Church which neglects if it does not despise civic ideals. It is not the distribution of capital— that can be distinctly proved to be an historical result and not a cause. No, it is not an exterior force, but something from within which has produced this passion, the soul (as it were) forming the body. 'La France a fait la France.'

Of this national character—and especially of its courage and tenacity—Danton was richly typical. Sometimes the love of the abstract, which is only another name for the love of the absolute, turns the French inhuman and sour. It did this to Robespierre. But Belloc might easily have met a Danton in his Battery. When he writes that 'in his dress he had something of the negligence which goes with extreme vivacity and with a constant interest in things outside oneself' we might be reading a description of Belloc himself. 'Rétif et sain, robuste et glorieux, il aima sa femme et sa parure'—the words were used of someone else by one of Danton's worst enemies, but Belloc borrowed them to strike the note of his hero's normality. And when, in cataloguing the weaknesses of Danton, he admits that 'he suffered from all the evil effects that abundant energy may produce—the habit of oaths, the rhetoric of sudden diatribes, violent and overstrained action, with its subsequent demand for repose,' those who knew Belloc best may feel that in choosing Danton among all the architects of the Revolution for his first historical portrait, he had chosen the man whose temperament was nearest to his own.

Danton represented the happy society that the Revolution intended—and failed—to produce. The tragedy of his death, which Belloc described with deep feeling and perfect control, was the symbol of that failure. One by one, the great phrases minted white-hot from experience and the natural command of words are recalled to us. 'I am leaving everything at sixes and sevens; one had better be a poor fisherman than meddle with the art of governing men'; 'nous avons assez servi; allons dormir'; 'I am Danton, not unknown among the revolutionaries. I shall be living nowhere soon, but you will find my name in Walhalla'; and the terrible, the Shakespearian retort to poor Fabre who had written a play and was afraid the police would get hold of it and steal the fame. 'Tais toi! Dans une semaine tu feras assez de vers.' And Belloc's pen, moving with an ease and majesty it rarely afterwards recaptured, was at hand to animate and recover the scene. There was the crowd seething round the guillotine 'like water moved by a strong wind'; the Louvre that 'flamed with a hundred windows'; the western sky glowing 'like a forge'; and high above the streets, in a shuttered room where the noise of the procession could not reach him, sat Robespierre—'the man who, by some fatal natural lack or some sin of ambition unrepented, had become the Inquisitor—the mad, narrow enemy of mercy and of all good things.'

By what Belloc may have regarded as a mischance, his *Danton* came out at the same time as another book on the same subject by A. F. Beesley. Both books were sympathetic to the theory of the Revolution and to its principal actor. They were generally reviewed together in lengthy and, on the whole, laudatory articles. For some critics Belloc's Republicanism was too fervent, and for one or two his style was too inflated. A certain 'Balliol' cocksureness was remarked upon. But at least one reviewer predicted that *Danton* would become a classic. The views expressed in it will always be open to dispute; how far was Danton responsible for the Terror; how far was the Revolution corrupted by its own *hubris*; just how inevitable was the welter of blood and tyranny into which it so quickly degenerated? And although the democratic doctrine, as Rousseau had defined it, may be proved perfectly compatible with Catholic doctrine, is there not something in the mood and mystique of democracy—a defiant *non serviam*—which is constantly at variance with the sense, if not with the expressed formulæ, of Catholicism? These questions will be argued until the end of time, and Belloc did not attempt to answer them all in this first book. But one thing, at least, he had proved: that a new historian had arrived in English letters.

What does *Danton* tell us of his method? To begin with, he does not quote his authorities. He tells us that he has read everything that has been written upon Danton—or at least that he has studied all the first-hand evidence for the facts that he adduces. But he does not give chapter and verse for the detail of his narrative. On the other hand, he devotes an Appendix to the exact location of certain sites mentioned in the book, and this proves that he had personally gone over the ground. A second Appendix clarifies his views on Danton's responsibility for the September massacres. Belloc concludes that by those 'who would regard public order and a security for life as being more important than the success of a political idea, of the integrity and defence of a nation, he can be accused of criminal negligence', but that although Danton would 'appear responsible to history for having been guilty of indifference at a moment when he might have saved his reputation by protesting', it was possible that 'his protest would not have saved a single life'. In a third Appendix Belloc published for the first time an important extract from the Report of the First Committee of Public Safety, read by Barrère to the Convention on May 29, 1793. This is given in the original French. Otherwise the book does not contain a single note and there is no Bibliography. The absence of notes is a great help to the narrative, but the reader who wishes to pursue his study of the subject would be grateful for a list of authorities.

In brief, *Danton* is not what is commonly described as scientific history. But then Belloc would have claimed that history is more than science. No less than fiction, its aim is to tell a story; and if that story is to live and to convince, it must be artistic as well as true. There must be emphasis and selection, proportion and form. If history is to be more than mere record, as Belloc believed it must be, then the imagination must be allowed its rights. A distinction must be drawn between the material and the work achieved. The researches of history are a continuing process; new facts are brought to light which modify or contradict our conclusions. No historical work is literally accurate. All we can ask of the historian is that he should not falsify the facts, as far as he has been able to ascertain them, in favour of a *parti pris*. In later years Belloc was often accused of wilful inaccuracy and purblind prejudice. But no such accusation was brought against his *Danton*. He had shown that he possessed the highest gift of the historian, as distinct from the chronicler; the power to reanimate the past.

The book was crowned by an award of twenty-five guineas from the *Academy*. Belloc appeared in company with W. B. Yeats whose *The Wind among the Reeds*, and G. M. Trevelyan whose *England in the Age of Wycliffe* had been similarly honoured.

Ten years later, in a letter to George Wyndham, he spoke of true history as

an integration of infinite detail as true sight is. But history differs from mere sight and is nobler in a way, because the acquaintance with the innumerable differentials of it involves labour. . . . There are also many—or at least not few—who deal with an accumulation of detail as rich men with a waggon load of furniture in a new house; careful only to put it into some 'scheme' and ready to consider any 'scheme' into which the whole will fit—but none of these is history. History is to know on one's first vision, but to confirm and build by an immense dual and coincident *work* of research and judgment one's original knowledge: modifying also a little as truth corrects and defines the whole.[1]

[1] Nov. 28, 1910.

These were the only standards by which he would have consented to be judged.

Looking back on the first, and as some would hold the greatest, of his historical studies, Belloc admitted some 'violent judgments and contrasts perhaps too strong for reality—though these can never be too strong for arresting the reader of a great historic story'. He also admitted the political disappointments which had lessened his faith in the democratic doctrine. But he concluded that

though perhaps this equal and just society, this ideal of democracy, be too great for man (at any rate in States ancient, varied and of millioned population) it remains the noblest. If it must fail, and perhaps it must, under the complexities of what the centuries have built up in our ancient Europe, it fails not from any baseness in itself, but in man.[1]

[1] Preface to the American Edition (1927).

CHAPTER VIII

THE PATH TO ROME

I

THE Bellocs had taken a lease of 104 Cheyne Walk on what was then an undisturbed corner of the Chelsea Embankment. The house stood upon a corner site only a few yards beyond Battersea Bridge, the brick washed with grey plaster. Small, elegant, three-storeyed and compact, it was a good example of a modest eighteenth-century home. The entrance hall was especially pretty with its fluted pillars sustaining the arch in front of the staircase and an alcove built into the wall on the right as you went in. On the first floor there was an L-shaped sitting-room, with windows facing south and west, across to the giant warehouses on the south bank or up river to Putney. They commanded all the traffic of the stream for a considerable stretch, and all those semi-tones of light and colour that Whistler had recently introduced into English painting.

The first thing the Bellocs did was to install the telephone—'1724 Kensington'. Theirs was the first house in the street to be fitted with this amenity; and the detail is worth remembering by those who suffered from Belloc's habit of asking to telephone as soon as he arrived in anybody's house and from his refusal, right up to the end of his life, to have the instrument at King's Land. Now, in the winter of 1900, he was eager for contacts; nor should his literary command over 'country matters' lead us to forget that he was generally happy in London. He needed the company of friends and the friction of opponents. He also needed money.

Do let me tell you again [he wrote to Mrs. Asquith] how much I think London, always available, in long stretches, is of advantage to one's own life and to (much more) children. It makes all the difference: experience, fullness, variety and, later, judgment. Our modern life is so organized that it is a necessity.[1]

He described the move-in to his mother:

Have fixed up a scratch bedroom where we sleep. I get in my work in the intervals of business and buying locks and keys —the kitchen-range is on my landlord's account. We have wonderful views up and down the river. I have written a good deal of verse, some of which will appear (I hope) in the next *Speaker*.

Many of his friends were already in London, grouped around *The Speaker*, which had been revivified by J. L. Hammond and F. W. Hirst. Hammond was editor, with Philip Comyns Carr as his assistant. Eccles was in charge of the book reviews and Phillimore was a frequent contributor. Both he and Eccles had an immense erudition, which they carried lightly; their essays on French and classical literature still make excellent reading. The young G. M. Trevelyan wrote on history. John Simon was associated with the group for a short time, but he left it in fear lest the paper's strongly pro-Boer opinions might blast the promise of his career. In this judgment he was probably correct. The contributors would read their articles to each other and benefit from mutual criticism. As Hammond's first number was going to press, the ultimatum had been sent to Kruger, and this dramatic coincidence gave the key to the paper's policy.

Hammond was living at this time with Lucian Oldershaw, a journalist who was in sympathy with his views. Oldershaw had been educated at St. Paul's and there he had formed a close friendship with G. K. Chesterton. He tried to persuade the *Speaker* group to publish Chesterton's articles, but Eccles declared that Chesterton's handwriting was the handwriting of a Jew, and when Belloc joined the group he prejudiced him, according to Oldershaw, against reading 'anything written by my Jew friend'. Belloc appears to have neglected this advice, for when the two

[1] Dec. 28, 1920.

men were at last introduced to each other by E. C. Bentley
outside the Mont Blanc restaurant in Gerrard Street, Belloc
remarked pontifically, 'Chesterton, you write very well'. His
arms and pockets, Chesterton tells us, were 'stuffed with French
Nationalist and French Atheist newspapers. He wore a straw hat
shading his eyes, which are like a sailor's, and emphasizing his
Napoleonic chin'.[1] They passed inside with Bentley, who had
been at Oxford with the one and at St. Paul's with the other, and
ordered a bottle of Moulin-à-Vent. So momentous a meeting
surely deserved no less; and they talked far into the night.

Chesterton was twenty-six at this time, four years younger than
Belloc; but as Maisie Ward has shrewdly pointed out in her
admirable biography of Chesterton, the disparity was greater
than the difference in age would suggest. Belloc had a wealth of
experience behind him, Chesterton had very little. Belloc already
knew the world; Chesterton was still angelic in an innocence
which he never lost. Belloc knew his classics, but Chesterton was
far more widely read in English literature. A journalist of genius,
he was less pure a writer of prose than Belloc and far less pure a
poet. But for all that he was a man of letters in a way that Belloc
never was or aspired to be. He relished the study and the midnight
oil, where Belloc needed human contact, the stimulus of history,
and the open spaces or the sea before his genius could expand.
Both men were interested in politics, but Belloc had a more
cynical view of politicians, because he had a far wider experience
of men. Both were fond of company and good cheer, but whereas
Belloc had a head of iron Chesterton was always tempted to drink
more than he could take. There was in both men a certain *fond*
of melancholy and Chesterton had surmounted an adolescent
crisis of despair. But both reacted sanely against the pessimism and
the 'greenery-yallery' affectations of the *fin de siècle*. Only, for
reasons which will become clearer, Belloc's melancholy deepened
with the years while Chesterton's was quickly dissipated.

Chesterton was a natural romantic, seeing things in the high-
lights of his imagination, inclined to be impatient of reality.

[1] Introduction to *Hilaire Belloc: The Man and His Work*, by C. Creighton
Mandell and Edward Shanks (1916).

'Belloc', he once wrote, 'suggests a classic temple, while I am only a sort of Gothic gargoyle.' His imagination was stronger than Belloc's just as his philosophical intuitions were more profound. But they needed the Attic salt of Belloc's realism; Chesterton's fantasy required Belloc's fact. In general, it would be true to say that they continued as they had begun; that Chesterton listened while Belloc talked. But when Chesterton wrote that what emerged from the Mont Blanc restaurant that evening was the monster afterwards to be known as the Chesterbelloc, he was blurring a little the distinction between two famous friends. For the differences between Belloc and Chesterton were at least as interesting as the similarities. Indeed what is remarkable in the long story of their effect upon English life and letters is that two men whose temperaments were so diverse should have thought alike on all important questions.

They were at one immediately on the issue of the Boer War. Their objection was not the pacifist objection—that, generally speaking, it was wrong to fight. It was the militant objection that the Boer Republics were right to fight on this particular issue. It was not the anti-patriotic objection that there was something slightly shaming in fighting for one's country. It was the passionately patriotic objection that the Boers were in honour bound to defend themselves. Here, as so often happened with the battles they fought together, they were a minority of crusaders within a minority of cranks. Chesterton has explained this very well in his *Autobiography*. They did not believe in anti-vivisection, reverent agnosticism, votes for women or total abstinence; but when it came to the rights of Boers or Irishmen, or the London poor, they found themselves, a little uncomfortably, in the same camp with people who did believe in these things. Chesterton described himself and his group as romantic Radicals, and there has never yet existed a political party in England where the romantic Radical will feel at home. 'They became a centre and an example for those who loved England but hated what England was trying to become, and still believed that most evil things could be proved to be silly.'[1] In many ways Belloc and Chesterton

[1] *English Literature and Life in the Twentieth Century:* H. V. Routh (1944).

were natural Tories, but there had long ceased to be a Tory party that was not a contradiction in terms.

Belloc had already begun to write for *The Speaker* before he left Oxford for London. His touch, which in *Lambkin* had never faltered, was here a little uncertain. There was a very feeble masque called *Error's No Crime, or Failing Goes by Fortune;* an affected essay on *The Valley of the Rother,* only interesting as showing that his roots were still in Sussex; and one or two other stories that missed their mark. Then, in December 1899, came two perfect quatrains:

> When you and I were little tiny boys
>   We took a most impertinent delight
> In foolish, painted and misshapen toys
>   Which hidden mothers brought to us at night.
>
> Do you that have the child's diviner part—
>   The dear content a love familiar brings—
> Take these imperfect toys, till in your heart
>   They too attain the form of perfect things.

There was an essay on *Manners,* or 'the folly of imposing aristocratic manners on the rest of the population'; a review of W. Graham's *English Political Philosophy – from Hobbes to Maine;* and an article on J. S. Mill, 'a man who gets greater and greater as we recede from him in time'.

It was mostly reviews that he contributed. In discussing the *Memoirs and Papers of the Prince de Ligne,* he remarked that 'the translation of French into short, jerky sentences is almost a test of the translator's disabilities', and he quoted with approval de Ligne's summary of Rousseau: 'There was no baseness in Jean-Jacques. There was only pride and a grain of madness.' Belloc's interest in the Boer War was no less military than political. He criticized G. M. Theal's *How to Read the War News* on the grounds that there was 'no insistence upon the fact that we possess no mobile guns heavier than the 15-pounder, whereas the Boers have certainly the Creusot 120-millimetre short and probably the 155 as well'. And a review of John A. Wyth's *Life of General Nathan Bedford Forrest* gives us his views on the American War between the States, still a burning topic in Europe as it was still a running sore in America.

> . . . that colossal fight which was not waged on the contention of the Confederacy for the upholding of slavery, but for the principle of State rights. The Republic is today facing fiscal problems, trusts, monopolies and a bastard dream of Empire. The critics would be less severe . . . if the South had not been goaded into a quarrel, if in that quarrel she had not struck for independence, or if some compromise could have been reached that would not have given the mercantile States so complete a power.[1]

French topics were generally reserved to Eccles, but Belloc discussed Pierre de Coubertin's *France Since 1814*. Here there was a valuable appreciation of Taine and a just estimate of why the Boulangist challenge had failed.

> The truth is that Taine is only odious because of the violence and bitterness of the reaction to which he gave himself up; and that his influence, which was imagined to have been wholly evil, was on the contrary a very salutary admixture in that French literary temperament which tended to make history a romance. Boulanger failed . . . because Boulanger allied himself with the contemptible 'high life' of Paris, which is to every honest Frenchman a danger-signal of corruption. The Jockey Club on the one side, the Intellectuals on the other—both symptoms of the same disease of vanity and exclusiveness— would ruin any cause.[2]

Belloc also published the first instalments of his satirical novel, *Emmanuel Burden,* and a pastiche of Rabelais under the appropriate synonym of 'Panurge'.[3]

On January 22, 1901, the reign of Queen Victoria came to an end, and behind the anonymity of the leading article Belloc's peculiar *gravitas* can be detected.

> It is a commonplace to call her good, and it is a little the fashion to be weary of the private virtues or to leave them

[1] March 24, 1900.   [2] April 14, 1900.   [3] *Ibid.*

unmentioned. But that commonplace has been of inestimable value to our nation and that wearying subject has appealed so forcibly to the world that we have received through her in these last days, a little to our astonishment and very much to our comfort, a universal benediction. At a time when the domestic foundations of the State have been so grievously weakened in every place, and especially among those who pretend to a peculiar eminence among civilised nations, she limited us, as it were from above, by the same persistent sense of duty as is found everywhere below in the humble basis of the State. Elsewhere the peasantry, here also the Crown, were the type of the family. If there are those who think it a light thing that the head of our society should have chosen a certain austerity for her surroundings and should have devoted herself so entirely to the great work which is the glory of women, they have but to ask at random any citizen of any European State what he would think of the value of such an example today in his own, or, better still, let them ask why every public print and every opportunity of public utterance have combined in her praise and ours since the news of last Tuesday. It is a commonplace and a little thing, but on such a spirit depends the vigour of a whole society.

Of all the obituaries of the Queen, Chesterton held Belloc's to be the best; and indeed we have only to measure the distance between the writer and his subject to realize the strength of the Victorian legend. The Queen, not without certain fumblings and a too gross indulgence of self-pity, had set a pattern for monarchy which would do something to redeem, or at least do something to rebuke, the vulgarity of the modern world. Belloc was too much a man of his moment to expend his sentiment on a retrospect of Victorian grandeurs; they did not, in any case, seem so grand to him as they did to most of his contemporaries. His mind was full of approaching perils.

In the difficult circumstances to which fate and—who knows?—perhaps the failure of the Queen's great influence have brought us, it is our business to recreate within our civic life, and to perpetuate in our political tradition, the spirit which she lent us in her maturity. We were threatened by these three evils: disaffection in every portion of our dominions, in Canada, in South Africa, and, above all, in Ireland; the corruption of the class that, in our aristocratic society, yet governs the State, and its conversion into a vulgar plutocracy; the influence in our Press, our markets, and our foreign policy of cosmopolitan finance.

This diagnosis of danger would have been signed by all those who were trying, through the renovated *Speaker,* to force a new realism and integrity into English politics.

Less than three months after the Queen's death Belloc bared his teeth in a second unsigned article showing, for the first time perhaps, his formidable controversial power. Sir Henry Colville, Commander of the Ninth Division in South Africa, had been dismissed from his post without a Court Martial or public enquiry. Belloc believed him to have been a victim of 'that abominable financial influence which is ruining our reputation upon every side', but it is a pity that the law of libel forbade him to be more specific; hints at mysterious and malevolent powers behind the scenes do not always carry great conviction. But it was to these forces of cosmopolitan finance that Belloc attributed the recall of Sir William Butler, the Press campaign against Sir Redvers Buller, and the more recent attacks against General Colville. It had been said that 'social influences' were supporting the General. But Belloc replied by asking:

What has put a man of Mr. Brodrick's calibre at the War Office except 'social influences'? What saved Lord Kitchener from the publication of his blunder at Paardeburg and from the publication of Lord Roberts' vigorous comment except 'social influences'? What put a mass of incompetent young men of title into various offices about the Commander-in-Chief in South Africa except 'social influences'? And what is it but 'social influences' that keeps the public in ignorance of the behaviour of the cavalry at Sanna's Post, of the name of a distinguished officer who was sleeping in a waggon when the convoy was attacked, of Lord Methuen's dispatch after Magersfontein, and of a hundred other matters that it concerns every elector to know? This Government is the Government of 'social influences'.[1]

Belloc's blood was up, and the article was followed a week later by the famous lines, 'To Dives'.

Dives, when you and I go down to Hell,
Where scribblers go and millionaires as well . . .

Here every couplet was designed to make the rich squirm between their linen sheets.

But it is already remarkable that in this group of men whom Belloc outshone in brilliance and personality, if not in certainty of judgment, he does not appear as a leader. At no time does he seem to have had a gift for the management of men. A certain rigidity of mind, an intolerance of compromise, a lack of sympathy for opposing points of view, a volcanic individualism— these precluded him from the rôle of a *chef de file*. He was an intrepid outrider, not the captain of a company. Intellectually he would always initiate and no artilleryman ever stuck more grimly to his guns. But he could not easily discipline, organize or persuade. He gave his opinions with such force that people expected from him an authority of which he was incapable. He was temperamentally a man of action, but he was a poor general; he did not really care for his troops and he had not the patience to concert his plans. The reason for this failure lay in the complexity of his character. For all his zeal in public causes, he had a perpetual hankering for the private life. He was devoted to his family and his friends—and his friends were not invariably his allies. He would be drawn increasingly into virulent debate, but his nature craved repose. It had depths which are rarely found in men who are public characters. But the principal reason for his reluctance to enlarge the rôle that his own genius had thrust upon him was one that did him nothing but credit. He had an insatiable appetite for the discovery of truth and the proclamation of it; but he had no appetite whatever for the exercise of power.

[1] March 16, 1901.

2

In May 1900, Belloc's book on Paris was published by Edward
Arnold. He was proud of it. 'It is a good, good book, explanatory
of the city as is none other.'[1] And indeed it was a little masterpiece
of historical topography. He knew the place by heart and loved
showing it to his friends. Mrs. Wilfrid Ward and her son Leo
used to count it 'as one of the great experiences of their lives to
have dined with Belloc in a small Paris restaurant (Aux Vendanges
de Bourgoyne) and then to have walked with him the streets of
that glorious city while he discoursed of its past'.[2]

The book belonged, wrote Belloc in his preface, 'to that kind
of history (if it can be called history at all) which is as superficial
and as personal as a traveller's drawing or as the notes of a man's
diary, but which has its purpose because, like such sketches and
memoranda, it serves to give just the necessary framework upon
which the memory and imagination may build'. More than half
the book was given to the origins of Paris, and nothing was said
of the development of the city after 1789. Belloc justified these
proportions by the belief that 'in history we ought not to look
down a perspective, but to travel along a road'. He had carefully
studied his authorities, and added to them from his own memory
and reading. The book is personal and charmingly dated. As Belloc
surveys the city from the height of Mont Valérien, he notes
that Montmartre is unspoilt and the Sacré Cœur is uncompleted;
he remembers the windmill that used to stand on the summit.
Now and then he is inaccurate; it is the Théâtre Sarah Bernhardt,
not the Opéra Comique, which stands on the eastern side of the
Place du Châtelet. But he had grasped the personality of Paris;
and though he had stopped on the eve of the Revolution, thereby
denying himself the Napoleonic glories and the glitter of the
Second Empire, he had understood the permanent character of
the place which outlives its continual transformations. He had felt

that unique suggestion which hangs about the autumn trees and
follows the fresh winds along the Seine; the riddle of her

[1] Letter to Maria Lansdale: Aug. 9, 1900.
[2] *Gilbert Keith Chesterton*: Maisie Ward (1944).

winter evenings and of the faces that come on one out of the dark in the lanes of the Latin Quarter. She is ourselves; and we are only the film and edge of an unnumbered past.

The publication of the book coincided with the great Paris Exhibition of 1900, and many people crossing to France found it a stimulating guide. There was truth, perhaps, in the *Academy's* criticism that it was 'poised somewhat awkwardly between the essayist's sphere and the historian's', but in general the Press was enthusiastic.

In August Belloc paid a visit to Porto Fino where the fourth Earl of Carnarvon had built a villa, with great skill and taste, on the summit of the peninsula. Belloc was a close friend of Aubrey, his eldest son by a second marriage. Aubrey was still at Balliol, and Belloc was coaching him for the History Schools. The inhabited rooms of the villa looked out on the sea and the peace was absolute. On November 17 a second daughter was born to Elodie, and christened Elizabeth Mary Yvonne. She was given the name of Yvonne after her godfather, Yvon Eccles. The nurse, writing to Madame Belloc a few weeks later, describes her as looking like 'a white flower'.

In the following May *The South Country* and *Sussex Drinking Songs* appeared in *The Book of the Horace Club*.[1] Raymond Asquith, Laurence Binyon, John Buchan, J. S. Phillimore and Owen Seaman were also contributors to the volume.

Belloc was now at work on *Robespierre*. He was impatient to get it finished because a new project was forming in his mind. On December 31, 1900, he writes to Maria Lansdale:

> I am going to walk on a kind of pilgrimage from Toul (which was my old garrison town) to Rome next Easter and on my way I shall write down whatever occurs to me to write— what proportion will deal with landscape, what with architecture, what with people and what with general subjects I can't yet tell—it will be as the spirit moves me. ... I don't know if the subject would attract anyone, it will be full of what I think that's recondite, peculiar and often unsympathetic. Also it will

[1] Blackwell, 1901.

be *décousu* and written anyhow of its essence. I should be glad if it could get a serial public in America before I publish it here in October.

The Bellocs were still poor and Hilaire was compelled by necessity, if not by choice, to forgo the amenities not only of transport, but of lodging, food and drink. He was well used to these hardships, and he had, besides, his own ideas about the best way to make a pilgrimage—'On foot where one is a man like any other man, with the sky above one, and the road beneath, and the world on every side, and time to see all.'[1] His mother was opposed to the plan; and Belloc once told the present writer how she had stood with him on Battersea Bridge, strenuously trying to dissuade him. She may have felt it was a mistake to drop so many of his new contacts and to absent himself for two or three months from London. He answered these objections in a letter on May 21, 1901.

> I am doing an enormous amount of work for the *Daily News*, which I cannot afford to neglect, as it comes sometimes to £14, and once to £20, in a week, but there is nothing permanent in that. . . . There is more of a future in good literature for me, even if the Bar does not pan out as it should, than there can be in journalism. Moreover, my literary work raises my journalistic prices immensely.

What Elodie thought of the project we do not know; her intuition probably told her that when Belloc had determined to do something it was his duty to do it. She may well have discerned, or he may have told her, the spiritual impulse which was driving him.

He left for Paris at the beginning of June (1901), meeting in the train a Californian by the name of Nott who struck him as the most ignorant man he had ever met. Belloc showed him Paris and found him rooms in the house where he was lodging. *Robespierre* was not yet finished and he was working at the last chapters in his spare time. He bought for nine francs a coat and pair of trousers to walk in, and hoped to start for Toul by the six o'clock express on the evening of June 5. But *Robespierre* still kept him sitting in cabarets, writing away indifferent to the

[1] *Hills and the Sea* (1906).

chansons, the chatter and the smoke. Like Georges Bernanos, he found this a congenial method of work. By the evening of June 5 all was finished, including the preface and appendices—all but six pages. Meanwhile the Californian was delighted with his sight-seeing and wanted to give his cicerone a big dinner. But Belloc had sterner business in hand and declined. On the following day he left for Toul and sent his wife a postcard of the Caserne de la Justice.

> This is the identical gate of the identical prison where I passed a year. But the 8th have all gone away, not a soul left and there are common linesmen in their place. The guns are at Nancy. The place pulls at my heart strings.

The morrow was the Feast of Corpus Christi. He went to Mass in the morning, which the priest managed to get through in seventeen minutes; posted the last pages of *Robespierre*; and started to walk up the valley of the Moselle in the early evening.[1]

It would be superfluous to describe a pilgrimage which Belloc has made immortal, but the postcards and letters that he sent home during his walk add a few details to the picture. There was the baker who had put a large wooden statue of the Blessed Virgin over his shop and professed a fear of clericalism. There was the village of Thaon that washed the clothes of the whole Départe-ment, and had a little railway to bring in the dirty clothes and take out the clean ones. There was the old man bellowing in the church at Le Thuillot. There was M. Thomassin who kept the Café du Commerce at Epinal and advertised it as follows on his note-paper: 'Siège de l'Association Commerciale. Marché aux Grains. Grandes Terrasses. Salles des Réunions, pianos, cercle universitaire.' M. Thomassin, observed Belloc, obviously thought 'no small beer of himself'. There was the mountain that reminded him of the mountains above Napa where Elodie was born, 'but with much deeper wood'. And at last, as he completed his two hundred and tenth mile, there were the Swiss with their wooden, unsmiling faces.

[1] The date of Belloc's departure from Toul is taken from the evidence of his letters at the time, not from *The Path to Rome*.

All the time he is anxious for his family; they were obviously living on a slender margin. He will get sixty-five pounds for *Robespierre* on delivery of the MS.; and he is owed six pounds from *Fun,* seven guineas from the *Daily News,* and twelve pounds ten from the London University Extension for whom he was now lecturing. These sums were not large, but Elodie cannot cash a cheque until they have been paid in; nor can she send him the five pounds he will need by the time he gets to Milan. He does not expect to have more than two pounds left when he arrives there. Meanwhile his heart is gay and his foot light. At Brienz, as he crosses the Swiss frontier, he enjoys 'a magnificent great meal' of six courses, with cognac, vermouth and a cigar, which costs him two shillings and eleven pence, and this extravagance is justified because he is rarely charged more than a franc for his night's lodging and sometimes not even that. As an earnest of his high spirits he sends Louis a picture of a man being run over by a train.

He hopes that Elodie is following his journey on a map; and on June 15, as he sits on the top of the Grimsel Pass, he remembers the anniversary of their wedding. But it is freezing cold and the sleet is falling; he is tired now after failing to cross the Alps by the Gries, and when he reaches Como he takes the train to Milan. The unseasonable cold persists as he slogs over the Lombard Plain with its 'wet rice growing out of stagnant water', and at Piacenza he would 'give sixpence for a fire'. He is happier when he gets into the Apennines, but he is never quite at home in Italy. The language bothers him and perhaps the people are too soft. He feels that the whole country is encumbered with its past; it has not renewed it, as the French had perpetually renewed theirs. He writes to Elodie of Lacordaire and of his hopes for Christian democracy, always menaced by reaction on the one hand and by revolution on the other. At last he is in Rome and hears Mass, as he had vowed to do, on the Feast of SS. Peter and Paul. The Mass was said by Mgr. Stanley, the uncle of his Balliol friend, and Belloc served it. Mgr. Stanley, he wrote,

is delightful. Just like all his family, as rude as a Pig, and the Church has given him in addition every virtue that is dormant in the others. He is a high Tory and boasts loudly of his rank. He is one of the nicest men I ever met . . . a priest to a ridiculous extent like the Priests in books.

Belloc spent the first day of his visit wandering round the city, and the impressions he then received were the ones that remained longest in his mind. The place seemed smaller than he had imagined it; he had expected the historical magnitude to be matched by mere size. He missed the Middle Ages, only discovering them in Bracciano's tower and in the recumbent statue in the Chapel of the Blessed Sacrament in St. Peter's. Like most other pilgrims, he found it difficult to realize the scale of St. Peter's; he grasped it from the size of the Holy Water stoup on the right-hand side, as you enter from the west end. He did not like, at first, the Travertine stone out of which so many of the monuments were built, although later this seemed to combine, as no other material could combine, the qualities of strength and beauty. Of modern buildings he was spared the eyesore of the Vittorio Emmanuele monument (which had not yet been built) and he admired St. Paul's Outside the Walls. But what struck him most of all, in the churches he visited, was the singing. Afterwards he grew to love (almost alone among things German) the church music at Aix and Vienna, but it never effaced from his memory the church music in Rome. He was surprised by the Renaissance mosaics in St. Peter's. With his blindness to the grandeur of Byzantium, he had imagined all mosaic to belong to a barbaric convention. And the tombs of the Stuart kings gave a sudden rude jolt to his historical perspective. Here—the truth dawned on him in a flash—were the rightful kings of England, and they were all part of that exile from which an earlier and a simpler England had not returned.

Belloc remained in Rome for a fortnight, staying with friends and hoping for an audience with the Pope. But to his great disappointment this project fell through, and he had to be content with a glimpse of Cardinal Rampolla—'a fine man, like a great horse'. Through all the joy in what he had accomplished, the note of anxiety creeps through. 'I wish money did not drive me

Hilaire Belloc at Oxford: a lithograph from *Oxford Characters*
by William Rothenstein

Hilaire Belloc on his arrival in Rome, June 29, 1901

so.' Later in the month he returned to Paris where Elodie met him, and they spent a short time together in Normandy.

Belloc had not only made the sketches for his book while he was *en route,* but he had written a good deal of the text. It came easily. ' This *Path to Rome* is a jolly book to write. No research, no bother, no style, no anything. I just write straight ahead as fast as I can and stick in all that comes into my head.'[1] The book was published in the following April (1902) by George Allen, and 112,000 copies were eventually sold. The reviewers were generally enthusiastic. The *Athenæum* saw Belloc as belonging to the same school as Sterne, Heine and Cobbett, and it was no small advantage 'for a man to be able to see with the eyes of two races'.[2] William le Queux praised him in the *Literary World* and others added the names of Burton, Butler, Walton and Rabelais to his literary pedigree. Chesterton, writing in *The World,* contrasted Belloc's high spirits with the anæmia of the æsthetic school.

The Path to Rome is written recklessly. The typical modern book of nonsense is written so as to appear reckless. *The Path to Rome* is the product of the actual and genuine buoyancy and thoughtlessness of a rich intellect; whereas the young decadent takes more trouble over his nursery rhymes than even over his sonnets. And this is the paltriest and vilest of all the many vile works of the ultra-aesthetic school, with its care for technicality and finish. . . . The dandies in *The Green Carnation* stand on their heads for the same reason that the dandies in Bond Street stand on their feet—because it is a thing that is done; but they do it with the same expression of fixed despair on their faces, the expression of fixed despair which you will find everywhere and always on the faces of frivolous people and men of pleasure. He will be a lucky man who can escape out of that world of freezing folly into the flaming and reverberating folly of *The Path to Rome.*

The *Daily Chronicle,* pursuing the comparison with Rabelais, found that both Belloc and Pantagruel *'sentent plus le vin que l'huile'*, and the *New York Times* admitted Belloc to the freedom

---

[1] Letter to E. S. P. Haynes: Sept. 9, 1901.   [2] Aug. 16, 1902.

M

of the Republic of Letters. 'Here is acclimatized in our tongue', remarked the *Manchester Guardian*, 'a French temperament, not, moreover, of that French type which is cosmopolitan and familiar to us, the type of Voltaire or Taine or Anatole France, but of that riotous and romantic type, that blend of optimistic Catholicism and high animal spirits, and, it must be added, of intelligence none the less clouded because the clouds are rosy, which finds its perfect exemplar in Rabelais.' A comparison with Heine's *Reisebilder* leapt to the reviewer's mind; but where in Heine imagination was subordinate to intellect, with Belloc the imagination was master and 'intellect and emotion are but its twin slaves'.[1] The *Pilot* thought that no book since *Travels with a Donkey in the Cevennes* came so near as this to the peculiar excellence of Stevenson, but whereas Stevenson was 'tolerance itself and found . . . engaging qualities in everyone', Belloc, when he met someone, was 'apt to pity him for a dull, soulless fellow'. [2] The *St. James's Gazette*, on the other hand, thought *The Path to Rome* 'a really far finer performance' than *Travels with a Donkey*, though its perfection was less clear and gem-like. Some reviewers thought the book uneven, and the *Spectator* thought it too long. But there was one notice which must have given Belloc pleasure at the time, and which he may have recalled with some poignancy in later years. This was by C. F. G. Masterman in *The Speaker*. Masterman was then a tutor in English at Christ's College, Cambridge; he and Belloc had not yet met, but they afterwards became close friends—and then, as we shall note in its proper place, there was a sundering quarrel. Masterman was lyrical in his praise of *The Path to Rome* and he ended his review as follows:

> To others, and especially those who have not forgotten Youth or the winds that blow beyond the city, the book will stimulate attraction towards that self-revelation of a personality which is perhaps the highest function of literature. To these the 'good-bye in charity' at the end will be meaningless; the volume itself will be placed amongst the scanty number to which no good-bye is possible; and the author, though

[1] May 27, 1902.   [2] May 3, 1902.

unknown, henceforth included among those few who through
the written word alone have been able to excite an almost
personal affection.[1]

More than any other book he ever wrote, *The Path to Rome*
made Belloc's name; more than any other, it has been lovingly
thumbed and pondered. It was a new kind of book, just as Belloc
was a new kind of man. It gave a vital personality, rich and
complex, bracing and abundant, to the tired Edwardian world.
Above all, it brought back the sense of Europe, physical and
spiritual, into English letters. Vividly and personally experienced,
the centuries returned.

The book is almost, but not quite, exempt from the change of
fashion. The humour is sometimes heavy and occasionally arch.
The reader is too insistently nudged, and there are passages where
the style lapses into mannerism. Rabelais is too evidently at the
author's elbow, and Belloc, though he had all, and even too much,
of Rabelais's heartiness, lacked the imagination and the large,
contemptuous anarchy of the French master. He was restrained by
the decencies and conventions both of his time and his upbringing.
But these limitations are incidental. The book is a classic, born of
something far deeper than the physical experience it records.

Sir Arnold Lunn, who knows much about literature and much
about landscape, has pointed out[2] that Belloc could do more than
describe a sunrise; he could convey the exact impression of a
southern sunrise in particular.

Then suddenly the sky grew lighter upon every side. That
cheating gloom (which I think the clouds in purgatory must
reflect) lifted from the valley as though to a slow order given by
some calm and good influence that was marshalling in the day.
Their colours came back to things; the trees recovered their
shape, life and trembling; here and there, on the face of the
mountain opposite, the mists, by their movement, took part in
the new life, and I thought I heard for the first time the tumbling
water far below me in the ravine . . . There, without any
warning of colours, or of the heraldry that we have in the

<hr>

[1] May 31, 1902.   [2] *The Tablet*: July 29, 1950.

north, the sky was a great field of pure light, and without doubt it was all woven through, as was my mind watching it, with security and gladness.

Equally fine is Belloc's description of his first view of the Alps as they rose above the mist.

> One saw the sky beyond the edge of the world getting purer as the vault rose. But right up—a belt in that empyrean—ran peak and field and needle of intense ice, remote, remote from the world. Sky beneath them and sky above them, a steadfast legion, they glittered as though with the armour of the invisible armies of Heaven. Two days march, three days march away, they stood up like the walls of Eden. I say it again, they stopped my breath. I had seen them.

This vision of the Alps struck from Belloc more than his descriptive power; it made articulate the piety which had impelled his pilgrimage.

> From the height of Weissenstein I saw, as it were, my religion. I mean, humility, the fear of death, the terror of height and of distance, the glory of God, the infinite potentiality of reception whence springs that divine thirst of the soul; my aspiration also towards completion and my confidence in the dual destiny.

Those who knew Belloc best believed that something in his character was achieved by the walk to Rome. In the deepest sense of all, he had come home. The return to California in 1896 and the crowning happiness it had brought him were now confirmed. The whole book, for all its humour and gusto, distils a mood of benediction and of peace. Belloc knew what the Faith had cost him—the intellectual pleasures of scepticism—but he also knew how good a thing it would be not to have had to return to it. When he stood on the summit of the last ridge along the Cassian way, he stood upon the summit of his youth; and in extreme old age he had this quiet comment upon a journey which had brought him more fame than he can ever have dreamt of: 'I am very glad I went.' [1]

---

[1] Conversation with the author.

CHAPTER IX

VARIETY

I

IN the same month as *The Path to Rome* appeared Belloc was granted a certificate of naturalization as a British citizen. This did no more than confirm a decision which had long ago been arrived at, but it reminded any who took note of the formality that Belloc was as fixed in England as he ever could be. Opinion has inclined to overestimate his French characteristics, because he had in many respects so warm an appreciation of France. We have seen his debt to French political thought and to much French historical writing; no one has ever more clearly understood what France has done for Europe. He had an abiding admiration for the French military temper, the French intelligence and energy. He liked travelling in France and he enjoyed French cooking and French wines. The French cuisine seemed to him the only tolerable one, and he would always maintain that the French alone knew how to cook meat. But he had surprisingly few friends in France, considering how often he went there. Looking back on his military service, he found his fellow conscripts 'an extraordinarily attractive lot of men. I called on one of them afterwards at his home, attractive, and very much of the bourgeoisie. I never saw him or any of them again. I wonder what would have happened had I married a Frenchwoman. There was one, of a family rich, cosmopolitan, civilised. I should probably have been very happy'.[1]

He might have been, but he liked French people in the mass better than he liked them as individuals. He had no sympathy with the French reverence for writers and he was at once terrified and repelled by the literary salons. No one was ever less of a *cher*

[1] Conversation with F. J. Sheed, 1944.

maître. He had an acquaintance with certain French authors—Molière, Racine, La Fontaine, the poets of the Pléiade—but there were huge gaps in his reading. Quite late in life his friend Duff Cooper sent him a copy of *The Atheist's Mass,* by Balzac, and Belloc was a little astonished that the author did not 'seem to care much about the construction of his sentences' and went on to ask if he had written any verse. He was always filled with 'the immensity of the French tradition, culture and mind. It is like turning the corner of a lane and coming upon the sea'. [1] But he enjoyed Voltaire and Diderot and Montesquieu; and of course he enjoyed, above everything else in French literature, the *Chanson de Roland.* This was the nearest Christianity had ever got to an epic, and Belloc's translation of two lines:

> High are the hills and huge and dim with cloud
> Down in the deeps the living streams are loud

makes one realize what a masterpiece we might have had if he had found time to translate the whole poem.

He wrote, and conversed in, French easily enough, but he found it difficult to lecture in what he insisted was not his mother tongue. In fact, he was in every way the reverse of the cultivated Francophil, and the France he knew and loved was not that France at all. Belloc took culture in his stride, and he was always capable of a resounding *gaffe.* A reviewer of *The Path to Rome* reminded him that Milan Cathedral was not 'the most renowned cathedral in the world'. It was the same with painting and sculpture. He thought, for example, that Virgil's *Bucolics* contained 'some of the most wonderful lines ever dictated by a human tongue. The last two lines of the first Eclogue a Poussin and a Claude, and I can't say more'. [2] But it was always chancy what he would admire. At Chartres it was the Smiling Child that captivated him (had he the patience really to study the place in detail?) and he considered the sculptures in the Eglise de Brou the finest in Europe—an extraordinary judgment. Among the later French sculptors Houdon was his favourite. But Belloc stumbled

[1] Letter to Duff Cooper : October 14, 1933.
[2] Letter to Mrs. Asquith: July 10, 1920.

on beauty; he did not go out in quest of it. And there were many things in France and elsewhere that were beyond his appreciation.

In April 1902 he was in Paris for the *Pilot,* sending home his impressions of the Nationalist reaction. He mixed with the students of the Sorbonne and found them quite indifferent to the spectre of clericalism. He drank with the workmen in the Rue Mouffletard, just outside the University; and in all his conversations he found the social and political solution being sought 'by way of art and emotion rather than by way of the hard, semitic logic of Karl Marx'. The younger people were feeling after 'a Socialism that may be brotherly and French—not Collectivism' and it was not so long since Professor Lemaître had looked forward to that 'voluntary association which will be the great French work of the next generation'. In the following March, Belloc was staying with Berthillon, who was head of the statistical bureau of the Municipality of Paris. This gave him the material for a series of articles in the *Daily Mail.* Danton's statue had just been erected on the site of his house; the old Roman amphitheatre had been uncovered and restored; Roman pillars had been preserved on Montmartre; and the foundations of the Bastille had been revealed during the construction of the Métro. All this and more, Belloc pointed out, was due not only to the *énergie Française,* on which M. Hanotaux had just written so eloquent a book, but to a municipal bureaucracy that Englishmen would hardly tolerate.

Whatever his views may have been on England—on her Protestant ethic and mercantile economy—England was his home and by now all his closest friends were English. But there remained in him enough of French blood and French formation, to make him seem a somewhat marginal kind of Englishman; just as in France the John Bullishness of his physical habit and his large unself-conscious Johnsonian manner would have made few people mistake him for a Frenchman. And it is a curious thing how little his work was known or appreciated in France; where Chesterton had a hundred readers, Belloc hardly had one. He did not make new friends easily, and with only a few exceptions the pedigree of his friendships can be traced back to the Balliol and the early

London years, though it sometimes goes through the female line. Even after he was settled in Cheyne Walk, he would pay frequent visits to Oxford. At Balliol, F. X. Kelly had followed Tovey as musical scholar and Belloc was among those who would gather round the piano in his rooms. 'Kleg', as he was called, was fond of playing Chopin's Etude in A, and then Belloc would ask for one of the Nocturnes. Later, he came to have a fixed, unreasoning hatred for the piano; so this early enthusiasm seems out of character. Among his older Balliol friends Kershaw was now a clerk in the Land Registry Office; Auberon Herbert was *The Times* correspondent in South Africa, where he was wounded and lost a leg; Anthony Henley, having been called to the Bar at the Inner Temple, had enlisted in Compton's Horse and received a commission in the Scots Greys; and Edmond Warre was studying architecture in London. Arthur Stanley was also serving in South Africa where he was awarded the Queen's Medal. Belloc and he acquired the *Nona* together during the summer of 1901.

All through this year he was contributing essays to the *Daily News* and his reminiscences of the French army to the *Pilot*. He was also teaching economics to Lord Henry Cavendish-Bentinck, brother of the 6th Duke of Portland and Conservative M.P. for South Nottingham; and the young Mervyn Herbert, brother to Aubrey, would come up from Eton for special coaching before passing into Balliol at Michaelmas (1901). On October 7 Belloc began a series of lectures on *France since the Great Revolution* for the London University Extension, at the Limehouse Town Hall. 'We are certainly', he had written on the last page of *Robespierre*, 'on the threshold of the Republic', and he was not yet prepared, in this doubtful dawn of the twentieth century, to abandon the dream.

2

Robespierre was published in November 1901. It was at once a complement and a contrast to *Danton*. Where Danton had embodied the concrete energy of the Revolution—its opportunism, its courage, its warmth, and its flash of phrase—Robespierre was the cold incarnation of its ideal. Where Danton reflected in so

many aspects the nature of Belloc himself, and in particular his
attachment to reality, Robespierre was in almost every way his
antithesis. Puritan and pedantic, inquisitorial and idealist, he was a
man whom only the eighteenth century could have raised up to
its own undoing. The classical periods of his rhetoric, his habit of
constant allusion, the order and the isolation of his mind, the
primness of his demeanour and the quiet elegance of his dress, all
these he inherited and preserved from the society he made it his
mission to destroy. Yet one quality he possessed, excessive and un-
corrected by experience, which Belloc was able to appreciate,
because up to a certain point he shared it. This was his devotion to
dogma. But where Belloc's dogmatism was at best a strength and
at worst an amiable weakness, in Robespierre it was a mania. The
sanity of Belloc saved him from the inhuman simplifications which
brought Robespierre to the guillotine, and conferred a lasting
infamy on his name. But there was still in Belloc enough of pure
logic—of what he called 'the hard crystal of the Enlightenment'
—to enable him to sympathize with what he was forced to condemn. When he speaks of the qualities which Robespierre lacked,
he speaks, quite unconsciously no doubt, of the qualities that were
his own salvation.

> That practical temper and those inconsistencies of affection
> which are the general tone of all mankind, he, on the contrary,
> imagined to be peculiar to some few evil and exceptional
> men . . .

or again:

> There can be no better corrector of intellectual extravagance
> than the personal love of friends, for this gives experience of
> what men are, educates the mind to complexity, makes room
> for healthy doubt, puts stuff into the tenuous framework of the
> mind, and prevents the mere energy of thought from eating
> inward.

The 'repeated personality' of Robespierre had the monotony of
a French road. It was incapable of deviation. It went straight to its
destination; to the precipice of that rude platform in a crowded
square on which the monarchy had perished and where the best

hopes of the Revolution foundered in a sea of blood. 'As the axe fell, the powder shook from his hair.' The idolater of Reason had himself become an idol; and as the idol was broken on the pavement there returned to the rescue of the Republic a few, at least, of those saving inconsistencies which the frozen integrity of Robespierre had proscribed. Intelligence had paid a tragic debt to the mystery it can never fully comprehend; Paris, which suffers, beyond all other cities, the double temptation of the facile and the absolute, was allowed a new margin for cynicism; and Danton was avenged.

But Belloc perceived in this story of Robespierre's fall a striking paradox. Robespierre had become the symbol and personification of the Terror, but he had not created it. It had been created, principally, by Carnot. Robespierre, however, fed upon the general illusion and when he intervened to save he did so secretly. He 'was killed for trying to do the opposite of the very thing which he was popularly supposed to be doing, and his death and removal largely achieved what he would have desired to achieve himself. He would not, indeed, have desired the social reaction which took place; but the end of the Terror would have been consonant with his ideas'.

The book is a masterpiece of perception, and it is also a masterpiece of pity. The man whom sheer abstraction had made the enemy of mercy, receives the benefit of a charitable doubt. He had thought to find all truth within the frontiers of his own fanaticism, and 'there was no exile in his eyes'. His career was terminated, but it was not broken; it left no jagged edges or imploring shreds, as is the way of broken things. Robespierre spoke, symbolized—and stopped. In so far as he stood for the revolutionary idea, he proclaimed in careful phrases that have not the fire of Danton's or of St. Just's, its high intellectual beauty; in his conduct and his character he showed its power both to exalt and to petrify the soul. 'He was thin,' writes Belloc, 'but he was not shallow.'

He stood, a pale exception, a man all conviction and emptiness, too passionless to change, too iterant to be an artist, too sincere and tenacious to enliven folly with dramatic art, or to save it by flashes of its relation to wisdom. Where so many loved and hated men and visions till their great souls turned them into soldiers, he knew nothing but his Truth and was untroubled.

At the end Belloc fears 'to have done him a wrong'.

Such men may be greater within than their phrases or their vain acts display them. I know that he passed through a furnace of which our paltry time can re-imagine nothing, and I know that throughout this trial he affirmed—with monotonous inefficiency, but still affirmed—the fundamental truths which our decadence has neglected or despised, and is even in some dens beginning to deny.

He saw God Personal, the soul immortal, men of a kind with men, and he was in the company of those who began to free the world. God have mercy on his soul and on each of ours who hope for better things.

If Belloc had never written anything but the opening chapter of *Robespierre*, these thirty-eight pages would deserve to rank among the finest historical essays in the English language. If history is indeed 'a resurrection of the flesh'; if historical judgment means an understanding of a man in relation to his time and circumstance, warmed by sympathy but not warped by *parti pris*; if exactitude and vividness of phrase, sonority and variety of rhythm, persuasiveness of argument, lucidity and sequence of thought—if these are the marks of good prose, then the claim that we have made will not seem extravagant. And when one has analysed the excellence of this writing, and pardoned the rare moments when Belloc's latinity becomes a mannerism—'exsanguine' for 'bloodless'—there is still something over which escapes the catalogue. One can describe it best by saying that where another writer paints, Belloc sculpts: words, with him, are a hard material and what he makes with them has more than the look—it has the feel—of work that will stand all weathers.

Robespierre will only be considered biased by those who would deny to historians the right to a point of view; and this is to reduce history to record. But it remains a very personal book. In his introduction to the new edition in 1927 Belloc apologized for a 'presentation of the French Revolution with a crudity which belongs to youth'. He went on to say that

> though my convictions upon the political principles of the Revolution have not changed, yet my judgments upon their applicability to human society have changed very much. In particular, when I wrote this book I had not, as I have now, a considerable and detailed acquaintance with what are called 'representative institutions'. When I wrote this book I was under the common illusion that it was not only possible but natural to combine these with democracy. I know now what a younger generation has thoroughly learned and experienced, that Parliaments are the negation of democracy, and can never work well in an ancient, complex and highly civilized society, save in a senatorial and aristocratic fashion.

The old bee was buzzing, and we shall see later what experiences disturbed the hive. But *Robespierre* had no need of apology. One other observation, however, is worth quoting from Belloc's retrospect. 'It was Robespierre', he writes, 'who said that if ever man should come to deny God, the initiative would proceed not from the poor but from the rich. Look at the world around you today, and remark the profundity of that truth.' Like its forerunner, *Danton, Robespierre* was indeed a young book, and it tells us even more than *Danton* about the associations and the reveries from which these glowing studies of the Revolution were born. Little as he resembled Robespierre, Belloc carried the story in his blood, for one of his French forebears had been released from prison by Robespierre's command. We see the young historian seated before a fire of logs in an apartment of the Rue St. Honoré, and we hear the dull, persistent rumour of Paris reaching him through the closed windows. We observe around us in the room that severity of furniture and ornament which composes the décor of lives given not to indulgence but to action and creative thought. Here he had imagined Condorcet and St Just; Carnot 'stretched out on the floor of the Committee, poring with candles over the large maps of the defence'. Danton and 'his soul that always recalled the Marne'. He 'had some communion with the Girondins; the gravity of Vergniaud, the fire of Barbaroux, the sombre anger of Isnard'. He followed 'Marat that was never himself and that carried a mad torch without a sequel, but just avoiding catastrophe'. And he heard La Diane, 'the bugle-call, waking the young men out of the trenches to the battle'.

He remembered his walks through the woods of Marly in the glow of a September dusk; the last days of the *grandes vacances;* and the autumn chill. Here the timeless trees, in their annual rhythm of renewal, re-echoed the deaths and resurrections of history.

The genius of these woods does not pass, or if it passes, passes in a slow transformation that infinitely exceeds the hurried movements of men and that lives the slow life of the sacred trees. It would seem as though the presence of the dead were native to the undergrowth and the neglected lawns, and as though whatever power preserves the past in its peculiar places, worked with a greater mastery under the veil of loneliness and sleep. Here the rare echoes are returned as though from a grave space of years, the springs have an older gaiety, the autumns a sadness more majestic, the summers are more profound, the winters have a more saturnian brooding because Time mingles with them all: and the half-forgotten human minds from whose clear vision proceeded, and in the framework of whose society was formed the chief enterprise of politics, visit these places again, I think, for their influence is certainly to be discovered here.

Nor here only: the courtiers whom Voltaire delighted, the women whose eyes caught the new enthusiasms of humanity, the swords and the youth that were to marshal the great wars, are found—or something more than their memories is found— wherever the scrolled gates and the severe avenues still lead to unspoilt manors.

Belloc remembered Villebouzin on the road to Orléans where he had so often stayed with the Redelspergers, and a certain inn, lonely among the meadows of the Boutonne, where the Girondins had dined as they went up to Paris in '91. He had talked to women whose fathers had been in the Palace Guard, and to men whose minds had been formed, not indeed by Diderot himself, but by the legend of diamantine logic that he had left. These were the influences which had created Robespierre and they were those by which Belloc's most impressionable years had been surrounded.

He was at work upon the book for two years. He had studied every one of the nearly 2,000 pages in which the industry of M. Hamel had amassed every fact and anecdote that can be discovered about the life of Robespierre. There was no pedantic avoidance of vivid presentation, but Belloc assured his readers that every detail he admitted could be proved true 'from the witness of contemporaries or from the inference which their descriptions and the public records of the time' permitted him to draw. If he only occasionally quoted these sources, it was because such an accumulation of footnotes would have made the book unreadable. For instance, he describes in his ninth chapter how the dawn came into the room when the Committee of Public Safety was in session on the night between the 8th and 9th Thermidor. By what evidence could he justify the description?

Because there remains at the Observatory in Paris a record of the sultry overcast weather of that morning, and of the increasing heat and distant thunder of the day; because Mercier has given us the details and the situation of the room; because many men still living have been able to describe to me the aspect of the two great halls in the Pavillon de Flore; because one may check upon the map the road that Collot and Billaud must have followed from the Jacobins to the great staircase of the Tuileries; because we have a record of the exact time when St. Just rose to leave and one can estimate how far the daylight was advanced.

These are not the methods of a careless or unscrupulous historian, and no reviewer of the book contended that they were. But Belloc still left himself open to contradiction on details. He had stated, for example, that Henriot could not have been there to ward off the crowd from the last tumbril because he was lunching with friends in the Quartier St. Antoine, a mile away. But we know from a letter of Dumesnil that the last tumbril did not leave the Palais de Justice till after 5 p.m., and even Henriot could have finished lunch by then. Belloc had said that Robespierre was driven to the Luxembourg in a cab with Chanlier (*sic*) and a single gendarme, whereas the man's name was Chanlaure and there was also an usher with them. Robespierre's assassin was Méda, not 'Merda', and he died of wounds received not at the Beresina but at the Moskowa. Belloc sometimes gave what the *Pilot* called an 'artistic abridgement' of Robespierre's actual words. For instance, Robespierre did not say of death, 'Believe me, it is not an eternal sleep. I would have it written upon all graves that they are an entry to immortality.' His words, on that occasion, were both clumsy and prolix. 'No Chaumette, no Fouché; death is not an eternal sleep. Citizens, efface from the tombs this maxim engraved by sacrilegious hands, which throws a funeral crape over nature, which discourages oppressed innocence, and insults death; rather engrave this: death is the beginning of immortality.' Belloc would have been on safer ground if he had covered his quotation by making it clear that he was only giving the sense of Robespierre's words, or if he had abridged them into *oratio obliqua*.

The book was widely and on the whole well reviewed, but it did not really receive its critical deserts. It was severely attacked in the *Athenæum*, and cautiously praised in *The Nation*. Frederic Harrison, in *The Speaker*, found that Belloc's portrait of Robespierre corresponded with the Greuze portrait reproduced as a frontispiece to the book, and that it had besides 'the repellent fascination of a fine Goya'. He wished that he would write a complete history of the Revolution from 1789 to 1795, for no Englishman had done this and none could do it so well. The splendour of the style was marred here and there by mannerism and rhetorical excess—a young man's faults—and the carping were quick to pounce upon them. He should not have spoken of the soul of man being 'adust', or of 'the last of violence grumbling in the streets'. The Gallicisms were growing more frequent; 'evasion' for 'escape', and 'deposal' for 'deposition', and when he wrote that Lebas 'gave himself death' he was clearly writing French in the English language, albeit a French based on the best models. But the more discerning reviewers agreed with Henry Murray in the *Sunday Sun* that Belloc

> would seem to possess in a most unusual measure all the principal gifts which go to the making of a really great historian; unwearied patience in the collection of his materials, the capacity of divining on what side lies the weight of truth amid conflicting contemporary judgments, the historic imagination which enables a writer to transplant himself amid the complex surroundings of a vanished epoch, and a strong spice of that dramatic sense which teaches him to move from point to point of a story without neglecting the medial links of minor events or wearying his readers' patience by an undue wealth of detail.[1]

3

We must now consider, briefly, six books published between June 1903 and November 1904. Belloc had not yet acquired the habit, or been forced to the necessity, of dictation; the creative effort and energy of these months was therefore all the more remarkable. Indeed they go far to disperse Belloc's later contention that good writing is generally slow writing; what they show, unmistakably, is that good books must be written with joy, whether or not they are spurred by necessity. In the case of Belloc both these pressures were operating. He was not yet disgusted with pen and ink, and he had a growing family to support.

Caliban's Guide to Letters, published by Duckworth in June 1903, was a series of literary skits, many of which had previously appeared in *The Speaker*. They bear the mark of occasional journalism; one or two read like a foretaste of 'Beachcomber'. Taken all together, they do not produce the artistic effect of *Lambkin* and are chiefly interesting as a further inventory of Belloc's *bêtes noires;* Rudyard Kipling imperialism, the Old Testament, titled Jews, legal casuistry, and the Anglo-Saxon myth. England was still smarting from the political vulgarity and mili-

[1] December 29, 1901.

Elodie Belloc

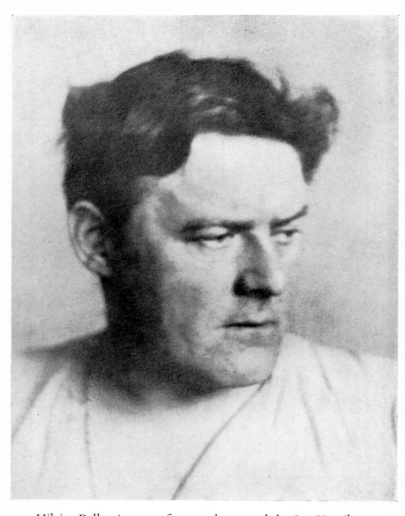
Hilaire Belloc in 1910, from a photograph by Ian Hamilton

tary ineptitude of the South African campaign, and the smart had
not been eased by the 'Khaki' election. Belloc's satire is lightened
by his invincible high spirits, but it reflects a spiritual malaise: this
dawn of the twentieth century was very much like a hang-over.
The book, he noted with pleasure, had 'glorious' reviews.[1]

Caliban was followed in September (1903) by The Great
Inquiry, a political squib on Tariff Reform published in paper
wrappers at one shilling. It sold only thirty-five copies and was
chiefly remarkable for the illustrations by G. K. Chesterton. The
'Chesterbelloc' had emerged, growling good-humouredly, from
its cage, and it would gather, as the years went by, an increasing
number of spectators. A month later (October 1903) Belloc's
translation of Bédier's Tristan and Iseult was published by George
Allen. A special edition of three hundred numbered copies was
issued at five guineas a copy. Bédier had retold the story from the
best sources, and Belloc's translation—the only considerable
translation he ever undertook, except those from Foch—was a
good example of what he called 'special prose'. The archaic
flavour of the original was preserved, but not tiresomely so, as the
following extract will illustrate:

And thus the Queen complained so long as the storm
endured; but after five days it died down. Kaherdin hoisted the
sail, the white sail, right up to the very mast-head with great
joy; the white sail, that Tristan might know its colour from
afar: and already Kaherdin saw Britanny far off like a cloud.
Hardly were these things seen and done when a calm came, and
the sea lay even and untroubled. The sail bellied no longer, and
the sailors held the ship now up, now down, the tide, beating
backwards and forwards in vain. They saw the shore afar off,
but the storm had carried their boat away, and they could not
land. On the third night Iseult dreamt this dream: that she held
in her lap a boar's head which befouled her skirts with blood;
then she knew that she would never see her lover again alive.

Belloc was always fond of this translation of Tristan and Iseult.
Epic was his natural home; and when the question was raised

[1] Letter to E. S. P. Haynes: July 17, 1903.

N

(abortively, as it turned out) of a Collected Edition of his works, he wanted *Tristan and Iseult* to be included in it.

In May 1904, *Avril* came out; this was a collection of essays on the poetry of the French Renaissance, some of which had already appeared in the *Pilot*. Duckworth was the publisher. Now it is generally assumed that Belloc was a poor critic. If it is meant by this that many sorts of writing were beyond his knowledge or appreciation, then the limitation must be admitted. He was not what is generally regarded as 'a great reader'. He had neither the curiosity nor the literary culture of a Maurice Baring or a Desmond MacCarthy, both of whom were his friends. But if a good critic is one who can detect and define the excellence of writing, then Belloc could be a very good critic indeed. He was incapable of admiring the second-rate. But he was limited, rather more strictly than the professional critic, by his intellectual and æsthetic sympathies. Either a book hit him, or it didn't. Now it so happens that *Avril* is about the best introduction to its subject in the English language. Belloc not only knew these poets, but he understood the civilization that produced them. He was inside them in a way that he could never have been inside—for example —the English Metaphysicals. His appreciation was certainly strengthened, but it was not distorted, by a cultural and religious *parti pris*. In a long and modest dedication to Eccles, he laid

... no sort of claim to that unique and accomplished scholarship which gives you a mastery of the French tongue unmatched in England, and a complete familiarity with its history, application and genius, yet I can put to my credit a year of active, if eccentric, experience in a French barrack-room, and a complete segregation during those twelve memorable months wherein I could study the very soul of this sincere, creative, and tenacious people ... But if you ask me why the Renaissance especially— or why in the Renaissance these six poets alone—should have formed the subject of my first endeavour, I can only tell you that in so vast a province, whereof the most ample leisure could not in a lifetime exhaust a tithe, Chance, that happy Goddess, led me at random to their groves. Whether it will be possible to continue such interpretation I do not know, but if it be so possible, I know still less what next may be put into my hands: Racine, perhaps, may call me, or those forgotten men who urged the Revolution with phrases of fire.

What a loss to us that he did not turn to Racine! He could see nothing at all in Racine until he was thirty-one, and then it came to him quite suddenly. But in his short essay on Villon he showed how well he understood that hard material out of which the greatest French poetry is made. It was through Villon that 'the great town—and especially Paris—appeared and became permanent in letters. . . .

Since his pen first wrote, a shining acerbity like the glint of a sword-edge has never deserted the literature of the capital. . . . The ironical Parisian soul has depths in it. It is so lucid that its luminous profundity escapes one—so with Villon. Religion hangs there. Humility—fatally divorced from simplicity—pervades it. It laughs at itself. There are ardent passions of sincerity, repressed and reacting upon themselves. The virtues little practised, are commonly comprehended, always appreciated, for the Faith is there permanent. All this you will find in Villon . . .'

Other poets considered were Charles d'Orléans, Clément Marot, Ronsard, and du Bellay. Each essay is followed by representative poems, and these, too, have their separate comment. Belloc perceived the national quality in Marot:

Whatever is new attracts him. The reformation attracts him. It was *chic* to have to do with these new things. He had the French ignorance of what was foreign and alien; the French curiosity to meddle with it because it had come from abroad; the French passion for opposing, for struggling. . . .

Marot was as untranslatably French as Wordsworth was untranslatably English. You could no more transpose the simplicity of

Glimpses that would make me less forlorn

than you could transpose the austere grandeur of

> Et arrivoit pour bénistre la vigne.

Belloc quotes, of course, the superb *Vineyard Song,* and as one reads his comment, it is easy to imagine that his own *Heroic Poem in Praise of Wine* was beginning, already, to form in his creative consciousness.

All the poem is wine. It catches its rhymes and weaves them in and in, and moves rapid and careless in a fugue, like the march from Asia when the Panthers went before and drew the car. The internal rhythm and pulse is the clapping of hands in barns at evening and the peasants' feet dancing freely on the beaten earth. It is a very good song; it remembers the treading of the grapes and is refreshed by the mists that rise at evening when the labour is done.

Set beside this:

> Sing how the Charioteer from Asia came,
> And on his front the little dancing flame
> Which marked the God-head. Sing the Panther-team,
> The gilded Thyrsis twirling, and the gleam
> Of cymbals through the darkness—

and it is not difficult to detect the germ of the *Heroic Poem.* When he came to discuss du Bellay—after Villon, perhaps the greatest of the circle—Belloc singled out the tremendous opening to the last stanza of the *Antiquités de Rome.*

> Telle que dans son char la Berecynthienne.

He would always take an appreciation of this line as a test for the understanding of poetry. Belloc had neither the complexity of Villon nor the *chic* of Marot, but he was French in the way that these men were French; in an early Renaissance or a late medieval, not in a modern, way. *Avril* did not pretend to be a work of scholarship or even of scientific criticism; but it was something more valuable than either. It was a work (too rare among Belloc's considerable *œuvre*) of perfect and spontaneous sympathy.

Its successor, *Emmanuel Burden*, was published by Methuen in October 1904, with thirty-four illustrations by G. K. Chesterton. This was an altogether more serious affair than *The Great Inquiry*; indeed it is a shining example of the essential seriousness of satire. Much of it had already appeared in *The Speaker*, but Belloc was in some doubt of his ability to complete it. These doubts seem to have been shared by his friends, for on October 28, 1903, he writes to Reginald Balfour:

> Do not have any fears for Mr. Burden. I also thought it could not possibly be continued and had done no more than the first two chapters and the two last, which is my way of writing a book. I thought it quite on the cards that the middle would never be finished, but the other day, sitting at eleven o'clock in some despair in my room alone without any children in the house or servants, the *Pneuma Hagion* fell upon me, and I wrote rapidly without ceasing till six in the morning.

It is true that *Emmanuel Burden* does not give the effect of easy writing. Belloc had little command of narrative or dialogue, and the book moves stiffly. Here a comparison with Mr. Evelyn Waugh, who is a satirist of equal power though widely differing method and intention, is not in Belloc's favour. But the total impression of *Emmanuel Burden* is at once unforgettable and not easy to explain. To begin with, the irony is sustained throughout, so that the passage is smoothly made from a mood very close to caricature to one very near to pathos. Then, Belloc never lowers his sights; the target is the same—the operations of cosmopolitan finance. Not being able to attack these men directly, Belloc is thrown back on satire. *Emmanuel Burden* could only have been written by a man who was very angry and by one whose anger was controlled by an over-riding moral and artistic purpose.

Burden is an exporter of hardware in the city of London and the book sets out to be a record of his lineage, speculations, last days and death. He is persuaded to join the Board of a Company to develop the M'Korio delta in Africa and he finally revolts against his associates when they resolve to destroy a commercial colleague and friend of his, Mr. Abbot, who refuses to come in on their scheme. Only a few hours after this act of self-assertion and saving integrity Mr. Burden dies at his home in Upper Norwood.

Loneliness caught him suddenly, overwhelming him; wave upon wave of increasing vastness, the boundaries leaping, more and more remote, immeasurably outwards with every slackening pulse at the temples. Then it was dark; and the Infinite wherein he sank was filled with that primeval Fear which has no name among men; for the moment of his passage had come.

And then we have the picture of Cosmo Burden, Emmanuel's son, coming home in the middle of the night.

His subdued, but rather husky voice, as he paid the driver, was carried on the rare morning; he dropped a coin to the pavement and it rang. Even the shaking key in the lock could be heard, though he turned it softly. He was careful of his father's repose, as he had always been when he came home after a night of pleasure with his equals. He pulled off his boots, not without many blunders, and went up the stairs noiseless, holding the bannisters well. He reached his room above, and lay down at once to sleep, half-dressed, the sleep he needed.

The whole book is written in the same key of murderous understatement, and the cumulative effect is profound. It contains two other portraits, each deliberately stretched to caricature, which remain in the mind: Lord Benthorpe, the limp and monosyllabic aristocrat, and Mr. Barnett, the Jewish financier, both directors of the M'Korio company. The scene in which Burden goes to dinner with Benthorpe in his mansion is charged with all Belloc's sense of dangerous fun.

Mr. Burden was a merchant worth at most but £257,000, and that locked up entirely in his business; but no difference of fortune affected the demeanour of the more illustrious man.

We have the painting of Lord Benthorpe's grandfather

standing in his robes against a fringed and tasselled velvet curtain of a rich purple hue with a broken pillar at his side,

while a sunbeam bursting through a distant cloud, threw into
fine relief the orator's gesture. The great Irishman was represented speaking in the House of Lords in favour of the reform
of the Poor Law. His left hand touched with the index finger a
map of Great Britain; his right was slightly raised to heaven in
dignified appeal. A wolf-hound nestling at his feet indicated
the domestic nature of his character, for the taste of that time
permitted the allegory in spite of the improbability of such a
creature's presence in such a place upon such an occasion.

And we have the painting of Lord Benthorpe's wife

seated writing at a superb escritoire, or writing-table, holding
a graceful quill in a hand of which the little finger emerged
coquettishly above its fellows. The frame was surmounted by
the ornament of a dainty coronet; upon the features an amiable
smile was recorded.

'My wife,' said Lord Benthorpe simply. Then, after a long
pause, 'by Marston . . .'; finally, in a deeper and more subdued
voice . . . 'from a photograph.'

The two men parted, and Mr. Burden dressed in profound
thought, wondering to have seen so much greatness united with
such native ease.

It was not for nothing that Belloc had been admitted, sometimes as a friend and sometimes as a salaried tutor, into the houses
of the English nobility. Lord Benthorpe, it seems, was in the
hands of his trustees but in spite of their generosity on this
occasion, he preferred

. . . with inbred tact, to call but one other guest to the table,
lest the merchant should be confused by too considerable a
gathering. This other guest, chosen with admirable judgment,
was Mrs. Warner, who lived as an honoured neighbour in the
seclusion of her widowed cottage near by. Lord Benthorpe
introduced the clergyman's widow, as is the custom among
men of breeding, in a voice so low and blurred as to leave
Mr. Burden under the erroneous impression that the lady, if
not a peeress, enjoyed at least a courtesy title. . . .

But if Belloc had a smile for Benthorpe, he has none for
Barnett. The creature, spawned in some Central European ghetto,
is at home in every metropolis and a native of none. With his
crudity and his cunning, he might have been inspired by some
savage anti-Semitic caricature of Forain's illustrating some diatribe of Drumont's. The truth is that too much has happened to
the Jews since *Emmanuel Burden* was written for Mr. Barnett to
make comfortable reading today. It is not thus that we now
conceive the anonymous masters of our destinies. But however
little we may share Belloc's bias in this matter, we must be fair to
him. He was growing up against a background of Edwardian
plutocracy, whose predatory vulgarity was evident on every hand,
and here Jewish financial power did, very often, cut a repellent
figure. Belloc had in him enough Gallic licence of speech not to be
daunted by the secrecy in which its operations were shrouded, or
deceived by the manœuvres with which it silenced any discussion
which it believed to be inimical to its interests. In Paris they
debated these matter more openly, and Mr. Barnett may almost
be said to owe his existence to *La France Juive*. Drumont's terrible
pen had pointed to the Bambergers and the Bichoffsheins, the
Ephrussis and the Camondos, whose irresponsible speculations
had placed in jeopardy the whole economy of France and whose
enormous fortunes had made them answerable to no one but
themselves. Belloc would have liked to name their counterparts in
England; but, as it was, Mr. Barnett had to represent the pride of
riches and Mr. Burden their pathos. The book that bears his name
is hard and sharp as a diamond; bitter, cutting, serious, profound,
momentarily tender, frequently amusing, and—the word cannot
be avoided—dangerous.

The response to *Emmanuel Burden* showed how difficult it was
to write for a public untrained to irony. Some people thought the
book a glorious lark; others were offended by Canon Cole's
'chivalrous attack on the Incarnation'; others again thought Mr.
Barnett too crude a caricature of imperialist finance. The most
interesting reviews were from William Archer in *The Morning
Leader* and by Edward Garnett in *The Speaker*. Archer greatly
admired the brilliance of Belloc's writing but doubted whether

sustained irony of this sort was really worth while. It would be easy, he said, to indict an attack against the Catholic Church which would be just as true and just as partial. Garnett admired the book almost without reserve, but at the end of his review he exclaimed: 'Will the book be understood? Only by those who have understanding.' *Emmanuel Burden* was widely read and widely praised, but not perhaps very widely understood. 'Not one woman in a hundred will extract a laugh from its pages', was the opinion of *Vanity Fair,* and indeed Belloc's popularity as a writer decreased in exact proportion to the growing influence of the woman reader. *Emmanuel Burden* was not enjoyed by the critic of the *Investor's Review.*

History and saga, criticism and satire—and now, topography. One day, late in December 1902, Belloc, Harold Baker[1] and Phil Kershaw set out from the site of the old North Gate at Winchester, walked up the right bank of the Itchen, and followed the traces of the Pilgrim's Way to Canterbury. It was a march of a hundred and twenty miles, and the day of their departure was chosen to correspond with the probable date of the first pilgrimage. Wherever the traces of the road were lost, they established it; nearly always to the south of a church porch and always on the southern slope of the great ridge which curves round in a gradual arc from Farnham to the Stour. When, at last, they approached the West Gate of Canterbury and the sacred maturity of all English things, it was at the same hour and on the same day of the year that Becket was felled by his assailants. The weather, clear and cold and windless, was also the same.

It was barely eighteen months since Belloc had entered Rome by the Flaminian Gate, tired, travel-stained and triumphant. He was less tired and less triumphant now. As he covered the last mile of Watling Street, the great Bell Harry Tower grew sharp against the sky. This 'was the last thing in England which the true Gothic spirit made'. Once it had drawn all Europe to Canterbury, but now its significance had gone. Bramante's dome which had beckoned Belloc across the Roman plain was a symbol of home-

[1] The Right Honourable Harold Baker, P.C.; sometime Warden of Winchester College.

coming, tender with the certitudes of home. It stood for an order and an affirmation that were unchanged. But now, as the pilgrim drew near to the spiritual heart of England, to the shores where Augustine had landed and the sepulchres of the Saxon kings, he could measure the distance of his exile. For the official cult which had arisen over the ruins of united Christendom he cared nothing. All he could do was to climb on to the top of an omnibus, in front of a hideous villa, and burst ironically into song.

There remained, however, the Cathedral and its tower, mournful and summoning in the dusk. Never before, 'save perhaps once at Beauvais', had Belloc known 'such a magic of great height and darkness'.

I received its silence for an hour, but without comfort and without response. It seemed only an awful and fitting terminal to that long way I had come. It sounded the note of all my road—the droning voice of extreme, incalculable age.

He went inside and waited, vainly, for the ghosts which should have been there to greet him. He had travelled the length of the Middle Ages between Winchester and Canterbury. At Winchester the Gothic arch, though it is already present, does not lift the long, low weight of the church as the Perpendicular of Chillenden raises the nave of Canterbury. To Belloc Winchester had seemed a wintry cathedral, consonant with the snow outside and the rooks cawing hoarsely in the trees. But at Canterbury the shrine of St. Thomas and the lofy, marble-pillared Romanesque of William of Sens had announced the summer of a sacred civilization; a civilization doomed, even so, to perish, though leaving its monuments behind to amaze, and even to appal, posterity. Belloc went inside and

. . . stood at the edge of the north transept, where the Archbishop fell, and where a few Norman stones lend a material basis for the resurrection of the past. It was almost dark . . . I had hoped in such an exact coincidence to see the gigantic figure, huge in its winter swaddling, watching the door from the cloister, and watching it unbarred at his command.

I had thought to discover the hard large face in profile, still caught by the last light from the round southern windows and gazing fixedly: the choir beyond at their alternate nasal chaunt; the clamour; the battering of oak; the jangle of arms and of scabbards trailing, as the troops broke in; the footfalls of the monks that fled, the sharp insults, the blows and Gilbert groaning, wounded, and à Becket dead. I listened for Mauclerc's mad boast of violence, scattering the brains on the pavement and swearing that the dead could never rise; then for the rush and flight from the profanation of a temple, and for distant voices crying outside in the streets of the city, under the sunset, 'The King's Men! The King's!'

But there was no such vision. It seems that to an emptiness so utter not even ghosts can return.

Here, in the last pages of *The Old Road,* the traveller and the historian meet together, in a personality already tinged with sadness. The book is as scientific as an atlas—who else would have demonstrated so clearly that the very existence of Canterbury and Winchester depended on the Channel crossings? And it is as individual as a human voice. The irony of the close is unflinching; already, in 1902, this was England.

In the inn, in the main room of it, I found my companions. A gramophone fitted with a monstrous trumpet roared out American songs, and to this sound the servants of the inn were holding a ball. Chief among them a woman of a dark and vigorous kind danced with an amazing vivacity, to the applause of her peers. With all this happiness we mingled.

For the rest of Belloc's lifetime the gramophone would continue to play, and the woman, ever more vigorously, to kick her heels.

CHAPTER X

POLITICS

I

BELLOC was a man of too varied gifts to content himself with the craft of letters. Besides, even at the rate that he was now writing and lecturing, he could with difficulty earn enough to support his family. Two more sons, Hilary and Peter, had been born to Elodie, and to the younger of these Chesterton was godfather. Belloc decided, therefore, to read for the Bar. He ate the dinners at Gray's Inn and was coached for the Bar Examination by Arthur Malcolm Latter, who had been a Brackenbury scholar at Balliol in 1893, and had recently returned from practising at the Bar in Shanghai. Belloc duly presented himself, took one look at the papers, and departed. His name remained on the books at Gray's Inn and he continued to incur an annual debt to the Inn. It does not appear that this obligation was either pressed on the one side or discharged on the other. Meanwhile he increased the circle of his acquaintances, meeting Mr. David Lloyd George at the annual dinner of the Palmerston Club in 1904. Belloc made a brilliant speech about nothing at all (his views on Palmerston would hardly have been popular on such an occasion) while Lloyd George, now a rising hope of the Liberals, played the heavy statesman. There is also a record of his appearance at the Pharos Club: 'a youngish dark man, with expressive eyes, a pointed chin, a frequent smile, and a conversational manner resembling his books'.[1] He was now widely regarded as that rather vague phenomenon—a coming man. 'Personally', wrote Shawn Bullock in the *Chicago Evening Post*, 'I do not think that

---

[1] Vincent Baynes: *Chic*, July 4, 1903.

Belloc's talents fit him for great public service, nor am I convinced that his convictions lead him in that direction; but no matter. Two full hours of his company convinced me of his genius. . . . He rose to speak on French fiction. Once or twice he sighted the subject— but a word turned him—and off he went rambling delightfully, talking about his experience as a conscript, his dealings with the French peasant, his adventures everywhere, his ideas, his opinions, his beliefs. And the talk was splendid . . . it flooded us all, just carried us off our solid British feet and left us gasping.'[1]

The writer was shrewd in his estimate of Belloc's gifts but he guessed his intentions wrongly. Having fled from the Bar, Belloc now decided to stand for Parliament. Mr. Balfour's Administration was growing daily more unpopular. The importation of Chinese labour into South Africa, the threat of Tariff Reform, and the Education Act of 1902, whereby the elementary schools run by the Church of England received subsidies from the State, had exasperated that Nonconformist opinion upon which the Liberals relied. This discontent was shown by the loss to the Government of several by-elections. Mr. Balfour loomed aloof from all this ferment, cultivated and charming, benevolent and bored. Joseph Chamberlain's hot-gospelling campaign for Tariff Reform was answered, in one constituency after another, by the cool logic of Asquith, whose rational cast of mind and Ciceronian turn of phrase balanced the fervour of Chamberlain on the one hand and of Lloyd George on the other. Belloc was also a nonconformist in his way, and the refusal of the Conservatives to consider the case for Home Rule threw him decisively into the Liberal camp, remote as he was from much of their mystique. Between the Puritans and the Imperialists he slightly preferred the former; and indeed he composed a 'triumphant ode to Mr. Chamberlain on his return from South Africa, but my wife wouldn't let me print it, wisely perhaps. It is very funny'.[2]

His religious beliefs were, of course, an obstacle in many places to his adoption as a Parliamentary candidate. He tried to challenge Akers-Douglas at Dover, but when the parish priest came forward

[1] May 2, 1903.
[2] Letter to Marie Lansdale: March 14, 1903.

to embrace him at the meeting, his slender hopes were shattered. Elsewhere he fared no better. By a fortunate chance, however, the constituency of South Salford was in need of a Liberal candidate. Salford was then an industrial suburb of Manchester with a large working-class population. It contained a model cotton factory—Richard Haworth and Co.—which was shown to visitors; some ironworks; and several docks serving the Manchester Ship Canal. It gave its name to a Roman Catholic diocese, and of its 8,645 voters about 800 were Catholic.

So the National Liberal Association in London recommended Belloc to apply. His credentials appealed to the Salford Selection Committee, who in turn recommended his adoption by the Executive and General Council of the local Liberal Association. On May 13, 1904, he presented himself for adoption.

In his speech, which was quite free from oratorical flourish, he stated his personal position on four live issues. He opposed the Education Act (1902) on the ground that 'there is no right more sacred than the right of a parent to have his children educated in the religious influence which seems to him the most important part of his life', and he maintained that the effect, if not the intention, of the Act would be 'that a number of children in the country whose parents are Nonconformists will be educated by the Church out of public money, some part of which will have been unwillingly paid by Nonconformists themselves'. This argument would of course equally hold good for Catholics. Belloc held that where there was only one school in a community of mixed denominations, that school should be neutral. He next tackled the problem of Temperance Reform. Here he showed himself fiercely opposed to the wealthy brewing interests, and determined to abolish the tied-house system once for all. The power of the magistrates to issue or withhold licences should not be hampered by the necessity of paying compensation on a scale dictated by the brewers.

Before the brewing monopoly arose England was not a drunken country. The power of magistrates to issue or to discontinue licences was absolute and unquestioned. The Press freely criticized the evil of excessive drinking where it appeared, and Parliament dealt with it under no compulsion or fear. In those days the publican managing his own house—the man, that is, who is now put forward as the victim of our policy—was the only person directly concerned in obtaining licences. At the present moment the vast majority of publicans throughout England are the servants, and probably the debtors also, of a small and very wealthy clique whose power it is our business to destroy.

On the question of Chinese Labour, Belloc believed that it would be the first business of a Liberal Government 'to bundle these people out if they ever get there'; on Home Rule, he did not believe there was a rational Unionist left in the country, and he claimed that the real opposition to a National Council in Dublin came from those who held mortgages on Irish land and were frightened of losing them. On Tariff Reform he proclaimed himself a militant Free Trader, subscribing to every article of Cobdenite orthodoxy. Before a Lancashire audience no further argument was necessary. Like many other Liberals he had detected a tendency, if not, as yet, a certain intention, to circumscribe the rights of Trade Unions—those 'essentially English things'. He believed that if legislation threatened the Trades Union funds, they should be guaranteed by positive law. Finally—or rather, firstly—he made no secret of his religious beliefs.

My religion is of course of greater moment to me by far than my politics, or than any other interest could be, and if I had to choose between two policies, one of which would certainly injure my religion and the other as certainly advance it, I would not for a moment hesitate between the two.

After he had spoken Belloc withdrew, and was then unanimously adopted as the Liberal candidate. He subsequently moved a vote of confidence in the Party at the annual meeting of the National Liberal Federation in Manchester, of which Augustine Birrell was the chairman. Belloc expressed his confidence that the Party would win and that 'the ancient soul of Britain, a thing in some peril, would thereby be delivered'. Afterwards he wrote to his mother:

> I was getting tired of being refused in so many places on account of my religion. . . . The chances are against me, but it has already done me a great deal of good that I should be standing. It has helped the sale of my books and has suddenly made the provincial press in the north of England acquainted with my name.[1]

2

In the same spring of 1904 G. K. Chesterton dedicated his *Napoleon of Notting Hill* to Hilaire Belloc and Elodie's reply not only shows how easily and happily she moved in the Chesterton circle, but it illustrates her power of expression, and her warm, decisive character. The Bellocs had just returned from a holiday in France.

> I am lost in my effort to choose which thing I must most thank you for—the book, the inscription or the glorious dedication! My loyalty to you and my memories of Slindon drive me towards the book; my egotism and my violence and my security in the soundness of my views in all things drive me towards the inscription in which you have so sweetly and so kindly included me; my passionate love of Liberty and my mild Irish belief in the final victory of all the good over the miserable muddy muggy streams of evil that drip under our unhappy noses (here and in Holy France) and the love for my beloved Man and the joy that I always have when he is recognised drive me to the dedication. I beg you and Frances to come and tell me which is the thing of all these three that should make me most happy.
>
> Meanwhile, my friend, let me tell you and Frances that for the first time in eight years I have been below the parallel of 45° North. And there, by God's grace, I found his Sun and hills and sheep and vineyards and happy blessed people who have

---

[1] May 18, 1904.

high horizons—away up in the air and purple at that—and who
work in the fields and who sleep at night and who go to Mass
and say their Rosaries in trains and behind their market-stalls.
May God give back to England some such strong hold upon
her own heroic soil—a great cable we shall need here! These
precious Frogs (I call them so lovingly) hold securely to their
land, their country, their very God by a silky film like a spider's
web. Alas for us all! We Irish are of the South. God planted us
in that little Island for your bane and for ours. But He knows
His business best. And I suppose some day there will be a
miserable, unhappy and discontented colony of Erin somewhere below the Mediterranean and above the Sahara, and
then England will get her due from us cross-grained, recalci-
trant, angry and wounded children who now feel ourselves
defrauded by God of the sun and by England of liberty.[1]

In January of the following year (1905) Belloc was taken
seriously ill with pleuro-pneumonia, and at one moment there
were grave fears for his life. An obituary in *The Times* was laid
down, beginning with the words 'Young as he was . . .'. Specialists were called in and trained nurses were in attendance. Both
his mother and his medical advisers were opposed to his being
told how dangerously ill he was, but Elodie insisted on a priest
coming to the house. Belloc, we are told, 'wept with gratitude
and begged for the Sacrament himself'.[2] Further light on the
illness is thrown by Charles Somers Cocks, writing from
Calcutta:

> I think it a good thing that part of your body was attacked,
> as it means that what was strongest in you, most capable of
> resistance has been placed in jeopardy. You will pull up at
> once. What you will have to be careful about is that you do not
> get bronchially inclined: it is easy to get into a state (in which
> you used to be before I came out here) of always having some
> sort of cold and sore throat.[3]

[1] April 5, 1904.
[2] Letter from Elodie Belloc to Mrs. Reginald Balfour: Aug. 20, 1907.
[3] Feb. 1, 1905.

And again, three months later, with a hinted doubt as to the wisdom of the Salford adventure:

> As you know, my view is that your real bent is intellectual mingled with physical pottering. Where you make a mistake is that you often do not potter enough physically. Hence your recent illness.

Belloc's affected lung was reconstituted and Somers Cocks sent him one hundred pounds towards the considerable expenses of the illness. A period of convalescence was necessary, and as soon as he was fit to travel, Belloc sailed for North Africa. The fruit of this journey was *Esto Perpetua*, which we shall discuss later. On February 2, 1905, he sent the following postcard to John Phillimore from Setif:

> If ever you have £20 to throw away go and see Africa. Rome sticks out of the earth at every step. . . . You will go and visit all the desert for the sum I mention. I am of course paying my expenses with a book. . . . The Churches are full. The press deplores the decay of Catholicism, or rejoices in it according to whether it is Christian or Jewish. Meanwhile there is no standing room in the Churches. . . . The Great Sahara (which is pronounced Sāhara) is deathly cold. Item, there are no lions in the Desert. Never has been. They live in Woods.

He wrote at greater length to Chesterton:

> The most remarkable things about the re-Europeanization of Roman Africa so far as I have seen it is or are: 1. The enormous number of Motor Cars which rush along the extremely good road into the most distant recesses of the land. 2. The appearance of green things, water, rain, grass, just as in Europe. 3. The High Mountains which are everywhere and in all shapes. 4. The equality of all races: this is most striking. Arab officers dine with French officers and in the railways everybody goes by the class he can afford. Rich Arabs go first. Poor Arabs go third. There are no middle-class Arabs. I go third. 5. The enormous extension of Agriculture. There are great plains now being ploughed for the first time. 6. The nasty

strength of the wine which is presided over, not by Bacchus, but by some Punic god such as Ashteroth or Baal-Zebub. 7. Its extreme and startling cheapness. 8. The cheapness of everything else: the hotel I am in costs 4s. 2d. a day and the meals excellent and wine thrown in. 9. The fact that *all* Arabs wear turbans on *all* occasions *everywhere*: this makes the whole landscape strange: some Arabs are porters in stations yet they wear turbans and burnooses like this (*Drawing*). 10. The sudden piety of European Catholics—for religion is here a badge. 11. Most Arabs are slightly tattooed. 12. All Arab women talk without stopping.[1]

The journey did him all the good that was expected of it, but he may have taken to heart Somers Cocks's admonition about 'physical pottering', for as soon as he returned to England he decided to leave Chelsea and move the whole family to Sussex. There were other reasons as well for this brusque decision—a decision he was afterwards, in some ways, to regret.

My going out of London in 1905 and keeping no house or flat there was disastrous. And yet I was driven by real—and even dangerous—poverty. I was earning not a quarter of the absolutely minimum income necessary to the meanest household of our sort, and my earnings were decreasing.[2]

The Bellocs took a lease of Courthill Farm, which stood on the northern slope of the hill behind Slindon. It was a pleasant Georgian house facing north-west in the direction of Halnacker Hill. Elodie, at least, breathed a sigh of relief at finding herself in the country. On May 25 (1905) she writes to her friend Grace Joel, a New Zealand painter and pupil of Renoir.

We have a great kitchen garden full of cabbages and cauliflowers ready for use now; the other beds are set out with peas, beans, French beans, radishes, lettuces, and for later times and such gross palates as mine, potatoes, turnips, carrots, parsnips and heaps of onions. We have gooseberries, strawberries and currants to come by the bushel if we have no frost.

[1] Jan. 28, 1905.   [2] Letter to Mrs. Raymond Asquith: Dec. 28, 1920.

Also in the orchard apples, cherries, pears, with a dozen great hazel nut trees as the place stands where once a wonderful forest was. We have no flowers! The last people let the lovely little garden go quite to bits—but we have put in some wall-flowers and so on, for next year, and planted nasturtiums, sweet peas, candytuft, etc. for this year.

The view is like heaven to me; but Nurse and Clara find it lonely. Great forests of wonderful beeches and firs and beyond the blue line of the Downs. We have two darling pigs whom we call Ruskin and Carlyle. Also 9 hens, 2 cocks and 17 chicks. In about 10 days we have had 46 eggs . . .

I wish that you could see your picture of Chelsea. It is quite charming and has the place of honour in our dining-room . . . I brought it here as a sort of memento of all my life in dear old 104, Cheyne Walk.

After they had settled in, Elodie escaped to France with her sister, and wrote to Frances Chesterton from the Hôtel de la Chaine d'Or, Les Andelys. Here it is easy to see what she had taken from Hilaire, and what the Irishwoman in her had given to him.

My sister has come to me from the Equator and I have brought her to France. I was a broken reed and Dr. Penny said I must go away, so I left Courthill under the regime of Hilairius Primus and came here a fortnight ago. We stayed a joyous week in Paris and we have been here a week. I have still a few days of paradise left me. We saw the Review at Longchamps on July 14 —Eleanor's birthday. How I wish that you and Gilbert had seen it. It shook my soul, and tell Gilbert that as the horsemen and the guns rushed over the shaken earth I felt like a terrible vision of the Angel Michael the emotion of a magnificent and militant patriotism. My patriotism, by the grace and will of God, has always been the obstinacy of the vanquished, the tragedy of the one who hopes. What a people are these Frogs! Homogeneous, amiable, powerful, joyous, tragic—they are Europe. And always my mind goes back to my Green Island, battered ignominiously, squalid, helpless, waiting and waiting for God to give the word when we may claim St. Michael for our patron. Oh! *When* will the blinded English see what we as a nation would do for them in return for a tardy, grudging, recriminating Justice! Never, I suppose, as He knows His business best; and, as the Italians say, He does not settle His bills on Saturday night.

When are we, my beloved friend, to have a week together in Paris? In the Name of God let us have it before we are much older or the grand crash comes. I can see the Frogs dilating with joy as we four or five would go by them. Let us complete these plans for some day before we die. It has been a miracle to me, to see Paris and the French as I have seen them during this fortnight.[1]

Meanwhile Belloc had been hard at work ever since his return from Algeria in March. He even tried his hand—as ever, unsuccessfully—at a play. He also found time to give lessons in French literature—at thirty shillings for an hour and a half—to Miss Dorothy Hamilton, a close friend of his wife. He started her off with Joinville and the *Chanson de Roland*. 'Don't fear the old French', he tells her. 'It is only a question of practice. It is like any other literature of a limited vocabulary. You spend two or three days thinking you can never learn it, and then it becomes quite plain all of a sudden.'[2] One could not appreciate the hard French of the seventeenth century unless one understood how the language had been formed during the Middle Ages. He made two important points about Montaigne: that he was the first writer who dared to be entirely personal and that he started the essay. The essay, like the sketch, was essentially a product of the Renaissance.

As a natural consequence of his adoption by South Salford, Belloc was elected to the Reform Club on March 9, 1905; he was proposed by Herbert Gladstone, M.P., and seconded by Francis Mowatt. The Reform became a second home to him. Here he could write and receive letters; here he wrote a large part of his *History of England*; and here he could meet those Liberals with

[1] July 23, 1905. [2] April 16, 1905.

whom he was in sympathy, as well as a few with whom he was not. He remained a member of the Club until the very last years of his life.

As soon as Elodie returned to Courthill, Belloc, now fully restored to his normal vigour, set out to walk in the Pyrenees. It was not his first exploration of those legendary hills, and it was not to be his last. Already he was comparing the civilizations he found on either side of the frontier.

> The government and all public affairs of Spain [he writes to Miss Hamilton] are about what you might expect from negroes. They are really inexcusable for laziness and utter lack of discipline. It would astonish you to see this place. It is a pity Napoleon did not get there earlier and stay longer; he might have re-invigorated it as he did the valley of the Rhine. As it is, positively *nothing* is done. All the French roads stop dead at the Frontier and even the mule paths up the passes often cease to exist when one gets over on to this Southern side. All the clocks are stopped, all the windows broken and all doors off their hinges.
>
> Catholicism (or mysticism in excess) has been made to blame for it and it might certainly have such effects, but as a fact it has nothing to do with it. The people are a good deal less Catholic than in France, the Church has more power, or rather it is less attacked politically, but the number of men who go to Mass is less than in France. I think a good deal more Catholicism would wake them up a little.[1]

3

Esto Perpetua [2] is vintage Belloc: he was always at his best on subjects where history and geography meet. Yet although he had set out to write a book about North Africa, what he wrote was more nearly a book about Europe. It was through uneasy contact with Islam that the genius of Europe here stood out in its full colour and complexity. The contrast was vivid; variety versus monotony, will versus fate. Belloc's was not one of those curious

[1] Aug. 8, 1905.   [2] 1906.

or dispirited minds which are tempted by the mystery, or subdued by the militancy, of Islam. For its militancy he had the professional respect of an opposing general; its mystery he discounted as a false and mathematical simplicity. In so far as he understood Islam at all, he understood it as a strategist behind a rampart understands the manœuvres of an advancing foe. And what really drew him to Barbary was not the permeating presence and creeping sterility of Islam: it was the ancient vestiges and the recent resurrection of Rome.

By 'Rome' we may read 'Gaul'. The French effort in North Africa moved him to an appreciation so exact in its insight and lapidary in its style that it demands quotation.

The vices and the energy of this people are well known. They are perpetually critical of their own authorities, and perpetually lamenting the decline of their honour. There is no difficulty they will not surmount. They have crossed all deserts and have perfected every art. Their victories in the field would seem legendary were they not attested; their audacity whether in civil war or in foreign adventure, has permanently astonished their neighbours to the south, the east and the north. They are the most general in framing a policy and the most actual in pursuing it. Their incredible achievements have always the appearance of accidents. They are tenacious of the memory of defeats rather than of victories. They change more rapidly and with less reverence than any other men the external expression of their tireless effort, yet, more than any other men, they preserve—in spite of themselves—an original and unchanging spirit. Their boundaries are continually the same. They are acute and vivid in matters of reason, careless in those of judgment. A coward and a statesman are equally rare among them, yet their achievements are the result of prudence and their history is marked by a succession of silent and calculating politicians. Alone of European people the Gauls have, by a sort of habit, indulged in huge raids which seemed but an expense of military passion to no purpose. They alone could have poured out in that tide of the third century before our era to swamp

Lombardy, to wreck Delphi and to colonise Asia. They alone
could have conceived the Crusades; they alone the revolutionary wars. It is remarkable that in all such eruptions they
alone fought eastward, marching from camp into the early light;
they alone were content to return with little spoil and with no
addition of provinces, to write some epic of their wars. . . .

The passage is among the greatest Belloc ever wrote—and it
was Africa that inspired him to it. Once, on the shores of the
Mediterranean, he had seen a man at work on two ornaments in a
builder's shop. Both had been ordered by a customer in Algiers,
and each was required to decorate a building. One was a crescent
and the other a cross. It was this contrast, and this historic conflict,
which moved Belloc to his African journey. One may fairly
comment that he saw only one side of the crescent and perhaps
only certain aspects of the cross.

'Their Faith', he writes of the Moslems, 'was like some plant
out of the solitudes; it was hard in surface; it was simple in form;
it was fitted rather to endure than to grow.'

Belloc's rational temper forbade him to understand, or to
investigate, the mysticism of Islam, and his Latin bias prevented
him from digging deeper into its origins. He was not able to
explain how far Islam was a Christian heresy; he only saw it as a
conquering horde. And in any case, his purpose was not theology,
but travel. Much of the journey he did on foot, in the thin
winter sunshine, crossing the Great Atlas to the edge of the desert
itself. Now and again he notices an Arab face, nobler in expression
than any commonly seen among European men. He acknowledges the Gothic debt to Arab architecture, though he finds
the Arab ogive finicky by comparison with the Gothic arch.

The ecstasy of height, the self-development of form into
further form, the grotesque, the sublime and the enthusiastic—
all these things the Arab arch lacks as utterly as did the Arab
spirit.

And when he is faced with the irremovable faith and inflexible,
though decaying, culture of Islam, he is forced to admit that the
European reconquest will not 'be accomplished until we have

recovered, perhaps through disasters suffered in our European homes, the full tradition of our philosophy and a faith which shall permeate all our actions as completely as does this faith of theirs.' The *Gesta Francorum* were no more persuasive in the twentieth century than they had been in the twelfth—and they were perhaps a shade less magnificent.

The contrast between the *nirvana* of the desert and the fertility of the plateaux and the seaboard was indeed the contrast between two cultures adjacent but eternally apart. Belloc accepts this separation. He is not haunted, as another Christian thinker might be haunted, by any dreams of universalism, by any passion for unity. He desires to reconquer, even if he cannot convert. He glories in the limitations of the European thing, because his eyes teach him that where so much else perishes, that thing endures.

This nameless character which is the mark of the Empire, and carries, as it were, a hint of resurrection in it, is as strong in what has fallen as in what stands. A few bricks built at random into a mud wall bear the sign of Rome and proclaim her title: a little bronze unearthed at random in the rubbish heaps of the Rummel is a Roman victory; a few flagstones lying broken upon a deserted path in the woodlands is a Roman Road; nor do any of these fragments suggest the passing of an irrecoverable good, but rather its continued victory.

He tells the story of the French officer who wanted to inscribe the name of his regiment on a wall of mountain rock only to find that a Roman officer had been there before him. Terse and graven, the words stood out to silence him. 'The IIIrd Legion. The August. The Victorious.' And there was that other epitaph carved upon a tomb in memory of some priestess of Isis who had served the divinities of the woods so well that when she died '*ingemuerunt Drayades*'. 'Twice I read those delicate words, delicately chiselled in hard stone, and I saw her going in black, with her head bent, through groves.' This was Pagan antiquity and Belloc was perfectly at home in it. Only the miniature acropolis of Hippo recalled Augustine writing from its summit: '*Ubi magnitudo, ibi veritas*'; the words might be taken as referring to

the Empire itself, or to that further *imperium* into which the
Empire was transformed.

Belloc returned from the desert to the coast, and as the train
vibrated down the slopes of the Dwijura he composed *The
Ballade of All the Heresies*. Then he embarked on a Spanish
steamer bound for Majorca. It was of Europe that he thought, as
he sat huddled in the bows; of the Latin order and the men and
women of his blood. Not for him the other-worldliness of the
desert, with its refusal of the grape and its fear of the image.
'The Faith is Europe, and Europe is the Faith'—the brave fallacy
may well have taken shape in his mind as the ship drove through
the Middle Sea and he exclaimed '*Esto Perpetua!*' to the Europe
he had left behind, and to the Europe that was waiting to receive
him.

4

In December 1905, Mr. Balfour resigned. Sir Henry Campbell-
Bannerman formed a Liberal Government and immediately
dissolved Parliament. All Belloc's energy was now concentrated
on the electoral campaign.

He had given his general views to a correspondent of the
Westminster Bud a few months after his adoption.[1] The interviewer
remembered him in his Oxford days, dominating the Union
with his oratory, like Camille Desmoulins. The years had not
damped his enthusiasm and they had given his energy a finer
point. His Liberalism was inherited and inbred; Joseph Parkes, his
maternal grandfather, had been called 'the last of the English
Radicals', but the grandson was resolved to continue the line. He
was not ambitious for office; he did not think office was important.
Cobden had never accepted office; yet he had moulded the legislation of his day. What Belloc desired to see in Parliament was 'a
strong Radical Party, who chiefly care for the results of their
political creed and who do not expect office'. He was asked for
his ideas on Imperialism.

It seems to me [he replied] that when people talk of
Imperialism they are thinking of maps, not of things. It was

[1] Oct. 28, 1904.

Chatham's reproach. It has a noble side, for with most it simply means patriotism, but with the few who control it it means money—and only money . . . It is common sense that any citizen of any country should wish that country to be strong, he should wish it to be self-respecting, powerful and happy. To this end I am for a strong Army and, by the way, a well-paid and a national Army. I believe that it is absolutely necessary that we should keep our possessions with pride and security. The Empire is there, and it is our duty to retain it. . . .

But he did not think that the colonies were a source of strength, and when people talked of 'federation', his reading of history told him that only one part of a Federation had ever fought in a common cause. This calculation was to be decisively belied twice in his own lifetime. He did not believe that common action was possible unless 'the naval and military forces of the Empire remained at the disposal of Westminster'. Nor did he think the non-European expansion of European people necessarily for their good, and he thought the forcible incorporation within the Empire of communities non-European in origin 'as being in hopeless conflict with the tradition of European civilisation'. There was in all this a kind of tacit assumption that only Europeans had rights, and also a kind of European provincialism. Once, in later years, he let fall the phrase 'Atlantic Europe'; it was one of the truest things he ever said, although he did not know it.

Questioned about Ireland, he replied that he did not regard Home Rule 'as dependent on elementary democratic principles'. He regarded it as a purely national problem, though it was in origin religious. The failure of any modern attempt to govern Ireland by English landlords was itself the strongest argument for Home Rule. The Irish, he maintained, with perhaps a shade of overstatement, were 'the most industrious, the most thrifty, and, what is more important, the most virtuous—by far the most virtuous—and the bravest of the mixed and rather unworthy races who speak the English tongue overseas'. It was folly not to make allies of them.

The current of popular feeling was running strongly in favour of the Liberals. But Belloc expected a hard fight at Salford. He thought the constituency excellent for a 'preliminary canter' and he expected to lose it by about four hundred votes. His own campaign was managed by Sir Edward Wood, Chairman of Edward Wood and Co., a large local firm of constructional engineers, and by Charles Goodwin, a soap manufacturer and prominent citizen of Salford. The sitting member was a Conservative, J. Greville Groves, who belonged to the wealthy brewing firm of Groves and Whitnall. He had won the seat at the previous election by a majority of 1,227; and the Liberals had held it since 1892. South Salford was therefore what is now called a 'marginal' constituency. Belloc had two things telling heavily against him; he was a French citizen by birth and he was a Catholic. Catholicism has never been a political asset in Great Britain, and the Tories were not slow to chant their slogan: 'Don't vote for a Frenchman and a Catholic.'

Belloc himself saw nothing incongruous between Catholicism and a Radical programme. As a Radical he wanted self-government for Ireland—and, incidentally, for England also. He wanted to prevent an increase in the price of food and an increase in the risk of war. It seemed to him natural enough for a Catholic, with an elementary sense of justice, to want all these things. He held his first meeting in the schools of St. John's Catholic Cathedral. The clergy had warned him that the religious question was going to be very tricky for him, and that he had better say nothing about it. He proudly disregarded their advice. He rose to address the packed audience and spoke as follows:

Gentlemen, I am a Catholic. As far as possible, I go to Mass every day. This [taking a rosary out of his pocket] is a rosary. As far as possible, I kneel down and tell these beads every day. If you reject me on account of my religion, I shall thank God that He has spared me the indignity of being your representative.

There was a hush of astonishment, followed by a thunder-clap of applause. He went on to describe himself as 'Liberal and Free Trade', and declared his intention of waging war on the clique of wealthy men at Westminster. He issued one hand-bill, accusing the Tory Government of spending one hundred pounds more per minute than the Liberals when they were last in office; and another with his photograph in the middle, surmounted with flags and supported by two illustrations. 'Protection and Poverty' was represented by a dejected trio from the slums; 'Free Trade and Prosperity' by a lady in a pink dress, carrying a red parasol, while her two children made mud-pies at her feet. A rather expensive-looking yacht occupied the horizon. Belloc addressed a circular to all the licence-holders in Salford, repeating his previous arguments that the contracts forced upon them were always hard and often unjust. A larger share of compensation should go to the man whose name was above the door. He went on to attack Groves's record in Parliament. 'He charges me with being a gunner, and I know how to shoot. Let the people say, "This man is no foreigner, but an Englishman who talks a Radicalism which is not talked in any other country but England."' Groves owned no less than one hundred public-houses in the district and claimed to be 'a Salford lad'. His supporters had scrawled up the following rhyme on the grimy walls of the town:

> A Frenchman there was named Hilaire
> And René—the names make you stare;
> He wished to be Salford M.P.
> But they wanted no foreigners there.

To this Belloc replied that he had as much French blood in his veins as Lord Lansdowne or Lord Edmund Fitzmaurice—and better blood because it was democratic blood. He had served in the French Army for the same reasons as Lord Kitchener—to see what it was like.

During the early days of the campaign he and Elodie stayed with Lord Stanley of Alderley, his Balliol friend. This relieved him of strain and got him back after his evening speeches to a house with books and leisure. J. W. Dulanty, later for many years Irish High Commissioner in London and first Irish Ambassador at the Court of St. James, was campaigning for the Irish Nationalists in Salford, and describes a week-end spent in Belloc's company. Belloc had been to see Miss Horniman's company at the Gaiety and came on to Dulanty's room, where he remained until 3 a.m. expounding the fallacies of Determinism. After Mass the following day they called on the Catholic Bishop of Salford, and on finding him out, bearded the Protestant Bishop of Manchester, Dr. Knox, whom Belloc entertained with the impersonation of a don lecturing on the Futility of the Final Utility theory.

In the evening . . . a friend motored us into the country. I told Belloc that he was a furniture manufacturer on a big scale, and also that his Irish horse, Rathlee, had lately won the Chester Cup. Belloc . . . told my friend how to make antique furniture and how to breed and train horses for the classic races. As he left me, my friend whispered: 'Isn't your Mr. Belloc a holy terror?' [1]

Polling day was January 13, and Belloc was elected by a majority of 852. Many workers voted for him who had voted Conservative in 1900, and who were angered by the proposal to import Chinese labour into the Transvaal. After the results had been declared, the victorious candidate had much difficulty in forcing his way to the Liberal Committee rooms in Egerton Street.

We have pulled it off [he declared]. Concerning everything in this world worth doing, the first thing is to determine it, and the second thing is to do it. And we have done it.

The next halt was at the Regent Liberal Club in Trafford Road. Here he emphasized that he was going to Westminster

on a whole-hearted and well-defined democratic programme, such as that on which Mr. John Burns was returned for Battersea twelve years ago. Liberalism of that kind will spread. It is like lighting a fire that you cannot put out. They cannot put me out of Parliament till Parliament is dissolved, and before that time comes, I intend to let the people at St. Stephen's hear a few truths in the interests of the working classes that will astonish them.

[1] Broadcast: Nov. 18, 1953.

To a representative of the *Manchester Guardian* he said that he had fought an artisan constituency on a very strong democratic programme, which 'some of my friends thought was too strong, but which was not quite strong enough for my convictions'. Then he went on with his wife to a reception at the Manchester Reform Club, where the jubilant Liberals had started to sing 'Praise God from whom all blessings flow', had then abandoned the attempt, and were now expressing their feelings with champagne. On being called upon to speak, Belloc asked for complete silence.

For this is all that is left of my voice. If you desire to hear that voice in Parliament for purposes on which we are agreed, you must spare it. You know how hard the fight has been in South Salford. It was especially hard because I chose to be, and shall continue to be, a thorough-going Radical. As I had the hardest fight, so it will probably appear I have the smallest majority. But I cannot tell you how hard the fight has been, and how thankful I am that we have won. It seems that Manchester and Salford are going solid for Liberalism and Free Trade. If there had been a black spot it would have been my fault and I am glad.

In fact, no Protectionist had pierced the ramparts of Free Trade in Manchester. Winston Churchill defeated Joynson-Hicks in the North-West constituency, and J. R. Clynes won the North-East for Labour. Belloc used to go over and listen to Churchill's speeches. Once he heard him say that men would forgive a man anything except bad prose; and then he knew that Churchill was much more than a politician. Belloc himself was a much better campaigner than politician, and he had unashamedly enjoyed the fight. 'Hoarse, mad and tired out,' he arrived at Euston where Chesterton and Dorothy Hamilton had been summoned to meet him. 'This is a great day for the British Empire' he remarked, 'but a bad one for the little Bellocs,' for he was wondering how he could be an efficient M.P. and an efficient father of a family at the same time. Meanwhile the routed Tories could find only two words to express their dismay:

'Belloc's in!'

CHAPTER XI

PARLIAMENT: 1906–1909

I

IN the new House of Commons there were 377 Liberals, 157 Conservatives, 53 Labour Members, and 83 Irish Nationalists. Since the Liberals could generally count on the support of the Labour men and the Nationalists, they could expect a working majority of about 400. Such an ascendancy of one Party over the rest had never been known before in British politics.

The Liberals were only loosely united. The right—or 'Whig'—wing of the Party was represented by Asquith, Grey and Haldane. These were the old Liberal Imperialists and belonged to the Liberal League, under the presidency of Lord Rosebery. They accepted Campbell-Bannerman as Prime Minister, but hoped that he might soon withdraw modestly to the House of Lords. In this hope they were disappointed. 'C.B.' remained at Downing Street until he died two years later. The chief posts in the Cabinet were distributed as follows: Grey to the Foreign Office; Haldane (a surprising appointment) as Secretary of State for War; Bryce in charge of Irish affairs, until he went as Ambassador to Washington; Morley to the India Office; Herbert Gladstone to the Home Office; John Burns as President of the Local Government Board; and Lloyd George to the Board of Trade. Asquith was Chancellor of the Exchequer, and Winston Churchill Under-Secretary for the Colonies. Churchill had entered Parliament in 1900 as a Conservative, and had then joined the Liberals on the issue of Free Trade. It was probably the most able Ministry that has ever been gathered together at Westminster.

Of the Labour men twenty-four were Trade Unionists; five—and these included Keir Hardie, Philip Snowden and Ramsay

MacDonald—were members of the I.L.P.; and twenty-nine had been sponsored by the Labour Representative Committee. But twenty-four others, 'Lib-Labs' and miners' representatives, accepted the Labour whip. Two-thirds of the Unionists were regarded as thorough-going Protectionists; the rest shared Balfour's polite scepticism about Tariff Reform and were opposed to any taxes on imported food. Joseph Chamberlain had a stroke shortly after the election and disappeared from active politics altogether. He died in 1914.

Nearly half the Liberals in the new House belonged to Non-conformist congregations. This was not the company that Belloc normally cared to keep, and when he supported a Bill against the manufacture of impure beer, declaring 'there are very few nights when I do not go to bed after drinking a pint or two of beer', it was rejected by sixty-five votes. He admitted that he had hope-lessly offended all the teetotallers in his constituency, and then added, amid gales of laughter, 'There are eight of them'. *Punch* had its comment on this.

> True, there are hardy souls among us still
> Convinced adherents of the foaming beaker,
> Like that M.P. who nightly takes his fill
> Two pints of bitter, as he told the Speaker.[1]

But the Nonconformists ensured that the Education question would be tackled without delay. Augustine Birrell, President of the Board, had the task of piloting a complicated Bill through the Commons. The intention of the Bill was that some Voluntary Schools, according to the number of children professing a particu-lar religion attending it, should have the right to appoint teachers all of the same faith. Other Voluntary Schools would have to admit a certain proportion of teachers not of the faith to which the school belonged. This meant in practice that Catholics would be able to get Catholic teachers for all the posts in their schools, whereas, in many cases, the Anglicans would not. The dream of every Minister of Education is a single system in which all children receive simple undenominational religious instruction.

[1] July 25, 1906.

P

This means the Bible and Hymns. It also means that no doctrine shall be taught which is in dispute between the various Protestant communities of the nation. The Catechism is replaced by the lowest common multiple of contemporary belief—and this may be very low indeed. To the Catholic minority such bargaining will always appear both abhorrent and nonsensical. They will demand nothing less than Catholic schools and Catholic teachers for Catholic children supported out of public funds to the same degree as everyone else, without discrimination.

The demand will always be unanswerable in reason and impracticable in politics. Birrell did his best to meet it, but it was impossible to give equality of treatment to Catholic and Council schools. 'Minorities must suffer,' he exclaimed regretfully, 'it is the badge of their tribe. But it is the duty of enlightened Liberalism to mitigate their suffering as much as possible.' What was to happen when there was only a handful of Catholic children in a district and no school for them to go to? It was to meet these cases, and similar cases affecting children of other religious minorities, that the Cowper-Temple clause had been devised to safeguard the minimum undenominational teaching. Meanwhile Belloc had made his maiden speech in February, soon after the opening of the new session. He looked, already, more like being a nuisance to the Government than to the Opposition. He writes as follows to Maurice Baring:

I have made my maiden speech. After it I was sick. This is true and not an exaggeration. My maiden speech lasted eight minutes. It was intensely Radical and would have pleased you. I said that if the Government made any pretence to be Liberal it would (a) deport the first batch of Chinese labourers from South Africa in the next three months; (b) fix the rate at which the deportation was to continue (I suggest five thousand a month); and (c) make the whole cost fall upon the mine owners. The *Morning Post,* naturally trying to hurt the Government, said that I alone of the Liberals had shown courage. *The Times* said in a leader that what I had said was 'dangerous rant'. The Liberal papers keep an ominous silence—being cowardly, but I, my dear Maurice, continue to dance in the sun-light and to sing like the gaslight. For instance, even today I leaped up in my seat and asked a question of the Government which gave them the greatest possible annoyance, to wit, whether it was not a fact that Kaffir labour was increasing steadily until the Chinese labour was brought in, and has since then been decreasing. It is a fact.[1]

He supported, however, the second reading of the Education Bill on May 7, because he thought it was certain to be amended by the Lords. He was at pains to point out not only the size but the nature of the Catholic minority. This was 'as large as Manchester and Liverpool combined; larger than Birmingham and its satellite towns'. The Member for Louth, he said, had made use of the word 'moderate' and he had also heard the word 'compromise' mentioned as regards the Catholic schools.

I cannot too emphatically point out that these two words are absolutely meaningless when the House of Commons is dealing with Catholic Faith. The House may tyrannically insist on their having less, but English Catholics cannot be content with less for their Catholic children than Catholic schools with Catholic teachers teaching the Catholic religion and impressing the children all the time.

No proper history, he continued provocatively, was taught in the Universities and Public Schools. Otherwise people would know

that since Diocletian nothing can compare with the persecution of the Catholic people of this country by the wealthy and official classes. It has not been a popular persecution, but a cold, deliberate and bloody persecution on the part of the men who got hold of the land of the country after the dissolution of the monasteries. Can you wonder after two centuries of such suffering we emerged a wholly distinct and highly homogeneous body? Right or wrong, all the rest of the country stands as a body of English Protestants unless I except the small body of the Jews.

[1] February 27, 1906.

Roman Catholics, he explained, accepted the Universities as distinct from the schools,

> because the effect of University teaching is vastly different from the effect of school teaching. The former is critical and falls upon a mature mind; the latter is formative and moulds a mind yet plastic. I never knew any Catholic who went to Oxford and was in any way influenced by the dominant doctrine of the place. But a little child must accept what it is told and that which it is told finds a permanent hold . . . It is true, not only of myself but of every Catholic in England, that the preservation of the Catholic schools is far and away the first of the political controversies in which he may be engaged. I should not hesitate for a moment, if I found it impossible satisfactorily to represent my constituency, and yet to stand, as I do, for my religion, as to what course I should take. A political career is nothing to us compared with our religion; nor is wealth. Catholics must have their rights on some general principle, and that principle is the right of the parent to have his child instructed, immersed in the religion for the glory and defence of which he brought that child into the world. The Catholics feel that they are in a sense exiles in this country, misunderstood both in regard to their vices and their virtues; and so long as they retain that feeling, they demand the right of maintaining the things for which they have struggled so long and so bitterly. . . . If you could devise a purely neutral and secular system, then you could logically say, 'We do not ask you to pay for our morals or our philosophy, neither should we pay for yours'; but when you ask us to endow the opinions of the vast majority of the people of this country, so long as we are a minority we can stand up and say, 'As we pay, so we must receive'.

To the argument that the multiplicity of sects would make this impracticable Belloc replied that only the Catholics and the Jews would, in fact, refuse to accept the simple Bible teaching. A single school area should be neutral, even if the school had been Catholic, because 'you have no right to teach even a small minority some-

thing they do not believe in.' Whenever four-fifths of the people
in an area demanded a particular, definite teaching, they should
have it. Teachers should be nominated or suggested by the body
which represented the views of the parents, subject to appeal to
the Board of Education.

Such reasoning was absolute, but in the nature of English
politics it could not be met; and on June 10 Belloc voted against
the Government. As the wearisome debates drew to their close,
he still found the Bill unacceptable. On July 30 he pointed out
some of its more gross anomalies. In Sussex there was a town
of 12,000 inhabitants, which would retain its Catholic schools,
although it had been strongly Protestant, even in the sixteenth
century. Another town, of under 5,000, with Catholic traditions
equally strong, would lose them. In this case a Catholic landlord
would have to hand over his rates not only for the support of the
local Protestant school, but in order to make Protestant a school
built largely out of his own money. Nevertheless, the Catholic voters would not throw themselves into the arms of the
Conservatives.

> There is a newer force arising in the country and it is already
> represented in the House. It is there that you will find the
> Catholic vote, which is not only a numerical but a moral force,
> represented in the future.

Augustine Birrell, winding up for the Government, denied that
Cowper-Temple religious instruction was a thing hateful to
Roman Catholics.

> I know many parents of Roman Catholic children who
> attended the Board Schools have admitted that their children
> have received advantage from the simple undenominational
> teaching which is given in those schools. There are in those old
> Board Schools also many scores of Roman Catholic teachers,
> devoted men and women, who give Cowper-Temple religious
> instruction every day of their lives and find it no injury either
> to their faith or their passion for the Church to which they
> belong.

Belloc abstained in the subsequent division. But the Bill was so mangled by successive amendments in the Lords that the Government dropped it. Belloc, however, recommended the rejection of these amendments on the grounds that

> no consistent Radical can be dependent even for a good thing upon the non-elected Chamber. The House of Lords consists of a small body of eminent men given a position in a sort of Senate for their services to the nation; a large body of men who sit there by hereditary right; and thirdly there is a body of men who have openly purchased their place in that Assembly. The Catholics of Great Britain will obtain the immunity and treatment they desire, but they will obtain it in other ways: they will not be defeated because they are infused with something that is never defeated, and that is Irish blood.

How inconvenient he must have seemed to the Front Bench, this obstreperous tribune, who was in such a hurry to take their election promises out of pawn! What an incomprehensible blend of French logic, Irish fanaticism, Conservative instincts, and plain Radical principle! A. G. Gardiner's neat sketch in *Prophets, Priests and Kings* gives a hint of the Liberal bewilderment. Those who had listened to Belloc at the Oxford Union may already have begun to wonder whether he would ever master the acoustics of the House of Commons.

2

Immediately after the election the Bellocs took a tiny flat in Victoria Street. This was essential for attendance at the House and Elodie would occasionally come up for the night. Courthill was not entirely a success, partly because the Bellocs both took an overpowering dislike to the inhabitants of Slindon. So, already, on March 9 (1906) we find Elodie writing to Grace Joel:

> We have bought a place of our own in Sussex. A lovely old long brick house. We have had to do a lot to it—but we hope to be settled in there during the summer.

This was King's Land, which was to be Belloc's home for the
rest of his life. They had bought it, with five acres and a mill
attached, for one thousand pounds, and it illustrated the cheapness
of a house which was

> exactly suitable to oneself, though of a kind that no one else
> would like. When I bought King's Land at such a bargain both
> these were combined. It went cheap because not every modern
> man would care to live in a house which was planned as it is,
> and also because most townsmen coming to it and finding no
> water supply and not appreciating that a full water system,
> well, pump, cistern, closets and all could be put in for £100
> were put off.[1]

The Bellocs moved in on August 22; a large caravan lumbering
down from Slindon. King's Land occupied a corner site in the
village of Shipley, seven miles to the south of Horsham. It was
far from the main road, close to the sources of the Rother, and a
walled garden, about an acre in extent, stretched out behind to
the village. Beyond it was the tower, squarely and perfectly pro-
portioned, of a superb twelfth-century church. The surrounding
country undulated, like a gently heaving sea, so that you could
never see as far as you expected, but from the top of an adjacent
field the spire of the Charterhouse at Parkminster was visible and,
on a clear day, the round copse of Chanctonbury.

The house had once been a village shop. In its oldest parts it
dated from the fourteenth century and the newest, and northern,
wing had been added in 1890. It had eleven gables, so similar in
aspect that you could not tell which were old and which were new.
It was held together by dark oak beams. There were iron railings along the front and you entered between two windows
straight into the living-room. The walls were lined with little
drawers, such as you will see in any village shop, and the shelves
had leather fringes, about one inch thick, to keep out the dust. A
narrow stone-flagged room, next door, with an open fireplace,
served as a dining-room; down the middle, and total length, of
this stood the polished oak refectory table which the Bellocs had

[1] Letter to Desmond MacCarthy: May 6, 1914.

bought for ten pounds from a second-hand dealer in Oxford during the first year of their marriage. It had once belonged to St. John's College. Out of the dining-room you passed into a small study. A large interior hall was added later, with a gallery and staircase leading to it from the first floor. Upstairs were several bedrooms, and a room which was used as a Chapel. The furnishings for this were bought from Mrs. Reginald Balfour, a close friend of the Bellocs who lived near Littlehampton. The house was lit by candles only and oil lamps, and Belloc, not wishing to be importuned by casual and unsolicited callers, refused to admit the telephone. At first there were only earth closets, but a bathroom and the usual amenities were afterwards installed.

It has become trite to speak of the 'atmosphere' of a house, but to those who were privileged to know it the atmosphere of King's Land will always be unforgettable. Like the house itself, it did not bear any trace of deliberate creation. It grew and matured, until it seemed to be impregnated with the spirit of Belloc and his wife. Nothing in it was planned, nothing self-conscious; yet everything was in the right place. It reflected the harmony of two lives which were perfectly in tune; not an easy harmony perhaps, but enduring and deep. King's Land was a house where nothing was ever destroyed. The papers, the pictures, the books, the souvenirs found their casual resting-place, and there they lay—or hung— undisturbed by circumstance or time. In a life which had little continuity, save for its inflexible purpose, King's Land became an image of the things that do not change: faith and love and the steady expectation of repose.

For immediate neighbours the Bellocs had Sir Walter Burrell, the principal landowner of the district, at Knepp Castle; Wilfrid Scawen Blunt at Newbuildings with his Arab stud and quixotic impulses—a Catholic by birth with leanings towards Islam, and a prolific minor poet. A little further away was Mrs. Wright-Biddulph at Burton Park, where Belloc wrote a good part of *The Four Men* and Barlavington Park where he had riddden her horses as a boy.

He had, however, small time for local society. The financial problem was pressing him hard. His election to Parliament had seemed a very off chance and he had made no provision for it. As a result of his success he was about half a year behind with his income. Lectures had been arranged, a series of very well-paid travel articles for the *Tribune* commissioned, and two very lucrative jobs in Paris (one for the American Encyclopædia) fixed up. Now they would all have to be postponed. The Education Bill tied him to Westminster and he had to meet the expenses of the move. His election would of course raise his price and increase his opportunities in journalism. But these prospects were of no immediate help; what he required was a regular salaried job. In a series of letters to Maurice Baring he poured out his heart on the subject.

Meanwhile things are getting very grave indeed. No one will give me any sort of salaried post, and it is extremely difficult to earn under the conditions of the House of Commons; my lecturing is cut off, and although, of course, I can get any amount of publication for, and good prices for, my imaginative stuff signed, no man can live by that. What apparently I cannot get from man or devil is quiet regular and salaried work such as all my inferiors get for the asking. This plunges me into the depths of gloom. Who on earth do the *Morning Post* want, or the *Tribune*, to edit their literary columns? It is perfectly intolerable. Neither could possibly have it done worse than it is done and I have all the credentials for doing it well. I feel as though there were a gulf between me and other men. For instance, this morning, a man asked me on what I could lecture in connection with the University of London. I suggested Descartes. He asked me, naturally, what I knew about Descartes. It turned out that he had never read a single line that Descartes had written and so it has been all through my life. . . .

I am tired out of piecing together a livelihood by little special efforts of the brain. I want regular work and regular pay. No one dreams of giving it to me. I try to start a good *radical* weekly which just now would boom. No one will hear of it. No one will even give me a literary page to review. It is like

being in a large room with fifty doors and all of them locked.
I lie awake at night full of black thoughts. I am miserable.

It is quite ridiculous. First Oxford wouldn't give me work and
now after all these efforts London won't.[1]

Six months later, on September 20, Belloc obtained the literary
editorship of the *Morning Post*. Fabian Ware was the editor and he
had been persuaded by Lord Glenesk to secure Belloc's services.
The appointment showed a refreshing absence of Party prejudice
on all sides. Belloc contributed regular essays to the paper, many
of which were afterwards republished, and sent out books for
review. But the strain was telling on him. On September 29 he
writes to Baring:

I am really ill and don't know what it is. At the least attempt
to work my head feels like a drum and I wake up every morning worse than I went to bed. On the top of this a payment of
some hundreds that was fixed to come on the 20th has failed
and has been put off for some indefinite time, so I stand
appalled.

And again, four weeks later:

I am doing more work than a man should. But it does not
hurt me. What does hurt me is worry and care and debt,
especially debt.

Sometimes he would escape from his duties and his worries into
the society of his Balliol friends. Auberon Lucas was now Under-
Secretary of State for War. He and his sister had a house near
Ringwood in the New Forest, built by Edmond Warre, and here
they would all relax over dinner beside a large bonfire. Warre
made Turkish coffee from a long-handled copper saucepan.
During the day they would swim in the artificial pool, wrestle
on the grass, and round up the forest ponies. From the ridge beyond the house you could see the spire of Salisbury Cathedral
and the towers of Christ Church Priory. Then, after a brief respite,
the round of politics, lecturing and journalism would begin all
over again.

[1] Feb. 27 and March 2, 1906.

The life of an M.P. before the First World War was not the servile drudgery that it has since become. It was understood that if a man was to be a useful Member, he must not be compelled to spend too much time in the House of Commons. Besides, the Liberal majority was so big that the life of the Government did not depend on a chance vote. At no time would the House have been Belloc's favourite club, and one imagines that the large Nonconformist representation must have sensibly diminished the Smoking-Room receipts. The truth is that Radical as he was in many respects Belloc was a good way removed from the *mystique* of the 1906 Election. The Liberal Party was full of people who wanted to reform the working-classes, just as it was full of people who wanted votes for women. Belloc thought that certain other classes were in more urgent need of reformation; and in spite of his mother's campaign for women's rights, he did not believe that these included the right to vote. He was a domestic diehard and thought that a woman's place was the home.

Two of the men he liked best in the House of Commons were on the Conservative benches. George Wyndham he got to know in the autumn of 1906, and their acquaintance was to ripen into a secure friendship. Henry Cavendish-Bentinck he had known for some years and always liked. Among the Liberals he had a warm regard for John Poynder.[1] But he never seems to have got on to easy terms with the leading men in the Party; and some of them, in particular Mr. Lloyd George and Sir Alfred Mond, he disliked intensely. A supporter who insists on keeping you up to the mark can be a good deal more embarrassing than an opponent with whom you may be in more or less amicable collusion. Mr. Asquith and Mr. Balfour were much closer to each other than they were to the doctrinaires of their respective Parties. This is something which often happens in English politics and Belloc never realized what a good thing it is.

Meanwhile Belloc did not add to his official popularity by a letter to the *Manchester Guardian* demanding a public audit of the Party Funds. He would return to this charge in Parliament, but

[1] Sir John Poynder Dickson-Poynder, Bart.; M.P. for North-West Wilts, 1892-1910; afterwards first Baron Islington and Governor of New Zealand, 1910-1912.

he was anxious to make the public realize that the Party Funds existed and that they were accumulated largely by the sale of public honours. He believed that 'whenever a Government makes a fool of itself, especially a Liberal Government, one may be pretty certain that it is due to the pressure of one of the big subscribers.'

3

In the session of 1907 Belloc made two important speeches. The first, on April 22, was on the Territorial and Reserve Forces Bill. Here he spoke as a gunner, desiring to impress upon a rather sceptical military opinion the overwhelming importance of artillery. He described how the action at St. Privat, on August 18, 1870, had been decided in the German favour by the superiority of the German guns. It may be doubted whether anyone in the House of Commons had heard of the action at St. Privat, but that did not deter Belloc from his lecture. He maintained that the recent campaigns of which the English had experience had been fought against opponents ill-equipped with artillery, and that a slight prejudice against the value of artillery had grown up in consequence. Only one popular objection against artillery would he admit; he admitted that it made a noise.

He was especially concerned to see that the British Army had a sufficient reserve of trained drivers. This was the branch of the artillery that he best understood. The British Army had the heaviest field-gun in the world, the 18-pounder, and this weight behind the horses only added to the importance of the driver. Artillery duels in any future war would be very severe, and if there were not a sufficient reserve, both the pieces and the battle would be lost. Belloc did not believe that this reserve could be raised from the Militia; it must be recruited on a professional basis. The British drivers were the envy and admiration of the Continent.

> During a period when foreign opinion was directed with peculiar bitterness against this country, I heard in a foreign town enthusiastic praise of the action of our drivers at Colenso.

There has hardly ever been a more gallant act than that of Lord
Roberts' son and his comrades. You do not get a thing like that
done unless there is a magnificent professional tradition behind
it.

This speech made an excellent impression on Haldane, and
indeed on the whole House. Belloc himself described it as 'an
exceedingly good little speech full of great square facts, carefully
cut from the quarry and larger than six oxen could shift.'[1]

The second important contribution made by Belloc to the
debates in 1907 was on the Prime Minister's (Sir Henry Campbell-
Bannerman's) motion 'That, in order to give effect to the will
of the people as expressed by their elected representatives, it is
necessary that the power of the other House should be so restricted
by law as to secure that within the limits of a single Parliament
the final decision of the Commons shall prevail.'

The House of Lords, as then constituted, was bound to be
overwhelmingly Unionist and would certainly reject any
measure of Home Rule. The Liberals were tied to Home Rule, and
in another Parliament they might depend upon the Irish Nationalists for their majority. It was essential, therefore, to remove the
veto of the House of Lords.

Belloc was a democrat but he was not a demagogue, and his
speech was a moderate one. The reform of the House of Lords, he
said, was a matter so pressing that any Government would be
bound to undertake it. He began by examining the arguments on
the other side, admitting that throughout the eighteenth century,
right up to the first Reform Bill, the greater landlords in the Upper
House had given more thought to the needs of the people than
the lesser landlords in the Lower. But the House of Lords had
changed considerably during the past thirty years. He took the
case of the Plural Voting Bill which the Lords had rejected; 186
Englishmen—Belloc could not resist pointing out that 'several
of them were not of strictly English blood'—had decided by a
majority of 100 that Plural Voting should continue. This meant
that a large number of constituencies—there were some in South

---

[1] Letter to J. S. Phillimore: April 24, 1907.

Lancashire—would be represented by the will of those living outside them. The majority had included ten dukes.

> May the day be far distant when any Duke should fail to do his duty in a matter of that sort! Everything in this world has its place and its nature and I hope I shall never see a Duke voting for ending any political abuse whatever.

Belloc next examined the argument that the House of Lords composed a kind of 'Grand Jury' of the nation. He did not deny that certain Peers qualified for the title of 'Grand Juror'. But what of the rest? In the first place, they were nearly all of the same, Anglican, religion; although not more than half of the nation were professing members of the Church of England. Belloc asked for what services had these noblemen received their rank? It was, of course, well known that in a large number of cases their titles had not been earned but purchased. The sale of honours was naturally repugnant to the political idealist, but it might be harmless and even beneficial if the moneys so subscribed were put to sensible public use. What was intolerable was that the purchase of titles should carry with it the power of legislation and veto.

Later in the same session Belloc, pursuing his campaign against secrecy in public life, asked for the names of the Directors of the Ayrshire Foundry Company which had supplied a defective rudder to H.M.S. *King Edward VII.*

During the recess Belloc crossed the Pyrenees on foot and walked doggedly to Madrid. His impressions of Spain are given in a further letter to Maurice Baring, written from a café in the Puerta del Sol.

> Yes, at last! Madrid! But at what a cost! All the way burning deserts from the Pyrenees onwards and my Christ! What cooking! Never again! Next time on a mule, or in a Litter, or even in a train. But never again on foot across those brown Sahara plains and those formless, treeless hills. I have added to my knowledge and I am a fuller man. I know now what is meant by 'Dura Iberiæ Tellus' as also by the 'Reconquista'. Great God what a march. I am off home. It is not to be endured.

I had meant to run to earth the great-granddaughter of Carmen in Seville, but it was not for me. The country has defeated me as it did Napoleon and sundry others. What an ugly country, a curious place, more like the moon than the earth. The Spaniards have in common with the English: Monarchy, Kindliness, Religious Manias, Megalomanias, Self-regard, *Sporadic* Art, *Atrocious* Cooking, Sexual Decency (exaggerated), Bad Army; with the French: Splendid Bodies, Sound Sleep, Careful Agriculture, Vivacious accent (*not* gesture), Cruelty, Sudden False judgment, Filthy whitewash, no appreciable Aristocracy; with nobody else: One train a day from large towns; said train starting at 2 to 3 a.m. and going eight miles an hour; use of mules, hardly any roads; with Everybody Else: Electric Light, stupid newspapers, chemical beer, the Providence of God.

I have had enough of Spain. I have crossed the Pyrenees by a difficult col that makes me sick to think of even now, so steep it was and so precipitous for one on foot and all alone. I have marched to Huesca, to Saragossa, to the hills of Teruel, to the hills of Cuenca and here.[1]

Meanwhile political opinion was becoming hag-ridden by the educational *impasse*. The *Tribune* proposed its own solution in the autumn of 1907. This was widely discussed and the essentials of the scheme were as follows:

1. In every district there must be within the reach of every child a public elementary school which the children of all denominations may attend without suffering any religious disability.

2. Every public elementary school must open and close with some form of religious service (consisting of a hymn, the Lord's Prayer, and the reading of a passage of Scripture without comment), in which all children may take part without objection on religious grounds.

3. In *every* public elementary school there must be opportunities for *every* child to receive such *special* religious instruction

[1] Sept. 27, 1907.

as its parents may desire. Such instruction must not be given in school hours, must not be given at the public expense, or by the publicly-appointed teacher. The arrangements as to the time and place when such instructions shall be given shall (subject to certain restrictions) be controlled by the local education authority.

4. No publicly-appointed teacher shall be permitted to give special religious instruction.

5. Any school now recognized as a non-provided school may be carried on as an elementary school recognized by the Board of Education (but not by the local education authority) in which it is shown to the satisfaction of the Board of Education that the parents of two-thirds of the children attending that school desire that it shall be so carried on. But no parent shall be compelled to send his child to such a school.

Belloc admitted that this solution would command the general assent of Radical and Nonconformist opinion, but from the Catholic point of view it had the disadvantage of presupposing a national system of religion and morals. To the Catholic the differences between Anglicans and Nonconformists were differences between Protestant sects. The Catholic Church was not a sect, and it stood radically distinct from any national system of religion or morals. It was

a body of people who regard the whole business of the common religion around them as a thing to be avoided and combated. They are not specially careful that their children should hear the Lord's Prayer, the Sermon on the Mount, or a translation of the Jewish Scriptures. They are specially careful that their children have about them emblems significant of the Faith, as the Crucifix, and statues of Our Lady and of the Saints; that they should thoroughly know the Penny Catechism; that they should regularly attend Mass; that they should appreciate from the beginning of consciousness and from their earliest years the physical presence of Jesus Christ on earth today in the Blessed Sacrament through the miraculous power of a priesthood, and the power of the same priesthood in the Sacrament of Confession to absolve from sin.[1]

In face of this foreign and convinced minority a Government had only two choices. Either it must recognize the special position of that minority and endow it according to its numbers, or it must persecute. Persecution is not a nice word, but it was characteristic of Belloc that he should have used it. All a Liberal Government could do, as Birrell had pointed out, was to mitigate the persecution.

On February 19, 1908, Belloc moved 'That this House regrets the secrecy under which political funds are accumulated and administered and regards such secrecy as a peril to its privileges and character.'

He raised no objection to the existence of such funds and he admitted that as the House of Commons became more democratic, they would be necessary to meet the travelling, postal and printing expenses of M.P.s. What he attacked was the secrecy of their administration. This was a peril to the representative character of the House of Commons, because the public were unable to judge by what influences and from what motives a particular candidate was chosen. These were only known to a wealthy and powerful inner circle of large subscribers. Secondly, the initiative of the Government was bound to be affected by the sources of its wealth.

Wealth when it acts publicly cannot dare to do what it would often dare to do when it acts in a secret manner. A man will bring influences to bear privately in favour of policies which he would never dare publicly to defend. The very names of certain contributors would be a warning to the public, just as the names of others would guarantee the independence with which the funds were used.

If it were argued that such pressure was not, in fact, brought, Belloc replied that the only intelligible motive for secrecy was to bring it with impunity. If a large subscriber, who favoured

[1] Letter to *Tribune*, 1907

Q

certain policies, threatened to withdraw his support from a Party on the eve of an electoral campaign, might not that threat have some influence upon the Party's programme? Might they not yield in private when they would not have dared to yield in public? It was one thing to conceal, from motives of delicacy, the financial support which might be given to a certain candidate; but there was a risk of extending the class of men whose disbursements were covered by this secrecy. Furthermore, it was difficult to draw the line between a man who could afford nothing, a little, the greater part, or the whole of his election expenses.

> Unless there be publicity, there is every danger that within a certain space of time the bulk of a political Party will have acquired the custom of obtaining such support.

There was also the danger of pressure being put on individual candidates. Belloc believed that such pressure was exceedingly rare, and that, if it had been exerted at all, it had not yet affected the workings of the British political system. Here he could speak from his own experience.

> It was from Party funds that my expenses were paid. It was my duty as a Catholic, speaking for the Catholics of Lancashire, to vote with independence upon the Education Bill, and I have adopted an independent attitude upon other occasions. On every occasion I have been absolutely free from pressure of any kind.

Still the risk remained; and with it, the further danger that an unscrupulous man of great wealth might exert pressure on a scrupulous man of no wealth, simply because he was a large subscriber to the Party funds. Belloc believed that this had come very near to happening in the life of the 1906 Parliament. He did not propose a specific remedy for these perils; he was only concerned to point them out. But he was not listened to. The Edwardian world was secure in its worship of wealth; it was simply not plausible to suggest that money was a moral danger. The Members of Parliament would disperse on Friday evenings to their country-houses, and the stiff ritual of the week-end would follow its prescribed course. There would be baccarat and billiards, hock and seltzer and riding to hounds; the gloved hands which were clasped conventionally at Matins would pat the sleek quarters of the hunters as the party proceeded round the stables before luncheon; and in the political houses politics would, of course, go on. Between teetotalism on the one hand and hock-and-seltzer on the other Belloc pursued his own undeviating course. What he thought of the *beau monde* and its moral vulgarity may have been scribbled on his knee during some tedious interlude in the House of Commons.

> The party will be large and rather free,
> And people will be given lots of rope;
> The Duke of Dorset, M.F.H., K.G.
> Will bring a *divorcée* in heliotrope.

Belloc had his own country-house and he was very happy to get back to it.

> Would that you were here, where, in this glorious air and surrounded by those who love you, you might forget the brevity of life and the disappointment of the Soul of Man.
> I am here in the cool night: the moon is on my garden. I am in harbour for a little while. This morning I was in Cardiff. I rose, prayed God, ate, took a train, wrote in it an article, came to town, went to the typewriter's, dictated twenty-three letters, wrote another article—not good— called 'Roncesvalles', went to the House, voted against the Government, gave ten shillings to charity, went to the *Morning Post,* put my page through, saw Ware, sent out eight books, ate a sole at Victoria, took the train and am here.[1]

And again, two months later:

> King's Land is in exquisite beauty. Last night my wife and Miss Beardsley [2] and I dined out of doors.[3]

[1] Letter to Maurice Baring: March 13, 1908.
[2] His secretary.
[3] May 22, 1908.

4

Belloc made four more long speeches in Parliament before the
recess. In the first of these [1] he spoke on the Army Estimates,
supporting the idea of an auxiliary artillery for the Territorial
Services, and insisting once again on the need for trained drivers.
'You cannot', he said, 'make a driver in 45 drills and you cannot
make a driver at all with lectures.' He went on to discuss the
pieces, maintaining that there was no advantage in exchanging
the 18- for the 15-pounder since the latter did not use fixed
ammunition.

> The whole feeling of a man who uses fixed ammunition is
> different from that of a man who uses ammunition in which the
> ignition charge and projectile are in three separate pieces. If
> you take men out of your Auxiliary force—which is not at all
> an improbable circumstance—and try to turn them into
> trained artillery, the fact that they are not in the habit of using
> fixed ammunition will be a very serious drawback.

Belloc believed that in the event of war rapidity of fire would
count for more than anything else, and here the personnel was
more important than the projectile.

On May 19 the new Education Bill received its second reading.
Augustine Birrell was now Chief Secretary for Ireland and
Reginald McKenna had succeeded him at the Board of Education.
Belloc admitted the value of a unified system of elementary
education and what this had meant for France and Germany; and
he emphasized again that the only obstacle to it in England was
the necessary and historic intransigence of the Catholic body. Here
he was not afraid to make a comparison with Jewry.

> Let those who are afraid to call a spade a spade ask them-
> selves who of their Jewish friends and acquaintances, upon
> making a considerable sum of money, hesitates to send their
> sons to an Anglican school, or who of the Jewish community
> upon achieving a place in society, hesitates to send their sons to
> Eton and Harrow. At enormous sacrifices, at the sacrifice of

[1] March 11, 1908.

the opportunity and advantage of community with the national life, my co-religionists maintained for three generations, two generations most actively, even amongst their wealthier members a system of a separate education. . . . Can you pretend that our differences in theological opinion compare in any way with the intense fervour which made poor men sacrifice five shillings a week and which made the poor in our industrial cities build their schools, endow their altars and beautify their churches?

Belloc held that the difficulty would have been met by the clause in the previous Bill which allowed four-fifths, or some very large proportion, of parents to give a school an exceptional position. It had been objected that this clause was introduced to please the Catholics; Belloc replied that it was 'a clause introduced for anybody who cared enough to send their children on a rainy day some distance to school instead of to the nearest school, for any body of parents who had a sufficient grip upon their fanciful philosophy to make it the principal thing in their lives'. Some people held that the clause had been rejected by the extreme Nonconformists; Belloc was not of that opinion; he held that it had been rejected by the House of Lords.

It remained therefore to decide how the exceptional position of the Catholics should be recognized. A purely secular solution would not work because the atmosphere of such schools would remain invincibly Protestant. The Member for Peterborough had described the discomfort he felt in being asked to believe the two stories about Elisha. Belloc replied that nowhere but in Protestant England would the difficulty have arisen because nowhere else would the stories have been told. It would be manifestly unjust to exclude the Catholics altogether from public assistance. They would be prepared to accept certain sacrifices, and if these were not made intolerable, Belloc would support the Bill. He realized the extent of public boredom with the whole question, and pending the necessary discussions with clergy and managers, he voted for the Second Reading.

The other measure which preoccupied him during 1908 was the

Prevention of Crime Bill, which had its second reading on June 12. In the first clause of the second part of the Bill there were two provisions utterly at variance with any doctrine of personal liberty that had ever been held in Christendom. One made it possible for a man convicted of violence and larceny to be imprisoned for life on the grounds that he was incorrigible. The other permitted the action of the Bill to be retrospective. Belloc protested against these infractions of natural justice with a warmth that he rarely allowed himself in the House of Commons. The poorer classes were to be penalized for the lesser crimes.

There are at the present moment men suffering imprisonment who are looking forward to the day when that will come to an end and they will again be free, and you are going to those men who have suffered three previous convictions, to tell them that the time to which they are looking for their release—when they are to make a re-entry into civilised life—is not to be the end of their detention. I can conceive nothing more inhuman. If there is one principle running through the law ever since it was made by Rome for the whole of Europe, it is that it should not be retrospective; and I have no doubt that if these clauses could be put before popular audiences on the platforms of the country there would be a storm of indignation which would wreck the measure. . . . For my part, and I care not how ridiculous my attitude may seem to the 'scientific', I cannot allow the provisions of such a document as this to pass without making against it the most emphatic protest possible.

When the Bill had its third reading on November 24, 1908, Belloc seconded an amendment to delete its objectionable clauses.

I remember during the second reading of the Bill that a member of this House, who is also a member of what are called the governing families of this country, made some jokes about an old lady who stole some bacon, and I wonder what the noble Lord thinks of those countries where they punish those who steal land. The noble Lord appears to think that because an old lady who stole bacon was a nuisance, therefore there should be an arbitrary right to put her in confinement for a period which might perfectly well, if she were guilty of any violence, extend throughout her life.

He reminded the House of the saying—'old as the Romans'—that a man 'purges' his sin. This conception which had run through morals and jurisprudence for three thousand years was not to be discarded at the bidding of 'pseudo-scientists with broken-down reputations like Lombroso's'. Belloc felt more strongly about this issue than upon any other which came before him in Parliament, and there was something of prophecy in his peroration.

When I hear appeals to new countries, America, and the Colonies and Heaven knows where—I fear that the members who use them have lost their sense of things European and traditional. The Bill will probably become law because there is not a single member in this House, and not even in the other House, who could in any conceivable set of circumstances be inconvenienced by its proposals. Will any man who regards these things lightly ask himself how his conscience stands in the matter of right and wrong? They of the well-to-do classes know that they stand in little danger from the law. If you could apply the indeterminate sentence to the type of evil which well-to-do men commit, there would be no chance of its passing into law in this House, and still less in the other. It is almost certain to pass into law and that is why I speak with violence. When it is passed into law you will have entered for the first time into that path which all modern pseudo-sociology is trying to force us into, at the end of which you have the tyranny of bureaucrats.

Belloc got the indefinite sentence reduced to five years. 'May God reward me for it', he exclaimed afterwards. But when it came to dividing against the Bill he could not find a single member to 'tell' with him.

Campbell-Bannerman died on April 22, 1908, and Asquith became Prime Minister. In July he was entertained to dinner by twenty-six (out of thirty) Balliol M.P.s. Lloyd George succeeded

him at the Exchequer, and the chief excitement of the following
session was the Budget of 1909. Mr. D. C. Somervell has described
this as the dividing line between Gladstonian and modern
financial policy.[1] Hitherto Chancellors had been content to allow
money 'to fructify in the pockets of the people', and the burden
of taxation was little heavier in 1908 than it had been in 1860. But
Lloyd George enjoyed spending other people's money as much as
he enjoyed making his own. Economically speaking, he liked
turning other people's other cheeks. His fertile and unprincipled
mind was full of bright ideas. Old Age Pensions, National
Insurance—the future was radiant with taxation. Meanwhile
£16,000,000 were required for eight new Dreadnoughts. 'We
want eight and we won't wait'—so ran the popular refrain. The
naval competition from Germany had got people seriously
alarmed, and although Lloyd George had no affection for the
Navy its needs gave him a pretext for what he called a 'people's
Budget'.

This, according to modern standards, was a very modest affair.
The increase of revenue required was only eleven per cent. on
the previous Budget, and although the grading of the Income Tax
was steepened, it never reached more than one and ninepence,
even on the largest incomes. There was a heavy tax on licensed
premises—the revenge of a Nonconformist who really only cared
for champagne; and additional duties on spirits and tobacco. A
bottle of whisky would now cost four shillings instead of three
and sixpence. There were also taxes on motor-cars and petrol. But
the Budget had a political as well as a fiscal purpose. Lloyd George
went to Limehouse in the hope that the House of Lords would
send him to the country. Like all supremely clever politicians, he
was a shrewd judge of other people's stupidity, and in this calculation he was correct. The Lords rejected the Budget, and Asquith
could go to the country, openly instead of covertly, on the issue of
the Lords *versus* the People. In December 1909, Parliament was
dissolved.

Belloc took little part in these debates, but his views are given in
letters to Maurice Baring.

[1] *British Politics Since 1900* (1950).

Lloyd George's Budget was a very remarkable thing. I will tell you about it. In the first place the speech both in matter and in manner was without exception the worst that has been delivered in the House of Commons. This is no violent or peevish criticism of my own: it is the universal opinion of all who listened to it. Lloyd George can make a shallow and vulgar but effective speech of a demagogic type, and why on earth he had gone to pieces like that no one can make out. He spoke like a man in the last stages of physical and mental decay. One could hardly hear his voice. His speech was read from beginning to end from typewritten notes and was simply deplorable. It lasted four hours, of which quite two and a half consisted of long stupid paragraphs about the rich being rich and the poor being poor.

Belloc thought that Asquith would have done the thing in an hour and a half and very much better.

Now the details of the Budget, that is the actual proposals, are perfectly excellent. It would be difficult to imagine a better Budget. The only drawback is the grave stupidity of treating Ireland the same as England. Ireland is already over-taxed in proportion to her wealth and population, to the extent of about two million a year; that is about two pounds got out from every Irish family on the average, more than the fair share according to wealth and population. But as I intend saying on Monday if I can get the opportunity, it is something much worse than that: when you overtax the poorer person, the hardship done is greater than the mere numerical surcharge. For instance if you and I had to pay 12 per cent. of our income while Jack Poynder only paid 10 per cent. it would be a much greater hardship for you and me than a 2 per cent hardship. The Budget overtaxes Ireland by a new heavy tax on Whisky, which is the national drink, and it has the same effect in Ireland as though you were to put 50 centimes a bottle on Vin Ordinaire in France, or a penny a glass on the working man's beer in England. The Irish are furious about it, and they are quite right.

But, as I say, in other respects the Budget is quite excellent; for instance, motor-cars are going to pay on a graduated scale. A little runabout such as a professional man can enjoy will only pay what it pays now. And big things worth a thousand pounds, of 60 h.p. and over, will pay £40. There is gradation in between. Then again, very great incomes will pay an extra 6d. Income Tax, and, the best of all, in future all automatic increase of values of Crown Land will pay 20 per cent. of the increase to the community. This is most just, and if it had been put on a hundred years ago, would have produced more than enough money to pay the National Debt without doing anyone the least harm.

Even the Whisky tax is an excellent thing so far as England is concerned because whisky is not the national drink in England; I am certain in our climate or at any rate with our inherited bodies it does harm.[1]

Philip Snowden, one of the new Labour members in the House, had written a pamphlet entitled *The Socialist Budget* and he claimed that several features of Lloyd George's Bill had been taken from this. Now, although Belloc insistently called himself a Radical—so insistently indeed that rumours quickly got around after his election that he was about to join the Labour Party—he was never within yards of Socialism and was quick to detect the Socialist sting in the Budget. This gave it the 'kick' that knocked the House of Lords off its mental balance. Belloc was no friend to the Lords, but, unlike so many of his richer Liberal friends, he did see the danger of attacking capital. 'Distributist' that he was (though the horrible noun had not yet been invented) he perceived the dilemma of distributism. He describes to Baring an evening at the Follies with John Poynder in which, during the intervals, he had tried to explain to him the peril of destroying the nation's capital:

Jack Poynder, like nearly all rich men who are jolly, has no objection to the part of the Budget that hits him and there he was with many thousands a year, arguing on the side that he did not mind capital being attacked, while I, who am much

[1] May 1, 1909.

more democratic and poor, was arguing on the side that it should not be attacked. It is an unhappy paradox in all economic legislation that if you set up a plutocracy you get a large and solid capitalisation with which to run the State; whereas the more well distributed your wealth is, the less chance you have of high capitalisation except after a very long period. The reason of this is perfectly simple. It is that rich men can afford to save more than poor men can. A man will save a thousand pounds in order to get twenty-five pounds a year, but he will not save a sovereign in order to get 6d. a year. Now, when in pursuit of a democratic policy a Government takes away some of the capital of the rich and distributes it among the poor in the shape of old age pensions, etc., the poor do not use that capital as capital. They consume it; therefore in a legislation of this kind there is a constant tendency to fritter away the capital upon which the material prosperity of the State is based; of course the popular policy is to take away some part of the capital of the rich and turn it into capital for the poor. That for instance is what Wyndham's Irish Land Act does. But if the action of the State simply turns over the capital of the rich to be spent by the poor as they choose, the nation must ultimately suffer impoverishment. Except in its tendency to touch capital in some portions of its provisions, I think the Budget excellent, as you know.[1]

It was the friendship of men like Poynder and Wyndham and Lord Derby that made Belloc understand the virtues of enlightened aristocracy. He could admit the achievement, even if he could not propound the ideal. He thought, for example, Lord Derby's comments on the Budget the most intelligent he had heard, and his personal generosity shook Belloc's belief that great wealth must necessarily corrupt. Did he really, looking across the Channel at the Chambre des Députés, think they ordered these things better in France? A week later, Poynder was speaking on the land question; Belloc admires, but the itch for equality is still nagging him.

[1] May 19, 1909.

It was a speech full of stuff and matter and to be listened to, every word of it. England has the rare boast that men of this great wealth can talk fairly about the taxation of wealth. Of course, it is self-evident that a plutocracy could not live unless the wealthy classes thus inclined to justice. Still, it is a noble thing to find them doing so, though it would be better that there were no dominating wealthy class at all.[1]

Belloc voted against all but one of the licensing clauses in the Budget, but he supported its other provisions. It was one of the few measures brought in by his own Party of which he generally approved.

5

During these three years Belloc had not neglected his constituents. He was constantly travelling between Manchester and London— too constantly for his comfort; so we find him asking Miss Hamilton to procure him a travelling rug and air-cushion, 'to save vibration in the train'.[2] He would go to any pains to be of service to the people he represented. There was a 'walking club' in Salford, and he would advise the members of this how to go from Boulogne to Paris or from Dieppe to Coutances. His versatility drew an appropriate comment from Punch.

Inquiries at the House of Commons elicited the fact that Mr. Belloc is the most hardworked of our younger Parliamentarians. The week-end brings him no respite from his labours, as he invariably spends it in the grimy heart of Salford among his constituents, where he conducts classes in military history, conversational French, mediaeval theology, and thorough Bass. As Mr. Belloc has expressed it in a touching couplet:

> French is my heart and loyal and sincere
> Is, and shall be, my love of British beer,

and Punch, which lost no opportunity of linking Belloc's name with Chesterton's, suggested as a title for his new novel, 'The Man who was Thirsty'.

These were jokes; but Belloc's agent, Charles Goodwin, had to

[1] Letter to Maurice Baring: May 26, 1909.　　　　[2] Nov. 15, 1909.

remind him that his vote on the Licensing Bill was no laughing matter for some of his supporters.

It is taking me all my time to keep the peace here. We had a meeting last night, and a resolution was passed regretting your vote on the Licensing Bill. The rank and file keep forgiving you your antagonism to the Government ever since you were elected, but the temper exhibited last night indicated that they are getting fed up with your policy—which they don't understand. What they want is to feel they are behind a man who supports their ideas in the House—and you don't.

I don't think you appreciate the position and how dependent you are on the 'workers'—without whom an election cannot be fought. It looked at one time as if we were not going to get a platform for you on Friday.

Of course if you are indifferent as to whether you sit again or not for the Division—all well and good, but even in that case you are not giving the men who helped to return you that support which they have both a right and claim to expect.

As for myself—well—it is somewhat disappointing after 15 years fighting the influence of the wealthy Brewer to have the weapon you used to hit him turned against you and used in his favour.

The enclosed letter suffices to show that matters are getting critical. He is one of our best working supporters.[1]

Belloc was quite undaunted by this:

Yes, I know they are on the War-Path but I pay little attention to it. The gang of rich women who are running this absurd business know perfectly well that I am an active opponent. It is nearly ten years since Lady Carlisle made the devil of a row about me because I prevented the agitations getting into one or two Liberal papers. I think they have been pushed into this particular appeal in my Constituency by people outside who do not understand the constituency. I am absolutely certain that a man representing a working-class constituency is safe in regarding a certain number of fads as poison to his constituents;

[1] Dec. 2, 1908.

Teetotalism is one, and without doubt Women's Suffrage is another.[1]

In October, shortly before the dissolution, Belloc was the centre of a sudden storm in the House. Francisco Ferrer, a Catalonian anarchist, was executed by the Spanish authorities for his supposed part in a popular uprising in Barcelona. The initial reverses of the Spanish-Moroccan War had been the ostensible cause of this, but they were really no more than a pretext for a violent campaign against Catholicism. Churches and convents were burnt down, graves violated, and the bodies of the dead dishonoured. Ferrer was a Freemason and an atheist, who had carried his anarchism into his private life, and he was believed to have instigated these excesses. He was an educational crank, and he had recently been in London, studying the text-books of the English elementary schools and mixing with Dissenters of his own way of thinking. He pottered about with his mistress in the progressive underworld; frequented the Reading Room of the British Museum; and was in every way cut out to impose upon English liberal opinion.

The evidence at his trial was conclusive. It was reported verbatim, and the verbatim reports were admitted to be accurate under the signatures of the accused and his accusers. There was no doubt that Ferrer had participated in rebellion and had sought to overthrow the existing Government. Nevertheless, his execution caused a furore of protest wherever the secret power of Freemasonry could influence the Press and the politicians—especially in London and Paris. A hostile demonstration was even staged outside Westminster Cathedral, and many of the English newspapers took up the hue and cry without a close examination of the facts. Much of this protest was instinctive liberalism or atavistic 'no Popery'; some of it was calculated untruth. When the matter was raised in the House of Commons Belloc shouted 'rubbish', and this brought down upon him a good deal of hostile comment in the Press and a flood of anonymous and threatening letters. Later he analysed the case very carefully in two articles for the

[1] Dec. 3, 1908.

Dublin Review [1] and in a pamphlet for the Catholic Truth Society. [2] When he wrote to the *Daily News,* asking for the production of proofs for and against Ferrer, that newspaper printed several violent letters in his favour. Belloc then sent a list of the hostile witnesses, with an abstract of their testimony, but the editor suppressed it. The fuss, however, soon died down. It was difficult to maintain the halo round the head of a man who had left his wife and three children; inherited fifty-thousand pounds from his mistress; and then embezzled such small part of her fortune as had been left for pious purposes. The campaign had revealed Belloc's force and courage in controversy, and his acquaintance with the realities of Continental politics; also his proud and combative isolation. Because English freemasons were generally benevolent people like the Duke of Connaught, the public could never believe in the machinations of the European lodges. Belloc knew better, and he was rather relieved that they had been forced out into the open. The knowledge certainly fostered a prejudice, and sometimes, as in the Dreyfus case, it led him seriously astray. But in the case of Ferrer he had traced the agitation to its secret and squalid source.

As a dissolution of Parliament became more and more certain, with Churchill and Lloyd George eager and Asquith, so it was said, reluctant, Belloc, in common with other M.P.s, was tied increasingly to the House. He felt the artificiality of this restriction.

> You must remember [he writes to Baring] that in normal years Peers and Commons go back to the country and live alongside their people (I mean Peers that count). The United Kingdom is infinitely diversified. That is its glory—and the various shades of feeling are quickly apprehended, e.g. though I am not a Northcountryman I quickly saw the temper of Salford the other day. Now this Session has been so abnormal that it has kept the political Peers and all the commons tied to London and London influences virtually for a year. I know lots of men who have hardly got on horseback during the whole time; racing men who have hardly been to a race, and shooting men who have had hardly any shooting. The holidays that were

[1] January and April, 1910.   [2] *The Ferrer Case.*

snatched were taken mainly abroad or rushing about in motors, and it is astounding to note how both sides talk in terms of London. I suppose such a thing has not happened in English politics before.[1]

Belloc thought that Asquith made a most excellent speech on the winding-up day of the Session:

a Lawyer's speech, making one roar with laughter of course when one considered its complete unreality, but exceedingly well delivered and with every word beautifully chosen. Balfour was all to bits.[2]

And so he braced himself for a new fight. He thought that a thorough reform of the voting system should precede any new election, but this was most improbable. Moreover, he had begun to detest politics.

I am very dejected about the approaching election. I don't want to stand. I detest the vulgar futility of the whole business and the grave risks to which are attached no proportionate reward. So anxious are most people to get into Parliament that they will do anything to oust an opponent, and I have really no desire to be mixed up with such hatreds, or to see myself placarded on the walls in twenty ridiculous attitudes, and with any number of false statements or suggestions attached to my name. It is a perfectly beastly trade.[3]

In a speech to his constituents in October he claimed his personal liberty at the next election; and then went on to Knowsley where Lord Derby had given him the run of his library. This was 'one of the most glorious libraries in Europe, and what is especially remarkable, really and properly kept up to date. I could spend in it any part of my life: a day, a week, a month or a year, without moving from it.' It was 'the most domestic, the most enwrapping library in Britain'[4], reminding Belloc that there was a world beyond Westminster. We must now turn back to look at it.

[1] Nov. 29, 1909.   [2] Letter to Maurice Baring: Dec. 4, 1909.
[3] Letter to Maurice Baring: Nov. 12, 1909.
[4] Letter to Duff Cooper: Nov. 1, 1925.

CHAPTER XII

GOOD LAND TO LEAVE

I

BETWEEN his election to Parliament in January 1906
and the dissolution of the same Parliament in December
1909—virtually four years—Belloc published his longest
biography, *Marie Antoinette;* four volumes of essays, most of which
had already appeared in the *Morning Post* and elsewhere; two
books of travel and topography; two satirical novels; one volume
of verse; and four pamphlets. The output would have been
remarkable for a man whose whole time was given to writing;
for a busy M.P. and lecturer, of sociable habits and diverse
interests, it was astonishing. How, one asks, did he do it?

Miss Ruby Goldsmith succeeded Miss Beardsley as his secretary
in September 1908. She had rooms in the village and could come
to the house whenever she was needed. Belloc, she tells us, was
an indefatigable but erratic worker. He had great energy but
little method. Sometimes he would impose on himself a strict
régime, resolving

> to sleep (if I can) before midnight, to work (excluding letters)
> not more than nine hours in the day, to read some part of
> a *story* all the hour's leisure before sleep (thus curing a voracity
> for mathematics and speculative history), to walk three miles or
> ride six, or chop one quarter of a cord of wood at the least in a
> day. To not drink save at meals, or beer, or (what is legitimate)
> as a prolongation of dinner.[1]

But these resolutions soon broke down. He might plan to start
work after breakfast, but if he had slept badly, as was often the

---

[1] Letter to George Wyndham: Nov. 28, 1910.

case, it might be after midday, or even as late as two o'clock in
the afternoon, before he got going. Then he would forget every-
things else, except his pipe and an occasional glass of beer. If he
began after dinner, he might go on till two in the morning.
Sometimes, when he dictated on through a meal-time, Miss
Goldsmith would have to remind him that her own meal was
probably getting cold and her landlady impatient. Young Louis
used to chant a refrain about 'Goldie, going to eat her cold
mutton chop, swimming in an island of grease'. The lines had
little poetry in them, but much point.

Belloc and his secretary usually worked in the small study. She
would sit at the little round table in the middle of the room, taking
her shorthand notes while Belloc dictated, often for hours on end.
Sometimes he would sit in the big green armchair, pulling at his
pipe, and dictate straight on to the machine. He knew that his
methods imposed a certain strain.

> I extemporised as I went along, and by the light of one small
> lamp poured forth my words in such profusion that my
> tongue outstripped my secretaries' pens and my volubility
> baffled the tricks of their shorthand.[1]

Most of his work demanded considerable research and this had
been done in London, either by himself or Dorothy Hamilton.
Contrary to the hostile legend, he was (at least in early days) most
punctilious in verifying his facts. Naturally he preferred to write
at King's Land, but he could write anywhere if necessary. Miss
Goldsmith describes taking his dictation in the train and in taxi-
cabs, jogging along over the cobblestones in London. At other
times, when he was tired, he would dictate from his bed, and she
would have to sit at the large round mahogany table in the darkest
corner of the room, fumbling for her pencils and paper.

> I recall very cold days when the trees were heavy with snow,
> and Edith would come up and stoke the open grate wood fire,
> and I would go down and get a sweater in an effort to keep
> slightly warm.[2]

---

[1] Letter to A. P. Ryan: Mr. Ryan's translation from the original Latin.
[2] Letter to the author: April 27, 1955.

Edith Fair had come as nursery maid to Nurse Drewitt in November 1906; later she took on wider duties and was one of the props on which the household rested.

The impression persists, as it always does with Belloc, of energy disorganized by restlessness. He had himself that power he admired in Ronsard—

that power that our anaemic age can hardly comprehend, of writing, writing, writing, without fear of exhaustion, without irritability or self-criticism, without danger of comparing the better with the worse.[1]

Even if one only wrote to make money, Belloc believed that

the whole art is to write and write and write and then offer it for sale, just like butter. The more one writes, the more one gets known. The more enormous one's output the more the publishers get to regard you as a reliable milch cow.[2]

Much of his restlessness was unavoidable. A lecturing programme might take him to Dudley, Manchester, St. Helens, Repton and Leeds in a single week. Or a week in Scotland would find him at Glasgow on a Monday, then at Edinburgh, Forfar and Aberdeen, finishing up at Newcastle-on-Tyne. The net profit of all this labour might be £50. And he had been working at the same pressure for years. The following itinerary of a week in 1904 is typical of a week in 1909.

This week I dictated two articles on Monday morning, lunched in the train, gave an afternoon lecture at Reigate, dined in Norwood with an admirer of *Emmanuel Burden*, and lectured at Dulwich the same night, wrote another article on Tuesday morning, took the express on Tuesday at 3 o'clock for Chesterfield, lectured in Chesterfield, left Chesterfield before eight on Wednesday, gave two political speeches Wednesday afternoon and evening in my constituency, went out to stop with the Barlows the night in Cheshire, came back to Manchester on Thursday; wrote two notes on the war for 'Outlook' and one

[1] *Avril* (1904).   [2] Letter to Maurice Baring: Dec. 5, 1909.

note for the Speaker, sent four telegrams and wrote eighteen letters; then I gave another longer and most effective political speech in my constituency in the evening, was back in London Friday afternoon, dictated some more stuff and more letters, and am now upon this blessed occasion ending my fifth letter after dictating a review of Rose's 'Napoleonic Studies'.[1]

It was little wonder that even so accurate a student of Bradshaw occasionally missed his train. Once the expectant audience at Loughton were regaled by lantern slides of Algeria and the river Wye, and by a local lady singing 'Where the Bee sucks', until Belloc arrived to speak on 'London'—and also to describe the acute congestion of its traffic! In Glasgow he would always spend a night or two with Phillimore, and for this pleasure he would snatch at almost any excuse. Even during the crowded last session of Parliament he is ready to come.

I received a telegram this morning from Glasgow unsigned saying 'Could you lecture on travel?' . . . I will lecture on the Proper Method of Milking a Cow, which I have never done, or of Mowing a Field which I can do jolly well. I will lecture on the Influence of the Jesuits on Europe, or of the Influence of Europe on the Jesuits. I will lecture in verse, like Milton, or in prose like old Bright of University, or in alternate verse like Apuleius in the theatre of Carthage. I will lecture on anything in any manner for money: and don't you forget it. I can lecture twice a day or three times. I can lecture on my hand, on my head or between my legs or with the dumb alphabet.[2]

But when Phillimore was not at the other end, he found the lecturing an increasing drain on his energy, his temper and his time.

Do you know the filthy village of Glossop? [he writes to Miss Hamilton]. It is inhabited entirely by savages. I tried every inn in the place and found each inn worse than the last. It stinks for miles. Rather than sleep in such a den I started walking back

---

[1] Letter to E. S. P. Haynes: Nov. 12, 1904.
[2] Letter to J. S. Phillimore: Nov. 14, 1909.

to Manchester with a huge bag. A horse and cart met me after some miles . . . I have a mind to chuck this lecturing.

He may well have had a mind to chuck it when he heard his oratory described in Leeds as second only to Charles Bradlaugh's. These years brought Belloc two large blessings beyond the acquisition of King's Land. In 1906 John Phillimore was received into the Catholic Church, and Maurice Baring followed him in 1909. What the conversion of these friends meant may be gauged by the following letter to Charlotte Balfour.

It is an immense thing. They are coming in like a gathering army from all manner of directions, all manner of men each bringing some new force: that of Maurice is his amazing accuracy of mind which proceeds from his great virtue of truth. I am profoundly grateful! I have no vision. I am resigned to it as a man might be to blindness; but in the absence of vision I feel with the grosser senses, and appreciate as a solid, the presence of the Catholic Faith . . . I express myself badly in the matter of religion, for in the matter of religion I am abominably alone. I feel sometimes like a sentry at night.[1]

It was a consolation, therefore, to have company on guard. Belloc had many intimate friends who were not of his faith, and this made no difference to his affection. But if, as sometimes happened, they became Catholics, intimacy deepened with the removal of the last barrier. Baring had a small house in Westminster, 6 Lord North Street, and here Belloc rented a room when he had given up the flat in Victoria Street. It was quiet at night and close to the House of Commons. The Phillimores had a house in Hampshire, and John was a frequent visitor at King's Land during the University vacations. Others who came were Somers Cocks, Auberon Lucas, Gilbert and Cecil Chesterton, and Desmond MacCarthy. Elodie was now at ease with all these men, receiving them in her own house; Cecil Chesterton, with his high voice (like Gilbert's), his smiling chubby face and schoolboy charm, was a particular favourite with the children.

[1] April 22, 1909.

A well-loved house is like a well-tried friendship; it is familiar and yet it is never finished. Even Belloc's local patriotism was put to a strain by the sloth of the Sussex workmen. They had taken nine months to bring the planks for the drawing-room floor, and the oak to panel the dining-room. This was veneer oak from Austria and John Phillimore helped to put it up. By May 1, 1908, there was a proper guest-room, and Mass was now said in the house every alternate Sunday.

Elodie was fond of gardening and Belloc, who was bored with flowers, had made her a brick path. He writes to Phillimore for advice.

If you desire peace in this transitory place of bewildering change (and God knows it is more like a kaleidoscope than what we were promised at 18!) write to the Mistress of this Honourable House and inform her of how *Lavender, Rosemary, Bergamot, Burrage, Anisette, Crême-de-menthe,* and *Grand Marnier* may be grown: as also *Old Man, London Pride, Angelique, Lemon Plant, Scented Poplar* and others . . .

Be good enough to write Elodie on Annuals, bi-ennials, perennials (the hardy things!) and even millenials—but anyhow, write to her on FLOWERS for BORDERING PATHS.

She is persuaded you know. I fancy you don't. But no matter. You are to say, how HERBS are bought, when, at what price, where; their kinds, their diseases, the remedy therefore. You are to speak of their burgeoning above, their stuffiness below . . . their brittle old age, their unlamented death. You are to enlarge upon their value to man and to hint at their debt to him. You are to do all these things.[1]

These were the happiest days of Elodie Belloc's life. She had, at last,

> Children for memory; the Faith for pride;
> Good land to leave and young love satisfied.

They were in comforting contrast to the materialism and snobbery of all that Edwardian world. 'It is almost impossible',

[1] March 1, 1907.

she writes to Father Russell, 'for anyone to whom God has not given it to suffer, to know what it is for two militant and convinced Catholics to live in our world in England.' But Hilaire's 'love and his companionship and the security of the Faith' constitute 'an unmerited reward'.

I never dress for dinner here [she wrote to Grace Joel], I just change my bodice or such-like. The days are long and quiet here. Most people would find it dull—but I adore it. . . . It is like Heaven, thank God. We have panelled our dining-room with oak and set in Eleanor's portrait.[1]

Eleanor Belloc had been painted as a little girl by Grace Joel.

Believing, as she did, that 'good food does only good to human beings', Elodie presided with a robust competence over the material needs of the family—and Belloc was as interested in vegetables as he was indifferent to flowers. But she found time to teach their Catechism to two Catholic boys from the immediate neighbourhood, to read a good deal, and to arrange her scrap-book. Here we find a *roundel* by Froissart, and gleanings from Whitman, Emily Brontë, Coventry Patmore, Ambrose Bierce, Matthew Arnold, Alice Meynell, Balmès and St. Bernard; and a portrait of Robert Louis Stevenson. Belloc had written out for her a few of his own verses and a line here and there comes to us loaded with a tragic, unconscious irony.

Oh! you that in this place gave life for love.

Occasionally the Bellocs would go away for country visits. While they were staying with the Wyndhams, near Chester, George gave Belloc his copy of Catullus. But there was too much to do at King's Land for these visits to be anything but rare. The following is typical of a day snatched from politics and lecturing.

I have today planted twelve rows of onions, eight rows of shallots, one bed of aubergines. I have written a review article on the export of capital. I have bought six flowerpots. I have drunk one bottle of Sauterne, half a bottle of claret and no port. Also one pint of beer.[2]

[1] June 4 and 15, 1907.   [2] Letter to Maurice Baring: Feb. 27, 1909.

If, after this, he felt the need for exercise, he could ride his chestnut cob, Monster, through the woods; a Cobbett *redivivus* with his hunting-crop and his sharp eye for country. The crop was a gift from H. A. L. Fisher, and it bore his name inscribed in Latin upon a silver band.

In a famous essay (*A Remaining Christmas*) Belloc has described how Christmas was kept at King's Land. The ritual may have varied a little, but the pattern was set from the start. The holly and greenery were brought from a neighbouring wood, and the house was decorated with these just before dark on Christmas Eve. Then a young pine tree, about twelve feet high, was brought into the raftered hall. (This was formally opened at Christmas, 1909.) Sometimes there were two trees, one for the family and Elodie's Catechism class, and another for the schoolmaster and his wife, the schoolmistress and her father, the miller and his boy, and other children from the village. As many as fifty might be invited from outside, and they were immediately given the refreshment suitable to their years. Then they came in to the Christmas trees, which had been separately lit, and presents were handed round. A silver coin was given to each child.

After that they dance in the hall and sing songs, which have been handed down to them for I do not know how long. These songs are game songs, and are sung to keep time with the various parts in each game, and the men and things and animals which you hear mentioned in these songs are all of that country-side. Indeed, the tradition of Christmas here is what it should be everywhere, knit into the very stuff of the place; so that I fancy the little children, when they think of Bethlehem, see it in their minds as though it were in the winter depth of England, which is as it should be.

Belloc would sometimes give a magic-lantern show with slides 'chiefly representing the most horrible animals but also many beautiful landscapes, and one amusing story for the children'.[1]

When the singing and dancing were over, they gathered round

---

[1] Letter to Maurice Baring: Dec. 26, 1909.

the Crib and sang their carols; and more drink was provided for the grown-ups before they went out into the night.

Later in the evening an immense log—oak like everything else at King's Land—was brought into the house, laid on the hearth in the dining-room, and ceremonially lit. Shortly before midnight the family and their guests would drive to West Grinstead or Storrington for Midnight Mass. As they rattled down the lanes in the trap the children would sing the King's Land 'Song of the Magi':

> There were three Kings and oh! what a sight!
> One was yellow and one was white,
> And one was as black as Epiphany night
> On Christmas Day in the morning.

There was a Premonstratensian Priory at Storrington and after Mass the older members of the party would go in to drink 'Arquebus' with the monks. This was an exceedingly strong liqueur, as its name suggests. The Prior was a Provençal, and just before he died, having received the last Sacraments, he dictated a Ballade which is one of the hidden glories of twentieth-century verse.

The Bellocs would rarely get back to King's Land until three o'clock in the morning. Then they would drink mulled ale and roll into bed. On Christmas Day they rose just in time for the midday meal, and when the plum-pudding was set on fire, all the other lights—for by that time the day was drawing in—were extinguished.

> After that one spends the rest of the day in drinking. It is no small feast, that in which we celebrate at King's Land the Nativity of Our Lord coupled with a Saturnalia.[1]

The rites were prolonged until the Feast of the Epiphany. On New Year's Eve, at about a quarter to twelve, every window and door in the house was opened, however cold the night, and the family, with their servants and guests, went outside. Meanwhile the bells of the neighbouring church were ringing out the old year. They ceased just before midnight and the New Year was

---

[1] Letter to Maurice Baring: Dec. 5, 1909.

proclaimed by the booming of a distant gun. Then the chimes would ring out again with a fresh tune, and Belloc, or one of his boys, would walk back into the house with a stone or lump of earth brought from outside. The doors and windows would be shut, and the household would drink to the New Year. On 'Twelfth Night'—or rather, 'Twelfth Day'—all the green and holly in the house would be burnt and the Christmas tree re-planted in the wood. The same tree would never be used twice and each lived on 'bearing witness to the holy vitality of un-broken ritual and inherited things'.[1]

The ritual was not always followed without irritation by members of the family, and at Easter there was much less of it. In 1908 Belloc tried the experiment of drinking no beer or wine during Holy Week,

> partly to see what this is like, partly in memory of the Passion, and partly to strengthen my will which has lately had bulgy spots on it; I have now gone through thirty-six hours of this ordeal, and very interesting and curious it is. I will describe it at length to you when we meet. The mind and body sink to a lower plane and become fit for contemplation rather than for action: the sense of humour is also singularly weakened.[2]

Later he extended his abstinence to the whole of Lent and would arrive at people's houses with a small crate of ginger-beer instead of pockets bulging with Burgundy. He broke his fast with Cognac, drunk after Mass and before breakfast, on Easter morning.

In 1907 the Modernist crisis in the Catholic Church was gathering to a head. Belloc's hard mind was always attracted by a total scepticism, but he was correspondingly impatient with the timidities of disbelief. His love of clear definition was well satisfied with the Encyclical *Pascendi*, issued by Pius X in October, 1907.

Have you seen the Pope's gentle remarks to Modernists? [he writes to Miss Hamilton]. They are indeed noble! I could

---

[1] *A Remaining Christmas.*
[2] Letter to Maurice Baring: April 13, 1908.

not have done it better myself. He gently hints that they can't think—which is true. The old Heretics had guts, notably Calvin, and could think like the Devil, who inspired them. But the Modernists are inspired by a little minor he-devil with one Eye and a stammer, and the result is poor.[1]

In September 1908 there was a kind of pan-Modernist Congress at Storrington, almost under Belloc's nose. Tyrrell and Brémond and Maud Petre were all there. Belloc claimed, in a letter to Baring, that Miss Petre had written a book to prove that God was not a 'Person' but a 'Vagueness'. The difference between the two conceptions was amusingly illustrated by a sketch; and once, in conversation with William Temple, he remarked, 'They think we've got the text wrong, and that what Our Blessed Lord really said was "Thou art Maud Petre, and upon this rock I will build My Church."' This may not have done justice to the niceties of Modernist hesitations and Belloc certainly did not grasp the tragedy of what was going on around him. It needed a mind more sympathetic and theologically trained—a mind like Wilfrid Ward's—to see that while the Papal condemnation might have been necessary, the handling of the crisis on the human side was both clumsy and cruel. When Ward remarked to someone at the Athenæum that the Pope was 'narrow', Belloc assumed that he was at least fellow-travelling with the persecuted trio at Storrington. Ward was as orthodox as Belloc, but he knew much more about the working of other people's minds.

2

Belloc was quick to turn his political experience to literary account, and the result was two satirical novels, *Mr. Clutterbuck's Election* (1908) and *A Change in the Cabinet* (1909). These were tossed off for a lark, and 48,000 words of the former were dictated at a stretch in Holy Week. They lack the gravity, and therefore the permanence, of *Emmanuel Burden*, although Burden himself is reincarnated in Mr. Clutterbuck, another honest and bewildered

[1] October 8, 1907.

representative of the English Middle Classes. Belloc's hold on
narrative always lacked the tightness of the born story-teller,
except when the narrative was historical, but there are many parts
of *Mr. Clutterbuck's Election* which still make amusing reading.
Mr. Barnett, having been raised to the peerage as Lord Lambeth,
has now become the Duke of Battersea. His repulsive aspect is
unchanged and he pulls more strings than ever. Other characters,
like Mary Smith, the Edwardian hostess who makes or mars
political fortunes, now appear among the *dramatis personæ*.
Belloc had met her, no doubt, in the fashionable circles which he
used occasionally to frequent but to which he never, in any
serious sense, belonged. Both she and her Prime Minister, Dolly,
reappear in *A Change in the Cabinet*. Where exactly was Habberton, the country seat of their conspiracies? Some people have
identified it with Mells, the lovely sixteenth-century manor house
on the borders of Wiltshire and Somerset. Here Lady Horner,
whose daughter Katherine was married to Raymond Asquith,
would preside over Liberal house-parties, and Belloc used occasionally to go there in later years. He was already a close friend of
Raymond Asquith, but their favourite meeting-place was with
Auberon Lucas at Picket Post. Later, as we shall see, Katherine
Asquith became one of Belloc's closest friends, but Lady Horner
did not find him sympathetic. Mention of the 'Somerset hills'
suggests Pixton Park, the home of Lady Carnarvon and Aubrey
Herbert, as the more likely model for Habberton. This was at the
opposite, and western, end of the county.

Nobody any longer writes funny books about politics, and if
these satirical novels of Belloc are less read than they used to be,
the reason is not only because most fiction is ephemeral. Politics
may or may not have become purer since Belloc wrote about
them; they have certainly become more professional. Cabinet
Ministers are no longer remote deities, lending themselves to
irreverent myth. They are plodding and anxious bureaucrats,
living in flats and travelling on the Underground. Most of them
are honest and very few of them are picturesque. Their motor cars
and expense accounts may give them a façade of momentary
glamour, but when their Party is out of office they relapse into

the anonymity of a voting cipher. The world of Mr. Clutterbuck, by contrast, had the freedom of the speculator and the amateur, and when Cabinets changed there was still a pretty opportunity for caprice.

On March 31, 1909, *Punch* published a cartoon of Belloc, with a caption borrowed from the Speaker of the House of Commons: 'Everybody knows that the Hon. Member fills a considerable space in the literary world.' Belloc's girth and sinew lent themselves easily to caricature, but the remark was true in more than a physical sense. Like other leading actors on the literary stage, he was stepping quite unself-consciously into the limelight. He did not greatly enjoy, and he rarely sought out, the company of literary people. Wilfrid and Alice Meynell lived not far off at Greatham, but here there was no more than a polite contact. 'Mrs. Meynell is a charming woman,' Belloc used to say, 'the only trouble is she's sick every time she sees me.' There may have been a grain of truth in this hyperbole. His work on the *Morning Post* brought him into touch with writers and publishers, since he was responsible for getting their books reviewed. Belloc had a considerable esteem for Conrad, and Conrad in his turn was always grateful for an article on *Almayer's Folly*. Later he sent Belloc a signed copy of *Nostromo*. The sense of honour and the sense of glory were active in both men, and Belloc would not forget that Conrad was a Pole. Of Edmund Gosse he wrote characteristically:

> Gosse was an excellent writer, a man of quite incredible literary erudition, a worthless critic save when he was repeating French judgements he had heard. He saw everything too much on a level and believed whatever he heard said around him— especially by the rich. The best thing about him was that he could quarrel.[1]

Belloc greatly admired Charles Whibley; he thought him 'not only a loyal and good man but also an excellent writer of peculiarly perfect English'.[2] Wells he had met at dinner with

[1] Letter to Mrs. Raymond Asquith: Jan. 6, 1929.
[2] Letter to Maurice Baring: Aug. 5, 1913.

A. M. Latter; on this occasion Belloc had recited some Homer and Wells had exclaimed 'What absolute rot!' In spite of this, the two men remained on speaking terms until Belloc exposed Wells's ignorance in a controversy which we shall discuss in its proper place. He thought Wells wrote excellent English and had a high degree of scientific imagination. Shaw he knew well and met, on and off the platform, over many years. He rather liked him, and summed him up in a lapidary definition: 'a witty, kindly man; lacks instruction'. Belloc regarded him as 'intellectual' in the pejorative sense of the word. He explained what he meant by this to Phillimore:

> I often use the word 'stupid' to indicate this intellectual attitude; for instance I should have said that Bernard Shaw's contention against me in Clapham a year ago, that the social institutions of the ninth century were Collectivist was stupid— by which I would mean not that he had not put a lot of brain-work into the study of them, still less that the defence of his thesis was not exceptionally ingenious, but that he was convinced that he was studying the thing in the cube when, as a fact, he was studying it in the square. Or to use another metaphor, it is as though a man were to go on about the chemical analysis of food when his wiser opponent was considering its general and integral suitability as food for a human being. Thus I should say of a man who wanted us to eat sawdust because sawdust contained certain chemical elements, that his attitude was 'stupid' or 'intellectual'.[1]

Of the other prominent writers of the period the one Belloc knew best was Max Beerbohm. The two men regarded each other with a certain satirical affection. 'When you really get talking, Hilary,' Max once remarked, 'you're like a great Bellocking ram, or like a Roman river full of baskets and dead cats.' On hearing the very surprising news that Belloc had been seen at a cricket match, Max observed drily: 'I suppose he would have said that the only good wicket-keeper in the history of the game was a Frenchman and a Roman Catholic.' And when Belloc died, he

[1] Nov. 16, 1909.

vrote that 'he wasn't merely a man of genius; he was a man of
many geniuses'. Belloc, on his side, thought Max had 'an excel-
ent heart and is at bottom a very sincere man'; though his art,
both as a writer and a draughtsman, was too well-dressed for
Belloc to appreciate it at its proper worth. Belloc's impact on
English letters—his ideas and his way of expressing them—can
best be understood in contrast to Max Beerbohm. Belloc was in
healthy, and sometimes in crude, reaction against the *fin de siècle;*
and the reason behind this reaction, which he shared fully with
Chesterton, is explained in the following letter.

It is very difficult for our generation to understand why our
elder brothers were, so to speak, so moved by the sporadic,
isolated epigrams and the mere verbal paradoxes of that time.
It was evidently some sort of reaction against another, older,
philosophy of which we know nothing by personal experience.
I remember as a boy of nineteen being bewildered by it when I
came up from the country, for it was not a reaction against any
philosophy I had ever held, and it seemed to be either obvious
or silly, but never new or valuable. When people said that
beauty thrilled them so much, it merely bored me because
beauty in my experience had thrilled everybody; and when they
pointed to the grotesque or the misshapen as examples of beauty,
I thought it simply silly. The whole thing was perhaps a violent
reaction against mere emotion. And you must remember that
the nation had no experience of warfare, was quite ignorant of
Irish or other influences, to which it is now open, and had
become isolated. On the other hand, I think the opposite side,
which was manly, was manlier than anything we have today.[1]

Max paid Belloc the compliment of parody in *A Christmas
Garland*, and some readers of *The Path to Rome* may think he had
found the chink in his armour.

There was a man came to our Inn by night, and after he had
called three times they should open him the door—though
why three times, and not three times three, nor thirty times
thirty, which is the number of the little stone devils that make

[1] Letter to Maurice Baring: Dec. 19, 1909.

mous at St. Aloesius of Ledera over against the marshes
Gué-la-Nuce to this day, nor three hundred times three
hundred (which is a bestial number), nor three thousand times
three and thirty, upon my soul I know not, and nor do you—
when, then, this jolly fellow had three times cried out, shouted,
yelled, holloa'd, loudly besought, caterwauled, brayed, sung
out and roared, he did by the same token set himself to beat,
hammer, bang, pommel, and knock at the door. Now the door
was oak . . .[1]

For the reader who had grown up with the Edwardians, *A
Christmas Garland* conferred a certificate of eminence, if not of
immortality; and Belloc's place in English letters towards 1910
can be measured by recalling the men with whom Max associated
him: Henry James, Rudyard Kipling, A. C. Benson, H. G. Wells,
G. K. Chesterton, Thomas Hardy, Frank Harris, Arnold Bennett,
John Galsworthy, G. S. Street, Joseph Conrad, Edmund Gosse,
George Bernard Shaw, Maurice Hewlett, George Moore, George
Meredith. To compare these reputations today in the light of their
Edwardian glory is to receive a sharp lesson in the whirligig of
literary fortunes. For some the halo has brightened; for others it
has dimmed; for one or two it has disappeared completely.

Among the younger writers of that time there was one who
acknowledged his debt to Belloc. This was Rupert Brooke.
Brooke knew many of Belloc's poems by heart and often quoted
them. Edward Shanks in his study of Belloc[2] sets the following
lines from *Grantchester* beside Belloc's *Dedicatory Ode*.

> In Grantchester, their skins are white,
> They bathe by day, they bathe by night;
> The women there do all they ought;
> The men observe the Rules of Thought.
> They love the Good; they worship Truth;
> They laugh uproariously in youth.

Brooke had a 'metaphysical' side to his verse—complexities of
thought and feeling—which were alien to Belloc. But if you read

[1] *A Christmas Garland* (1912).
[2] *Hilaire Belloc*, by C. Creighton Mandell and Edward Shanks (1916).

Brooke's *Letters from America*; it is easy to imagine that the two men might have become friends.

The *Morning Post,* as we have seen, was a natural point of contact between Belloc and the literary world. He did not read many new books, but at least he knew what was being written. His own column brought him fame as an essayist at a time when the essay was still a recognized and popular branch of formal letters. Belloc had a respect for the paper which is rather surprising. He thought it 'with all its faults, a really English paper and one of the very few left'. He had been introduced to it by Oliver Borthwick, a Balliol contemporary, whose father, Sir Algernon Borthwick, was then in control of the paper. When Borthwick was raised to the peerage as Lord Glenesk, in 1895, his son took over control, but died in 1905—just before Belloc joined the staff. The management then passed to Lady Bathurst, Oliver Borthwick's sister. Belloc's relations with the paper were easy while Glenesk's influence was still active among the staff, but there was constant friction with the editor, Fabian Ware. Differences between Ware and his more distinguished reviewers, like W. H. Hudson, often had to be settled by Belloc; and Belloc was much more apt to excite differences than to smooth them out.

It is exceedingly difficult to work under Ware. A week ago he simply wouldn't print one of my articles because he thought it was disrespectful to the wealthy. It is impossible to hammer into his head the fact that the wealthy like to read articles against themselves. The one thing the wealthy won't stand is being bored, and goodness knows the front page of the *Morning Post* is enough to strike the whole Governing class dead with boredom. The hearts of its readers sink the moment they open it. He is unable to give any coherent account of why he suppressed one of your articles. He said it had something to do with the game of Bridge. I don't know whether he includes Bridge with the House of Lords and other institutions which must be treated as half divine in his columns, but anyhow he is a pestilent bore and has made me miss five guineas. Meanwhile I am having offers of work on every side at higher rates than the *Morning Post* is willing to pay and I am beginning to accept them.[1]

It is clear that the two men did not get on, and there may well have been faults on both sides, as the following letter from Ware will illustrate.

March 23, 1909

DEAR BELLOC,

I owe you an apology for the way I shouted at you this afternoon; but *please* don't, on your rare and unexpected visits to the office (about which I shall say more on another occasion), stand in my door and wag a finger at me when I am engaged on private and difficult business.

Yours,
F.W.

Matters were moving to a crisis in June of the following year; Belloc writes to Baring:

The *Morning Post* have now played the second trick in the series that I foresaw: the Literary Page being founded, they put me on to a lower salary with less frequent attendance in order that I might train to a sufficient degree of competence an assistant. This being more or less done, they now propose to sever my contract with the literary side of the paper altogether. I should probably have done better to take your advice in the original place and have told them that if they didn't keep me on I wouldn't do any work for them at all, since their game obviously was the one I had seen so often played in English journalism, to wit, getting a man to start a thing at a fair salary under the verbal promise of continuing and when he had put in his very best in order to obtain such continuance, ceasing payment after they had got the fullest results out of him. It is, however, too late to go back on that. I was very frightened then, because it was my only large source of income at the time. At present this is not the case, and I propose to tell them that as long as they leave me the title of Literary Editor (which is

<hr>

[1] Letter to Maurice Baring: Dec. 19, 1909.

essential to me) and do not pay me less a year as a whole, and make that payment regular, I shall be content to make up the difference in other forms of work for them, which I am well able to do.[1]

Ware refused to make any regular arrangement. All he wanted was Belloc's weekly article; apart from this, he merely said that he would see what other work he could give him from time to time. Belloc replied that this was not good enough; that he could sell his articles at better prices elsewhere; and that what he needed was a small regular salary. He asked for six hundred pounds a year, but gave Ware to understand that he would accept five hundred. He offered to write an agreed number of leaders on non-political subjects, so many columns of book reviews, so many articles on military subjects at home and abroad. But Ware would say nothing definite. Belloc accordingly wrote that if he did not hear from him by the first post on September 2, he would sever his connection with the paper. Ware still said nothing, so Belloc wrote to Lady Bathurst regretting his inability to continue. The letter left it open to her to insist on Belloc's terms, but she did not do so; indeed she did not even answer his communication.

Belloc was miserable at the break. The *Morning Post* had given him a quarter of his total income; but the loss was more than financial, it was a loss of milieu and occupation. Nor did he find a substitute. The truth would seem to be inescapable; he was not made for regular employment. He did not understand what it meant to work with other people. When the publishing firm of Sheed and Ward was founded many years later, he expressed a desire to join it. He was asked politely what kind of work he proposed to do; but he was quite unable to give an answer which would justify the salary he expected to receive.

3

Belloc's literary affairs were handled by A. P. Watt. 'This man,' he told Phillimore, 'is a Scotchman of enormous shrewdness. He

[1] June 19, 1910.

forces publishers to take books and gets you admirable terms, seizing himself 10 per cent. Not only does he force publishers to take books, but he forces them to advertise them and sell them.'[1] Belloc had proposed forty pounds as an advance on *The Old Road*, and Watt had secured him one hundred and fifty pounds the following day. The two men were in almost daily contact during this period of intense literary output.

In July 1906 Adam and Charles Black published a book of seventy-five coloured plates by Wilfrid Ball, illustrating the county of Sussex. There was a caption to each plate; these and a few additional notes had been contributed anonymously by Belloc. The book appeared in Black's twenty-shilling series. On October 11 *Hills and the Sea* was published by Methuen. These essays had already been printed in *The Speaker*, the *Pilot*, the *Morning Post*, the *Daily News*, the *Pall Mall Magazine*, the *Evening Standard*, the *Morning Leader*, and the *Westminster Gazette*. The list gives a good idea of Belloc's wide market in daily and weekly journalism. For many people *Hills and the Sea* will be their favourite among Belloc's collected essays; certainly, if we only had this book to go by, we should place him among the finest essayists in the English language. For the most part, the book is personal and 'unbuttoned'; the essayist, like the short-story writer, can waste no time in catching the reader's attention. The decline of journalism over half a century can be judged by the space that editors, fifty years ago, were prepared to give to the essay. How much literary or dramatic criticism is now long enough to be reproduced between the covers of a book? Who are the leading essayists today? The question resounds hollowly.

The best essayists—Addison and Steele, Lamb and Hazlitt, Max Beerbohm and Montaigne—give us their personalities as well as their subjects; indeed there is a sense in which their subjects are themselves. Belloc, as we shall see, could be a coldly impersonal writer. Everything he wrote carries the signature of his style; he could not have been anonymous if he had tried. But there is a clear distinction between the books where he put himself in and

[1] 1905.

those where he kept himself out. The essay, except when he was dealing with history or topography, gave him an opportunity to unbutton. Here, and in *The Cruise of the 'Nona'*, is the nearest he comes to reminiscence.

In the case of a writer so prolific and various as Belloc, it is tempting to ask oneself which of his books one would choose to keep, if one had to sacrifice all the rest. For the welding of his personality into a closely-knit, original, and nearly perfect composition one might choose *The Four Men;* for sheer splendour of style and vivid presentation of history, *Danton* or *Marie Antoinette;* for craftsmanship, *Belinda;* for seamanship interspersed with opinions, *The Cruise of the 'Nona'*. Or some people might take his *Verse* and be content to leave it at that. But if one wanted a glimpse of his many-sidedness—the traveller, the historian, the conscript, the pilgrim, the seafarer, and the natural philosopher that went into all of these—then one would surely have to go to a volume of the essays. And of these collections *Hills and the Sea* is perhaps the best.

The book was dedicated—though of formal dedication there was none—to himself and Phil Kershaw; for Kershaw was the other of the two men of whom Belloc speaks in the preface. This, for all its affectionate mockery, throws a sudden light on the quality of Belloc's friendships. Kershaw had been his companion on recent explorations of the Pyrenees; he had accompanied him, as we have seen, along the Old Road; and they often sailed together.

They loved each other like brothers, yet they quarrelled like Socialists. They loved each other because they had in common the bond of mankind; they quarrelled because they differed upon nearly all other things. The one was of the Faith, the other most certainly was not. The one sang loudly, the other sweetly. The one was stronger, the other more cunning. The one rode horses with a long stirrup, the other with a short. The one was indifferent to danger, the other forced himself at it. The one could write verse, the other was quite incapable thereof. The one could read and quote Theocritus, the other read and quoted himself alone. The high gods had given to one judgment, to the other valour; but to both that measure of misfortune which is their Gift to those whom they cherish.

In some of the essays—*The Wing of Dalua* for example—we see Belloc and Kershaw together; lost in a haunted valley of the Pyrenees. But in most of them Belloc is alone, or driving the guns with his fellow-conscripts. He lands from the North Sea at King's Lynn, and the individuality of the houses reminds him that England has never known the power of strong, centralized government and the august, monotonous architecture which is its fruit. Belloc only realized later—if, indeed, he realized at all— how lucky England had been. He sees the whole history of Europe vividly incarnate at Arles, and he feels the air of Paris electric with essential conflict as he comes out on to the *parvis* from a great ceremony in Notre Dame. There are frequent glimpses of the Pyrenees—Roncesvalles, the Canigou, the Cerdagne—and then he will explain to us the technique of mowing a field. We catch the mood in which he set out along the path to Rome, and are subdued to reverie by his meditation on autumn and the fall of leaves.

At this season a sky which is of so delicate and faint a blue as to contain something of gentle mockery, and certainly more of tenderness, presides at the fall of leaves. There is no air, no breath at all. The leaves are so light that they sidle on their going downward, hesitating on that which is not void to them, and touching at last so imperceptibly the earth with which they are to mingle, that the gesture is much gentler than a salutation, and even more discreet than a discreet caress.

They make a little sound, less than the least of sounds. No bird at night in the marshes rustles so slightly; no men, though men are the subtlest of living beings, put so evanescent a stress upon their sacred whispers or their prayers. The leaves are hardly heard, but they are heard just so much that men also, who are destined at the end to grow glorious and to die, look up and hear them falling.

This is only one example of how Belloc's observation and his careful record of it become fused into what literary Puritans call purple patches and other people call great prose.

Two other similar collections appeared in 1908 and 1909: *On Nothing* and *On Everything*. In the first of these there are two interesting glimpses. One is of Belloc bicycling through the Vendée on his tour for the *Pall Mall Gazette* and listening to an innkeeper discourse on death. The man had no clear belief in revelation, but he had arrived in his old age at the point to which Belloc himself came when Hubert Howard was cut off in his early manhood.

It was incredible to him that a Sentient Being who perpetually accumulated experience, who grew riper and riper, more and more full of such knowledge as was native to himself and complementary to his nature, should at the very crisis of his success in all things intellectual and emotional, cease suddenly. It was further to him an object of vast curiosity why such a being, since a future was essential to it, should find that future veiled.

This was Belloc's natural position on the great and anxious question of immortality, for he would always refuse a facile optimism. He returned to the subject in the following essay, *On Coming to an End*. Here he quotes the poets for consolation; Keats's 'Or cease upon the midnight with no pain', and Ronsard's 'Je vous salue, heureuse et salutable mort'.

The noblest or the most perfect of English elegies leaves, as a sort of savour after reading it, no terror at all nor even too much regret, but the landscape of England at evening, when the smoke of the cottages mixes with autumn vapours among the elms.

To this mood Belloc himself wished to contribute, and it is here that we catch a glimpse of that *Ode to the West Wind,* which he was never able to bring to completion. A good deal of it must have been written, since Belloc quotes from three stanzas in the

essay we have been discussing. These give us a clear taste of what
its quality might have been.

> For now the Night completed tells her tale
> Of rest and dissolution; gathering round
> Her mist in such persuasion that the ground
> Of Home consents to falter and grow pale.
> And the stars are put out and the trees fail.
> Nor anything remains but that which drones
> Enormous through the dark . . .

Belloc prays that he may at the last be fed with beauty

> . . . as the flowers are fed
> That fill their falling-time with generous breath:
> Let me attain a natural end of death,
> And on the mighty breast, as on a bed,
> Lay decently at last a drowsy head,
> Content to lapse in somnolence and fade,
> In dreaming once again the dream of all things made.

The writing here is careful, and Belloc infers that more of the
poem was written than he quotes. Fragments survived among
his papers from which it is now possible to reconstruct the first
and third stanzas.

I

> From what known hills, in what remembered skies
> Or over what familiar, following seas
> Or in what bowls of morning did you rise
> West wind of the contented? That to these
> Dull shores lethargic an appalling Breeze
> Quick with the remembrance and the power
> To stir the unburied dead you wake th'accomplish'd hour.

III

> Why will you vex me? I have paid the debt,
> Which all to the inexorable pay;

The mortal's dues of numbness and decay
That do enfranchise from this olivet
Of purposeless but passionate regret
For those deep hills and that strong youth of mine
When I was raised in light and kissed of lips divine.

Why was the poem never completed? One reason may have been that it did not come easily enough for a man who was too busy to give much of his time to verse. There are two notes in the margin of the fragments quoted above. 'Belloc, old boy, this has got to be finished!'[1] and 'That's all right, but you must jog the Muse.'[2] Another answer is suggested by Belloc's own description of the poem as 'touched with despair'. Certainly the note of Christian hope—the triumphant note of the Resurrection—is nowhere sounded. All the poet can speak of is

> . . . that outer place forlorn
> Which, like an infinite grey sea, surrounds
> With everlasting calm the land of human sounds.

This is vague enough for the mistiest agnostic, and Belloc may well have scrupled to complete and publish a poem which was more consonant with his temperament than his beliefs.

If there was one quality that Belloc possessed in a far greater degree than any other writer of his time, it was the quality of historical imagination. Macaulay had it and so had Carlyle. Belloc's interpretation of history, like theirs, will always be open to dispute; but there can be no disputing the vividness and, let it be emphasized, the accuracy with which he reconstructed the past. His imagination was visual and the famous book of essays which was published by Eveleigh Nash in October 1908 was appropriately named *The Eye-Witness*. Belloc placed himself at certain key-points of history and re-imagined them on the basis of evidence patiently collected. He showed how the course of history had turned on minute accidents: if Burgoyne had not delayed along the Hudson, if Drouet had not taken that particular path through the Argonne. Here and there he might invent a character to bring

[1] Sept. 28, 1906.   [2] July 17, 1907.

a situation to life, but more often the characters were real:
Napoleon in the biting December cold of the Guadarrama, James
Stuart on the night of his exile, the Barons at Runnymede and the
Guns at Valmy. The Guns! How that word reverberates through
Belloc's life and work! With the exception of certain marching
songs, certain immemorial chants, certain simple airs, and 'the
Christian innocence of Mozart', they were the only music he
ever really understood.

What the 'eye-witness' saw were not fancy pictures; they owed
nothing to the licence of the historical novelist. If Belloc described
a place, he had been there; if he stated that the weather was fine
or cloudy, he had evidence to back his assertion. And one of the
scenes—an episode of the 1906 election—he had witnessed at first
hand. There was nothing new in this method; he had practised it
in *Danton* and *Robespierre*. But here his imagination ranged over
the whole course of European history, lighting up some phase of
a story, or some aspect of a man, that he might wish to treat in
fuller proportion or more elaborate detail later on. The book,
rather strangely, was not an immediate success, but it has helped
many candidates in a History Sixth on their way to a scholarship;
clothing the dry bones of record—the dates, the treaties, the
edicts, and the campaigns—with the substance and the variety
of life.

4

As we have already noted, Belloc's political views were considered so radical that rumours began to go round that he would
accept the Labour Whip. The truth, of course, was quite the
contrary; he was moving, all the time, further away from
Socialism. A reading of Arthur Ponsonby's book, *The Camel and
the Needle's Eye*[1]—and Belloc regarded Ponsonby as the most
sincere Radical he had ever met—showed him how far he had
travelled in another direction. The pressure of Catholic philosophy may have had something to do with this, for he published
two pamphlets for the Catholic Truth Society, defining his

[1] 1909.

attitude to Socialism.[1] Belloc had a warm sympathy with the emotional roots of Socialism, and his opposition to it was coldly intellectual. The Socialist State was a State in which all the means of production—transport, land and machines—would be owned by the politicians. The politicians might be democratically elected, or they might not; that was irrelevant to the Socialist thesis. They might enforce their distribution of wealth equally, or at least equitably; or they might not. The point was that the moral responsibility of ownership would be exercised not by the people but by the politicians. If it were objected that the people were anyhow deprived of ownership, Belloc replied that it was better to heal a limb than to amputate it. He admitted that one-quarter of the means of production in England was owned by about two hundred families, and that a second quarter was owned by about two thousand families. These were rough calculations, but they pointed to a society that was mortally diseased. Belloc, however, saw that the Socialist, though he might be at war with the capitalist, had much in common with him. Both wanted to accumulate and concentrate wealth; Belloc wanted to divide it.

The Socialist did not object to people possessing goods for personal enjoyment, but he objected to them possessing the means of production. He opposed the principle of well-divided property because he believed such division would be impracticable and inefficient. Here Belloc pointed to the experience of Catholic Europe. Wherever a society was informed by Catholic philosophy—Ireland, Quebec, France and the Southern Germanies—a determining proportion of the people were owners in one form or another. It was in Protestant societies that the modern proletariat had arisen. Belloc looked forward—and heaven knows there were few who shared his vision—to a time when the medieval idea of free co-operation between free owners would return, because this was the only form of society where personal honour and personal freedom would be safeguarded; the only form of society natural to western man. He would elaborate his ideas as time went by and the Distributist movement got, rather crankily, under way to propagate them; he would suggest practical means

[1] *An Examination of Socialism* (1908); *The Church and Socialism* (1909).

by which property might be restored. These two pamphlets, which were little noted outside Catholic circles, were his first statement of principle.

They had the defects of Belloc's dogmatism; not in the sense that his principles were too clear, but that he attributed an equal clarity to other people. He never made sufficient allowance for other people's inconsistencies, perhaps because he was so oblivious of his own. If people were as logical as Belloc wanted them to be, the world might have fulfilled his prophecies more exactly; but it would be an uninhabitable asylum. When he was attacking Socialism, he was really attacking Communism, and he would not have it that there was any difference between the two. He could not envisage a mixed economy in which certain sections of the nation's productive power would be taken over by the State and others left in private hands. This ideal, which has become the practical policy of the Labour Party, was, of course, open to criticism—but Belloc did not criticize it. His mind was so impatient of any *via media* that he never really looked at the Labour Party; or if he looked at Ramsay MacDonald or Jimmy Thomas he very quickly looked away. Nevertheless, if he had listened to men like R. H. Tawney, he might have looked again more attentively, and recognized in British Socialism a common concern for equality. But he would also have seen that equality, as they understood it, and liberty, as he understood it, were incompatible. Just as there was a wide discrepancy between Marxist or Fabian doctrine and any Socialist policy which has proved feasible in any society of the West, so there was a similar divergence between Catholic social philosophy and the practice of Catholic societies. You could not hold up Poland and Spain as examples of well-divided property: each had a vast peasant proletariat. Nor was it at all accurate to say that peasant societies produced better soldiers. The proletarian from Dusseldorf or Manchester fought just as well in two great wars as the peasant proprietor from Champagne. Indeed, war itself has become so mechanized that the mechanic sometimes found it easier to master its technique. If Belloc was concerned with the real but very abstract conception of military honour, he would have done better to attack the principle of conscription; an idea abhorrent to Christian societies until the regicides of the Revolution introduced it.

Belloc wrote these pamphlets in full disgust with 'practical politics'; but politics are of their nature practical and they cannot be discussed in a void. The political theorist always oversimplifies, and what the future held in store was just that compromise between a planned and a free economy, now tending one way and now the other, which was most congenial to the English temper and most difficult to classify under any heading of *idées générales*. Nevertheless, it was most unlikely that either of the two great political parties in 1909 would have proposed to the electors the nostrum of a 'property-owning democracy' and when at last, in 1950, the Tories staked their fortunes on the phrase, one asks oneself whether they realized their debt to Belloc? In any case, they knew better than to acknowledge it.

Two more studies in what we may call historical topography were published during these years: *The Historic Thames* in 1907, with coloured illustrations by A. R. Quinton, and *The Pyrenees* in 1908, with forty-six sketches by the author and twenty-two maps. In *The Historic Thames* Belloc showed the historical importance of the river from medieval to modern times. It is a rather dry, deeply informative essay. *The Pyrenees* was written at top speed, and the last chapters were polished off in four days. When it was finished Belloc escaped to the New Forest and rode hard for twenty-four hours. The book resumes his personal exploration of the mountains. He had tramped them on various occasions, from end to end, and the book is still much the best guide to them that exists. It is packed with valuable details and generally sparing of description. It tells you what equipment to take, how to make a difficult passage from one point to another, and how to drink wine from a gourd. It estimates your costs (in terms of currencies picturesquely outdated) and the time it should take you to cover a particular stretch. It is pessimistic about the precipices and the weather, and assumes that you will make every possible mistake. Where the inns are concerned, it is not always to be relied on, for many of these have changed hands. A special *amende* should be

made to the primitive but hospitable inn at Bujuarelo on the
Spanish side of the Pass of Gavarnie. Sophistication had already
invaded these hills at Gavarnie, and elsewhere, when Belloc was
writing. It has since made drastic inroads upon their peace. They
remain the most fascinating and most easily negotiable of European mountains for those who are not technical mountaineers.
Yet they still constitute a barrier which is all but absolute. France
and Spain—not least in their interpretation of a common religion
—continue to go their separate ways. In some respects it would be
true to say that Belloc started his life on one side of the range and
ended it on the other.

In this same year of 1907, *Cautionary Tales for Children*,'designed
for the admonition of children between the ages of eight and
fourteen years', was published by Eveleigh Nash, with pictures
by Basil Blackwood. Neither Belloc's hand, nor 'B.T.B.'s', had
lost its cunning since *A Moral Alphabet*. The misfortunes of
Matilda and Godolphin Horne, of Henry King and Charles
Augustus Fortescue, reminded all those outside the author's
private circle that the Member for South Salford still knew how
to play the fool. The book was greatly helped by Clara Butt, who
sang the *Cautionary Tales* to immense audiences up and down the
country.

5

Publishers are like theatre managers, they want their artists to
repeat themselves. It makes for tidiness all round if the same man
goes through the same hoop with the same astonishing somer-
sault. Now Belloc was not this kind of performer; indeed he hated
the very idea of performance. But like other actors who find
themselves pigeon-holed into repetition of the same part, he
needed to earn his living. He had written two successful biographies about the French Revolution; let him now write another.
Or rather, let him write about one of the great figures on the other
side. Who could be more appealing than Marie Antoinette—she
who had moved Burke to one of his most splendid flights of
rhetoric; she who still symbolized the sweetness of life as it was

lived before the Revolution; she whose name was a synonym for pleasure and whose fate might be trusted to draw tears? Belloc was insensitive to this appeal; he was the last man to let himself be bullied by Burke, whom he regarded as a hypocritical Whig and whose political insights he quite grotesquely misjudged. Marie Antoinette was not his subject; he wanted to write about St. Just. Nevertheless, under pressure of poverty—for he was in debt to Methuen—he agreed, 'in the conviction that a certain minimum of good work will float a man's bad work'. But he still felt that literary work 'is better done when the writer is at least free as to his method and his subject, though it may be true, and I should say is true, that it ought to be written for money and that men who do not need the money do not usually write well.'[1]

The book took him five years to write and was published in October 1909. King Edward VII was heard discussing it. The frequent allusions to the Catholic Church were thought to be out of place, and Belloc received a number of letters criticizing him for dragging it in. For his own part he found the book 'stodgy with good passages just like a suet pudding with plums, which is the very worst thing one can say of anybody's style. It is more learned than I had imagined myself to be.' The writing of it had been a 'prolonged, minute and tiresome labour'.[2]

I have but to open any page to find in the very adjectives used and even in the arrangement of the punctuation memories of fatiguing research, long waiting in the British Museum, the bad taste of former years of peril, during which the writing of history seemed to me a desperate interference with what I ought to earn for my family, and especially that sort of nausea which rises in men of an impatient temperament when they remember the slow misunderstanding of attendants in public libraries and the miserable work of verifying important details.

I have just opened the book at random and found on Page 272 the fifth paragraph beginning with the word 'Already'. That is based on quite a page of very packed notes: the number

[1] Letter to Maurice Baring: Nov. 12, 1909.   [2] Ibid.

of the troop, the colour of the wall of the Posting House, its position adjacent to the road, the fact that the stones of the road came right up to the wall without a pavement; the fact that there was more than one ostler, and that I worried to find whether the number were exactly three; the fact that peasants came up from the fields and joined the enquiring group at the post house—all that is contained in those few lines. And I might take any number of such small paragraphs indefinitely, and they would remind me of the same weary business; on this account it is impossible for me to judge the book. Therefore your letter is a great consolation to me. I agree with your criticism, especially with regard to the personality of the Queen. The fault proceeds from the conditions under which the book was produced. I particularly did not want to write on Marie Antoinette; I only got to know her character towards the end of my five years' work. And indeed my appreciation of the anti-revolutionary position has become very strong in the last two years. But the book was not written consecutively and therefore there is not, as there should be, a crescendo in which the Queen gets better and better known to the reader until in the last catastrophe love aids comprehension. The last two things I wrote in which her character in any way appears through the print was the passage upon Page 394, and the end of the episode of the Dauphin upon Page 357; the paragraph beginning 'She stood up by the little bed' on that page was written months months months and months after the paragraph at the end of Page 356.

All this means that I ought to have rewritten the book as I could indeed now rewrite it if I had any leisure, but there is the rub! Ever since the idiotic Dons turned me out of doors, not only leisure but even regularity of employment has been denied me, and I had not the courage to do more than put my voluminous writings together and publish the book. I have two great boxes of notes which make me sick to look at, and I can assure you that having the thing out at last and being free of the debt it involves, was like waking after a nightmare.[1]

[1] Letter to Maurice Baring, Nov. 12, 1909.

Belloc disagreed with one of Baring's criticisms. Baring had denied that the French aristocracy thought the Queen theatrical.

I don't think she was theatrical, but I think that certain mannerisms of hers *seemed* theatrical to the French. You probably know how the perfectly natural manner of an English middle class tourist, which I think is usually full of humility, seems to Italians nothing but the most disgusting and calculating rudeness proceeding from pride. Marie Antoinette came from an aristocratic community where the upper class, I understand, are as in England quite natural, and regard their superiority as natural; the French, you must remember, long before 1770 had lost all conception of aristocracy properly so-called; it had become an elaborate sort of religious ritual, but the French were already so egalitarian that you could hardly tell the different classes apart (spiritually, I mean, for of course they had differences of locution and table manners) and that is what accounts for the complete success of the new generals who were raised from the ranks and who had to work side by side with the old gentry in the revolutionary wars. No one, for instance, ever noticed the social difference of Jourdain who was a small linen draper, and Carnot who was of the very highest professional family, when both were in command at Wattignies, and the letters and diaries of the officers who were noble in that same campaign show a complete oblivion to rank. Now the Queen must have betrayed rank perpetually, and that I think would have been odious to the French nobility who loved their elaborate ritual (which she despised) but hated the vivid note of reality in connection with rank, a note which was for her part of the very air she breathed—just as it is with the English plutocracy today.[1]

This is full and candid self-criticism; how far was it justified? Certainly *Marie Antoinette* does not move with the rapidity and impulse of *Danton*. But then Danton was a man who had captured Belloc's imagination and an idea which had captured his mind; Marie Antoinette was an idea imposed on him by a

[1] *Ibid.*

T

publisher. His heart was with the determined Commons, with their kindling phrases and their debates which changed society; but he had to penetrate the core of a corrupted Court with its august hypocrisies and its strategic conventions. At the best, he had to desert the fresh air for Arcadia. Still, he made the effort; and although the effort is too perceptible, it cannot be written off as unsuccessful. Some of the pages are strained, but none of them is dull. It was impossible to trace a guiding principle through all the caprices and affections of Marie Antoinette; in that sense, but only in that sense, she was an unprincipled person. But it was possible to discern the process of an irresistible fate. This process, as distinct from the character of the Queen herself, gives unity and excitement to the book. It seemed providentially determined that at every crisis of her story she should do the wrong thing. Belloc would have been more at home with her grandfather-in-law, Louis XV, for whose frailty he had a large and clear comprehension; or with her mother, Maria Theresa, whose vigour and wisdom stand out warmly from the opening chapters. But he could not help being more interested in the fate than in the personality of the Queen; the personality was small, but the fate was enormous. And so it is with the summoning of the States-General to Versailles in 1789; with the storming of the Bastille; with the escape to Varennes; and with the emergence of Mirabeau that the book begins to gather that passionate momentum which takes it to its tremendous and its tragic close.

We can sympathize with certain complaints of the critics. Parallels with modern plutocracies are dragged in by the heels and disturb the flow of the narrative; the reader is far too insistently nudged. Belloc admitted his fault to Baring, comparing himself (though modestly) with Swift, whom he would rather have resembled than any other English writer. Swift had dragged in Dryden and denied him any literary merit. Belloc also admitted that where the Church was in question there were certain passages where he 'might very well have let the Old Lady take a rest'.[1]

Again, the anti-Semitic gibes grew monotonous and even the

[1] Letter to Maurice Baring: Nov. 12, 1909.

unfortunate Dreyfus was not allowed to rest in his rehabilitation. The idea of representation is paraded as the first principle of revolutionary action and then (as Belloc crosses the Channel) condemned as the cement of oligarchic tyranny. He is not insensitive to the grandeur of the monarchy, though here, as always, he is impatient with ritual divorced from reality. The Capetian monarchy becomes 'that great, once good and very ancient thing which God now disapproved'; and he does not hesitate to assert that 'God intended the Revolution'. 'Permitted' would be more theologically exact; but it was not in Belloc's nature to set any limits to the action of any will. It was one thing to assert that the Revolution had set Catholicism free by saving it from the embarrassment of privilege; to contrast the cynical décor of a national cult with the spiritual renaissance of the twentieth century. But this was the last thing that the Revolutionaries intended; and indeed Belloc is forced very near to admitting the paradox that whereas in the matter of politics they destroyed a stability and a sanction which the French have never been able to recover, in the matter of religion they helped, quite unintentionally, to bring an Institution that looked like dying back to life. The mistakes of Marie Antoinette were her principal misfortunes, and Belloc sets them out plainly as the origin of a conflict whose most picturesque and pathetic victim she became. The scales are held evenly, and through all the virtuosity of the final chapter the thud of the hammers erecting the scaffold is answered by the guns at Wattignies.

Upon that scaffold before the gardens which had been the gardens of her home and in which her child had played, the Executioner showed at deliberation and great length, this way and that on every side, the Queen's head to the people.

Marie Antoinette was the height of Belloc's achievement during these crowded years. The book has remained deservedly popular, and its climax was adapted, very successfully, for broadcasting by Mr. Val Gielgud. But neither this, nor any other of the books we have been discussing, exhausted his creative energies. He maintained a tireless correspondence with his friends, of which we

have only found the space to give short and relevant selections.
But he always had time to be trivial, and his triviality was
tremendous. This is how he announces his arrival in London to
Maurice Baring.

> Dear Maurice
> You write better than Horace,
> For you at your worst write madly
> Whereas *he* at *his worst* wrote badly
> But neither of us
> Writes as well as Theocritus.
> This is Sunday,
> I shall come up at noon tomorrow, Monday,
> And hope to see you at 12.35
> If you are alive.

And on two pages of note-paper sent to Evan Charteris we find
drawings on the following themes: death, coffins, tombstones,
hearses, devils; the House of Commons, the House of Lords; the
Boys of the Bull-dog breed; two Prime Ministers selling peerages
and two peers looking on at Lords; twenty-five very old Com-
moners going out for a walk; a baronet shooting a rocketing
pheasant; and some partridges winged by a marquis's second son.
Such was the largesse of this man, not yet forty years old, who
now, for the second time, asked the electors of South Salford to
return him to the House of Commons.

CHAPTER XIII

PARLIAMENT: 1910

I

AS we have seen, Belloc's independent action in Parliament had cost him some support in Salford. Already in January 1909 a group of local Liberals were writing to the Press, giving their reasons for opposing his candidature. Belloc replied to them; he could distinguish between constituents and cranks. He delighted his audience and dismayed his caucus by declaring:

At present my tongue is tied because I have to represent so many different interests; but if at the approaching election you restore me to freedom, you will hear from me things much more direct and moving than any that I can speak to you tonight.

But it was another matter to accept financial aid from people and then act in a way that was distasteful to them. The burden of Belloc's election expenses fell upon Goodwin and Wood; if, therefore, these two responsible citizens wished to support someone more securely attached to the Party line, he was prepared to withdraw.

This does not mean that I should necessarily disassociate myself from candidature for Parliament, even in South Salford. But it means that if another candidate were chosen and put forward as the official Liberal, I would not, in opposing him, regard myself as having been in any way given away by the local Liberal people of influence.[1]

[1] Letter to Charles Goodwin: Jan. 16, 1909.

Goodwin reassured him, but the difficulties remained.

The Election was fought on the House of Lords and Tariff Reform. Belloc's Conservative opponent was C. A. M. Barlow, a lecturer at the London School of Economics. He was a good man and Belloc sympathized with him for having to talk Tariff Reform in Lancashire. There were only three trades in Salford which would benefit from Protection and the chief of these was paper. Belloc thought, privately, that there was no good economic argument against protecting paper, but he swore to invent one— or perish in the attempt! If you artificially raised the price of paper, you would handicap anyone who wrapped up anything, and that meant most of the manufacturers. This was dangerous in principle, but it need produce no immediately disastrous effect. It was a very different matter from introducing Colonial preference on raw materials—especially cotton—which would damage the whole of British trade. Belloc estimated that Colonial preference would increase the working-man's budget by 1s. 6d. a week; 8d. on bread and meat, 10d. on the rest. It would be necessary to tax wool, wheat, butter, meat, bacon, eggs and cheese. If the Colonies (by which Belloc meant what we now call the Dominions) were struggling communities with a precarious grip on the needs of life, and if social conditions in England were what the radical reformer desired them to be, then the working-class might reasonably be asked to make this sacrifice. But, in fact, the Colonies had social conditions infinitely better than our own. Belloc thought that politicians

> made a great mistake in under-estimating the brains of the ordinary working-man; he has brains like everybody else, a little sharper than the business man because he has had more need for sharpness in his precarious life.[1]

Belloc issued a pamphlet advocating certain forms of Protection, and Barlow was quick to seize upon this. Belloc replied that Protection would not, in fact, be so limited, and that in existing circumstances it represented

[1] Letter to Maurice Baring: Dec. 4, 1909.

a danger greater than the danger of war with a first-class power. . . . A nation whose whole existence is based, as ours is, upon a vast import of raw and partly manufactured materials, is cutting its own throat when it interferes with that import.

He pointed to the example of Germany, a highly protected country, where the working-man paid 2s. 5d. on rent and food compared to 2s. in England. And Germany had been compelled to borrow sixty millions.

Belloc had seen too much of the House of Commons not to feel a certain fondness for the House of Lords. Here there had been a definite shift in his feelings since the 1906 election. But since the Lords had thrown out the Budget, they had challenged the whole democratic spirit in English politics, of which the Budget was the partial expression. 'It is not enough; it is not nearly enough; but it is a beginning.' The trouble with the wealthier classes was not that they were inhuman, avaricious or cruel. The trouble was that even the best of them did not understand the conditions that were asking for reform. Belloc declared that something was very soon going to be changed in the nature of England, and the first seed of this change was the Budget. Where was the working-man with a weekly wage who opposed it? What were they to think of Lords Rothschild and Rosebery who came down to the House of Lords and declared that, although they were lifelong Liberals they could not swallow it. 'Hang it all', exclaimed Belloc, 'if a man can't pay extra taxation with £100 a week, what are we coming to?' The only time when taxation of the rich could ultimately hurt the people was when the rich were seriously hampered by it. But the Budget would not make them go less often to the theatre, or drink less champagne, or lead less luxurious lives.

England is at a turning-point. Society is trembling with the desire to produce a new and a better England. But it cannot be done without raising great sums of money and without putting burdens on the rich. If it is going to be done at all, it is going to be done in the next few weeks. An old man said to me the other day, 'This is the first election I remember in which something is going to happen'. That is true. You are either going to push the great weight of social reform and democracy over the edge and send it down the other side, or you are going to allow it to slip back on yourselves and crush you.

This sort of peroration was naturally popular, but Belloc was on trickier ground when he came to defend his own record in Parliament. Here he distinguished between vital and less vital divisions. He had voted with the Labour Party on the Trades Dispute Bill in the interests of the working-classes and the Bill had passed the House of Lords. He had abstained from voting on the Third Reading of the Education Bill, because he knew the Lords would make the Government give way on the disputed points. When it came back amended, sixty-four out of sixty-seven Catholics in the House of Commons had voted for it. This was generally enough to satisfy the Catholics, but the Nonconformists remembered that Belloc had voted against the Licensing clauses in the Budget; and he had to meet a *fusillade* of questions about Ferrer, whom the Liberals had taken to their hearts. Others regretted his attitude to votes for women.

I am opposed to women voting as men vote. I call it immoral, because I think the bringing of one's women, one's mothers and sisters and wives into the political arena disturbs the relations between sexes.

Belloc thought that the election would be decided by the small Labour minority within the nation, and these would be swayed either by their general dislike of the Government or by their particular partiality for the Budget. He believed that London and all the counties, except East Anglia, would go Tory, and that the North, with the manufacturing towns in general, would remain attached to Free Trade. A visit to his constituency had convinced him of the unpopularity of Tariff Reform, and he thought that, on balance, the North might just save the Government. Nevertheless, he was extremely dubious about his own chances; he thought he would be defeated by a little over 900.

I really cannot see where my chance comes in. I bewilder so many people by not being 'party'; I directly offend so many more by refusing to have anything to do with teetotalism, vegetarianism, suffragism, Buddhism, and Scientific Monism, that whole belts of people who voted for me last time will vote against me this time. There is no corresponding gain. For the healthy people, who like my opinions in these regards, will nonetheless vote Conservative, saying to themselves, 'Though he *is* quite sound, with the Conservatives one is *absolutely* safe'. For instance, the publicans, who last time voted for me, will vote against me this time because they will say, 'Though he is sound on the liquor question, he is mixed up with people who are not, whereas the Conservative man is straightforwardly pledged not to touch my interests in any way'.[1]

Little as he had wanted to stand again, he still relished the prospect of a fight; but this was spoilt by illness. Very early in the campaign he lost his voice and was obliged to husband his resources, spending a few days with the Stanleys at Alderley. He sent the following appeal to Baring:

I stand here upon the platforms and shout and shout
And shout, shout and shout and shout and shout
Elodie and my eldest son come up onWednesday to see the fun
And on Thursday and Friday they will see all there is of it, will
    she and my eldest son.
You, if you have any sense, will come up on *Friday* and I will
    put you up at the hotel.
And on Saturday will be the Polling, the Huzzaing, the
    Brickbats, the Eggs, the Cheering and all Hell!
It is really worth seeing, come and see it. It moves the Soul.
Come and see an election for once in your life: *And help me
    count the Poll.*

This was irresistible; Baring came post-haste and rubbed his forehead with an emerald. On January 5 the doctor ordered Belloc to keep to his room, and it was not until the 8th that he was allowed to return to the fray.

Specialists made of gold did all manner of things to the very inmost of my being and hurt like the devil. The Election became

[1] Letter to Maurice Baring: Dec. 26, 1909.

a race. I had the safest seat of the six to begin with but I was so groggy in the shouting match that the odds crossed and then lengthened damnably . . . Moreover I could not think and force my throat at the same time, so that at the point three days before the Poll it was heavily against me. You know how I hesitated to stand again, but my backers forced me to, and I went on. I inhaled. I was painted and sprayed . . . I had two days, I made two speeches of loud power to thousands . . . It was as exciting as a Prize-fight—and I! who would not touch it with a barge pole, I had said![1]

There was no doubt of Belloc's personal popularity. He had advertised a single meeting at the Egerton schools in Tolton Street and this became three crowded demonstrations. A photograph shows him, in several different attitudes, addressing the workers at Platts and Mills. He wears a billycock hat with a curled-up brim, and an unbuttoned overcoat. He uses a folded umbrella to drive home his points. Beside him the Chairman, heavily bearded, sits impassive at a table draped with a thick and hideously patterned cloth. In front of him stand the rows of operatives. Such were the simple hustings and Belloc thought them a good deal more dignified than the House of Commons. At his last meeting at the Central Hall he addressed 4,000 people, and this was his message to them:

When I went back to a University I went back plunged through and through with this conception—that the first duty of a man who knows, who has travelled, who has read, who has met men, is to change the social condition of England so that the rich of England shall be made less rich and the poor shall be made less poor . . .

He admitted, a little sensitively perhaps, that 'pure accident has made me the friend of many in every rank', but he maintained that 'all those who have the right to call themselves democrats desire Englishmen to sit round one table and to be brothers'.

The excitement mounted during the last two days. By the 11th *The Times* political correspondent regarded Belloc's as the safer

[1] Letter to George Wyndham: Feb. 5, 1910.

of the two Salford seats, but the *Manchester Guardian*, obedient to the Party orders, would admit no comment on his meetings. Belloc and his wife drove around in an open carriage. Some threw mud at them and others cheered. Even the children of Salford proved the truth of Gilbert's famous tag. One little Tory of tender years ran after the carriage shouting, 'Tear him oop! Tear him oop!'; whereupon a lifelong Liberal of about the same age called out from a doorway, 'Ah'll stick thee in tha bahels!' These were politics and this was Lancashire. Polling day was January 15. While the count was being taken Belloc amused himself—and perhaps others—by ragging his opponent. Barlow, with his trim, dark moustaches, was a High Churchman, but not even this had prevented the Bishop of Manchester, Dr Knox, from sending him a telegram of good will. The result was declared on placards pasted on the upper windows of the Town Hall in Bexley Square; below, the crowd waited in a downpour and blew tin trumpets. When it was known that Belloc was just in by 314 votes, red lights were burned in a neighbouring street, and Irishwomen in the crowd mobbed and kissed him as he reached the Exchange Club with victory in his eyes and practically no voice.

Balfour had sent a telegram to Barlow, but Belloc had won without any official support. The Catholic vote was split. Out of 800 Catholic voters in the constituency, about 500 had voted for Belloc, 200 against, and 100 had abstained. He had lost all the Irish publican vote which had supported him in 1906. These people liked and trusted him personally, but they were nervous of the Nonconformist company he was compelled to keep. They felt safer with the Tories. Within four days of the election Belloc had received more than one hundred and fifty telegrams; and these showed that the people who claimed to be 'in the know', on both sides, believed that the seat would be won by a Protectionist candidate. When it was all over, Belloc escaped to the Continent. This is how he described his rest-cure to George Wyndham:

I went to Paris where I hobnobbed with soldiers and renewed my youth; sat for my bust with artists and renewed my vanity (not of beauty but of fame); ate clams and oysters with no collar on and renewed my gluttony; mixed with equals and renewed my pride; heard Mass in Notre Dame des Victoires and renewed my faith.[1]

At the 'Ecu de France' at Gisors he 'drank an amazing Burgundy and renewed my belly'; at the 'Ecu d'Or' at Beauvais he 'ragged the aged and *passés* anti-clericals and renewed my guts'; at the 'Univers' at Amiens he 'talked learnedly to Commercial Magnates and laid hands on my friends and blessed them and walked all over the roof of the Cathedral with a jolly old man who stank'. Having done all this, he came home in a French boat, visited his son at school (with the Ropers, then at Bournemouth), returned to King's Land and slept for ten hours on end.

2

The results of the General Election satisfied none of the three English Parties. The Liberals had lost one hundred seats, and their 1906 dream of a more or less permanent majority was abruptly shattered. In Manchester and Salford there had been one Liberal retirement in favour of the Labour candidate, and one Conservative gain from Labour. But in the country, as a whole, the Conservatives, though they had recovered a good deal, had not recovered enough. The Labour representation was reduced from fifty-three to forty-one. Only the Irish Nationalists were happy, since they were once more in a position to insist that the veto of the Lords—which appeared to be the sole remaining obstacle to Home Rule—should be removed. For the Liberals could now only govern with the Irish support.

Lloyd George remained at the Exchequer, and his first task was to get the Budget passed by both Houses. But here the Irish intervened. They disliked the new duties on whisky and would only vote for the Budget if the Government laid down their policy for dealing with the House of Lords. This was embodied in three 'resolutions'. The Lords' veto on Bills certified by the Speaker as money Bills was to be abolished; other Bills were to

[1] Feb. 5, 1910.

become law, in spite of the House of Lords, if they had been passed by the House of Commons in three successive sessions; and the duration of Parliament was to be reduced from seven years to five. These 'resolutions' were adopted, and the Budget was passed rapidly through both Houses. Belloc took little serious or constructive part in these debates, merely making a number of short, waggish speeches exposing the hypocrisy of politicians. These were unlikely to have endeared him to either side of the House. Elizabeth Haldane described his speech on the King's Address as 'full of wit, but irresponsible'[1] and the *Evening Chronicle* came out with a cartoon of Asquith, dressed as a huntsman, driving his hounds into the kennel for an important division. Underneath was the caption: 'Mr. Asquith's previous experience with Mr. Belloc suggests a little difficulty'.

He was, however, extremely active behind the scenes. He, with 'Loulou' Harcourt and the small Radical group who felt as he did, regarded the 'resolutions' as a blind, forced on the Cabinet by the Prime Minister and Haldane. He thought they would be voted on in the Commons, rejected by the Lords (who had already put up their own proposals for reform) and that a new election would be forced on the country in June. He believed that Asquith and Balfour, who were known to be personally on the best of terms, were already in collusion on this point. So he wrote a letter to *The Times*[2] to the effect that 'Curfew should not ring tonight', and further explained his views in an article for the *Saturday Review*[3]. Belloc believed that any shelving of the problem of the House of Lords and any appeal to the country without electoral reform would be fatal to the Party. By electoral reform he meant a wider suffrage, a shorter residence qualification, and an alternative vote. He was irritated that one or two Whigs in a Cabinet of Radicals could frustrate the wishes of a democratic majority of 124. That was why he had written to *The Times* and started the ball rolling. These private interventions caused the Conservatives to fume and the Liberals to frown. But since the Party had not supported him at the recent election he felt free to

[1] *From One Century to Another* (1937).
[2] Feb. 1910.   [3] Feb. 19, 1910.

say what he pleased. He was worried, however, by the prospect
of appealing to Goodwin and Wood for further help if an election
should be forced on the country in the summer. If he and his
fellow-independents got their way, they would be all the stronger
for having acted independently. But if Asquith's policy prevailed
and the Party put up an official candidate against him—'whether
he calls himself Woman's Suffragist, or Vegetarian, or Devil
Worshipper'—Belloc warned Goodwin that it would be foolish
for him and Wood to involve themselves in heavy expense over
what was certain to be a losing fight. Nevertheless, it was quite
on the cards that the Radical group would get their way. They
had helped the Irish to push the House of Lords question to the
front, and Belloc could boast that their success had been 'closely
connected with my own action in the beginning of the Parliament', and it was important 'to connect both those facts with the
fact that the strongest people inside the Cabinet warmly approved
of the Radical action so taken'.[1]

These calculations were upset by the death of King Edward VII
in May. Belloc attended the funeral which he thought

> a most impressive sight marred by not a few bits of detestable
> music-hall business the worst of which was the King's dog.
> The Queen Mother went on just as though she was on the
> stage, which was very unpleasant to see. Of the Kings not many
> could ride, but the young King of Portugal could.[2]

Parliament stood adjourned until the autumn, while four leading
members from each Party met in private conference to settle, if
they could, the problem of the House of Lords. Lloyd George even
proposed the formation of a 'national Government' to contain
the leaders of both Parties and settle the Home Rule question as
well. This scheme broke down over Lord Lansdowne's insistence
that Home Rule should be excluded from the Liberal scheme
already outlined in the 'resolutions' and shortly to be embodied
in the Parliament Act. Lansdowne wanted any 'constitutional'
measure rejected by the Lords to be submitted to a referendum;

[1] Letter to Charles Goodwin: April 6, 1910.
[2] Letter to J. S. Phillimore: May 22, 1910.

but a referendum was a far more revolutionary proposal than any put forward as yet for the reform of the Upper Chamber.

Belloc, of course, had no part in these discussions. They were secret and no formal account of them had ever been published. But they smacked of the collusion which he hated. He blamed the new King for the very sensible course of persuading the Party leaders into conference, and he thought that the Liberals would be wheedled by Balfour's charm into making concessions which would wreck them with their rank and file. Meanwhile he asked inconvenient questions in the House about what firms had the opium monopoly from India, and helped Maurice Baring run the *North Street Gazette*. Only one number of this remarkable periodical ever appeared. It was edited, printed, and mainly written in the west wing of 6 Lord North Street. It described itself as 'a journal written for the rich by the poor', but since Baring had been able to afford a new printing press the statement was not to be taken quite literally. Belloc gave it his intermittent attention and escaped to France after the King's funeral to study the battlefield of Valmy.

Let me ask you [he writes to Wyndham] whether you have ever pleased yourself with that garden of pleasure called Military History.

By God! I know of nothing like it! Not only does the writing—or better, the study—of it put one into communion with well accomplished things, peril, the seasons, and the fate of what one loves, but also the science itself is more absorbing than cooking, or the laying on of colours.

Valmy has latterly been my duty for £10—but I have threshed £23 out of it. I found a Squire from Norfolk holding Les Islettes in the rear of Dumouriez, two German regiments breaking on the *French* side in the worst of the cannonade: and (what surely would please *you*) a groping of cavalry towards each other in the early morning before the positions were occupied, of which Massenbach (writing of the Prussian side) says—'In another half hour we should have been caught in the flank and the whole force enfiladed—upon what a *thread of silk*

hang the fates of a people!' Dumouriez making a record
march with a rout taken (in the French Manner) as a matter of
course: Dillon—le Beau Dillon (differing therein from the
modern) ordered to march right across the Prussian flank and
calling it mad (which it was) but escaping untouched. Poor
young Ligne killed at Croix aux Bois so charmingly, with an
unfinished letter in his pocket: the Volunteers racing like sheep
from Verdun but carrying dead Beaurepaire with them and
burying (him) in a solemn manner because he chose to die
rather than witness *their* surrender. . . .

There is in this a countryside. One sees the Argonne and the
dusty waste of Champagne—Pouilleuse beyond and above
them the skies, full of leaden and persistent rain, the Providence
and the Genius of Europe. All moulds in together when one
reads right or makes a battle-history and it is the only true
history in the world: men are then so alive![1]

More than thirty years later, in the middle of the Second World
War, General Bedell Smith, Chief-of-Staff to General Eisen-
hower, asked for a copy of Belloc's *Six British Battles*. 'That is the
man I want to read,' he said, 'he has studied the thing on the
spot.'

Soon after his return Belloc was off again to Berlin which he
found as vulgarly vicious as he expected. He grotesquely under-
valued the German organization, science and skill; bias had blinded
him. He knew the Germans made the only good and cheap
gramophone records and were to the front in the manufacture of
aniline dyes and certain forms of metallurgy. He also suspected they
had bad teeth. But he did not look any deeper than that, and was
more interested in trying to grow aubergines in the Sussex weald.

Have you seen this spring? I hope you have! At last—at
long last—there is a chance for *Aubergines*. All things grow in
clay and if Aubergines shall at last flourish in England I shall
have achieved a little conquest of my own. Less than Agricola,
and not so noisy as William of Falaise: but Aubergines are
Aubergines and if the vine was made to grow by force and

[1] May 29, 1910.

authority on the Garonne, why not the Aubergine upon the Adur?[1]

In August he spent three days in Burgundy, walking with George Wyndham.

> Personally I shall travel as light as possible [Belloc wrote to him]. All the best journeys I have taken have been taken like an animal who travels with nothing but his fur. This time I shall take a little bag with two soft shirts in it, four collars and two changes of sock, the whole thing weighing perhaps five pounds and being fourteen inches long by nine.[2]

They travelled third-class, visiting Beaune and Chambertin, Avallon and Vézelay, and ending up at Auxerre. On the way back Belloc called at La Celle St. Cloud, where he found his mother and his nephew sitting in the midst of the wilderness which had been his home. He then saw the French Torpedo Station at Dunkirk and was shown the inside of the boats; but he was not allowed to go inside a submarine.

The first part of September was spent building a stable at King's Land, with brick walls, hard blue-brick floor, two stalls and a loose box. The total cost of this was less than eighteen months' rental of the stable he had hired hitherto. On the 10th he set out with Kershaw to follow the French manœuvres in Picardy. Eighty thousand soldiers were engaged in these, and it renewed his youth 'to hear the French infantry cursing their officers and prophesying immediate disasters'. Aeroplanes were used; the main problem was whether they could be hit by rifle fire when they were flying at a height to do effective scouting. If they could not be so hit, the whole art of war—Belloc believed—would be 'immediately and fundamentally changed'.[3]

He sent his impressions of the manœuvres to Wyndham.

> What a day! Slept in straw till 5. Up in my boots, walked 12 miles, found by following the fire of the 74th, the 39th and a group of artillery. Left the guns. Marched with the 39th.

[1] Letter to George Wyndham: May 29, 1910.
[2] Aug. 23, 1910.   [3] Letter to Maurice Baring: Sept. 8, 1910.

Passed a ravine, saw them capture Feuquière . . . a captain stuck a barricade at the last moment across the entry to the village, but no use! Village taken. Then they went on without stopping, curling round the other Army corps and taking anything. Great rolls of men over a plateau with high *islands* of beech woods. The men were amazing! Good humour and jollity for 13 hours of marching, rushing, hiding and firing. At 6 p.m. 3 aeroplanes, one after another (for the first time in the history of arms!) shot out of the North East, came up like huge dragon flies, flew above the victors, spotting their last dispositions before night, and then sped homewards, buzzing. What a day! Such days—rarer as life proceeds—do not console me but make me forget the warning uncertainty of my life and the 'strong blows but on the void and work without reward.' For such days healthy souls were made. What a day! I thought I would scribble and tell you so at the end of it. Waves of men over a high rolling plateau . . . great art (by Meunier) in the management of three divisions and 120 guns, all the picture of war. The subtlest infantry, the most *maniable* in the world.[1]

Meanwhile a German officer was arrested sketching the dismantled fortifications at Portsdown. Belloc had done his best, in the teeth of the 'Blue Water' school, to see that Portsmouth was fortified on the land side; but nothing could persuade the War Office to reverse their policy.

Belloc had now passed his fortieth birthday and the future filled him with alarm. The break with the *Morning Post* (as we have seen) was a severe blow. He tried to get a similar job with the *Observer* or the *Saturday Review*, but without success. In the course of about fifteen months his articles for the *Morning Post* had brought him in three hundred pounds, and when they were published in book form he could add another two hundred pounds to this. The world at large might imagine that he had a great literary position, but this reputation did not reflect any financial security. He was therefore thrust back upon lecturing, and for the growing fatigue of this there were only rare compensations:

[1] Sept. 12, 1910.

the feather beds in the New Inn at Gloucester, and the company of
Bishop Hedley at Cardiff. A new volume of essays, *On Something*,
came out in October (1910) containing the very beautiful
Portrait of a Child. This was full of a mature and slightly melancholy wisdom, and one is surprised that it should have given
Elodie 'the hump'. Lady Ottoline Morrell, whose literary taste
was infallible, greatly admired the essay; Belloc had it separately
printed and gave her a signed copy during the war. *Pongo and the
Bull* had appeared in the same month and *Verses* was published
by Duckworth in December. This contained most of the poems in
Verses and Sonnets (1896)—now long out of print—and several
new ones which had since appeared in various periodicals, or in
The Path to Rome. They defined Belloc's personality, without
perhaps greatly adding to his stature. His new poems were for the
most part merry or satirical—Sussex rhapsodies and drinking-
songs—but one of them at least revealed the lyric gift which
placed him, at moments, among the masters of English verse.
It must be quoted in full.

> *Song Inviting the Influence of a Young Lady*
> *Upon the Opening Year*
>
> You wear the morning like your dress
> And are with mastery crowned;
> When as you walk your loveliness
> Goes shining all around.
> Upon your secret, smiling way
> Such new contents were found,
> The Dancing Loves made holiday
> On that delighted ground.
>
> Then summon April forth, and send
> Commandment through the flowers;
> About our woods your grace extend
> A queen of careless hours.
> For oh, not Vera veiled in rain,
> Nor Dian's sacred Ring,
> With all her royal nymphs in train,
> Could so lead on the Spring.

Among the new additions was *The Prophet Lost in the Hills at Evening*, where Belloc evokes his experience with Kershaw in the Pyrenees. The last quatrain is as good an epitaph as any that is likely to be written on him.

> I challenged and I kept the Faith,
>   The bleeding path alone I trod;
> It darkens. Stand about my wraith,
>   And harbour me, almighty God.

3

In November Belloc visited Ireland, staying with Sir Bertram and Lady Windle in Waterford. He saw and admired the new technical school, which seemed to compare favourably with the same kind of institution in Lancashire, and he spoke to the very young at the Ursuline convent. It was a revelation to revisit Ireland after ten years and to see the effect of Wyndham's Land Act (1902). He had always regarded this as the one historic and creative piece of legislation passed by a British Government for the benefit of Ireland, and he wrote to Wyndham to tell him so. Many people go to Ireland because they find in it the haunting traces of an older world; for Belloc it carried all the promise of a new. He even thought the railway tracks better laid than in England, and he looked forward, with superb optimism, to the day when express trains would rush along them at record speed. He debated at Trinity with the Bishop of Down and Connor, of whose intelligence he formed a poor opinion, and he compared Trinity with a second-class Oxford college. Worcester was rather unkindly singled out to illustrate this comparison.

He felt in Ireland what he had recently felt in France—the salutary pressure of reality. He was now resolved to have done with the Party game, if not with politics, for ever. A new and, as many felt, an unnecessary election was clearly looming, and he wrote to his caucus to tell them that he would only stand again as an Independent and that he would rather not stand at all.

I can't believe the Grocers and Pawnbrokers who control the caucus in Salford will stand a candidate pledged to ridicule and criticize the Party System, and if they won't have me independent they shan't have me at all: if they *will* have me they will be idiots, for I shall be defeated and they will have paid for nothing.[1]

The caucus, as he expected, would not accept these terms, but there were some, outside Salford, who regretted his decision. A Socialist, A. C. Tait, wrote to him asking him to contest the seat.

. . . your courage, your outspoken desire for straight politics and your advocacy of the democratic ideal have not gone unregarded in this land.[2]

Belloc replied to him as follows:

Without a second ballot, without proportional representation, nothing but a very great expenditure or some particular hold upon the locality can give a man a chance against the two official candidates. Had I fought South Salford an official Liberal would have been put against me, and the sum of £600 to £1,000 would have been put at his disposal, and a sum of £600 would have been necessary on my side. The official Liberal would have received anywhere from 1,000 to 2,000 votes, proceeding from convention, tradition, Nonconformist opposition to a Catholic and so forth. My quarrel would not have been that the Conservative would have got in, for it does not matter in this election who gets in, but that £600 on my side would simply have been thrown away. Moreover one must be inside the House to see how utterly futile is any attempt at representative action. It is all very well as advertisement, but it is without any practical consequence whatever, and it is like trying to feed on air to attempt to satisfy the appetite for action under such conditions. I agree with you that realities may enter politics soon, and when they do, I shall re-enter politics with them . . . You are right in your surmise that I am a Democrat.[3]

[1] Letter to George Wyndham: Nov. 14, 1910.
[2] Nov. 20, 1910.   [3] Nov. 28, 1910.

Parliament was dissolved in the last week of November; never before had two General Elections been held in the same year. Asquith had promised to obtain from the King certain guarantees that, if the Liberals were returned to power a second time, the will of the Commons should prevail over the House of Lords. Neither Belloc, nor anyone else, knew what these guarantees were, nor whether they had in fact been obtained. He would have been surprised to learn that the King had consented to create such new peers as were necessary to give effect to the will of the Commons in the Upper Chamber. He spoke in the concluding debate to a rather empty House. It was the longest and the most important of the speeches he made in the House of Commons, and it held the core of his attack on the Party System. He believed that the Election was being forced on the country to save that system; the question was whether it was worth saving. His visit to Ireland, with its reminders of political reality, was still fresh in his mind, and he chastised the Government for its failure to tackle a problem which no educated person any longer believed to be incapable of settlement. He ended as follows:

You cannot prevent the resurrection of Ireland; the truth is that the nation is springing again to life, no thanks unfortunately to the English statesmen who might have left so great a record if they had chosen the right path. Even their internal quarrels are a proof of vitality which we unfortunately lack. Nothing, not even the vacuous and inept conception which the Party system still imposes on us can prevent this development. I must close by a remark, in which I do not wish to reflect on any of my colleagues. I believe there are to be found among them, even perhaps among the comparatively few who are listening at this moment, a certain number who, whether from circumscription of their personal experience or family tradition, or from great attachment to some one part of the supposed Party programme, still attach a certain reality to the words 'Government' and 'Opposition', 'Liberal' and 'Federation-Unionist'. It may be that there are such men. I always act in conversation with my colleagues on the supposition that there may yet linger somewhere in their minds some small remnant of the old true Party feeling. I have never found it yet, but if anyone listening to me still has that feeling, and does feel, in the really extraordinary words of one of the recent acquisitions to the Party system that there was an 'unbridgeable gulf' between himself and the opposing 'Party', let him not be offended when I say I do not see how, in this coming Election, any man not of a definite section such as is represented by the Socialist Labour Party, or such as is represented by two sections of the Irish Party—I do not see how any other type of my colleagues can put himself forward under any general Party programme whatsoever. For my part I shall be quite unable to meet my constituents unless local opinion is so indicated and local machinery is so controlled that I may come forward in complete independence of the system which I now fully understand and which I now clearly believe to be both unreal and dangerous to the country. I do not see how anyone can stand in an English constituency today and say: 'If you return me I will vote in favour of this or that set of men, self-appointed, who are going to bring forward some programme I know not what.' If it were possible, which it is not, to fight against this, we might in the new Parliament have achieved something for the country. For myself, I repeat my own intentions as a declaration of faith, that I shall not be at pains to play the Party game. I shall not go to my constituency and talk about the wicked leader of the Opposition and the good Prime Minister—angels here and demons there. I do not act like that, and I do not believe my constituents think like that. If the machine will not let me stand as an Independent to represent my constituency and to do what my constituents want done in this House, then I think everyone will agree with me that even the most modest pen in the humblest newspaper is as good as a vote in what has ceased to be a free deliberative assembly.

Such was Belloc's farewell to Parliament, and in a speech at Worthing he put the matter less politely. 'Perhaps', he exclaimed, 'they did not bribe me heavily enough, but in any case

I am relieved to be quit of the dirtiest company it has ever been my misfortune to keep.' Many of his warmest admirers were also relieved; they had long agreed with the journalist in *Black and White* that there was surely no need for him 'to waste his fine talents in the arid atmosphere of the House of Commons'. But it was not in the nature of this Republican ever to say farewell to politics. The fight went on.

CHAPTER XIV

THE PUBLIC THING: 1911–1913

I

TO anyone who asked him why he had refused to stay in Parliament Belloc would have given the answer that he gave to Baring.

I left, Maurice, because it was up to me (A) to make a definite sacrifice of honour for a particular end or (B) to refuse it and work for the same end more round about. It is an *invariable* rule in human life to do (A).[1]

And if he were asked how he had left, he would boast that he had gone 'blowing a huge trumpet and banging the door behind me'.[2] But since there were not more than twenty or thirty members present to hear the blast and the bang, he had to contrive other methods to make himself heard. *The Party System* was already in preparation with Cecil Chesterton before Parliament was dissolved, and it was finished before the end of the year. It appeared in February 1911, less than two months after the election had taken place.

There were probably only two men who had any influence over Belloc after he had reached maturity. One of these was Father Vincent McNabb; the other was Cecil Chesterton. It is possible that he overrated Cecil Chesterton. Cecil was not a deeply educated man. A brilliant debater and a superb stylist, resolute in action and intrepid in controversy, he was too thoroughly a journalist in the literal sense of feeling and thinking from day to day to give at all times a balanced judgment on the complicated problems of an ancient and a subtle society. He had immense virtues of which

---

[1] Undated.　　　　　　　[2] *Ibid.*

the chief were loyalty, candour and courage; these endeared him to Belloc as they had endeared him to his brother, Gilbert. He was a man of action in a way that Gilbert was not. Following the history of the two brothers up to 1910, one would imagine that Gilbert would have become a Catholic before Cecil. There seemed nothing to stop him. But joining the Catholic Church is an act, not a reflection or a tendency. It is a conclusion (as it is also a beginning) but it is not, principally, a conclusion of the mind. It is principally a conclusion of the will. And where acts of the will were required—acts requiring decision and energy—Cecil was the more prompt to take them. In fact he became a Catholic in 1913, quite suddenly and decisively, in the middle of the Marconi crisis. His widow suggests that Elodie Belloc had a good deal to do with his conversion.[1]

Now Belloc was before everything a man of action, a man of physical action, a man active to the point of restlessness; and it was among men of action that he found the majority of his friends. He was closer to Cecil than he was ever to come to Gilbert. Like Gilbert, he was happily married, and he had a family—which Gilbert, to his sorrow, had not. But whereas Gilbert would remain happily at Beaconsfield, dictating in his study for days on end, and craving no other society but his wife's, Belloc had an itching desire for companionship. This desire Cecil, who was then un-married, was able to satisfy. Gilbert was a contemplative in his fantasies before he became a contemplative in his faith. But Cecil was a pure extrovert, never happier than on the hustings. Where Gilbert hated to wound, Cecil fought to kill. Here Belloc, who never ceased to proclaim that the truth was hard and necessarily hurt, was naturally at his side.

There was a wide, though not an absolute, agreement between the two men. Cecil had been an official Fabian, where Belloc had merely appeared on Fabian platforms. Paradoxically, Cecil was always attracted by Tory democracy, and if the Conservative Party had been faithful to these principles, he might have belonged to it. He had never, like Gilbert, been associated with the *Speaker* group of Liberals, and he used to say that Gilbert was a Tory

[1] *The Chestertons* (1941).

without knowing it. It is, indeed, a chronic *malaise* of English politics that the Tories who do not know it are so often better than the Tories who do. And there was a further reason which attracted Belloc to Cecil; he thought him a far better writer than his brother. He did not, it is true, read many of Gilbert's books; but he could not help reading his articles, and these often wearied him by their verbalism and paradox. Where prose was in question, Belloc was always looking for a Swift, and here the clean, incisive style of Cecil was immensely to his taste. Gilbert was temperamentally a Franciscan, generous even when he was forced to take up arms. By contrast, St. Dominic was Belloc's favourite among medieval saints; he called him 'that hefty Spaniard' and visited his tomb in Bologna whenever he got the chance.

The friendship of Cecil Chesterton cost Belloc several years of embittering controversy. Such controversy, with its technique of direct personal attack, is dangerous for the soul. It is one thing to kill a man, anonymously, in battle for what you believe to be a just cause. Such action is violent, but it is not personal. If you dislike Mr. Lloyd George or Sir Alfred Mond as much as Belloc disliked them, it is much better not to think about them too much. But Belloc thought about them incessantly. This is what his admirers mean when they say that Cecil Chesterton was bad for him. They are thinking of another *Danton* or *Marie Antoinette*, a better *History of England*, that he might have written if he had been content to sit quietly at King's Land. But the answer is that, with or without Cecil Chesterton, he would never have sat quietly at King's Land. To sit quietly anywhere, he would have had to be a quite different sort of man.

The Party System contains a good example of how controversy can hurt the character. C. F. G. Masterman had entered Parliament in 1906, as a Liberal of independent views, and had for two years freely criticized the Ministry under which he served. He then accepted office and was silent. On March 13, 1908, he voted for the Right to Work Bill introduced by the Labour Party; and on April 20, 1909, he voted, as a Member of the Government, against the Bill he had previously supported. Belloc and Cecil Chesterton

knew Masterman well, and Masterman had taken every opportunity of praising Belloc's work in print. But the authors of *The
Party System* never forgave his change of face. They attacked him
in the book and set on their followers to secure his defeat in two
by-elections. No one with any sense of Ministerial responsibility
and the discipline of silence which it must always impose, can
help feeling that their persecution was quite disproportionate.
Gilbert Chesterton took a more comprehending and charitable
view. As a matter of fact, the paragraph in *The Party System*
which so wounded Masterman was written by Cecil; but Belloc
was too loyal ever to disown it. 'I would have written it differently,' he said many years afterwards, 'because I know the
world. Cecil didn't.'

We have said, at the conclusion of the last chapter, that Belloc
was a Republican; and we have suggested elsewhere what this
meant. It meant that he cared for the Public Thing, and cared
that it should, in fact, be public. What goaded him beyond
intellectual discretion was the conviction that England was
governed in secret. We must not underestimate, even where we
dispute, the intensity and the sincerity of this feeling. At the
height of the Edwardian complacency, and suffocated by the
illusions of a society too prosperous and padded, he perceived
the peril of decline. On May 29, 1910, he had written to George
Wyndham:

> The destiny of a people seems to shine backwards and
> forwards at any moment: as one reads—knowing what is to
> come—one sees also that those contemporaries whom one most
> trusts also perceived it. When the old King died and was buried
> it seemed as if the crowd perceived the extreme peril and
> doubtful chances of the future . . . At any one of these pageants
> men go about saying that something has ended for many
> because one man has died. *That* is not true: but it is true that in
> fifteen years things have changed appallingly.
>
> Those who care most for things most easily understandable
> note that the wealth of the nation is failing in contrast to its
> rivals. Those who care most for the things least evident have most

hope but they base that hope upon very distant and intangible things: that a province of Europe does not perish: that one ounce of good seed outlasts centuries: that neglected virtues survive when proud and evident vices have met their due catastrophe. The nation will live, but the road by which it has chosen to continue its life will not continue.

Those who care for such games may try to determine which sections of *The Party System* were written by Cecil Chesterton and which by Belloc. The opening is clearly by Chesterton, and then, as the book proceeds, we have the impression that Belloc takes over. Yet there is no disunity; two pens are writing as one.

> Cecil Chesterton wrote one half and I wrote the other, just as the Hail Mary was written half by the Church and half by St. Gabriel—a personal and individual author . . . Dual authorship is seldom a success, but the Hail Mary pulled it off all right.[1]

The thesis of the book is as follows: that England is not, in fact, governed by one Party, or alliance of Parties, having a majority in Parliament, but by a series of understandings between the two Front Benches, ensuring that, turn and turn about, they may enjoy the fruits of office; and secondly, that the Party in power, instead of being able to ensure that the Cabinet carried out the policy for which it had been elected, had in fact no influence on policy at all. The Members of Parliament represented, or were expected to represent, no one but the Party chiefs who had proposed them to their constituencies. This was a mockery of the democratic process. You could only have pure democracy when the village elders sat round the village tree and decided the affairs of the village. In larger communities the village had to be represented. Belloc and Cecil Chesterton contended that in England it was not represented at all.

The book opened with a note on the recent election, and its initial criticism is a little blunted for us (in the light of our subsequent knowledge) by the fact that Asquith did not feel that he could ask the King to implement the guarantees to create a host of

---

[1] Letter to George Wyndham: Dec. 27, 1910.

new peers unless he had an irrefutable mandate from the country. It might be argued that since the Lords had thrown out the Budget, and the Budget had been confirmed by the electors, the Government (though returned with a much reduced majority) had a clear mandate to remove whatever obstacle prevented the Budget from passing into law. The most responsible Liberal paper, the *Manchester Guardian*, had proclaimed this to be the main issue. Asquith may be criticized on two grounds: firstly, that he had no right to ask the King to take a certain action in a hypothetical contingency—this point has been lucidly examined by Sir Harold Nicolson in his life of *King George V*; and secondly, that he quite needlessly put the country to the expense and bother of an election, when it had clearly approved what he wanted to do. But it was grotesque to pretend that he was acting in collusion with the Conservative Party in seeking a mandate, which would, he knew, in one way or another, clip the Conservative majority in the Lords. If ever a politician concealed his motives from his opponents, it was Asquith in 1910; although he also concealed them from his supporters. It was one thing to complain—if you thought it matter for complaint—that the two Front Benches were on speaking and drinking terms with one another. It was quite another thing to pretend that any political Party acquiesces beforehand in the loss of an election because 'it is Buggins's turn next', or because Buggins is its brother-in-law.

Belloc and Chesterton were obsessed by the fact that the two opposing hierarchies in the House of Commons were in some measure interrelated. This undoubtedly favoured a certain degree of collusion; but the collusion was largely unconscious and it was surely preferable to a chronic and paralysing conflict. Belloc and Chesterton seemed to think it an exceptional enormity that Liberals and Conservatives should dine in each each other's houses. They put it wittily:

We are not surprised at Romeo loving Juliet, though he is a Montague and she a Capulet. But if we found in addition that Lady Capulet was by birth a Montague, that Lady Montague was the first cousin of old Capulet, that Mercutio was at once the nephew of a Capulet and the brother-in-law of a Montague, that Count Paris was related on his father's side to one house and on his mother's side to the other, that Tybalt was Romeo's uncle's stepson, and that the Friar who married Romeo and Juliet was Juliet's uncle and Romeo's first cousin once removed, we should probably conclude that the feud between the two houses was being kept up mainly for the dramatic entertainment of the people of Verona.

In a letter to Baring, Belloc had translated this into Parliamentary terms.

On Thursday is the big Division which will wind up the Session I suppose: the Division which will give the Resolution of the Commons defying their brothers-in-law, stepfathers and aunts' lovers in the Lords. Thus Geoffrey Howard will defy Lord Carlisle while the more dutiful Morpeth will acquiesce in his father's power. Kerry will similarly support the privilege of Lansdowne but Fitzmaurice (oddly enough) will be of an adverse opinion. Alfred Lyttelton will think the power of the Peers reasonable; not his sister's husband, Masterman, who will, however, be supported by his wife's first cousin, Gladstone; while the Prime Minister will not find his brother-in-law, Mr. Tennant, fail him, nor need he doubt Mr. McKenna, since he had married the daughter of the Tennants' chief friend. Oddly enough, however, while Pamela Tennant's husband will support the Government, her brother Mr. George Wyndham will not find it possible to agree with them. His stepson, the Duke of Westminster, has privileges not to be despised, and it is curious that that young gentleman's wife's step-nephew, Mr. Winston Churchill, should be found in the Liberal ranks. However, it is some compensation to this member that his aunt is the mother-in-law of the Tariff Reform League in the person of Lord Ridley, called by the vulgar Fat Mat.[1]

The second thesis of *The Party System* was more tenable: that the rank and file of M.P.s had no means of enforcing the wishes

[1] Nov. 29, 1909.

of their constituents on the Executive. If the Liberal victory of 1906 meant anything, it meant that the Chinese labourers imported into South Africa should leave at once. But they had not left. The South African mine-owners—Belloc was careful to point out that most of them were Jews—had obtained permission for the Chinese to work out their contracts; by which time the wages expected by the Kaffirs would be sufficiently depreciated. This was only one case of the people's will, and the Party's will, being frustrated by secret bargaining. Let us be clear; Belloc's objection was the pure democratic objection, and the debatable question (which Belloc and Chesterton did not debate) is how far this kind of democratic purism is possible when you are guiding the policies of a Great Power. It is obviously impracticable and undesirable that every Member of Parliament should know everything that is going on behind the scenes. A Party may come into office with a specific programme and then discover, in the light of government, that portions of it would be impolitic or impossible to carry out. A government must be guided by its conscience, as well as by its nostrums; and its conscience is its sense of the common weal. There may be occasions when it is more important to secure the assent of its opponents than its supporters, or the people whom its supporters represent. To say this is not to say there was no excuse for Belloc's frustrations; it is only to say that a considerable measure of secrecy is essential for effective government, and that if the Executive is to be continually at the mercy of the Legislature, the result may be purer democracy, but it will also be pandemonium and paralysis. Belloc even went so far as to appeal to the French example in this matter, little as he liked it. The shorter Parliaments and continually shifting Executives seemed to him preferable to the English stability.

The authors of *The Party System* were oddly at fault in not seeing who was really the architect of the Party machine, as they had seen it developing and as it has continued to develop to this day. The architect was not Asquith or Balfour; it was Parnell. The political genius, the superb Parliamentary generalship, the cold dominating personality of Parnell had imposed on his followers a discipline which the English leaders were compelled to imitate. *The Party System* was the protest of a back-bencher, and the day of the back-bencher was already passing. Every one of Belloc's complaints—the wearisome Parliamentary procedure, the severe rationing of private members' time, the stifling of personal initiative—all these might be echoed by any M.P. who has sat through the post-war Parliaments and whose independence of mind has excluded him from the inner circle of government. In a world dominated by large concentrations of power, the individual counts for less and less—unless he happens to possess political genius of a high order. A Roosevelt, an Adenauer, a Churchill—men of this stamp can still be thrown up by the more or less representative democracies of the western world. But Belloc did not possess political genius of this kind. An understanding of other people's minds and motives; the capacity to compromise and wait; the sense of the feasible; an occasional ruthlessness—these are not among the highest virtues, just as politics is not among the highest arts. But it is an art, none the less, and exacts its separate skill. Belloc entered politics at a bad moment, though to him and the other enthusiastic Radicals of 1906 it seemed radiant with hope. He had reason to complain of the corruption he saw around him, and his experience of Europe made him more alive than most to the envy of Continental powers. Nor did he expect politicians to be perfect; he merely thought the Parliamentary system had decayed too far for him to be able to work inside it any longer. The only hope of acceptable reform had been sketched out in a small pamphlet by William Jowett, the Labour Member for West Bradford. This suggested the abolition of the Ministry with its collective responsibility, and the substitution of a number of Departmental Committees of the House. All Parties would be represented on these, and the permanent officials would be responsible to them. The Minister would be retained as chairman of the Committee, where he might be outvoted by his colleagues, and the decision of the Committee might be reversed by the House of Commons. In neither event need he resign, and in neither would a dissolution be imperative. Belloc warmly approved of these proposals, but he thought they should be accompanied by a provision fixing the duration of

x

Parliament and withholding from the Front Bench the right to force a dissolution. It need hardly be said that Jowett's proposals never stood the slightest chance of consideration, still less of acceptance.

In some ways Parliament declined, or at least developed, in the direction that Belloc foresaw. In other ways it recovered. As the Socialists replaced the Liberals, it became impossible to maintain that the Government had intermarried with the Opposition. The sale of honours, which was to reach the proportions of a scandal under Lloyd George, was reduced if it was not abolished altogether. There was a recurrent tendency, hastened by the crisis of war or bankruptcy, towards the coalition which Belloc had predicted as the logical outcome of the 'conference' of 1910. But at no time did the common voter manifest the least desire for a change in the system of British representative democracy. A New Party was founded—and foundered. A few cranks, here and there, talked about increasing the power of the Crown. The British Union of Fascists knocked a few people on the head and smashed a few windows in Whitechapel; and an occasional educated voice was heard belauding the virtues of the Corporative State, or advocating the Communist Revolution. Steadily, complacently, absurdly if you like, the common voter determined to maintain the House of Commons. His reasons might have seemed flimsy enough against Belloc's unswerving logic; but if the two had ever engaged in open debate, the vague spokesman for political England might have remarked that his opponent, for all his brilliance and his patriotism, still spoke with a foreign accent. The accent grew more and more foreign as the years wore on, and the champion of democratic liberties in 1910 became the champion of whoever, in any corner of Europe, decreed or threatened the death of Parliamentary institutions.

2

The Party System made a considerable stir and it was followed by the launching of a new independent weekly, *The Eye-Witness,* of which Belloc was the editor, with Cecil Chesterton as assistant.

Belloc motored all over the country to collect contributors, and returned with Shaw, G. K. Chesterton, H. A. L. Fisher and Algernon Blackwood in his pocket. He had hopes of Yeats and Walter Raleigh. The paper was financed by Charles Granville and the first number appeared on June 22, 1911. There was a profit on this of between thirty and fifty pounds. The paper was boycotted by a large section of the Press, and notably by those journals under the control of Harmsworth; but both *The Times* and the *Westminster Gazette* were friendly. It was quoted, without acknowledgments, in several leading articles. The contributors were paid on receipt of MS.; a golden editorial rule.

In the first issue there were essays by Baring, Wells and Blackwood, dramatic criticism by Desmond MacCarthy, and a Coronation Ode by Wilfrid Blunt. Belloc himself had written the first of a not very effective series of 'Conversations'[1] and the commentary on Foreign Affairs. This was unsigned. It dealt with the situation in Morocco, preceding the crisis of Agadir. Belloc believed that a tendency was at work towards a Franco-German understanding, and he was concerned that British foreign policy should forestall it. Cecil Chesterton, under the pseudonym of 'Junius', contributed an *Open Letter to the Prime Minister* on the subject of the sale of honours. In subsequent numbers there were articles or poems by G. K. Chesterton, A. C. Benson (whom Belloc had met and liked earlier in the year), E. S. P. Haynes, Edward Thomas, F. Y. Eccles, John Phillimore, and Quiller-Couch. It was the *Speaker* group, with additions, and the paper maintained an astonishingly high standard of intelligence and taste. It was independent, but seldom reckless; serious, but generally readable.

Belloc, as we have already suggested, was not a natural editor, and the responsibility fussed him.

> I find that I have to do the thinking, and the adding-up, and the judgment, which in a regiment would be spread among seven or eight men, and above half my energy is spent in something unknown to armies, which is the undoing of the ineptitude of others.[2]

[1] *The Conversations of Mr. Bailey.* [2] Letter to George Wyndham: July 2, 1911.

His judgment could be very capricious. An anonymous critic had written on Barrie's *Twelve Pound Look* and Belloc quite unreasonably blamed himself for letting the article appear,[1] on the grounds that Barrie was divorced, and had no children. He seemed to imagine that the play in question—which has since charmed many a Women's Institute—was an attack on marriage. Even if it had been, that was no reason why it should not have been discussed.

Already, before the paper was launched, Belloc was referring to it as 'the wretched thing'. After six months, in spite of a sustained boycott, its circulation was still rising and was larger than that of any other weekly except the *Spectator*. John Burns bought two copies weekly and forced them on his Cabinet colleagues, among whom he encountered stiff resistance from Mr. Herbert Samuel. But the advertisements were insufficient; and without advertisements it needed to sell 100,000 copies in order to pay its way. In June 1912, Belloc, bored and heavily overworked, resigned the editorship to Cecil Chesterton and sold his shares. In November, Granville's financial support collapsed altogether and Cecil Chesterton carried on the paper under the title of the *New Witness*. The running costs were drastically reduced, and the literary standards were only fitfully maintained. Even before the paper had changed its name Belloc was writing to Baring:

> The *Eye Witness* continues to be conducted by Cecil Chesterton, always with vigour, not always with discretion; and his friends who desire to succour him in his gallant efforts contribute for nothing to his largely printed but somewhat irritant pages.[2]

They were meant to irritate, for Chesterton was now hot on the trail of Mr. Godfrey de Bouillon Isaacs, a spectacularly unsuccessful financier, and co-director of the 'Marconi Company', to which the Government had, rather surprisingly, given the contract to establish wireless telegraphy stations in Britain. The Minister responsible for this was the Postmaster-General, Mr. Herbert Samuel. Those who wish to form an unbiased judgment

---

[1] Oct. 19, 1911.   [2] Oct. 26, 1912.

on the scandal of the Marconi shares should read the chapter on
the case contributed by F. J. Sheed to Maisie Ward's biography of
G. K. Chesterton. There is no need to recapitulate the story here,
since Belloc was not directly involved in it. But his views were
known to be so nearly identical with Cecil Chesterton's that his
comment on the successive phases of the affair must be recorded.
The first of these was in a letter to Maurice Baring on October 26,
1911. We can clearly read, beneath the bias and the banter, what it
was that made so many people raise their eyebrows at the sudden
popularity of the Marconi Company.

Of this company Mr. Marconi, his father an Italian Pantheist,
his mother an Irish Protestant, was director. Nor did it pay any
dividends nor had it any prospect of doing so. Mr. Marconi,
therefore, approached Mr. Godfrey de Bouillon Isaacs and
begged him to become a co-director. This gentleman accepted
the post and shortly afterwards emerged as sole director, with
Mr. Marconi occupying the honourable position of Chairman,
the leisures of which he beguiled by touring upon the Continent
where only the other day he had one eye poked out in a motor-
car accident.

Meanwhile Mr. G. de B. Isaacs discovering that the shares of
the Company fetched no more than 14s. approached the Post-
master General of England and suggested that a monopoly
should be given him for establishing round the world an All
Red Chain of Wireless Stations. Fired as the young patriot was
(I refer to Mr. Herbert Samuel) by so splendid a conception, he
drove the hardest possible bargain in the public interests and the
shares of Mr. Godfrey de Bouillon Isaacs only rose from 14s. to
one hundred. An extraordinary example of the secrecy and
honour with which such affairs are conducted today is the fact
that Sir Rufus Isaacs, though the very born brother of de
Bouillon Isaacs (the one being named after the second Norman
King of England, the second after his contemporary The Great
Crusader) never heard of the negotiations at all until the day
before the contract was signed! To the truth of this Sir Rufus has
himself testified amid the cheers of the House of Commons and

what is more proclaimed it for a second time in a loud voice
before two battalions of the Royal Marines drawn up in Hollow
Square for the purpose of the ceremony. Unfortunately foul
tongues are at it again and suggesting that Mr. Lloyd George,
our popular Welsh Chancellor, though sprung from the
people, had fallen into the aristocratic vice of fluttering and,
having inside knowledge, had made no small profit upon the
difference between the 14s. and the 100s. No one, I am assured,
gives credence to his vile tale with the exception of a couple of
hundred gossiping bankers in the City and some eight or ten
thousand in the West End. It is even asserted, I am glad to say,
that the poorer and more contemptible of those who have lent
themselves to this abominable slander will be sent to prison at
the discretion of some judge appointed by the Chancellor
himself.

Here it is important to note that the Ministers had bought
shares in American, not in British, Marconi, and the net result of
Rufus Isaacs' deal was that within a year he had incurred a loss of
£1,300.

A Parliamentary enquiry was instituted and both Rufus Isaacs
and Lloyd George appeared before it. The nature of this appearance was described by Hugh O'Donnell in the *New Witness*:

... While the simile of a panther at bay, anxious to escape,
but ready with tooth and claw, might be applied to Sir Rufus
Isaacs, something more like 'a rat in a corner' might be
suggested by the restless, snapping, furious little figure which
succeeded.

When Mr. Lloyd George replied that 'there was no time on a
Friday afternoon' to mention his purchase of Marconi shares in
the House of Commons, popular suspicion was not appeased. On
January 9, 1913, an article in the *New Witness* listed the twenty
bankrupt companies of which Godfrey Isaacs had been a director,
and sandwich-men paraded up and down outside his office with
placards bearing the words 'Ghastly Failures'. This had not been
done on Cecil Chesterton's instructions, but he did not disclaim it;
and when he refused to give a promise to cease his attacks, Isaacs

brought an action against him for criminal libel. The case was opened at Bow Street at the end of February.

Belloc recognized his moral responsibility in the affair.

My own mind is clearly made up on the matter and I shall do everything I can for Cecil Chesterton, whose position I support, and whose attitude is largely due to my own action.[1]

There were, however, weaknesses in Chesterton's position, which Belloc was quick to notice.

You are quite right about your view that Cecil has not put himself in the best posture for meeting an attack. I have been with him largely throughout the matter and I have specially regretted the recent and increasing way the *New Witness* has got into of hitting blind. For instance, the detestation of the Jewish cosmopolitan influence, especially through finance, is one thing, and one may be right or wrong in feeling that detestation or in the degree to which one admits it; but mere anti-semitism and a mere attack on a Jew because he is a Jew is quite another matter, and I told him repeatedly that I thought the things he allowed O'Donnell to publish were unwise and deplorable. There is nothing easier than to make out to an English Jury that your adversary is fantastic, for Englishmen naturally suspect exaggeration, and indeed usually go to what may paradoxically be called the other extreme of not allowing *enough* for enthusiasm. When, therefore, an opponent can be pointed at as quite irrational about something, and as having brought in utterly extraneous matter it does him more harm in England than anywhere else. This is just what O'Donnell's letters have done and many other passages unsigned in which the national term 'Jew' has been used simply as a term of abuse, much as Lower Middle-class Americans will use the term 'Irish'.

I have also thought it very bad policy and have told him so, not to keep his hands off people who are morally upon his own side. It is asinine to attack McKenna and still more stupid to have notes against a thing like the Board of Agriculture! The truth is that the conduct of such ticklish business requires more

[1] Letter to Maurice Baring: Feb. 21, 1913.

knowledge than he can have of the nuances inside of the various rings. He has not got the flair for isolating an enemy. On the other hand there is one aspect of this business in which he has a stronger position than one can judge anywhere save on the spot and this aspect has been especially prominent since the proceedings opened at Bow Street. It is this: his opponents have chosen to fight upon one particular ground, to wit, an accusation of having so maliciously attacked one particular person, Godfrey Isaacs, as to warrant that person in getting him not to pay damages but to suffer the consequences of *crime*.

Belloc thought that Chesterton's attack on Godfrey Isaacs was more easily defensible before a judge and jury than his attack on Rufus Isaacs and Lloyd George, though it was less important from the point of view of exposing political corruption. Rufus Isaacs and Lloyd George were in the heart of politics; Godfrey was only on their fringe. Belloc was present at the Bow Street hearing, when Chesterton immediately took his stand on the original article in the *New Witness*. Isaacs' counsel tried to prove that this was not in the indictment, but—to Belloc's surprise—Chesterton won his point. Everything would depend upon how far he was allowed to press it in cross-examination. In fact, he was committed for trial, and the case came up before Mr. Justice Phillimore at the Old Bailey on May 27. Edward Carson and F. E. Smith appeared for Isaacs and Ernest Wild for Chesterton. The conduct of the defence was puzzling, for Chesterton withdrew his charges against the Ministers. Furthermore, no single shareholder was forthcoming to complain that he had been defrauded of sixpence through the failure of Godfrey Isaacs' companies. The Judge summed up heavily against Chesterton, and the jury were out of court for only forty minutes before returning their verdict of 'Guilty'. Chesterton was sentenced to a fine of one hundred pounds. Belloc was among the friends and relatives behind the dock, to whom he smiled and waved in his jubilation at what he, and they, regarded as a moral victory. But since he had withdrawn the charges which had been the chief ground of his attack, it is difficult to see what they all thought he had defeated. Sir Rufus Isaacs and Lloyd George were more likely to have trembled for their careers when the Conservative motion was brought forward in the House of Commons a few days later: 'That this House regrets the transactions of certain of its Ministers in the shares of the Marconi Company of America; and the want of frankness in their communications on the subject to the House.' But the motion was lost; the two Ministers expressed their regret for any indiscretion of which they might have been guilty; Mr. Balfour behaved like the perfect gentleman that he was; and his right honourable friends relaxed on the Bench opposite, as the cloud passed which had darkened, so briefly and yet so incredibly, the prospect of their fortunes and their fame.

Chesterton was a man of boundless courage, but he had struck in the twilight if he had not exactly struck in the dark. Whether or not the Marconi affair proved the case for political corruption —and at the very least, it left a nasty smell in the lobbies of the House of Commons—it surely went some way to disprove the case for political collusion. The *Outlook* and the *National Review*, both Conservative papers, were as eager as the *New Witness* to bring the charges home against the Liberal Ministers. It was a Conservative who first raised the question in the House, and it was a group of young Conservatives who paid the cost of Cecil Chesterton's defence; it was the Conservatives who went on trying to ferret out the truth in Parliament; and it was a Conservative on the Committee of Enquiry, Lord Robert Cecil, who issued a minority report damning for the Ministers in question. If the Front Benches were still in collusion, the Back Benches certainly were not.

3

Belloc took no satisfaction in the passing into the law of the Parliament Act of 1911. He thought the Bill had been dictated by the will of the Party machine and not by the will of the people; and that the House of Lords had been robbed of 'just those powers which were either traditional or valuable'.[1] The squires would be

---

[1] Letter to George Wyndham: Aug. 11, 1911.

replaced by the experts, and the House of Lords would be used
as a bogey when the Government did not want to pass a measure
and as an excuse when they did. Men would buy their titles as
gaily as ever, and the hereditary peers would be confirmed in
their indifference. Belloc was not afraid of revolutionary change,
but he did not think the Parliament Act revolutionary. We may
remark in all this confused and disgruntled comment a rather
paradoxical shift of front from the Radicalism of 1906, and even
of 1910. And, indeed, a man with a fraction of Belloc's intelligence could have foreseen that the more faithfully the 'people'
were represented in the Commons, the more they might need,
on occasion, the Lords to save them from themselves. One of
the purposes of a Second Chamber was to provide time for
second thoughts. A House of Lords that was not aristocratic was
a contradiction in terms. And Belloc observed that, as aristocracy declined in England, a great many other good things were
declining with it: manners and morals and learning. He was not
blind to the virtues of the hereditary principle, and one of these
was to confer a certain decency upon wealth. It does not require
any exceptional sensibility to see that money which is inherited is
very often cleaner than money that is made. And it was the way in
which he saw money being made by South African millionaires
and London stock-jobbers that tempted Belloc, on occasion, to
the vocabulary of the Popular Front.

He had little sympathy, however, for the popular politicians, of
whom Lloyd George was the most cunning, the most uneducated
and the most successful. Belloc confessed to Maurice Baring that
he felt himself, already, to be an exile; he had wished to live at
ease in English society and to find a place in the University
which he loved. But his temperament forbade him this—or any
other—repose, and when Lloyd George introduced his Insurance
Bill of 1911 Belloc was immediately in arms against the advent of
the Servile State. For this reason, among others, he rejoiced in the
victory of his friend Aubrey Herbert in the South Somerset by-
election in November of the same year. He thought this would be
'a smack in the eye for the Insurance Bill, which is a vile enslaving
measure', for Herbert had beaten 'the most odious type of man

imaginable, a sham workman, loud-mouthed reformer on the make'.[1] Anyone old enough to remember the Insurance Bill will recall the indignation of the people it was supposed to benefit. Little boys in middle-class households were invited to mount the kitchen table and declaim against a measure, and a man, which would compel the working-classes to insure their health. In these days of universal insurance such indignation is difficult to understand. We are all used to doing as we are told. But there was, in that protest, a primitive instinct of liberty and a passionate rejection of servile status, which showed that Belloc's apprehensions were not those of a solitary crank.

Meanwhile, he spoke at public meetings against the Bill, without much faith in the efficacy of a merely rhetorical resistance. He debated with Ramsay MacDonald before the South-West London Federation of the Independent Labour Party, and their speeches were afterwards published verbatim in a pamphlet entitled *Socialism and the Servile State* with a foreword by Mr. Herbert Morrison. Belloc defined the Servile State as 'one in which a portion of the inhabitants of the State, dispossessed of the means of production, are secure in sufficiency, without the dispossession of the capitalist or means-of-production-owning class'. This was the State to which he believed the Socialists were involuntarily moving. They were confiscating income—or rather, Lloyd George whom they generally supported was confiscating it; they did not even propose to confiscate capital. Belloc did not believe that collectivism was possible without confiscation. If the Socialists wanted a revolution, they would not get it by making the proletariat contented with their servile status. But Ramsay MacDonald did not want that sort of revolution at all; the last thing he desired was furious and semi-starving artisans seething behind the barricades in Whitechapel. He and Bernard Shaw (who was sitting in the front row at the debate) wanted an educated, white-collar minority infiltrating into public life and tidying up the waste and anomalies of capitalism. They looked forward to a planners' paradise in which no bones—and no bottles—would be broken. By and large, they have had their wish.

[1] Letter to Maurice Baring: Nov. 23, 1911.

The debate was a good example of the cross-purposes at which Belloc talked with most of his contemporaries. His point of departure was historical and his audience was not composed of historians. Like Henry Ford, Socialists are apt to dislike history. Ramsay MacDonald, at any rate, was clearly irritated when Belloc dragged him back to the Middle Ages and Pagan antiquity. Belloc was not primarily concerned to attack the Servile State; indeed, he was at pains to emphasize what high civilizations had been built upon it. Nevertheless, it was not in the long run compatible with a widespread belief in the Incarnation. But then Ramsay MacDonald and his fellow-Fabians did not particularly want to be dragged back to the Incarnation either. They did not think the Incarnation was relevant to anything very much, and they could not see what it had to do with twentieth-century economics. Belloc, who interspersed his speech with several ironic apologies for bringing in the Name of his Redeemer, thought it had a great deal to do with everything. Living as he did in the absolute, he was continually nonplussed at finding the Socialist living in the contingent, and so what he wanted to be a real, though friendly, debate became shadow boxing in which no one really came to grips.

We start [said MacDonald] as a critical organization, very crude at first, using absolute expressions, which we by-and-by apply under capitalism, not under Socialism, which we by-and-by apply in the actual world, not in the ideal world which we have constructed in our own minds; and in the application of those ideas of ours we are limited, not by ourselves but by you. We are limited, not by Socialist opinion, but by opinion outside, by Mr. Belloc, for instance, who is not a Socialist at all.

In winding up the debate the Chairman, A. G. Gardiner, editor of the *Daily News,* expressed the hope that the dialectical battle would be resumed later. He need have had no fears on that score; Belloc was the last man to lay down an argument. In fact he pursued it, magisterially, in *The Servile State.*[1] This book has been

[1] 1912.

described as one of the most prophetic pamphlets of the twentieth century, and it resumed, more exactly and methodically, the thesis he had argued with MacDonald. The debate and the essay should be read side by side, for they show not only the outline of Belloc's thought, but the kind of opposition it encountered. He had proposed the Middle Ages as the chief example of a Christian society in which the determining mass of the population owned, co-operatively or individually, the means of production. Indeed you may say that while Belloc was very far from being a State Socialist, he was very near to being a Guild Socialist. This brought him into friendly association with Orage and the *New Age,* to which he often contributed. Orage and his group really were men of the new age in a way that Belloc was not. Their psychology was modern, even when their ideas were traditional. But Belloc was more at ease with them than he was with the Fabians. And the reason is clear; the members of the Medieval Guild really did own the means of their production, whereas in the Collectivist State these were owned by the politicians. Here Belloc's experience of the House of Commons crucially affected his economic theories. He could not, by any stretch of sophistry, equate the People with the People's representatives. His anti-Parliamentary bias seemed to Ramsay MacDonald a tiresome red herring thrown across the trail of their discussion, for it had not occurred to MacDonald—as it would later occur to Shaw and many Continental Socialists—to doubt the intelligence or the integrity of Parliaments. Belloc himself had stated that Socialism might be 'democratic', or it might not. In 1911 this sounded like a wilful paradox, but time gave it proof.

The Servile State did, indeed, fulfil the minimum condition of prophecy, in so far as it saw through a glass darkly. It saw that men in modern industrial societies would willingly give up their freedom to secure sufficiency and security. It doubted—and with good reason—whether the instinct of property was sufficiently vigorous in these societies to enforce that distribution of productive wealth (not of income) which Belloc believed to be the only social doctrine consonant with a Christian philosophy. The moment, he feared, had passed.

Within the memory of people still living a sufficient number of Englishmen were owning (as small free-holders, small masters, etc.) to give to the institution of property coupled with freedom a very vivid effect upon the popular mind. More than this, there was a living tradition proceeding from the lips of men who could still bear living testimony to the relics of a better state of things. I have myself spoken when I was a boy to old labourers in the neighbourhood of Oxford, who had risked their skins in armed protest against the enclosure of certain commons, and who had, of course, suffered imprisonment by a wealthy judge as the reward of their courage; and I have myself spoken in Lancashire to old men who could retrace for me, either from their personal experience the last phases of small ownership in the textile trade, or, from what their fathers had told them, the conditions of a time when small and well-divided ownership in cottage looms was actually common.

Where the prophecy of *The Servile State* was inexact was in not seeing that the State itself would become the more or less benevolent slave-owner. Belloc believed that the rich would organize the poor with the poor's consent. He did not believe that the rich would allow the State to step in and take over the organization of servility. Or rather, he refused to admit a distinction between the State and the rich; and when he found his rich friends being progressively impoverished by successive Governments, whether they called themselves Conservative or Socialist, no one was more annoyed than he was. The book also raised a number of questions which it left unanswered. What exactly did Belloc mean by the 'determining' mass of men, whose ownership of productive wealth conferred, as he believed, essential freedom on a society? Obviously there must, in any State outside Utopia, be employers and employed. Under what conditions could the employed man —perhaps a very highly employed man, like a diplomat or an admiral—be described as 'free'? Belloc might have answered that a man was free when he was able to change his master. But while a mechanic may be free to go from one employer to another, this is impossible for a civil servant. Yet it would be paradoxical to suggest that, in any serious sense, civil servants are slaves. Indeed it is difficult to resist the conclusion that, according to Belloc's definition, a great number of important and skilled employments are of their nature servile.

The answer to this in terms of Christian philosophy is that service has a special dignity, and, put in this way, Belloc would hardly have denied the proposition. He had described the transformation of society, which he believed to have been the result of the Reformation, as the change from status to contract. But in so far as the man who made a free contract with his employer was freer than the man who lived and worked within the limits of an inherited status, then there could surely be no doubt that under the centuries of what is loosely described as capitalism the area of liberty had been enlarged. One is not disparaging the achievement of the Middle Ages when one says that no man accustomed to the personal liberties of the modern world would willingly go back to them. History cannot stand still, and the central problem of the twentieth century is how the individual energies released by the Renaissance (and by that we must include the Reformation) can be controlled for the common good. The common good was a very medieval notion, and the Middle Ages were as united as the modern world is divided about what is meant by it. But while Belloc rightly perceived that the condition of free contract was being transformed into the condition of compulsory status, he did not perceive that in this respect, though in this respect alone, society was returning to the Middle Ages, and not drawing further away from them.

Again, the reader of *The Servile State* may ask, as Ramsay MacDonald had asked during the debate—how were the monopolies of capitalism to be broken up? Belloc had said that the Socialists ought to confiscate the railways; what other portions of the national economy did he think should be brought under public ownership? What were the limits of a decent distribution? How were they to be guaranteed? Could property be restored? Belloc gave the short answer to these questions that where there was a will there was a way; his detailed prescription was reserved for a later book. His immediate aim was to define the Servile

State and to prove that the England of Lloyd George's Insurance
Act was moving rapidly in that direction. If Belloc had been
writing satirically, he would no doubt have substituted the word
'welfare' for the word 'servile'—for 'welfare' distils a certain
odour of political anæsthetic. No one now living under the com-
pulsions of the Welfare State can reasonably deny that Belloc's
prophecy was a true one, although the way in which it has come
true has been different from the way that he foretold. He did not see
that an aristocratic society was the best preparation for Socialism,
because it is a society in which government is respected; although
the reason why he disliked the radicalism of Lloyd George was
because it was inspired by the society at once aristocratic and
proletarian of northern Germany. The truth is that this prophet
of equality was the least egalitarian of men; and that this teaser of
the rich could only expand to the full size of his personality in a
society where inequality was accepted as the condition and
corollary of freedom.

The other matter of acute political interest during these years
was the protracted crisis over Home Rule. Belloc, proceeding
from his rather doubtful premiss of Front Bench collusion, believed
that a Home Rule Bill would be brought in by the Liberals and
dropped, and that the matter would eventually be settled by the
Tories. He thought, with good reason, that any settlement should
exclude the Protestant North; this, of course, was not at all the
same thing as Ulster—or even as Ulster minus Donegal. Belloc
tended to see Ireland in terms of a romantic antithesis between
North and South; between a prosperous peasantry and a degraded
proletariat. But there were plenty of proletarians in Dublin, and
they lived in slums just as bad as the worst slums of Belfast. He
was right, however, in seeing that the general mentality of the
North favoured industrial capitalism, while that of the South
tended always towards an agricultural economy. But he did not
believe that the exemption of the North would last long; he
thought that the Ulster Protestants would desire, in their own
interests, to join the National Government. In this prediction he
was not correct. The division between North and South was only
hardened under the spur of southern separatism. Belloc listened to

F. E. Smith in Crewe and to Carson in Manchester, and then wrote to George Wyndham of the danger of allowing the situation to drift.

> That will simply mean a practically autonomous peasant state, contemptuous of England and doing all the harm she can in the approaching perils.[1]

His fears were only too well justified. And he did not envisage at this time the almost complete degree of autonomy which was subsequently granted to the Dublin Parliament.

What preoccupied him beyond Irish discontents was the certainty of the approaching perils. Whether the custody of the Panama Canal, or naval bases in the South Atlantic, or the strength of garrisons overseas were in question, his thoughts came back to a war, or a partial disarmament, which he believed to be inevitable within two years. He agreed with Wyndham that only the Royal Navy could be trusted to hold the gates of the Canal and he emphasized the importance of Simonstown.

> I do not believe that the great modern fleet will hold the Narrow Seas in time of war, and I can perfectly well conceive a Fleet (so long as it depends on coal) supreme in the Atlantic, but crippled by the distance of stations in the South Pacific and unable to enter the Mediterranean, especially as all our domestic stations which are virtually Atlantic are at the gates of our own great coal supply.[2]

[1] Jan. 27, 1912.   [2] Letter to George Wyndham: March 7, 1912.

CHAPTER XV

BEREAVEMENT

I

THE break with the *Morning Post* had all the consequences that Belloc had feared. He tried in vain to persuade the *Observer*, the *Daily Telegraph*, the *Graphic*, and the *Saturday Review* to give him a weekly column. His quarrel with the Liberals had cut him off from the *Daily News*. The *Academy* and the *Century* would generally print his essays, and the *Pall Mall Gazette* published his articles on Napoleon's 1812 campaign in Russia. These afterwards appeared in book form,[1] and thus helped to commemorate the centenary of the great disaster. But his only certain income was a ten-pound-a-month article for the Catholic Press in New York. Of course he could always write for the Catholic Press in England; but this was readier to use than to reward his services. More than ever, therefore, he depended on his books and his lecturing.

He would sometimes give as many as four lectures in a single day. He talked on Marie Antoinette at Eton and was given a bad dinner by Edward Lyttelton. Harrow was better and he liked Lionel Ford. At Repton the Barsac was good, the masters agreeable, and Mrs. Temple conspicuously intelligent. He spoke for Father Waggett in Cambridge and tried to explain the nature of property to undergraduates who did not seem to have heard of it. A galaxy of Professors took part in the discussion afterwards at Waggett's house. He spoke for the East London College on Bacon, Keats, Pope, Shelley, the English Historians, the Minor English Poets, the Decline of Rhetoric, English Metrical Romances before Chaucer, and Characteristics of Seventeenth-Century Prose. These lectures were not always well attended and

[1] *The Campaign of 1812 and the Retreat from Moscow* (1924).

322

once he found himself with an audience of only two students. Then there were visits to Oxford where he addressed the Alpine Club at Balliol and spoke on Rabelais to 600 undergraduates in the Schools. This lecture had been arranged by Walter Raleigh, and it was never forgotten by anyone who heard it. Belloc crossed to Ireland and addressed the seminarians at Maynooth, where the President, who was a cousin of Elodie, gave him champagne. In Dublin Jim Larkin's men were on strike and Belloc watched their hungry procession through the streets. In Scotland he could earn as much as one hundred and thirty pounds in a single week, but the constant travelling exhausted him. He was worried by the new system of steam heating in the trains and asked Dorothy Hamilton if she could find him a small metal hot-water bottle. The india rubber ones were no good to him; they burst.

In the autumn of 1910 H. A. L. Fisher was appointed general editor for the Home University Library (Williams and Norgate), and invited Belloc to contribute a short essay on the French Revolution. An advance of only fifty pounds was offered, but Belloc obtained one hundred pounds, which was half to a third of what he would have received elsewhere for a book of the same length. The scale of royalties, too, was thirty per cent. less than he could normally expect. Nevertheless the book was well worth writing, and well worth the little trouble that it cost him. He passed on his recipe to Phillimore.

Don't sweat up your facts. Out of the abundance of your knowledge, tell the ordinary man generally what you want him to know in a spout, and there comes out a perfect little essay of the length they want. So I did with the French Revolution, not opening a reference book half-a-dozen times, and dictating the whole thing off-hand, with the result that I have already sold 27,700. If I had worried in the least about it I should not have sold half the number.[1]

Fisher had insisted that the book be free from bias, as distinct from legitimate opinion, and the result was a splendidly objective

[1] April 19, 1912.

study; probably the best short account of the Revolution in the English language. Here is the bare skeleton of analysis, which Belloc had clothed with living flesh in his earlier and longer biographies. He contributed a second volume to the Home University Library—*Warfare in England*—in which he discussed the principal campaigns fought on British soil between the Roman Conquest and the Jacobite Rebellion of 1745.

But his imagination had not yet deserted the Revolutionary theme. He returned to it in *The Girondin*, published by Nelson in 1911 also. This was an historical novel, and it was for that reason the best novel that Belloc ever wrote. It is imagination—a much larger thing than invention—that makes fiction live; and Belloc's imagination was as keen when he was coping with the past as it could be clumsy when he was coping with the present. His invented characters were as real as those handed to him by history because his imagination had entered, equally, into both. It is worth noting that the book is dedicated to Pacte and Basilique, the two horses that had been under his charge in the 10th Battery. Here, transmuted in time and place, is the annealing discipline of arms as Belloc had himself experienced it.

What gives the book its special flavour, and sets it apart from anything else in the same *genre*, is the sustained irony. We get the realism of the conscript: 'soldiers are always cheated'; or again:

> . . . if there was one thing the army hated it was politics. To be seized round the neck by market-women and told that you were adored for opinions you never held; or, when what you most needed was sleep after a long day and drinking, to be cheered before a company of singers and told that you were the bulwark of the country; or worse still, to receive a violent blow in a dark passage and to have yourself called a traitor by some-one whose views upon the State you did not know and who might very well be in agreement with you—these were the things that young soldiers could not bear.

The book grinds no axe. It merely tells the story of Boutroux, a young Bordelais Republican who kills one of his own side to protect his uncle's house; flees the city; falls in love; is recruited for the army of the Revolution; and is crushed to death by his own horse after the victory of Valmy. The victory is not overplayed. We sense, although we do not see, 'the strict and brilliant army of the invasion'; we share the bewilderment of the battle, as we do in *War and Peace* and *La Chartreuse de Parme*; we are surprised, with Boutroux, by the sudden new note of the artillery—'the un-bugled boom of guns'; we do not quite know what it is all about.

> Horse [says Boutroux to his faithful Pascal], this is a battle. Do not forget it. Things are not in manhood what boyhood imagines them! . . . This has been a battle. We shall have to boast of it by and by.

And when a sergeant comes up with the news that there has been a victory and that there is now a Republic, Boutroux asks: 'What is a Republic?' 'I don't know,' replies the sergeant, 'but it sounds bloody good.' Boutroux, however, observes that all is not mended by a Republic, when he is made to pay for his wine.

Belloc was paid £300 for *The Girondin,* but his hopes of a further £800 from America were disappointed. No American publisher would touch it.

In March 1912 Belloc finished a book on which he had been at work for five years. It was originally called 'The County of Sussex', and in 1909 he told Maurice Baring that it would describe 'myself and three other characters walking through the county: the other characters are really supernatural beings, a poet, a sailor and Grizzlebeard himself: they only turn out to be supernatural beings when we get to the town of Liss, which is just over the Hampshire border'.[1] This book became *The Four Men*. It had been ordered by an American publisher—Scribner— and then refused because of its 'religious tone'. Nelson published it in the summer of 1912. In answer to the objection that the Poet did *not* throw beer at the Philosopher ('as you shall later read'), but was, on the contrary, the means of bringing grace to him by baptism, Belloc replied that the book had taken so long to write that it was small wonder the characters had turned inside out. He was consoled by the example of Marryat who had killed a

[1] Dec. 4, 1909.

character and then brought him to life again in the same book. Belloc had made his own illustrations in wash and composed the tunes for the Sailor's songs. These he would often sing for the entertainment of his friends. Described as a 'farrago', the reader might expect *The Four Men* to be formless; but in fact, it has a singularly perfect form. Indeed, 'fugue' would have been a better description than 'farrago'. It has been suggested that each of the three characters that accompany Myself are aspects of the author—the mature and melancholy pessimist, now naked of illusion; the sailor with his high spirits and his itch for travel and the far horizons in his eyes; and the poet chiselling away at words. This is certainly true even if it was not intentional. The book obviously invites comparison with *The Path to Rome*, for it is a journey through the author's other *patria*. Where in the earlier book he adventured into the unknown and discovered the familiar, in *The Four Men* he adventures into the familiar and discovers the strange. Far more profoundly than in *The Path to Rome*, he adventures into himself; and the introspection is touched with irony. Where *The Path to Rome* was a pilgrimage, *The Four Men* is an exploration. It is the mixture of the real with the imaginary that gives the book its unique flavour. These are real places—the 'George' at Robertsbridge, the Brightling Beacon, the inn at Bramber and Washington, and Harting on the Hampshire border beyond which are 'shapeless things'—and they are seen and discussed by characters invented and even fantastic. The journey is diversified by story and song—the Battle between the men of Kent and the men of Sussex, Mr. Justice Honeybubble, the Sailor's 'On Sussex hills where I was bred', and the superb lyric which closes the book. *The Four Men* belongs to the *genre* of the *picaresque*, but it does not straggle. It is defined by the county boundaries at either end, enclosed by the rampart of the Downs, firmly supported by its four characters, and limited by the four days' duration of their march.

This takes place at the end of October and the book, for all its occasional high spirits, is tinged with autumnal melancholy; the *malaise* of early middle-age when the mind comes to grips with mortality. This is the message of Grizzlebeard's farewell, as it was the message that Myself had dreaded to read in the inn at Bramber, if he had dared to return to it.

There is nothing at all that remains: nor any house, nor any castle, however strong; nor any love, however tender and sound; nor any comradeship among men, however hardy. Nothing remains but the things of which I will not speak, because we have spoken enough of them already during these four days. But I who am old will give you advice, which is this —to consider from now onward those permanent things which are, as it were, the shores of this age and the harbours of our glittering and pleasant but dangerous and wholly changeful sea.

This was not the whole of Belloc, but it was a large part of him —and the part which would grow more and more predominant in the years that lay ahead. The book stands at the watershed of his life and work. Here, again, a comparison with *The Path to Rome* is revealing. *The Path to Rome* is full of spring, radiant with a natural hope. Only ten years divided it from *The Four Men*, and in those ten years many illusions had been lost and many hopes had been disappointed. The future was now uncertain and dark. It was on November 2—the Day of the Dead—that Myself went up alone into the high woods, and the memories crowded round him—memories of La Celle St. Cloud and the annual pilgrimage to the graves, his mother enclosed in her grief, and his sister walking at his side. But his roots were no longer there among the woods that encircle Paris like a necklace: they were here in Sussex where he had founded his home. He would not speak of immortality as his faith had taught it to him, but as some pagan forebear might have conceived it—not as a personal survival but as a memory intimately mingled with the soil which had bred him and the sights among which he had moved.

> The spring's superb adventure calls
> His dust athwart the woods to flame;
> His boundary river's secret falls
> Perpetuate and repeat his name.
> He rides his loud October sky;
> He does not die. He does not die.

The beeches know the accustomed head
Which loved them, and a peopled air
Beneath their benediction spread
Comforts the silence everywhere;
　For native ghosts return and these
　Perfect the mystery in the trees.

So, therefore, though myself be crosst
The shuddering of that dreadful day
When friend and fire and home are lost
And even children drawn away—
　The passer-by shall hear me still,
　A boy that sings on Duncton Hill.

The lines are prophetic, not only of a lonely and enfeebled old age, but of a steady fame. In the summer of 1951 the Festival of Sussex presented a dramatic version of *The Four Men* as a contribution to the Festival of Britain. This was skilfully made by Viscount Duncannon, and was performed in town and village halls, in barn theatres and on school platforms, throughout Sussex. Audiences of every sort—the schoolboys of Christ's Hospital and Lancing, the schoolgirls of Mayfield and Roedean—responded to Belloc's humour and rhetoric, as if there had been no change in popular fashion since the book was written. Everywhere—except, perhaps, for its single excursion into whimsey—it touched a chord which still vibrated. Miss Elizabeth Belloc wrote to Lord Duncannon afterwards:

All the really memorable and valuable parts of the book are presented in the play and 'come over' miraculously—especially the Inn at Bramber (so difficult to say) and the concluding passage where the four men are parted from each other... Long ago I heard my father say, 'I put my whole heart into that book, but no one cares about it.' How delightful for him now to know how many people care for it, and how much.[1]

[1] Nov. 18, 1952.

2

Belloc continued to work on his monographs of British Battles, and these were afterwards collected into a single volume.[1] They found a ready sale among a public slowly awakening to the importance of arms. Crécy, Poitiers, Blenheim, Malplaquet, Tourcoing and Waterloo were each discussed in considerable detail, with due regard for their political as well as their military aspect. Waterloo, in particular, has never been more clearly treated; it was only by going over the ground himself that Belloc understood how a small accident of terrain had prevented Blücher from coming up sooner to Wellington's support. He described to George Wyndham [2] how he had risen at 5 a.m. and walked eight miles to Malplaquet, measuring the distances; and his pleasure at discovering in Calvert's Journal the exact position of the Coldstreams at Tourcoing.

> What a fight it was! Fame is with armies almost what it is with individuals, capricious, tardy, insufficient, or exaggerated. If it were not so, that defeat ought to have made the Guards more famous than any of their victories.[3]

And then he goes on to speak of the three books he really wanted to write.

> First, a really good history of the Revolutionary and the Napoleonic wars; secondly, a thorough examination of the way in which modern taxation was exhausting the State. That is of capital practical importance. Every civilisation there has ever been has ended in that way; and people ought to be warned; it is like socialism, the product of the very evil which it promises to cure. It is the product of an ill-distribution of wealth. Thirdly, I would write a description of the Normans, the active little men with round heads and broad shoulders . . . But of course if I really had leisure I should not write at all, so it is all in the Providence of God, like so many other things, including Mrs. Sidney Webb and the rules of the House of Commons.

[1] *Six British Battles* (1931).   [2] April 22, 1911.   [3] April 16, 1911.

As it was, he was compelled to write books

> just like a man searching the hillside to draw fire. If they won't
> buy one kind of book, then I write another; but there is one
> kind of book I cannot write for the life of me, and that is an
> epic. I wish I could, for it is much the finest kind of book to
> write.[1]

So it had to be another novel, *The Green Overcoat*, begun in
Holy Week, 1911 (Belloc generally dictated a novel during
Holy Week), and *More Peers* (1911), again with Basil Blackwood;
and *The River of London* (1912) describing the long *mariage de
convenance* between London and the Thames; explaining why it
had been so necessary and so successful; and hinting at the further
reasons beyond history which had helped to cement it. To
obtain a general perspective for this book Belloc sailed up the
river in a motor-boat from Sheerness to Westminster Pier. At
the same time he was at work on a short history of France for
John Buchan (Nelson), most of which he wrote in long hand;
and a book on *The Stane Street*, which Constable published, with
photographs and maps, in 1913. He had followed the Street with
Harold Baker; not, this time, on foot, but in Auberon Lucas's
motor-car, liberally provided with cold chicken and champagne.
He toyed with the idea of turning *A Change in the Cabinet*
into a play, with the collaboration of Hubert Foss. Foss was to
provide the scenario and Belloc the dialogue. But the idea
got nowhere. The best plays, like the best novels, are made out
of private emotions, and of private emotions Belloc was
curiously shy.

During the first week of June 1913 George Wyndham visited
the Bellocs at King's Land. He and Hilaire walked in the woods
and talked at length about the problem of immortality. Wyndham
declared his firm belief that the soul was immortal, and Belloc,
for his part, naturally believed this to be true; but he believed it
upon authority rather than upon feeling. A few days later he
received a letter from Wyndham in which the affirmations of
their walk were repeated.

[1] April 16, 1911.

It is clear [wrote Belloc to Maurice Baring] that the whole conduct of human life must depend upon a man's decision in this matter. Those who are so blessed as to feel (and personally know) the high destiny of man I have always sought (those few whom I know well, those very few) and importuned them with questions as I have also you. I like to hear from the lips of others, as though it were a thing seen, that which I know I must defend but to which I have no access of my own.[1]

The day after he had received this letter from Wyndham, Belloc and Baring were walking in the streets of London, and saw the news that he was dead. The blow was a heavy one; it was the first bereavement that Belloc had suffered since the death of Hubert Howard in 1898. The loss haunted him through a journey to Lourdes and the Pyrenees.

I cannot get the Dead Man out of my thoughts ... Today in rattling through the prayers for the living in my head, at Mass, his name halted me suddenly and abominably: I remembered, or rather stumbled, and left it unspoken: it has to come later now in the much longer list of names one runs through in a chain night after night and at Mass, too; for whom we ask the three things, Refreshment, Light and Peace. We agreed and were continuing to agree more nearly in everything; he was the only man older than myself whom I sought, and I sought him eagerly always. I loved him with all my heart, and so surely as I have no horizon beyond that plain horizon of this world, so surely will some years of mine to come be full *desiderio tam cari capitis*.[2]

Soon after their return from France Belloc was motoring with Elodie past Halnacker Hill and was appalled to see the mill in ruins. The observation met his mood exactly and resulted later in some of the most beautiful verses he ever wrote. You cannot put your finger on their poignancy, but they may stand as an epitaph on all that England which he had striven so passionately to serve; an England which refused to be saved in the way that he had wished to save it.

[1] June 15, 1913   [2] *Ibid.*

Sally is gone that was so kindly,
    Sally is gone from Ha'nacker Hill.
And the Briar grows ever since then so blindly,
    And ever since then the clapper is still,
    And the sweeps have fallen from Ha'nacker Mill.

Ha'nacker Hill is in Desolation:
    Ruin a-top and a field unploughed.
And Spirits that call on a fallen nation,
    Spirits that loved her calling aloud:
    Spirits abroad in a windy cloud.

Spirits that call and no one answers;
    Ha'nacker's down and England's done.
Wind and Thistle for pipe and dancers
    And never a ploughman under the sun.
    Never a ploughman. Never a one.

He set the words to a high, plaintive melody, and a record exists of him singing them many years later. The tired voice may not do justice to the music, but it faithfully reflects the mood.

3

The ceaseless round of work and lecturing, resisting the Insurance Act at public meetings up and down the country, dining, wining and dictating, was interrupted by constant travel. Sometimes it would be a brief visit to Belgium to visit a battlefield, to Bayeux to study the tapestry, or to France to attend the manœuvres. On these Belloc would generally go alone; and it is painful to recall that a third-class ticket from London to Boulogne then cost only 12s. 9d. But on his longer trips he was often accompanied. In the summer of 1911 Auberon Lucas and his sister took the Bellocs for a long motor tour through France and Spain. They followed the valley of the Rhône, crossed the Pyrenees, went down the Ebro, and came back through Normandy. A year later Belloc was at work on his study of the 1812 campaign and he wanted to see the country which had defeated his hero. A closer study of this journey shows us how and why he travelled.

He started with Evan Charteris, on August 27. Having lunched, very badly, at the Savoy, they caught the 2.20 from Victoria. A heavy gale forced the Folkestone boat to Calais, where they dined in the station, arriving at Brussels the same night. The next morning they took the train to Liège, noting as they went the battlefield of Neerwinden. At Liège they hired a motor which took them to the battlefield of Laffeldt, where it got bogged down in the mud and had to be pulled out by horses. Later, on the Maestricht road, it caught fire, which the mud was now called in to extinguish. To crown the day's disasters Belloc overpaid the chauffeur. They took the tram into Maestricht, and thence proceeded by train to Aix where they missed the Cologne express and gaily hired another motor instead.

Belloc left Charteris in Cologne and caught the night train to Berlin where he was met by Somers Cocks. Dismissing Germany as 'an odd filter through which civilization gets to the Slavs', he went on the same afternoon to Frankfurt-on-Oder, and on the next day to Posen—a town so thoroughly Polish that the cooking seemed possible again, with a speciality of crayfish. These, done in white wine, were always his favourite dish. He reached Thorn the next afternoon and crossed the Vistula by ferry, going on by train to the Russian frontier town of Alexandrovna. Here the formalities were interminable, and for the remainder of his journey to Warsaw he had nothing to eat and nowhere to sit. The distance was no further than from London to Birmingham but the discomfort was extreme.

Warsaw reminded him of Omaha and he left it after twenty-four hours. He heard Mass at St. Joseph's Church, but saw nobody—except the people dredging the Vistula. He booked a first-class ticket on the midnight express for Moscow; but the noise under the carriage was like a gong, and he had to console himself with *The Wreck of the Grosvenor*. All next day he could observe the country of the campaign; the Beresina,

like the Upper River at Oxford; the extraordinary dead flat of the whole landscape . . . the trees occasionally tall but not usually so. Smolensk. The considerable height on the right bank of the Dnieper ... Borodino in a perfectly clear position ... the Moskowa.

Having reached Moscow he stayed there exactly six hours, dismissing the Kremlin as 'quite insignificant' and boarding the afternoon train for Krakow where Somers Cocks was awaiting him at the Hotel de Saxe. Krakow might be 'the backbone of Poland', but it did not detain him any longer than Moscow. By 2 o'clock the next afternoon he and Somers Cocks were in the train for Vienna. It was 3 a.m. before they had found a room, and by ten the following morning they were *en route* for Salzburg. A single glance at Salzburg convinced Belloc (though not perhaps Somers Cocks) that it was no better than Earls Court, so he stopped on the train and proceeded to Innsbruck. The superb scenery struck him as 'practically Switzerland' and therefore 'detestable'. An hour was enough for Innsbruck and he caught the night train on to Zürich which he disliked more than any town he had ever seen. It was not improved by the German Emperor who was stopping at the same hotel. The next halt was Geneva, and by September 5, nine days since he had left England, Belloc was back in France looking at the *miséricordes* in the Eglise de Brou. It was evidently a relief to be able to look at something without impatience, boredom or disgust.

He took a boat—a dirty old barge—up the Saône from Mâcon to Tournus, and went on by train to Châlons. Here a regiment of soldiers, marching over the bridge in full kit, gladdened his heart, and sending on his luggage to Bourges he set out along the main road to Autun. He arrived at Bourges at 10.30 p.m. and by the following noon he was in Tours. Having visited the cathedral and the shrine of St. Martin, he was off again the next morning, lunching off crayfish at Orléans, catching an early afternoon train to Paris, and dining at Prunier's. A message reached him that his mother was at La Celle St. Cloud, and he took her out to lunch at Versailles. Later he dined with a friend at Prunier's and failed to sit out a farce at the Palais Royal. He spent one more day in Paris, buying a carving-knife for Elodie at the Bon Marché, and paying his first visit to Laperouse in the evening, where Mounet-Sully was among the *clientèle*. In the morning he caught the train for England after an absence of no more than sixteen days.

The bare record of such a journey reads like lunacy. What did Belloc hope to gain from it? Certainly not rest, since he had never been still for more than a few hours, and he returned ill and exhausted. Not company, since, apart from a day or two with Charteris and Somers Cocks, and his short stay in Paris, he had been alone. Not scenery, since he had dismissed the Tirol as 'detestable', and not architecture since he had confused Salzburg with Earls Court. The satisfaction, perhaps, of a single curiosity, since he now knew what the Beresina looked like; but, all in all, how little curious he had been! Not until he got back to France did he pause to gather the impressions that depend upon casual conversation and reasonable progress. But what was the point of travelling from Tours to Paris by way of Orléans (a dull town) merely to eat the crayfish that he could have got at Prunier's? And even in France it is astonishing how few people he really knew. He visited Drumont when the lion-hearted old anti-Semite was breaking up; but there is no evidence that he had heard of Péguy.

Nevertheless, it is possible that if Belloc had not made this absurd and exhausting journey we might never have had his pages on the Retreat from Moscow. He needed a physical contact with the *genius loci*; to see for himself the peril of those appalling plains; to grasp the width of the rivers, the receding horizons, and the distances immeasurable as fate. He was never to write the classic life of Napoleon, which he alone among contemporary historians could have achieved, and which Desmond MacCarthy always maintained would have crowned his fame. But his book on the campaign of 1812 gives us, already, a great deal. Admiration had not blinded him to the *hubris* which had brought about the downfall of Bonaparte, and he could now imagine him, monumental and solitary against the snow.

It was just as the late winter dawn was greying the fogs above the snowfields that Napoleon so decided, and gave the order to go forward. He stood under that dull half-light, a Polish cap of marten-fur upon his head, and, covering all his short stout body, a green velvet-lined coat trimmed with fur and marked by gold braid. He had in his right hand the thick birchen staff which he so carried during all the last days of the Retreat, and which all saw and remembered the next week at the Beresina. This was the figure of the man, bearded with the mist and sodden, when he took under the grey sky of that morning the determination to advance, even though it should cost him the bravest of his friends, and one whole fraction of what was left of his army.

Belloc had made his visit in the brief intense heat of the summer, but he could evoke the winter nightmare of the Retreat.

No snow fell on that day, and the very low and heavy sky, all even and motionless grey, did not mix with the horizon, but rather afforded along the horizon a background for the sharp rim of white so many miles around. All the world was white except four things which were black: the trees, here and there the burnt huts by the roadside, the long marks of water by the hollows of the land, and the enormous stippled belts of the Retreat.

Here, as surely as anywhere in his prose writings, is Belloc's power of exact visual description. 'The enormous stippled belts of the Retreat'—how good it is; how clearly it suggests

. . . a vast number of little black isolated things that cast no shadow (for there was no sun), and these were either creeping through the snow or lying still. The moving and the unmoving alike were not linked out upon the line of any road (for no road was marked at all through that white expanse of glare and cold), but the whole was scattered right and left upon half a mile of front or more; waggons abandoned, and dying men and little groups still going forward by themselves, and here and there an oblong of guns pushing and pulling as it could through such deep and half-frozen stuff.

In May 1913 Belloc was again in France with Elodie and the two girls. He showed them his birthplace and the more obvious sights of Paris. Elodie only just stood the pace of the journey—for it was very hot—but they eventually reached Toulouse. From here he sent his impressions to Maurice Baring.

I took the daughters to Mass this morning. All they have seen of a Catholic country hitherto was a short time in a Norman village, and they were hugely moved. I never saw such crowds! And it was particularly remarkable here in Toulouse where the attack on the Faith has been so violent and was, until quite lately, so successful. The gap, as one might expect, was of the men of middle age. The old men were there, not in great numbers, but the striking thing was the shoals of the younger men, from my age and less, the men of thirty or so, the men born since the war. It was remarkable also to see the floods of people coming in relays to one Mass after another making the big nave of St. Sernin what I had never seen it, though I have come to Toulouse again and again during the last fifteen years. These reactions of the Faith always give me—in this last year or so—the effect of a campaign or a battle. The masses of human beings all crowded and perpetually arriving and recreated; and I have the issue so much at heart that my interest in watching such sights is perhaps too strong.[1]

They went on into the High Pyrenees; to Gabas and the Oak Grove and the Pic du Midi; then to Lourdes where they were happy mixing with the Belgian Pilgrimage; and so back through Narbonne and Nîmes (where Belloc was annoyed to see a *plaque* erected to Bernard Lazare),[2] Lyons, Dijon, Langres, and Troyes to Paris. The holiday had been so successful that it was repeated, with variations, four weeks later! Belloc went down through Brittany and Cognac by himself, and met Elodie and the children at Bordeaux. They revisited Lourdes and on their return through Paris went up, and not merely alongside, the Eiffel Tower.

4

His work on and for *The Eye-Witness,* and his regular lectures for the University of London Extension, took Belloc to London a

[1] June 15, 1913.
[2] One of the most eloquent champions of Dreyfus, cf. Péguy's *Notre Jeunesse.*

great deal, and his naturally sociable inclinations tended to keep
him there. He would generally stay with Auberon Lucas, the
Chestertons, or Somers Cocks, until he found a tolerable lodging-
house in Wellington Square. When Elodie came up, they would
stop together at the 'Windsor'. He was able to meet his old friends
like Basil Blackwood and Maurice Baring (except when Baring
was away reporting the Balkan War). He also met a number of
people a good deal younger than himself, whom he would soon
count among his intimates: Duff Cooper, who was just going in
for the Foreign Office examination, Lady Diana Manners, Lady
Juliet Duff, and Mrs. Raymond Asquith. He used the Reform Club
to write and receive his letters, but he generally ate at restaurants.
At the Café Monico for Barsac and oysters; at Princes Grill for a
good marrow-bone; at the Holborn or Gow's for a steak; at
Gatti's or Pagani's, Romano's or Jules, the Mont Blanc or the
Gourmet's, the Cavour or the Café Royal; or at Overton's when
he was catching a train from Victoria.

He also made a host of new acquaintances, like Father Martin-
dale and Arnold Lunn, whose copy of *The Path to Rome* he signed.
Then there were the public dinners: with the Men of Sussex at
the Cannon Street Hotel, where everyone made speeches about
the Duke of Norfolk, to which the Duke of Norfolk responded
with delicate distaste; or with the Catholic students, when he sat
between Cardinal Bourne and Robert Hugh Benson. He got to
know Harry Preston who would take him to prize-fights, and he
met Mrs. Kendall and Granville-Barker without pursuing their
acquaintance. His theatre-going was generally confined to the
Follies, at the Apollo, which he thought 'a triumph of English
genius' or to the Music Halls—the Oxford or the Tivoli. He liked
to occupy a gangway seat in the Dress Circle so that he could
escape if he found the show unbearable; on these occasions he
would generally insist on paying for his companion's seat as
well as for his own. He walked out after the Second Act of
General John Regan; and when Lady Juliet Duff took him to see
Chesterton's *Magic,* he thought the play got worse as it went on
and that many of the speeches had nothing to do with the stage
at all.

Lord Islington asked him to dinner to meet the Prime Minister, with H. A. L. Fisher, Ramsay MacDonald, Sir George Schuster and Samuel Montague. Everyone was immensely cordial, but Montague wrote to Islington afterwards that he thought him a very brave man to have invited Belloc. At other houses he met Bonar Law and Lord Hugh Cecil, Ben Tillett, Cunninghame Graham and John Dillon. When he could spare an hour from work or society, he sat to Neville Lytton for his portrait.

This was one side of the picture, gregarious and convivial; the late nights over the port with Bron Lucas, Somers Cocks, or Cecil Chesterton; the irritations and the interest of public affairs; laughter and the love of friends. But it must be seen in contrast to the peace and refreshment of King's Land. Here there were visits to neighbours; to Mr. Blunt at Newbuildings where there was a constant coming and going of interesting guests—Yeats, Sturge Moore, Ezra Pound, Richard Aldington and Sydney Cockerell in his peaked velvet cap; to Mr. Graveley at Cowfold, with his great oak-tree which had grown from a sapling in a single life-time; and to the Burrells at Knepp, where the Bellocs frequently dined. There were long bicycle rides with John Phillimore to the Spread Eagle at Midhurst, or shorter ones to the inn at Billings-hurst, which had been so horribly spoiled. There were expeditions with the children—to the pantomime at Brighton, where Eleanor was frightened by the King of the Rats in Dick Whittington; to the Downs with a view of Courthill in the distance; to Steyn-ing to order a weekly barrel of ale from the brewery; or to Littlehampton, returning up the river with the tide. And some-times a friend would be taken as far as Handcross to see the lake where the Arun rises.

Louis was at Downside; this was not due to any special dis-content with the Oratory, to which Hilary and Peter were sent later, but a concession to Elodie's love for the Benedictines. Belloc would meet Louis as he passed through London on his way back from school, and there is record of a visit to the Admiralty where they studied the charts. He also showed the boy his birth-place at Oxford, and they spent a long day punting down the river to Abingdon in the rain and staying at the 'Rose and Crown'.

Meanwhile there was plenty for everyone to do at King's Land.
The runners must be cut off the strawberries, and the thistles—
some of them with roots two feet long—pulled up from the
flourishing asparagus bed. It was a relief how well the French
artichokes resisted the May frost. The carrots must be thinned,
the flints properly laid in the back-yard, and the little dam constructed so that the children might have a pond. The wild bees,
swarming outside the window of Elodie's room, must be coaxed
away. In September 1913 the 'Trolls' Hut was built at the end of
the garden. One wall of this was covered by an immense Ordnance Map of England, fourteen feet by twenty-two feet, the gift
of Auberon Lucas; and Maurice Baring's printing-press stood in
the corner. Belloc used the hut as a study. He had one gardener,
Laker, and two indoor servants, while additional help would
sometimes be provided by a passing tramp. There were ponies
for the girls, and in the afternoons Belloc liked to ride with them
through the old green way behind Edwards' farm and back
along Blunt's hunting road. He would amuse himself and the
children by flying an enormous kite, or building houses with toy
bricks—and even these had been specially made for him out of
seasoned oak. In the evenings they would play cards or jig-saw
puzzles, with Belloc drinking his beer from a 'magical mug'
given him by Evan Charteris. This played a tune each time you
raised it to the lips.

He had now started the practice of bottling his own wine. A
barrel of Burgundy was bottled in two and a half hours; three
hundred bottles all filled and corked. Later he got his wine—
Bordeaux slightly fortified by Algerian—from a shipper at
Nantes; good, rough stuff, costing only 4d. a bottle on the table
before 1914. One day a couple of Oxford undergraduates
arrived uninvited at King's Land and said they wished to see Mr.
Belloc, whom they regarded as their teacher and prophet. Belloc
informed them that there was an amusing occupation known as
bottling wine, and proposed that they should all go and do it while
he discoursed to them on politics and religion. The two youths
were then compelled to bottle a hogshead of Rhône wine, as
Belloc superintended and talked. On another occasion Mr.

Winston Churchill remarked to him that he had bought a barrel of wine abroad and was proposing to have it bottled by the Army and Navy Stores. Belloc implored him to do no such thing. He came over to Lullenden, where the Churchills were then living, and the two men bottled it themselves. Generally, however, he required about six pairs of hands if the operation were to be performed expeditiously.

On December 23, 1913, Elodie Belloc fell suddenly ill, being unable to swallow her food. She grew worse over Christmas, and Belloc was up with her for several hours in the night. The doctor came on Boxing Day and gave a serious report on her condition. Two nurses were in attendance and leeches were applied. By the 28th she was a little better and could take nourishment in extract, but she had a bad night on the 30th and was again unable to take food. She improved slightly in the New Year, but the nurses remained in the house and the doctor came regularly from London.

Life went on as normally as possible through the holidays, with a visit to *Mother Goose* in Brighton, and the solemn inauguration of the Trolls Hut on January 13, the Eve of St. Hilary. Belloc had himself painted up the motto outside: 'St. Hilary my kith and kin bless this hut and all therein.' The girls went back to school on the 19th, and on the 20th Gilbert and Frances Chesterton came over for the day. On the 21st Belloc was writing to Baring:

> Elodie gets no worse and no better; certain of the symptoms have improved, but others are more distressing and I am bound here very anxiously . . . Elodie is stronger *functionally* i.e. in digestion and nutrition but weaker *nervously*. She eats almost normally but she can see no one, she can read but very little and she sleeps more and more ill. I cry and pray God to take her to the *Sun*. The doctor won't let her move—not even out of bed— and it will be long, long. Priez pour elle et pour moi.

It was not long. There are no further entries in Belloc's diary after January 27. Elodie grew steadily worse during the last days of the month and a new weakness appeared in her hands. She passed into unconsciousness on February 1 and as her speech wandered it was suddenly touched with the old Californian accent of which Hilaire had cured her in the first years of their marriage. On Tuesday, February 3, he sent the following telegram to Gilbert Chesterton:

Elodie entered immortality yesterday the Purification a little before midnight unconscious blessed and without pain. Pray to God for her and for me and for my children.

Her body lay in the large hall at King's Land before the burial at West Grinstead, and many people came to pray beside it. Her room was closed and never again used during Belloc's lifetime; but as he passed it on his way to bed, he would always pause outside the door and trace upon it the sign of the Cross.

5

The shock was terrible. It is sometimes said too glibly of a man that 'he never got over the death of his wife'; but in the case of Belloc this was literally true. He was only forty-three when Elodie died and he had many years of useful work, and even of reasonable enjoyment, in front of him. His family grew up and his friends rallied round him. But the spring of his life was broken, and when he took it up again he was a different man. He now looked forward to nothing but the hardly imaginable moment of reunion in a beatitude which he firmly believed in, but of which he had no sensible intimation.

In the first crisis of bereavement he was sustained by Father Vincent McNabb, who came down to King's Land. The two men walked together in the garden among the flowers that Elodie had loved, and up and down the brick path that Hilaire had made for her. It was sometimes said that he over-dramatized his grief, not through any lack of control but through the outward symbols of his mourning. He dressed to the end of his life in the same black broadcloth, and the King's Land writing-paper was from now onward edged with black. Every year Mass was said for the repose of her soul, sometimes on the Feast of the Purification and sometimes on their wedding day in June; there was the

constant tending of the grave, and the money disbursed for
Masses in whatever part of the world he happened to be. But in
all this there might have been no more than the very Catholic,
and the very French, feeling for the companionship of the dead,
the very ancient and pagan sense of the *pietas* which the living owe
to them.

In the case of Belloc, however, there were also the gnawings of
remorse. 'Never', he would say to his friends in after life, 'give
yourself occasion for remorse.' He felt that he had left his wife
alone too much; that his vitality had worn her out. He himself,
though subject to headaches and constant sleeplessness, had an
iron constitution and he did not understand the meaning of
delicate health. If only they had given him the fellowship at All
Souls—the regret now rose with a new bitterness, for he had not
even been able to offer her security. Small occasions for remorse,
we may object; but this man had loved immensely, with a love
that leaves the conscience raw. There were few, even in that
astonishing circle of his friends, to whom he could speak the fullness of his mind. Belloc was a man not only of rich communication, but of deep reserves: he spoke the intimate thing with
difficulty and only after long hesitation. But he wanted to visit
the places where he had been with Elodie and to see the people
she had known. It was characteristic of him to feel that such
grief as now overwhelmed him should be met not with an
emotion but with an act; and characteristic, too, was the feeling
that he could not stay still.

So within three weeks of Elodie's death, he set out by himself
on his second journey to Rome. Before leaving he sent twelve
mortuary cards to John Phillimore, asking him to distribute them
where they would be seen by the Irish and the poor—for these
were Elodie's compatriots. In Rome he saw his old friend, Mgr.
Stanley; had an audience with Pius X; and left money for Masses
to be said for Elodie, in the city which she loved beyond all other
cities but which they had never visited together. The weather
was warm and sunny, and he went on to Naples; lingered there
for a day or so; and then took ship for Sicily. He had thought of
going to the Holy Land, but 'feared the miles of featureless

journey by sea and back alone.'[1] So he walked through Sicily instead; crossed to Tunisia; went to the edge of the desert, where the intense heat repelled him; and returned by boat to Marseilles. He walked in Provence (always alone); crossed the pass of La Croix Haute into Dauphiné; went north into Lorraine to visit the house and village of Jeanne d'Arc; came south again to Toul to see the soldiers; and on St. Patrick's Day, March 17, he was writing to John Phillimore from Lyons.

> I write you this brief line because I know no one else intimately on earth who is fully possessed of the Faith. I desire you to take such means as should be taken, whether by prayers or by Masses, or any other means for my preservation in this very difficult task. I am in peril of my intelligence and perhaps of my conduct and therefore of my soul, which deserves little through the enormity of what has happened . . . It is not as though I had any vision, comprehension or sense of the Divine order. All that was done for me as by another part of me: therefore I find myself without powers, like a man shot in the stomach and through the spine. I was content to keep the door and fight the crowd outside the church and now my office is valueless to me. I wish to God it were the body that was in peril. For I must take a third journey, as I took those two others in my boyhood and early manhood, but those were to California and in the known world: for the third journey, in which I must also do all to succeed, there is no plan and no knowledge in me. The body will, I fear, be strong and will keep me too long from that start upon that journey.

He returned to England and the days passed. Six weeks later he still confessed to an 'increasing doubt whether I can live my life'.[2] But his soul was secure in its humility, and his courage did not fail him when at last he took up the burden.

---

[1] Letter to Dorothy Hamilton: March 10, 1914.
[2] Letter to J. S. Phillimore: May 6, 1914.

CHAPTER XVI

THE GREAT WAR

I

BELLOC resumed his diary on March 28 and the family were together at King's Land for Easter. Auberon Lucas had lent Belloc a motor-car and chauffeur, and insisted that he should take the children and Miss Goldsmith for a tour through England and Wales.

Mr. Belloc put up a good 'front' of joviality and sang lustily as we travelled along; when we returned to London, we stopped first at Lord Lucas's town house and then went on to . . . his country home in Hampshire. There Mr. Belloc and I tried to answer the many hundred letters of sympathy and condolence which he had received.[1]

The holidays were enlivened by a large sheep-dog, which a friend had given to the children, and Louis spent the last week-end with his father at Picket Post, tracing the Roman Road. The literary work was taken up again.

Belloc was now completing his continuation of Lingard, and was also in correspondence with Feakins, the American lecture agent, about a tour of the United States in the autumn. He did not want to go, but the financial prospect was compelling.

One day, not long before Elodie's death, he had overheard the following conversation in the train coming down to Horsham.

'Terrible news from the Balkans.'

'Yes, but they're only barbarians.'

[1] Letter from Miss Goldsmith to the author: Feb. 16, 1956.

This measured the distance of public opinion from any immediate fear of war. Even Belloc himself was not particularly apprehensive. He had recently acquired Lord Stanley of Alderley's yacht, the *Nona*, for fifty pounds and on May 22 he arrived at Holyhead with Phil Kershaw for the purpose of sailing her round to a Sussex harbour. The story of this cruise was afterwards told in *The Cruise of the 'Nona'* (1925), and in fact the journey was interrupted a good deal more often than a reader of the book might imagine. Belloc and Kershaw returned to London for shorter or longer periods from Portmadoc, Fishguard, Appledore, Newquay and St. Ives. From St. Ives they had the boat sent round to Plymouth. During the week-end of June 29 Belloc was again at Picket Post. He motored in to Mass at Salisbury and there the congregation was asked to pray for the soul of the Archduke Franz Ferdinand, who had just been murdered at Serajevo. Belloc admits that he 'had never heard the name, and I had but a vague idea who this archduke was, of his relationship to the Emperor, and of his heirship to the throne of Hapsburg-Lorraine'.[1] He was in no doubt that the subsequent ultimatum from Vienna was of Prussian dictation, but he thought that all but the most humiliating points in it would be accepted by Serbia, and that these points would then be waived. He did not believe there would be a war, and Somers Cocks, whose judgment in foreign affairs he trusted, did not think so either.

On July 20 the cruise of the *Nona* was resumed at Plymouth, and it was in the morning mist, as they were crossing Start Bay, that Belloc and his companion saw the Grand Fleet, 'like ghosts, like things made themselves out of mist',[2] hastening eastward. Looking back more than ten years later, Belloc said that at that moment he knew there would be war. But at the time, as the hesitations of the Cabinet became known, he was not so sure. He was in London with Auberon Lucas when war was at last declared on August 4, and his first care was to stress on all around him the importance of knowing the exact position of every sack of flour in the British Isles. He saw General Macdonough at the War Office and offered his services; but Macdonough replied that he did not quite know where to send him. Belloc persisted in his attempts and on September 12 he was writing to Lady Juliet Duff:

> Not a sign of a staff for me to go to yet, not even a divisional one. It is an abominable shame, and when I chuck it in disgust and try through the French, it may be too late—they will wonder why I didn't ask before.

There was a suggestion that he should join the staff concerned with transporting the white troops from India, but this also came to nothing. The failure to get an appointment was no doubt a legacy of the Marconi case; officials evidently regarded Belloc as a man difficult and unpredictable to work with.

During August, Paul Déroulède came to London, a few weeks before his death, and Belloc took him to see Marie Belloc-Lowndes. Shortly afterwards the first frontier post pulled up from the Vosges in a vain and premature offensive was driven into the ground above his grave in the cemetery of La Celle St. Cloud. Meanwhile Belloc got to work with his pen. An article on 'The French Soldier' appeared in the *Sunday Chronicle* and another on 'Modern French Temper' in the *Dublin Review* (October 1914). He was explaining the necessary and unpopular alliance; and he was remembering his youth. The strength and the weakness of the French lay in their appetite for reality, with its emphasis on the concrete and its distrust of the extravagant. This was why they had consistently neglected moral effect in military matters.

> They directed their whole energy to discovering what sort of boot it was in which a man could best march; what sort of saddle it was that saved the horse best from sores; how best the weight of the pack would be distributed, and all details of this kind. They did perpetual violence to those appetites of military pride or vision which seemed to them divorced from and inimical to military reality.

On September 9, Belloc was visited at King's Land by a rich Australian, Murray (commonly known as 'Jim') Allison, who had

the main control of *Land and Water*. Allison was advertisement
manager on *The Times* and later on the *Daily Telegraph*. He
became a close friend and neighbour of Belloc, at Rodmell near
Lewes, until his early death between the wars. *Land and Water*
was a new weekly journal, as yet only projected, to deal exclusively
with the war, and planned to appear on August 22 (1914). After
a discussion lasting three hours Belloc signed a contract to write
a weekly article on the military situation. These were completed
on a Wednesday evening, corrected or amplified up to noon on
Thursday, and were in the hands of the public by Friday morning.
Later, the paper went to press earlier and the copy had to be in by
Monday. The naval articles were contributed by Fred Jane and
afterwards by Arthur Pollen. Belloc's articles brought him a
wider fame than any earned by his previous writings. *Land and
Water* reached a circulation of 100,000 and the articles were
discussed by men in every street, club, railway train or mess.
People read Belloc on the war who had never read him on
anything else. Yet there is no aspect of his public life on which
it is more difficult to get an objective valuation. The articles
were at once a tonic and a corrective to the layman, who still
hoped that the Allies would be in Berlin by Christmas but who
could not help observing that the Germans were making it unexpectedly difficult for them to get there. They were richly informative for the same layman who had not the slightest idea
what Continental war was really like, and they were based on an
exact knowledge of the terrain over which the western campaign
was being fought.

Of the many walks I have taken alone in Europe none has
more filled my memory or moved my mind to more conjec-
ture of the past than those walks, three or four of which I have
taken, cutting the Ardennes from east to west, and taking in
that line the central gorge of the Meuse ... I wonder, as I write,
whether there will be any more an opportunity for quiet men
seeking their souls to camp alone in that woodland as I have
camped, and to cross the lonely majesty of those valleys.[1]

[1] *Country Life* : September 19, 1914.

Belloc had a personal acquaintance with the methods, and also with the men, of the French Army, not only through his service as a conscript but through his following of the annual manœuvres. Of course he was occasionally wrong, but this generally happened when he was ignorant of the lie of the land; the *wadis* of the Egyptian desert were less familiar to him than the valleys of Champagne. He was accused, later, of lending himself to ludicrous prophecies. But if you study the articles, you will find that his prophecies are nearly always conditional. He never states categorically that this or that will happen; he only says that *if* this or that happens, a certain result will follow. His chief mistake was in underestimating the man-power of the Central Alliance. It was surely rash to say in October 1914 that 'the Germanic powers have put their last recruits and their last reserves into the field'; but when he freely declared, in April 1917, that the Allies would be fighting on German soil before the year was out, he was not alone in failing to see the completeness, or the consequences, of the Russian collapse. However, the day came when the readers of *Land and Water* were disconcerted to realize that Belloc was not infallible. The soldiers fighting the battles made a ribald play upon his name: a mysterious note-book, *What I Know about the War*, by Blare Hilloc, was circulated by a business house and was found to contain nothing but blank pages; and some people wondered why the war was still going on if as many Germans were being killed as he pretended. On September 6, 1915, posters appeared in the streets bearing the words 'Belloc's Fables'. These advertised an article in Northcliffe's *Daily Mail*, which convicted Belloc of various errors. Belloc, replying in *Land and Water*, not only admitted the mistakes but added, for the benefit of his readers, a number of other points on which he had been proved wrong. The point about these admissions was not the degree to which Belloc had been misled, but the fact that under the conditions of war such errors were unavoidable. Every writer on military affairs was calculating in the twilight, and for much of the time in the dark.

Now a distinction must be drawn between military journalism and military history. The man writing from day to day, or from week to week, is at a disadvantage compared with the man who can see the campaign in retrospect, check the rumours and distortions of the moment, rely upon assembled documents and collated evidence, and discuss the part in relation to the whole. Belloc, in these first few critical weeks of August–September 1914, had nothing to go on but the official communiqués and his own military common sense. The science of public relations was still at a rudimentary stage, and there was the further difficulty of translating the communiqués of the respective combatants. The French announced, for example, that the British line had been nowhere *'réellement entamée'*, and when this was translated as 'really pierced', justifiable alarm was excited. Belloc was able to point out that *'entamée'* does not mean 'pierced', or anything like it. Again, the Press Bureau announced that in their advance over the Marne the French had captured the whole of a 'corps artillery' and estimated this at 160 guns. Belloc, as an artilleryman himself, was able to remind his readers that a 'corps artillery' did not mean all the artillery belonging to a corps, but only those guns not allocated to a particular division. The numbers captured, therefore, were more likely to be 36 than 160.

The articles were a weekly warning against wishful and ignorant optimism. Belloc expressed an unstinted admiration for all that was remarkable in the German advance—'few finer things have been done in the history of war'; for the courage of the massed infantry attacking the Liège forts; for the rapidity of movement which he thought it would be 'folly not to admire and pedantic not to be astonished at'; for the skill and mobility of von Kluck's retirement to the Aisne. On September 18 he was writing to Chesterton:

This is the most extraordinary war that has ever been fought in the history of the world, and the Germans are conducting it with surprising activity. They marched a million of men over a triangle 120 miles by 100 in a week, and then marched them back again over a triangle measuring 120 miles by 60 in four days. Their weakness seems to me to lie in the extreme simplicity of their plans and the lack of alternatives. But they have

thought out exceedingly thoroughly the half dozen main
points which were in their minds; for instance, they are
occupying at this moment the very best defensive position that
could possibly be found. There was a great deal of carelessness
on the French side in the North; political carelessness as must
always be expected of democracies . . .

Belloc admitted himself partially mistaken on three aspects of
the German theory of war. First, the Germans had proved that
modern forts could be reduced by siege artillery, but could they
be reduced quickly enough for the needs of German strategy?
Manonvillers had held out for ten days and, in the event, the
crucial line Verdun-Toul held out indefinitely. Secondly, the
Germans had proved that it was possible for highly trained units
to digest a certain number—though not more than a certain
number—of unskilled recruits. And, thirdly, they had proved that
it was possible, through iron discipline, to launch infantry in mass
attack on a heavily fortified position; although the strain of this
would not bear repetition. Belloc stressed the accuracy of the
German war communiqués and the perfection of their Intelligence
service. He could not resist pointing out that the second Dreyfus
Court Martial at Rennes had disclosed the French plan of an
offensive through the Vosges in the event of war between France
and Germany. But the advantage of superior Intelligence, like the
advantage of superior numbers, which the Germans could boast
in 1914, was an initial advantage only; it would be neutralized
as time went on.

The British public were shocked by 40,000 German soldiers
goose-stepping through the streets of Brussels, but Belloc
reminded them that this theatrical parade was designed to destroy
Belgian morale, and that the destruction of morale was a legitimate object of warfare. Naturally, he did not approve of the
atrocities by which the Germans were already enforcing their will;
and the reported destruction of Rheims Cathedral, though in
fact this was only partial, drew from him a noble protest in the
Daily Chronicle. If contemporary evidence were correct, he
believed that the destruction must have been deliberate; if so, it

was against all true military instinct and at the same time in tune with the Prussian character.

It is already half-mad. Before long we shall see it run amuck. And if we do not kill it, it will kill us. Prussia can no longer think widely, she cannot paint, she cannot write. And most of what Germany had patiently learnt from the civilised west and south through centuries of industrious pupillage, Prussia has tarnished or got rid of in no long interval of time.

For Belloc the Cathedral of Rheims

was at the very summit of one of three, and only three, great movements in which European art has risen. The first was in Greece at the greatest time of Athens; the second was in the Italian Renaissance; the third was in the end of the twelfth and the beginning of the thirteenth century. . . . If you knew Rheims you knew all that past of Europe better than if you knew any other of the great cathedrals. For myself only I would say that the figure over the southern of the three western portals has more appeal—or had—than anything in Europe, much more than the dead Pagan, much more than the self-criticising Renaissance, more even than anything at Brou . . . the nucleus of France.[1]

Belloc went beyond the evidence in his warning that the Germans would probably treat their prisoners as hostages unless there were an approximately equal number of German prisoners in Allied hands. But this was not likely to be the case for some considerable time. Again, he prepared his readers for the possible loss of the Channel ports, and for the fall of Paris—although he believed that the capture of Paris was only incidental to the main German strategy. In his summing-up of the Battle of the Marne on September 19—two weeks after the tide had begun to turn—he emphasized how inexpensive had been the German retreat, and how much greater, proportionately, had been the Allied losses in men and material. The French use of their strategic reserve did, however, illustrate his point about the French passion for reality.

[1] September 23, 1914.

This use of a reserve goes with the determination only to act upon certain knowledge. It corresponds to secure investment in finance and to the positive spirit in philosophy. I do not say for a moment that this is the rule of victory; it may be, as precisely the same spirit is so often in financial affairs, the mark of over-caution and of consequent defeat. It leans towards materialism, a philosophy fatal to courage, and it leans towards the extinction of enthusiasm. It might destroy the cohesion of an army under a strain. But such a spirit, when it succeeds, succeeds in a fashion singularly solid in whatever sphere that spirit manifests itself.[1]

When people talked about 'the Russian steam-roller' Belloc reminded them that there could be no threat to Berlin until the Russians had reached the Oder. The Russian offensive in East Prussia had been repulsed, and although the Russians had won an important victory against the Austrians at Lemberg and now menaced the industrial basin of Silesia, there could be no movement on Berlin until the Germans had been driven out of East Prussia. The German commanders in the West would not need to worry about the Russians until the end of October; in the event, they did not have to worry about them at all. Generally speaking, Belloc stuck to his military brief; he discussed the moral and political aspects of the war elsewhere, particularly in the *Illustrated*. But he would always emphasize, as he had emphasized in his military history, that, since war is an extension of politics, the success of a campaign must be judged by its political results. Waterloo, for example, had destroyed Napoleon, but it had not had the political effect desired by Wellington and Blücher. Only very occasionally did Belloc betray his deeper feelings. The French army was 'engaged in this war upon the stupendous task of saving the culture of Christendom from dissolution and historic France from final disaster'; the sacrifice of Belgium promised the redemption of Europe since it had imposed a delay of ten days upon the German advance. Belloc knew in his bones, as well as in his heart and mind, what was at stake when the German pressure

---

[1] *Dublin Review:* October 1914.

2 A

at Vitry-le-François threatened to break the French line before the mass of manœuvre from behind Paris could threaten von Kluck and force a general retirement. It was along these river valleys— the Marne, the Meuse, the Grand and Petit Morin—and across the bare plateau of Champagne-Pouilleuse and looking eastward to the wooded ridge of the Argonne, that he himself had driven the guns in the summer manœuvres of '92, a conscript in the same army that was now battling for survival. He could imagine it all, as clearly as if he had been there; the trees untouched by autumn, the harvest gathered. And as he imagined it, history took hold upon him.

It must have been about the 4th September, Friday last, that once more men from Brandenburg saw before them south of the great camp at Châlons the half-starved rolling plain of the Champagne-Pouilleuse, utterly bare save for dwarf lines of newly-planted firs. And as they looked over that mournful country, which is like a tumbled sea of hillocks and rounded dips with the dull, low line of Argonne crossing the eastern horizon, one crest and roll over which they marched bore the tomb of Kellerman, and was the lonely position of Valmy. Whatever column it was that crossed this field, some man among them as he crossed the high road rested for a moment where young Goethe rested, and if he glanced back during a halt, may have wondered, as Goethe wondered, whether he were not at the beginning of a new world . . . Even as I write these lines upon the Wednesday of the week I do not know, for there is no immediate news in England, whether this effort of the invader upon the French centre at Vitry has succeeded. But I know that he is marching over sacred ground where there rise against him the influences of the dead. Not so far away, a day's march behind the defending line, is the house that nourished Danton. If that line is pierced the invader may burn the house, still standing, where Joan of Arc was born.

The effort, as we know, failed and a week later Belloc imagined himself on a certain hill, called 'Mont Aimé', which formed part of the escarpment bounding the Champagne-Pouilleuse on the west.

On this height I could wish to have stood last Friday in the south-westerly gale watching the long lines threading northward across the flats and knowing that these were the columns of the invaders in retreat.

But such passages were rare. For the most part Belloc's articles were pure analysis, and only descriptive when description was necessary to aid an understanding of the campaign. They were clear by dint of hard repetition and numerous maps and diagrams. They were also exceedingly long, often running to 8,000 words in a single number.

The vogue of *Land and Water* remained steady all through 1915, and in July Belloc was receiving forty pounds for his weekly contribution. Later, as the war became bogged down, the sales decreased and he was ready to accept twenty pounds for a summary and editorial. The circulation continued to fall, but he made up for this by an article at fifty pounds a week for the *New York American*. His articles for *Land and Water* appeared right through the war, although they became much shorter towards the end. Already, by March 1916, he was becoming critical of those parts of the paper not written by himself!

The non-Belloc part of *Land and Water* gets stupider and stupider every week. Even March Philipps, who is a first-rate man, is only allowed to write in it on condition that he talks of Prussia as a great big strong man, while everybody else is kind, good, and weak. Notably, I take it, the Senegalese. My feelings about *Land and Water* are mixed. If it went to pieces it would not be able to pay me my contract money. On the other hand, if it became a large and permanent fortune I should regret having taken cash instead of shares.[1]

The paper was, of course, subject to censorship, and it was always made clear where a passage of Belloc had been deleted. Sometimes he found it necessary 'to lie damnably in the interests of the nation. It wasn't only numbers that lost us Cambrai, it was very bad staff work on the south side. Things like that oughtn't

[1] Letter to Maurice Baring: March 17, 1916.

to happen.'[1] He did not at all object to a rational censorship and he put the case for it in the *Daily Chronicle*.[2] It was necessary to prevent panic and to conceal information from the enemy. The French Government had been right not to divulge their losses in the retreat from Mons, and they were right to allow no correspondents at the front. Belloc held that any government was justified in concealing bad news to prevent a run on the Banks, and he pointed out that a strict censorship was always tolerated by military nations.

In September 1914, Belloc signed a contract with Nelson to publish his *Land and Water* articles in three-monthly instalments under the title of *A General History of the War*; and as the details of the Battle of the Marne became available, he wrote a separate book devoted to this battle alone. But he was still hampered by lack of material. He maintained a close contact throughout with people who were vaguely, or precisely, 'in the know'. There were week-ends at Mells, with walks up the 'Iron Valley' which reminded him of California. There were other week-ends at The Wharf, Sutton Courtenay, with the Asquiths and, on at least one occasion, Mr. Balfour. Here Belloc would entertain the company with lawn tennis 'which I play like an elephant, and song'. He often stayed with Sir Herbert and Lady Jekyll, near Godalming, where Reginald and Pamela McKenna, their son-in-law and daughter, were constant guests. 'The politicians', he remarks in his diary, 'say that England is all right and everyone else is in the soup.' He noted a particular dislike of the French and a conviction that the war would not 'cost so much as to burden the finance of the country'.[3] But McKenna showed him confidential documents which explained the strength of the German forces in Poland, and gave him the details about Verdun just after they had been given to the Cabinet. On other visits to the same house he would discuss politics with Haldane, whom he found 'comfortable and cynical'; or walk through the woods with Harold Baker, listening to his views on Hesiod. Early in the war he had lunched at Downing Street for the first time in four years, and when he met Winston Churchill at Wilfrid Blunt's in April 1917

[1] Letter to G. K. Chesterton: Dec. 12, 1917.
[2] Unsigned article: Nov. 27, 1914.   [3] Oct. 24, 1918.

he found him still thinking of an offensive against the German ports. Churchill told Belloc that plans for this were being made when he came out of office. There were meetings with Lord Fisher, who harangued him on naval strategy, and with Colonel Repington, military correspondent of *The Times*, whose later articles he admired. And there were visits to Cliveden and Hever, where he would walk with old Mr. Astor through the park, talking of the *Chanson de Roland*.

His chief friend among the military was General Sir David Henderson, who was in command of British Aviation H.Q. in France. Belloc paid several visits to these H.Q., to which Maurice Baring was attached; and on one of them he lectured to the officers. He was frequently in Paris where he would dine with Berthelot, head of the Quai d'Orsay, and obtain information from the Press Bureau. In February 1916 he had an interview with Joffre at French G.H.Q. at Chantilly and was given secret documents by the Deuxième Bureau. He saw the Arsenal at Le Creusot and was lent a staff car to visit the battlefields of the Marne. Two further visits followed in December 1916 and in June 1917. On the second of these he went to Compiègne, where the French had moved their H.Q., and saw Pétain at some length. He again had the fullest information from the Deuxième Bureau, and dined at Moricourt with General de Castelnau, whose son was a gunner in Belloc's old regiment. In Paris he met Foch at the Invalides.

A *really* delightful man, full of genius and movement. He confirmed me in what I had said of the Marne and drew a little rough plan for me, which will be the most precious possession when I have it framed in my house.[1]

The sketch was hung in Belloc's study, and remained there until the end of his life. It bore the following inscription:

This sketch was drawn for me in the Invalides by General Foch on Saturday the 23rd June 1917 to illustrate his manœuvre when he brought the 42nd Division down and broke the German centre at 5 p.m. Wednesday 9th September 1914.

[1] Letter to Mrs. Reginald Balfour: June 26, 1917.

The sketch shows, in rapid and simple diagram, the Prussian Guard advancing in rectangular formation, and Foch moving to meet it from behind the marshes of St. Gond.

Belloc made two journeys further afield in his efforts to know what was going on and to give his news to those who only knew a particular sector of the War fronts. The first of these was to Lyons, where he lectured to the University at the request of the Foreign Office; and the second was to the Italian front in June 1916. Here he saw the new 305 gun in action; lunched with General Caputo at Cortina; and went up to Crustallo over the wire bridge—a terrifying experience. Then he went on to Rome. There had been general discontent in Allied circles over the lack of sympathy shown for their cause by the Vatican, and neither the efforts of Sir Henry Howard, head of the British mission to the Holy See, nor those of Cardinal Gasquet, the only English-speaking Cardinal in Curia, had modified this hostility. Little as it liked the Hohenzollerns, the Vatican had some reason for holding to the Austrian connection. Neither the Masonic governments of France and Italy, nor the Liberal government presided over by Mr. Lloyd George, gave much ground for hoping that the rights of Catholic populations would be respected in the post-war settlement, should the Allied Powers prove victorious. Quite early in the War, a Catholic friend in the Foreign Office, J. D. Gregory, had mooted the idea that Belloc should go out and see the Pope. He was at all times ready to do what he could, and the visit to the Italian front gave him an easy opportunity. He arrived in Rome on June 3, and two days later he was writing to Miss Hamilton from a room in the Vatican, on Vatican notepaper, with the complaint that he had just had fifty-three pounds stolen in a Post Office. As he was finishing this letter, Mgr. Pacelli came into the room; and the man whom he was later to see crowned as Pius XII informed him that Benedict XV would receive him in private audience. He gave his impressions of this in a letter to Charlotte Balfour, written from Paris on July 11.

I had a long, long talk with him. He is a *thoroughly good man*, which is not what I had been led to expect! I had thought to see

one of those rather subtle and very *bornés* Italian officials—
bureaucrates. Instead of that he has something like Holiness in
his expression and an intense anxious sincerity. He spoke of
individual conversion as opposed to political Catholicism in a
way which—with my temperament all for the Collective
Church—profoundly impressed me. I was exceedingly glad to
have seen him and to have got his blessing.

. . . I spoke to him at great length *on Poland*; that is the key
after the war. Only, as all plain wisdom demands clear action
and the re-erection of Poland, it will be too much to expect of
the modern world. But such as men are they may do something
towards that end. Such conditions make me long for momentary power.

All this talk about Poland presupposed that the Allies would
win. 'But do you think they will, Mr. Belloc?' the Pope asked
with kindly scepticism. It was proposed that Belloc should pay
him a second visit in 1917:

I shook him badly and took many thousands of prisoners and
guns from him a year ago, and some think I might, by repeating
the attack under the much more favourable conditions of this
moment, compel a general retreat.[1]

But this idea came to nothing.

2

The mission to the Vatican was the only official work on which
Belloc was employed during the Great War. Various projects
were mooted from time to time. The Duke of Westminster was
arming six Rolls-Royce cars; what these were supposed to do is
not clear, but the Duke proposed that Belloc should join his staff
because he knew the roads in Northern France. There was also
question of Winston Churchill forming a personal staff at the
Admiralty and Auberon Lucas suggested that Belloc should be a
member of it. But this idea obviously lapsed when Churchill
went out of office. It is an extraordinary thing that he should not

---

[1] Letter to Maurice Baring: April 12, 1917.

have visited British G.H.Q. until February 1917; a terse entry in
Haig's Diary records a lunch with the C.-in-C., who seems to have
had only a vague idea who Belloc was. He met John Charteris,
who was chief of Intelligence, and dined with General Percival at
the H.Q. of the 49th Division. There he was taken up into the
trenches, and had a clear view of the German positions opposite
from an Observation Post. He paid a second visit in May (1917)
when he was able to note 'the overwhelming character of British
artillery and air-work'. Both the pleasures and the responsibilities
of looking after Belloc on these occasions are conveyed by the
following letter. He was on his way back from Italy in 1916, and
had been invited to give a lecture to the 2nd Army School of
Instruction near Boulogne.

We had a good Mess and he liked good things and late that
Saturday night on bidding him good-night I asked him if he
had all he required. His answer was 'I always like a bottle of
champagne by my bedside'. He had it and was up at 5.30 a.m.
next morning for early Mass—I saw him on to the boat a day
or so after and never have I been a gaoler to a more charming
and interesting man.[1]

On one of these visits he found a number of Tommies telling a
woman in the market that she ought to have more children. 'Not
'arf', she replied. The Entente Cordiale, he observed, was really
beginning to take effect.

As soon as the first American contingents arrived in France
Belloc went over to Paris to meet General Pershing, of whom he
formed a very high opinion. He also paid tribute to the American
quickness to learn. 'We owe to the American temperament and
the American form of government a very deep debt of gratitude.'[2]

The immediate effect of *Land and Water* was that Belloc was in
great demand for lectures, not only to military units but to schools
and general audiences. In the first months of 1915 he was delivering up to ten a week. From the outbreak of war until the end of
1915 he paid five visits to Winchester, two to Eton, Harrow,

[1] Letter to the author from Colonel R. A. C. L. Leggett.
[2] *Daily News:* July 17, 1918.

Rugby and Repton; and he also spoke at Bradfield, Clifton, Cheltenham, Charterhouse, Haileybury, Epsom, Lancing, Shrewsbury, Wellington and Ampleforth. The Godolphin School for Girls at Salisbury and the Ladies College at Sherborne also had him down to speak. He lectured three times in the Queen's Hall in London, and on the first of these occasions six hundred pounds was taken at the doors; at the Colston Hall in Bristol more than 2,000 people came to hear him; and there were several visits to Scotland, Wales and the industrial North. In May 1918, accompanied by Eleanor Belloc, he visited the Grand Fleet in the Firth of Forth, where they were the guests of Admiral de Robeck. He lectured to the officers on H.M.S. *King George V* and H.M.S. *Marlborough*, and learnt how the guns were sighted on the big turret. 'I have seen many things', he told Lady Juliet Duff, 'in the last blazing days: the British and the Americans, the great hills of the West Coast and the torpedoes burrowing like white lightning in blue water and the huge ten miles of ship-building all the way from Glasgow to where St. Patrick was born.'[1] In the summer of 1916 he gave the Lees-Knowles Lectures in Military History at Cambridge. This was an annual professorship, and four lectures were required to be given. It was the first academic distinction Belloc had received since he left Balliol. An entry in his diary throws a vivid light on the whirl of his activities about this time. 'Sent a number of telephone messages from the Union to various parts of England.'[2]

He was now getting as much as twenty to thirty pounds for a lecture, and the fatigue of constant travel was mitigated by visits to his friends; to Phillimore in Glasgow; to the Goodwins at Altrincham; to Vaynol, with its little port and its little railway, looking across the Menai Straits, and Juliet Duff, 'timeless as ever among the trees'; to Stone, where he would take out his daughters from their school; and to the Oratory, Edgbaston, where he was allowed to sleep in Cardinal Newman's bedroom. Private hospitality was not easy on account of rationing, but Belloc professed himself 'utterly indifferent to meat, so that solves half of the problem, and I care nothing at all about

---

[1] June 7, 1918.   [2] May 13, 1916.

butter, so that solves the other half. As for sugar I snap my fingers at it.'¹ When he was lecturing in the West Country he would stop at Downside. Here the Community had their own farm and rationing was less rigorous than elsewhere. Belloc was never happier than with bacon and eggs, and on one of these visits he is recorded as having consumed at least half a dozen eggs, disposing at the same time of lashings of bread and jam. Louis was still at Downside when the war began, but in the summer of 1915 he passed eighteenth into Woolwich. He was only seventeen, among the youngest of several hundred competitors. His tastes had always been mechanical, and railways were among his favourite hobbies. Returning to the school for a visit, he was asked what had been the high-light of his leave. 'Oh,' he replied, 'a most interesting journey from London to Edinburgh with my head out of the window most of the time, and after a short wait there I took the next train back to London.' He still had time, though, for short visits to King's Land, and when he went out to France in July 1916, Belloc had more than one opportunity of seeing him there.

Although so many of Belloc's friends were scattered on active service, he never wanted for society. Somers Cocks was in London and the two men were constantly together. Although their friendship was so close, they were always 'Cocks' and 'Belloc' to each other, as in Oratory days. Cecil Chesterton was still editing the *New Witness* and Belloc was writing for it pretty regularly. This association caused him some embarrassment. Much as he liked Cecil as a man and warmly as he sympathized with many of his ideas, he did not think he was a good editor. Belloc's own reputation as a responsible critic of public affairs had been not a little compromised by his connection with the paper in the past. In August 1913 he had written to Maurice Baring:

I am a little in doubt whether the *New Witness* will manage to survive. No one takes any trouble to make it:
(a) Broad;
(b) Diversified and witty;
(c) Even moderately business-like.

¹ Letter to J. S. Phillimore: May 21, 1918.

They do not seem to know who they pay, nor when they pay him. And Cecil never seems to get anybody in from outside a very small clique. Without the Marconi to feed on it may easily perish. I cannot give my time to it unrewarded; I have to catch up the arrears of months of ill-health; but more important still is the fact that if I dabbled in it people would make me responsible for its enormities; not enormities of daring, but enormities of mis-judgment.[1]

Those who are too ready to accuse Belloc of an atavistic anti-Semitism should take note of a subsequent letter, also to Baring, provoked by Hugh O'Donnell's excesses in the same paper.

The irritation against Jewish power in Western Europe is partly the friction between the two races, but much more the annoyance of feeling that non-national financial power can restrict our information and affect our lives in all sorts of ways. It is legitimate to point out, if one does not grow wearisome, the fact that Jewish financial power has prevented people from knowing the truth about most famous foreign trials where Jews were concerned. But just because these matters so nearly verge upon violent emotion, it is essential to avoid anything like the suspicion of fanaticism. It destroys all one's case and weakens all one's efforts. . . .

. . . I think it is particularly silly to turn the one independent paper we still have into a monotonous mass of repetition upon the one single question of the hundred it should deal with. Supposing one were to fill a paper entirely with the danger to England of the German Fleet—which is a very real and practical question calculated to interest a vast number of people—how deadly the paper would become in three weeks. As for any influence of mine, I have decided not to exercise it. I have done my best in the past, but the only effect has been that, while my advice was not followed, outsiders thought I was still in some sort of control and that of course is intolerable. Sometimes I have thought of writing a letter which would testify to my disagreement in policy. I have had it in mind to do so now for

[1] August 27, 1913.

six months, but I have always hesitated because it would look disloyal. Certain cardinal points which I emphasised as long as I *was* in control, have been quite abandoned: as for instance that you must never attack without knowledge. That you must never emphasise an unimportant point, and that you can never effect anything against one section of people in any department of life in which you are friends with others in the same department. There ought to be a regular scheduled list of people in politics whom Cecil should keep off.[1]

Belloc did succeed in dropping out of the paper for a time, but the publication of E. S. P. Haynes' *The Decline of Liberty in England* (1916), and the criticism this drew from Wells in the *Daily News*, showed how deeply Belloc was implicated in the fanaticism of his friends. Haynes was no fanatic, but he was still tarred with the *New Witness* brush and Wells bracketed him with Belloc. According to Wells, reading the *New Witness* was 'like eating spring onions, a present excitement with a sort of afterwards'; its teaching had 'the simplicity of the taproom'; it relied not on 'reason but reiteration'; and it should have had for sub-title 'the art of stirring mud'.[2] G. K. Chesterton intervened in his brother's defence and Wells replied that public exposure would defeat its own end unless it were exercised with a sense of proportion. Belloc refused to answer Wells 'because I do not think that this enormous time is the right moment for literary gents to quarrel. I think also that his outburst was a sign of the enormous strain which everybody is subject to just now.'[3]

When, however, Northcliffe started his attacks on Asquith in 1915, Belloc found a platform in the *New Witness* at a time when he might with difficulty have found one elsewhere. He had already refused to write for *The Times Literary Supplement* because the paper belonged to Northcliffe, and his articles against him were so strong as to move the printers to censorship. Belloc regarded Northcliffe as a public menace, and among the specific charges he brought against him the following may be singled out.

[1] October 30, 1913.　　　　[2] July 24, 1916.
[3] Letter to Maurice Baring: August 6, 1916.

He had threatened the delicate negotiations going on for the cutting off of cotton supplies to Germany; he had attacked the Government over the lack of munitions when provision for increased supply had already been made; he had done everything he could to lower the reputation of Kitchener at a time when Kitchener's popularity was a national asset; he had refused to print the Government's appeal for recruits and betrayed their scheme for registration; he consistently dramatized the worst news and played down the good. Belloc urged that Northcliffe should be privately warned; that legal notices and public announcements which normally appeared in *The Times* should be withdrawn; and that special information should be withheld from it. 'I am going to keep him worried, dancing round and round at the end of his rope. He is in a panic and likely to go mad with it.'[1] He did.

Belloc had accused Northcliffe of wishing to influence the Government to his own advantage. Belloc, for his part, had a just appreciation of Asquith's qualities; he had

shown himself to be an excellent patriot throughout the war and he has now become a physical necessity to the maintenance of England among the Allies. The King said the other day that he was indispensable and he was right. He has never enriched himself, though he might have done so, and he has always considered the public good.[2]

When Asquith had been displaced, Belloc met him one day in Cavendish Square. Asquith asked him if he had any intention of returning to Parliament, and warmly approved his determination not to do so. Belloc took away the impression of a man thoroughly disgusted with the degradation that had come upon the House of Commons. In so far as Asquith had played the Party game according to the rules which he had inherited, Belloc did not exempt him from a certain responsibility for this. But his fall had done something much worse than split the Liberal Party to its eventual destruction; it had placed in supreme authority

[1] Letter to E. S. P. Haynes: Sept. 20. 1915.
[2] Letter to Maurice Baring: Sept. 14, 1916.

over English affairs a political revivalist who not only left public
life infinitely more corrupt than he found it, but went far to ruin
by his ignorance what he had achieved by his exertions. Asquith
may not have known a great deal about Europe, but he had at
least heard of it. And when other knowledge is lacking, it is
something to know one's Thucydides.

Belloc believed that Asquith had given way over conscription
under pressure from Northcliffe, lest worse should befall him;
and he was himself strongly opposed to the idea when it was first
mooted at the outbreak of war.

> We shall get all we can possibly want, and more than we can
> officer or gun—far more in any useful time—by a voluntary
> system properly paid, and above all by not nagging the wives
> and families of the men as they are now doing. A man should be
> absolutely certain of what will happen to his wife and family if
> he gets killed, and the allowance should be generous. To talk of
> conscription in a country organised as England is, and un-
> touched as to her soil, is to have quite lost grip of reality.[1]

Belloc still held these views in 1916. He was not particularly
excited by the proposal to apply conscription in Ireland, because
he thought the idea Pickwickian. The Southern Irish farmers
would refuse to drill, just as they had refused to lick Lloyd
George's Insurance stamps; and no one would be so foolish as to
force them. Belloc thought it a capital mistake (as it obviously
was) to shoot the leaders of the Easter Rising; they should have
been treated as prisoners of war. But he thought Roger Casement
should be shot because he had helped the enemy privately and
taken money for doing so, and he did not think the Irish cared
what happened to him. If he were spared, they would accuse the
British Government of favouring an Ulster Protestant and Freemason at the expense of Catholic patriots who had rebelled openly.
The Government hanged Casement after smearing his character
with what many people believed to be forged diaries, and some of
the Irish—and even a few of the English—minded quite a lot.

There was some talk of Belloc founding an independent—and

---

[1] Letter to Maurice Baring: Nov. 9, 1914.

mainly literary—weekly during the summer of 1916. This would be very different from the *New Witness*. Belloc, whose nose was very sharp in these matters, seemed to scent, already, the revolutionary *malaise*.

The moment for violent political action is past. What will be wanted now and for some time after the war will be just the other thing, restraint and direction; for people will be at sixes and sevens and so far from having to shake people out from too great sense of security or acceptation of evil one will have to keep them to common sense and save them from panic and exaggeration. The strain for the re-adjustment of industry after the war will be something really tremendous and there is no doubt that the beginning of the breakdown of the great institutions which appeared just before the war will make it worse. It would be an enormous advantage if one could strengthen Parliament a little. They want a good stiffening of aristocrats, a pinch of professional men outside the lawyers, and some new, well-organised party; the latter I think is coming, but not until well after the war.[1]

Meanwhile he grew more and more disgusted by the political cabals.

One would think [he wrote to Lady Juliet Duff] that the agony of England only served to give opportunity to vulgar politicians and still more vulgar millionaires with their newspapers and their intrigues. Their vices are the great asset of the enemy. It is a terrible thing when the government of the country breaks before the rich and when it has no King . . .

The Republican had long ago returned to the altar; he was now returning to the throne.

When the movement for an agreed peace gathered strength in 1916 Belloc analysed and refuted it in six 'letters' addressed to an imaginary peacemaker, and published in the *New Witness*. The movement, he maintained, was inspired by a belief that the war was not really national; that it was destroying many things

[1] Letter to Maurice Baring: April 13, 1916.

essential to the nation; that its objects were undefined; that it was
being waged at an excessive price; and that complete victory was
impossible. Belloc began by demolishing the heresy that the
British and Germans were cousins; he had been fighting this
illusion ever since he first met it at Oxford. 'Kingsley shouted and
screamed it; Freeman hallowed it; Carlyle and Coleridge and all
the lesser men knew nothing else; the genial and learned Stubbs
ponderously reinforced it.' The Angevin parliaments had not
been born in the Thuringian forests; England had been founded
on 'age-long traditions of a civilised past . . . upon ineradicable
doctrines of chivalry, adventure and honour—and irony, the salt
of it all. You do not find even the opposite of these things in the
Germanies—they are not there at all.'[1] British intervention against
Germany was 'abnormal, new and necessary', because German
sea-power would 'continue to increase and must be directed
against this country unless the German Empire is completely
defeated in the present campaign'.[2]

3

Early in 1916 Belloc acquired a small house in Knightsbridge
which he afterwards exchanged for another near by. He christened it 'Orthodox Hut', and it was, in fact, within a few yards of
the Oratory Church. For occasional diversion he would go to the
theatre—anything from *Henry V* to *A Little Bit of Fluff*—and he
discovered a sudden passion for French and Italian opera. When
he had a free day at King's Land he would take the *Dreadnought*—
his old sailing-boat to be distinguished from the *Nona*—up the
river to Stopham or Timberley Bridge; and he would see about
the reconditioning of the *Nona*, which had now been brought
round to Littlehampton. In September there were short holidays
with the children in the West Country, staying with friends,
which he enjoyed, or in an hotel on Exmoor, which he hated.
Edith Fair had remained on at King's Land after Elodie's death to
keep house for the family. She was a remarkable cook; and in the
garden Laker, with whom determination only just fell short of

---

[1] April 27, 1916.   [2] *Ibid.*

For Miranda

New Year: 1929.

Do you remember an Inn, Miranda?
Do you remember an Inn?
And the speeding and the tedding
Of the straw for a bedding,
And the fleas that tease
In the High Pirenees,
Do you remember an Inn, Miranda?
Do you remember an Inn?
And the cheers and the jeers of the young Muleteers
(Who hadn't got a penny
And who weren't paying any)
And the wine that tasted of the Tar?
Do you remember an Inn, Miranda,
Do you remember an Inn?

And the cheers & the jeers of the young Muleteers
(Under the Vine of the dark Verandah)
Do you remember an Inn Miranda)
And the hammer at the doors and the Din?

And swirl and the twirl
Of the girl
Gone chancing
Glancing
~~Clapping of a snapper~~
Backing and advancing
Clapping of a snapper to the spin
Out and In.
And the Ting Tang Tong of the Guitar.
Do you remember an Inn, Miranda?
Do you remember an Inn?

* * * * *

Never more! Miranda. Never more!
Only the High Peaks Hoar,
And Aragon a torrent at the door.
No sound
But the fall
Of the fread
Of the dead
To the ground
Of the Hall.
No Sound:
But the Boom
Of the far waterfall like Doom.

H. Belloc.

This is the original version with
its erasures: the end of the "No
Sound" is best. But "And the
Wine that tasted of the Tar"
Should come after line 6
& form line 7. ⁓

the tyrannical, insisted on growing the sour Sussex cucumbers that Belloc disliked. Thanks to a legacy of £4,000 from Auberon Lucas, he had acquired a further twenty-five acres of farm-land, with a large wood, and in August he could boast of seven calves, five cows, four bullocks, five pigs, three horses, and fifty-three fowls. One of the pigs (called Rufus Isaacs) the Government permitted him to kill for his own consumption. There was also a family of rabbits which perished from eating old carrots. 'Eleanor', he tells Miss Hamilton, 'cuts down trees with a huge axe and enormous vigour, swinging herself about like a whirlwind and bringing down oaks with a crash.'[1]

Meanwhile he had resumed work on his *History of England* and a neighbour, Mrs. Frank Collin, was teaching him to etch. He had made one or two new literary friends who lived near by—J. C. Squire and 'Raffles' Hornung—but, in general, his diaries give a sense of continuity, the same habits and the same hobbies, which impresses one as a proof of courage.

He had need of courage, and the need would not grow less. The casualty lists told their dreadful story, week by week. The men who might have remade the public life of England—the generation of Belloc's friends, men only slightly younger than himself, and the generation that came after them—were being mown down in senseless offensives or in stubborn defence. Raymond Asquith was killed in September 1915, and Edward Horner in 1917. Basil Blackwood was staying at King's Land in March 1916 and Belloc read aloud to him, eight times over, the last line of the *Æneid*:

vitaque cum gemitu fugit indignata sub umbras.

Fifteen months later he was dead. Worse was to follow. Auberon Lucas was lost, flying, on November 3, 1916. Belloc wrote to Chesterton from Boulogne:

Pray for Bron Herbert continually and he will help you from heaven. I do not know how these things are. (Neither does any man outside dogma, which is mathematical, therefore of God),

[1] Aug. 14, 1918.

but in human words he was the most chivalrous, the bravest and the best, and will help us all out of heaven. God has received him with the fighting men of the Pyrenees whom he loved.[1]

And again to Lady Juliet Duff, more briefly, in words that grief had carved into an epitaph:

He was the noblest and the best and therefore they took him from this vile world, and our lives are changed.[2]

None of these men were Catholics, but every year Belloc arranged for a Mass to be said for Bron Lucas. Although he was exalted by his, and their, example, he was depressed when he considered the world which had bred them, with its immense natural virtues and its dearth of supernatural faith.

. . . here is all England [he wrote to Baring] taking for granted either no soul or (what is worse) some drug of easy transitions and perpetual communion between them and us: a falsehood of a vile and weak kind . . . the absence from the Faith of such souls in England turns us all into exiles—a few exiles alone.[3]

Cecil Chesterton was called up in 1917 and served in the ranks. Belloc was present at his wedding to J. K. Prothero soon afterwards. At the end of the year he was discharged from active service with a septic hand and was stationed for some time in Scotland. In the crisis of March 1918 he volunteered for active service again; was accepted; caught trench fever shortly before the Armistice; and died in the Military Hospital at Wimereux. A Requiem was celebrated at Corpus Christi, Maiden Lane. Father Vincent McNabb preached the panegyric and Belloc always held this to be the finest piece of sacred oratory he had ever heard.

Desmond MacCarthy had described Cecil Chesterton as the best pugnacious journalist since Cobbett, but it was not upon his pugnacity, nor upon his power of expression and rapidity of synthesis, that Belloc dwelt in his own tribute. What he emphasized was his courage. It was this that had drawn the two men together.

[1] Dec. 7, 1916.   [2] Dec. 3, 1916.   [3] Sept. 22, 1916.

His courage was heroic, native, positive, and equal: always at the highest potentiality of courage. He never in his life checked an action or a word from a consideration of personal caution, and that is more than can be said of any other man of his time. . . . He was incapable of neglecting an act from lack of courage or even from a modification of courage, as most men are incapable of a public act which would involve them in danger, and by the measure of the one you may take the measure of the other. Courage possessed and displayed in that degree is by definition heroic. . . .

There are private things which are the more important in the decline of a State. The qualities I have described are less than the things which I have not said of such a friend and of such a companion in arms: *tam cari capitis*.[1]

Tam cari capitis—it was five years since Belloc had used the same words of George Wyndham. Some fate decreed that this soldier of the forum should lose his allies while the battle was still hot around them, and the issue still perilous and undecided.

Louis Belloc, who had started his active service as a sapper on the Somme, was mildly gassed in August 1917 and sent home to hospital in Manchester. Belloc and all the children went up to see him. The skin of one leg, both calves and the lower part of his right arm were blistered. The gas had sunk into the ground, and these injuries were the result of lying on it five hours after the attack. He quickly recovered, but his heart was now set on flying. General Trenchard's influence assisted his transfer into the R.F.C.

I parted from him with a heavy heart but . . . like myself at his age there was no escaping what youth so intensely desired.[2]

Louis did his training at Reading and Lincoln, and then went out to the front. On August 26, 1918, when the war had already entered its victorious phase, his squadron set out to bomb the German transport columns. Those machines flying slightly higher

[1] *New Witness:* Dec. 13, 1918.
[2] Letter to Dorothy Hamilton : Aug. 14, 1918.

than the rest were just able to glide back to the English line; the others, among which was Louis's, were forced down a little short of them. He was immediately reported missing. For a time it was thought that he had been taken prisoner, and in December his death had not been confirmed, although Belloc had by then given up hope. His body was never found, and it was a long time before the children would believe that their brother had been killed. There had been a certain lack of confidence between father and son, but during the days and weeks of suspense all the boy's life returned continually to Belloc's mind. He remembered the boat they had built together in 1913 and the day when he was first sent to school in Bournemouth and had cried so bitterly—the day when they had borrowed Auberon Lucas's car to impress the schoolmaster—and 'especially his early childhood and the days before any disasters came.'[1] Belloc often now wished he could get back to these things and to the poverty he had once thought so hard. He would get back to the poverty in time, but there was no way back to the rest—'except the roundabout way perhaps, through death.'[2]

In 1924 Belloc had a tablet erected in Cambrai Cathedral to the memory of his son. It was placed at the entrance to the Lady Chapel, and he had arranged for a similar plaque to the memory of Edward Horner to be fixed opposite. On a pillar in Amiens Cathedral, just behind the tablet to the British and Canadian dead, a third plaque was put up to Raymond Asquith, and here again Belloc had used his influence with the civil and ecclesiastical authorities. It cost him many months of wearisome negotiation and delay. For Belloc these memorials had a representative value; for behind the names which they commemorated may be read the names of all those others whom the war had taken from him.

[1] Letter to Mrs. Reginald Balfour: Sept. 6, 1918.
[2] Letter to Lady Juliet Duff: March 11, 1915.

CHAPTER XVII

DEFENDER OF THE FAITH

I

THE moment has now come to desert chronology, and it is precisely the moment when we have to consider, in more detail, the attitude of Hilaire Belloc to those things which are not answerable to time. The central importance of the Catholic Faith in his life and work will already have been made clear. But whereas, up to 1920, this had been an integrating principle and a recovered habit, after the Great War, as the years grew upon him and his private dereliction became harder to bear, it became the chief purpose of his writing. To proclaim, and where possible to prove, the truth of Catholicism; to show the Church as the salt and savour of such civilization as survived in Europe; to demonstrate the price paid by his own country for the loss of Catholic belief—these now became a single, urgent, public task to which he addressed himself with all the force of his will.

Most people, even those who were already converted to his beliefs, regarded Belloc as a religious propagandist; as a man logically, and sometimes perversely, possessed by a *parti pris*. They knew little of the personal life on which his convictions were based and in which it found private expression. Because he would generally separate objective truth from personal feeling, they did not always catch the warmth or the quality of his faith. It was the opposite with Chesterton. Long before Chesterton became a Catholic, his readers felt themselves in contact with an *anima naturaliter Christiana*; with a man who was a Christian before he was a Catholic; with a man who would have lived and died a Christian even if he had never become a Catholic. For Belloc the Church came first. If he had not been convinced that the Church was a divinely appointed and, in its essence, a divinely governed institution, he would have been a sceptic; hardening, as sceptics generally do, with the diminishing capacity for faith. This was his natural temper, and he had perpetually to be converted out of it. If we want to understand his approach to religion, at least in his later years, we cannot do better than turn to his letter to Chesterton, when Chesterton became a Catholic in 1922. Much of this was reproduced by Maisie Ward in her life of Chesterton, but the following is relevant to our enquiry and some of it is published here for the first time.

If the ordnance map tells me that it is eleven miles to Wookey Hole then, my mood of lassitude as I walk through the rain at night making it *feel* like 30, I use the Will and say: 'No. My intelligence has been convinced and I compel myself to use it against my mood. It is *eleven* and though I feel in the depth of my being to have gone twenty miles and more, I *know* it is not yet eleven I have gone.

I am by all my nature of mind sceptical, by all my nature of body exceedingly sensual. So sensual that the virtues restrictive of sense are but phrases to me. But I accept these phrases as true and act upon them as well as a struggling man can. And as to the doubt of the soul I discover it to be false: a mood: not a conclusion. My conclusion—and that of all men who have ever once *seen* it—is the Faith. Corporate, organised, a personality, teaching. A thing, not a theory. It.

To you, who have the blessing of profound religious emotion, this statement may seem too desiccate. It is indeed not enthusiastic. It lacks meat. It is my misfortune. In youth I had it: even till lately. Grief has drawn the juices from it. I am alone and unfed. The more do I affirm the Sanctity, the Unity, the Infallibility of the Catholic Church. By my very isolation do I the more affirm it as a man in a desert knows that water is right for man: or as a wounded dog not able to walk yet knows the way home. . . .

But beyond this there will come in time, if I save my soul, the flesh of these bones, which bones alone I can describe and teach

I know—without feeling (an odd thing in such a connection) the reality of Beatitude : which is the goal of Catholic Living.

> In hac urbe lux sollennis
> Ver eternum pax perennis
> Et eterna gaudia.[1]

We have seen, or surmised, how much of his religion Belloc imbibed from the Oratory Fathers or at his mother's knee—and this should not be underestimated. We have seen how nearly he lost it during the Balliol years, though he probably kept a good deal more than he admitted. We have seen how humbly and how surely he received it back from his wife; how—in a manner of speaking—he was content to fight while she prayed; and how helpless he felt when she was taken from him. He had lost more than a comrade; he had lost a comrade-in-arms—and in the battle he would always feel essentially alone. This loneliness, which was also part of his incapacity either to lead or to work in a team, gave a certain sadness to his polemic; and this in turn produced the aridity of which he so often complained. Yet we must not be betrayed into asserting, as Belloc in his humility would assert, that he was without experience. We must distinguish between experience and feeling. A man may have all kinds of Christian feelings and yet be without sensible Christian experience. Or he may, like St. Thérèse of Lisieux, have the supreme experience of sanctity and yet have, for long stretches of time, no feelings whatever. The Christian experience is precisely the exercise of the theological virtues—faith, hope and charity— and we estimate a man's Christianity by the degree to which he appears to practise them. Judged by these standards, no one who knew Belloc would say that he was without experience of the religion which he preached. His expression of it was highly personal. He was a man living at constant tension and beset, as the years brought their toll of physical decline, by material worries of which he might have hoped to be relieved. He was reduced, at the end, to a sad dependence on the care of others. But as the body failed him, his spirit became more luminous, and he

[1] Aug. 1922.

acquired the difficult virtue of patience. Like every other man, he had his faults. But it is not often that one can say of a man of genius, quite simply, that he was a good man. One can say of Belloc not only that he was good, but that he was supernaturally good. The 'experience' that was not apparent to him was apparent to other people—and that is the test.

On one occasion, in the hospitable common room of Campion Hall, Oxford, the conversation turned on the doctrine of transubstantiation. A sceptical guest asked Belloc how he could possibly believe that the Bread and Wine of the Eucharist were changed into the Body and Blood of Christ. Belloc replied that he would believe they were changed into an elephant, if the Church told him so. The answer shocked some of the younger Jesuits present; this, they felt, was faith degenerated into fideism. But it gave the quality, uncritical and uncompromising, of Belloc's belief in the Church. If once this belief had been shaken, nothing would have remained. But it would be wrong to assume from it that Belloc never thought for himself. He was neither a trained philosopher nor a trained theologian. He knew bits of Descartes and St. Thomas, and he knew enough theology to explain the course of history. This was certainly more than most historians possessed. But he had also a strong and subtle (not too subtle) mind. He had a quick eye for analogy, a powerful logic, and an entire trust in reason up to the point where it stopped short of mystery. He had large gaps of knowledge and large defects of sympathy, but his intelligence worked with great speed and precision within the limits of what he felt and knew.

It would therefore be a gross oversimplification to suggest that he took no pains to certify and confirm his beliefs; that within those beliefs his mind was inactive. Sometimes discussion with a friend would force him to think out his acceptance of Catholicism afresh. In a letter to Mrs. Asquith, which is too long for extensive quotation, he lets us see the process of his mind, and his words are not those of a man who has taken refuge from scepticism in credulity.

Scepticism—the belief that any religion is the creation of man himself—seemed to him 'the normal youth of a healthy mind', but he had found by experience that scepticism grows sceptical of itself. The initial assumptions of the mind—that the earth is flat, for example—are found to be insufficient, and the intelligence looks for support to that which confirms and expands common knowledge. It proceeds from the blank declaration that men fabricate their own gods in the image of the visible universe to the mysteries of Personality and Evil, and to the admission that some one religion might be true even though many may be false. The mind reasons from the known to the unknown and discovers a purpose and a unison. But it has reached, by now, a point beyond demonstration and well beyond experience. If certitude in the major things be attainable to man, then it can only be attained in a transcendental system, in some affirmation of non-demonstrable things, in some religion.

The question remained—which? And for Belloc it was easier to say why one particular religion was true than to say whether such truth were attainable at all. He concludes his argument as follows:

There might be such a system, such a religion. Only *if* there is, do I discover replies to the only questions worth asking. But *is* there one? That is another matter. Now the reply is in the concrete and the particular. The Faith, the Catholic Church, is discovered, is recognised, triumphantly enters reality like a landfall at sea which at first was thought a cloud. The nearer it is seen, the more is it real, the less imaginary: the more direct and external its voice, the more indubitable its representative character, its 'persona', its voice. The metaphor is not that men fall in love with it: the metaphor is that they discover home. 'This was what I sought. This was my need.' It is the very mould of the mind, the matrix to which corresponds in every outline the outcast and unprotected contour of the soul. It is Verlaine's 'Oh! Rome—oh! Mère!' And that not only to those who had it in childhood and have returned, but much more—and what a proof!—to those who come upon it from over the hills of life and say to themselves 'Here is the town.' The true is proved by analysis and demonstration where these are to hand—where they are not, by direct vision: as is our proof of daily things and their reality. When vision again is lacking, how can it be proved? By its other aspect in the triune definition: by Beauty and by Goodness.

The Faith has Beauty and nothing has it so fixedly, permanently, pointingly. It is a Beauty ambassadorial and determinant, a proving Beauty. And it has Goodness, in this time of ours more marked than ever by contrast. It shines with, produces, supports, promises and reveals Goodness. I say again, it is a person to be discovered and not to be merely loved: a plenitude of excellent experience. Not only satisfaction, but conscious satisfaction. Satisfaction reasonable and final. You know the phrase 'Sero cognovi?' It expresses it all. And that other phrase the little teacher wrote me years ago which was a revelation to me and which I have quoted too often: 'Secure within the Walls of the City of God'.

Here, then, is the meeting of Belloc's mind with his experience. Of the difficulties he had to overcome the most formidable was the fact of mortality. Indeed mortality runs like a refrain through all the thinking of this man who was so ardently in love with life. Here, as always, Belloc preferred ignorance to illusion, and where knowledge—or even imagination—failed, dogma came to his aid.

I do not think myself that any positive evidence will ever appear in favour of the immortality of the soul such as would convince any reasoning man. It does not seem to me susceptible of positive proof by deduction or experiment. There is nothing in the spiritualist phenomena which cannot be explained either by illusion or in extreme cases perhaps by the action of spirits. But there is no sort of evidence of the human dead being at work.

St. Thomas is very good on the different kinds of proof required for the different kinds of truths, and I have learnt from him that hardly any of the truths of the Faith admit positive evidence. It would be like trying to prove the existence of a scheme of colour by measuring the outlines.[1]

[1] Letter to E. S. P. Haynes: Nov. 8, 1923.

In further letters to Mrs. Asquith he compared faith to 'the knowledge of the real coloured visible world to a man half blind';[1] and, deeply moved by a return to Lisieux where he had been with Elodie in the year of their marriage, he tried by analogy to define the nature of holiness. The sanctity of St. Thérèse shone out by contrast with her hideous shrine; such manifestations were rare, but they were 'intense actualities of promise'.

> Not only does a soul in beatitude inhabit this modern small ungraceful thing and roof, but brings into it such universal influence as floods the mind. . . . Of its nature such evidence escapes measurement and the control of an experience daily and common to all. It is but the more real.
>
> Landscape, which is to all who were bred in South England the nearest road to the appreciation of the ultimate beauty, is common if not to all at least to many. If, of these, any deny the glory beyond this world, and Paradise, he may be half convinced or rendered doubtful by the sight of the Severn Valley on a still summer sunrise from the height of the Cotswolds, or of the Weald from Gumber Corner. There is a common appeal therein and an argument from mind to mind. Music, which is a more general ground in our relaxed, undisciplined times, gives moments of the sort—and on that account is too much run after as a drug. High verse, which is more removed and nobler, some few can still admit: and others the inspiration of carving or line or even (much too uncertain) of colour. But all, at least, are susceptible to some admitted test: they are not opinions but certitudes. With the highest and most determinant of influences, the unseen presence of Holiness, it is otherwise. It is subject to unanswerable challenge and stands always accused of illusion—but only because it is a direct shaft into the individual mind, and by that character in it it is the more absolutely sure. There is something behind the senses which appreciates with violence and completely:—but how rarely![2]

This sixth sense of holiness was for Belloc a sixth proof of the existence of God. He did not in the least run after holy people, but

---

[1] Dec. 2, 1929.   [2] *Ibid.*

when he met them he felt the contact—as hard and as real as rock. It was the conviction of sanctity which bound him to Father Vincent McNabb and he would go anywhere to hear him speak.

That last conference of Vincent McNabb's has inhabited my spirit all these days. It had certain profundities deeper than I ever heard: notably the transition of Death. It is well to have emphasised the enormity of the Affair—for to turn the mind away from its enormity is always one of the forms of falsehood (hypocrisy, or drugging or deliberate suppression). It is no derogation from its enormity that the Faith calls it a transition. It is catastrophic. All is involved and the foundations are shattered. It is so, not so much in the prospect of death as in the separation. How well he said that its enormity was best seen in this: that we cannot conceive it. We cannot imagine what is the other half of the broken sequence. I have known that from my thirtieth year, but I have never so meditated on it as since last Wednesday. It was well to say that on the dust of the crash and ruin rose 'the piping of a lark'. I like the violent metaphor: the small but beatified beginning of a new thing. Well: it's wise to think on these things and I am enormously grateful when they are—once or twice in many years—made alive. . . . It seems to me that there are three truths: of the body, the intelligence or mind, and of the soul: and that a Spiritual truth stabs home to the core of reality as does not either of the other two. It is (as it were) ultra-true, 'Archi-vrai'. It is well to hear that sleep is good and it is well to learn the consonance of philosophy and numbers: but to hear 'beati humiles' or 'Blessed are the Poor' is to those other truths as music is to noise, or a lost, and recovered, voice to the common talk of men.[1]

Here is the essential and intimate Belloc, the spirit behind the sword. The first business of man was beatitude, and it was the task of religion to lead him to it. We are a long way from 'Europe and the Faith'.

It is strange that with this nostalgia for Paradise, which filled him with humble hope but also with the melancholy of an un-

[1] Letter to Mrs. Raymond Asquith: Nov. 30, 1929.

certain love-affair, he should have had so little understanding of mysticism. Mystical experience, guaranteed by the authority of the Church, he, of course, accepted; but he seemed to feel that it was dangerous, abnormal, and generally unsuitable to man. On one of his visits to Spain he had been recommended to study El Greco, because El Greco was 'the painter of the supernatural', but he found El Greco 'a repulsive lunatic'. Or again, advised to read an essay on St. John of the Cross, he

> found the whole thing *repulsive*. I don't say—I am not so foolish as to say—that it is false. But I do say that I was never made for understanding this 'union with God' business: St. Theresa and the rest. I don't know what it is all about and the description of isolation and detachment, 'the necessary night of the soul', disgusts me like Wagner's music or boiled mutton. Good for others: not for me. I am no more fitted to it than is an elephant for caviare, or a dog for irony.[1]

When his son Peter was fifteen years old, he told his father that he thought he had a vocation to the religious life and would like to enter the novitiate of a Benedictine monastery. Belloc replied immediately: 'Put that idea out of your head. You're not meant for that. No Belloc can do that sort of thing.' This was not quite true. Two of his grandchildren are now members of religious orders.

Belloc's practice of his religion was simple and customary. He went, whenever he could, to Mass, but he confessed that the 'modern habit of very frequent Communion for the laity came too late to capture me'.[2] He liked to remember his Communions and to associate them with a particular place; with the Chapel at King's Land and the obituary cards of Elodie and Louis fixed to the walls; or with the chapel that Lady Phipps had made in her house at West Stowell among the Wiltshire downs. He always carried a rosary which had belonged to his wife, and he once became nearly distraught in the middle of Holborn because he thought he had lost it. If he wanted something for himself or a

---

[1] Letter to Mrs. Raymond Asquith: Feb. 23, 1927.
[2] Letter to Lady Phipps: Aug. 15, 1934.

friend, he would put up a candle before the statue of a saint, like a child or the humblest of the faithful. He had little sense of the Liturgy, and if a priest took more than twenty minutes over his Mass he suspected him of modernism. He never read 'spiritual' books, but the essential passages of Scripture were familiar to him from their reproduction in the Missal. He did not read them elsewhere. There is no record of his ever making a retreat since he left the Oratory, and a single visit to the Carthusian Monastery at Parkminster was enough to revive the anti-clericalism of his youth. No, indeed he was not 'made for such things'.

He conducted himself in church with a complete absence of self-consciousness. A Catholic church, whether it were Notre Dame or a tin hut, was a place where he always felt at home, and at home in exactly the same way. Nothing would ever stop him saying exactly what came into his head. At West Grinstead he would occasionally interrupt the priest as he was beginning to read out the notices by asking him in a loud voice which Sunday after Pentecost it happened to be. When his son-in-law, Reginald Jebb, was being received into the Church and was reciting the Creed in Latin, Belloc tapped Father Vincent McNabb on the shoulder and enquired: 'Excuse me, father, is there a telephone in the sacristy?' Another time, he was attending the wedding of two friends, rather early in the morning. As the Nuptial Mass was proceeding, the newly married pair heard Belloc's voice lifted behind them in conversation with his family. 'On this day, my children, in 1066, William of Normandy landed at Hastings. The wind was blowing in a south-westerly direction . . .' And the story is often told of how he was standing at the back of a church during Mass and was motioned to a seat by the verger. Three times the man tried to persuade him to sit down, until finally Belloc exploded 'Go to hell!' 'I beg your pardon, sir,' the man replied, 'I didn't know you were a Catholic.'

Belloc had a soldier's sense of discipline and he was too conscious of the English Catholics as a minority with their backs more or less permanently to the wall to allow himself to give rein to his feelings when they were ruffled by his co-religionists. He had been attacked in *The Tablet* over an article on Gibbon for the *Dublin*

Review (April 1917); and Wilfrid Meynell, who was then editing the *Dublin,* offered him space for a reply. He declined on the ground that the English Catholics could not afford an open division in their ranks. He did reply indirectly, however, in *Studies,* the Irish Jesuit Quarterly; and in private he would sometimes give vent to his irritation.

> I have been having my bellyful of clerics lately. I always like to associate with a lot of priests because it makes me understand anti-clerical things so well. They have been making me give for nothing addresses on subjects where I usually command 15 or 20 pounds outside and at the same time they have been treating me with contempt, a thing I do not forgive. *Caveant sacerdotes.*[1]

After one such gathering he arrived to lecture at Repton, and banging his hat down in the hall remarked to William Temple: 'The Catholic Church is an institution I am bound to hold divine —but for unbelievers a proof of its divinity might be found in the fact that no merely human institution conducted with such knavish imbecility would have lasted a fortnight.' Another time, when he was due to attend a christening as godfather, the authorities of Westminster Cathedral refused to allow the ceremony to take place before 3 p.m. This prevented Belloc catching the 4.30 to Taunton. 'In a Catholic country', he wrote to Mrs. Mervyn Herbert, 'they would be drilled into better manners.' When he was among Catholics he would sometimes ride lightly to the rules. He never failed his Lenten fast from drink—an heroic imposition—but on coming down to breakfast one Friday morning in a country house he was heard to ask, 'Are we all Catholics here?' and on receiving an affirmative answer, he added, 'Very well, I shall help myself to a large slice of ham.' Yet perhaps the nearest Belloc ever got to religious feeling, as we have distinguished it from religious experience, was in a romantic attachment to the Church. He grew very fond of the popular service of Benediction, and the concluding lines of the hymn, '*O salutaris hostia*', would often bring tears into his eyes.

[1] Letter to E. S. P. Haynes: Nov 9, 1909.

2

Belloc's apology for the Catholic religion was a single work, but it may be seen under two aspects: first, as it affected his co-religionists, and then as it affected his Protestant opponents. It may be said at once that in contrast to a man like Baron von Hügel, or even to a man like Jacques Maritain, Belloc had more effect among Catholics than among Protestants. No one did more to give the English Catholics confidence in themselves and to make them feel part of a European tradition. And who were they, these three million-odd people, mostly of the poorer classes, to whom Belloc revealed the Faith as the thing which had made them, and the only thing which could preserve their civilization from decline? First, there were the Irish, and Belloc's Catholicism, except that it bore no taint of Jansenism, was very Irish in its devotional simplicity and its militant zeal.

Warmly as he sympathized, however, with Irish nationalism, he did not think it was a good thing for the Church; particularly in England, where the Church was so largely officered by Irish clergy.

I wonder whether there will not be in the future some new arrangement for getting Irish priests trained on the Continent? It would be an extremely good thing. Pitt never did a worse thing for Ireland (though he was not intelligent enough to intend the result) than when he subsidised a centralised training for the Irish clergy and thus closed the door upon their foreign travel.[1]

Belloc reckoned the Irish as three-quarters of the Catholic population of Britain, counting marriages and descendants, and nine-tenths of its energy.

But the Irish are difficult. They were never in the [Roman] Empire, and therefore their discipline is an external constraint and not an acquired inheritance. Thus they make excellent soldiers and incomparable monks and nuns—but socially they are as quarrelsome as dogs and their minds go off at tangents.[2]

The rest of the English Catholics could be grouped under two headings: the converts and the members of the old Catholic

[1] Letter to Mrs. Reginald Balfour: March 20, 1929.
[2] Letter to Mrs. Reginald Balfour: March 6, 1933.

The *Nona*

Hilaire Belloc at Sea, from a photograph by James Hall

families. Belloc's opinion of them was given in a further letter to the same correspondent.

All efforts to sow any seed of the Faith in England are necessarily heroically hard and 9 out of 10 must fail. This is not mainly due to the hostility of the national spirit but to its increasing lethargy, *which has especially affected the Catholic body.* They have no idea of using what they have and they prefer the inert to the active. It is like a stagnant pool (or puddle) of stinking water in which the most vigorous freshet of clear light water is always coming through conversions, but which *never* gets any better through that addition. The Catholic converts are the most intelligent and strong of the English. They are very few, but they are each of an *élite*. But they are not appreciated by the woeful mass of old Catholicism. *C'est à pleurer.* When I consider their [the Old Catholic] attitude towards Europe, towards literature, towards history, I am tempted to think that it would be to the moral advantage of the body if it were to turn septic.

But it is a subject on which I exaggerate because it exasperates me. During the whole of the Irish struggle they sided with the vilest form of Protestant hostility to the Catholic culture, during the whole of the Dreyfus struggle they sided with the filth of Zola and the anti-Catholic Freemasons, and in the present crisis, though England is manifestly going lower every year and the Protestant culture throughout the world is stricken, they are the most convinced that the Catholic culture is inferior. I see as little of them as possible.[1]

Since Belloc himself admitted the exaggeration in all this, we may as well admit it, too. The historical situation of the Old English Catholics had made them anxious to prove that it was possible to be a good Catholic and a good Englishman at the same time. They were proud of their tenacity through the penal centuries and of the martyrs they had given to the Faith. But they were also proud of their modest achievements in the armed and

[1] March 19, 1932.

2

civil services of the Crown. They were certainly not intellectual, certainly not international, and they were inclined to be exclusive. No doubt, at times, they gave the impression of excluding Belloc, and this he naturally resented. But the Old English Catholics were right in refusing to confound religious and political issues, however closely they might seem to be entangled. There was no necessary connection between Catholicism and Sinn Fein, and the English Catholics were not original in holding murder to be a mortal sin. It is really desperate to find Belloc, in 1932, still unable to see the innocence of Dreyfus through the smoke of his more unsavoury supporters. Where the interests of the Catholic Church were plainly involved in a political struggle, as in Mexico or Spain, the English Catholics were quite prepared to take a line which was nationally unpopular. But they were right in seeing that on a moral issue the Protestant may be right and the Catholic may be wrong. Protestant and Catholic 'cultures' had nothing to do with it.

From the way Belloc sometimes talked and wrote one would imagine that he was a lonely and rejected prophet instead of a revered protagonist. Lonely, in a sense, he always was, but when one looks back on his long and practically unquestioned ascendancy over English Catholic thought one is inclined to make quite a different criticism. Did not his co-religionists take him too literally? Did they not fail to distinguish what was sound from what was exaggerated, what was permanent from what was personal, in his teaching? In fact, he formed a whole school of disciples, and a book like Christopher Hollis's *The Monstrous Regiment* was a tribute to his power. He welcomed the adhesion of Hollis and Arnold Lunn to the ranks of his fellow combatants. They did something to relieve his loneliness. But their fidelity did not guarantee the truth of every private attitude or interpretation. His disciples created an orthodoxy, which was their manner of being Catholics, as it was his, and there is no need to reproach them for it. Genius will always produce its hero-worshippers. But the hero-worship bred its reaction in the later twenties, as English Catholicism grew more self-critical and came under Continental influences very different from Belloc's.

A mood developed of awakening and of welcome to the modern world; a sense that history continues and must be continually redeemed; a conviction that Catholics must keep step with it, a step in front rather than a step behind; a readiness to change, not indeed the essentials of doctrine, but the accidents of expression. In contrast to this *disponibilité*—the lightly accoutred cavalryman ready to set out on his reconnoitre—Belloc sat tight behind his rampart and his guns. Not for him a religion of 'becoming', altering its shapes and its habits and even its language —what would he have said to a vernacular liturgy? The Faith was a beloved and familiar City, with its turrets and its walls and its spires; always recognizable and eternally the same: a thing made, permanent and enduring. His vision was a noble one and true within its limits. But there was more to Catholicism than that. He too readily confused the walls that man had made with the ramparts of eternity. For all his hunger for Paradise, he did not always distinguish between the gates of porphyry and the portcullis which had defied the barbarian. The Faith established and defined, the cultural city of Christendom, magnificent and crumbling—these are what he set out to defend. But his sailor's eyes, though they were accustomed to wide horizons, lacked the evangelist's audacity, and he did not even want to imagine what Catholicism would be like when it had been preached to all peoples, nor what expression it would wear when it had expanded to the uttermost ends of the earth.

Belloc had only himself to thank if his name became associated with the European aspect of a universal thing. But, in justice, we must give his reply to the accusation.

I have never said that the Church was necessarily European. The Church will last for ever, and, on this earth, until the end of the world; and our remote descendants may find its chief membership to have passed to Africans or Asiatics in some civilisation yet unborn. What I have said is that the European thing is essentially a Catholic thing, and that European values would disappear with the disappearance of Catholicism.[1]

[1] Letter to the *Catholic Herald*, 1936.

3

It was not primarily, however, to his co-religionists that Belloc addressed himself. He was anxious to convert his Protestant fellow countrymen, if not to Catholicism—for he rarely argued the essentials of doctrine—then at least to a Catholic view of history. He certainly did not exaggerate the ignorance opposed to him; an ignorance all the more culpable because it was fostered by the academies of English learning. Here was this immense, ubiquitous thing—the Catholic Church; the thing that had made the Europe we know; the thing that was loved or hated wherever it had taken root—and yet educated English people could go on as if it did not exist. 'The *ignorance* of the Catholic Church'—the present writer can remember the aged Belloc exclaiming thus in a taxi, as he drove up to the funeral of Father Vincent McNabb. It was the point of departure for all his apology.

The Church revitalised the dying fourth and fifth centuries— that is the point. It gave new life. If you read the literature of the time you see that all was tired out, *except* this new interest. *Nothing* could have preserved the excellence of sculpture, architecture and letters: they had gone long before the Church counted. But the power to revive was saved. It was like a belated love-affair saving a man from drink.[1]

Belloc's dearth of religious feeling went hand in hand with an attachment to the Church which was like the loyalty a man feels to his regiment. How did he set about curing the vision of those who could not love as he did because they could not see?

When he abused the ignorance of dons, Belloc was not only indulging a petulant resentment. As early as 1910 he had informed the young Arnold Lunn of a don who had written, or undertaken to write, a history of the Middle Ages without ever having heard of Gregory of Tours; a don in Holy Orders who did not know that Mormons still existed in Utah; a don—a Master of his College—who had asked Maurice Baring in what language the Russians wrote their books; and yet another don who had written

[1] Letter to E. S. P. Haynes: Dec. 25, 1923.

to the *Saturday Review* to say that 'very beautiful' in French was *beaucoup belle*. Beside a sub-human ignorance of this kind a knowledge of Catholicism—of its doctrine and history—was perhaps hardly to be expected. Nevertheless, Belloc set to work.

Now it is a first rule of apologetics not only to know your own mind but also the mind of the person you are hoping to convince. Belloc was never in doubt of his own mind, but he was not clever at getting inside other people's. This made him, at his best, superbly uncompromising; at his worst, needlessly provocative. His method and objective were set out in a letter to Charlotte Balfour.

Most people waste their time either explaining things to the already converted, or telling the non-converted things that they like to hear and which are therefore useless. The conviction of people who do not want to be convinced is a victory and the result of an attack; therefore hard to be achieved. The third miserable error in English Apologetics (such as they are) is the fiddling about with what may be called ecclesiastical details: making out every piece of Papal policy to have been wise: every congregational decision to have been just: every national policy where it clashed with some temporal Papal policy to have been wrong. These things are quite unimportant, and it is a terrible waste of time to worry over the five or six stock questions like Galileo and the French Revolution quarrels. The real business is to present the Catholic Church to people who either do not know of its existence, or cannot be got to see it in perspective, and above all to make the opponents of the Church understand that they are in the inferior position: less developed and less acquainted with the soul of Europe.[1]

He had made the same point in the magnificent *Open Letter on the Decay of Faith*, addressed to C. G. Masterman (1906). This may be read as the opening shots in his campaign. He saw the Church in an attitude not only of defence but of counter-attack. Admitting 'those visions of nothingness which I have twice suffered in the last five years, even in my own shrines',

[1] March 20, 1920.

he went on to look beyond the political and social controversies of 1906.

> The enormous evils from which we are suffering, the degradation of our fellow-citizens, the accursed domination of our plutocracy is in the act of settlement. But after that? Will there not remain the chief problem of the soul? Shall we not still smell what Chesterton so admirably calls 'the unmistakable smell of the pit', shall we not still need salvation with a need greater than the need for water upon a parched day? And will there not remain among us—since we are a civilised people, possessed of printing and careful of our monuments—the record of the faith?

Insistently the note of pride is struck.

> I desire you to remember that we are Europe; we are a great people. The faith is not an accident among us, nor an imposition, nor a garment; it is bone of our bone and flesh of our flesh: it is a philosophy made by and making ourselves. We have adorned, explained, enlarged it; we have given it visible form. This is the service we Europeans have done to God. In return He has made us Christians.

Already in 1906, to Belloc's quick mind, the positivism of the nineteenth century was *passé*, and its anti-clericalism as *vieux jeu* as an antimacassar.

> Do not, I beg you, be oppressed by forces already dissolved. You have mistaken the hour of the night. It is already morning.

Belloc did not often write so personally or so rhetorically as this, and here the date of the letter to Masterman should be noted. He still had the habit of rhetoric, and he had not yet despaired of the Republic. The letter is notable, too, for a theme which Belloc was to make all his own; Europe and the Faith.

The book bearing this title was published by Constable in 1920, and it was an expansion of lectures he had given to the Catholic students of London University during the war. On May 16 he writes to Phillimore:

My book 'Europe and the Faith' is now passing through the press and will be out very soon. It is quite abominably ill written. I did not know that I could write so badly even if I tried. For the first time in my life I feel that I am making a sacrifice, and like Danton, may my style be *flétri* but may the book do good! Every bit of work done for the Faith is of enormous importance at this moment, and though there is not the least chance yet of England's conversion—many disasters must come upon her first—still the immediate future is going to be a chaos of opinion, and in that chaos the order, the civility of the Faith will make a deep impression *if it is presented,* but it has to be presented. The difficulty just now is that English Catholics do not present it at all. They fiddle about with unimportant things of detail or fill the air with their hymns of praise of Protestants for being allowed to live. It is essential for us to impress it upon our contemporaries that the Catholic is intellectually the superior of everyone except the sceptic, and the superior even of the sceptic in all that region cognate to and attached to that which may be called 'Intellectual appreciation' —pure intelligence.

Four powers govern man, avarice, lust, fear and snobbishness. One can use the latter. One cannot use the first three. Blackmail is alien to Catholic temper and would cut little ice. Pay we cannot, because we are not rich enough and because those of us who are will not use their money rightly. Threaten we cannot, because we are nobody, all the temporal power is on the other side. But we *can* spread the mood that we are the bosses and the *chic* and that a man who does not accept the Faith writes himself down as suburban. Upon these amiable lines do I proceed.

This, then, was the mood; not a particularly good-tempered one. Indeed, one cannot do better than compare the letter to Masterman—Belloc never did a finer or a more formal thing— with the introduction to *Europe and the Faith,* to realize the change which had come over his style. Rhetoric has gone, and with it he joy and care of writing. Henceforward, apart from a few exceptions that we shall note, Belloc would regard writing as a labour; a labour not of love but of duty. He had written about the Revolution, or about this or that military campaign, because he wanted to write about them. He wrote in defence of the Catholic Church because he felt himself morally obliged to. The Catholics had twenty years of his all but undivided energies, and they had the full power of his intelligence. But of his re-creative imagination they only had the lesser part.

The theme of *Europe and the Faith* is stated in the introduction: that only the Catholic 'sees Europe from within'. This is the 'Catholic conscience of history', and what the Catholic brings to the study of the past is something more precious than research; it is self-knowledge. So far so true. But it was only a step from this to the perilous fallacy—'The Faith is Europe and Europe is the Faith', words which have come to define Belloc to his disadvantage. He was not afraid of them:

> I say again, renewing the terms, the Church is Europe: and Europe is the Church.

Obviously, to a reflective mind, the Church is more than Europe, and Europe is at once much more and much less than the Church. Europe is what she is because the Church helped to make her; so much is true. But the truth requires qualification. The Revolution and the Enlightenment, the Renaissance and the Reformation, the witness of the sceptics and the heresiarchs—all these have had their part in forming the soul of Europe. Again, none of these would have exercised their peculiar character, if the Church had not been there to provoke them. They belong to the Church with the intimate interdependence of historical things. But interdependence is not identity. 'When I see a warped piece of metal', Belloc once remarked, 'I do not knock it straight, I warp it in the other direction.' This was a dangerous principle. The aim of the historian should never be less than the dead straight of accuracy. 'But then I am not an historian', Belloc replied to the young Philip Hughes, on being asked why he refused to give references, 'I am a publicist'. The refrain of *Europe and the Faith* was a good example of warping in the other direction.

Because so many people underestimated what the Faith had done for Europe, Belloc knocked them on the head to bring them to a juster appreciation of the truth. It is possible that he knocked them too hard.

Belloc was fond of saying that truth lies in proportion. Yet take the following passage, and it will set you thinking, *mutatis mutandis,* of some passage by a Protestant or a sceptical historian where the Church is condescendingly mentioned as a minor influence or a competing sect.

> The Catholic understands the soil in which that plant of the Faith arose. In a way that no other man can, he understands the Roman military effort; why that effort clashed with the gross Asiatic and merchant empire of Carthage; what we derived from the light of Athens; what food we found in the Irish and the British, the Gallic tribes, their dim but awful memories of immortality; what cousinship we claim with the ritual of false but profound religions, and *even* [1] how ancient Israel (the little violent people, before they got poisoned, while they were yet National in the mountains of Judaea) were, in the old dispensation at least, central and (as we Catholics say) sacred: devoted to a peculiar Mission.

There is nothing wrong here except the word in italics; but this, and what follows it, implies so blind an inability to see that the Catholic is a son of Israel—'spiritually we are Semites' as Pius XI reminded the Third Reich—in a profounder sense than he is a son of Greece or Rome, that we may well ask ourselves how Belloc's Mediterranean mind can ever have come to grips with a Protestant psychology formed by the Old and New Testaments.

It might easily be deduced that the only kind of Protestant that he really respected was the Calvinist. 'I . . . am full of Calvin,' he tells Mrs. Balfour, 'a violently interesting Frenchman of the wrong sort, full of energy and will wrongly directed.' [2] For the Church of England he had little sympathy, though its dogmatic absurdities amused him; and he was always driving home the point that the doctrine and discipline of the Church of England depended

[1] Author's italics.　　　　　　　　　[2] Jan. 23, 1934.

upon English law, whatever individual Anglicans might or might not believe. It was not 'a *creed* or a *communion* but a national and therefore civil *institution*'.[1] He viewed its controversies from afar, and summed up the expected passing of the Revised Prayer Book into law with the succinct prophecy: 'So there shall be two folds and 47,896 shepherds.'[2] For Belloc 'Christianity' had practically no meaning; he was impatient with Christian sentiment unless it were controlled by dogma. But here, again, he had one standard for his friends and another for everybody else. He was scrupulously careful not to hurt the feelings of those he knew and liked. Wherever he found a sincere Christian faith he respected it, and he always held his old Wesleyan nurse, Sarah Mew, to be one of the saintliest people he had ever known. Belloc was as delicate with the individual as he could be rough with the mass; if his opinion or advice were asked, he gave it—at great length and with great diffidence.

One thing, however, about the Church of England he did understand, and it is a thing which can never be understood too thoroughly. He knew that a great part of its power was literary. The same ear which had been enchanted by the *Contrat Social* responded to the solemn music of Cranmer's prose. Cranmer might have 'carried his wife about in a tub bored with holes to let the poor German pudding breathe', but Belloc thought he 'wrote better English than ever had been or has been since'.[3] In so far as the mind of the Church of England, and to that extent the mind of the English people, had been moulded by the Book of Common Prayer, Belloc was not tempted to underrate its resistance to Catholicism. Those who thought him un-English mistook the depth of his affections, for he had himself become the memory, angry and tender by turns, of so much that had seemed to be forgotten. Looking at the contemporary decline of all good things, he exclaimed:

Dear England! After what disasters do you think these accretions shall be eliminated? By what fires? And if only the natural ease in acceptance which this climate of 'grasses and

---

[1] Letter to Maurice Baring: April 10, 1913.
[2] Letter to Mrs. Raymond Asquith: May 26, 1928.   [3] *Ibid.*, April 3, 1928.

green boughs' innumerable leaves' breeds and its love of fellow-ship and trust to luck and all that goes with these rivers and old walls, had not allowed the Faith to be jockeyed out of them by men who themselves hardly knew what they were doing—and did it idiotically for money—for huge sudden sums of money, which never gave men happiness . . . You know all the lovely stuff of the early lyrics and the great ballads. Do you know this —put into the mouth of Richard III at Bosworth in a contem-porary verse?

> Set you the crown upon my head
> Set it upon my head so high,
> For by Him that made the sea and the land,
> King of England today would I die.

And again:

> Put my foot in the stirrup's iron
> And put me my sword into my hand
> For by Mary that is so bright
> I will die King of England.[1]

To those who complained that Catholicism had become an un-English thing Belloc may not have brought much present com-fort, but he could re-imagine a time when it had been as English as a rose in June.

Among Anglican controversialists the one he crossed swords with most sharply was Dean Inge. Inge had questioned the authenticity of the miracles at Lourdes in an article for the *Evening Standard,* and Belloc wrote to the paper in protest. But his reply was not printed; a consequence of the Beaverbrook boycott. He admired, however, the Dean's 'well-knit prose' and he praised him publicly in a speech at the Guildhall. It is fair to add that he enjoyed praising Inge because he knew that this annoyed Dr. Coulton. He liked to infer that Inge was a scholar and a gentle-man, and so let Coulton nurse his exclusion from those who could debate these matters on equal terms. More than anything else that Inge had written Belloc admired the Latin poem inspired by the

[1] Letter to Mrs. Raymond Asquith: Sept. 17, 1927.

death of his daughter. He thought it 'a marvel that such a thing should appear in 1939 and in England'.[1] And we owe to Inge's provocation one of the noblest passages he ever wrote in defence of the Faith.

> For what is the Catholic Church? It is that which replies, co-ordinates, establishes. It is that within which is right order; outside, the puerilities and the despairs. It is the possession of perspective in the survey of the world. It is a grasp upon reality. Here alone is promise, and here alone a foundation.
>
> Those of us who boast so stable an endowment make no claim thereby to personal grace; we are not saved thereby alone. But we are of so glorious a company that we receive support, and have communion. The Mother of God is also ours. Our dead are with us. Even in these our earthly miseries we always hear the distant something of an eternal music, and smell a native air. There is a standard set for us whereto our whole selves respond, which is that of an inherited and endless life, quite full, in our own country.[2]

4

Apart from his desire to expound the true causes and effects of the Reformation—and this was a question of history no less than apologetics—Belloc did not waste his time in controversy with Anglicans. His personal relations with them, though remote, were friendly, and occasionally teasing. Once at a public dinner in Toronto he turned abruptly to the vaguely agnostic Vice-Chancellor and exclaimed: 'Tell me, Sir Robert, do you believe that Christ died on the Cross?' He used to take Protestant visitors into the Catholic church at Horsham on the plea of going to confession and as he came out of the box he would exclaim in a loud voice: 'Thank you, father; there's five shillings till next time.' He drank Cognac with the Modernist Vicar of Shipley; and when a clergyman from Brighton asked permission to set to music his quasi-pagan poem about Our Lady standing on the

---

[1] Letter to Guy Dawnay: June 21, 1939.
[2] *Evening Standard;* reprinted in *Essays of a Catholic* (1931).

moon, he gave an astonished consent. And he was even commended in *The Church Family Newspaper*. But it was not difficult to see, as the post-war world, so restless and so uprooted, began to assume its hideous shapes, that the choice now lay between a hectic and despairing materialism on the one hand and Catholicism on the other. In England, with its established Church and its competing sects, the issue might seem to be disguised; to anyone acquainted with Europe it was clear.

Belloc did not readily find the antagonists he desired; no one since the great Huxley had really been worthy of his steel. Angrily, he looked round for a mind; but all he discovered was a mood. Still a mood was better than nothing, and when H. G. Wells published his *Outline of History* (1920) Belloc pounced upon it like a pugilist. To be sure Wells had a mind, though the mind might be no more than the reflection of a mood—and the mood suburban. But in the Britain of the twenties the suburbs were spreading far and wide, and the suburban errors were spreading with them. Wells also had imagination, and he could write. The duel that ensued may be described as a duel between a European mind and a provincial imagination; and both were of the first order. The mind won, because it had forced the imagination to fight on ground of its own choosing.

The campaign—if we may enlarge the metaphor—was opened with restraint. Belloc had known Wells for some years and rather liked him. They frequently met at the Reform Club, and they had both been Liberals in the days when Liberalism still had a meaning for Belloc. But the acquaintance did not get any closer; Wells's shoddy morals were no more to Belloc's taste than the Cockney amateurishness of his thought. In 1922 Wells put up for Parliament in the Liberal interest and the *Daily News* invited both Belloc and Chesterton to give their comment on his candidature. Their replies not only explain why Wells loved Chesterton and hated Belloc; they explain why a great many other people loved the one and heartily disliked the other.

G. K. Chesterton: I wish Wells all possible luck, but I can't say that is exactly the same as wishing he will get into Parliament.

The question is not whether Wells is fit for Parliament, but whether Parliament is fit for Wells. I don't think it is. If he had a good idea, the last place in the world where he would be allowed to talk is the House of Commons. He would do better to go on writing.

H.B.: Of the effect of election upon Mr. Wells's style I am not competent to pronounce. But in morals, temperament, instruction, and type of oratory, I know him to be admirably suited for the House of Commons.

Belloc believed that the truth was hard and inevitably hurt, and this gave to his quarrels the 'sundering' quality that Chesterton remarked upon. The battle with Wells was a sundering quarrel indeed.

Belloc opened the attack by praising the clarity of Wells's style; his sense of historical time; his imaginative power, which allied him to Michelet; his verbal accuracy which Belloc contrasted with his own carelessness; and his patent, if provincial, sincerity. The charge of provincialism was the kernel of Belloc's accusation. He defined it as 'satisfied ignorance: a simple faith in the non-existence of what one has not experienced'; for Wells really did believe that 'his doctrines of good-will, vague thinking, loose loving, and the rest' might ensure the salvation of mankind. Belloc defended his opponent against the charge of brevity—it was the shape, not the size of the *Outline* that was wrong; and of superficiality, which was not the same thing as limitation. The essence of superficiality was indifference. 'Mr. Wells means to say all that is in him, and if there is not very much in him, that is not his fault.' Even Wells's provincialism was an aspect of his patriotism; and patriotism, even when carried to lengths which were intellectually absurd, had something to be said for it. Thucydides had been none the worse historian for being patriotic.

The trouble with Wells was not that he loved his country too well but that he knew it too little. All he knew were the prejudices of the Home Counties and the outer suburbs. Belloc proceeded to demolish them. Wells was driven frantic by the thought of an English gentleman, because a gentleman was associated in his mind with lineage, tradition, nobility and military honour—all four concepts which he reviled. He was associated with the Classics rather than with the positive sciences, with the Public Schools and not with the Board Schools. Belloc was perfectly prepared to admit that an English gentleman could be dislikeable— he had disliked quite a few of them in his time, though now he looked on them more fondly; but it was the unreasoning violence of Wells's reaction—the 'instinctive kick'—which disqualified him from the writing of History.

Wells disliked the Catholic Church more than he disliked anything else—even more than he disliked the English governing classes—because he felt that the Church would like to stop him doing a number of things that he enjoyed. In this feeling he was correct, although he probably exaggerated the interest taken by the Church in his proclivities. He was also correct in feeling that the Catholic Church had some connection with God, and that if one wanted to have a good time—with public life as tidy and private life as untidy as possible—it was just as well to get God out of the way. This was the impulse, the fiercely emotional impulse, behind *The Outline of History*.

He began doing it with the dogma of Natural Selection because Natural Selection, as it was preached when Wells was a boy, had relieved creation of the horrible encumbrance of a creator. Belloc had no difficulty in riddling the notion that Natural Selection was the inevitable agent of Evolution, and he was able to quote the names of fifteen important scientists with whose work Wells showed no acquaintance whatever. Again, when he assailed the doctrine of the Fall of man, he betrayed his ignorance of any position between fundamentalism and unbelief. The unbelief of the suburbs and the garden cities was the paltry descendant of Lucretius, and Wells assumed it as a universally admitted fact. Even in its majestic origins it had never been more than a disputed theory; Wells, in his provincial innocence, did not suspect that in 1926 it was being disputed more loudly than ever. Having got rid of God he was naturally anxious to get rid of sin, and especially of original sin. His notion of this doctrine was quaintly biological: 'many believers feel it is more seemly to suppose that man has fallen rather than risen'. Belloc could reply that *all* Catholic believers affirmed that man had fallen, not because it was more seemly but because it was true.

Like so many Protestants who no longer believe in Protestantism Wells called in the pacific Buddha to beat the Christians over the head. Buddhism, he declared, pure and spiritual in its origin, had caught 'almost every disease of corrupt religions; idols, temples, altars and censers'. Belloc pounced on the incongruity of the list; he could get on quite well, he said, without censers. It was over-simplified, perhaps, to affirm that Buddhism was founded on despair, but Belloc had no time for the syncretism which was the staple substitute for people who could not bring their thoughts to a conclusion. Wells was a good example of the emotional flux which passed for thinking in the modern mind. His 'stuffed Nicean God' had evolved into a species of Santa Claus; Wells had all the Modernist's desire to combine 'what his feelings craved with what his creed denied'.

If there was one thing that he disliked more than the Roman Church it was the Roman Empire. Popular government had failed towards the end of the Republic owing to the lack of Board Schools; the Roman victory over Carthage was an example of supreme cowardice; the ignorance of the Roman citizens was contrasted with the enlightenment of British Trade Union leaders; Julius Caesar was 'bald and middle-aged', and his affair with Cleopatra was shocking in an elderly sensualist of fifty-four; so the diatribe went on against all those things, majestic or mean, of which Belloc and Wells were alike the children and the inheritors. Naturally Belloc was quick to stigmatize this as 'degraded rubbish'; but it was only a prelude to his assault on Wells's muddlement of the Incarnation. Here Wells betrayed all the Modernist's refusal to face the consequences of his disbelief. Jesus, stripped of His Divinity, had to become 'a great Teacher'; the 'seed' rather than the founder of the horrible thing called Christianity, and of the still more horrible thing called the Catholic Church. But the difficulties in proving that Christ did not believe in His Divine origin were as nothing to the difficulties of proving that His followers did not believe that He believed in it.

It was not for His Beatitudes but for His blasphemy that He was put to death; and Belloc's criticism was not assuaged by Wells's picture of the 'Three Crosses on the Red Evening Twilight'. Better the old robust English atheism than sentimentality masquerading as scepticism; better vigorous denial than nervous doubt.

The 'very little' that, according to Wells, was known about the early Church might have been 'very little' in quantity but it was comprehensive in extent. The witness of Ignatius, Justin Martyr, Irenaeus, Papias and others was quite clear on the essentials of the Creed. Ignatius stood to the contemporaries of Jesus Christ as Wells stood 'to men like Huxley and Matthew Arnold', and what he had heard about the effect of the Resurrection was analogous to what Wells had heard about the effect of the *Origin of Species*. To suggest that St. Paul got his doctrine of the Atonement from the mysteries of Mithras was about as sensible as suggesting that Wells got his ideas about Natural Selection from the *Contrat Social*; and to suggest that the disciples did not witness the Resurrection but were afterwards persuaded that they had witnessed it was to run away from any plausible explanation of the event. The belief in the Resurrection might have arisen from hearsay; from falsehood or conspiracy; from individual or collective hallucination; or from affirming (long afterwards) as a fact what had at first been affirmed as a metaphor. Each of these hypotheses was arguable, and had been argued by the Higher Critics. But Wells was as ignorant of the Higher Criticism as he was ignorant of the Orthodoxy it attacked. All he knew were the catch-penny and discredited versions of it current in the semi-educated circles in which he moved. His theory of the Resurrection was the one theory which will not hold any water at all; and he gave the impression of holding it because he did not want to be rude to the Apostles.

The Outline of History was as easy game for Belloc as Kingsley's unfortunate article had been for Newman; and both resulted in a classic, although they were classics of a different kind. But there is in each the same mastery of material, the same subtlety of thrust and parry, the same irony, the same conviction and verve. In his first review of the book Belloc had said: 'It will have a vast circulation, especially in the New World—and an early grave.' But these ephemeral fallacies—religion without dogma; the Catholic Church invading Europe like an alien and holding it down; Wycliffe flaunting his vernacular; a priesthood of conspiring conjurers and a laity of servile dupes—these were the mental stock-in-trade of a whole mass of the English middle-classes who imagined they were in the vanguard of progress. Wells was their prophet; sharing their shallow antinomianism and their bumptious hopes; a typical product of the Protestant underworld, and tempted by his native genius to venture into territory where he could neither read the signposts nor understand the language. Poor Wells! In *The Outline of History* he was not at his happiest, and he had the misfortune to meet Belloc at his best. 'I am a writer, a biter and a fighter'—and Wells discovered it to his cost.

Belloc's answer to Wells had first appeared, serially, in the *Universe*, and was then published by Sheed and Ward (*A Companion to Mr. Wells's 'Outline of History'*; 1926). The fight was prolonged with a riposte from Wells, *Mr. Belloc Objects* (1926) and a reply from Belloc, *Mr. Belloc Still Objects* (1926). Wells was aggrieved that Belloc had paid him only 'oily' compliments; he confused the doctrine of the Immaculate Conception with the doctrine of the Incarnation; boasted that he now knew all about Catholicism because he wintered on the Riviera; boasted, again, that he knew five European languages, including Portuguese; and declared that 'Existence impresses me as a perpetual dawn'. Belloc could only express his surprise that anyone who knew so many European languages should know so little about Europe. As for Wells's 'dawn', he did not think it would last very long, and he did not think it was the precursor of the day. It was 'the shoddy remnant of the Christian hope, and when it is gone there will return to us, not the simple paganism of a sad world, but sheer darkness: and strange things in the dark.' Wells and Belloc both lived to see them; and they were strange indeed.

Wells, for all his faults, was a man of warm affections and he could not understand how Belloc could attack him so violently and yet bear him no personal ill-will. He was bitterly resentful and there was a painful scene at the Reform Club. No, he had not enjoyed the game. The controversy has demanded discussion because at the time it was so well known; now, beside it, should be put Belloc's duel with a far greater antagonist, which is hardly known at all.

5

It would be scarcely an exaggeration to say that, outside of Homer, Gibbon was Belloc's favourite writer.

I have not read all the books in the English language, but of such as I have read, Gibbon's *Decline and Fall* is far and away the most readable . . . Certainly there is not a dull page. For wit, for concision, for exactitude of expression, for *meat* (the right word) I know not his equal.[1]

Belloc was not one of those nervous partisans who can only enjoy the books of people with whom they agree. He was immensely fond of Macaulay. But Gibbon came out of a greater tradition than Macaulay. He was a child of the Enlightenment, and the men of the Enlightenment were of all the adversaries of the Faith those to whom Belloc was most temperamentally akin. He would have been uneasy and impatient with Chateaubriand, but perfectly at home with Voltaire. The difference—or one of the differences—between *The Decline and Fall* and *The Outline of History* was the difference between a book which could be 'picked up anywhere at any hour and read with pleasure; with satisfaction; for any space of time, short or long',[2] and a book which could only be enjoyed intermittently and, once enjoyed, would certainly never be returned to.

But what moved Belloc to exert himself was the paradox that while Gibbon was a great writer, he was a bad historian. He had chosen to deal with those centuries in which the Catholic Church was slowly, painfully, but triumphantly moulding the mind and institutions of Europe. Belloc did not reproach Gibbon for disliking the Catholic Church; he never asked of an historian that he should be entirely without bias. But he blamed Gibbon for allowing his bias to betray him into culpable falsehood. What

---

[1] *A Conversation with an Angel* (1928). [2] *Ibid.*

first drew his fire was Gibbon's misleading account of the
execution of Priscillian. He had exposed this in an article for
the *Dublin Review*.[1] Then, the rejoinder in *The Tablet* showed
him how far the Catholic public was under the spell of Gibbon's
reputation, and in four articles for *Studies* [2] he proceeded to attack
Gibbon on a number of vulnerable points. He seems to have had
the idea of expanding these into a book, and it is a pity that he
never did so.

The trouble with Gibbon, he quickly saw, was that he had not
read his originals. He had taken over from Mosheim the ludicrous
notion of the Catholic Hierarchy evolving 'out of a jealously
republican congress of presbyters'; which was like an opponent
of Socialism collecting his ammunition from the Primrose
League, and omitting any reference to Karl Marx. Secondly—
and here the *lacuna* was astonishing—he had not even mentioned
the Eucharist. This was 'the supreme criterion, the distinctive act',
and Gibbon had simply left it out. Belloc next examined his
account of the veneration of the True Cross in the reign of Constantine. Here Gibbon had inserted the mendacious word 'perhaps' before the name of Cyril of Jerusalem, in citing the supposed witnesses of the rite. Belloc had no difficulty in showing
that St. Cyril was the only witness to have been of age to 'follow
the whole thing *on the date of the discovery*'; that no contemporary,
pagan or heretic, protested against it; that the 'universal belief'
alleged by Gibbon in the miraculous growth of the wood was
attested by only one authority, and that untrustworthy—for St.
Paulinus was a man well known for his extravagant credulity.
Belloc did not commit himself to the belief that the wood so
venerated was in fact the Cross on which Christ had died, but
when Gibbon suggested that the True Cross could not have
remained hidden underground (and the ground was dry and
rocky) for three hundred years, he answered that the wood of the
table on which he was correcting the proofs of his article had been
felled in the reign of James I and was still going strong. Having
quoted Gibbon's passage in full, Belloc proceeded to rewrite it as
it might have been written by an impartial historian with no

[1] April 1917.   [2] Dec. 1917, June and Sept. 1918, and Dec. 1919.

sympathy for the Catholic Church but an honest regard for his materials.

The Christians of the early fourth century (some 300 years after the rise of their society) worshipped as God a Man who had been put to death by crucifixion upon a wooden Cross somewhere about the year 29–33 A.D. There is ample evidence that they had so worshipped from the beginning. They had been at first a small, and for long a persecuted, body who had to hide what they thought sacred; and they further had enemies who would try to deprive them of their sacred objects. Among these sacred objects the Cross upon which the Object of their worship had suffered had naturally always been held in the highest veneration. Imitation of its form by a motion of the hand was one of their earliest and most regular practices, and their very first documents speak of the Cross continually as the emblem of salvation. When the Christians had grown powerful, this most venerated of all objects was sought for. It is clear that no general knowledge remained of exactly where it lay, though there is some evidence of its having been in their possession much earlier and having been lost again. At any rate a Cross was found and the relic was publicly exposed and venerated in Jerusalem from about 326. Whatever the circumstances of its discovery, none doubted its authenticity. Miraculous powers were ascribed to it.

A better example than this could not be found of Belloc's controversial method. In subsequent articles he considered Gibbon's treatment of the Donation of Constantine and Julian the Apostate. Gibbon had glossed over the cruelty of Julian's execution of Florentius by omitting any mention of Julian's debt to him, and by inferring that Florentius had been guilty of some crime whereas he had been guilty of none. Gibbon had also, among a great many other statements equally misleading, confused the rather nebulous George of Cappadocia who became the Patron Saint of England with the perfectly historical and wholly disreputable Arian Bishop of Alexandria who bore the same name and was stoned to death two centuries later. Gibbon's purpose was always the same—to discredit the Catholic Church by implication, innuendo and controversial sleight of hand when he could not do so by a frank and frontal assault. Belloc's refutation of his errors does not make such exhilarating reading as his refutation of Wells. But then he was dealing with a stiffer antagonist; and the last thing he would have wished for *The Decline and Fall of the Roman Empire* was an early grave.

Already, as the relaxed twenties passed into the grimmer thirties, Wells was becoming a back-number. In an article contributed to the *Evening Standard* Mr. Evelyn Waugh tried to define the mood of the generation to which he belonged; the generation which had grown to maturity immediately after the First World War. He described it as reacting from a woolly Liberalism, both in behaviour and belief. The climate was changing, and the new challenge to the Faith did not come from the suburbs. The New Paganism, as Belloc defined it, was advancing 'over the modern world like a blight over a harvest. You may see it in building, in drawing, in letters, in morals.'[1] It was apparent in the prevalence of divorce, and here Belloc was at odds with his old rationalist friend, E. S. P. Haynes. He saw that when the social argument had been pushed a certain distance, there was an unbridgeable gap between the social and the sacramental view of marriage. Both men had written on the subject in 1918.

I have got your pamphlet and am just reading it. You are right when you say that when Western Europe was all Catholic, men in daily life (*not* the Church) discovered many a way of getting round the rigidity of the doctrine of marriage, but the doctrine still stands for us like all other doctrines and has not itself ever changed. You are also profoundly right when you say that if the English choose to have a new religion they are welcome to it, and that is exactly the line I have taken up in another pamphlet I am writing about divorce for a Catholic body, to wit, that it is no business of ours. But I still think the underlying fallacy is that which regards the mere ceremony

[1] *Survivals and New Arrivals* (1929).

of marriage as in some way 'respectable'. The analogy of polygamy exactly applies. If a man's having two or three households comes to be tolerated and even thought normal, why should one bother to imitate the old state of affairs?[1]

And again, later:

The more you look at the divorce question the more you will see that the real debate is on the abstract point on whether it is to the benefit of man that marriage should be permanent. There is no debate on the sacramental idea because there is no common ground between the sacramentalists and the non-sacramentalists, but there is common ground on the matter of human beings. The real argument on your side is that an institution can be normally established in spite of a certain degree of exception and negation. That argument is unanswerable, as witness a non-sacramental society such as the Mahomedan: or at least it is only answerable after a further debate upon the sacramental idea.[2]

Belloc was not insensitive to the sacrifices which the sacramental view of marriage might enforce. He knew its victims. But anarchy of any kind was abhorrent to him.

The liberty of the individual is not only rightly but necessarily limited by his organic connection with society. The society of which he is a part made him; but for it, he would not be himself. He may rightly be summoned upon in a grave matter even to sacrifice himself wholly for it, as in war.[3]

The breakdown of marriage was only part of the breakdown of morals, and this in turn was only one aspect of the new paganism. Belloc analysed perfectly the post-Christian or, more exactly, the post-Protestant mood. He saw that England and America were full of people who called themselves pagans, without having an ounce of that *pietas* which was the root and the strength of paganism. He saw how quickly the repudiation of belief was leading people to despair. He naturally had himself no

---

[1] March 24, 1918.   [2] Undated: 1919.
[3] *Manchester Evening Chronicle:* July 10, 1925.

illusions about the Brave New World, and here he was closer than he guessed to writers with whom he had no personal contact or sympathy, like Aldous Huxley and T. S. Eliot. What he looked for in the new paganism were the seeds of a new religion, and he only found them in spiritualism. Little as he liked spiritualism, he noted its ancient lineage, and he came to admit that, when fraud and illusion had been allowed for, it contained some proof of transcendental experience. But it did not answer the great questions of Why and Wherefore, and it could only palliate —it could not exorcize—despair.

Belloc gave his own reply to these questions in a little book, *The Question and the Answer* (1938). This was no less than the answer of the Church, but it was lucidly and personally argued. It summarized, without any resort to polemic, arguments which he constantly advanced, even more vividly, in letters to his friends. The neo-paganism of the post-war years was shot through with a memory of Christendom, as the paganism of the past was shot through with an intimation of it. Even in its confusions and uncertainties it was Messianic.

> The expectation of better things—the confident expectation of their advent—affects the vileness and folly of our time everywhere. Let one individual appear with the capacity or chance to crystallize these hopes and the enemy will have arrived. For anti-Christ will be a man.[1]

He was, indeed, and he had now arrived, bearing the double name of Hitler-Stalin. Belloc was at one with all the best of his time in preparing to resist on the political plane what presently showed itself to be a vast spiritual aggression. As the years passed Manning's great dictum came back to mind; that all human conflict is ultimately theological.

[1] *Survivals and New Arrivals* (1929).

CHAPTER XVIII

VERSUS THE WHIGS

I

IN correspondence with his friends Belloc often wrote, a
little wearily, of the burden he had assumed in writing
'Catholic history'. But in print he was more cautious. There
was no such thing, he told the readers of the *Universe*, as 'Catholic
history'. His business, and the business of any Catholic historian,
was 'to restate things as they were; to give the events of the past
in their right order of emphasis, as well as in the accuracy of their
outline; to see to it that things which had been suppressed or
slurred over and which were essential should be put well into the
foreground and that myth should be exploded. They must tell
their story so that a man who was indifferent or hostile to the
religion of the writer should accept the story as true.' But this
was more easily said than done, and much more easily said than
believed. Inevitably Belloc stood before the world, and especially
before the academic world, as a man with a *parti pris*. He was out
to destroy what was arguably a legend and what sometimes
appeared to be a vested interest.

Belloc's writings, if we include his continuation of Lingard,
covered the whole of English history from the Roman Conquest
to 1910. His *History of England* was published by Methuen in four
volumes; these appeared in 1925, 1927, 1928, and 1931, and took
the reader down to 1612. Three further volumes were projected,
but never completed. It was not a labour of love; such a work
demanded the whole of a man's time, and Belloc was too finan-
cially harassed to give his heart to it. He also placed himself at a
quite unnecessary disadvantage by his refusal to provide a bibliography and references. At least one of his friends, Somers Cocks,
begged him not to give this handle to his opponents. He would

also ask to read the proofs of Belloc's historical works, in order
to forestall the usual criticism. But Belloc would never let him
do this, in spite of their long friendship and of his high regard for
Somers Cocks's judgment. No doubt he was afraid that niggling
criticism would spoil the sweep of his work, and it was true that the
reinterpretation on which he was engaged did not always lend
itself to chapter and verse references. He argued that if he were
writing for a learned journal, he would quote his sources; but he
was writing for the general reader, for whom such a parade of
scholarship would be merely a waste of printer's ink. Nevertheless his refusal did not help the student who wished to propagate
his ideas. If an undergraduate served up an essay to his tutor,
which contradicted the official teaching on the Gunpowder Plot
or the Great Rebellion; and if, on being asked where he had
found his ideas, he admitted that he had got them from Belloc,
then he would probably be asked for Belloc's authorities, and
could only reply that Belloc had not given them. An impression
was created that Belloc was much less erudite than in fact he was,
and it was an impression that Belloc did a good deal to encourage.
The present writer asked an eminent contemporary historian
for an opinion of Belloc's history and received the following
answer:

> Of course, he was sometimes wrong, but then it is impos-
> sible to write history without occasionally being wrong. When
> Belloc was wrong, it was generally because he had overlooked
> some quite obvious source, whereas he would have the more
> recondite authorities at his fingers' ends.

But which authorities? That was the question one could never
answer with certainty. In the preface to the first volume of his
history he refers to Fustel de Coulanges, but this great scholar
had died in 1889. In the preface to the fourth volume he refers
only to Pollard. What about the others? Who were they? Lingard had won respect from a Protestant public by the studied
moderation of his views and the extreme accuracy of his statements. He had felt no need to warp the metal in the other direction. Belloc had himself discovered small errors in twenty articles

from the *Dictionary of National Biography*, and he would quote Stubbs's saying that there was no historical book of any size in which one could not find a score of such things. What mattered, he maintained, were not the misprints and the inaccuracies, but the emphasis and the proportion. If these were just, the errors—sometimes so glaring as to be excusable—were of little consequence. For an advocate pleading an unpopular or an unfamiliar cause they were of much greater consequence than he at first suspected. But here, as so often, he would admit in private what he would deny in public. After correcting the proofs of his first volume, he writes to Mrs. Asquith:

. . . at the end one is always sure that there are a hundred elementary errors. With official history that doesn't matter, but with opposition history the smallest mistake is a peril.[1]

To another friend he remarked 'Tait and Tout may have been dull dogs, but at least they had their dates right'; and in a letter to Douglas Woodruff he distinguished between mortal and venial howlers.

If you say and really think the Battle of Ligny took place on a Saturday while alluding at the same time to Waterloo as having taken place on the Sunday it shows intense ignorance of the campaign; but if in writing casually about this countryside you say that the battle was fought on a Saturday, it would not matter a tinker's curse.[2]

Belloc felt that the moment you began to worry too much about detail, you missed unity.

The ideal thing is for the historian to write his history, and then to have a gang of trained slaves who can go through the proofs from various aspects. That is why, take it all in all, gentlemen have made the best historians.[3]

Belloc was not so biased as to condemn all academic history, but he did not keep up to date in his ideas of the Oxford dons.

[1] Jan. 4, 1925.   [2] Dec. 17, 1939.
[3] Letter to Arthur Pollen: Nov. 19, 1931.

He was thinking of men like J. F. Bright and Arthur Johnson; some of their successors, however, appreciated him more than he suspected. He, for his part, admired Oman for his research, and H. A. L. Fisher for his power of synthesis. Nor did he forget the impression made on him as a boy by Stubbs's character-sketch of Henry II, and his own companion portrait is worthy to be set beside it.

See him moving feverishly about, restless in gesture, impatient, desiring quick Masses from his chaplains and short meals from his cooks; with scant tufts of red hair on a pate nearly bald; prominent but keen eyes, glancing everywhere, observant; ready for anger.[1]

But, in general, Belloc was out for the blood of the official historians. The phrase, of course, begged a pretty big question. Is there such a thing as English official history, and if so, what is meant by it? Belloc would have answered that the English governing classes (in his day they mercifully still governed) were educated at Oxford and Cambridge, and that the only history they knew was what Oxford and Cambridge dons taught them. Historical truth was confined within a vicious circle of mutual advantage. If the dons had begun to teach what their alumni did not like, they might have to quit their quadrangles. At all costs a national myth must be upheld.

This was how Belloc would have argued, and if you had asked him for the contents of the myth, he might have summarized them as follows:

The English people derive their character and their institutions from Saxon tribes settled in these islands during the fifth century A.D. In spite of being conquered and converted by the Romans, they retained only a small part of these foreign influences and it was not until they cast them off that they became a united and powerful people, and eventually a great imperial power. In throwing off the yoke of the Roman See they established the national character of their religion, and in

[1] *History of England:* Vol. 2 (1927).

getting rid of the Stuarts they laid the foundations of that Parliamentary and social democracy which is flourishing today, both in the British Commonwealth and in the United States.

If the reader still doubts whether any version of history can be called 'official' in a free country, it may be well to remind him that when John Fisher and Thomas More were canonized in 1935 the British Legation to the Holy See received instructions from the Foreign Secretary (Sir John Simon) to pay no attention to the event. It was a pretty insult from one Lord Chancellor to another. Belloc wrote many books, pamphlets and articles to controvert the myth, and it would require another book to summarize them. We have only the space to indicate the main trends of his teaching. The most eminent and respectable of official historians was G. M. Trevelyan, and the most readable was his great uncle, Thomas Babington Macaulay. Belloc returned to Macaulay when he was at work on his *James II* (1928):

> It is as fresh and vigorous reading to me in the decline of life as it was to me in youth, and it is as fresh and vigorous reading to the man of today in the London of petrol and an immense income-tax and cads in control as it was in the London of the great Whig houses and the carriages and pairs, and a government of gentlemen. Is that not a remarkable thing to say of any man?[1]

And the remarkable thing was that Macaulay did not date. His philosophy was dead and his falsehoods were discredited, but almost alone among the early Victorians he was still abundantly alive. He was

> like a man visiting and eating with friends in a circle of some dozen houses, each of which will mirror exactly his own self-satisfied vanity, and as exactly his own raw and absurdly insufficient convictions.[2]

Nevertheless, a few of these convictions were still in circulation, though their value was much depreciated, and Belloc thought

---

[1] *A Conversation with an Angel* (1928). [2] *Ibid.*

them worth attacking when even so revered an historian as Trevelyan tried to pass them off as genuine coin. Belloc took the matter of the Boyne, which had become the Lepanto of the Protestant myth, and William of Orange who was its Chevalier Bayard. He claimed that no one reading Trevelyan would have suspected that William's army had a 400 per cent. superiority in guns, a 180 per cent. in numbers, and a 300 per cent. in fully equipped and trained men; that his army was largely officered by Frenchmen; and that he so bungled the battle as to allow James to get away with a loss of only 6 per cent. in men, one gun, and hardly any unwounded prisoners, and to keep up the war for two years. Again, Trevelyan had written, 'The army of Monmouth was identical with the rural population of Somerset'. Belloc answered that it was largely composed of hired miners from the Mendips who could most easily be recruited for pay, and that Jeffreys' 'Bloody Assize' was in no way exceptional in severity. Trevelyan had followed a garbled account, written later, for the purpose of discrediting James. He had not taken into account that James's own father had been beheaded, that his throne and dynasty were in danger and the principle of monarchy was at stake. Trevelyan had then gone on to write that 'the way was cleared for the acceptance by all English Protestants of William as their only champion', whereas it was even chances for some years whether James would not be reinstated in spite of his Catholicism—so greatly were William and his perverted morals detested by the bulk of the population; and Trevelyan had missed (or avoided) the point that James's policy of toleration was designed for the advantage not only of the Catholics, but of all those who refused to worship under the State Church. James would have been justified in giving the Catholics at least one-eighth of the commissions in the Army and Navy and in making one-eighth of the Universities Catholic. In fact, he had imposed Catholicism on only one Oxford College. Trevelyan had said that Catholics were 'freely' placed upon the Bench, whereas Belloc went to great pains to discover that James had appointed only one Catholic judge and a mere handful of J.P.s.

In these, and similar, controversies Belloc put his case in the

Universe. He did a great deal to increase the circulation of that paper, but it was not an adequate platform for one who wanted to change the national habits of reading history. It did, however, give him the opportunity of contradicting the cruder statements of the Press. How could the 1549 rebellion be understood without reference to the imposition of Cranmer's Prayer Book? Was it not highly disingenuous to refer to Lord Baltimore's sailing in *The Ark and the Dove* without mentioning the fact that the expedition was a Catholic expedition, fleeing from the Penal Laws; or that the settlement of Maryland was the first settlement in America to establish complete religious toleration? Was it not ridiculous, on some naval occasion, to launch out in eulogy of Drake and Hawkins, and make no reference to James II? The reason was clear; the picturesque piracy of Drake formed part of the national myth, whereas James II was only a gloomy Roman Catholic monarch who had lost his throne. Nevertheless it was James who

> first drew up a line of battle as against the old chaotic fighting of ship to ship; first manœuvred in line during a fight; invented signalling, without which it would have been impossible when fighting in line to maintain formation; formed the first body of regular naval officers; won the battle of Sole Bay, keeping command on deck for seventeen hours, standing unmoved while his closest companions were killed at his side.[1]

Belloc never made any bones about preferring the company of educated people, but when a friend of his could remark, on hearing the *Adeste Fideles,* 'I didn't know you had a Latin version of that', and when a man of eminence in the State could volunteer, during a discussion of the Johannine comma, 'Why don't they look it up in the original MS. in the British Museum?', he concluded that there was no limit to educated ignorance. Sometimes, however, he had to come to grips with formidable learning, and of these opponents Professor G. G. Coulton was the most dangerous. Coulton was a self-made historian who by dint of prodigious

[1] *Universe.*

industry and mastery of MS. sources had obtained academic recognition late in life. He was a Fellow of St. John's College, Cambridge. He professed a strong love for the Middle Ages, but he was opposed to their idealization by Catholic historians, particularly by Cardinal Gasquet. Coulton's reputation, however, always stood higher with the reading public than with other medievalists who understood more about the Middle Ages than their misdeeds.

Belloc attacked him in season and out of season, and notably in a pamphlet, *The Case of Dr. Coulton* (1938). He took considerable pleasure in writing it, and was satisfied with 'the mixture of learning and insult which I hope I have achieved'.[1] And again, to Dorothy Hamilton:

> It is amusing to chastise the insolent and this time he has got it good and hot. The trouble is the getting of it sold. But Coulton is a figure at Cambridge; 30 people may buy it for the joy of seeing him brought down, though they themselves be indifferent to history and theology and all the rest.[2]

Coulton was in the habit of deluging his opponents with telegrams and solicitor's letters, until at last they broke off the engagement from sheer weariness. But with antagonists of this sort, said Belloc, 'one should never let go. One should get them on the run and, having got them on the run, one should keep them on the run. But it is an awful strain'.[3]

The controversy began with a letter to the *Daily Telegraph* from Mr. A. S. May on June 26, 1937, containing the following words: 'In the early Church divorce with remarriage was permitted.' Father Ronald Knox then wrote asking Mr. May 'to provide some justification with contemporary references for this extraordinary statement'. Coulton subsequently intervened with a letter, both violent and prolix, of which only thirty-one lines out of 190 were on the point at issue. Six documentary references were given in support of Mr. May's statement, but of these only one had any connection with the Early Church. Coulton affirmed

---

[1] Letter to Guy Dawnay: Sept 4, 1938.
[2] Sept 4, 1938.   [3] *The Case of Dr. Coulton* (1938).

that the Council of Arles (314) had permitted the remarriage of divorced persons. Only one out of the twenty-nine canons of the Council—supposing that all those commonly quoted were genuine—had dealt with the general doctrine of marriage, and this was unequivocal in its prohibition of the marriage of divorced persons. Now Coulton had omitted all mention of this canon, and when challenged by Belloc admitted that he considered it spurious. Belloc answered that 'debatable' would have been a more honest word. The canon was perfectly compatible in style with the date ascribed to it; it contained no anachronism; and there was no proof of forgery or interpolation. If Coulton had been writing history from the Bench instead of from the Bar, he might have said: 'Canon XXIV of Arles may be quoted in support of the Catholic position, but its date is not certain, and for my part I reject it, for it occurs in only one Codex.' But he had simply left it out.

The article upon which he rested his case was Canon X. This said that if the unfaithful wives of *youths* are divorced, and the youths are forbidden to marry, then every effort should be made to dissuade them from remarriage. On the face of it, this made nonsense. Did it mean that minors could not legally remarry till they came of age, and that the Church must, nevertheless, dissuade them from doing so then? Did it mean that the Church forbade them to remarry, and therefore dissuaded them—a corollary which might have been taken for granted? Did it mean that if a marriage had not been consummated owing to the youth of a husband, he should still be bound by the promised contract, even if his wife had left him? Had a transcriber dropped out the word 'not' before the first 'forbidden', so that the sense of the article was as follows: 'though they are not legally forbidden to remarry, let every effort be used to dissuade them from doing so'? Canon X might have meant any one of these things, but it was a flimsy basis for the assertion that remarriage was permitted in the Early Church.

Coulton, resting on the massive scholarship of A. F. Pollard, had questioned Henry VIII's infatuation for Anne Boleyn as one of the principal causes of the Reformation. Pollard, armed with an array of footnotes, had maintained that Henry had been contemplating divorce long before he met Anne Boleyn. Belloc replied that this 'new evidence' was no more than a doubtful rumour circulated 1,000 miles from the spot, and that it was unconfirmed from any contemporary source close at hand. And when one of Coulton's colleagues had asked whether it was credible that a mere infatuation for a woman should have such enormous consequences, Belloc retorted that if this professor had seen even a corner of the real world, he would have known what nonsense he was talking. The infatuation of men for women accounted for half the calamities of the world; it was 'a force almost irresistible'. Coulton himself had suggested that the whole story was invented by 'Farmer' Cobbett. Now Belloc, though he sympathized with Cobbett's ideas and greatly admired his prose style, did not think him a good historian of the Reformation. But he answered Coulton as follows.

It was known that Catherine had been incapable of bearing children for some years before there was any question of a remarriage; that Anne Boleyn was the cause of Charles V's anger; that she was praised by Henry's envoys to the Pope; that Henry admitted that he had been 'bewitched'; and that Cranmer was chaplain to the Boleyn family. Coulton came back with the argument that the best historians of the Roman Church—Lingard and Henri Constant—lent no excuse to Belloc's view. Constant had described it as 'simple, facile and brief; but truth is generally more complex'. Belloc had himself written a laudatory preface to Constant's book, and he did not need to be reminded that truth was complex. But it was one thing to say that Henry's infatuation was among the contributory causes of the Reformation, and quite another thing to say that it had nothing to do with it. So the acrimonious controversy, and others like it, dragged on, with Coulton describing Belloc as a bully and a coward, and boasting that on at least ten occasions when they had met in open controversy in print, he, Coulton, had been left in possession of the field.

One famous evening the adversaries met face to face. It was on November 15, 1924, at the Cambridge Union. Belloc and Ronald

Knox were debating, quite frivolously, the motion 'That History should serve patriotism rather than truth'. Belloc opposed, and suggested that a little truth might be introduced here and there. It was all mildly funny and facetious. Then Coulton who was present, rose and accused Belloc of falsifying history. He said there should be some method of ostracizing people who deliberately and persistently evaded historical truths. Belloc replied hotly, and the debate developed on somewhat personal lines. Only the President's tact prevented the two men from calling each other liars, but, according to the *Granta*, the more irate they became the more the House enjoyed it. 'It was first-rate pantomime.' Later the President apologized to Belloc for the discourtesy to which he had been subjected.

Belloc, like the good general he was, could always respect the qualities of an opponent, even when he was as personally offensive as Coulton. He admired his sincerity, his accuracy, and his erudition, rather cavalierly admitting his own carelessness.

> I am the most inaccurate of men, writing 'north' for 'south', 'Richard' for 'Henry', transposing order, misreading my own voluminous but very badly written notes, etc., to an unpardonable degree.[1]

These were large and damaging admissions, but unlike the academic historians Belloc lacked the support of a professional income. He was compelled to work in haste.

> The few—very few—who can do historical presentation ought to be free to do it. It would be an advantage to the State. Endowments are there for that, but they would never give me one. How wise was old Salisbury when he compelled Oxford to endow Thorold Rogers! But for that we should never have had that foundational work on the Middle Ages which has *only* been done in England and *only* by that one man.[2]

Careless in some respects Belloc may have been, but how many other men, sitting down to write an account of the Battle of

[1] *The Case of Dr. Coulton* (1938).
[2] Letter to Mrs. Raymond Asquith: May 31, 1921.

Hastings, would have taken the contours of the field at 25-foot levels with their own hands? Or have asked for the wardrobe accounts of the Kings of England for 1346 when they were writing about Crécy? Or have examined, most carefully, the upper part of Sedgemoor to see if it were firm enough in normal weather for troops drawn up in line?

There were Catholic scholars as learned as Coulton, and we must in justice point out that Belloc's theories about the settlement of Britain were countered by Father Herbert Thurston, S.J., as vigorously as his ideas about the Reformation had been attacked by Coulton. Thurston was no Teutonist, but he argued in the *Month*[1] that Belloc's *romanità* had been pushed to impossible lengths. He quoted modern authorities like Maitland and Vino-gradoff to prove that the typical English village was neither Roman nor Celtic in origin but 'very purely and typically German'[2]; and that if the speech of the Saxon invaders could be dismissed as 'local jargon', 'then the popular speech at the same period in Gaul, Italy and Spain—the later French, Spanish, Portuguese, Catalan, Ligurian, Venetian, etc.—was equally a jargon'.[3] The only modern authority on whom Belloc appeared to rely was Professor Wiener, whose theory that half the German dialects were debased imperial speech had been discredited by the best contemporary scholars, and whose books had been described by one of the greatest experts in the philology of Romance languages, Professor Guilio Bertoni of the Royal University of Turin, as containing 'little or nothing at all which is accurate, sane or true'.[4] Like Belloc, Thurston had been brought up on John Richard Green's *Short History of the English People,* and had reacted against its absurdities; but he was anxious that Catholics should not feel themselves committed to Belloc's very uncertain scholarship, exercised in the opposite sense.

In other respects, too, Belloc's judgment was disproportionate. It was not the murder of Becket but the jealousy of Eleanor of Aquitaine which raised up against Henry II the coalition of his sons and broke the moral authority of the English Crown. There

[1] July, 1925.   [2] Maitland.   [3] Thurston.
[4] *Archivo Storico Italiano*, 1916: LXXIV.

was no reason why the profligacy of Edward IV should be more leniently treated than the sins of the Lancastrians—Belloc had always regarded the Lancastrian usurpation as 'the irreparable disaster of English history' [1]—or why Henry VIII should be represented as the mere tool of Thomas Cromwell. The Reformation Parliament had already put in train its revolutionary legislation before Cromwell became important. The King had been acknowledged as Supreme Head of the Church in England, appeals to Rome had been forbidden, and the King empowered to appoint Bishops without reference to Rome. All this had been done on Henry's initiative. In the same way Belloc is out to prove that Elizabeth was the tool of Cecil. This view, which Belloc had arrived at by intuition, was in some degree vindicated twenty-five years later by the independent and exhaustive researches of Professor J. E. Neale.

What is valuable in the four volumes of Belloc's History, and what largely outweigh its defects, are the vivid portraits and the detailed descriptions. The recumbent effigies rise from their tombs, animated and often peculiar. We hear Strongbow's squeaky voice, and see the puckered forehead and half-open eyelid of Henry III; William Rufus, half-atheist, with a strong vein of superstition, vicious, intelligent and brave; Henry I, short and broad-shouldered, with the black hair falling over his large forehead, versatile and rapid, gazing on the porcupines and camels at Woodstock. And the Middle Ages themselves, with their social customs, their architecture, their economy and their military techniques, are traced from their Norman origins to their summit and their elaborate decline—'the quaint English interspersed here and there with fragments of French', the grotesque sculpture and the complicated stained-glass, the sophisticated fashions and the ill-distributed wealth. All this is a resurrection of the flesh.

2

In addition to his *History of England*, Belloc covered a part of the same ground, and considerably added to it, with a series of

[1] *Avril* (1904).

biographies which came out, at regular intervals, between the two wars. With the exception of *James II*, these were all published by Cassell. They were designed to illustrate a single theme: the snatching of the Catholic religion from the English people by the Crown in league with a new oligarchy; and then the snatching of power from the Crown by that same oligarchy when it was established more firmly. The Crown which had failed to defend the religion of the people was seen as the last protector of their liberties; and when he had described the 'last rally' of Charles II, Belloc's conversion to the principle of monarchy (not legitimism) was complete. A book might be written to refute or support this thesis, and it might well be longer than the present biography. It must suffice, in the space of a few pages, to suggest the main lines of Belloc's approach.

He had chosen the biographical method in dealing with the English transition for the same reason as he had chosen it for dealing with the French Revolution, because he believed that men, rather than forces and tendencies, were the main architects of history. He did not underestimate, of course, the general tendencies of the times. He saw how the Black Death had cut right into the beginning of the Middle Ages; these had started with the English gentry all French-speaking and ended with most of them English-speaking. He saw how this change was made easier by the resentment against the State of the Papacy at Avignon and the consequent irritation against the French Crown. He perfectly appreciated the abuses of the later medieval Church, and seized the capital point about the witness of St. Thomas More. More had chosen to die for a single article of doctrine, about which he had long been uncertain in his own mind, and to which he gave no sort of emotional assent. It was, however, characteristic of Belloc that he should have thought St. Thomas More's ideas on toleration (so far as they went) 'ruined . . . the Church in England' [1]; here he was in disagreement with the great authority of R. W. Chambers. Again, Belloc understood the economic causes of the Reformation, the jealousy of ecclesiastical wealth, and the close connection of this with the rise of modern capitalism. But he

[1] Letter to Douglas Woodruff: 1928.

chose to emphasize the personalities who had been the catalysts,
or the victims, of so great a change.

It will be convenient to look at these figures in their historical
order rather than in the order in which Belloc wrote about them.
Wolsey and his power politics bored him, and there is no account
of his administration and his reforms. Belloc concentrated, almost
exclusively, on the Divorce, and the argument is spoiled by
avoidable mistakes. The birth of Henry VIII is twice given as in
1489; the portrait reproduced of Anne of Cleves was really of
someone else; the fifth Earl of Northumberland is confused
with the sixth, and Cardinal Campeggio with Cardinal Adrian
di Castello. All these were hostages to unfriendly reviewers.
Wolsey, in Belloc's portrait, had many of the right ideas
and all the requisite ability. He saw that Christendom was
in danger of imminent disruption, but he was too ridden with
a purely personal ambition. Belloc defined ambition as the
'putting of oneself before one's chief task', and it was a vice
which particularly repelled him. Whatever might have been said
against his *Wolsey*, no one disliked the book as much as Belloc
himself.

> . . . it is supremely bad. I say so with full knowledge of how
> bad writing can be. Many of the sentences don't make sense,
> and whole passages are repeated. Yet he is an entertaining dul-
> lard. He was always being duped and made a fool of by the
> more subtle Italians and by the saturnine Anne Boleyn, the
> Howard woman. Also he made the brother of his mistress and
> therefore the uncle of his illegitimate son his *official confessor*.
> Also he used to write to Rome asking for the latest fashion in
> Cardinal's get-up, whether they wore crimson Sarcenet or
> ribbed silk; it occupied his mind. . . . [1]

It had not occupied Belloc's, but Cranmer was more interesting.
Here was a man, academic in all except his horsemanship; flirting
with the latest heresy; the theorist of the Royal Supremacy and
ignominiously dependent upon the Royal favour; a great artist
but not a great intellect; conferring upon drastic innovation the

[1] Letter to Lady Lovat: Aug. 31, 1930.

dignity of a perfect style; meeting death with difficulty; and hating, above all things, the Mass.

The jolly thing about Cranmer, as about Luther, was that he really did like the ladies. It is always a point in a man's favour. But having that to his advantage, it was silly of him to revile the best thing in the world, or at any rate what leads to it.[1]

In so far as the genius of the Church of England had come to birth in Cranmer, he was the spiritual father of Charles I. Belloc was as bored with Charles as he had been with Wolsey, but he did not make the mistake of turning him into a crypto-Catholic. Charles was rigidly and rather coldly Anglican, conscientious and chaste. 'I had written "too chaste", were not the phrase bad in morals.' One passage in *Charles the First* made Arthur Pollen, who was a naval expert, raise his eyebrows. Belloc had written:

England was to take up the weapon which made her progressively greater and greater and at last invincible; until modern conditions, even in our own time—the change in weapons and transport—were to make invincibility at sea no longer possible, nor, even if it were possible, of decisive utility.

Pollen thought this 'the worst heresy since the Albigenses'. But Belloc, while admitting that sea-power, even under present conditions, was of high value over great distances, did not think that it could be decisive in the Narrow Seas against an enemy of equal culture.

In opposition to Charles I stood Oliver Cromwell, with whom Belloc amused himself immensely. He saw through the homespun. Cromwell was

a man on whom the official English history has lied more freely than on anybody else. He came of a gigantically wealthy family and was connected by marriage and blood with about a dozen millionaires of his day. It is great fun to see how bewildered he was by finding that it was necessary that he should

[1] Letter to Miss Pauline Cotton: Jan 1, 1934.

take on the boredom of government which he didn't like one little bit. He was a great cry-baby, always breaking out into a loud Boo-Hoo upon every occasion that lent itself to sentimentality.[1]

Belloc wrote a short preliminary study for Benn's sixpenny series, and followed this with a fuller biography. In the first he emphasized Cromwell's uncanny aptitude for intrigue and his genius as a cavalry leader; in the second he did him a larger justice. It was on a visit to the Fens in 1904 that he had first appreciated with his own eyes the naked wickedness of the Whigs.

> It is astonishing to read of the villainy of the Russells when they drained the Fens. The first Duke of Bedford was perhaps as villainous a skunk as ever lived—at least so it seems to me. . . . By the way, in my reading I found that Oliver Cromwell's real name was Williams. More shame to me that I did not know that before.[2]

Belloc was reasonably satisfied with his *Oliver Cromwell*. 'It is one of the very few things I am proud to have written.'[3]

His study of Charles II—*The Last Rally*—was also the last of this series to appear. It was published in 1940. Characteristically, and rather sadly, it bore a misprint on its title page; the 'study' was called a 'story'. A story, nevertheless, it was, and it told of Monarchy's last successful wrestle with the Money Power. It was conceived as a companion and sequel to Belloc's book on Louis XIV; but whereas Louis had won his campaign, Charles had only won a single battle and the campaign was to be lost under his brother. Now at last despairing of the Perfect Republic, Belloc reposed upon Napoleon's dictum that 'the only institution ever devised by men for mastering the Money Power in the State is Monarchy'. He was not so simple, however, as to see the struggle between them as a struggle between good and evil. The triumphant plutocracy of 1689 had ensured the material greatness of modern England; the colonial expansion, the naval supremacy,

---

[1] Letter to Miss Pauline Cotton: Feb. 13, 1934.
[2] Letter to E. S. P. Haynes: April 12, 1904.
[3] Letter to Mrs. Raymond Asquith: Nov. 18, 1927.

the industrial power. It had united the nation and fostered, as Belloc was at last prepared to admit, a climate of individual liberty. But these triumphs had been bought at a cost. The peasantry had been destroyed, and the sense of human equality had been lost. The peasantry was not likely to return, but the sense of equality was coming back with all the crudity of a political nostrum, and with very insufficient emphasis on the metaphysical doctrine which sanctioned it.

Meanwhile Belloc was fully at home with the character of Charles II and with the Nemesis that overtook him; the Nemesis that by no means always punishes wrong-doing, but is so often found attached to men of right intention who, for reasons of personal or political advantage, act against their better instincts.

In the case of Charles it was certainly so. He allowed a monumental wrong to be done to the Irish nation. He lived a whole life in contradiction with his profound perception of religious truth. He sacrificed the victims of the Popish Plot in general, and Stafford in particular. He was guilty of all these three major evil deeds for the sake of restoring their Monarchy to the English: and he did not restore it. He paid the highest possible price for that which he legitimately desired, and failed to obtain what he had thus thought to have purchased.

But the book that Belloc had always wanted to write was his *James II*. He had been approached by the American firm of Lippincott with a request to do a life of Richelieu. The subject did not interest him, but he agreed to write about Richelieu if he might first write about James II. This suggestion was agreed to, and the book came out with Lippincott in America and with Faber in London (1928). In spite of occasional and playful complaints, he enjoyed writing it fully as much as he had expected.

James II . . . is most attractive to me. He was a thruster and loved ships and was sincere. He had 300 affairs with ugly women. He couldn't bear the beauties. They made him weary. What he liked was character, go, wit, buzz, solidity, charm with black tints and affection. He got it. He was also exceedingly brave, but he underestimated the power of wickedness—especially in organized wealth.[1]

Belloc wrote his *James II* in long-hand, staying in a small hotel at El Kantara, on the fringe of the African desert. It took him eight days; and here is a picture of him at work.

> I wake at six. I get down by 6.30. I write this mud from seven, after coffee, till twelve. I eat till 12.30 (oh! the vile food!) very little and read articles in old magazines left behind by tourists of the flood: especially the Revue Hebdomadaire of 1922. I then drink coffee and brandy and smoke. At one I begin again the horrible sing-song of the tenacious and brave—but ill judging—Jacobus. It goes on till four. I then take the air for half-an-hour. Then I write again till seven. Then I eat an ounce or two of nauseating food; then I do nothing for an hour but read or write a letter—as I do now—with *empressement*. Then by 8.30 I go to bed and pass the night in dreams of trying to telephone and not getting through, or of trying to read small print by a bad light. Then I wake at six and begin all over again. What a book poor old James will have! He was dull. He never smiled again. But he deserves a better book.[2]

The book was finished on November 27, and he writes to Mrs. Asquith again with triumphant relief.

> James is dead! . . . Poor Devil, what a time he had! Worse than my own. I have harried him for eight mortal days, holding on by the teeth and never letting him go, eight hours (or seven) for eight days. And now I have brought him down.
>
> He may complain that I have jerked him and mutilated him and given him in little pieces. So I have. But I have achieved him. Now (when I get back to England, whither I send him to be typewritten out), now to re-write it; as is my custom. For there is no book of mine which I do not first write bits of, then dictate, then re-arrange, then write up, then have typed, and then re-write. Hence a certain viscosity of style. But no

---

[1] Letter to Mrs. Raymond Asquith: October 5, 1927.
[2] *Ibid.*: Nov. 22, 1927.

matter: he is completed: and to the day and the hour. I said
that on this day of God I would have the last word with him
and I have—poor Devil! There he lies in a heap of manuscript
and scored pages: 75,300 words long and the Dies Irae sounds.
I am determined to tell you the great news before I sleep.

In fact Belloc took a great deal of trouble over the book when
he got back to England, searching the county records to discover
the religious opinions of the J.P.s holding office in 1687. James II
summed up the last episode of active monarchy in Britain; but
he was the first, as Charles II was the last, of these tragic or
triumphant protagonists to be considered by Hilaire Belloc in his
assault against the Whigs. The book, whatever its mistakes, was
written with the zest of an initial attack. But take the series as a
whole; see Wolsey and Cranmer at odds in the Henrician schism;
watch Cromwell move towards the killing of the King; pierce
the deceptive façade of the Restoration; follow James down the
estuary into exile—and what does it all add up to? A vivid
picture, certainly, wide in its grasp and sharp in its detail. The
vacillating Cranmer facing the ordeal of the faggots; Cromwell's
despair and doubtful trust in his Election; the royal chamber,
with the tapestries and the spaniels and Louise de Kérouailles,
where Charles was reconciled to his Redeemer; the high dignity
of his father's beheading—all this, and much more, lives before
the reader's mind. If Belloc had enjoyed the leisure and endow-
ments of a professional scholar, he might have written a con-
secutive history of the period which would have stood as a
corrective to Gardiner and Trevelyan, to Macaulay and Pollard.
This he had not been able to accomplish; all he had undertaken
was a series of raids on territory where his opponents seemed to
be in complacent possession.

Looking back in an article for the *Universe,* Belloc counted his
gains. Nobody any longer believed that seventeenth-century
England was solidly Puritanical (but had they ever believed quite
that?). It was understood that seventeenth-century England was a
battlefield, and that if James II had remained upon the throne, the
country would have remained divided, like Holland, with a

large and tolerated minority of Catholics. Nobody any longer regarded as a reliable historian a man (Macaulay) who described as 'filial' the relations between Keppel and William of Orange. It was now better understood that in the transition between Henry VIII and Edward VI, 'the religious revolutionaries, though serious and intense when they were sincere, were few and formed no more than a clique'. Many people also realized that 'what is repulsive cruelty in one age may be the commonplace of another. People always tend to read history backward.' Looking forward Belloc foresaw 'the materialistic misconception of history', and he believed that this would appeal to the 'economically disinherited and oppressed'. It has appealed to quite a number of highly paid professors and publicists, and it has proved equally difficult to convince them that 'the age-long tradition of the Catholic Church, though it proclaims authority, also proclaims justice'.

Belloc's boasts may have been exaggerated, as his prediction was certainly correct; but when he looked deeper, he was filled with discontent.

> Shall I before I die have strength or leisure to write real history all aflame with life? I could do it, but I haven't done it yet and probably I never shall.[1]

It was his sense of history, even more than his writing of it, that was remarkable: 'Charlemagne left his soul to Gaul and his clothes to Germany.' He was the first President of the University of London Catholic Students Society, and some of his best historical lectures were given for them. He took some part in the discussions of two historical societies—the St. Thomas More and the Lingard. The first was a private group, in which Mrs. Warre-Cornish, widow of the Vice-Provost of Eton, her daughter Charlotte Balfour, and Mrs. Leigh-Smith, a very old friend of the Bellocs, were prominent. They met in each other's houses, and their approach was literary rather than historical. Later, the Society was put on a public basis and changed its name to the Lingard. A number of professional historians—Maurice Wilkinson and Outram Evennett—then joined it, and Belloc who had been

[1] Letter to Mrs. Raymond Asquith: Aug. 8, 1929.

the Prophet of the St. Thomas More soon gave up attending the meetings. He found the Lingard insufficiently 'European'. This was nonsense, and he would have gained a lot by discussion with men who possessed, in certain fields, a wider and more exact scholarship than his own. When he had delivered his paper, he would leave hurriedly, without listening to the observations of anybody else. He could not even talk, let alone work, in a team. Mrs. Leigh-Smith, who was a woman of high intelligence, often said—she said so to the present writer shortly before her death— that Belloc would never be *accepted* as an historian. Time has not yet proved her wrong.

CHAPTER XIX

THE OLD WORLD AND THE NEW

I

IT was in the winter following the Armistice—so Belloc told Duff Cooper—that he first felt his energies were lessening; and when he climbed to the top of the Jura through deep snow in March 1920, he found the effort too much. But his mental strength was not exhausted by the re-writing of history and the defence of the Catholic Church, though the effort wearied and often discouraged him. It was not merely that he was at cross-purposes with his antagonists as a thinker; he was at cross-purposes with them as a man. He was a different sort of human being. Sir James Frazer was a case in point. Belloc saw that the fallacy in Frazer was his artificial arrangement of facts, but when he met Frazer he wondered whether Frazer himself was not somewhat artificially arranged.

I have often noticed that people who write books which are interesting and yet show a lack of intellectual grip, turn out when one meets them in private life to be mad. It is perhaps their madness that starts them on their wild and interesting theories, and at the same time prevents them from exercising intellectual power, for a madman's writings never show intellectual grip and indeed a man of tenacious intellect is the opposite to a madman.

This chap Frazer goes on precisely as I have seen lunatics go on in Asylums. He sits in a corner muttering and mumbling to himself with a terrified and surly look in his eye. His wife who leads him about is a sort of lion-tamer, and fears him no more than the hunter does the Denizen of the forest. But all others fear him and keep well out of reach of any sudden plunge with a cutting instrument. For my part the contrast between him and his book kept me in subdued laughter almost the whole time I was with him.[1]

Belloc had propounded, with infinite repetition and unwavering zeal, a body of social and political doctrine which the English temper and tradition were unable to digest. He had chosen the rôle of Jeremiah—and Jeremiah is not a popular prophet. At the same time, he had made the English cause his own in the fearful conflict which had been brought to a victorious close. Out of his writings and propaganda he had made, and invested, a good deal of money. He was standing, to all appearances, on the crest of his renown. But there were changes going on in the world around him which he was too inflexible to appreciate. He did not understand the rise of the British Labour Party. He did not grasp the significance of Kerensky's defeat, or estimate until much later the dangers of a new power in the east, anti-European and dogmatically anti-Christian. There was more to the Russian Revolution than a group of Jewish agitators in control of a population inured to serfdom. This was a new Islam on the march, and Belloc did not believe that it was capable of marching. Or again, when the Germans sank the *Lusitania*, they did more than bring America into the war; they brought it into Europe. But Belloc went on believing that America had said 'Good-bye' to Europe for ever. He looked at the United States with the eyes of an Irish-American, and the appearances of isolationism were too strong for him.

He remained, of course, strongly political to the end of his days. The commentaries and the articles continued to pour out, but his politics no longer had quite the relevance, nor the effect, that they once had had. Because he lacked in himself the power of renewal— the power that Yeats had to an astonishing degree—he could no longer surprise, though he could still powerfully impress. But the world was moving away from him, and what separated him from it most sharply was his belief in reason. The flight from this divine faculty in man was already in full swing, and he warmly approved the book in which Sir Arnold Lunn had analysed it.[2] The new

---

[1] Letter to E. S. P. Haynes: June 3, 1907.
[2] *The Flight from Reason* (1930).

irrationality was noticeable in the nearest approach to a new religion: the widespread belief in a rapid and inevitable progress. This had been gathering force for some time, and even so intelligent a man as Mr. Gladstone had congratulated a certain railway company on getting rid of second-class carriages on the ground that such an action was a step towards 'enlightenment and progress'. This was arguably the most idiotic remark ever made by a British politician. The superstition took two forms. Either you believed (if you had sunk so far in idolatry) that the present was a realized ideal, and that every step that led towards it was necessarily progressive. Or you formed an ideal of temporal good and found it more comfortable to imagine that you were marching towards it. The first conception was refuted by its own nullity; the second could only be held by omitting all the facts you didn't like. Belloc did not believe that man was made for intellectual or emotional comfort, and he offered no drugs (though he did undertake to provide reasonable satisfaction) to those who took the pains to listen to him. He could remember a time when people thought it enormously important to know whether the Resurrection had really happened. A time was now approaching when they would be content to accept it as a significant myth. The reason why Belloc did not carry wider conviction in his controversy was not, principally, the bluntness and occasional carelessness of his methods. It was because many of those who were in search of religious truth were not prepared to use their minds in the way that he insisted on using his.

Up to 1918 Belloc had been an active, though restless, participant in English politics. His influence had persisted even when he had withdrawn from the House of Commons; but from now on he would become increasingly isolated, and his views generally unpopular. If you believed that parliaments were the instruments of plutocracy, and that plutocracy could only be controlled by despotism, then you were bound to sympathize, more or less, with what liked to call itself the Counter-Revolution. The name was a little too respectable for what the anti-parliamentary movements generally became. Belloc met Mussolini in 1924 and gave his impressions to Charlotte Balfour.

I had a long talk with him alone. He has read assiduously and has good judgment on the whole. I bade him not exaggerate the decline of British power, which he is somewhat inclined to do. On the other hand he fully understands that Parliament is no longer serious with us and that a 'Labour' gang is just the same as a 'Liberal' or 'Unionist' or any other. He appreciates the fact that the International Financiers govern us, but he is puzzled at our yielding to that power when its aims are obviously at issue with the good of the country: e.g. in trying to avoid reparations payments. I have no doubt at all that he means to keep in the middle of the see-saw and advantage whichever side seems to him to be lowest at the moment. But a sudden rise in power on either side, Paris or London, might take him unawares. He is not ambitious and that is always a great asset in governing men. His driving power is first disgust with Parliamentarianism, which he shares with pretty well everyone in Europe—and next Patriotism. He will do a great deal to confirm the already established religious peace—but I doubt whether he has much faith himself. The point is that his régime will help it to return to the younger generation.[1]

Belloc disagreed, however, with Mussolini's contempt for majorities; he believed that there were conditions in which a decision by a majority might be just.

(1) When the question arises from a homogeneous community; (2) When there is an active popular demand for its settlement; (3) When the matter under discussion is reasonably familiar to all; (4) When it concerns all, or nearly all, directly, and in much the same degree; (5) When the majority is substantial.[2]

Belloc had warmly supported the Italian claim to Fiume, which he had visited in 1919, and he was quite untroubled by Austrian grievances in the South Tirol. He believed that the tide had turned and that the future lay with Italy, France and Poland. This belief, which had its obvious bias, conditioned all his com-

[1] Feb. 21, 1924.   [2] The Cruise of the 'Nona' (1925).

ment on foreign affairs between the two wars. It was the ideology of the Latin *bloc*. When the Italians attacked Abyssinia he thought the policy of sanctions idiotic, but his views were not so *simplistes* as he sometimes made them appear.

> I have no doubt that I exaggerate a little on the Italian side—but there is always a tendency to do that when one is playing a lone hand, otherwise one is not heard. What I regret is the possible disappearance of an old native Kingdom, the last one left. The end of anything ancient is always to be deplored, unless it were the Devil.[1]

Belloc was not, of course, alone in holding the views he did. Many intelligent people—Winston Churchill among them—thought there was more to Mussolini than the Pontine marshes and punctual trains. Many people doubted whether liberal democracy could flourish in a Latin soil. It was only later that Fascism revealed all the corruption attributed to democracy, and an irresponsibility that was not answerable to electoral checks. Duff Cooper, who generally thought Belloc's politics fantastic, fully shared his disapproval of sanctions. Later, Belloc came to weary of Fascism's monotonous self-praise, though he never faced up to the dilemma of despotism; the dilemma of power grown incompetent or corrupt which cannot be constitutionally removed.

With Germany it was a different matter. Belloc did not like Hitler, but he did not understand him. He took him for a Prussian militarist instead of a Bavarian romantic; for the tool of the General Staff, not their master. Belloc was too civilized and reasonable a man, too steeped in the Latin tradition, to imagine the power of paranoia raised to the pitch of maleficent genius. His incapacity to sympathize with mysticism made it impossible for him to appreciate its parody. He was in Weimar for the elections of 1932, and described the populace 'grouped round a Hitler placard with large grins'. It was no more exciting than 'the sheep-fair at Findon'.[2] He did not guess to what lengths this

---

[1] Letter to Maurice Baring: Sept. 24, 1935.
[2] Letter to Duff Cooper: March 14, 1932.

gemütlichkeit would be transformed. Meanwhile the 'Erb Prinz' was as good an hotel as you could find in Europe with its 'garden, thick wall shutters, thick curtains, and all kinds of old traditions',[1] and it was only five miles away to Jena with its memory of a greater man than Hitler.

But the country where he was most at home, outside England, was naturally France. He was there visiting the battlefields in February, 1919. He contrasted the ruined churches with the crucifixes all intact by the roadside, and as he looked upon the scene of so fearful an apocalypse, he was stirred to a deep anger. Somewhere beneath those cratered fields his eldest son and many of his friends lay buried. But it was not of them that he now spoke.

The battlefield of the Lys, which I crossed today, is like a white sea. No trees, no houses—nothing. The ground is a mass of shell holes, like waves: and there is complete desolation. It is almost incredible to me that even Protestantism can produce such vile morals as the attempted saving of the authors of such ruin.

I feel the horror of that destruction more than I did during the war. It is so also with grief: it becomes clearer and more weighty with time. The War overshadowed its own evil. It was a vast activity which filled me with vigour. Now it is over the mind is aghast at what has happened. It has a curiously weird effect upon my mind to approach the battle front *for the first time in four years to hear no sound*. It was as though the world had died. As one got near Béthune one used to hear the guns louder and louder and then filling all the sky: and the roads were filled with the movement to and fro of war. Today I passed Béthune, crossed the trenches—over to the German side: all is snow and absolutely silent. Behind what was until so lately the German front there are still a mass of notices in German: huge signs and orders. Certain places which they turned into bandstands or beer halls still have their vile colours painted over them. The false tooth-on-edge colouring of the Germans. And

---

[1] Letter to Mrs. Reginald Balfour: March 19, 1932.

I passed the cemetery of theirs with a huge 'Modern Style' marble monstrosity that was appalling. I hope it will be *soon* destroyed. The association of their degraded paganism with death is intolerable: even with the death of Germans.[1]

He went on down the Rhine to the recovered provinces. At Metz the huge bronze statue of William I had been melted down, and a *poilu* of equal size had taken its place. Then to the Palatinate with Mangin in control—'intelligent, violent, rather strong, and full of the knowledge of war'[2]; Frankfurt 'full of movement and light and—as I thought on a short visit—covert insolence'[3]; Strasbourg, wholly French, resisting Germany better than Metz because it was German-speaking.

It was in this mood, a bitter one, that he looked at the problem of France and Germany. On the question of the Ruhr and Reparations he was, of course, ranged with French nationalist opinion, and the bolstering of Germany by British financial interests seemed to him yet another example of the English passion for Prussia, and its 'particularly sterile brand of Protestant Atheism'.[4] Poincaré had the right ideas, but still he was a politician and was afraid to liquidate his own kind. 'What all Europe wants is a young soldier in France and that quickly. But it won't be granted.'[5] It was granted at the *vingt-cinquième heure*; and although the soldier's name was Charles de Gaulle, Belloc was not alone in failing to recognize him.

Meanwhile the French continued to stoke the smouldering fires of their civil war, and then to damp them down when they threatened to blaze into a *coup d'état*. Belloc rushed through the country in third-class carriages, his pockets bulging with the *Action Française*. On one occasion Eccles introduced him to Maurras in the Rue du Dragon, but Maurras was too deaf to converse easily and Belloc was not the best of listeners. He remained fixed for three-quarters of his mind in the orthodoxies of the old French Right—the Parnassian in poetry, a crudely applied

---

[1] Letter to Mrs. Reginald Balfour: Feb. 6, 1919.
[2] *Ibid.*: Feb. 15, 1919.   [3] *Ibid.*
[4] Letter to Mrs. Reginald Balfour: Jan. 21, 1922.
[5] Letter to Mrs. Raymond Asquith: Feb. 20, 1921.

Thomism in politics, the *Revue Universelle*, Louis Bertrand and Bernard Fay—it was not a very inspiring company, and it all came to rather a sticky end. Belloc had not the faintest notion of what was happening to French Catholicism; and here Péguy, with whom he had much in common, could have helped him more than anyone else. When he met the subtle and deeply contemplative mind of Jacques Maritain he was quite unable to come to terms with it. The intransigence of Claudel was more to his taste, and *L'Annonce Faite à Marie* moved him deeply.

Although he came to find Paris hardly habitable, he still went there a great deal. He would revisit La Celle St. Cloud where all his cousins lived 'in Palaces crowning the heights, while my poor little dusty ancestral house which bred the whole boiling lot of them lies down below like a slum with a pocket-handkerchief of a garden all in ruins'.[1] Among his more distant relatives living at La Celle St. Cloud was Charles du Bos, and it is amusing to think of him in conversation with this pontiff of literary criticism. The two men had nothing in common except the same religion, a similar ancestry, and an admiration for Maurice Baring. More to his taste were evenings spent with his English friends—J. B. Morton and Bevan Wyndham-Lewis—roaming about the Quartier Latin, in search of restaurants and history. Mr. Wyndham Lewis describes a rainy night when they tried to find an obscure restaurant near the Halles where the *tripes à la mode de Caen* were said to be incomparable. They proved to be nothing of the kind; but the disappointment

> evoked neither fury nor mourning but an *excursus* on Illusion, with special reference to tripe and official propaganda, which ended some three hours later in a spirited defence of Blanche of Castille, having touched on and discussed *en passant* the proper cookery of frogs, the decline of British Liberalism, Arab horses, St. Thomas on alchemy, Collective Security, Parisian taxi-cabs, bimetallism, Danton's second marriage, the virtues of elastic-sided boots, the technique of controversy, and a dozen more cognate topics I forget.[2]

[1] Letter to Lady Juliet Duff: Nov. 24, 1919.
[2] The *News Chronicle:* July 26, 1953.

Belloc would sometimes stay at the Hotel St. Romains, just behind St. Roch, where he had often been with Elodie; or at the Récamier in the Place de Saint Sulpice. At one point he took over Henri Brémond's flat in the Rue Chanoinesse within a stone's throw of Notre Dame. According to the Abbé Dimnet, he

> paid his rent punctually for a long time without spending a single night in his property, finally appeared with his friend Warre, and started keeping house on two cots, a kettle and two French soldiers' mugs, which his loyalty to barrack life showed to him as indispensable. After two months he decided he could not sleep in the place, not, as I was afraid, because the clock of Notre Dame chimed too loudly, nor indeed because of any noise in particular, but because of 'the expectation of noise'. [1]

In fact Belloc and Warre slept there for two nights, and the noise was rather more than expected. The *fracas* of the local dust-bins being emptied disturbed the sleepers, and they were hardly consoled when the concierge explained to them that it was the '*ménage d'ordure*'. In 1938 Belloc took over a room from his former secretary (Miss Soames, then married to Mr. Hoffman Nickerson) and when Sir Eric Phipps was Ambassador in Paris he often stayed at the Embassy. A room was set apart for him where he could work undisturbed. Belloc liked the permanent officials of the Foreign Office and the Phippses in particular. He had stayed with them in Vienna, when he was in search of Central European battlefields, and had celebrated Sir Eric's appointment to the Legation (with other aspects of the diplomatic general post) in a series of triolets.

> Sir Austen Chamberlain, K.G.,
> Returns this morning from Geneva,
> It is indeed no less than he—
> Sir Austen Chamberlain, K.G.
> A lady told me so at tea,
> I had no grounds to disbelieve her.
> Sir Austen Chamberlain, K.G.,
> Returns this morning from Geneva.

[1] *My New World* (1938).

Claud Russell is to go to Berne,
It's also news I have to send you,
It is from Eric Phipps I learn
Claud Russell is to go to Berne;
(And let me tell you in your turn
That all the Hosts of Heaven attend you)
Claud Russell is to go to Berne,
It's all the news I have to send you.

Sir Eric Phipps himself, I hear
Is nominated to Vienna.
So, early in the coming year
Sir Eric Phipps himself, I hear
Will take the train to Belvedere,
And carry on across the Brenner.
Sir Eric Phipps himself, I hear
Is nominated to Vienna.

The Paris Embassy will go,
And soon, to somebody or other,
To whom indeed I do not know
The Paris Embassy will go.
Perhaps t'will be the Rumbolds? (No,
The man in Holland—not his brother)
The Paris Embassy will go,
And soon, to somebody or other.[1]

In fact, Belloc was better known and better appreciated in
Belgium than he was in France. He lectured in Brussels a good
deal, and was given an official banquet at Mons with the Governor
who looked like Poincaré, and the *député* who looked like a rabbit,
and a woman with a voice like a gramophone who asked him
repeatedly what he thought of the League of Nations. What
Belloc thought of the League of Nations was not mentionable in
mixed company. In 1925 he took the chair in Louvain for a
lecture on Thomist economics. But the richest reward of his visits
to Belgium was the friendship of Cardinal Mercier whom he

[1] Letter to Lady Lovat: Dec. 14, 1927.

took every opportunity of seeing, and to whom he introduced his sons. Belloc admired everything about Mercier except the Malines Conversations; finding him 'full of truth, irony, justice, and (what hardly ever goes with these) peace'.[1]

Belloc could never resist the great cities, because it was in the city that history was made. If one side of him—the deepest side—was happiest at sea, or in the high sanctuaries of the hills, another side demanded the company and the conflict of men. This is what we mean when we say that to the end of his days he was political. Moreover there were moments in these post-war years when landscape no longer satisfied him; and it was characteristic that he should discover in this deprivation a new source of steadfastness. He knew it for a mood; and moods pass.

And now I want to say what I thought on the top of Masbury hill that early morning, overlooking the Vale of Glastonbury in the clear weather after the night's gale, with the mist between the hills. . . . In the flood of thought on that hill, on that morning, I noticed most how little landscape meant any more: how it had grown to be outside the soul. It is not very long ago that such a landscape would have been more to me than any sound, of music or of verse. It was the vision of the world and its past that fulfilled me, and I shared it; and it did so because I shared it. Everyone has his own appeal, and perhaps I was odd in this: but I would travel to the ends of the earth and take any deprivation to have a prospect of the world: and the pictures of it moved me as colours do some and others music. Now I knew that I was deprived of it: like a colour-loving man gone blind or a music-loving man gone deaf. If mood could break despair, I would despair quicker than others and once for all. But the intelligence is supreme and is the master of mood. I know, no matter what I feel.[2]

2

Belloc had to go to North Africa to find the France that he most admired; the Roman inheritance; straight roads cutting the desert;

[1] Letter to Mrs. Raymond Asquith: Nov. 6, 1920.　　[2] *Ibid.*, Jan. 12, 1920.

soldiers and Christian shrines. In September 1920 he visited
Morocco for the first time. He saw Lyautey who was then
Governor-General, and formed a high impression of that attractive and remarkable man. Everywhere, the army looked after him
and he noted, shrewdly, the results of French rule. Lured by
civilization, the tribes were coming down into the plains.

> They are like children with toys. They adore railways, but
> cannot believe it just that they should have to pay for tickets.
> They quite easily learn the telephone and how to drive motors,
> but they get more easily tired and distracted than do Europeans
> and they won't work long at a time. They all pick up enough
> French to get along with—but no more, and all can read a few
> words of Arabic. They *loathe* the Catholic Church and it will
> not convert them. But it is now their master which is the next
> best thing.[1]

This makes sad reading in 1956. Further visits to North Africa
followed in 1927, to finish *James II,* and again, early in 1928 with
Edmond Warre, to get material for a book. Each time the impressions of *Esto Perpetua* were renewed.

> A wind and sun both bitter and with a sort of steely edge; a
> place that made the Donatists and the ebony of Tertullian and
> the terrors of St. Augustine—but also his elevation. I marvel,
> enjoy and fear it.[2]

He goes on to describe a drive into the Tunisian desert.

> It was over 150 miles with but one piece of life: a strange
> huddled quadrilateral of white-washed huts, the natives
> huddled in circles in the midst and a fire of dead branches
> from Lord knows where. After that a grandiose descent
> into a valley of dead salt, with the last rock wall (rather
> higher than the Moorlands—hardly as high as the Welsh
> mountains, but all one serrated edge) beyond. No wonder the
> men of these solitudes are haunted by implacable things! Into

[1] Letter to Mrs. Reginald Balfour: Sept. 30, 1930.
[2] Letter to Mrs. Raymond Asquith: Feb. 23, 1928.

that wall we climbed by a track not perceptible to my untrained eye and sometimes lost by the driver, till it became clearer where men had shaped it somewhat to the contours, in order to make the ascent possible. We reached the stone hut of the mine we were to visit, just as darkness fell: and it fell suddenly (did the night) in ten minutes. There we passed the night, huddled in too few and very lousy blankets. But we had wine and tinned food and coffee. Only no stars. Next day we went on across the plain Northward, leaving behind us the great sheets of salt and going into the more rounded hills where the Romans founded their great towns. Of these—in land now all gone bare and sterile—huge ruins stand at strangely short intervals. You pass the ruin of a portico, of an aqueduct, of a wall or shrine, every ten miles: at Feriance the scattered remnant of Thelma and at Kasserine a Triumphal Arch hardly ruined, and below half of a great theatre. At Sbeila there is a mile of fallen column and rampart and paved streets, in short remaining sections, and three august Temples standing crippled —and still noble. It is an awful thing to see how that great civilization—which is ourselves—was murdered by the wild reaction of Islam and even its fields turned to nothing: and most impressive of all are the poor mosaic floors of the Christian churches and baptisteries which have heard no music for a thousand years. All that! I hope some day you will see it. It haunts the mind . . . and still the cold goes on, as though of a grave, and still the grey sky without a sun mourning that utter death.[1]

In the spring of 1935, on his return from America, Belloc made the journey to Palestine which he had thought of undertaking at the time of Elodie's death. He desired to receive Communion in the Church of the Holy Sepulchre, and to see the country of the Crusades. His book on the subject (*The Crusade*) was published by Cassell in 1937. The treatment was neither romantic nor ideological; Belloc confined himself to tracing the military effort and the military errors which frustrated it. The voyage tired him,

[1] Letter to Mrs. Raymond Asquith: March 2, 1928.

but the classics—his great companions—returned to life and
refreshed him, as the ship steamed past the plains of Troy and he
saw 'Mount Ida like a cloud, and on the other side of the sea, a
long way off, Athos standing up enormous'.[1]   He came down
through Syria, pausing by the tomb of Saladin. He was almost
tempted to pray there, as he might have prayed by the tomb of
Charlemagne; not because he believed the romantic legends
about Saladin, but because 'Saladin was a very great soldier and
that is something never to be despised'.[2]

Islam now appeared more threatening and Belloc formed a
more realistic estimate of its future. It gave him the impression of
'a strong animal held in leash by a man who has captured it
indeed; but who is still afraid of it and has neither its tenacity nor
its health'.[3] It would soon acquire mechanical techniques, and
it had retained its morals as well as its religion; notably the freedom
of its justice and its comparative freedom from usury. Belloc was
moved, of course, by the sanctity of the places he visited, but even
more by their sadness. When he came to Galilee ruin was all that
he could see.

It was not beauty which affected me when I saw it; the
landscape is stern, and I will maintain of this great site, as of all
else southward, down to Bethlehem itself, of all else in this land
save Nazareth, that it carries more the air of tragedy than any
other. I can only believe that the Passion has chiefly imprinted
itself on all that land wherein our Lord taught, gave the signs
from Heaven and suffered, at last, the Agony . . . Tiberias
was stately and splendid, with the Grecian column everywhere,
and the marble statuary and colonnades which you may still
see overthrown, lying in ruins, of city after city from Palmyra
in the desert down to Petra in the far south. All that loveliness,
all that dignity, has gone; and the squalor has replaced it which
follows everywhere at last the sweep of the Mahomedan
conquest. Magdala has been wiped out; a few stones and a
house or two of no presence, a tree or two, and the reeds along
the lake are all that remain.[4]

[1] Letter to Lady Juliet Duff: Good Friday, 1935.   [2] *Universe*.
[3] *Ibid.*   [4] *Ibid.*

To this *tabula rasa* of Mahomedan decay there was a strong contemporary challenge. Belloc was not unsympathetic to Zionism. Palestine was the natural home of the Jew, and his presence there in increasing numbers offended no civil right. He bought his land at a high price, and Belloc could find no evidence of coercion put upon the native farmer. His superior skill was tapping new sources of power, light, transport, and mineral productions. Through Jewish money the British had built the harbour of Haifa, which was the only modern and secure port in the Eastern Levant between the Turkish boundary and Alexandria. It was also the only one capable of fortification. But in improving the country the Jew was coming to dominate it. The position was, therefore, unstable to a dangerous degree. Belloc compared it to a Pyramid standing upon its apex,

> only prevented from falling if the natural effect of gravity is counteracted by someone holding up the sides. . . . For hundreds of miles in every direction there is a Mahomedan world which regards the Zionist experiment as temporary and is determined to destroy it. . . . The quarrel is not to be appeased: it is permanent: and that is why the Zionist experiment, *in proportion to its success*, will be an increasing anxiety to this country.[1]

It would be hard to find a more lucid analysis or a more accurate prediction. Certain things had a way of coming far truer than even Belloc foresaw.

3

Belloc paid three visits to America between the two wars. The first was in 1923. He had not been there since 1898, and he was to find the country much changed. He was in the hands of the lecture agent, Lee P. Keedick, and he sailed on the French ship *Roussillon* (the old *Goeben* transformed and rechristened) on February 5. He had never had much contact with Americans outside their own country, and he was quickly reminded of how different they were

[1] *Universe.*

from other people talking the same language. There were ten of them on board and they discussed Europe with a naïveté which Belloc described as 'renversant—like sudden thunder and the house catching fire unexpectedly'.[1] One of them was reading a book called *The Life of the Soul* and Belloc rashly asked if he might look at it. His eye fell on such sentences as these: 'Who has seen with the Mirror of the Enlightened Mind through which and in which the Self of the Soul is seen', or 'Trust in the in-dwelling Self and have boundless faith in the Self-Soul and the Soul-Self'. A fellow passenger remarked to him that the Americans were getting to think almost as much of Wells as they had thought of Kipling; they thought him 'fine'. Belloc fervently wished they would come to the same conclusion about himself during the eight weeks of his lecture tour; for he was often heard to growl: 'There are 25,000,000 Catholics in the United States and none of them will buy my books.'

What irked him as he started his travels was the American disrespect for privacy and the American toleration of noise.

A host always honours a guest of consequence by giving him the best bedroom over against the electric tram, and possessing a telephone even if no other bedroom in the house has one.[2]

Whenever the visitor sat down to write, or set out to look at something by himself, somebody else sat down beside him and walked beside him, talking incessantly. These complaints are a little comic coming from this most gregarious of men; and Belloc realized how much the American friendliness—the greatest single virtue of a great people—owed to the Colonial isolation and the covered wagon, when the conversation of another human being was like sweet music in the silence of hardly inhabited space. He was also struck by the lack of variety; toast, for example, was exactly the same in every house, hotel or restaurant throughout the United States. Indeed it was not what Belloc understood by toast at all. It was 'grilled bread'. He was continually finding one word in America doing the work of fifty anywhere else.

[1] Letter to Mrs. Reginald Balfour: Feb. 11, 1923.
[2] *Ibid.*, March 17, 1923.

Thus to blame, to criticize, to curse, to suggest modifications, to rave against a thing, to disapprove, to find unusual, to detest, to despise, etc. etc. etc. are all under one head 'To score'. Papers put huge headlines such as 'Premier Bonar Law scores Opposition'. Or 'Bishop Hobo scores Divorce'. Or—of a literary opinion slightly revising an older view of Tennyson—'Prominent Harvard Man scores British Poet'. In the same way 'stress' is used for every nuance of emphasis from the least recommendation to the loudest shouts. 'Raps' is used for any form of adverse decision or punishment by any authority. 'Judge raps Clubman' means that a man of means has got a verdict against him in a Court of Justice. 'Pope raps British Lord' means that an argument against the Halifax claim to Orders has been issued in Rome. 'Mussolini raps Railway Chief' means that Mussolini has fined or dismissed a Station Master. It is a funny word ultimately deriving in the distant past, I suppose, from our idiom to 'rap over the knuckles' but now grown from that humble seed to be a vast growth. All this does not mean that they think *less* than us but differently. They are prodigiously foreign and getting more foreign every day.[1]

But in all this alien world the Church was familiar, although nothing is more American than American Catholicism; the legitimate price for the Church's considerable conquest in a part of the Western hemisphere which she did not help initially to form. It was

like coming across the Faith in China, or meeting a black Bishop. The Mass in an American small town, and a convent of nuns all talking American is the most striking proof of the Church's universal character conceivable.[2]

This was putting it strongly; but it was a victory of observation over bias that Belloc could at last see the Catholic Church as the bridge between the Old World and the New, bringing 'the general tradition of that ancient civilization from which the New World ultimately derives as much as does the Old'.[3] He

---

[1] *Ibid.*   [2] *Ibid.*   [3] *Universe.*

addressed Catholic audiences in several of the big cities, and found
many Catholics who knew Elodie's family; this brought him 'a
great consolation and feeling of home'.[1] He particularly enjoyed
a visit to a Girls' School run by the Sisters of Charity—the Order
to which Elodie had tried to belong.

> The host of young wenches demure and respectful, the Holy
> Women authoritative and efficient: an oasis in the desert of
> American education as I knew it in non-Catholic households
> and schools years ago.[2]

In other places he was bored with having to speak on Modern
English Literature, of which he admitted he knew nothing.
All he could do (though he might have done a little better)
was to read aloud from Masefield and Rupert Brooke. Why, he
wondered impatiently, didn't the Americans want to hear about
the eighteenth and early nineteenth century classics? They wanted
to hear about quite different things; a young journalist came into
Belloc's hotel in Boston and asked him what was his rule for
happiness. 'I have none', replied Belloc. 'You can't be happy.
Don't try. Cut it out. Make up your mind to be miserable.' The
audiences varied in size, for Belloc's reputation in America never
stood as high as Chesterton's, and the tour was not under Catholic
auspices. Sometimes he would make as much as one thousand
pounds above his expenses, sometimes five hundred pounds, and
at other times nothing at all. He had no fixed fee, and all money
passed through his agent. At Pittsburg four hundred pounds was
taken in entrance money, but of this he did not expect to get
more than fifty pounds except indirectly through the future sale
of his books. He went up into Canada for a few days and wrote
to Desmond MacCarthy from Toronto.

> I have just got your letter after a meal of tepid beef with
> grease over it, vegetables boiled in water without salt, some
> stale bread and a cup of water with ice in it. The air is heated to
> 75 degrees, with hot water pipes, and is dry. Outside there is a
> blizzard. The country is made of mud and the trees are very

---

[1] Letter to Mrs. Reginald Balfour: Feb. 25, 1923.
[2] Ibid., March 17, 1923.

rum, like umbrellas turned inside out and stripped of their covering so that only ribs remain sticking up all round. The trees do not hang together in lumps but grow anyhow. The Houses are of planks, of iron, of bright red brick and of stone. They stand anyhow, but all in a line, some big, some little, side by side. Often a patch of land in between. The people are happy. The trains are twenty-five per cent. late always i.e. six hours on 24 hours, a quarter of an hour on one hour, and so on. There are hardly any cats or dogs. The women stare at the men, the men look nervous when a woman passes. The expression of the face is fixed; the mouth hardly moves. Happiness everywhere.[1]

He was glad to get home, stunned by the contrast between Europe and America; and he immediately sat down to write the book which bears that name.[2] This is one of the most intelligent, because it is one of the most honest, essays ever written about the United States. Where it exaggerates it does so to the detriment of Britain. It was asking for trouble, with Winston Churchill still at large, to assert that 'the great function of Prime Minister is dead'; and the thesis of *The Party System* was rather tediously rehashed. But these distortions do not seriously spoil the synthesis, which showed Belloc thinking and writing at his best. He had already seen that the essential mark of the American social spirit was publicity; but anyone can see that, and many people find it as irritating as Belloc found it. Nevertheless he could so far conquer his irritation as to see that publicity is the spirit of the market-place; and that when you have the market-place, that is to say the continual pressure of corporate opinion, you have the distinguishing mark of democracy. Democracy was becoming confused with things that had nothing whatever to do with it; with a belief in the infallible wisdom of majority decisions; with calling everyone by their Christian name; with a contempt for lineage and tradition. Democracy simply meant the belief that political power, which Belloc called the Prince, derived from the community, which he called the Sovereign; and it meant that the

[1] March 27, 1923.   [2] *The Contrast* (1923).

2 G

Sovereign kept a permanent but not a paralysing vigilance over the Prince.

It was of course no news to the Americans, or to anybody else, when Belloc called them a democracy. But it would have surprised some of them a good deal when he called them a monarchy. Now monarchy has nothing, essentially, to do with a man sitting on a throne. Monarchy simply means that executive power is vested in one man, for a limited period or a specific purpose; a man known by, and answerable to all. Belloc found this principle at work not only in the Presidential office but in the Universities and in the mayoralities of the great towns. Anyone with the most superficial knowledge of American life will know what he meant. It is possible that he exaggerated a little. It was hardly true to say that 'at the death of Mr. Harding the character of the national mourning, the novel and peculiar depth, emphasis and exaltation of the moment was observed by all'. President Harding, when he died, was in imminent danger of impeachment. But it was certainly true that America illustrated the virtues of monarchy, its simplicity and truth, far better than any European State. They were virtues of which Europe had need, but they were not to be had by robbery.

The principles of monarchy in the United States were guaranteed—and this is where Belloc did not quite fit together the two parts of his synthesis—by the American worship of their Constitution. In any State, and particularly in a State still new and founded upon a dogma of equality, there has to be a fixed point of sanctity. Something must be untouchable. In America this thing was the Constitution, and its visible symbol was the flag. The opposition aroused by the policies of President Roosevelt was not always respectable, and indeed it was not always comprehensible to the English visitor; but the visitor would have missed the whole point of America if he did not realize that the mere suspicion that the President was tampering with the Constitution—and this is what he appeared to be doing when he tried to pack the Supreme Court—was enough to mobilize against him the mystical reverence of Americans for the thing that the Founding Fathers had made. Now Belloc understood the meaning, the quasi-sacramental depth, of the American Constitution, and it marked the maturity of his political thinking that he did so.

Americans—especially at the time when Belloc paid his first visit after the war—were freely accused of worshipping money. He had no difficulty in showing that they did no such thing. They enjoyed making money; he enjoyed making it himself. They enjoyed the things that money could buy; he enjoyed that even more. They occasionally envied people who were richer than themselves; he was not above envying them either. But they did not invest the possessor of money with moral qualities; they did not bow down and worship him. Now this, and this alone, was what Belloc meant when he talked about the worship of the rich. His language often seemed exaggerated to people who did not know, or did not remember, the background against which he grew up. In England this servility towards wealth had been odious at the turn of the century; by the outbreak of war in 1914 it had become intolerable. Rich people were somehow regarded as good, and poor people as less good. The thing amounted to a total transformation of moral values. It was an evil thing and Belloc discovered it to be quite absent from America. There were more rich men in America than in England; but they were not worshipped—they were watched.

Of American literature he knew very little and he hardly touched on it in his book. But Arthur Pollen had sent him the story of a prize-fight in verse, and his reaction to this indicates what he would have felt about the strong realism which marked so much American writing.

I know the manner. It is very powerful when they pull it off as this one does. But it is incapable of dignity or beauty. At least I have never seen anything in it, not even a poem called 'The Congo', which achieved dignity. It seems to me to have power without dignity; and that is top heavy in art of any kind for the absence of dignity goes with fun rather than with power. On the other hand it is an achievement. Anything which is of effect in its own kind and at the same time very difficult to do is worth close attention.[1]

[1] April 22, 1929.

He thought the Americans happier than any other people he knew, although he did not think this happiness would last. It was in the nature of all societies to grow, and in growing to become more complex. With complexity would come cynicism and discontent; even, at the last, despair, But he saluted this present innocence, as he had saluted it more than thirty years before in a California seen through an aureole of romantic love. The Faith alone might preserve it, but then the Faith would eventually come into conflict with the Civil Power. That was the crisis that Catholicism, when it was organized in sufficient strength, always brought into society; not peace, but a sword. Belloc saw the Faith in America surrounded by the Opinion, into which Protestantism had dissolved; an opinion which thought you could believe as you liked, so long as you behaved in the way it wanted you to, in opposition to a Faith, inflexible and received upon authority, claiming a wide freedom of behaviour outside a restricted field of morals. For the one, Prohibition or compulsory secular education was an intolerable affront to liberty; the other saw an equal threat in the Catholic doctrine of marriage and the sacredness of human life. Belloc foresaw, not altogether fantastically, a time when Opinion, clothed with the sanction of Law, might demand the removal of the incurably insane and forbid the marriage of the physically unfit. In either case the Catholic Church would be bound to resist the Law; and Americans, who are naturally a lawless people, do not expect the Law to bend for fear that it may break. It is an essential safeguard against themselves.

In a word, Belloc foresaw Mr. Paul Blanshard and he would not have worried in the least to hear the Catholic Church described as a 'pressure group' in the United States. He believed that it was the business of Catholics to make themselves a nuisance. But he devoted a chapter of *The Contrast* to discussing the other strongly organized minority in the United States—the Jews. His book on this subject had recently appeared [1] and the matter was uppermost in his mind. Indeed, as we have seen, it was a chronic preoccupation. *The Jews* was anything but an anti-Semitic tract, and it is a tragedy that for a hundred people who know the rhyme

[1] *The Jews* (1922).

about Lord Swaythling or the 'little curly-headed men' there is
not one who has read Belloc's sober examination of the problem.
The fault was partly the unfortunate people's whom he wanted to
warn and to protect. He had submitted the proofs to a Jewish ad-
viser, who declared the book to be unjust and told Belloc that his
own people would refuse to read or sell it. This saddened Belloc,
for he had put the case as justly as he could. He had many Jewish
friends; and his desire was constant—'that Israel may have peace'.

To say that he had put the case justly is not to say that he had
put it incontrovertibly. He had seen the Jewish problem, but he
had not solved it. He had saluted the virtues of Israel; the special
Jewish courage, the *pietas* of their family life, and their particular
indifference to money. He thought them 'the people least grasp-
ing of small sums and most ready to lend or give'.[1] What he was
concerned to analyse and, if possible, to cure was the friction set
up between Jews and the communities in which they lived. This
was the burden of his book, and he was only translating into
careful and qualified argument what he had written to Baring
many years earlier.

My own attitude is quite clear. The Jewish nation ought
to be recognized as a nation in some way or another, with
all the advantages and disadvantages that follow from the
recognition of any truth. I express that policy in the word
privilege. Where there is conscription the obvious bargain
would be not to submit Jews to military service. In England,
where there is no conscription, I would have registration
and charters, Jewish Courts and so on. But all that is mere
Utopia. The wretched misunderstanding will work its way
fatally as it has worked its way twice before in European
history. The simple solution of absorption neither has nor can
succeed. There is some fate against it. After every great period
of financial power in the hands of a few Jews (the mass of
the nation is absurdly poor) that power wanes and then there
is no check upon the bad passions which the friction between
the races allows. Not one educated man in a hundred has any

[1] Letter to Maurice Baring: Jan. 1, 1916.

appreciation of the past history of all this and that is why it is so difficult to give an effective warning. Most to blame in my opinion are those, especially in England and France, who say the vilest things about the Jews behind their backs, never make a real friend of a Jew, gloat over their misfortunes, and yet accept their hospitality and pretend to mix with them as though there were no racial or cultural problem at all.

I have come across a very good book indeed written by a Jew called Ruppin. I recommend it to you. I can only read it in a translation which has just come out (George Bell & Sons) but you could easily get the original German. Get it. Excellent as the book is it suffers from one error which vitiates its value. It believes absorption to be possible. That seems to me no more possible than it would be to make the English shallow and cynical, the French unmilitary or the Germans delicate and the Irish orderly.[1]

Now this was the policy of *apartheid* and it reeked of the *Action Française*. Belloc was too humane and reasonable a man to express himself with the crudity of Maurras and his disciples; he was too careful of words to deliver himself to their vile invective. But the solution was the same and it was contradicted by the facts of common observation. Anyone can quote examples of Jews who have been perfectly assimilated to the society in which they live, and have worked, fought and died for it. Belloc did not see how easily his arguments could be turned against the Catholics. Here, too, was a society highly, though less secretly, organized and, in a measure, set apart; conscious of its superiority; alien to some extent to all that stood outside it; international, and in certain matters of moral consequence challenging civic authority; persecuted and perpetually resurgent. If Europe had not taught him this obvious parallel, he might have learnt it from America. But where the Jewish problem was concerned, there was a difference between England and America which he was quick to notice.

The Jew question is a fearful bore over here. People talk of it morning noon and night. Those who know I have written a book on it take it for granted that I am in approval of a general massacre—which is the usual extreme confusion Americans reach when they have worked themselves up on the matter, while the very much smaller number who have *actually read* my book, disagree with its judicial tone: they want blood and thunder. But much the greater part of those I hear talking have no idea I have written about it—and all in Toronto and Montreal, Buffalo, New York, Pittsburg, Boston, everywhere rave and howl against the Jews. It may or may not come to an outbreak—on the whole I think not—but it makes the life of the mass of Jews here—who are poor—very hard. Magistrates are . . . biased against them—they are insulted in public and refused entry to Clubs and even hotels and in general made to feel that they are enemies. What a life! Fancy some wretched man coming with his family from, say, Poland, and landing into this! For the American has no tradition or habit in the matter and never appreciates complexity. He feels the racial friction and reacts in the shape of violent revulsion.[1]

On page 54 of *The Jews* Belloc wrote as follows:

The first to enlist from the United States was a Jew, whom I had the pleasure and honour of meeting on Mangin's staff at Mayence. I hope he may see these lines.

The man in question was Major Louis Henry Cohn, and his story is an interesting one. Born of Alsatian parents, who had long since emigrated to America and had little feeling for the land of their birth, he was sent to school in Cleveland. Here he had the misfortune to come under a German teacher whom the recent abolition of corporal punishment had deprived of her favourite occupation. Instead, she would take her revenge on the pupils by refusing to let them leave the room when they pleaded a natural necessity. The cruelty of this left an indelible mark on the mind of Louis Cohn, and he conceived a hatred for Germany which he was later able to turn to good account. As soon as the news of the Serajevo murder in 1914 was made known, he went to Washington, obtained an interview with the French Ambassador, Jusserand,

[1] Letter to Mrs. Reginald Balfour: March 17, 1923.

and offered his services to France in the war which he believed to
be certain. The Ambassador was sceptical, but when war broke
out Cohn was accepted by the French, employed on special services in the United States, and later fought with great distinction
in their army. At the Victory Parade in 1918 he stood with a small
company of the most highly decorated soldiers beside the Arc de
Triomphe.

This was a very good example of the Jewish passion for abstract
justice and Belloc acknowledged it, though he did not know all
the details of his friend's life related here. When Belloc came to
New York in 1923 Major Cohn gave a luncheon for him at a
Jewish Club. There was some indignation that one who was
generally regarded as an anti-Semite should be admitted as an
honoured guest, and one eminent Jewish judge had made a
speech saying that he ought to be deported. Belloc, let us repeat,
thought popular anti-Semitism a violent and vulgar absurdity,
and in correspondence with Major Cohn he was at pains to
dissociate himself from it.

The Cause of the World Unrest is a book written by a woman
called Webster. In my opinion it is a lunatic book. She is one
of those people who have got one cause on the brain. It is the
good old Jewish revolutionary bogey. I think people are great
fools who do not appreciate what a part the Jew has played in
revolutionary movements, but people are much bigger fools
who get it on the brain and ascribe every revolutionary movement to Jews and secret societies. The prime cause of revolution
is injustice, and the protest against injustice, when it becomes
too violent, produces revolution. But there is a type of unstable
mind which cannot rest without morbid imaginings, and the
conception of single causes simplifies thought. With this
good woman it is the Jews, with some people it is the Jesuits,
with others Freemasons and so on. The world is more complex
than that. Many of the facts quoted are true enough, but the
inferences drawn are exaggerated. It is perfectly true that the
Jews were the leaders and remain the leaders of the Russian
Revolution, but there was much more in it than that. I am

afraid it has done your people a great deal of harm that they should have been so prominent in it, but it is mere lunacy to regard the Jewish race as a whole as the sole instigator and prime mover against Social Injustice; though I do think their detached position makes them neglect the national interests in favour of an abstract ideal.[1]

Yet it was the abstract ideal which had brought Major Cohn to a position of confidence on Mangin's staff.

Belloc was not, however, above teasing the Jews, as he would tease the Protestants, when an occasion presented itself. Once he bought a little table for five pounds at an auction and a Jewish bidder remarked to him: 'It won't be worth much to you at that price.' Belloc turned and recited to him the Jewish profession of faith, as Disraeli had recited it on his death-bed. The man went quite white. At other times a prophetic judgment would shine through his banter.

> The poor darlings, I'm awfully fond of them and I'm awfully sorry for them, but it's their own silly fault—they ought to have let God alone.[2]

The defect of Belloc's discussion of the Jewish problem, both in public and in private, was that he could not take the Jews naturally.

He paid further visits to America in 1935 and 1937, and on the second of these he had a personal interview with President Roosevelt. He sent his impressions to Duff Cooper.

> He seems to me to have more integrity than most men and plenty of intelligence as well and considerable knowledge of the past—which is a good test of a man's cultivation.

> He perhaps exaggerates the danger of civic trouble everywhere (except in England) from the clash of the huge modern Proletariat with its taskmasters. But, if anything, that is an error on the right side. He is certainly an asset to the policy of England, for England of which he has, like most travelled and wealthy Americans of any lineage, some vague idea, is for him (as for most tr: and w: A of any l) an idol. . . . He wants

---

[1] Feb. 6, 1924.   [2] To the author.

someone to write about the Occident of 350–750. . . . Also
he has enough knowledge to know that it has never been properly done—for the great Fustel studied and described all the
main facts but had no vision of it. Miss Waddell has a partial
glimpse of it. He has been so long in politics . . . that he
worries too much about the intrigues of men: one has to in
such a post. But he keeps a fairly solid judgment. I don't think
he knows how far France has gone down hill and he is oblivious
of the Catholic philosophy and its effect on society—though
he does see that it is increasing in effect over here: but he puts
it down to the greater wealth of the 3rd generation of Immigrants: which is but one factor and not the greatest. The greatest
factor is the decay of all other certitudes over here: even the
dogma of majorities, even the dogma of Equality. So much for
him. I liked him. I was closeted with him over an hour and it
was not wasted.[1]

During this last of his visits he stayed with his former secretary
and her husband, Mr. and Mrs. Hoffman Nickerson, at their
home on Long Island, going in twice a week to New York for
his lectures at Fordham University. These were subsequently
published by Cassell as *The Crisis of Our Civilisation* (1937), and
they were a *résumé* of Belloc's teaching on history and politics.
But he had come to feel that being in America was 'like living
in a railway station'.[2] Genuinely as he liked the people, it would
be insincere to pretend that America saw Belloc at his best. He
made it too clear that he had come there to make money. Now
and again the inextinguishable temperament flashed out, as when
he kicked off his slipper at a boring dinner in Philadelphia and
proceeded to dance the hornpipe. But, in general, he did no
more than fulfil his obligations, and he often did that with a
rather poor grace. He was invited to give a Memorial Lecture to
Chesterton at Fordham, and a very big audience came to hear
him. He began by saying, 'Of course it would be bad taste to say
anything about Mr. Chesterton which I knew through our long
friendship', and then proceeded to enlarge on the information

[1] April 14, 1937.   [2] Letter to Lady Juliet Duff: April 22, 1937.

which his audience could have found for themselves in *Who's Who*. Not a word suggested that he had ever set eyes on his great ally. On another occasion the Editor of *The Commonweal* gave a luncheon in his honour at the Waldorf Astoria to which he had invited about forty rather distinguished people, including the presidents of all the New York Universities. The host made a few graceful remarks about the guest of honour, after which Belloc half rose and growled: 'When I accepted the invitation to come here, I had no idea there'd be such a large group. These unremunerative speaking engagements are killing me. I simply cannot speak.'

At Fordham he did not take easily to the seminar idea; avoided meeting the students; and was impatient if he were asked for proofs and references. Yet in the end the very few to whom he spoke at all intimately grew to like him, as he dropped his aggressive manner and gave some idea of the fatigue and financial anxiety under which he laboured.

Nor was his theory of the 'contrast' always acceptable to Americans in the form in which he put it. Some years before the Second World War an American priest and publicist, known for his strong English sympathies, came to London. A dinner was arranged for him at which he pleaded for a common front between English and American Catholics in face of the growing international dangers. Belloc, who had not been briefed about the purpose of the dinner, bluntly declared that American and English Catholics had nothing in common but the Mass. This speech was never forgotten by the guest of the evening. A few years later he became one of the most powerful and unrepentant isolationists in the United States.

4

As the crisis of 1938 gathered to its climax, Belloc had no doubt that Germany must be resisted, and said so, with loud emphasis, in *The Weekly Review*. Many people who opposed the Munich agreement did so because they admired the Czechs and did not want to see their democracy destroyed. Belloc had no such feelings. He had only been once to Bohemia and had detested it.

Bohemia is a horrid disappointment! It's the only European country (excluding the Balkans and Hungary) which I had never seen, and I imagined it to be of an opera bouffe Drury Lane character such as I delight in, with highly complicated Gothic and ultra Rococo and deep gorges and odd rocks. Instead of which it is like the worst parts of America and is inhabited by some of the beastliest people I ever saw. *No Gentry*. For the Gentry were all Austrian. Also it pullulates to-day with anti-Catholic propaganda of the Yankee type due to the odious Masaryk and his Yankee connections. There are Y.M.C.A. and Y.W.C.A. all over the place and boy scouts and horrors. All the churches quite empty. Also the Landscape is vile. Also the beds are full of Bugs and the food bad. I was indeed glad to get out of such a hole. It makes me love the Germans! [1]

Nevertheless, when it came to the point, he did not love them as much as all that. He saw the further threats—to Danzig or Alsace-Lorraine—and he believed that the English and the French had agreed to Hitler's demands at Munich because they were afraid of what he might do to them. When Duff Cooper resigned, Belloc warmly approved the action of his friend; and the approval was justified by the events.

. . . Meanwhile you are in the rare position of having been proved right—not only in temporal judgment but in morals. The event has proved you right in your estimate of the German attitude and doubly right in resigning as and when you did.

You know how a man's action stands separate from the general action around him. Sometimes it is in direct contradiction to the general mind, nearly always unattuned to it in some degree. The same is true of judgments. The judgment of the many is always somewhat at issue with that of the wisest individual, and when the individual is right it often takes a very

[1] Letter to Mrs. Reginald Balfour: March 19, 1932.

long time—nearly always more than a lifetime—to justify a sound appreciation.

I think that in your case coincidence of right judgment and actual event has come with quite exceptional rapidity. How long the full appreciation may take to come, no one can tell. But it's already manifestly on its way. As for the rewards of such wisdom they are usually denied and never tangible. But those who know you have been advanced beyond measure in what was always their very high appreciation of your prescience through universality of vision.[1]

Belloc would often say that Duff Cooper was the most intelligent man of his acquaintance.

For most people Poland was the occasion of the Second World War, but for Belloc it was its cause; and the survival of Poland would be the test of victory in the second war against the Germans, as its reconstruction had been the test of victory in the first. The peacemakers of Versailles had just passed that test, although Lloyd George had never heard of Teschen. There were no peacemakers after the Second World War; only a divided triumvirate —and the desecrated body of Poland lay between them. For Poland Belloc had a kind of historic passion and it was one of the few subjects that could rouse him, in these later years, to an exalted rhetoric. His speech at the Caxton Hall in July 1927 was a shining performance.

Those who listened to Belloc on these occasions were sometimes heard to remark that Poles were not invariably angels, and there were unlovely episodes in recent Polish history, like the pacification of the Ukraine, which Belloc would have dismissed as Byzantine propaganda but which did something to lessen English sympathy for the Polish cause. Indeed Poland was an extreme example of the type of landowning aristocracy which Belloc would have been the first to condemn if the landowners had been Lutheran Junkers. In private, he could admit that 'Poles, like Irishmen, say everything with an object'.[2] But he became their foremost champion in Britain, and when their leaders visited

[1] Oct. 3, 1939.   [2] Letter to Maurice Baring: Dec. 31, 1916.

this country he was generally invited to meet them. These occasions were not always exhilarating; here is a picture of a dinner at the Rembrandt Hotel, when Cardinal Bourne was entertaining the Polish Minister, Cardinal Hlond and other Polish prelates.

It was all crimson moiré silk, pectoral crosses, crimson skull-caps, decorations, big ribbons across the Shirtfront and the glories of this world. For the tenth time I said to myself that I *must* get a white waistcoat. I am stuck fast in 1890 and people will begin to think me affected. What you really would have liked to see was his Eminence of Westminster *writhing* with boredom under the ponderous utterance of his eminent brother of Warsaw. I never saw a man writhe with Boredom—but he did. It is truth and no lie. I have seen men snappish with boredom, peevish with boredom, rude with boredom, and raving at the reminiscence of boredom—but I never saw actual writhing before. He of Warsaw sat in a gilded arm-chair on my left after Dinner. He of Westminster in a similar chair on my right. I on a sofa between them. He of Warsaw spoke execrable almost incomprehensible French, *very* slowly for an incredible time and though I eagerly followed, nodded, grunted, assented, flashed an occasional kindly, an occasional enthusiastic eye, murmured 'Est-il possible'? 'Que c'est intéressant!' 'Ah! Jamais je n'ai su cela!'—and so on—to keep the machine in motion my ordinary sat suffering in silence till he could suffer no more and the spiritual heir of 100 Primates was, I tell you, at last driven to real, physical, open *writhing*. The Bishops . . . were less persistent. They were all—including their Chief—enormous men, placid and contented.[1]

Shortly after this dinner Belloc travelled to Poland on a pilgrimage only second in importance to his pilgrimage to Rome. His destination was the shrine of Our Lady of Czestochowa and he had with him the ballade which bears her name:

> Lady and Queen and Mystery manifold
> And very Regent of the untroubled sky.

[1] Letter to Mrs. Raymond Asquith: May 28, 1928.

After hearing Mass in the great church of the monastery which dominated all the surrounding country by its situation and all Poland by its legend, Belloc took the Ballade, mounted in a black frame, to the chapel where the tear-stained face of the Mother of God looks down upon the multitudes who pray before it. He then hung it on the wall on the Gospel side of the altar among the swords, medals, gold ships, and golden arms and legs which bore witness to Our Lady's intercession. Afterwards he made a translation of the verses into dog-Latin and deposited this with the archives of the monastery. If any Polish pilgrim to Czestochowa today looks closely enough at those sacred walls, he will see that an English poet was the first among his country's friends.

What Belloc admired in Poland was the flame of a military Christendom not yet extinct, and he found the same fire alight at the opposite extremity of Europe, in Spain. Mervyn Herbert was attached to the Embassy in Madrid in 1924, and Belloc set out with him and his wife to motor there across the Pyrenees. By an extraordinary mistake Belloc was arrested on the frontier by the French authorities. Exasperated by some formality, he had exclaimed 'C'est idiot', and the official, mishearing, thought Belloc had called him a 'salaud'. The wires were set buzzing and the British Ambassador in Paris received the following telegram from Herbert.

> Very urgent. Hilaire Belloc travelling with me has been arrested and detained by passport authorities Cerbère on false and quite fantastic charge invented by minor official please do everything possible to get him liberated at once. . . .

Belloc was released just as he was being taken off to prison. He had not been to Castile since he walked there in 1909; now he travelled in comfort, and he sent his impressions to Mrs. Asquith.

> I have seen the Guadarrama, so like California and the west that it had the odd effect of halving my life for an hour and I have gone all along the road to Toledo between vast plains without hedge or tree and the southern mountains, a county away, dark against the blue of this January sky, all powdered

with light. It is sheer space. There is nothing like it in Europe and I never saw it so well. The whole of the vision of this earth is on a larger scale. One sees small ruins on isolated rocks in the plateau—one marks them against the sky—and they are 50 miles away. In the midst of that endless flat roof of Castile, bordered by its edges of mountains, the gulf of the Tagus cuts a broad shadow of indigo in the yellow glare—and, just peering above it, the marble of Toledo. I am glad I came. I wish you could see these things now. You will. The world is not small, it is too large, just as life is too long.

It is 15 years since I last went alone over these vast plains and under these bare and strange Sierras. The effect of such a gulf of time is curious, not frightening, not even melancholy: solemn. It is like stopping on a pass and looking back miles away to a group of houses where, at midday, one had rested, and now it is evening.[1]

When the Spanish Civil War broke out in 1936, there was, of course, no doubt where Belloc's sympathies lay, but he had an exact appreciation of the spiritual forces engaged on either side. On the one hand 'intense indignation against the social injustice of a system under which a proletarian mass were compelled by economic circumstances to work under the exasperating conditions of mechanized industry for the profit of interests with whom the workers had no sufficient human bond'; on the other hand 'patriotism, the traditions of an independent peasantry and, more important than either, religion'.[2] For Belloc himself the religious factor outweighed all others; the fate of Europe hung upon the Spanish man-at-arms. Belloc visited the battlefields during the concluding phase of the war and had an interview with Franco, whom he did not hesitate to describe as 'the man who has saved us all'. The generalissimo's H.Q. were at Petrola in a castle of brown-pink stone, with a wide courtyard. It belonged to the Duke of Villahermosa, and it was here that Cervantes had imagined Don Quixote staying. Franco was tired after a long Cabinet meeting, but he gave Belloc ten minutes of his time; and

---

[1] Jan. 19, 1923.   [2] *The Tablet:* July 15, 1939.

when they had finished said to him, evidently much moved, 'Come and see me again when it is all over'. The journey—long miles of motoring over bad roads with at least one breakdown—had tired Belloc a good deal; but here were soldiers, the furnace of creative conflict as he had felt it long ago coming out on to the *parvis* of Notre Dame, the *reconquisita* of which he had all but despaired.

5

Some of Belloc's happiest days abroad were spent with Edmond Warre, with whom he walked through the Haute Fugue of the Ardennes in 1932. This was a walk he had longed to do since 1897. They travelled over great parts of Europe and Africa together, and Warre executed drawings for *Many Cities* (1928) and *Return to the Baltic* (1938). They were a devoted and incongruous pair. Warre (known as 'Bear' to all his friends) was, and is, elegant and trim as an officer in the Brigade of Guards; Pall Mall rubbed in garlic. Belloc would say that this had given him 'a sense of Europe and reality', and, indeed, he spoke admirable French and had a sharp appreciation of architectural detail. Warre liked to travel in reasonable comfort, but he gallantly put up with Belloc's preference for going as cheaply and as roughly as possible. At sea they would usually sleep on deck or in the steerage; and a journey from London to Tunis, taking nine days, might cost them no more than £7 16s. apiece for their fares, four guineas for their food and lodging, and 30s. for extras. On another occasion they travelled 4,011 miles in five weeks and spent £60 a head.

Warre was a botanist as well as a draughtsman and his eyes were open to things to which Belloc was blind. In all Belloc's correspondence and in all his writing upon landscape there is hardly a reference to flowers or birds. But Warre was quick to notice the *salvin pratensis* flourishing south of Neufchatel; the asphodel and yellow irises, and the hedges of *marguerite geranium*, in Tunis; and the first primrose in Tuscany. It was he who caught the note of the nightingales and blackcaps at Las Palmas, and

2 H

recognized the dusky petrels at the entrance to the harbour of La Goulette. Both he and Belloc would have noted the huge umbrella held over the Bishop of Narbonne, but it was left to Warre to observe that it bore the colours of the M.C.C. And then there were the meals at the end of a long day's wandering and sketching— the clams at Prunier's; the dish of tripe at Chaux des Fonds; some *plat régional* at the 'Haute Mère de Dieu' at Châlons; or the favourite liqueur of Belloc's old regiment produced at Marsa by the Duc de Charente Tonnerre. And there was Belloc raising his hat to a priest in Linz with the words 'Ubi est ecclesia?'; and Belloc stamping out of a hotel in Danzig because the attendant, rubbing his hands with glee, told him that the music in the *jardin d'hiver* would go on till three a.m.; and Belloc in a third-class carriage scribbling down verses with a gold pencil which he had exchanged for a silver goblet with his companion.

> Lord Grampas full of his unworthiness
> Was covered with confusion and distress
> And shouted loudly as the Gate was slammed
> 'God bless my soul, I'm certain to be damned
> For once, at Tilbury, I committed fraud
> By not declaring knickers bought abroad'.

This was the private life; and if a good travel book resulted from it, literature had fulfilled one of its more important functions which was to pay for the pleasures of living.

CHAPTER XX

HOME AFFAIRS

I

IF we want to see Belloc at the height of his renown, we should
turn to the study by Edward Shanks and Creighton Mandell,
already referred to. This had appeared in 1916 and Belloc
used to say that whenever he was depressed he would dip into it.
Here he would find himself described as 'the greatest writer of
English prose since Dryden'; as a fine, though uneven poet; as a
rather casual literary critic; and as a superb essayist. He would see
a man who had instructed and influenced popular opinion; a
man who seemed at last to have come into his own. Very soon
the decline of his reputation would set in, as he became separated
from his time, confirmed in a solitary vocation. But he was
fixed, monumentally, in his niche and certain recognitions were
offered to him.

In June 1920 he was made an honorary Doctor of Law at
Glasgow University. The offer came to him through Phillimore's
initiative, but even so, he accepted it with reluctance.

My feeling about titles and honours, academic or other . . .
is that in the time in which we are living they have become
ridiculous. Except the Garter and the Victoria Cross and the
regular commissions of the regular Services one has, in such
labels, anyone at all as one's colleague. I would not, for instance,
accept the Legion of Honour, though it has many material
advantages attached to it. Nor would I dream of taking as an
old man a Knighthood or anything of that sort or other. In
the same way during the war, I would certainly not have
accepted one of those disgusting sham titles of Colonels,
Admirals, etc., the recipients of whom were no more soldiers

and sailors than greengrocers. It was this great rule about *all* modern distinctions that made me hesitate. But I do sincerely think it a great honour to be thus recognised by the Glasgow University which has never done me anything but kindness, for I do not count it an unkindness in old Caird to have written me as he did that he was torn between his affection for me and the utter impossibility of allowing a Catholic to teach history. . . .[1]

He did, however, accept the ribbon of an officer of the Légion d'Honneur in 1929, for the material advantages of this were not to be gainsaid. It gained you respect abroad and made people think 'you belonged to the secret police'. But when the Pope made him a Knight of the Order of St. Gregory the Great in 1934, Belloc neither paid the fee nor claimed the medal and ribbon. He thought they would make him look an 'official' Catholic. However, as soon as he realized that a refusal of the Glasgow doctorate would do harm to those who had proposed him for it, he put his scruples behind him. The ceremony was embellished by a certain amount of Presbyterian ritual which Belloc, a little unreasonably, found offensive.

The Irish, too, liked to honour him whenever they could. A luncheon was organized for him in Dublin[2] with the Governor-General, Tim Healy, present, and Sir Thomas Grattan-Esmonde in the chair. W. B. Yeats proposed Belloc's health, remarking that he and Chesterton had 'checked the depravity of a revolutionary epoch'; and Tim Healy presented him with the Irish blackthorn stick which became one of his most treasured possessions. A dinner at the Dublin Arts Club was less fortunate. This took place during Lent, and Belloc, arriving after a tempestuous crossing on the day boat, would drink nothing but ginger beer. The President of the Club did not help matters by observing that most of those present had doubtless read Mr. Belloc's story of his conversion, *The Road to Rome*. The evening ended in some disorder with a prominent local dramatist, well in his cups, shouting 'Walrus!' after Dr. Douglas Hyde.

[1] May 13, 1920.   [2] June 20, 1923.

Belloc was elected to the very exclusive 'Sussex Club' in 1929, and to the Literary Society in 1932. Another celebrated occasion was his oration at the first dinner of the Saintsbury Club on October 23, 1931. It was Professor George Saintsbury's eighty-sixth birthday and an august senate of gourmets had been founded in his honour. The dinner was held in the Vintners Hall. Belloc's words have been lost with the Latour 1878 which prompted them; only his high voice calling across the table to Maurice Healy has come down to us: 'Healy, Healy, this is wine!' But an idea of his performance is given by M. André Simon.

Jack Squire was in the Chair and Hilaire Belloc had been asked to deliver what we called the 'Oration', in honour of the Professor. I shall never forget the truly awful feeling of dismay that came over me when Hilaire rose, swayed, and there were but three words he uttered: 'I am drunk.' And he was. There was an awful silence and long faces all round. Then he hummed and coughed and pulled himself together, and within a matter of minutes he had us all absolutely fascinated by the most exquisite description of the importance of slight differences between good and bad writing, good and bad wine: a comma wrongly placed or a cork a little loose. It was really a magnificent piece of oratory, and we were all spellbound, but nobody was there to take it down. When I asked Hilaire Belloc the next day to put down on paper what he had said, he told me quite truthfully, I am sure, that he had not the slightest recollection of it and could not possibly oblige me. That was a lesson, and most of the other 'Orations' delivered since then have been duly recorded, and some of them have been printed in very limited editions for members of the Club.[1]

Belloc also spoke as a guest of honour at the Oxford Union Centenary Banquet on February 19, 1924. He replied to the toast of Letters proposed by Mr. Christopher Hollis, one of the three Presidents of the centenary year. Among the other speakers were Curzon, Asquith, Simon, Birkenhead, William Temple and Cosmo Gordon Lang. All these men had achieved high positions

[1] Letter to the author: July 12, 1956.

in Church or State, and the oratory was pompous in a political way. Belloc's speech was much shorter than the others. It took the form of a conversation between himself and his muse on their being invited to reply for Letters in the place of the Postmaster-General. The prospect of so many politicians, not to mention two archbishops, had given him a bad cold and put him in a bad temper. He reminded his listeners that when the Union was founded Liverpool was Prime Minister and Keats heard a nightingale singing. Today nobody remembered anything about Liverpool, but the nightingale was universally remembered because Keats had written about it. This proved that writers alone had the power of conferring immortality.

> I said to myself—if you want to be remembered after you are dead, you must get a poet to write about you. But then I said to myself, why should you want to be remembered after you are dead? And to that question I said to myself, I can't imagine.

The well-fed faces at the High Table looked glum; some of them could very well imagine. Opinions were divided about Belloc's speech. Some thought it an exquisite gem; others thought it tasteless and unkind of him to rag the politicians in public.

Meanwhile the books and essays poured out. Belloc had translated Foch's *Principles of War* and *Precepts and Judgments* (1918 and 1919) and he returned to military history himself with *Napoleon* (1932) and *The Tactics and Strategy of the Great Duke of Marlborough* (1933). He could have done a great book on Bonaparte, for Bonaparte alone, he believed, had the vision and genius to reconstruct the unity of Europe. But *Napoleon* was hack-work and Belloc was so discontented with it that he refused to let it be translated into French. He had visited all the battlefields, except Eylau and Friedland. He held that it was not sea-power but the Russian campaign of 1812 which had really destroyed Napoleon. He had also visited the battlefields of Marlborough's campaigns, and had made one discovery which he believed to be his own. He had carefully examined the ground in the mile and a quarter south of Folx, for it was Marlborough's use of this slight depression which had made possible the victory of Ramillies. Belloc detested most things about Marlborough, as he admired most things about Napoleon, but he thought him 'one of the very great captains recorded in the history of the western world'. In writing this book Belloc had the use of the library and documents at Blenheim, and he dedicated it to the ninth Duke of Marlborough.

With his new sense of the necessity of kingship, it was natural that he should be drawn to the character and the career of Louis XIV.[1] He was always attracted by the quality in others which was the strongest in himself—will. Louis illustrated on a larger scale the same principles of monarchy as Charles Stuart— the deft diplomacy and the long, uncertain contest with the Money Power; and he illustrated on a lesser scale the same private failings. Louis's women were important to him in a way that Charles's never were; and the last of them led him to his repose. Belloc faithfully visited the battlefields of Louis in the Low Countries, but there was one question that he did not answer in this book. How far did the centralizing policy of Louis assist the revolt against monarchy a hundred years later? If you reduced aristocracy to a décor, and to a frivolous décor at that, what would happen when the ruler's touch failed him? Having robbed the *élite* of responsibility while maintaining them, rather too magnificently, in the public eye, had not Louis XIV prepared the downfall of the monarchy and the nobility together? When his great-grandson took a prostitute for his mistress, there was no strength in the reaction of an outraged court, and for the public no alternative symbol of supreme power.

Belloc turned again, under strong pressure from his publishers, to French history for his *Richelieu*. He could not refuse an advance of eight hundred pounds. But he wrote it against the grain. He was bored by the intrigue and mind-reading, which were the two qualities in which Richelieu excelled, even when they had such enormous results. He visited the town from which Richelieu took his name, because 'the physical contact with a man's habitat is essential to his history';[2] and went on to Luçon and La Rochelle.

---

[1] *Monarchy* (1938).   [2] Letter to Mrs. Raymond Asquith: Jan. 6, 1929.

He thought Richelieu was at his best as a soldier, and when he studied his portrait in the Louvre, he was struck by a certain resemblance to Bonaparte in the forehead, nose and eyes. This was the first of Belloc's books to have a substantial success in America.

A short biography of William the Conqueror, in which he took little pride, was published by Peter Davies in 1933. More satisfactory than any of these was *Miniatures of French History* (1925). This was a companion to the *Eye-Witness* and quite as good. The title gives the key to Belloc's excellence in this kind of writing; he was a miniaturist in his prose as he was a miniaturist in his verse, just as successful with the detail delicately wrought as with the large sweep or the dogmatic exposition. He had the draughtsman's sensibility to the shape of things, and the artist's power to impose shape upon confusion. Here we have the deathless epic of Roncesvalles:

Before the shock came upon him he had looked down into the road, which he could well survey from such a place, and he saw in a moment what had come. He saw the summer sky of the afternoon, blue but misty above them, and the deep forest which had been so silent all about, and he saw, high in heaven, between the peaks, one great bird and then another, slowly circling upon black wings. And he saw the whole body of the rearguard stretched out upon a mile of the way, of the narrow way, and everywhere dark masses of men not in the accoutrement of the host, livelier, striking with knives, not sworded; and perpetually as men fell, and as traces were cut and teams destroyed, these enemies would leap off into the undergrowth again laden with booty. All the while there rang in that echoing place cries in a tongue he did not know, and that no man knew—the Basque tongue, the oldest tongue of the world. And urging the mountaineers on and on, in rush after rush from the heights, in charge after charge from the depths, was the little bagpipe of the mountains, screaming its war scream—the little bagpipe of goatskin, with its two flutes, which the mountaineers threddle with their fingers, while their eyes gleam. That was what he saw—the destruction of all for which he stood responsible to his young king who, in the plains below, had already camped his great army after the passage of the mountains.

And set beside this the fixing of the frontier post from the Vosges above the grave of Déroulède in the cemetery of La Celle St. Cloud, which Belloc knew so well and where he might have been buried himself if he had not chosen to be an Englishman.

Up this track, with a ritual dear to the French people, did certain delegates bear that frontier post, as we bear dead men for whom we proclaim the resurrection. They took it through the rustic gate into that small neglected place, and put it upon the grave of the man who had lived so strange and inartistic a life; who stirred and was gladdened in his sleep.

Or the glimpse of von Moltke at the crisis of the Marne, leaning upon the railings of a public square.

A group of boys playing in the square ceased from play to gaze at the old boy, timidly approaching the railings, and stared at that poor broken figure. They could know nothing of the traditions of the Prussian army, nor of how strange a sight they saw, but they felt its enormity. He, for his part, had forgotten what was around him—the place, the children; he stared at the ground, remembering as in a vivid dream his urgent appeal to his emperor, his agony at defeat, his intelligence too great for his heart, and the knell still ringing there: 'The campaign has failed. . . . The campaign has failed.'

These miniatures were drawn with all the old imagination of the past, reminding the modern reader who still had an ear for rhythm that Belloc was

that thing more rare than a first-rate tenor singer, and more precious than all the coroneted bald heads in the House of Peers; a really excellent writer of English prose.[1]

Belloc continued to turn out his satirical novels, for which Chesterton provided the illustrations. Belloc would go down to

[1] Robert Blatchford: *The Clarion*, Nov. 26, 1909.

Beaconsfield for luncheon, and the drawings would be done in an afternoon. These books began to lose their satirical bite, and this may have been the reason why they were translated into German and not into French. *Mr. Petre* was serialized in the *Berliner Tageblatt*. Nicolas Bentley, the son of Belloc's Oxford contemporary, E. C. Bentley, had now succeeded Basil Blackwood as the illustrator of his comic verse. Belloc would give him lunch at the Norfolk Hotel or the Carlton Grill, and after the meal they would consume together a bottle of white port. Belloc had exact ideas of what he wanted. For the lines

> Your lordship is perfectly right
> He can't go on rhyming all night
> I suggest . . .' (He is led away to a dungeon)

he asked for 'a silly, officious little man with flat hair', and Henry Malone Sandiland Keanes must look 'big and heavy like Henry James'.

The most effective of these satires was undoubtedly *The Mercy of Allah* (1922). Here Belloc returned to his old bugbear of usury, imagining an oriental financier explaining to his seven nephews how he had become so rich. The irony is imperturbable and deadly from the first page to the last, with a Swiftian formality and grace which Belloc had never quite recaptured since *Lambkin*. The Islamic setting deceived no one and the real origin of the book was betrayed on the dust-cover, where Mahmoud was described as a Jewish merchant millionaire. This greatly angered Belloc, and the publishers, Chatto and Windus, who had so negligently allowed the Semitic cat to get out of its bag, wrote round in consternation to the reviewers, hoping that no allusion would be made to a fact which was patent to everybody, and the dust-cover was withdrawn. Even the reader who is bored by books about money and finds Belloc's obsessions on the subject a little tiresome, can admire the skill with which he wields his whip-lash. The figure of Mahmoud invited an urbanity which would have been wasted on the Duke of Battersea, though the target is in each case the same.

The Cruise of the 'Nona' (1925) was the nearest Belloc ever came

to an autobiography. It is an invaluable source for his opinions on
a variety of subjects, many of which we have already discussed.
But it is a book quite without temporal hope; mature, disillusioned and—the word is apt but cannot be avoided—salt. Its
form is quite original, and achieved with considerable art;
England looked at from her coastal waters by a man whom the
sea could always move to a profound reflection and hush to a
momentary repose. It was not, however, solitude that Belloc
craved when he went to sea; that would have moved him too
much. For practical reasons he needed three hands on board, and
for personal reasons he needed company. He sailed without a
motor, not even an outboard motor for the dinghy. There he
would sit in the stern, clad in his blue seaman's jersey, and sometimes wearing a mackintosh and a peaked cap; giving directions
as required; shouting 'Bring up some wine, boys'; or observing,
quite calmly, as disaster threatened off St. Alban's Head, 'My
children, we shall all be drowned'; or, suddenly and disconcert-
ingly, demanding that they make port because he must send off
some telegrams.

Instead of going to the nearest Post Office, he would insist
on appearing at possibly the largest and most expensive hotel,
which was sometimes very large and very expensive. The
liveried porters would observe the stocky figure, black half-
Wellington boots, old blue trousers, frequently done up with a
huge safety-pin, old blue sweater, seaman's hat, and a blue coat
with possibly a very few buttons remaining, approaching, with
myself almost as disreputable, trailing a few paces behind. You
could see the hostility of the reception staff rapidly mounting
as we approached until Hilaire arrived within speaking distance,
just as the Head Porter was about to suggest we went round to
the back entrance or got to hell off the premises altogether,
when he would let out a great roar: 'Send for the Manager—
I want some telegraph forms—send me a boy to take them to
the Post Office—bring me a bottle of Bubbly. I want a pen
and paper'. He always got what he wanted.[1]

[1] James Hall: Broadcast, Nov. 18, 1953.

He had his own sailing fraternity—Peter Belloc, Dermot MacCarthy, W. N. Roughead, James Hall, A. D. Peters, J. B. Morton, and Lord Stanley of Alderley. Sometimes he would ask them to bring round the boat from Poole or Folkestone to whatever harbour he wanted to sail from. They would cross the Channel to Dunkirk, or Montreuil-sur-Mer, dining in the trellised courtyard of the Hôtel de France; or sail up the river to Rouen; or round as many English capes as they had time for. July and September were the favourite seasons for these expeditions. Belloc's habits and behaviour at sea have been vividly described by Mr. Morton and Mr. Hall, and by Lord Stanley in his excellent preface to the new edition of *The Cruise of the 'Nona'* (1955). Lord Stanley tells how his father acquired the boat in 1901 and Belloc told Mrs. Asquith how at last he was forced to abandon her.

I am in Abbeville. I have long abandoned the sea. It was impossible, or rather the Nona was. Alas! She has lived her life, and all the rest is mere waiting for dissolution and the end. I have loved her well; I love her still. But there is no more sailing in her. Her age is upon her. With every season she costs more and more to keep her afloat and now her Appel has found her. She takes me out into the salt no more. She leaks very remarkably, decks and all. Her counter breaks at a heavy sea. Her noble lines still lift through it beautifully. A better sea boat never was. But teak and oak are mortal and must pass. Do you think I shall find her in the quiet river-mouth of Heaven where the South Wind blows? I doubt it! The theologians would tell me she has no rational soul—yet that is no reason why she should not be preserved on my account and translated, yet wooden—into beatitude—as witness the chariot of Elias and the veils of the Pleiades—material, yet granted immortality. There she lies now alone. But I shall go back to visit her from time to time—unless she sells herself: and she is capable of that. Lord! What times I have had with her! She also enjoyed it, though she never confessed as much (a modest craft) and we understood each other very well. But now that great friendship is interrupted and the end has come.

It was about fifteen miles out that I made the determination —a fog coming in and yet—what is rare with a fog—too much wind from the N.W. She already rolled with bilge. She complained of the sea. Then did I determine for harbour.

With great difficulty harbour was made. It was a matter of seconds because there is violent tide at the Springs racing past the harbour and one has to nip in. This done—just as darkness came—she reached smooth water and so lies at rest: in the custody of Moosoo Lehaut. Alas for mortality! This news—the passing of the Nona—is so enormous that I can add no other news. I fill my parchment with the threnody of so many years. It was in 1901 that she appeared—in one of the East Anglian creeks, a boat worth a hundred oxen at £1 an ox. What had been spent on her since then I tremble to think of. But now her expense and cherishment are over, and all the naiads deplore so dark a day. St. Wolfram stands above me as I write, and if I were rich I would order a Knell at 1,250 frs. But then, if I were rich, I would have the Nona cased in thick gold and set up in a porphyry in King's Land, but then, I am not rich. The kind of people who love Nonas (and who Nonas more discreetly love) never are. And so, good-bye, Nona. Good-bye, my dear.

I do wish everyone who has had pleasure from reading of the Nona would subscribe one shilling—then would there be ample to buy a new Nona, water-tight, seaworthy, young, buoyant—on her own divine lines—to give me during what few remaining years the illusion of the better years and to take me out into the seas gain. But such a gift there will not be. Such things are for Arnold Bennett, Sir Henry Meyer (of the Hippodrome), Sir Thomas Lipton, Edward VII (of pious memory) and other great mariners. Not for me.[1]

Belloc was in fact given another boat, the *Jersey*, by his friends; this was the oldest ship in Lloyd's Register when Belloc acquired her, a generation older than himself. She had been launched in 1846. But he never really loved more than one boat, just as he

---

[1] Letter to Mrs. Raymond Asquith: June 8, 1927.

never loved more than one woman. His love for the sea was permanent and inexhaustible, outlasting his love of landscape. At one moment it was 'a huge powerful capricious thing, loving and hating alternately. A coquette-virago',[1] and it was also 'the common sacrament of this world'.[2] Some of his writings about the sea were collected by W. N. Roughead and published by Methuen in 1939,[3] and his feeling for it is illustrated by the following story.

It was late in the year 1932 and I was a young man who had been following the sea. I had been in sail and had just returned from some experiences in trading schooners in the Pacific. I was caught up in the whirl of London and, at a luncheon party in the home of P. G. Wodehouse, I was presented to Belloc and introduced as a young man who was writing his first novel, had written poetry, and had literary ambitions. He took most of this in silence. We chanced to meet at the door when leaving. He looked at my hat (bowler), umbrella (correctly furled), gloves, and carnation (of the correct hue). 'So you wish to write,' he said in something resembling a growl. 'Yes, Sir,' I replied. 'Get rid of those things,' he said, pointing to the uniform just mentioned, 'and get back to the sea.' 'But I wish to write, Sir,' I replied. 'What better place to write than on a ship?' was his answer. And then, as an afterthought, 'Conrad left too soon.'[4]

2

The sea, in all its moods which he knew so well, responded to Belloc's sense of the insecurity of human life. The years continued to take a premature toll of those he loved. His old sailing companion, Phil Kershaw, died in 1924 and *The Cruise of the 'Nona'* was dedicated to his memory. John Phillimore died in 1926.

The superabundant value of virtue is not known until a man of that quality dies. Then it is revealed: for indeed Death reveals all things and is to be welcomed though with awe. In John

---

[1] Letter to the Hon. Mrs. Mervyn Herbert: July 23, 1933.
[2] *The Cruise of the 'Nona'* (1925).   [3] *On Sailing the Sea.*
[4] John Farrow: Letter to the author, April 28, 1954.

Phillimore's Death there is an amazing confirmation and solidifying of faith. I have felt no grief (only some addition to loneliness) but instead of it a conviction of the Faith which is rare with me. I cannot describe the process. It is organic, not logical. But his passing makes me feel of the Faith as an ignorant man feels of a scholar's explanation of a hexameter. Like saying to oneself, 'Ah! then yes; of course it is so, and that is final: for you know'. It is also a sort of feeling that he now has experienced and is himself confirmed. It is also a sort of time-less experience; as of repose in home. The light shines fully upon such souls at last and it all comes of doing what one ought to do: nothing more.[1]

Phillimore had used to say that life after death 'began as a rest-cure, and went on to new senses even fuller than the old'. Certainly Madame Belloc had earned her rest-cure when she died on March 29, 1925. She was ninety-five years old. She had said that the years between sixty and ninety were the happiest in a human life, if it lasted so long: 'all cares resolved or despised, and judg-ment serene'. In spite of the numbing bereavement of her husband's death, she believed that life was normally happy. Belloc had believed so, too, until he was well into middle age, but then he came to doubt it. His mother died without any pain or dis-cernible disease in a kind of prolonged sleep, which lasted for three days. It was an enviable passing. She was buried at Slindon with the family and a few people from the village to mourn her. Arthur Pollen, on hearing of her death, wrote that it was 'as if St. Paul's had really fallen, a masterpiece has gone that we shall not see again',[2] and Belloc replied that hers 'was a great generation, strong in its own knowledge of itself. We are living on the capital it accumulated, and the process is anxious'.[3] Others might have said of Madame Belloc what Belloc himself had said of Pollen's mother when she died seven years before. She 'had the supreme glory of women, that she could show the world so much in her children. No work any man does is comparable to it.'[4]

[1] Letter to Mrs. Raymond Asquith: Jan. 3, 1927.
[2] March 24, 1926.   [3] March 26, 1926.
[4] Letter to Arthur Pollen: Jan. 29, 1919.

On July 27, 1930, Belloc celebrated his sixtieth birthday. A dinner was organized at the Adelphi Hotel by A. D. Peters, and the occasion has already passed into the legends of immortal feasts. Chesterton was in the chair and presented Belloc with a tankard

> Open, golden wide
> With benediction graven on its side.

This was quite literally a loving-cup and everyone drank from it as it was handed round. Chesterton said that 'such a ceremony might have been as fitting thousands of years ago at the festival of a great Greek poet', and that he was confident 'Belloc's sonnets and strong verse would remain like the cups and carved epics of the Greeks'.[1] Belloc replied that he did not care very much whether his verse remained or not, but added: 'I am told that you begin to care again frightfully when you're seventy.' An Horatian Ode, composed by Ronald Knox, was printed on the back of the menu, and this was recited by Maurice Baring, standing with a glass of Burgundy balanced on his bald head. Certain irreverent guests threw pellets of bread in a vain attempt to dislodge it. It had been agreed that there were to be no speeches, but somebody whispered to Chesterton towards the end of dinner that it might be as well to thank Peters who had organized the evening. He briefly did so, but Peters replied that the real author of the scheme was J. B. Morton. Morton, by now well inhabited by wine and mischief, solemnly answered that he owed the idea to Sir John Squire who was sitting on his right. The joke was now in full swing, and every single member of that great company passed on the compliment to his neighbour in a few well-chosen words. A. P. Herbert impersonated a Town Councillor; Duff Cooper pretended to be a Liberal politician; E. C. Bentley proclaimed his intellectual debt to Professor Eccles; and so it went on with Douglas Woodruff, D. B. Wyndham Lewis, Edward Shanks, Edmond Warre, and every one of the forty present rising, as best he could, to the challenge. At one point Mr. Wyndham Lewis was found hiding under the table, but that did not save him. The mere list of the people present at this dinner is a tribute to

[1] *Autobiography* (1932).

Hilaire Belloc in late Middle Life, from a photograph by James Hall

The back of the Menu Card for the dinner given to celebrate
Hilaire Belloc's Sixtieth Birthday, July 27, 1930
(For names see List of Illustrations)

the variety, and also to the quality, of Belloc's friends. Chesterton died in January 1936, and Belloc was, of course, prominent at the funeral. He was heard muttering distractedly to the mourners, 'Chesterton will never occur again'. He wrote a noble tribute in the *Observer*, and this did something to offset what he rightly described as a 'crapulous' obituary in *The Times*; perhaps the most insufficient obituary that has ever been written of a great man. Belloc affirmed that it was a 'benediction' to have known him, and the quality of this benediction—the benediction of holiness and humility—was conveyed in the tribute. It could really be said of Chesterton that his pleasure in controversy came from the appreciation of his opponent, and that he had the rare capacity of hating ideas while loving the people who held them. There was no doubt of Belloc's affection and admiration for his friend; they had stood bravely for the same good things. But when he spoke of him in private, certain qualifications made themselves felt. Generally speaking, he was over-indulgent to the writings of his friends. But while he thought *Lepanto* the 'summit of high rhetorical verse in all our generation', he was irritated by the tricks of Chesterton's prose. Yet on another occasion he was strangely moved when he heard that Chesterton admired one of his poems, and he once exclaimed: 'Chesterton expresses everything so much better than I do.' Nor did any of his private reservations interfere with the fullness of his tribute when he published his essay, *On the Place of Gilbert Chesterton in English Letters*. Here he noted the intensely national quality of Chesterton's work, his power of reasoning, and his gift of illustrating his point by parallels. The essay has the generosity of a great epitaph, but it does not quite conceal the fact that Belloc had little knowledge of Chesterton's more important books.

The death of Chesterton left the fate of *G. K.'s Weekly* in suspense. This was the old *New Witness* which Chesterton had taken over from his brother and renamed; and just as Gilbert had assumed its cares out of loyalty to Cecil, so Belloc felt obliged to assume them out of loyalty to Gilbert. Maisie Ward has given her opinion that Chesterton made a mistake in so immersing himself in political controversy when he had greater matters to write

2 I

about; and Belloc was surely mistaken in following his example. No paper—and especially no personal paper—is so important that it cannot be allowed to die when its nourishing flame is extinguished. But Belloc had never underestimated the power of the small review or broadsheet:

> Some of the thought that has most profoundly influenced the recent history of our civilisation has appeared (and still appears) on paper that hardly holds together, printed in blurred type on little newspapers of one sheet and sold for half-penny— to the men who followed Garibaldi, or the men who followed Lacordaire.[1]

But the world was becoming a difficult place for little things and nothing was any more sold for a half-penny. Belloc valued G. K.'s because it provided an independent platform for the expression of views on all sorts of matters which he believed to be of public concern; and particularly because it was the only paper to advocate the wider distribution of ownership. But he knew its limitations. He knew that it was a platform with too many cranks addressing itself to too many cliques in a hall that was never more than half-full. Yet he bravely took up the task of editorship.

> I am sweating blood to get the little review really interesting and readable and to put it on its legs again, but I have to write about half of it myself because there is no capital and no one is paid. I do it all for nothing. The great thing was not to let it die when Chesterton died.[2]

Belloc could not long afford to do so large a thing for nothing; the paper presently changed its name to *The Weekly Review* and was edited by Hilary Pepler and Reginald Jebb. It was a small, and sometimes a shrill, voice in English journalism, and Belloc constantly wrote for it. For a long time its views seemed to have little effect, but a day would come when the Conservative Party proclaimed its ideal of a 'property-owning democracy', and when Englishmen, to ensure their bare survival, were forced to go 'back

---

[1] *Daily News*: April 16, 1903.
[2] Letter to Evan Charteris: Oct. 21, 1936.

to the land'. Belloc himself had never shared the anti-mechanical
bias of so many ardent distributists. 'My own attitude', he tells
Father H. E. G. Rope, 'is not so much anti-machinery as anti-secret
control by a few.'[1] Also even the most inveterate enemy of
Fascism began to wonder whether the imposition of sanctions
had not hurt the schoolmaster considerably more than it had hurt
the culprit. The paper struggled against increasing difficulties; it
was hard to get good writers to contribute to it unpaid.

> There are hosts of second-rate cranks who will write their
> fingers to the bone for nothing, but who first of all cannot
> write, and secondly see everything quite out of proportion,
> especially when they are on the right side. Many people who
> agree with us on one point or another are shocked by the rest
> of the points. The idea of supporting small property and inde-
> pendent farming and saving the country from being prole-
> tarian is vaguely regarded as Communism; and we get lots of
> complaints from people who say that they seem to discover a
> Catholic tone about the paper. We also get complaints from
> Catholics who want it to be a sort of sacristy organ; and we
> get complaints from people who hate the Italians and have an
> admiration as well as a horror of Berlin.[2]

Belloc had always been asked how he proposed to divide property in a highly industrialized and highly concentrated economy.
George Orwell, in an article for *Time and Tide*, had made a very
flattering reference to *The Servile State* but had gone on to say
that Belloc had no remedy to offer for the present disease of
Capitalism. Belloc replied that 'Ownership of shares in small
amounts, a very wide distribution of the interest upon National
and Municipal debt, free men owning and farming their own land
or holding it on low customary leases, artisans working with their
tools in their own shops' were to be discovered 'in all the civilized
countries of the West from Ireland to Italy; the proportion of
families economically free is in some countries so large as to determine the whole character of society.'[3] This answer had already

[1] March 13, 1929. [2] Letter to Lady Phipps: June 27, 1939.
[3] *Time and Tide*: April 20, 1940.

been expanded in a series of articles for *The English Review* and the gist of these was subsequently published as *An Essay on the Restoration of Property*.[1] This essay is important though little known, and it should be read as a sequel to *The Servile State*. Already, in 1912, Belloc had doubted whether enough Englishmen still desired property for its restoration to be possible. He had many more doubts in 1936; the task seemed to him *almost* impossible of achievement. Every current trend would have to be reversed, and they could not be reversed without strong legislation to enforce the change of gear. Two means of restoring the principle of well-divided property were by differential rates of interest and differential taxation. In this way the large distributor, the chain store or the multiple shop could be handicapped in favour of the small owner. It should be made possible for a man to accumulate, but not to accumulate too much. Again, the small craftsman should be protected by a charter and a guild. It might cost more to buy a well-made piece of furniture, but such an article was no more 'uneconomic' than many of the luxuries enjoyed by the rich. If you paid a little more for your good chair, you were paying for 'citizenship and the escape from slavery'.

Such arguments were, of course, moonshine to the urban mentality of modern England; but they would have been commonplaces to the French. Not because mass-production in France is less vulgar than it is in England—in fact, it is rather more so—but because the peasant and the craftsman and the small family business are more favoured by the French economy. Belloc had no dogmatic objection to large economic units when they were necessary; and he thought that State ownership was better than ownership by a few very rich individuals, or even than ownership by many small shareholders who were at the mercy of many rich ones. But he saw no reason why electrical power and road transport should not be decentralized, and he thought that the smaller millers might be aided by a subsidy provided by differential taxation of the bigger ones. He recalled the Wyndham Land Act in Ireland as an example of legislation which encouraged the small man to buy from the great and for the great to sell to the small.

[1] 1936.

Belloc's proposals all rested on the clear principle that a man living under his own roof and working his own land or running his own business should have the advantage over one who used his property to exploit others. It was a final criticism of modern society that so plain a truth should have seemed so impracticable to apply, and that Belloc himself almost despaired of its application.

The theory of distribution, as he preached it, met two obstacles, the first of which he took insufficiently into account. The responsibilities of property had become so onerous that men no longer equated ownership with freedom. Secondly, the necessities of the modern State demanded a rate of taxation so high that the money had to be found from the pockets of the rich. If wealth were more widely distributed where would the money come from? It stood to reason that you could tax a man with twenty thousand pounds a year more heavily in proportion than you could tax a man with two thousand pounds. Belloc saw that high taxation was inevitable and he was not opposed to a capital levy on industrial shares. What he was anxious to do was to protect the middle classes, which he described as the 'fly-wheel' of society, to the disadvantage of the gambler. The opponents of distributism often described it as a reaction rather than a revolution. For Belloc it was both. 'We are attempting a reactionary revolution'—and then he went on to admit, for the tenth time, that what he desired was now 'perhaps impossible'. There was no question of felling the trunk, or even of cutting the branches of capitalism. But he thought a start might be made with 'clipping the leaves'. This he may have done. One day, Chesterton had written, the world might wake up and find 'a new democracy of distributists' and 'at the fountain of that river, at the root of that genealogical tree, your figure will stand in the history of England'.[1]

It is fair to say that Belloc liked distributism better than he liked distributists. He had played a great part in the founding of the Distributist League, but he rarely addressed it, and ignored its official publications. This may have been due to his chronic reluctance to become a leader; or he may simply have been bored.

[1] An Open Letter to Hilaire Belloc: *The New Witness*, April 27, 1923.

He was certainly wearied by the distributists' quarrels and dogmatism; and where Chesterton would try to make peace between the contending factions, Belloc held carefully aloof, only meeting them now and then at a bar in the City where they used to gather. Even then he would keep his distance. One day he was sitting apart in conversation with his literary agent and a faithful disciple was overheard to remark: 'It's a sad thing when a man prefers to drink gin and French with his agent to drinking honest beer with his friends.' It was the kind of remark that popular legend would have ascribed to Belloc; but Belloc, though he could drink most people under the counter, was always more subtle and surprising than his legend. In fact, he disliked the beer-swilling legend quite particularly. Once at a meeting to discuss Monopoly at the Essex Hall the chairman incautiously announced that 'Mr. Belloc will speak about beer, about which he knows a good deal'. Belloc rose and, glaring down at the reporters, declared:

Let me warn you, gentlemen, that if any of your masters prints any vulgar sneer about me and beer, they will live to rue it. The men who own the Press in this country were born in the gutter. They are my inferiors intellectually, they are my inferiors socially, they are my inferiors morally. Take it down [he concluded], take it down.

And the representatives of the Press did as they were told.

In 1920 Belloc had made his first open plea for a strengthened monarchy to counteract the decay of the House of Commons. *The House of Commons and Monarchy* should be read as a sequel to the *Party System*. Its plea became the familiar one that Parliaments were only effective when they were the instruments of oligarchies and that in the degree to which England was becoming egalitarian she would need responsible government by a single man. Such ideas were interesting but unrealistic, and by 1937 he had begun to wonder whether England was changing as quickly as he had thought.

In his *Essay on the Nature of Contemporary England* he defined the country under three headings—Protestant, Commercial and Aristocratic. The first two of these might be taken as read; it was the

third which provoked argument. Now it was a curious limitation
in Belloc that very often he could see the thing in the distance—
the distant past or the distant future—much more clearly than
the thing under his nose. A French visitor of high intelligence
was taken to see him once, when his powers were failing, and remarked afterwards: '*J'avais l'impression d'un prophète qui se trompe
toujours.*' Later, when this man had travelled widely in America,
he came to see the force of something Belloc had said, to the effect
that the Irish tenacity in keeping their religion had been one of
the most important *political* facts of the nineteenth century.
Or, again, Belloc predicted in conversation that if the Danzig
problem were not settled on the right lines, Great Britain would
lose most of her possessions in the Far East. But this prescience
must be seen in contrast to an extraordinary blindness to what was
going on around him. England had certainly been an aristocratic
state since 1689, although aristocracy had latterly degenerated
into mere plutocracy. This aristocracy had at first been imposed
from above and then ardently accepted from below. The Englishman had almost no feeling at all for social equality. So much
might be granted, and Belloc himself granted the benefits deriving from it—notably an intense unity and patriotism. But it was
surely clear by 1937 that a violent wind was blowing in the
opposite direction. The crude Jacobinism of the Left Book Club,
a strident hatred of class distinctions, a repudiation of all that was
not radical in the political past, an irritation with tradition and a
contempt for lineage—these were the signs of the times and they
were flagrant long before the social revolution was won on the
playing fields of Haileybury. It was strange that Belloc should
not have read them.

The Englishman was inventing his own brand of equality; an
equality of mitigated socialism imposed by politicians and
bureaucrats. It was strange, too, that Belloc should not have seen
how easily an aristocratic state, with its habit of respect for
government, lent itself to this transformation. The docility with
which the English governing class gave up its privileges was
matched by the devotion with which they had exercised them.
When Belloc moved, as he constantly did, in the houses of the

well-to-do he could see for himself the results of a crippling taxation. Long ago, in 1910—and here was prescience indeed—he had
foreseen them.

> If in anger at seeing some great barn used only to store the
> superfluity of a rich man, reformers dispossess him of that barn
> and hand it over to a group of poorer men, the Capital repre-
> sented by the barn remains intact, and—so far as its use is con-
> cerned—may continue to make the whole community as rich
> as it was before. But if, in their indignation, the reformers *burn
> down* that barn, then there will be no place in which to keep
> food from the weather, either for the rich or the poor. Nearly
> every civilisation has, in its old age, suffered from this disease;
> it has dissipated its capital by taxation. . . . The State takes
> what was intended by the former owner to be used reproduc-
> tively, and, having taken it, consumes it in direct enjoyment.[1]

Much the most important thing to be said about the nature of
contemporary England in 1937 was how quickly the politicians,
with the active encouragement of the people, were burning down
the barn.

Only on two occasions did Belloc reappear on the hustings of
professional politics. In 1929 he campaigned for Duff Cooper at
Oldham. The future of the Catholic schools was once more at
stake. 'As between the Hankey and Pankey Parties—and Swanky
too' he made no distinction, but on the survival of his religion
through education he set great store.[2] He addressed meetings in
his old constituency, and in Manchester, Bolton, and 'the rest
of the Fairyland'. Two years later he spoke again for Duff Cooper
in the by-election at the St. George's division of Westminster.
The issue here was Baldwin versus Beaverbrook. Belloc had no
very high opinion of either, but Baldwin had at least made a
first-rate speech on the classics, and Belloc disliked Beaverbrook
as much as Beaverbrook disliked him—which was saying a good
deal. His contempt for the House of Commons remained unbounded, but he thought it would be all the better for Duff

---

[1] *Fortnightly Review :* Aug. 1, 1910.
[2] Letter to Charles Goodwin: May 7, 1929.

Cooper, if Duff Cooper thought he could stand it. In the event, the Beaverbrook nominee was defeated.

It may seem odd that a man so disgruntled with politics as Belloc had become should have given so much time and thought to them. But to this extent, at least, he remained the true republican. Many of his admirers, however, regretted that public affairs, which he had lost the power to influence, should have deflected him from formal letters.

3

Little as Belloc liked being forced to write for money, he was quick to perceive the one great advantage of the writer's trade—its freedom. A man can write where and when he likes. When the *Illustrated Review* was launched by J. S. Crosthwaite-Eyre, Belloc agreed to edit it. This was intended to be a well-written, well-produced, illustrated monthly record of events in Great Britain; but Belloc was quite unable to tie himself down to regular attendance at an office—not even to the two or three times a week necessary for minimum editorship. The paper was a complete failure.

Belloc gave four warnings and four practical rules to any young man setting out to be a writer. He warned him first against discouragement; *The Path to Rome* had been offered to several firms before it was accepted. Next he warned him against fatigue.

I have done many things in my time from ploughing to earning my passage on a tramp steamer, but nothing which compared with creative writing for taking it out of a man.[1]

The third warning was not to expect any relation between the excellence of the work and its material reward; this was already the period of the best-seller with its ephemeral reputation and its gigantic sales. And the fourth warning was not to take reviews too seriously, whether they were adverse or favourable. The practical rules were as follows:

First, to do something every day, however little, on whatever piece of work the writer has in hand; second, to cherish the freedom

[1] Broadcast.

which is the chief good of his profession; third, to keep records of
every contract, letter or review connected with his trade; and
fourth, to let an agent handle his affairs. Belloc himself kept these
rules pretty well, though his press-cuttings were generally left
unsorted.

In 1926, A. D. Peters became his literary agent. Both he and
his partner, W. N. Roughead, became close friends of Belloc,
who never doubted that they placed his books and articles in
the most advantageous way. They would get him a sizeable
advance on a book—four hundred to six hundred pounds, for
his need was always for ready money—but this was rarely earned.
His market was falling and, with certain exceptions that we shall
note, his later books were not as good as his earlier ones. 'Your
books sell better than mine', he once remarked to Maurice
Baring, 'because nobody in them has less than £5,000 a year.'
He might have added that they dealt, discreetly, with those intimate themes of private life which Belloc was reluctant to discuss.
The fortunes of a book were now made by the woman reader
and women liked novels about adultery even, and perhaps especially, when religion was mixed up with it. The gentle but inflexible
spiritual advisers who drift through Baring's novels had certainly
not reduced his sales.

Belloc was at ease in the literary circles presided over by Sir
John Squire and Sir Desmond MacCarthy—both his friends—
and represented by the *London Mercury* and *Life and Letters*. He
also wrote for the *Week-End Review*, when it was edited by Sir
Gerald Barry, and for *The Tablet* when it was taken over by
Douglas Woodruff in 1935. But his contacts with the literary
world were still remote. On one occasion Sir John Squire introduced him to Thomas Hardy.

I had been sailing (about 1932) up the Channel with Belloc.
We were weatherbound in West Bay by Bridport. I took a car
to Dorchester to see Thomas Hardy, with whom I regularly
stayed, and said I would like to bring Belloc to see him.
'What,' said he, 'do you mean that Catholic journalist?' I
said 'Yes,' and he agreed. I returned to the ship and told Belloc.

'What,' said he, 'do you mean that atheist novelist?' I said 'Yes,' and he agreed. Hardy had probably never read anything of his junior Belloc's; Belloc had probably never set eyes on Hardy's Napoleonic masterpiece 'The Dynasts'. But when I got them together, I faded into the background and they, both passionate about history, got talking about a great legendary storm which, possibly in the early nineteenth century, had swept ships across the narrow isthmus which divides Portland Bill from the mainland.[1]

Belloc read, as we have seen, little contemporary literature, save that written by his friends. Here is his judgment on Duff Cooper's *Talleyrand*.

I've just finished the Talleyrand. It is exceptional. I am very proud to have it dedicated to me. I can't exaggerate the effect of 'serrée' which it has on me; the packing of stuff clearly into an exactly necessary compass and no more. It is exceedingly impressive. There are many passages in the book which make it quite different from any contemporary work and most excellent as history. Notably those close resumés of motive, incident and character which you construct better and differently than I have seen done by anyone else. It is a really remarkable book.[2]

He read all Maurice Baring's novels with great care, and although he did not profess to be a judge of fiction, he regarded *Cat's Cradle* as a masterpiece,

presenting with exact economy and one proportion of silence and void for a background, the cross-purposes and despairs and maimed effort of human life; its very core. Yet he managed to suggest the Fatherhood of God and the Incarnation and Redemption behind it all. Masterpiece—masterpiece—masterpiece![3]

Readers of Baring's *C* will find certain aspects of Belloc in the character of Andrew Burstall.

Belloc also admired the beautiful writing and exact judgment

---

[1] *Illustrated London News:* May 28, 1955.
[2] Letter to Duff Cooper: May 26, 1932.
[3] Letter to Lady Lovat: Oct. 30, 1926.

of Mr. Evelyn Waugh's life of Campion, and he enjoyed, for different reasons, the same author's *Scoop* and the novels of P. G. Wodehouse. He thought Ronald Knox's *Memories of the Future* 'entrancingly funny,'[1] and returning to Douglas Woodruff's *Plato's Britannia* for the third time, he thought it more remarkable than ever. Satire was more to his taste than any other kind of writing, except history and high verse. Of contemporary poets he greatly admired Ruth Pitter. He thought her in the true line of Elizabethan lyricism and wrote a preface for her *Persephone*. He also contributed prefaces to *The Diary of a Nobody*, and the translations from Kai Lung. But in so far as he read for pleasure, it was generally the Classics and these remained his standard. Homer, above all, the 'foundational poet of our race'; then Catullus, packing it all into a single line; and Virgil whom he remembered with particular pleasure at sea, lying out on deck '*subter silentia lunae*' and gazing at the stars.

> When I was a boy I used to think the Latin 'nova sidera norant' meaningless, but now I know its meaning, for they are hardly the same stars.[2]

Among the English classics he was devoted to Gray's *Elegy*, which he had learnt as a child from an edition with steel engravings of 'Protestant angels brought up on milk pudding'.[3] But his favourite poets were Milton and Keats, and, for his satire and mastery of the heroic couplet, Dryden. He wrote a biography of Milton (1935) and this was a book with which he said he took special pains. It is more interesting in what it tells us about Milton as a poet than about Milton as a man. Belloc sympathized with the one as he could never have sympathized with the other. Milton had three qualities which made him supreme: rhythm, which released the innate and for ever inexplicable mystery of the word—the word which is dumb or eloquent according to where you put it; intense visual imagination, which Belloc always saw as a predominantly English quality, created by and even, in a

---

[1] Letter to Lady Lovat: March 2, 1926.
[2] Letter to Mrs. Raymond Asquith: Nov. 14, 1927.
[3] Letter to Mrs. Wansbrough: Jan. 6, 1926.

sense, creating the whole landscape of southern England; and the classical form—unity, proportion and restraint—which some people wrongly supposed to be alien to the English genius. Where Belloc surely exaggerated was in claiming Milton as the creator of English blank verse because he had 'lifted it from stage use to pure literature'. It would be much truer to say that he had killed it. The model which he set was highly artificial when he used it himself, although his genius justified it. It was fatal to his imitators. Belloc had, of course, no sense of the theatre as a fine art; but the fact remains that a large part of the world's greatest poetry, Sophocles no less than Shakespeare, had been written to be spoken on the stage, and derived its greatness not only from the qualities of rhythm, vision and form, but from the emotions it expressed and the situations it brought to life. Belloc had little admiration for Milton's prose, except for some rare passage of good rhetoric. The book is valuable for its analysis of Milton's method, his highly deliberated art; and it showed, once more, that Belloc's literary judgment was rarely warped by his dislike of a man's opinions. On one occasion the boys of the Latymer Upper School at Hammersmith were studying *Paradise Lost,* and on being asked to write down the names of the three devils who took part in the Infernal Debate, one of them wrote 'Belloc, Belial and Mammon'. The answer was sent to Belloc who promptly gave the perpetrator of this howler a signed copy of his poems.

He admired Byron rather in the way that the French admire him, for Byron struck the note of experience; an experience still familiar to Latin Europe. He combined magic and intelligence, emotion and reason, in a way that Shelley and Wordsworth had only fitfully combined them. Shelley had a more subtle rhythm and, at moments, a greater 'lift'. His peaks were higher than Byron's. But Byron never flagged; he had the sense of continuity, which was only another way of saying that he had the sense of form.

We have already spoken of Belloc's admiration for Swift, Gibbon and Macaulay, but of all the single masterpieces of English prose his favourite was Johnson's *Rasselas*. This had come out a few days before *Candide*. Belloc compared Voltaire's style of 'polished jade' with Johnson's style which was 'like the rhythmical swell of deep water'. Voltaire's economy was 'like a sphere; the maximum content for its surface'. Johnson's was 'like strong soup; a concentration of nourishment'. Belloc believed that Johnson was more nourishing than his French contemporary. 'No good man is the better for having read *Candide*, but every man is the better for having read *Rasselas*.'[1] Sensitive to beauty when it appeared in classical proportion, Belloc was impervious to the novel and the strange. Someone persuaded him to read Gerard Manley Hopkins, but he could make nothing of him. Of the modern French he admired Anna de Noailles and the little he knew of Claudel.

Meanwhile he worked slowly, and as the mood took him, at his own verse. He had always wanted to write six poems of considerable scale: *The Ode to the West Wind*, *The Dream of Charlemagne*, *The Renewal*, *The Dream of the Conscript of '93*, *The Battle of Val-es-Dunes*, and *The Heroic Poem in Praise of Wine*. Of these only the last two were completed. The writing of *Val-es-Dunes* caused him great difficulty.

I will show you the proof of Damnable Val-es Dunes which haunts me. The old bits are just good yell-verse, but the new bits are appalling! They are to the old what a diseased ape is to a reasonably healthy man. What a pity it is that the faculty of verse dies under the burden of life! It is not as though it died naturally like other faculties. We all go ga-ga at last if we have the misfortune to live long enough: at least, my half of the race does. But not to be able to write verse any more, when one can still write prose and add up sums and read clear print in spectacles, that is, oh Age, thine intolerable victory. And to see one's name set at the foot of bad verse—that is shame indeed! I never thought I should come to it. But one drinks all waters before Lethe.[2]

Val-es-Dunes first appeared in the *New Statesman* in February 1921. It is a good enough poem, but it is not one of Belloc's best. He should have been more capable than Chesterton of writing a

---

[1] *Short Talks with the Dead* (1926).
[2] Letter to Mrs. Raymond Asquith: Jan. 15, 1921.

great poem of action, but he never did so. Nevertheless, its completion beckoned him on to the *Heroic Poem*. There were, he would say, three kinds of poets: those who worked in clay with their fingers; those, like Homer and Theocritus, who worked in marble with bronze; and those, among whom he classed most of his contemporaries, who worked in butter with their toes. With the second category every stroke was sure,

> But those who work in clay with their fingers—ah! those are the problems on which Apollo and The Nine of his harem sit up all night debating jadedly! For they (the clay-workers) push out and in and bulge the clay and scrape it, and leave something just worth looking at, but no more.[1]

Here Belloc did himself less than justice. The best of his verse— certain of the sonnets and the epigrams and parts of the *Heroic Poem*—have exactly the quality of marble; the strength and delicacy of a frieze. The *Heroic Poem* was finished in 1928 and published in the *London Mercury*. Fragments of it had appeared earlier in an essay, 'The Good Poet and the Bad Poet', from *Short Talks with the Dead* (1926). If you compare the following couplet:

> Or where, festooned about the tall elm-trees
> Etrurian grapes regard Tyrrhenian seas

with the later version of the same couplet:

> Or where, festooned about the tall elm-trees
> Tendrils are mirrored in Tyrrhenian seas

you can see the effect of Belloc's polishing. Rhetoric has been transformed into poetry. No other poem so resumes Belloc's personality and spiritual lineage; his high spirits and his sense of exile; his courage and his near despair. Nothing so fine in the heroic couplet had been achieved by a modern English poet, if we except certain poems by Mr. Roy Campbell. For most people it will stand as Belloc's monument; the quintessence of a European mind, at once humble and combative.

But the poem can hardly be set, for literary perfection, beside certain of the epigrams published for the first time in *Sonnets and*

---

[1] Letter to Mrs. Raymond Asquith: Aug. 24, 1924.

Verse (1938). The deliberation of the *Heroic Poem* is clear, but in some of his short verses you cannot see how it is done; and that, as Belloc would have said, is the test. Three of the many may be taken as matchless in their kind.

ON A SLEEPING FRIEND

Lady, when your lovely head
Droops to sink among the Dead,
And the quiet places keep
You that so divinely sleep;
Then the dead shall blessèd be
With a new solemnity,
For such Beauty, so descending,
Pledges them that Death is ending.
Sleep your fill—but when you wake
Dawn shall over Lethe break.

This was set to music by Belloc himself and published by the Oxford University Press.

THE STATUE

When we are dead, some Hunting-boy will pass
And find a stone half-hidden in tall grass
And grey with age: but having seen that stone
(Which was your image), ride more slowly on.

Note, again, the genius of the proper names in the following, which was first published in *The Tablet* (1939).

DECAMERON

Maia, Ridalvo, Brangwen, Amoreth,
In mountain-guarded gardens vainly gay,
Wasted the irrecoverable breath,
And sought to lose in play
The fixed, majestic, questioning eyes of Death
By turning theirs away.

All these epigrams have the combination of density, lyricism and deep feeling which belongs to the highest poetry. They lie like rubies in the desert of ephemeral verse-making.

Hilaire Belloc at French H.Q. in January 1940

Hilaire Belloc in Old Age, from a painting by James Gunn
in the Hall of the Oxford Union

Desmond MacCarthy used to surprise people by saying that
Belloc was not only the most various of living authors—that was
not surprising—but the most underrated of modern poets. People
found it hard to believe that the author of *New Cautionary Tales*
(1930) could write verse of the quality we have just been illustrating. His satirical rhymes (not all of them printable) were
stored in the memory of his friends and were shared with anyone
who could see the joke. In his letters he would break out into
verse on the slightest excuse; on the baptism of his god-daughter,
Miriam Wansbrough (December 14, 1932):

> I know the place is Spanish Place
> An honest temple full of grace,
> But have no power
> To know the hour.
> I bring her Missal
> With Gospel and Epistle
> To fill her with spiritual bone and gristle
> Till the hour of her dismissal.

In 1917, Mr. Christopher Hussey who was then editing the
Eton Red Cross had asked him for a poem. He replied:

> Certainly I will send you a contribution and do so here and
> now. It is very short and not very grand. I wrote it last April
> under the threat of submarines, which I always fear when I
> cross the sea, being by nature cowardly upon that element.[1]

A triolet followed.

> De sous-marins la mer est pleine,
> Et j'en suis tout horripilé;
> Ma vie est ténébreuse et vaine
> De sous-marins la mer est pleine;
> Faites Justice Souveraine
> Que je n'en sois pas torpillé!
> De sous-marins la mer est pleine
> Et j'en suis tout horripilé.

[1] July 23, 1917.

The poems to Lady Juliet Duff and the sonnets to Lady Diana Cooper are well known from the published collections of Belloc's verse; and some verses, also in French, contained in a letter to the second of these devoted friends, placed him among the men of the Pléiade who were his brothers.

> Diane chasseresse
> Déesse enchantresse
> 　Et secourable encor
> Dont secrète et divine
> La Lueur illumine
> 　Les grands silences d'or.
>
> Percez tout en tournante
> Votre course indolente,
> 　O Régente des Mois,
> Lors de votre passage
> Fenestres de nuages
> 　Sur nos hyvernes bois.[1]

After poetry there was prose; and a passage from Charles Péguy, in which he is discussing his own poem, *Eve*, illustrates the quality which was constant both in verse and the prose of Belloc.

> Il en résulte que le mot est constamment juste, d'une justesse technique, non point que l'auteur ait fait des vers de prosateur, mais il a fait des vers de poète avec une sorte de marbre de prose . . . la plupart de ces quatrains en arrivent à se présenter comme des inscriptions lapidaires et même funéraires—

and another judgment by the same author is perfectly applicable to Belloc. He speaks of

> un certain comique qui est peut-être la plus profonde marque d'une certaine pureté de coeur, d'une innocence. Un comique grave et d'autant plus profond qu'il prend appui sur un fond d'une invincible mélancholie.

[1] For Christmas, 1932.

There were three prose works which Belloc wrote with particular care and joy in his later years. One was his *Joan of Arc*.[1]
This was an example of what he called 'special prose'. Once, at
King's Land, there was a discussion with Maurice Baring and
Max Beerbohm as to what constituted good prose; and Belloc,
to illustrate his point, fetched an old guide-book of 1850 from his
study and began reading the description of an English harbour.
This was what he normally meant by prose; exact information
conveyed in the right number of words, placed in the right order.
But 'special prose' had its special dangers; 'nothing is worse than
high-falutin manqué'.[2] The prose of Belloc's essay on Joan of Arc
is not 'high-falutin' but it is deliberately, though slightly, archaic.
In the case of *Tristan and Iseult* he had the excuse that he was
translating from the recension of an ancient text, and that he was
justified in maintaining the flavour of the period in which the
original story had been told. But the story of Joan of Arc could
have been told just as well in a more flexible and modern style;
a style which could adapt itself to rhetoric when rhetoric was
required, but could also be relaxed to meet the normal demands
of narrative or disquisition. There is a little too much of Viollet-
le-Duc in Belloc's *Joan of Arc*. We feel that the writer has assumed
a tone of voice, and his recital becomes something of a recitative.

To find Belloc's prose at its best the reader should turn to the
magnificent but little known Taylorian lecture *On Translation*,
delivered at Oxford in 1931 and published by the University
Press. This was the first honour that Belloc had ever received
from Oxford and he felt 'like a boy getting the 3rd prize
for spelling, or better still, like a rosebud at her first ball on
coming out'.[3] Nothing better than Belloc's Taylorian lecture
has been done in English criticism. Here he made the valuable
distinction between verse and prose: 'prose appeals through the
reason, verse through the emotions; the one to the Intelligent, the
other to the Appetitive in Man'. Translation was important
because it permitted one province of Europe to communicate
with another. But there were no 'identical equivalents'; that was

[1] 1929.   [2] Letter to Mrs. Raymond Asquith: March 30, 1929.
[3] Letter to the Hon. Mrs. Mervyn Herbert: 1931.

the difficulty. How, for example, should one translate Michelet's sentence about the Girondins singing? '*Quelle était cette voix?—C'était la Révolution même.*' If one said 'What was that voice? It was the Revolution itself' the effect was grotesque. Belloc suggested 'One might have said, on hearing such a voice, that one had heard the Revolution itself in song'. Or again, the difference of emphasis in two languages had to be kept in mind. If a French writer said of a certain law, '*Voilà ce qui a perdu le pays*', he really meant 'This law had grievous consequences for the country'; or, conversely, if he said that something was '*parfaitement incorrect*' he really meant that it was 'utterly false'; or where an Englishman said 'You can't believe a word he says' the Frenchman would probably say '*On ne peut guère toujours le croire*'. Belloc gave his listeners two valuable pieces of advice: to transmute boldly and never try to embellish. Also he thought that verse was generally better translated into prose. Neither Pope nor Chapman had quite succeeded with Homer; but Church had very nearly done the trick. Only very occasionally had a satisfactory verse translation been achieved, and Belloc read aloud Du Bellay's sonnet, *Liré*, followed by Chesterton's rendering of the poem into English.

On July 20, 1928, Belloc wrote to Maurice Baring:

I have finished *Belinda*—a fearful sweat—like sawing marble—but worth it. It is the only thing I ever finished in my life and the only piece of my own writing that I have liked for more than 40 years.

He had been at work on it since December 1923, and most if it had been written on the backs of envelopes.

I go over it word for word, like a mosaic; changing, fitting in, adapting, dictating, erasing, spatch-cocking, caressing, softening, enlivening, glamouring, suppressing, enhancing and in general divinising this my darling treasure.[1]

Of all Belloc's works in prose *Belinda* is the most perfect, the most original, the most timeless, and therefore perhaps the most

---

[1] Letter to Mrs. Raymond Asquith: July 1, 1928.

secure. It is also the most difficult to define. If we call it 'pastiche',
we realize at once that we have employed too light and artificial
a word. Artificial in a sense it is, and no one could describe it as
heavy; but deep feeling underlies the artifice and the humour has
the weight of Belloc's own *gravitas*. The book grinds no axe and
proves no point. It is a gratuitous, disinterested and quite impersonal essay in romantic irony. Small in scale and purposely
conventional in subject, it still leaves an impression of grandeur;
fine, not finicky; hard as a diamond and delicate as wrought
iron.

Described as a 'tale of Affection in Youth and Age', and
dedicated to 'The Eros of Keir', it does no more than tell how
a Victorian youth, Horatio Maltravers, and maiden, Belinda
Montgomery, inhabiting neighbouring estates, fall in love; are
separated by the malice of interested persons; are reunited, married, and presumably live happily ever after. The book has the
optimism of a fairy-tale, and yet is still rooted in reality. It is at
once a satire and an appreciation of Victorianism from one who
looked back on the century of his birth and upbringing and found
it much better than he had once thought it. Two passages will
give the flavour of the book; the first describes how Belinda and
Horatio fall in love.

She saw him as he came through the bracken, with active
carriage, with uplifted face. It seemed to her that there was
something there inspired; and her imagination put courage
and adventure into his advance, as though he were setting out
upon a quest. He turned a corner of the path to cross the rustic
bridge, and was aware of one scarcely known yet deeply known
whose airy figure among the solemn pines arrested all his being.
When he had approached and discovered her face, it was not
the familiar feature of a friend, but Radiance personate. In him,
for her, approached a god.

The moment was magical. It was as though some music had
transformed the world.

Breast deep in fern, the small and laughing fauns, who love
the awakening of life, hid tip-toe, sidling, peeping, benevolent;

but in the heart of the high wood a Presence, shining in a shaft of light, triumphantly let fly the arrow from the bow.

The second passage describes the wedding.

> In the room which had been set aside for the chapel of the ceremony, and recently furnished by the Chatelaine for that purpose with assiduous care, the household was assembled, the Reverend Mr. Atkins vested and prepared. He had required, he had demanded, he had obtained, a glass of port wine and a biscuit, which it was his invariable custom to consume before a Celebration, in protest against the Romish novelties of certain colleagues. As, with practised intonation, he recited the profound phrases of the Marriage Service, the Marquise, who had missed for so long the beautiful Liturgy of her youth, was deeply moved; while old Fauchette, the only French domestic not a Papist and, therefore, privileged to attend, was equally affected by the sacred scene, though, being ignorant of the English tongue (a Huguenot from the Vaudois) she could do no more than reverently follow the rhythms of the sacred office.

Belinda was first published by Desmond MacCarthy in *Life and Letters* and then by Constable (1928). Belloc had attached his own conditions to the printing and binding of the book, and he was delighted with its success among discriminating readers.

> My stock is going up. Hal Fisher wanders about England telling everyone that *Belinda* is the best novel written in English and the summit of all prose and lyrism. It is also (I may say) the best homage to the Little God.[1]

John Buchan once recorded his conviction that no man had attained more perfectly than Belloc to the 'piety of speech' of the seventeenth-century lyrists and that no man had written purer and nobler verse in the great tradition. Maurice Baring compared Belloc's prose to the mellow tones of a violin, and it is not surprising that one whose practice and appreciation of prose was based on rhythm should have had music in his bones. He had

---

[1] Letter to Mrs. Raymond Asquith: Jan. 6, 1929.

small practical knowledge of it, however, and his tastes were limited to Mozart, Gilbert and Sullivan, and a few old songs, mostly French. He composed settings for two poems by Clément Marot—*Une Pastorelle Gentille* and *A Sa Dame Malade*. On the MS. of this he drew the picture of an enormously fat lady in evening dress, singing, with her mouth wide open, 'to a vast audience'. He could never take soloists seriously. A letter comparing Beethoven and Mozart gives the clue to his appreciations not only of music, but of sculpture, painting and poetry.

It has been said that Beethoven added a third dimension to music—and it may be so, but to an ear more expectant of unity, it seems rather as if he plays for parallax; putting in sounds first from one side and then from the other in order to be stereoscopic. It seems almost as though he desired by such a method to force substance into that which he could not make substantial from within, and of itself: like a man who makes a tragic moment poignant by the contrast of something comic alongside of it, or like a man who suggests silence, not by its plenitude, but by the contrast of a single sound breaking in upon it. The effect is large, but carpenter's work; the structure imposes itself, but has too conscious a diversity of plan.

When, after this, the Divine quality of pure melody, the quality of Revelation, comes in with Mozart, it is the difference between the pure lyric—Theocritus, Keats, du Bellay—and a wilful thoughtlessness, an attempt at depth, not final and therefore unsuitable to man.[1]

An inexpugnable *parti-pris* ran through Belloc's judgments on music and painting. Rembrandt was 'a powerful painter and etcher, but on the wrong side of the cultural hedge; unlike Rubens'.[2] Yet he found the Dürer drawings from the Albertinum 'a source of revelation', and when he read of Dürer's adoration of Luther, he came a little nearer to understanding the Reformation. For a long time he was blind to the Primitives, and then he woke to them quite suddenly, at the age of forty. But he was

[1] To Mrs. Raymond Asquith: Nov. 26, 1930.
[2] Letter to Mrs. Raymond Asquith: March 8, 1927.

happiest with the high Renaissance, and he can explain why he does not think the wax bust at Lille is by Raphael.

It has something elusive in its Divinity which he had not: no, not even when he got well over the borders of this world as in the Heavenly eyes of the Child in the Sistine Madonna. He is *carré*: four square, and straightforward: but there is in the bust of Lille something that you get in Irish hills, in faint music half heard and in the unexpected scents of flowers, coming in to land from the sea in spring.[1]

Belloc could always be struck dumb by great sculpture. He never tired of returning to a certain bust of a woman's head in the Victoria and Albert Museum. The artist was unknown, though it reminded him of Houdon, and to say that of marble was like saying 'by Theocritus', of verse.[2] He would have been struck dumb more often if he had not been so bored by museums.

> I hold in absolute abhorrence
> The parson-ridden town of Florence
> But that is something I shall never say to
> The heavenly town of Orvieto.

Of the moderns he knew little, but he admired Frank Brangwyn and most of the English work in black and white. His own drawings and woodcuts were carefully executed, and we catch a glimpse in them, here and there, of the miniaturist that composed the epigrams.

Unlike Chesterton, Belloc was not successful as a broadcaster. He could evoke the forum more easily than the fireside. The broadcaster, like the actor, must be above all things anxious to please; Belloc was above all things anxious to instruct. If the B.B.C. had ever lost its desire to please, it would soon have lost its monopoly. Belloc was persuaded to do a 'turn' with Desmond MacCarthy, called 'Conversation in a Train', and he was afterwards invited to talk for half an hour on 'How to drink in Youth and Age'. For this he asked the not unreasonable sum of fifty

[1] Letter to Mrs. Raymond Asquith: Feb. 23, 1927.   [2] *Ibid.*

pounds. The B.B.C. official shook his head and urged Belloc to think of the publicity. 'That's what I hate about it most', was the reply. 'Very well', said the official, 'I'll try to make them pay.' 'I hope they won't,' replied Belloc—and they didn't. A rigid Calvinism then reigned at Broadcasting House, and one wonders how Belloc ever came to be asked to talk on such a subject and what would have happened if he had done so. It is only fair to record that the B.B.C. was not neglectful of Belloc's eminence and merits. Lord Duncannon's version of *The Four Men* was given over the air; and on Belloc's eightieth birthday, and after his death, generous tributes were paid to him.

4

Belloc suffered from recurrent ill-health as he grew older; no serious illness, for he had a constitution of iron, but chronic sleeplessness, severe headaches, eye-strain, prostrating attacks of influenza, at least one alarming 'black-out', and general fatigue. He made much of all this in letters to his friends; perhaps a little too much. He was anxious because he needed, at all cost, to make money. The complaint was monotonous, but it must be examined. Most of the money he had earned during the War was invested in French securities, and as the value of the franc fell the value of these securities naturally fell with it. Meanwhile he owed considerable sums to the Inland Revenue and he was the last man to sit down easily under the rapacity of tax collectors. In fact, he seems on the whole to have been kindly treated—but the moment he lost his capacity to earn, a whole pack of wolfish bureaucrats would be on his heels. Consequently he was never able to relax. He no longer had the strength to refresh himself with violent exercise, and he generally came back from his brief holidays more tired than when he had set out. Only at sea—and he was rarely at sea for more than a few days—did he find a real replenishment and repose. He had sold the remaining lease of his Knightsbridge house in 1920, and for a time occupied a room in Edmond Warre's house in Little Stanhope Street. When Warre moved to Chelsea Belloc established a claim on Mrs. Arkwright's guest-room in Brompton Square. Mrs. Arkwright was the sister of Somers Cocks.

The devotion and virtuosity of Edith ensured that the bounty of King's Land should not fail. Some idea of Belloc's hospitality is given by Mr. H. S. Mackintosh:

> At most times he liked several courses of very rich food, particularly jugged hare, and when we had imagined that there was no more to come and were feeling fairly replete, we would find ourselves faced with a sudden course, such as a dozen hot Cornish oysters each, to eat after all that had gone before. Again, after drinking heady wines all through the meal, at least one bottle of port had to be finished before we went to bed. In due course we found it best to starve throughout the day before tackling these sumptuous repasts. During the meal he would talk on a hundred subjects. On one occasion he delivered an extraordinary lecture on places where the food was bad—a sort of antithesis to a 'Gourmet's Guide'.[1]

When he was alone, however, Belloc was not a very big eater; he was generally satisfied with ham or bacon and eggs, and he once came into the Old Palace at Oxford exclaiming, 'I will have sherry and bread!' and took nothing else.

His financial responsibilities did not lessen as his family grew up. Hilary, after leaving Balliol, had gone to America where he did well in engineering. Peter was for some years a problem. As Father Vincent McNabb wrote many years later, he was a 'seaman by baptism and birth'. He had much of his father's temperament and many of his tastes. For a time he travelled and then Belloc found him a job with a firm in Barcelona. When he married in 1927 Murray Allison had him taken on to the *Daily Telegraph,* for he now needed regular employment not too far from his home. But he lived 'in a perpetual half-amused and half-baffled reaction against the whole world of modern commercial journalism'[2] and the world which it represented. He had considerable skill in the writing of short stories. *Below Bridges* was a

---

[1] Broadcast: printed in *The Listener:* Oct. 8, 1953.
[2] *The Tablet:* April 12, 1941.

worthy successor to W. W. Jacobs, for Peter had the same
knowledge of the water-front. Belloc was devoted to his wife
Stella and their three beautiful daughters, often visiting them at
South Moreton, and helping them with generous gifts both of
money and wine.

Elizabeth Belloc had developed a genuine lyric gift, in which
her father took a natural pride. Already, in 1921, Eleanor was
'replacing her mother; maturing, of spiritual wisdom, full of life
and altogether my household'.[1] But in the following year she
married Reginald Jebb, and for immediate practical purposes was
lost to King's Land. For twelve years Belloc had to do the work
of master and mistress combined.

> The main thing I have to consider in obtaining a new servant
> is to get them *young* so that they are thoroughly under the firm
> authority of Edith, and *local*, so that I know all about them and
> also so that they do not gad about but have a mother in the
> background. This is not always easy to combine, but I seem to
> have got one now and one must see how it works. She will be
> shoe-horned in her work more easily while I am away and my
> great object is always to train them to accuracy in time and
> cooking. But it is not a man's job. It is for the Lady of the
> House to do all that and much else.

> How right you are when you say that each sex *alone* is lame
> in the management of domestic things! The household, a
> *familia*, is the product of both, and each unsupported and
> unadvised in what is not of its province is at a loss. It is very
> much so with the bringing up of children, and you don't know
> how grateful I am to you for the advice and example you gave
> me in that during the critical years. Indeed I ought, in one or
> two particulars, to have asked you for further advice—it was
> so useful and good! For daughters a man is at sea. It is no bad
> rule to treat boys and girls much the same, but there is always
> the differing developing character as time goes on.[2]

Two circumstances compelled Eleanor's return. Mr. Jebb, who
had won the M.C. in the First World War and had then returned

---

[1] Letter to Mrs. Reginald Balfour: Jan. 25, 1921.   [2] *Ibid.*, Aug. 30, 1934.

to his work as a preparatory schoolmaster, was forced to give up
his school when he became a Catholic, and an attempt to start a
second school of the same kind for Catholic boys failed after
heroic efforts in which Belloc and many of his friends played their
part. Then, in 1934, Edith and her husband, George Rance, on
whom the running of King's Land depended, left his service and
Mr. and Mrs. Jebb, who had returned to Shipley a month earlier,
stayed on to take their place. Reginald Jebb looked after the farm
and Eleanor kept house.

The Jebbs had four children, and the cost of maintaining the
family largely fell upon Belloc. But his grandchildren brought
him an immense joy; here was the communal life recreating
itself under the roof where Elodie had created it; the ritual
Christmases and New Years; something of the old hospitality; a recovered home. Belloc had a great love for children,
whether they were his own or his friends'. *Economics for Helen*
was written for Lady Helen Asquith; he assiduously taught
mathematics to Gabriel Herbert; and for her brother Auberon
he composed in his own hand a juvenile *History of England*.
In the holidays he would give them lectures with slides, for he
had considerable experience of what was then known as a
'magic lantern', or take them to the pantomime. *Aladdin,* at the
King's, Hammersmith, was always his favourite. Burdened as
he was, he would put himself to fantastic pains; pages would
be written on the specifications for a sailing boat or the
programme for a journey. And as the children grew up, he still
remembered them because they were the children of his friends.
When Mrs. Balfour's daughter was entering religion Belloc
asked if he might give her a thimble, because he understood
that a thimble was the only thing one could take into a convent.
But his own grandchildren were closest to him and his letters are
full of them. Here is his grand-daughter, Marianne:

> My grand-daughter fills my heart with joy. When she stands
> by the picture of her mother as a child, it fills my heart with
> despair, so transient are the only things we know.[1]

[1] Letter to Lady Lovat: Jan. 12, 1926.

And here is his grandson:

> I further have news that before I left home I saw my grand-
> son Philip smiling simply and wholly in his crib like the
> blessed of God . . . I am ungrateful when I mourn over the
> years. Every new generation is a manifestation of God, and
> innocence is the mark by which they show it; yes: and joy.
> After all, what does it matter which end of life happiness
> comes? It is there; and therefore a promise of its own eternity.
> But I want it soon. Anyhow, Philip (Vincent) is three-quarters
> in Paradise all the time.[1]

In December 1955, Philip Jebb was married to Lucy Pollen,
the grand-daughter of Belloc's old Oratory friend, in the same
church at Napa where Hilaire and Elodie had been married in
1896, and their names are inscribed in the same register.

Belloc was often accused of caring too much about money.

> I'm tired of love, and still more tired of rhyme,
> But money gives me pleasure all the time.

He had, indeed, a certain Gallic realism where money was concerned. Once, in America, he had been handed the usual fee for a
lecture and his clerical host was disconcerted to see him pause
underneath a lamp-post, open the envelope and count the notes.
On another occasion he had promised to write an article on Dante
for an American magazine. The article was overdue and he received a telegram asking for it when he was on holiday in France.
He went into the village post-office, wrote 4,000 words straight-
way on a very large number of telegraph forms, and cabled them
to America 'wire-collect'. He might be in debt, but his personal
accounts were scrupulously kept and he always knew how much
he had in the Bank. If he borrowed money it was punctually
repaid; and he was generous in lending it or giving it away. He
rarely put less than a pound into the church collection, even
when he was hard up. On a visit to St. Edmund's, Ware, he met a
seminarian who wanted to spend his holidays in Sicily. Sympathiz-
ing with this desire, he collected small sums of money from his

[1] Letter to Mrs. Raymond Asquith: Sept. 16, 1927.

friends so that the young man could go. He did the same thing for a poor woman who was educating her son with difficulty, collecting twenty-eight pounds for her in small amounts. On a visit to the Oratory School, in 1919, he met a convert clergyman who had recently joined the staff. He, with his wife and family, had gone through a very difficult time since his conversion and Belloc wanted to help them. When the master had left, Belloc turned to Gerald Headlam, in whose room he happened to be, and said, 'I want to give that man fifty pounds, but you must arrange things so that he never associates the thing with me'. He then handed Headlam ten five-pound notes, which were later given to the master without his ever discovering their source. This may not have been easy for Headlam, but in a letter written shortly afterwards Belloc explained why he had acted as he did.

The importance of not letting people know who does this sort of thing (save in the case of an intimate friend) is that such secrecy saves the recipient from all embarrassment. It is absolutely impossible to avoid an actual burden to the recipient under any other system. This I know from a long course of borrowing and taking of gifts myself in the days of my poverty which are now about to return.[1]

They did return; and this explained the occasional appearance of cupidity. Indeed, he often wondered if he should not have thought more about money. The arts were an adjunct, he maintained, and man was never meant to live by them. A business, by contrast, was such a sane occupation. If he had run a business (but then he could never have run a business) he might have made more solid provision for his dependants. It was easy to say that Belloc lived beyond his means; that the cocktails at Bucks and the crayfish at Kettners were a luxury. Such arguments are priggish; Belloc could have answered that, in nine cases out of ten, the money he spent on himself was also spent on other people.

Dead Lucre; burnt ambition; wine is best.

[1] Dec. 11, 1919.

He was quite without the vanity that is so often found in literary people. Once a little boy was introduced to him at King's Land, and he replied gravely, 'Now you will be able to tell your grand-children that you once shook hands with Rudyard Kipling'. Although nothing could ever have turned Belloc into a *cher maître*, nothing could prevent him becoming a G.O.M. Modern taste might be turning away from him, as the emasculated palates of the 'twenties demanded a thinner diet, but he still had the power to impress. In 1933 a number of young men recently down from Balliol formed a Wednesday dining club under the presidency of Mr. Richard Usborne. They were bound together by a common conviction that *The Modern Traveller* 'was about the best and funniest thing ever written of its kind of nonsense'.[1] They were right about the fun but wrong about the nonsense, as they no doubt discovered for themselves when the wickedness of the world grew plainer to them. Their ambition was to have Belloc as their guest and the opportunity presented itself when they found him one evening dining in the same restaurant. Mr. Usborne sent a note down by the waiter to say that the seven members of the Wednesday Club—'founded somewhat in your honour (Sir, we are all recently of Balliol) and dedicated to the glowing memory of the Chaplain and Mate, who perished, you will recall, on June 7, after dark, in a (now regrettably out of print) classic entitled *The Modern Traveller*'—desired Mr. Belloc to take wine with them. The note was returned with a message in pencil, 'In ten minutes. H. B.'; and presently he came up. Wine was brought and he talked to those young men as no one had ever talked to them before. Walking and wine, France and Spain, Balliol, poetry, dons—the legend came to life. As the restaurant closed its doors and they passed out into the street, Belloc invited the Seven Men who were Wednesday to be his guests on a future occasion—and they were. Something in their simple approach— an echo of Balliol perhaps, a ghost of past carousals—had awoken his geniality. Nor was this the only Balliol Society founded in his honour. There was one in the early 'twenties which used to lunch in the College gardens off bread and beer and cheese.

[1] Richard Usborne: Broadcast, July 1950.

Belloc gave his books away very freely and sometimes received rather curious thanks. A man to whom he had presented his *Wolsey* replied: 'Your esteemed book to hand, by this post, as advised, and many thanks for same'. He would lecture or recite his verse, resignedly, when required to, in London drawing-rooms, and for charitable purposes. Thus we find him at Lady Anglesey's, improvising on the 'Art of Boring', and instructing the Somerset Nursing Association in 'The Art of Lying'. This homily raised one hundred pounds. For anyone called upon to open a bazaar he suggested the following speech:

Lots of things have to be opened: Oysters, Cases (both in law and of wine), Battery Fire, discussions, the heart—rarely—the way to repentance—always; and railway carriages, often in slow trains and now and then in fast ones. Bazaars also must be opened, so I open this one.

Some things are hard to open, such as safes, some impossible, such as the lips of the dead, but some quite easy. Bazaars are of these last, so I open this one, with an air.

Some things remain open, like an offer to sell a large London house. Some don't: like a snapshot shutter: some for a day or two—like this bazaar. So I open this one for its brief life.[1]

Although King's Land had his soul in it and he prayed that it might be preserved for him in his age, he never remained there for long stretches at a time. This was his home, and these his family, but they could not lighten the memories that oppressed him. 'For my part', he tells Mrs. Balfour, 'my cancer of loss gets worse and worse with every year and I grow fixed in the void of my wife and my son; to this, new poverty and anxiety for the home add greatly.' This was in 1922; and as the burden grew heavier, he craved the society of his friends. He moved from one to the other in his huge black cape, designed by an Edwardian *couturière*, the pockets stuffed with maps and newspapers, bread and wine, French mouthwash and an old felt hat. On the rare occasions when he dressed for dinner, he would wear a tail-coat, black waistcoat, black tie and stiff shirt; latterly he took to wearing

[1] Letter to Mrs. Raymond Asquith: Nov. 17, 1932.

false cuffs which he had difficulty in controlling. Once he asked himself to dinner with the Sheeds at Horley and insisted on bringing his own food: a loaf of bread, a lettuce, a tin of bully beef, and two bottles of Burgundy. When the maid took the lettuce to wash it, he exclaimed, 'No, you must always br-r-ush a lettuce. The water prevents the salad dressing from properly impregnating the leaves.' However, when the Sheeds' own repast of liver and bacon arrived on the table, Belloc eagerly devoured it and the bully beef remained in its tin.

Desmond MacCarthy used to say that when Belloc arrived it was like an express train tearing through a quiet country station. 'Old newspapers, paper bags and dust would be whirled frantically into the air and sucked along with the train for a few seconds. Then he would be gone and everything would settle into its habitual quiet.' Certain traces, however, might be left behind. Mr. John Somers Cocks describes a visit to a house where Belloc had been staying:

> Once I succeeded him in one of the guest-rooms, and found in the chest of drawers a long narrow strip of white starched linen, which I could not identify as anything but one of those starched belts that stiff Edwardian nurses used to wear round their middles. On exhibiting the object and asking who the Nurse was, I was told 'That must be one of Mr. Belloc's collars.'[1]

He was an unconventional but not an inconsiderate guest. A succession of postcards, letters and telegrams would explain, announce, and finally confirm his arrival. When he came he would invariably telephone and invariably pay for his calls. When he left, his thanks were never formal; delicacy, humour and affection, often adorned with a sketch or a poem, turned the briefest note into a treasured literary possession. He was certainly the greatest writer of Collinses in English social history. A single sheet to Elizabeth Wansbrough contained portraits of Arthur Balfour, Leo XIII, Ramsay MacDonald (moustache only), the Pope, St. Paul, the Archangel Michael and Queen Victoria. In

[1] Letter to the author: May 31, 1955.

1924, when he had been the guest of Lady Sybil Graham at the Embassy in Rome, he made up for her an entire scrap-book of quotations, grave and gay, his own and other people's, and sent it to her as a thank-offering.

He was sensitive to any inconvenience he might have caused. If for example he had talked too loudly about the Reformation before a country vicar, he would abase himself with a *mea culpa* for 'Hilary the Hound'. His friends could testify that his occasional aggressiveness came from the simplicity of saying just what was in his head, and that his violent individuality of dress and demeanour was the result of a perfect unself-consciousness. He preserved, to the end, the formal courtesies of another age and was slow to call people by their Christian name.

He wrote more easily away from home. Already, in 1925, he could describe himself to Mrs. Mervyn Herbert as 'a man driven by necessity to work for more than he can live on . . . so nearly at his end'. But he only spoke thus to his intimates, and at Tetton, on the southern slopes of the Quantocks, he wrote more enjoyably than anywhere else. He would sit there in the library while Mrs. Herbert, whom he would call 'my hostess', typed to his dictation; and then, suddenly, he would pull off his half-Wellington boots and rush out on the tennis-court in stockinged feet with a heavy gold watch-chain across his black waistcoat. At other times he would sit bottling wine for the household, a baize apron across his knees and his sad, strong face lit up by the candle which was the only light permitted in the cellar. Round him the others would fetch and carry and fill, each at his appointed task. There were visits to Mary Herbert at Pixton, on its wooded, hilly island, between the Barle and the Exe, looking up on to the moors; to Beaufort in the wilds of Inverness—'It will be a long time before I get Friendship and the Faith again under one roof'[1]; or to Guy Dawnay's on the banks of the Test, rapid and crystal-clear, like a poem by Ronsard or Du Bellay. There were continental tours, with Mary Herbert driving him down through France to Porto Fino; the seas of the Æneid *subter silentia lunae*; the places and the faces that he loved; children growing

[1] Letter to Lady Lovat: Aug. 13, 1926.

up and marrying; the Faith no longer a separation but a native air. Nearer home, he could rush off in his own 'T' Ford car to Maurice Baring at Rottingdean or to the Duff Coopers at Bognor; to the Mortons at Henfield; or to Charlotte Balfour at Ford, while she was still living. Often he would return early to be sure of his sleep, and sometimes he would fall asleep at any hour of the day, and in whatever house he happened to be. Sleeplessness and failing eyesight were among his worst troubles. Of the second he wrote to Mrs. Wansbrough:

> I wish you had sent me some new eyes for Christmas. When you do send them let them be of a liquid brown, for I am tired of having pale green eyes. I got them when I was quite young and did not know how unfashionable they were.[1]

And of the first he wrote that

> not fighting for sleep is a sound rule. I used to get myself into a frenzy of effort to seize on sleep, but now I just lie awake and bear it and I find it wearies me less.[2]

It was altogether in the character of this man and of this life that he should live most intensely and most happily in the company of his friends. Of the women who offered him the hospitality of their country houses some were the widows of his old companions and many were converts to his faith. Now, as the years drew on, they enclosed him like a bodyguard; good angels of privacy and peace.

[1] Jan. 1932.   [2] Nov. 14, 1932.

CHAPTER XXI

VALE

I

IN February 1939 the reign of Pius XI came to an end. The
Malachite Distich had prophesied, in Belloc's gloss, that he
would be 'a kicker and biter',[1] and so he had proved. Belloc
had seen him at some length with Eleanor, in 1922, soon after his
election. The Pope had spoken about the conditions of labour in
England and about the importance of the peasantry. Belloc took
away the impression of 'a highly cultivated upper middle-class
man of great energy and clear ideas'.[2] He attached a vast importance to Papal audiences, finding 'something sacramental in direct
contact with the Apostolic See and the Vicar'.[3] When the Pope
died Belloc went to Rome, as representative of the Hearst Press,
to report the election of his successor. He stayed at Porto Fino
with Mary Herbert, and with the Woodruffs visited the Etruscan
tombs in Tarquinium. It was these, he would say, which first
gave Europe the idea of personal immortality. He caught a mild
attack of influenza in Porto Fino, and this got worse when he
reached Rome. He stayed at a quiet hotel in Albano, coming in
for the ceremony in St. Peter's.

The crowd stretched all the way from St. Peter's to the Tiber
and beyond—just like a vast flood, and the inside of St. Peter's
was choc-a-bloc. One had to get up at half past four and the
doors were open at six and the thing wasn't over until after
one. But it was worth it.[4]

[1] Letter to J. S. Phillimore: Feb. 6, 1922.
[2] Letter to Madame Belloc: April 4, 1922.
[3] Letter to Mrs. Reginald Balfour: March 9, 1922.
[4] Letter to Evan Charteris: March 30, 1939.

He crawled home through Paris, where he stayed at the
Embassy with Sir Eric and Lady Phipps, in time for the Private
View of the Royal Academy on April 18. Here the latest portrait
of him by James Gunn was on exhibition. It represented him
'swaggering along with a big thorny stick and glaring horribly'.
He thought it an extraordinarily good picture—'the handling
of the black is astonishingly good'.[1] Gunn was a close personal
friend of Belloc, and this painting, even more than the famous trio
with Chesterton and Baring, revealed a rare fidelity of insight.

Throughout the spring and summer of this year Belloc had one
great preoccupation; would the British create an army in time to
meet the challenge that was close upon them? Would they realize
that Britain was no longer, strategically, an island?

> They are to this matter of an Army, as to a hundred other
> things, like young men in good health considering mortality.
> They know they are mortal, but they don't grasp that truth as
> do old men, and especially old men who are beginning to
> suffer from the last ailments of age.[2]

England was still to this extent an aristocratic State that the
people expected to be told what to do by the governing classes
whose palsied hands had brought them to their present predica-
ment. Given a lead, they would follow it. Belloc proposed to
Dawnay the idea of a round robin, signed by a few weighty names,
suggesting a detailed plan for eliminating private profit from
armaments. He thought that many people would support this
who would not support conscription. During his visit to France
and Italy, he had been appalled by the decline in British prestige.
This was not to be gradually—it must be immediately—remedied.
One official pronouncement would be enough, and even then
it would take two years to put an adequate force into the field.

> You were listened to in the Great War [he writes to
> Dawnay]. I think you would be listened to now. But the race
> is hot and a few days may decide it.[3]

[1] Letters to Evan Charteris: April 17 and May 14, 1939.
[2] Letter to Major General Guy Dawnay: Dec. 1, 1938. General Dawnay was a
distinguished soldier with some influence in military circles.
[3] Palm Sunday, 1939.

He had been to Brussels and had a long talk with Van den Bergen, Chief of the Belgian General Staff. He gathered from him that Russia was quite incapable of providing munitions for Poland, since no two calibres in the two armies were the same. At the same time the Poles could not manufacture them for themselves; eight weeks would probably be the limit of their resistance in the field. Belloc had no illusions about the value of the Russian alliance which the British Government were vainly trying to conclude.

> I am dreadfully afraid that the mortally dangerous alliance with Moscow is going through. Everybody whose opinion is worth having knows that it is murderous folly, but what can be done to stop it?[1]

In June he was at Pixton, lecturing to the Somerset Nursing Association on the nature of lineage,

> which is not 'as you vainly imagine,' said I 'in your crass suburban ignorance a mere inheritance of money for a whole 60 or 70 years but knowing *who you are*: a dimension in time appreciable to anyone who knows all about his 4 great grandfathers and his 4 *great grandmothers*: who they were and what they were in social habit and knows that they were all of his own kind and he of theirs. *That* is lineage,' said I.[2]

Belloc would claim to be 'the flower of the bourgeoisie' because he knew the maiden names of his four great-grandmothers.

Regularly, in the *Weekly Review*, he urged the necessity of conscription and the importance of honouring the Polish guarantee. When war was declared his pamphlet, *The Catholic and the War* (1940) gave the moral basis of the Allied cause.

All his fears of Russia were confirmed by the Nazi-Soviet pact, and by the common action of the two powers against Poland which it had clearly implied. By November the Communist danger was an open threat, and once again Belloc realistically read the signs:

> I am pretty sure that the real danger now is from Communism having been let in by a back door. It was German

---

[1] Letter to Guy Dawnay: May 23, 1939.   [2] *Ibid.*, June 29, 1939.

barbarism that let it in but German barbarism might have been recivilised again, or partly recivilised, through Western Europe: but once Communism catches on it is like a fire for which the fuel is laid already and inexhaustible. The only thing that could have checked the flood of disaster would have been the barrier of Poland.[1]

In the same month he crossed to France and, escorted by Henri Massis, visited his old regiment in the Maginot Line.

> . . . At the front I found my old regiment and my old battery, which brought me to the verge of tears, especially when I met my old gun. It had just come out of the front line, and there were all the young men, looking as fresh as daisies and as muddy as an old-fashioned London street. The Colonel made a speech and assembled the officers, so I had to make a speech and then I stood the men huge masses of wine. The regiment gave me champagne, but I gave my piece nothing but gallons and gallons of red wine, which they far prefer. It is an astonishing thing to come back to the same atmosphere and tradition after a gap of just on fifty years. It is the only pleasant accident to mortality I have known, and had an air about it of the immortal.[2]

Had anyone told them, these men who gulped their wine so gratefully, that the elderly stranger in the dark broad-cloth had immortalized their regiment in English verse?

> The sword that was the strength of the poor is broken;
> The wrath that was the wealth of the poor is spent;
> Witless are all the great words we have spoken—
> But you my regiment!

He went on to Belgium and had a long talk in private with the King.

> I took to him enormously. I think you will like him when you know him, which in the course of time you are bound to do. He is really intelligent and sincere, and he has been annealed.[3]

---

[1] Letter to Duff Cooper: Nov. 6, 1939.   [2] *Ibid.*, Nov. 27, 1939.   [3] *Ibid.*

Early in 1940 Belloc was in Paris again, working at a book on
'England and France'. But this was no more than sketched out;
private and public events would make its completion impossible.

The Belloc of *Land and Water* had not been forgotten and
throughout the winter of 1939–40 he was contributing a weekly
commentary on military affairs for *The Sunday Times*. Here, and
elsewhere, he continued to proclaim that Poland was the test.

It may be too late to awake opinion to the key position of
Poland in the present mortal struggle. It may be that, through
the impossibility of teaching men who have no grounding in
the past, the fatal compromise will be carried out which will
mean that the West is defeated . . . there is one central
criterion of value and success: the resurrection of Poland.[1]

When the break-through came in May, Belloc was at pains to
insist that the crucial failure was the failure to hold the bridge
over the Meuse north of Maastricht. The whole catastrophe was
due to that. By July the danger of invasion was apparent, and
Belloc's comment on this may be read as his last (it was, in fact,
very nearly his last) message to the English people. Few of them
may have read, or heeded, it at the time, but the central truth
which he proclaimed stands luminous behind the intervening
years. The truth was this:

that upon the defence of Great Britain from successful invasion
depends the whole future not only of the island itself but of the
general inherited culture of European men.[2]

That culture was partially recovered, though it survives under
mortal threats. But the part of it that Belloc knew best, after his
own country, was engulfed in 1940. His attitude to the fall of
France was the attitude of many Frenchmen; the British had let
them down. Pétain he had known during the First War, and
Pétain would have seemed as venerable in his eyes as he seemed
to many Frenchmen. In so far as he had got rid of Parliamentary
forms; proclaimed the virtues of *travail, famille, patrie*; liqui-
dated the anti-clerical caucus; and restored the monarchical prin-

---

[1] *The Weekly Review:* Jan. 4, 1940.   [2] *Ibid.*, July 18, 1940.

ciple in public affairs—Pétain was a man after Belloc's heart and
he did not hesitate to say so. These were not very popular things
to say just then; and when Maisie Ward challenged him outright
—'If you were a young Frenchman, wouldn't you be with
de Gaulle?'—he was constrained to admit that, well, perhaps he
would have been. His attitude was not, in fact, very different
from what is now known to have been the attitude of the British
and, more decisively, the American Governments. In supporting
those Frenchmen who were still fighting with us, it would be
fatal to alienate those who, for one reason or another, held aloof.
If we had made an army in time, the French might have been able
to resist the superior forces opposed to them. The French alliance
was still essential to us; and meanwhile

> the most unintelligent (and therefore ruinous) political attitude
> possible is to think that the uncertain issue of French opinion
> in the immediate future does not count. It is all-important.[1]

Belloc no longer had a permanent secretary. Sometimes he
would borrow a room in London and dictate all through the day
to Miss Stephens, who was secretary to A. D. Peters. After a large
meat breakfast he would lunch off bread and wine. In one house
there only appeared to be a single glass; so he remarked, with shy
delicacy, to Miss Stephens: 'I shan't mind drinking out of your
glass, but you won't like drinking out of mine. So you drink
first.' In the winter of 1941 Dorothy Collins would come for
short periods to King's Land and type for him. He was working
on his *Elizabethan Commentary* (1942), and she would take down
his dictation in shorthand. He also did a number of articles for the
German and North American services of the B.B.C., and for the
Ministry of Information to be reproduced in Latin-America.
These he dictated straight on to the machine.

The French collapse broke one half of Belloc's heart. The
earliest theme of that long and turbulent lifetime—the theme of
invasion, disintegration and defeat—echoed mournfully from the
barely recollected past. Another theme, the insistent reminder of
mortality, was presently to break in. On April 2, 1941, his son

[1] *The Weekly Review:* Feb. 27, 1941.

Peter died on active service in Scotland with the Marines. He was
thirty-six years old. Belloc was lunching in Horsham when
Eleanor and Reginald Jebb, with Miss Collins, who was staying
at King's Land, motored out to tell him that a telegram had come
with the news that Peter was dangerously ill.

> . . . The Boy did not fall in action. What happened was
> this. He went out with the Fleet in the boat to which his Bat-
> talion of Marines—the Vth—was attached. When it got back
> into the Clyde a telegram was sent me saying I should have
> news. I telephoned at once to Glasgow whether the ship had
> returned. There was a delay of some hours. When I got
> through it was only to hear that he was dead. It came thus; in
> a sort of flash and a stroke of lightning. It was sudden pneu-
> monia.
>
> He has been buried here next to his mother. His Battalion
> sent a detachment and rendered full honours. . . .[1]

Belloc stood apart at the funeral, stricken but very brave.

2

He did not completely recover from the shock of Peter's death.
His memory and his physical strength began to fail. On July 27
a dinner, postponed from the previous year, was held at the Savoy
to celebrate his seventy-first birthday. He walked up to the high
table, leaning on the arm of Reginald Jebb. Brendan Bracken,
who was then Minister of Information, presided; Duff Cooper
spoke of Belloc's verse; and Desmond MacCarthy said how much
he enjoyed his novels. Belloc replied briefly, saying how happy
he would be to have contributed anything to the sum of English
lyric poetry. It was a rather melancholy occasion and many of
those present must have looked back to the previous birthday
party, eleven years before. The anniversary was also marked by
the publication of *For Hilaire Belloc,* a collection of essays, edited
by Douglas Woodruff and published by Sheed and Ward. Only

[1] Letter to Duff Cooper: April 10, 1941.

one of these, by Mr. Douglas Jerrold, was concerned with Belloc himself, showing how the author of *The Servile State* had become the prophet of the Counter-Revolution. A state of war is not conducive to clear thinking, and in 1942 the Counter-Revolution was as unpopular as it was widely misunderstood.

On January 30, Belloc had a slight stroke at the Reform Club, where he was found unconscious by Sir William Beveridge, and was brought home to King's Land the next day. His heart was affected and he developed pneumonia. A Sister from the Order of the Bon Secours came to look after him and he received the Last Sacraments of the Church. He was not expected to live through the night. But his strength rallied, helped perhaps by a glass of wine which he had insisted on drinking, much to the Sister's disapproval. She did not find him an easy or a likeable patient. He remained in bed until the end of April, but on February 12 he was strong enough to dictate three articles to Dorothy Collins. When at last he came downstairs his mind was still confused. The War, with all its problems, had receded far into the background and he remembered only the past—the failure of All Souls, the marching-songs of the French Army, and Elodie beckoning him to beatitude.

> Most things pass [he had written to Lady Lovat], but certain forms of human affection do not pass; they seem to be of another stuff from the common fabric of life.[1]

Candlemas came round; twenty-eight years—'long in one way, short in another.'[2]

Although he occasionally wrote an article for *The Weekly Review*, he could now no longer concentrate for long, and his powers of expression quietly faded, like music lost on the breeze. He sat reading the newspapers and marvelling at their folly. 'What's all this nonsense about some new bomb?' he would exclaim, as the skies released their latest terror. 'All newspaper talk, all newspaper talk.' And he returned to Rabelais. When the Government took away the iron railings from in front of his house, he cursed them as he alone knew how to curse the audacity

---

[1] Jan. 28, 1941.   [2] *Ibid.*

of elected persons. He would go occasionally to London, and
meet his friends in Lady Phipps's house in Tite Street. In a letter
to Maurice Baring, Desmond MacCarthy describes one of these
occasions in the summer of 1944.

> Last Tuesday we had another Hilaire luncheon at 31, Tite
> Street. Frances, the Bear, H. and myself. After drinking to you
> a glass or so of Bear's brother's port, Hilaire sang:
>
> > 'My Bonnie has tuberculosis,
> > My Bonnie believes in Couee;
> > She's awfully bucked by the process;
> > So send back my Bonnie to me.'
>
> Sang it in a voice perhaps a little less resonant that we can
> hear in imagination still, but with the perfect rhythm and
> wagging of head and finger we remember so well. Wouldn't
> you like, Maurice, to have over again one of those luncheons
> at the Mont Blanc or elsewhere?
> Part of the music of heaven—not the most celestial part of
> course—consists of 'records'—humble happy tunes played
> over again when we want one; illuminated of course by being
> at last in their proper relation to life.[1]

But the journey to London became too great a strain; if one
had escorted him it was all one could do, physically, to get him
into a train at the end of the day. Fortunately, he was well known
at Horsham, since the days when he had given the porters a shilling to call out 'Horseham' which was the way he held the name
should be pronounced. He used to be much annoyed by the advertisements on Horsham station, declaring that a certain well-known
meat essence was made of old horses and animals that died at the
Zoo. There was a special arrangement, he maintained, between
the Railway Company and the Zoo officials. He would also declaim at length against the advertisement of a military and naval
tailor, because the faces used to illustrate the uniforms were the
faces of bounders. 'They've straightforward eyes, which gentle-

[1] June 19, 1944.

men never have. They're brought up not to have them.' In the train he would astonish the passengers by exclaiming in a loud voice: 'Nothing will ever cure the English of their unconquerable love for the Prussians.'

In 1943 the Prime Minister asked him if he would accept the Companionship of Honour, but he begged to refuse. Yet here surely was a public recognition which he could have accepted with dignity, and many of his friends wished that he had been persuaded to do so. It was a sign of Winston Churchill's quality of mind that he should have offered Belloc this honour as soon as it was in his power to recommend it. Many years later he was also offered an Honorary Fellowship at Balliol, but Balliol had spoken too late. On November 30, 1950, his portrait by James Gunn was unveiled by Duff Cooper in the Debating Hall of the Oxford Union. This had been exhibited at the Academy and presented by an anonymous donor. It showed an unfamiliar, bearded Belloc seated in his armchair at King's Land. The likeness was admirable, but many people felt that if Belloc were to be commemorated on the walls of the Oxford Union he should appear there in a portrait more evocative of his vigour and youth. Belloc was too infirm to attend the ceremony, but Duff Cooper interpreted his feelings in saying that 'he would like to think that here in this hall—where there were still the ghosts of men who were boys when he was a boy—this honour should have been done him'. A motion framed in Belloc's own verses was then carried by acclamation.

> The question's very much too wide
>   And much too deep and much too hollow,
> And learned men on either side
>   Use arguments we cannot follow.

In so far as he could get about he did so. He went once or twice to Oxford, lunching at Blackfriars and spending the night at Campion Hall. He surprised his hosts by talking in rather a kindly way about Queen Elizabeth I. At lunch he merely crumbled the bread on his plate and declined the wine which had been set before him. Afterwards he sat with the Community, speaking very little and dozing off to sleep in his high-backed chair.

He liked especially to see the children of his friends, many of them grown to manhood and serving in the war of which he knew so little; some of them to be killed. He wondered at the reason for this increased affection. 'Is it because we feel we are going away and wish to be remembered as guests or passers-by?' With those who had died young he felt an intimate communion; and nothing, after the loss of his own son, moved him more in these last years than the death of Rose Fraser in 1942.

> Thinking of her presence is as of the daylight. . . . What an immeasurable gift is the serene contemplation of Beatitude! Nowhere is it fuller of completion and substance than in the memory of the young and innocent who die in the full presence of God.[1]

His friends were scattered and petrol was scarce. Vincent McNabb died in 1943 and Belloc insisted on coming to London for the Requiem. Maurice Baring died in 1945, after a long illness heroically borne, and Marie Belloc-Lowndes in 1947. When the war was over Belloc's friends came down to see him at King's Land whenever they could: Douglas Woodruff, whose conduct of *The Tablet* he so much admired; 'Bear' Warre; and Duff Cooper, now Ambassador in Paris. Nearer neighbours, the Mortons and Sir Merrik Burrell, were constant visitors. Bishop Mathew and Monsignor Knox would come to say Mass in the house; and the Christmases followed, as far as possible, their traditional pattern. The children of the village gathered round a new crib, which had been given to the household by Elizabeth Herbert. When the war was over, she and other friends from the West Country would fetch Belloc in their cars, and pass him on, one to the other. He would sit in the drawing-room at Broughton Poggs and ask Elizabeth Wansbrough what the man in the Chinese glass picture in the drawing-room was doing behind the tree; for a small, strong flame of curiosity was alive in him to the last.

[1] Letters to Lady Lovat: May 8 and July 12, 1942.

By now he had grown a patriarchal beard and when he came in to Mass at King's Land, wearing his thick brown dressing-gown and slippers, he reminded one of St. Joseph in some old picture of the Nativity. One day, motoring through the main street of Marlborough with Lady Phipps, he decided to have his beard shaved off. But no local barber would undertake so considerable an operation, and he had to be taken to the hospital where presumably the surgical scissors did the job. But he soon found it less trouble to let it grow again. Escorting him was always a responsibility. On one occasion Dorothy Collins was driving him in her car and left him for a moment to go into a shop. When she came out she found him placidly sitting in a Rolls-Bentley on the other side of the street. On another occasion, before the end of the war, she had taken him out to lunch in Beaconsfield, and on asking for something off the menu he was told that, for that, points were required. 'Points,' roared Belloc, 'what are points?' He would still go in to Horsham for lunch at the Black Horse. There was never enough bread for his needs, and he would wander across to other people's tables and calmly take their loaves, murmuring that the lack of bread was the result of false religion.

The years passed, and he did not distinguish them one from another. He still remembered many details of his youth and early manhood and his historical judgments were still acute; but his body was failing him and it was evident to all who came to King's Land that there was only one thing left—the tremendous business of eternity. He moved very, very slowly, from room to room, and he now slept late into the morning. How far away they seemed, the days when he had wrestled with 'Bear' Warre on the pavement of the Brompton Road, and Warre had thrown him! His face grew paler, and more transparent; his eyes had a searching and yet a tranquil look. All his life he had relied on doctrine, 'as a man who had fallen into the water can rely upon his foothold when he has put his foot on the ground and knows that the depth is not enough to drown him'.[1] The doctrine of immortality belonged to that core of truth which was not

[1] Letter to Lady Lovat: Jan. 28, 1941.

normally confirmed by experience; yet the less vividly it was imagined, the more firmly it could be grasped. And there were moments now when flashes of sensible feeling seemed to lighten the aridities of belief. The words of the old Provençal hymn came back into his mind: *E ades sera l'Alba*—'And soon will be the dawn'.

He became more silent and would sit apart, pulling at his pipe and leaving a débris of 'Four Square' (yellow). Visitors generally brought him wine, though he could no longer drink so much as formerly; and this was poured into the silver tankard which he had kept by him since Balliol days. After the meal one would sit in his study, or in his bedroom beside the fire. There was the plaster statue of Our Lady on the dressing-table; and the water-colour of Naworth, where he had ridden and wrestled on the fells with Hubert Howard; and the coloured print of Mirabeau. His grandchildren were growing up. Marianne Jebb left to join the Canonesses of St. Augustine, a teaching order of enclosed nuns at Haywards Heath. Her departure saddened him greatly, but he was able to attend her clothing and to kiss her hand through the grille. That other theme of vocation—the vocation which had so nearly robbed him of Elodie, which had tested him as it had tested her—came to mingle with the memories and the great anticipation. Anthony Jebb entered the novitiate at Downside and Belloc remarked that that was 'a pretty good bore'. But still his daughter and his son-in-law kept faithful guard.

In July 1950 he celebrated his eightieth birthday. A great party was given in the Sparta field opposite the house and the lane was lined with cars. (Belloc would say that the reason why there were so many winding lanes in England was because the rich thought straight roads were French and therefore Catholic.) There were three special luncheons at King's Land, one with Duff Cooper; another, on the birthday itself, with A. D. Peters, W. N. Roughead and James Gunn; and a third with Douglas Woodruff, J. B. Morton, D. B. Wyndham Lewis and the present writer. We brought him a cold bird from London and several bottles of Moulin-à-Vent—the wine he had drunk at the first meeting with Chesterton. Belloc was bewildered by the number of his guests and by the occasion of their coming. If a man was eighty that was nothing to make a fuss about. He only knew that life was much too long on the one hand and much too short on the other. 'I have one foot in the grave', he once remarked to Elizabeth Herbert—and then added, shooting out his leg—'*this* one.'

He was not dismayed by the thought of death, because, although he had loved the world to the limit of his large capacities, he did not love it any longer. It was now some years since he had bidden it a 'tender farewell'. He had looked back to a stone house by a river in Normandy, where food was served on the terrace, and the slow carts moved along the further bank; to the 'wolds almost innocent of man' close to the Northumbrian shore, and the road leading up the glen; to the cities where in one gateway 'an arch proclaimed the decay of the Empire', and in another 'survived some small and venerable fragment of the Roman time'; to the carousals and the feasts 'intensified by quarrel, blown through with laughter, lifted by sudden perceptions'; to the conflict of mind with mind, and the eternal challenge of the sea; 'the headland that might be a low cloud save that it does not move; the headland behind which are the stone piers and the sheltered water and the roofs of home'; and the furniture of home itself, the laughter and the love of friends—must he leave them, too? Yes, he exclaimed, with a *saeva indignatio* worthy of his master Swift, he must—and he would leave them without regret because they were no longer what they once had been.

If there were a feast, what would he find at the end of it but 'one poor ugly, naked bulb, hanging by a fly-blown wire near the office door, while a lousy serf, eager to be off to his gutter-joys, was bawling "Time, gentlemen, time", through the deserted hotch-potch of dirty table-cloth, broken glass, and stale tobacco?' If he returned to the house of stone in the Norman forest, he would find the wine reduced to chemicals and the house rebuilt in jazz, and along the road where the carts had passed so slowly, the Rastaquouères and their women would be tearing along to the casinos which defiled the oily sea. And to Literature he said farewell more fondly than to anything else.

The glories of the past are destroyed, they are no longer understood, and language is forgotten. Letters, you have gone down in a cataract from depth of folly to further depth, from obscenity to obscenity, until you have reached the inane. For whom should any man now write? What ears remain to hear?[1]

By the time Belloc had passed his eightieth birthday the *saeva indignatio* was spent; and, although he did not know it, there were a few ears left to hear. In the summer of 1951 all those responsible for the dramatized version of *The Four Men* were invited to King's Land on their way to Chichester where the first performance was to be given. Belloc was much gayer than he had been on his eightieth birthday. His conversation entirely matched his legend. One of the actors, W. E. Holloway, a Fabian diehard, tried to persuade him of the social benefits of television. 'Oh, do you think so?' Belloc replied, with a grave and sceptical courtesy. He did not know what we were all doing, but he was glad to see us.

In March 1953 his friend Hugh Mackintosh took Sir William Haley, who had recently been appointed Editor of *The Times*, down to lunch at King's Land. Haley had admired Belloc's work for years, but the two men had never met. Belloc's strength was now known to be declining and his guests hardly expected that the meal would be a gay one. However, before lunch had started, he was reciting his own verse and singing his own songs.

During lunch he discussed a wide range of topics with us (including wine, California, and M. Thiers) and, though his memory was failing and he became abstracted from time to time, his courtesy never faltered.[2]

The feebleness grew and the fits of abstraction became more frequent. On Sunday, July 12 (1953), Belloc went into his study before luncheon. Shortly afterwards his daughter, who was preparing the meal, caught a smell of burning and hurried into her father's room. The place was full of smoke and Belloc was lying

[1] *The New Keepsake* (1931).
[2] H. S. Mackintosh: Broadcast, printed in *The Listener,* Oct. 8, 1953.

near the fireplace beside a piece of coal which he had evidently dislodged from the grate in attending to it. The family threw a rug round him; the village nurse was sent for; and a bed was put up in the study. The doctor arrived soon afterwards. It was clear that Belloc was suffering from severe shock and burns, and a room was engaged for him in the Mount Alvernia nursing-home of the Franciscan Missionaries at Guildford. He was taken there later in an ambulance, very pale but not seeming to be in pain.

The following evening he received the Last Sacraments for the third time in that long and sacramental life; and the statue of Our Lady from King's Land had now been placed in the room where he could see it. He was alternately conscious and unconscious through the next day and on the Wednesday he rallied a little. James Hall, who had brought so many bottles of wine to King's Land, brought a last bottle to the Nursing Home and the Matron willingly allowed the dying man to drink it. Lady Phipps also came to visit him. On Thursday, the Feast of Our Lady of Mount Carmel, he became unconscious again, and some of those who were nearest to him gathered round his bed: Eleanor and Reginald Jebb, Elizabeth Belloc, Peter's widow Stella and her sister, J. B. Morton and his wife, and Edith Rance. They all recited the Rosary and Philip Jebb read aloud the prayers for a departing soul. Up-stairs, the nuns at Benediction were singing the hymn that Belloc loved beyond all others; but there was no sign that he heard them or that his mind now rested upon any mortal thing. Yet he may have been dreaming of the *douceur Angevine* and of a certain meadow on the Boutonne where the Girondins had halted on their northward march; or of a Californian valley, long ago, where he had rested under the incredibly tall trees. He used to say that such places carried a foretaste of beatitude, and to wonder whether, at the moment of his death, he would be granted a vision of them for viaticum. Outside the window a thrush was singing and the skies were strewn with cloud. Once, at the end of a long day's plodding on the path to Rome, the man who there lay dying had fallen asleep dreaming of 'the shapes of clouds and the glory of God'. It was easy to imagine that he did so now; and that in the skies of his awakening there rose the 'piping of a lark.'

*   *   *   *   *

The national Press was generous in its tributes. Men who had not always agreed with what Belloc said admired the way that he had said it. To those of a younger generation, deeply involved in the contemporary adventure, he had receded far into the background, rooted in the certitudes they had lost. But he still belonged to the landscape of the century, and when he died it seemed as if a slice of England had suddenly been cut away. After the formal inquest his body was brought home to King's Land and lay in the hall, where Elodie had lain, beneath the portraits of his military forebears. Six tall candles stood beside the coffin, and although the room was draughty and there was much wind outside, the spear-points of flame burned steadily throughout the vigil.

The funeral was at West Grinstead on the following Monday. Hilaire Belloc was buried beside his wife and son, and a great company of friends came from long distances to mourn and to salute his passing. Some were of his Faith, others were not; but they filled the nave of the little village church where he had worshipped. In the choir were large numbers of clergy and religious, and monks from Downside Abbey chanted the Requiem. Among them was Anthony Jebb in the habit of a Benedictine novice. The Bishop of Southwark celebrated the Mass, pronounced the Absolutions, and gave a short address. A few days later Westminster Cathedral was packed to its doors for a Solemn Requiem at which the Cardinal Archbishop presided and Monsignor Knox preached the panegyric. Instinctively, it seemed, the Church came forward to honour the man who had fought her battles, and the tremendous petitions which accompany the passing of a Christian soul took on, in the case of Hilaire Belloc, a special note of assurance and thanksgiving. After the committal a number of those present returned to King's Land. They moved about the rooms, noting the familiar details: the picture of Elodie, very faded now; the photograph of Father Vincent McNabb;

Leo XIII in the gardens of the Vatican; the red wallpaper on the staircase; the refectory table—oaken, like the man whom they had buried. The mourners talked to each other with a quiet unconstraint, as if the living Belloc were sitting on the edge of the sofa or in the depth of the armchair, and might at any moment enter the conversation. The rooms were serene with his presence; and the tribute of Chesterton came back that no man of our time had fought so consistently for the good things.

THE PANEGYRIC

preached by Monsignor Ronald Knox at the Requiem Mass for Hilaire Belloc in Westminster Cathedral (August 1953) from the text: 'Up, then, gird thee like a man, and speak out all the message I give thee. Meet them undaunted, and they shall have no power to daunt thee. Strong I mean to make thee this day as fortified city, or pillar of iron, or wall of bronze, to meet king, prince, priest and common folk all the country through.'
Jeremias i. 17-18.

THE other day, in a curiously moving country church at West Grinstead, we laid to rest, not without the tears of memory, an old and tired man. It was a funeral of circumstance; the Mass was Pontifical, the habits of many religious Orders graced the sanctuary, and schoolboys' voices lent an intolerable beauty to the *Dies Irae*. But in essence it was a country affair; some of Hilaire Belloc's friends had met to see his body lowered into the grave—there, in Sussex earth; there, beside the wife he had so long mourned; there, with the house he had lived in for forty years, till it became 'like a bear's fur' to him, only a few miles away. Today, as if humouring that other side of him, which loved stateliness and the just proportion of well-ordered things, we gather with muffled footfalls among the echoing vaults of a great cathedral—we, lesser men, who have lived so long under the shadow of his championship, to remind ourselves what it is we have lost, and to do him honour.

We ask foolishly what such a man would have wished to hear said in his praise if he were alive; perhaps still more foolishly, what he is wishing to hear, if the dead know so much, care so much, about transitory things. It was a question that exercised him greatly, especially at the end of his life; the appetite for fame was, he said, at once the most irrational and the strongest of all appetites; of fame itself he told us, 'It is but a savour and an air'. For his friend Chesterton he prophesied enduring fame only on condition that the cause for which they both did battle should

534

ultimately triumph, and England should return to a happier way of living. Whether that was right may be a matter of dispute; but I think it gives us a clue to Belloc's own feeling about such matters. What he cared for was not the good word of posterity taken in the gross, but the praise of Christendom.

Only such praise concerns *us*, here before his catafalque. Let others remember him—have no fear, he will be remembered—as a great master of English prose, that virile, nervous English prose which he shares with men like Sterne and Cobbett; or as a satirist to be mentioned in the same breath as Swift and Molière; or as a historian who had the rare quality of making the past live. For us, these are but the trappings of his greatness. Here was a man that interpreted divine things for us, under homely images and in our common speech. He was a prophet.

When I say that, I do not mean to suggest that he had any special skill in forecasting future events; he made mistakes there, like the rest of us. I mean he was such a man as saw what he took to be the evils of our time in a clear light, and with a steady hatred; that he found, or thought he had found, a common root in them, and traced them back, with that light God gave him, to their origins in history. In this, he resembled a great man whom he was proud to claim as his master, Father Vincent McNabb, of the Order of Preachers. Father Vincent, who has left us so little record of his splendid gifts, was an inspiration to all that brilliant circle of Catholics among whom Belloc moved; men like John Phillimore, the professor of humanities at Glasgow, and Maurice Baring, whose novels we shall read again. But only two accepted from him the mantle of prophecy, Belloc and Chesterton. And of these, Belloc had the double portion; he was a prophet by destiny and by temperament.

A prophet, by derivation, is one who speaks out. He must not wrap up his meaning; he must not expect success. 'To brazen-faced folk and hard-hearted thy errand is, and still from the Lord God a message thou must deliver, hear they, or deny thee a hearing; rebels all, at least they shall know that they have had a prophet in their midst.' There is the double tragedy of the prophet; he must speak out, so that he makes men dislike him, and he must be content to believe that he is making no impression whatever. Such is the complaint of Jeremias: 'An ill day when thou, my mother, didst bring me into the world! A world where all for me is strife, all is hostility; neither creditor I nor debtor to any man, yet they curse my name!' He would be rid, if he could, of the prophet's burden; and there were moods, at least, in which Belloc would indulge in the same complaint. Even when he wrote *The Path to Rome*, he was conscious of the strain: 'We are perpetually thrust into minorities, and the world almost begins to talk a strange language. . . . And this is hard when a man has loved common views, and is happy only with his fellows.' And in his tribute to Chesterton, one of his last works, you will find him exclaiming, half in envy, half in reprobation, at the man who took part in so much controversy, yet never made an enemy: 'Without wounding and killing', he said, 'there is no battle.' With Chesterton, as with Johnson's friend who tried to be a philosopher, 'cheerfulness was always breaking in'; Belloc's destiny was conflict, and he did not love it. He was 'a prophet lost in the hills':

> I challenged, and I kept the faith;
> The bleeding path alone I trod.

Why must he always be different, not thinking the thoughts of common men?

A sad life? You would not venture to assert it; as a young man, he would sing in chorus, and ride, and sail the seas; nor did he lose, to the end, the pleasures of old memory and of tried friendship. But he was melancholy by temperament; the undercurrents of his mind were sad, and his face never looked happy in repose. And because this melancholy was fed, at all times, by a sense of intellectual loneliness, he stood, mentally, a confessor to the faith that was in him. Many, who shared that faith, would not go all the way with him in following out its implications. Was the story of the Reformation really so simple as he made it out to be? Were financial interests so powerful, were modern politics so corrupt, in real life, as in *Emmanuel Burden*? But *his* vision was prophetic, and therefore integral. If you could not trace every link in the chain of historical causation, still you could not doubt the logical sequence of events; it was no mere accident that the world which accepted the Reformation drifted, after a few centuries, into being the world we know. If we had lost good fellowship and good craftsmanship and a hundred other things which the natural side of him regretted, it was, it must be, a nemesis, traceable to the loss of certain other things, which the supernatural side of him regretted inconsolably.

Does the prophet do good? No such promise is made when he sets out with his message. His task is to deliver that message to the men of his time, whether they hear or refuse him a hearing. It may be, the stark language he talks to them, the unconventional gestures by which he tries to thrust it home, will produce a reaction, and wed them all the more firmly to their old ways of thought. There are one or two terrible passages in the Old Testament which almost seem to imply that the prophet is sent out, not to inspire repentance, but to redouble the guilt of his unbelieving audience. What is important, it seems, is that they should know they have had a prophet in their midst. Must that be the epitaph we pronounce today over a man so widely read, so greatly loved? That the violence of his protest defeated itself, and left England less kindly disposed than ever to a propaganda so crude, so exaggerated?

To be sure, he was prophet rather than apostle; he did not, as we say, 'make converts'. You do not often hear it said of Belloc, as you hear it said of Chesterton, 'I owe my conversion to him.' But the influence of a prophet is not to be measured by its impact on a single mind here and there; it exercises a kind of hydraulic pressure on the thought of his age. And when the day of wrath comes, and that book is brought out, written once for all, which contains all the material for a world's judgment, we shall perhaps see more of what Belloc was and did; how even his most irresponsible satire acted as a solvent force, to pierce the hard rind of self-satisfaction which, more than anything, kept Victorian England away from the Church; how the very overtones of his unostentatious piety brought back to us memories of the Faith, and of the Mass, and of our blessed Lady, to which English ears had grown unaccustomed.

2 N

Have I represented him as a figure of marble? No one who knew him, no one who has read the more intimate of his writings, can picture him otherwise than as a man essentially human, twinkling with fun, rippling with vitality. Even as we commit his soul into the hands of his Creator, with those severely impersonal prayers the Church dictates to us, we are haunted by a thousand human memories of him, recall a hundred endearing characteristics of him—his undisguised admiration for lesser men than himself, the punctilious care with which he would bestow charity on a beggar, his rather stiff courtesy to strangers, his fondness for company and good cheer. Human? God knows he was human. For human frailties, may he receive the pardon he always desired. For the wideness of his human sympathies, may he find reward.

And yet, you who loved Hilaire Belloc, you who read him, and found inspiration in the reading, do not imagine that he would be satisfied if we wrote for him the epitaph, 'This man endeared himself to his fellows.' He was a prophet; men thought him a fanatic, and he has written his own epitaph, I think, in a poem of that name. A fanatic, he says, is one who keeps his word —not merely this or that casual promise, but

> That great word which every man
> Gave God before his life began:
> It was a sacred word, he said,
> Which comforted the pathless dead,
> And made God smile when it was shown
> Unforfeited before the Throne;

an undertaking (that, surely, is the sense) that he will be true to himself, that he will carry out faithfully the mission God gave him to perform, that he will challenge the men of his age with his own characteristic protest. No human flattery, no love of ease, no weariness of conflict, shall make him retract the pledge he has given. 'I have fought the good fight, I have finished the race, I have redeemed my pledge'—that is what Hilaire Belloc would wish us to say of him, and there are few of whom it could be said so truly.

May his soul, and the souls of all the faithful departed, through the mercy of God, rest in peace.

BIBLIOGRAPHY

I. Books and Pamphlets by Hilaire Belloc

The following list of Belloc's publications is taken from *The English First Editions of Hilaire Belloc* by Patrick Cahill, from whom the complete text may be obtained at Lye End, St. John's, Woking, Surrey, price 10s. 6d. It is a fine piece of bibliographical scholarship, and should be consulted by anyone who wishes to have a full picture of Belloc's literary activity.

1896   VERSES AND SONNETS. Ward and Downey.

1896   THE BAD CHILD'S BOOK OF BEASTS. Oxford: Alden and Co., Bocardo Press; London: Simpkin, Marshall, Hamilton, Kent and Co.

1897   MORE BEASTS (FOR WORSE CHILDREN). Edward Arnold.

1898   THE MODERN TRAVELLER. Edward Arnold.

1899   DANTON. James Nisbet and Co.

1899   A MORAL ALPHABET. Edward Arnold.

1899   Extracts from the Diaries and Letters of HUBERT HOWARD with a Recollection by a Friend. (Edited by H.B.). Oxford: Horace Hart.

1900   LAMBKIN'S REMAINS. Oxford: The Proprietors of the *J.C.R.*

1900   PARIS. Edward Arnold.

1901   ROBESPIERRE. James Nisbet and Co.

1902   THE PATH TO ROME. George Allen.

1903   CALIBAN'S GUIDE TO LETTERS. Duckworth and Co.

1903   THE GREAT INQUIRY. Duckworth and Co.

1903   WHY EAT? A Broadside.

1903   THE ROMANCE OF TRISTAN AND ISEULT. Translated from the French of J. Bédier by H.B. George Allen.

1904   AVRIL. Duckworth and Co.

1904   EMMANUEL BURDEN. Methuen and Co.

1904   THE OLD ROAD. Archibald Constable and Co.

1906   ESTO PERPETUA. Duckworth and Co.

1906   AN OPEN LETTER ON THE DECAY OF FAITH. Burns and Oates.

1906 SUSSEX. Adam and Charles Black.

1906 HILLS AND THE SEA. Methuen and Co.

1907 THE HISTORIC THAMES. J. M. Dent and Co.

1907 CAUTIONARY TALES FOR CHILDREN. Eveleigh Nash.

1908 THE CATHOLIC CHURCH AND HISTORICAL TRUTH (Catholic Evidence Lectures, No. 3). Preston: W. Watson and Co.

1908 ON NOTHING. Methuen and Co.

1908 Mr. CLUTTERBUCK'S ELECTION. Eveleigh Nash.

1908 THE EYE-WITNESS. Eveleigh Nash.

1908 AN EXAMINATION OF SOCIALISM. Catholic Truth Society.

1909 THE PYRENEES. Methuen and Co.

1909 A CHANGE IN THE CABINET. Methuen and Co.

1909 MARIE ANTOINETTE. Methuen and Co.

1909 ON EVERYTHING. Methuen and Co.

1909 THE CHURCH AND SOCIALISM. Catholic Truth Society.

1910 THE FERRER CASE. Catholic Truth Society.

1910 ON ANYTHING. Constable and Co.

1910 PONGO AND THE BULL. Constable and Co.

1910 ON SOMETHING. Methuen and Co.

1910 VERSES. Duckworth and Co.

1911 THE PARTY SYSTEM, by Hilaire Belloc and Cecil Chesterton. Stephen Swift.

1911 THE FRENCH REVOLUTION. Williams and Norgate.

1911 THE GIRONDIN. Thomas Nelson and Sons.

1911 MORE PEERS. Stephen Swift.

1911 SOCIALISM AND THE SERVILE STATE. A Debate between Messrs. Hilaire Belloc and J. Ramsay MacDonald, M.P. The South West London Federation of the Independent Labour Party.

1911 FIRST AND LAST. Methuen and Co.

1911 THE BATTLE OF BLENHEIM. Stephen Swift and Co.

1911 MALPLAQUET. Stephen Swift and Co.

1912 WATERLOO. Stephen Swift and Co.

1912 THE FOUR MEN. Thomas Nelson and Sons.

1912 THE GREEN OVERCOAT. Bristol: J. W. Arrowsmith; London: Simpkin, Marshall, Hamilton, Kent and Co.

1912 TURCOING. Stephen Swift and Co.

1912 WARFARE IN ENGLAND. Williams and Norgate.

1912 THIS AND THAT. Methuen and Co.

1912 THE SERVILE STATE. T. N. Foulis.

1912 THE RIVER OF LONDON. T. N. Foulis.

1912 CRÉCY. Stephen Swift and Co.

1913 THE STANE STREET. Constable and Co.

1913 POITIERS. Hugh Rees.

1914 ANTI-CATHOLIC HISTORY. Catholic Truth Society.

1914 THE BOOK OF THE BAYEUX TAPESTRY. Chatto and Windus.

1915 LAND & WATER MAP OF THE WAR, drawn under the direction of Hilaire Belloc. *Land & Water.*

1915 THE HISTORY OF ENGLAND (in eleven volumes). Vol. XI is by H. B. Sands and Co.; New York: The Catholic Publication Society of America.

1915 A GENERAL SKETCH OF THE EUROPEAN WAR: THE FIRST PHASE. Thomas Nelson and Sons.

1915 THE TWO MAPS OF EUROPE. C. Arthur Pearson.

1916 THE LAST DAYS OF THE FRENCH MONARCHY. Chapman and Hall.

1916 A GENERAL SKETCH OF THE EUROPEAN WAR: THE SECOND PHASE. Thomas Nelson and Sons.

1916 THE SECOND YEAR OF THE WAR. Reprinted by permission from *Land and Water*: Burrup, Mathieson and Sprague.

1918 THE FREE PRESS. George Allen and Unwin.

1918 RELIGION AND CIVIL LIBERTY. Catholic Truth Society.

1919 THE PRINCIPLES OF WAR, by Marshal Foch. Translated by Hilaire Belloc. Chapman and Hall.

1919 PRECEPTS AND JUDGMENTS, by Marshal Foch. Translated by Hilaire Belloc. Chapman and Hall.

1920 THE CATHOLIC CHURCH AND THE PRINCIPLE OF PRIVATE PROPERTY. Catholic Truth Society.

1920 EUROPE AND THE FAITH. Constable and Co.

1920 THE HOUSE OF COMMONS AND MONARCHY. George Allen and Unwin.

1921 PASCAL'S 'PROVINCIAL LETTERS'. Catholic Truth Society.

1922 CATHOLIC SOCIAL REFORM VERSUS SOCIALISM. Catholic Truth Society.

1922 THE JEWS. Constable and Co.

1922 THE MERCY OF ALLAH. Chatto and Windus.

1923 ON. Methuen and Co.

1923 THE ROAD. Manchester: Charles W. Hobson.

1923 SONNETS AND VERSE. Duckworth and Co.

1923 THE CONTRAST. J. W. Arrowsmith (London) Ltd.

1924   ECONOMICS FOR HELEN. J. W. Arrowsmith (London) Ltd.

1924   THE CAMPAIGN OF 1812. Thomas Nelson and Sons.

1924   THE POLITICAL EFFORT. True Temperance Association.

1925   THE CRUISE OF THE 'NONA'. Constable and Co.

1925   A HISTORY OF ENGLAND: Vol. I. Methuen and Co.

1925   MR. PETRE. Arrowsmith.

1925   MINIATURES OF FRENCH HISTORY. Thomas Nelson and Sons.

1925   ENGLAND AND THE FAITH. A Reply published in the *Evening Standard* to an article by Dean Inge in the same journal. Catholic Truth Society.

1926   THE HIGHWAY AND ITS VEHICLES. The Studio Ltd.

1926   SHORT TALKS WITH THE DEAD. The Cayme Press.

1926   MRS. MARKHAM'S NEW HISTORY OF ENGLAND. The Cayme Press.

1926   THE EMERALD. Arrowsmith.

1926   A COMPANION TO MR. WELLS'S 'OUTLINE OF HISTORY'. Sheed and Ward.

1926   MR. BELLOC STILL OBJECTS. Sheed and Ward.

1927   THE CATHOLIC CHURCH AND HISTORY. Burns Oates and Washbourne.

1927   A HISTORY OF ENGLAND: Vol II. Methuen and Co.

1927   THE HAUNTED HOUSE. Arrowsmith.

1927   OLIVER CROMWELL. Ernest Benn.

1928   MANY CITIES. Constable and Co.

1928   A HISTORY OF ENGLAND: Vol. III. Methuen and Co.

1928   JAMES THE SECOND. Faber and Gwyer.

1928   HOW THE REFORMATION HAPPENED. Jonathan Cape.

1928   BUT SOFT—WE ARE OBSERVED. Arrowsmith.

1928   A CONVERSATION WITH AN ANGEL. Jonathan Cape.

1928   BELINDA. Constable and Co.

1929   SURVIVALS AND NEW ARRIVALS. Sheed and Ward.

1929   JOAN OF ARC. Cassell and Co.

1929   THE MISSING MASTERPIECE. Arrowsmith.

1930   RICHELIEU. Ernest Benn.

1930   A PAMPHLET. (Privately printed for H.B.'s sixtieth birthday.)

1930   WOLSEY. Cassell and Co.

1930   THE MAN WHO MADE GOLD. Arrowsmith.

1930   NEW CAUTIONARY TALES. Duckworth.

1931   A CONVERSATION WITH A CAT. Cassell and Co.

1931   ON TRANSLATION. (The Taylorian Lecture). Oxford: The
       Clarendon Press.

1931   ESSAYS OF A CATHOLIC. Sheed and Ward.

1931   A HISTORY OF ENGLAND: Vol. IV. Methuen and Co.

1931   CRANMER. Cassell and Co.

1931   TRAVEL NOTES ON A HOLIDAY TOUR IN FRANCE, by James
       Murray Allison, with an introduction and commentary by
       Hilaire Belloc. Privately printed.

1931   THE PRAISE OF WINE. AN HEROIC POEM to Duff Cooper. (1) No
       imprint. Presented by H.B. to his friends for Christmas, 1931.
       (2) *An Heroic Poem in Praise of Wine*. Peter Davies (1932.)

1932   THE POSTMASTER-GENERAL. Arrowsmith.

1932   LADIES AND GENTLEMEN. Duckworth.

1932   NAPOLEON. Cassell and Co.

1933   THE TACTICS AND STRATEGY OF THE GREAT DUKE OF MARL-
       BOROUGH. Arrowsmith.

1933   WILLIAM THE CONQUEROR.   Peter Davies.

1933   BECKET. Catholic Truth Society. (Published also by Sheed and
       Ward (1933) in 'The English Way', a collection of essays by
       various authors.)

1933   CHARLES THE FIRST.   Cassell and Co.

1934   CROMWELL. Cassell and Co.

1934   A SHORTER HISTORY OF ENGLAND. George G. Harrap and
       Co.

1935   MILTON.   Cassell and Co.

1936   THE BATTLE GROUND. Cassell and Co.

1936   THE COUNTY OF SUSSEX. Cassell and Co.

1936   AN ESSAY ON THE RESTORATION OF PROPERTY. The Distributist
       League.

1936   CHARACTERS OF THE REFORMATION. Sheed and Ward.

1936   THE HEDGE AND THE HORSE. Cassell and Co.

1937   AN ESSAY ON THE NATURE OF CONTEMPORARY ENGLAND.
       Constable and Co.

1937   THE CRUSADE. Cassell and Co.

1937   THE CRISIS OF OUR CIVILIZATION. Cassell and Co.

1938   SONNETS AND VERSE. Duckworth. New edition, with addi-
       tional poems.

1938   THE GREAT HERESIES.   Sheed and Ward.

1938   RETURN TO THE BALTIC. Constable and Co.

1938   THE QUESTION AND THE ANSWER. Longmans, Green and Co.

1938   MONARCHY: A Study of Louis XIV. Cassell and Co.

1938   THE CASE OF DR. COULTON. Sheed and Ward.

1939   ON SAILING THE SEA. Methuen and Co.

1940   THE LAST RALLY. Cassell and Co.

1940   THE CATHOLIC AND THE WAR. Burns Oates.

1940   ON THE PLACE OF GILBERT CHESTERTON IN ENGLISH LETTERS.
       Sheed and Ward.

1941   THE SILENCE OF THE SEA. Cassell and Co.

1942   ELIZABETHAN COMMENTARY. Cassell and Co.

1942   PLACES. Cassell and Co.

1954   THE VERSE OF HILAIRE BELLOC. The Nonesuch Press.

1955   ONE THING AND ANOTHER. Hollis and Carter.

                    II. Books about Hilaire Belloc

1916   HILAIRE BELLOC, by C. Creighton Mandell and Edward
       Shanks. Methuen and Co.

1945   HILAIRE BELLOC, by Robert Hamilton. Douglas Organ.

1954   HILAIRE BELLOC: NO ALIENATED MAN, by Frederick Wilhem-
       sen. Sheed and Ward.

1955   HILAIRE BELLOC: A MEMOIR, by J. B. Morton. Hollis and
       Carter.

1956   THE YOUNG HILAIRE BELLOC, by Marie Belloc-Lowndes.
       New York: Kenedy and Sons.

1956   TESTIMONY TO HILAIRE BELLOC, by Eleanor and Reginald Jebb.
       Methuen and Co.

INDEX